Economics

A Tool for Critically Understanding Society

EIGHTH EDITION

August 29

July 1 - 7th August 7th

July 28-August 7th

Economics
A Tool for Critically Understanding Society

EIGHTH EDITION

Tom Riddell
Smith College

Jean Shackelford
Bucknell University

Steve Stamos
Bucknell University

Geoffrey Schneider
Bucknell University

With Contributions by Bill Cooper

PEARSON
Addison
Wesley

Boston San Francisco New York
London Toronto Sydney Tokyo Singapore Madrid
Mexico City Munich Paris Cape Town Hong Kong Montreal

Publisher: Greg Tobin
Editor-in-Chief: Denise Clinton
Sponsoring Editor: Noel Kamm
Editorial Assistant: Courtney E. Schinke
Managing Editor: Nancy Fenton
Supplements Coordinator: Heather McNally
Senior Marketing Manager: Roxanne Hoch
Marketing Coordinator: Ashlee Clevenger
Rights and Permissions Advisor: Dana Weightman
Senior Manufacturing Buyer: Carol Melville
Cover and Interior Design: Gina Hagen Kolenda
Project Management and Page Make-up: Elm Street Publishing Services, Inc.

Cover image is a detail from an original quilt created by Jean Shackelford © 2005.

Library of Congress Cataloging-in-Publication Data

 Economics : a tool for critically understanding society. — 8th ed. / Tom Riddell ... [et al.]
  p. cm.
 Includes bibliographical references and index.
 ISBN 978-0-321-42358-0 (pbk.)
 1. Economics. I. Riddell, Tom, 1944-
HB171.5.R43 2008
330—dc22
2007023754

1 2 3 4 5 6 7 8 9 10—RRD—11 10 09 08 07

BRIEF CONTENTS

PART 5

International Economics and Finance   477

CONTENTS

PART 1

Economics as a Tool for Critical Thinking in a Changing Global Economy   1

CHAPTER 1   Economics as a Social Science   3

CHAPTER 2   Exploring the Emerging Global Economy   17

PART 2

Economic History and the Development of Modern Economic Thought   39

CHAPTER 3   The Evolution of Economic Systems   40

CHAPTER 4   Adam Smith, Classical Liberalism, and the Division of Labor   57

CHAPTER 5   Karl Marx and the Socialist Critique of Capitalism   71

CHAPTER 6   The Rise and Fall of Laissez–Faire in the U.S. Economy   87

PART 3

Microeconomics   109

CHAPTER 7   Scarcity: "You Can't Always Get What You Want"   111

CHAPTER 8   The Theory of Markets   124

PART 4

Macroeconomics   311

CHAPTER 14   Macroeconomics: Issues and Problems   313

CHAPTER 15   Macroeconomic Theory: Classical and Keynesian Models   338

CHAPTER 18   Aggregate Demand and Aggregate Supply   434

CHAPTER 19   Unemployment, Inflation, and Stabilization Policy in a Global Economy   455

PART 5

International Economics and Finance   477

FOREWORD

Entering the twenty-first century, the U.S. economy found itself in excellent shape following a period of record-setting economic growth that featured both low unemployment and low inflation that began in 1995.

Increases in worker productivity (worker output per hour) and budget surpluses produced the longest recorded period of economic growth in U.S. history. However, following the September 2001 terrorist attacks on the United States and the continuing wars in Iraq and Afganistan, budget deficits returned and political, economic, and foreign policy agendas turned toward domestic policies centered around military expenditures and homeland security.

Shortly after the Bush administration took office in 2001, a series of economic scandals were uncovered involving large-scale corporate fraud in companies including Enron, WorldCom, and Arthur Andersen. An "overbought" technology sector—hyped by misleading reporting—plummeted, wiping out billions of dollars of corporate and personal wealth and depleting the retirement funds of others. A decade earlier the banking system went through a similar period of turmoil. In the late 1980s, hundreds of savings banks around the country failed; in the 1990s and in 2003, bank mergers literally changed the face of the industry. Increased international competition and one-stop banking increased. Today, banks face dwindling shares of financial intermediary expansion and thus less control over financial assets and the fallout from a housing bubble.

In the labor force, there are relatively fewer high-paying jobs and more low-wage jobs. Increasingly, families rely on multiple wage earners to make adequate family incomes. Despite some reforms, discrimination against women and minorities continues to rob them of the chance for full economic advancement. As the population and labor force become increasingly diverse, job and wage discrimination will be an even greater challenge.

On the international scene, the United States continues to run persistent trade deficits and to face sharp competition in domestic and international markets from other advanced nations and from some of the newly industrializing countries. International debt problems pose potential threats to the stability of the international financial system. Extensive poverty and hunger throughout the world assault our sensitivities and responsibilities. Environmental problems such as climate change, the disposal of toxic wastes, deforestation, and the depletion of the ozone layer require truly global solutions. In the post–Cold War period, we have seen events that challenge peace and lead to uncertainty, including the dramatic changes sweeping Eastern Europe, the rise of nationalism in many areas of the world, continuing regional conflicts including those in the Middle East, along with a worldwide terrorist threat.

This list of problems is not all-inclusive, but it is suggestive. It highlights the economic importance of the U.S. and global economies at the start of the twenty-first century. This combination of strengths and weaknesses provides fertile ground for politicians, the media, and the public at large, as economists try to understand what is going on. What accounts for economic successes and failures? How can we address these economic problems and preserve long-run economic growth and stability? How can we utilize the resources at our disposal to respond to human needs? How do you make your way in this world and find gainful employment?

The recent experiences of the U.S. economy and its historical roots have produced ferment in the field of economics. There are many competing explanations for U.S. successes and failures. Economists even disagree about what to call a problem. Conservative economists have their explanations about what is wrong with the economy and how their policies will correct it. Those further to the right chime in with their own theories and suggestions. Keynesian and neo-Keynesian economists focus on the limitations inherent in these approaches and offer their solutions. Further to the left, based on their own assumptions and economic perspectives, other economists argue for industrial policy, public ownership, democratic economic planning, and increased attention to economic equity.

These debates are not sterile. They are a part of the public dialogue in this country—in the media, in political campaigns, in communities—about important problems and what to do about them. An informed position—indeed being an informed citizen in a liberal democracy—requires following events, paying attention to the discussion, and developing an understanding of how the economy works. In this context, the study of economics can contribute to our efforts to develop a critical understanding of our society and to work actively toward improving its performance in the future.

This introductory economics textbook is dedicated to promoting that effort. It attempts to develop fundamental economic tools of analysis in clear, simple, and understandable terms. It is designed to encourage the application of those tools to analyzing the most important economic issues facing the country, the world, and its peoples. And it emphasizes the variety of theories and ideas that economists and others have developed to explain U.S. and world economic events. We believe that the approach of this text helps students develop their critical ability to understand and analyze economic problems. It is readable, emphasizes relevant concerns, and does not avoid controversy. It is "user friendly."

The Eighth Edition

This edition of *Economics: A Tool for Critically Understanding Society* builds on the success of the first seven editions, as well as the need to update economics textbooks regularly with current information and changing economic issues. To guide our revisions, we have also relied on feedback from colleagues, students, and faculty who have used the text. Their criticisms, suggestions, and advice have been instructive and helpful.

In the eighth edition, we have updated economic data and commentary on policy and critical issues. Part 1 begins with a chapter on economics as a social science and a chapter on the global economy and growth. We have substantially reordered the presentation of economic history and the history of economic thought in Part 2, which continues to focus on the historical development of the modern economic system and the economic thought that accompanied it. Part 3 covers microeconomics and includes a number of additional problems to help students work through economic models. It continues to highlight issues of race and gender, globalization, and the environment as they relate to markets. In addition, we have added "The Big Picture" feature to microeconomic theory. These segments present an overview of the theoretical development in Part 3. Part 4 covers macroeconomics, where we have continued to simplify the Keynesian model and emphasize the operation of the macroeconomy in an international context. Part 5 maintains its focus on international trade, finance, development, and transition economies, and also adds "Big Picture" segments.

Economics: A Tool for Critically Understanding Society is still basically a one-semester text, although it may be appropriate for use in some full-year introductory economics courses. The scope of the book is less than that of most full-year texts. It does not try to cover everything. We emphasize the fundamentals of economics and focus on relevant applications of those concepts. In our experience, too much information, too much qualification, and too much supplementary material can get in the way of a solid foundation in the essential and relatively simple concepts. Furthermore, adequate examples from contemporary economic events are reported in the press every day to complement and enrich textbook economics.

Our objective through eight editions has been to retain simplicity while at the same time adequately covering the basic micro- and macroeconomic concepts. Consequently, we are convinced (both in theory and in practice) that this text is suitable for use in either one-semester or full-year courses. The Preface to the Instructor contains suggested outlines for one-semester and two-semester courses. Obviously, in a full-year course, there is more time to use supplementary material on issues or themes in modern economics.

Throughout the text, we have continued to supplement the development of basic economic concepts with cartoons and articles. We have reduced the number of reproduced articles based on the conclusion that a multitude of examples is available from following current economic events and requiring (or encouraging) students to read a newspaper. To emphasize the development of critical thinking and the controversial nature of economics, each part of the text ends with a "Thinking Critically" section with different views of important issues. In addition, the chapters contain questions for students to answer as they read through and review the text. We introduced this concept in the fifth edition, and we are delighted to see that it has been adopted by other economic principles texts. We feel it continues to provide a strong pedagogical contribution.

Acknowledgments

Once again numerous staff members at Addison-Wesley have been supportive in their assistance, advice, and cooperation in this edition of *Economics: A Tool for Critically Understanding Society*. We appreciate their contributions. We are particularly indebted to Denise Clinton for her encouragement and perseverance. Bucknell University has continued to provide support for our work.

Colleagues who offered helpful criticisms and suggestions for improving the text include Dean Baker, Adrienne Birecree, Greg Krohn, John Pool, Charles Sackrey, Frank Slavik, and David Wells. For past editions of the text, we appreciate the work of Teresa Amott, David Black, Jeffrey Blais, Victor Brajer, Paul Briggs,

Fikret Ceyhun, Norris Clement, James Cobbe, Thomas Cook, E. R. Dietrich, Anthony Dukes, Robert Drago, Cynthia Foreman, Gary E. Francis, Lorenzo Garbo, John R. Garrett, John A. Hansen, Richard B. Hansen, Steve Hickerson, Mariam Khawar, Stewart Long, Tom Maddox, Claron Nelson, Ned C. Pearlstein, Bruce Richard, Bruce Roberts, Edward A. Sayre, Philip Schuchman, Harry George Shaffer, Larry Simmons, Donald C. Tetmeyer, Mariano Torras, Dale Warnke, Stephen L. Widener, Edward Young, and Michael Zweig. For the eighth edition, we are grateful to Kace Chalmers, Heather Grob, John S. Heywood, Christine B. Lloyd, Charlotte A. Price, and Robert Sonora for their comments. Over the course of eight editions, we have received valuable research and preparation assistance from Brian Brinkman, Bob Brown, Chad Brown, Elizabeth Buchanan, Diane Collins, Lauren Ewald, Seth Foreman, Beverly Griffith, Karen Guarino, Patricia Hohl, Tony John, Jenae Johnson, Sharon Killian, Susan Lehman, Stephanie Metz, Pam Paaso, Stephanie Quinn, Jill Pompeii, Christie Rowe, Kaitlin Shepard, Letitia Sloan, Michell Walborn, Meagan Willits, and Ruth Wynkoop. We would also like to acknowledge the continuing contribution of Alice VanBuskirk.

We dedicated the fifth edition of this text to William Hawley Cooper, who passed away in 1997. Bill was our department chair, mentor, and friend. He brought Tom, Jean, and Steve to Bucknell in the early seventies and proceeded to convene meetings to produce a book of readings for our introductory economics course. Those readings eventually turned into the first edition of this text. Tom Riddell decided to "retire" from this text's production after the fifth edition. Certainly the first five editions reflected his commitment to challenging students to think for themselves in their quest for economic literacy. We continue to benefit from his ideas and inspiration.

Dedication

We would like to dedicate this edition to our families.

J.S., S.S., G.S.
Lewisburg, Pensylvania

PREFACE

TO THE INSTRUCTOR

Throughout the past several decades, teachers of introductory economics have expressed a good bit of dissatisfaction with the available textbooks. Not surprisingly, this discontent has led to the continual development of new textbooks for both one-semester and two-semester courses. Many of the new books, but not all, have attempted to cut down on the encyclopedic nature of the prototypical Samuelson text, and many have introduced readings and problems that are up-to-date and relevant to the current population of introductory economics students. This book is in that tradition. It also offers many singular contributions:

◆ It is intended primarily to be a one-semester book.
◆ It focuses on a particular set of basic economic concepts.
◆ It emphasizes active learning by the student.
◆ It includes different perspectives.
◆ It places a good bit of responsibility for teaching the course on the instructor.
◆ It encourages the development of critical thinking.

Many of the textbooks that were popular in the 1950s and 1960s were relatively easy to teach from; the material was all there, it was generally straightforward, and it was all familiar to anyone with a graduate degree in economics. Certainly, there was room for classroom innovation and experimentation to make learning economics exciting and lively. But the form and content of the two-semester textbook made it only too easy to lecture on the development of the theory in the text.

However, in the context of the continuing turmoil and confusion of the 1960s and 1970s, many economics teachers became dissatisfied with this approach to introductory economics. They wanted more relevance and applicability of economic concepts. Many were concerned with the lack of balance in the texts—one particular "brand" of economics would be emphasized to the exclusion of others. These teachers wanted their courses to provide more controversy and exposure to different points of view. They wanted less scope and less depth in the development of theory. They wanted to take a more active role in teaching their courses. These kinds of concerns originally inspired us to begin the effort of writing this textbook.

Most textbooks today continue as they have in the past. This text differs from those by introducing a variety of perspectives and providing real-world applications. This revised edition of *Economics: A Tool for Critically Understanding Society* maintains its commitment to focus on some of the most important, essential, and useful economic concepts. It provides up-to-date coverage, but not at the expense of overkill, and it includes additional "Big Picture" segments designed to help students understand the logic behind the economic models without technical details.

This text obviously does not cover every possible topic or economic concept that one might want to teach in the ideal introductory course. Nor are the articles and examples we have chosen the ones that everyone would select. The questions for the students as they read through the text might not be the ones that you would choose to emphasize the essence of a particular concept. However, our experiences with this book indicate that it will help students to learn and practice economics and the economic way of thinking as they progress through your course. We believe this book leaves room for and, indeed, requires a substantial amount of imagination, work, and dedication on the part of the instructor. You will have to teach economics, and we hope this text will help you in your task.

One of the most important innovations we have made in teaching our courses is to require the students to read a daily newspaper. Because of our location and the college service it offers, we have used *The New York Times* in this way. *The Wall Street Journal*, th*The Christian Science Monitor*, *The Economist*, *The Financial Times*, and *The Washington Post Weekly* are also good supplementary resources and are mailed all over the country. Reading the paper helps students use and reinforce economics—to inform themselves, formulate questions in class, discuss controversial events or proposals, and gain insight into real, current examples of economic problems and the light that economics can throw on them. Combining current events and economics can enable students to develop a critical understanding of the world. Using a newspaper allows the instructor to keep the course relevant and up-to-date. It also confronts the results of a 1990 survey that revealed very low rates of newspaper readership by seventeen- to twenty-nine-year-olds in the United States. (And, while online newspapers are readily available, we find students often miss the larger economic picture.) A more recent study by Princeton economists Alan S. Blinder and Alan B. Krueger found that most Americans rely on television as their most common source of economic information. Unfortunately, they also found those relying on television as their primary source were among the least informed.

We hope this text will encourage you and help you continue to be creative and imaginative in the way you teach introductory economics. It has been a lot of work for us—including many headaches and failed experiments. But then it has also been fun, exciting, and rewarding. Teaching's like that, isn't it?

Suggested One-Semester Course Outline (Fourteen Weeks)

Part 1	Chapters 1–2	Week 1	
Part 2	Chapters 3–4	Week 2	
	Chapters 5–6	Week 3	
Part 3	Chapters 7–8	Week 4	
	Chapter 9	Week 5	Exam 1
	Chapters 10–11	Week 6	
	Chapters 12–13	Week 7	
Part 4	Chapters 14–15	Week 8	
	Chapter 16	Week 9	
	Chapter 17	Week 10	Exam 2
	Chapters 18–19	Week 11	
Part 5	Chapter 20	Week 12	
	Chapter 21	Week 13	
	Chapters 22–23	Week 14	Final Exam

Suggested One-Semester Micro Course Outline (Fourteen Weeks)

Part 1	Chapters 1–2	Week 1	
Part 2	Chapters 3–4	Week 2	
	Chapters 5–6	Week 3	
Part 3	Chapter 7	Week 4	
	Chapter 8	Week 5	Exam 1
	Chapter 9	Week 6	
	Chapter 10	Week 7	
	Chapter 11	Week 8	
	Chapter 12	Week 9	
	Chapter 13	Week 10	Exam 2
Part 5	Chapter 20	Week 11	
	Chapter 21	Week 12	
	Chapter 22	Week 13	
	Chapter 23	Week 14	Final Exam

Suggested One-Semester Macro Course Outline (Fourteen Weeks)

Part 1	Chapters 1–2	Week 1	
Part 2	Chapters 3–6	Week 2	
Part 3	Chapters 7–8	Week 3	
Part 4	Chapter 14	Week 4	
	Chapter 15	Week 5	Exam 1
	Chapter 16	Week 6	
	Chapter 17	Week 7	
	Chapter 18	Week 8	
	Chapter 19	Week 9	Exam 2
	Chapter 20	Week 10	
	Chapter 21	Week 11	
Part 5	Chapter 22	Week 12	
	Chapter 23	Week 13	
	Review	Week 14	Final Exam

Supplements

For each chapter in the text, the *Online Instructor's Manual* provides teaching suggestions for class and answers to end-of-chapter questions, as well as additional true-false and essay questions. The *Online Test Bank* provides sample exams for each part in the text for use in the classroom. Both the *Online Instructor's Manual* and the *Online Test Bank* are available via a secure, password-protected Instructor Resource Center Web site (www.aw-bc.com/irc).

On the *Companion Web Site* (www.aw-bc.com/riddell), you will find chapter-by-chapter web links to additional readings and economic data, an online glossary, and tips on how to use the Internet in your economics course. If you wish to supplement your course with newspaper subscriptions or economic news sources, ask your local sales representative for details about Addison-Wesley's special offers.

TO THE STUDENT

Economics: What's in It for You?

More than 230 years after the United States became an independent nation, it is one of the most technologically and economically advanced countries in the world. Its complex economic system produces and distributes goods and services daily and provides one of the world's highest standards of living. Yet we are not satisfied, because we, personally and collectively, have many economic problems. Can people find and keep jobs that provide them with the income to support themselves and their families? What are the prospects for improvements in people's economic well-being? Can you find a job that you like? What's more, the United States is not isolated from the rest of the world. Other peoples face similar, as well as different, problems. Inflation, unemployment, energy problems, downsizing, discrimination, deficits, debt, poverty, pollution, resource shortages, underdevelopment, and corruption in business and politics are problems that dominated global headlines in the last third of the twentieth century, and continue into the twenty-first century.

Economics, as one of the social sciences, helps us understand, think, and form opinions about and develop responses to these economic aspects of our social reality. Economics can be a tool that aids us in defining our successes and our failures, as well as in preserving success and correcting failure. It can contribute to our awareness. In an increasingly complex and confusing world, this tool can serve us personally and collectively as we strive to be responsible citizens of our communities, our nation, and our world. This book is dedicated to helping you to acquire that tool.

> We want to make economics as important as baseball and football scores. The minds are out there. It's a question of getting the attention.
>
> —Robert P. Keim, president of the Advertising Council, commenting on a public service campaign to "improve public understanding and awareness of the system," 1975

> Acting is a business—no more than that—a craft, like plumbing, or being an economist; it's been a good living.
>
> —Marlon Brando, actor, in a television interview with Dick Cavett, 1973

> An inhabitant of cloud-cuckoo land; one knowledgeable in an obsolete art; a harmless academic drudge whose theories and laws are but mere puffs of air in face of the anarchy of banditry, greed, and corruption which holds sway in the pecuniary affairs of the real world.
>
> —A definition of *economist* that won an award from the *New Statesman* in England, 1976

The questions in this book are not rhetorical. Each is intended to make you pause and think. Try to answer each question as you go along. Or use them to review each chapter after you have finished reading it.

1. Would you like to be an economist? Why or why not?
2. Why are you taking economics?
3. "Economics has [usually] been a countercyclical discipline; it flourishes when the economy flounders, and vice versa." Why do you suppose that is so?

Objectives, or What We Have Designed This Book to Accomplish

Before you begin your formal study, we would like to share the following list of what we consider the most important objectives of an introduction to modern economics:

◆ To produce some "cognitive dissonance." By this, we mean that we hope to present you with some ideas, facts, and ways of thinking that are new or different to you. Our hope is that these will challenge you to think, to work a little, and to learn. Is capitalism better than socialism? It might be, but then again, it might not be! We hope to open your mind to thinking about alternatives. What is "investment"? It is *not* simply buying a share of stock in a corporation or the stock market! Introductory economics may shake up some of your preconceived ideas and beliefs. And it may reorganize them into a *system* of thought.

◆ To give you perspective on the historical changes in the material conditions, economic institutions, and social relations of human society. The United States has not always been affluent, and capitalism has not always existed.

◆ To introduce you to a system of economic theories and ideas about the economic institutions of societies—and how those ideas and theories have changed over time. Even the conservative Republican Richard Nixon became a Keynesian in the 1970s. (We will learn more about Keynesian economics in Part 4, but basically it is an economic theory that suggests an important role for the government in guiding the overall economy.) But in the 1980s, Ronald Reagan's economic policies were based on a harsh critique of Keynesian economics; he emphasized the primary importance of business activity as opposed to the government. Bill Clinton's economic policies in the mid-1990s relied on an eclectic mixture of market-based, Keynesian theories and monetary policy that emphasized a positive role for government in influencing economic growth. The challenge of Newt Gingrich and the Republican Congress in the mid-1990s over the role of government and taxes and spending was based primarily on conservative thinking. George W. Bush has in part continued this conservative tradition.

◆ To convey to you *some* of the economic theories that economists, or groups of economists, regard as accurate descriptions and predictors of economic activity.

For example, how do the two sides of a market, the buyers and sellers, interact to determine prices? We do not intend to give you a survey of all of economics, but to expose you to some of the most basic and useful economic concepts. There is too much of economics to try to do all of it in one semester or even a year; time is *scarce* (that's an economic concept).

♦ To focus on some contemporary economic issues—inflation, unemployment, growth, resource shortages, international trade, climate change, poverty and income distribution, multinational corporations, economic growth and development, and others.

♦ To expose you to the various, and contending, schools of economic thought. Not all economists agree on which theories or even on which problems are the most important. We hope that you will at least appreciate the variety of economic analysis—no matter which, if any, particular set of economic ideas appeals to you.

♦ To give you practice using economic concepts. We don't want you just to "input" the concepts in your head and "print them out" on tests. We hope that this text gives you opportunities to use economic concepts in solving real-world problems. Our intention is to provide you with case studies that allow you to apply economic concepts, ideas, and theories so that you may come to better understand the world you live in (and perhaps to change it!). We enthusiastically recommend that you read a daily newspaper. Regularly reading the newspaper will provide numerous real-world examples of economic problems (to integrate theory and reality). And applying economic concepts will help you understand them and figure out their implications. We may even be able to suggest solutions to some of these problems. How would you eliminate poverty?

♦ To give you a foundation in economic "literacy." You should be able to interpret some of the jargon of professional economists. You should also be able to identify the variables, ramifications, and possible explanations of and solutions to a variety of economic problems. We hope you develop a facility to evaluate economic ideas critically.

♦ To demystify economics so that you do not feel that the economy and its problems are too complex to understand and solve. Economics and economic policy ought not to be left only to the economists.

◆ To provide a foundation for future and continued learning. The world is complex. But economics will assist you in thinking critically and independently about our world. It can be one more tool that allows (and encourages) you to assume active citizenship in your community, your society, and your world.

Our hope is that we can excite you about economics, and that the insights you develop will make useful and creative contributions to your pursuit of a rich and meaningful life.

4. Are there any objectives we have missed? What are they? Do these objectives make sense to you? Why? Why not? In what ways are these objectives consistent with (different from) what you expected from introductory economics?

Part One

Economics as a Tool for Critical Thinking in a Changing Global Economy

Will capitalism continue for another century? How did the United States come to have a capitalist economic system? In the near future, how will the U.S. economy change? Will it retain world economic leadership? Or will it begin to lag behind Western Europe and China? With the collapse of the Soviet Union, will socialism survive? Can something be done about the estimated billion people who live on less than $2 per day?

Why does the United States have such an advanced economy? Yet, in the midst of relative affluence, why do child hunger and poverty continue? Is there a reason that a black person is more likely than a white person to be poor and unemployed? Why do women continue to earn, on the average, about 80 percent of what men earn? When there is a boom in the U.S. stock market, who benefits? How does the United States produce so much food when less than 5 percent of the population is involved in food production?

Can global hunger and starvation be eliminated? Are the threats of environmental degradation—global warming, the depletion of the ozone layer, deforestation, and the buildup of toxic wastes—irreversible? Will there be another energy crisis?

How will *you* be employed in the future? Will you be rich? Poor? Will you have health insurance? Will the average U.S. workweek continue to rise while those in Europe fall?

These are all predominantly economic questions that affect each and every one of us in our day-to-day lives—either directly or indirectly. We read about these problems in the newspapers, we hear about them on the radio and the television, we listen to politicians talk about them, and we discuss them with our friends and neighbors. They are important and interesting. We have opinions about them—and answers to some or all of them.

Economics is essentially an organized body of knowledge about all of these issues, some of which are current and some of which are perpetual. It seeks to understand and explain these problems and to assist us in solving them. It helps us to think about these problems by indicating important variables and relationships. We hope that, in this course, you will learn to use economics to consider the problems that interest and affect you.

CHAPTER ONE

Economics as a Social Science

◼ Introduction

*W*hat is economics? And what can it do for us?

Economics *is the study of how the productive and distributive aspects of human life are organized. The productive aspects include the activities that result in the goods and services that satisfy our day-to-day demands as human beings—for automobiles, cereal, clothes, movies, and so on. The distributive aspects are the ways a society makes these goods and services available to people in the society who are willing to pay for them. Economics studies the history of production, distribution, and consumption of goods and services in different societies and countries, including the ways these aspects have changed over time. It seeks to help us understand the complexities of economic systems in the modern world.*

Economics, as a social science, is thus an accumulation of human knowledge about one particular segment of social life: production, distribution, and consumption. Like the other social sciences, including geography, political science, psychology, and sociology, economics focuses on only one part of a rich and complex social reality.

Definitions in This Book

Key economic concepts are indicated in the text by **bold type.** In addition, a glossary at the end of the text defines these important terms.

In this chapter, we examine economics as a social science. We will be concerned with its goals and methods, as well as its relevance to our lives. In addition, we will introduce briefly different fields in economics and the kinds of things that economists do. Finally, we will see that economists have some disagreements about what economics is and ought to be.

What Is Economics?

Teachers of economics are concerned about how best to teach economics. Their concern stems from the importance of economic knowledge in the modern world and the difficulties of teaching that knowledge to students in a way that will prove useful to them. Out of this concern, many economists have attempted to define precisely what the key elements of economic understanding are and to concentrate on teaching these. A reasonable list of key elements of economic understanding would include the following:

- Practicing a reasoned approach to economic issues
- Mastering basic economic concepts
- Possessing an overview of the economy
- Identifying important economic issues
- Applying the concepts to particular issues
- Reaching reasoned decisions on economic issues

These elements provide some insights into the nature of economics as the study of the productive and distributive aspects of human life. Economic understanding encompasses both a body of knowledge and a way of thinking about the economic aspects of social life. It is concerned with practicing a reasoned approach; that is, economics presents an organized and logical way of thinking about economic reality. It uses many basic concepts that focus our attention on key variables in economic activity. It provides us with an overall appreciation of the structure and complexity of the economic system in this country as well as those in other countries and in the global economy. It should help us identify the issues that will be important to us in our individual and social lives. In addition, economics helps us to reason and to draw conclusions about specific economic problems, their ramifications, and possible solutions.

In attempting to accomplish all of these tasks, one of the central concerns of economics is the development of **economic theory.** This task relates to the *method* of economics. While economics is concerned with social life and the vagaries of human beings, the development of theory requires that economics be as scientific as possible. An economic theory, for example, would try to explain why the prices of agricultural goods change from year to year as well as to predict how prices might change in the future.

Economists attempt to measure and collect facts about economic activity. In doing so, they try to discover certain patterns in the relationships between different components of economic life. When the facts suggest that these patterns express a constant relationship (in normal circumstances), economists may use them as the basis for economic theories. An example of such a theory is the theory of supply and demand. This theory emerged out of observations of the behavior of prices of goods in markets and the ways prices changed over time. The theories developed from efforts to explain these changes. We can use this economic theory to gain insight into how goods and services are valued by society's members, how costly they are to produce, and what price they will sell for in the society, given different circumstances.

The function of economic theory, therefore, is to allow us to examine certain aspects of economic life, discover more or less constant relationships between different economic variables, and predict possible economic events. For example, the theory of supply and demand tells us that, most of the time, a desired article in short supply will command a relatively high price. From this we can conclude (theorize) that if the supply of that article is reduced, then its price is likely to go up even further.

Note that such statements are based on an **assumption**—an *if* statement—followed by a conditional conclusion. Economists love to make assumptions. Much of their theory is based on similar assumptions. In the final analysis, however, their theories must be judged by whether their conclusions and predictions conform with what actually happens in economic reality. In the case of supply-and-demand theory, frequent examples enable us to check the validity of the conclusions and predictions of this economic theory.

For example, in 1973, when the Middle Eastern oil-producing countries embargoed shipments of oil to the United States, Western Europe, and Japan, the supply of oil decreased, and the price *did* increase. Likewise, when there are good crops of wheat in the United States, the price of wheat is likely to go down; when crops are bad because of the weather, the price of wheat goes up. Whenever a freeze occurs in Florida, it sharply reduces the supply of Florida oranges, and this is followed by an increase in the price of oranges. In 2000, oil

European motorists responding to fuel price increases in 2000.
(© Virginia Mayo/AP/Wide World Photos)

prices rose again as oil companies raised prices and the Middle Eastern oil-producing countries, now fearing lower returns, reduced supplies to Europe and the United States. Higher gas prices prompted protests in Europe and complaints in the United States about the cost of filling cars, trucks, and fuel-guzzling sport utility vehicles. From 2004 through 2006, demand by Chinese and Indian industry and growing concerns about Middle East oil supplies sent prices skyrocketing. In each of these cases, economic reality conforms with economic theory.

These examples highlight the *relevance* of economics. Economics and economic theories are concerned with problems and activities that are important to all of us as individuals and to our societies. The scope of economics can be international, national, regional, local, or personal. The problems and activities that are the subject matter of economics include such pressing concerns as inflation, productivity, supplies of natural resources, efficiency, debt, unemployment, technological development, product distribution, advertising, poverty, alienation, the allocation of scarce resources, income redistribution, taxation, war, and a host of others. Economics identifies such economic problems, describes their ramifications, hypothesizes about their causes, predicts their future development, and prescribes solutions to them. In so doing, economics can build our understanding of the fundamental economic aspects of our social lives.

One Method for Economic Theory

Milton Friedman, a Nobel Prize winner in economics, has argued for a particular method in the construction of economic theory. This methodology, which he calls "positive economics," has four basic components:

1. The process begins with a set of reasonable *assumptions* about some aspect of economic behavior. For example, in Part 3, one of the most important assumptions that we will make is that the primary objective of firms is the maximization of profits.

2. Next, we try to identify some important economic *concepts* and construct some variables to measure them. For the firm, we will measure profits, costs, revenues, marginal costs, marginal revenues, and other variables. These are all functions of the economic activity of the firm.

3. Based on the assumptions we have made and the concepts we have identified, we develop some *hypotheses* and logical deductions about economic behavior. In the case of the firm, we theorize that the firm maximizes profits at a rate of output where its marginal costs equal its marginal revenues. In Part 3, we will demonstrate this in more detail.

4. The final step is to *test the theory*. Does the hypothesis conform with observable events? When marginal costs do not equal marginal revenues, does the firm alter its decisions so that it can increase its profits?

Friedman emphasizes that this method produces abstract economic theory; it simplifies and generalizes. The purpose, however, is to create a model of the economy that will help us evaluate and analyze the real-world economy. A model is an abstraction, or simplification, of the economy, not an exact replica of it.

Source: "Four Basic Components of Positive Economics" from Friedman, CAPITALISM AND FREEDOM. Copyright © University of Chicago Press. Used with permission.

Economics and Economists

There are many fields within economics, some of which will be introduced in this book. Economic history, reviewed briefly in Chapter 3, focuses on how and why economic activity has changed over time. Urban economics focuses on analyzing the economic operation and problems of cities. Microeconomics is concerned primarily with the activities of smaller economic units, such as the household or the firm, and markets for goods and services. Macroeconomics has the much broader subject of the operation and health of an entire national economy. International economics deals with economic relationships and activities on a global scale. Economic thought treats the development of ideas by economists through the years. Economic development concentrates on theories and problems associated with the economic growth and maturation of national economies. Public policy economics is concerned with the analysis of proposals for dealing with public problems. Political economy highlights the relationships between economic and political institutions and how they affect each other. This by no means exhausts the list of the different fields in economics.

Given this wide variety of fields in economics, economists do many different things. Many people trained in economics as a discipline become teachers of economics in high schools, colleges, or universities. Many work in businesses, informing decision makers on current and future economic realities. Since World War II, an increasing number of economists have found employment in government at the local, state, and federal levels. Economists also work for consulting firms, labor unions, public interest or lobbying groups, and international organizations.

With this diversity of employment experiences (and hence allegiances and perspectives), it should not be very surprising to find a healthy amount of "controversy" within the social science of economics. Economists, despite their efforts to build economic theory, often disagree with one another. They may differ about which problems are most important (or even, sometimes, that there are problems!), what the causes of a problem are, and which solutions to a problem are the best. Controversy in economics reflects controversy in life.

Nevertheless, most economists accept a large core of economic ideas. We will study many of these ideas in this book. In addition, economists are unified by the goal of economics: building knowledge about the economic aspects of life.

Much of the debate among economists about what economics is and should be concerns its scope. The famous English economist Alfred Marshall (1842–1924) thought economics could be one of the most precise and scientific of the social sciences because it deals with observable and measurable data in the form of prices, quantities produced and sold, and incomes. In his *Principles of Economics*, he wrote:

> The advantage which economics has over other branches of social science appears then to arise from the fact that its special field of work gives rather larger opportunities for exact methods than any other branch. It concerns itself chiefly with those desires, aspirations and other affections of human nature, the outward manifestations of which appear as incentives to action in such a form that the force or

quantity of the incentives can be estimated and measured with some approach to accuracy; and which therefore are in some degree amenable to treatment by scientific machinery. An opening is made for the methods and the tests of science as soon as the force of a person's motives—not the motives themselves—can be approximately measured by the sum of money, which he will just give up in order to secure a desired satisfaction; or again by the sum which is just required to induce him to undergo a certain fatigue.

Other economists, however, have been less convinced by this argument. They point out that economics, as one of the social sciences, cannot divorce itself from the society in which it exists. The efforts of human beings to understand reality must necessarily be influenced by morality, ideology, and value judgments. In other words, economics cannot be totally scientific because the economist's understanding of the subject matter is affected by his or her evaluation of, opinions about, and conclusions concerning social issues. Economics as a body of thought functions to preserve, protect, and/or challenge existing social reality—as well as help us to understand it. For some economists, then, economics should be a part of the effort to understand *and to improve* social existence. Joan Robinson (1903–1983), another English economist, wrote in *Freedom and Necessity:*

> The methods to which the natural sciences owe their success—controlled experiment and exact observation of continually recurring phenomena—cannot be applied to the study of human beings by human beings. So far, no equally successful method of establishing reliable natural laws has been suggested. Certainly, the social sciences should not be unscientific. Their practitioners should not jump to conclusions on inadequate evidence or propound circular statements that are true by definition as though they had some factual content; when they disagree they should not resort to abuse like theologians or literary critics, but should calmly set about to investigate the nature of the difference and to propose a plan of research to resolve it. . . . The function of social science is quite different from that of the natural sciences—it is to provide society with an organ of self-consciousness. Every interconnected group of human beings has to have an ideology—that is, a conception of what is the proper way to behave and the permissible pattern of relationships in family, economic, and political life.

For Robinson, then, economics must attempt to be scientific and rigorous, but since it is also concerned with the effort to create a better society, it must also devote itself to exploring areas that are more philosophical. It must recognize its ideological elements, and that, as one of the social sciences, it is also involved as a tool of analysis in the formation of public policy.

Along these lines, economists often divide their discipline between "economics" and what is called **political economy.** Economics in this sense is more concerned with explaining what can be measured and with developing theories about "purely" economic relationships. Political economy, on the other hand, is more concerned with the relationships of the economic system and its institutions to the rest of society and social development. It is sensitive to the influence of noneconomic factors such as political and social institutions, morality, and ideology in determining economic events. It thus has a broader focus than economics.

1. "The function of social science . . . is to provide society with an organ of self-consciousness." What does this mean? How does economics do this?
2. What, according to Robinson, is an ideology? What role do ideologies play in social development?
3. What does Robinson think is the task of economics as a social science? Do you agree with her or not? Would Alfred Marshall?

Paradigms and Ideologies

Not only do economists disagree about what economics is and should be, they often disagree about which economic problems are important, which theories are correct, and which economic policies are best. This is especially true over time, as the economic problems a society is likely to face change with changing conditions. Along with changes in economic problems and economic institutions, economic theories have also changed. The changes in economic theory and the differences among economists have two results that are useful to keep in mind while studying economics: First, there are different and sometimes contesting kinds of economic theory. Second, different economists begin their study with different assumptions.

The Realm of Theory

Different periods of economic history (and different economic systems) have given rise to different types of economic theories. New types of economic conditions and economic institutions have required different systems of thought and explanation. Stated slightly differently, as crises have developed in economic matters when the old gave way to the new, economic institutions changed. The previous theories and notions became inadequate to explain the new conditions and problems, so economic thought also changed.

Thomas Kuhn, in *The Structure of Scientific Revolutions*, refers to such changes in scientific theory as changes in **paradigms.** A paradigm structures thought about a certain aspect of nature, life, or society. It delineates the scope of a discipline (the questions to be asked about a certain subject and the phenomena to be explained), as well as the method of the discipline (the criteria for accepting explanations).

Paradigms are usually widely accepted as providing a coherent and correct understanding of some aspect of life. However, as time passes, natural and social conditions may change, and new interpretations and new facts may become known. If so, the existing paradigm may be challenged or may be inadequate to explain reality, and a new and more widely accepted paradigm will eventually be developed. An example of this in the field of astronomy was the replacement of the Ptolemaic by the Copernican paradigm. The Copernican paradigm is now widely accepted, because it conforms with what we now know and observe—that the planets revolve around the sun. Another example is the explorer Christopher Columbus, who was sure (along with others) that the earth wasn't flat!

Likewise, as economic crises occur and economic conditions change, one economic paradigm replaces another. Before the Great Depression of the 1930s, the dominant economic theory was classical economics, which argued that a laissez-faire, self-regulating market economic system would eliminate economic instability through the flexibility of markets. If overproduction of goods led to a decrease in production and an increase in unemployment, then the markets would respond to correct the situation. Prices would fall and stimulate consumption of those goods, thus eliminating the surplus. Wages would fall and stimulate the hiring of unemployed workers. To explain why overproduction or underconsumption would be unlikely in a laissez-faire market economic system, classical economics relied on Say's law, developed by the French economist J. B. Say (1767–1832), which held that supply creates its own demand. Say theorized that incomes paid out in the process of production of needed goods would always be sufficient to buy what was produced. The flexibility of prices and wages in self-regulating markets would ensure this result. However, when economists observed the severity and persistence of the Great Depression, they questioned Say's law. Consequently, they turned to a new paradigm, Keynesian economics (about which we will learn more in Part 4), which offered an explanation for why depressions occur and what can be done about them.

Not only do paradigms change over time, two contending paradigms sometimes seek to explain the same aspect of reality. Examining the same events and facts but differing in the use of key concepts and relationships, these contending paradigms offer conflicting (or at least differing) interpretations. At one time or another, or in different places, one or the other might be dominant.

An example of conflicting paradigms is the contrast between orthodox economics and Marxian economics. **Orthodox economics** accepts the assumptions of a competitive market economy and builds a theory around those assumptions. **Marxian economics** assumes a critical stance toward the existing market economic system and attempts to discover how it will and can be changed. Orthodox economics accepts capitalism, and Marxian economics criticizes capitalism and argues for socialism. A third paradigm, **institutional economics,** bridges Marxian and orthodox economics by focusing on the role of changing institutions and power in influencing economic affairs. Throughout this book, we will encounter these different paradigms as they attempt to explain economic reality.

The Realm of the Economist

Economists are human beings with differing ideas, theories, assumptions, and ideologies. As economic conditions and institutions have changed, so have economists' ideas, theories, assumptions, and ideologies. In different times and spaces, economists have differed. And in the *same* time and space, economists disagree. One way of clarifying this is to examine **ideology.** E. K. Hunt, in *Property and Prophets*, defines an ideology this way:

> [A set of] ideas and beliefs that tend to justify morally a society's social and economic relationships. Most members of a society internalize the ideology and thus believe that their functional roles, as well as those of others, are morally correct,

and that the method by which society divides its produce is fair. This common belief gives society its cohesiveness and vitality. Lack of it creates turmoil and strife—and ultimately revolution if the differences are deep enough.

At different times, different ideologies may dominate. At one time, Confucianism was the ideology of China. Later, the dominant ideology in China was that of Maoism and socialism. Catholicism and a concern with the next world was at the core of an ideology that dominated Western Europe; later, individualism and materialism held sway.

Ideologies influence the development of theory. For example, the ideology of individualism promoted the development of the economic theory of classical liberalism, and both accompanied the emergence of capitalism as an economic system. More recently, the combination of the ideologies of liberal democracy, the benevolent state, and individualism promoted the acceptance of Keynesian economics along with the emergence of welfare or state capitalism. In the 1990s, with an increasing government presence in the economy, some economists (and politicians) with a conservative ideology argued for greater reliance on market forces.

Different ideologies concerning the goals of a society and an economic system may conflict. For example, differences in ideology underlie the division of Western economists today into three broad groups: liberal, conservative, and radical. Each group has its own ideas, theories, and ideologies. These are described in the next section.

4. What is your ideology?

5. Compare and contrast Hunt's definition of ideology with that of Joan Robinson.

Conservative, Liberal, and Radical Economics

Milton Friedman (1912–2006) was a prominent conservative economist. John Maynard Keynes offered a liberal solution to the 1930s crisis of capitalism. Adam Smith, in his day, was a radical, as was Karl Marx.

What are some of the essential elements of conservative, liberal, and radical ideologies and theories? What are the differences among them? How do they interpret different economic issues, and what different solutions do they offer for economic problems?

Conservative economists focus on the operation of markets in a capitalist, free market economic system. They argue that private ownership of resources under capitalism assures economic and political freedom for individuals in that society. Individuals make their own decisions for their own private gains. Markets, where goods and services are exchanged, will then operate to produce economic well-being and growth for the society and the individuals within it. Markets, through the action of competition, enforce a result that is the best for everyone and uses resources efficiently. Consequently, conservatives see the profit motive as being one of the most important and positive aspects of capitalism. Firms, to meet their own interests in competitive markets, must produce exactly what consumers want at the lowest price. One further implication of conservative economics is that, since markets operate efficiently and produce economic growth, the government need not take an active role in the operation of the economy (beyond some important, fundamental obligations—see Chapter 13). In fact, most conservatives argue that excessive government intervention in the economy is the source of many of our economic problems.

The roots of conservative economics can be found in eighteenth-century classical liberalism. Beginning in Chapter 3, we will encounter the emergence of this body of thought and explore this theory in more detail. Modern examples of conservative economics include "free market" economics, supply-side economics, and monetarism. Conservative economists include Milton Friedman, author of *Capitalism and Freedom* and a Nobel Prize winner; Alan Greenspan, former chairman of the Federal Reserve System; and Robert Barro, *Business Week* columnist and Harvard economics professor. Ronald Reagan and John McCain are examples of politicians who believe in the ideas and the theories of conservative economics. Much of the advertising and educational efforts of corporate America utilize the logic and conclusions of conservative economics. *The Wall Street Journal* and *The Economist* newspapers take a consistently conservative position in their editorials.

Liberal economists accept the structure of the capitalist economic system and its basic institutions of private property and markets. They also agree with conservatives that, for the most part, this free-market system tends to produce efficiency and economic growth and that it protects individual freedom. However, they admit that the operation of the market system may produce problems. For example, it fosters an unequal distribution of income and economic power, often neglects some of the by-products of economic production and exchange such as pollution, sometimes fails to provide necessary goods and services that can't be produced profitably, and can't guarantee economic stability. Liberals then usually point out that there is a solution to these problems that does not interfere with the basic structure of the economic system; they give the responsibility for addressing these problems to the government. The federal government, in particular, can attempt to redistribute income, and it can attempt to regulate the production of pollution in the economy. All levels of government can provide "public" goods such as parks, roads, schools, and police and fire protection. Finally, the federal government can take responsibility for trying to achieve economic prosperity and price stability and to avoid economic depressions. For liberals, the market works economic wonders, but they are qualified wonders; the active involvement of governments in some aspects of the market economy can improve its performance.

The theoretical underpinnings of most liberal economists can be found in Keynesian economics. Some liberals also find the ideas of Thorstein Veblen and other institutionalist economists to be helpful in framing their understanding of the economy. We will encounter these theories again in Parts 2 and 4. John Kenneth Galbraith of Harvard University wrote a number of important books about economics and the economy from a Keynesian and institutionalist perspective. Paul Krugman, who teaches at Princeton University, is another liberal economist and the author of *The Great Unraveling: Losing Our Way in the New Century*. Jimmy Carter, Bill Clinton, and John Kerry are politicians who utilize the ideas and theories of liberal economics. *Business Week* magazine usually presents a relatively liberal editorial policy.

Radical economists tend to be very critical of the structures, institutions, operation, and results of capitalist economic systems. They do not deny that capitalism has been quite successful over the past several centuries in increasing the productive capacity of Western nations and the average standard of living for their inhabitants. However, radical economists suggest that the very operation of a market system based on private ownership creates different classes of people in capitalist societies. On the one hand are those who own productive resources, organize and control productive activity, and have the goal of earning profits for themselves. On the other hand are people who do not own any productive property and who rely on the sale of their mental and/or physical labor to earn a living. Radicals are quick to point out that there are inherent conflicts between these two groups over wages, working conditions, product safety, and economic power. It is this basic class structure of the society, radicals argue, that produces economic inequality, exploitation, and alienation. In addition, they conclude that capitalist production and growth are inherently unable to provide for public goods, ignore the social costs of productive activity, and lead to eco-

Lower East Side of Manhattan, New York
(© SuperStock.)

nomic instability. Consequently, the efforts of the state (all levels of government) to deal with these problems are merely Band-Aid solutions because they do not address the root causes—private ownership, production for profit, and a class society.

In the view of radical economists, solving modern economic problems such as poverty, income inequality, discrimination, and pollution requires alterations in the basic economic institutions of the society. Many radicals believe in nationalization, and many want to limit the existing power of corporations. Many would advocate much more significant redistribution of income in the United States (and the world). Some even call for social ownership and control of productive resources in pursuit of social goals of production.

Radical economics finds its roots in both institutional and Marxian economics. Although many radicals find the ideas of both Keynesian and conservative economics useful in understanding how capitalism and markets work, radicals depart in their evaluation of the operation and results of capitalism. For them, the negative aspects outweigh the positive. Samuel Bowles, David Gordon, and Thomas Weisskopf are radical economists who wrote *Beyond the Wasteland: A Democratic Alternative to Economic Decline*. This book contains their analysis of U.S. economic experience and presents a radical economic program for restructuring the economy and addressing many of its long-run problems. Barry Bluestone and Bennett Harrison, authors of *Growing Prosperity: The Battle for Growth with Equity in the Twenty-first Century*, have focused on the problem of plant closings and runaway shops from a radical perspective and have offered some solutions. Similarly, in his book *Contours of Descent: U.S. Economic Fractures and the Landscape of Global Austerity*, University of Massachusetts economist Robert Pollin argues that free-market policies have produced extensive poverty and increasing inequality. Along with Robert Pollin, writers for periodicals such as *Mother Jones*, *Z*, and *Dollars and Sense* express a radical point of view. Many of the ideas about economic priorities and policy articulated by Ralph Nader in his 2000 and 2004 presidential campaigns—for instance, increased income redistribution, significantly reduced military spending, and the promotion of environmentally responsible economic policies—are compatible with radical economics. The Green Party has a radical platform.

Conservatives, Liberals, and Radicals on Poverty

From these brief descriptions of conservative, liberal, and radical economics, it should be possible to identify the basic approach that each would take to understanding a particular economic problem and suggesting solutions for it. But let's develop a single example: poverty. Conservatives tend to argue that poverty exists because of the particular attributes of individuals and their inability to earn high incomes in labor markets. Either they have the wrong skills or few skills, or they don't try or work hard enough. The solution, then, is either "It's appropriate that their economic rewards are low," or "They need to develop their marketable skills." If the society decides that it wants to facilitate the reduction of poverty, the most appropriate way might be through education. Individuals have to develop skills and work harder. Conservatives would not support anti-poverty programs because they represent government interference with markets. Conservatives think that poverty can be reduced effectively only by the participation of responsible individuals in free markets.

Liberals maintain that, very often, the poverty of individuals is a result of circumstances beyond their control. Consequently, not only would liberals support a public role for education (and job training) to increase people's marketable skills, but, in addition, they would favor direct income redistribution to increase the purchasing power of poor people. This would reduce the burdens of poverty, but it also might create the chance for people to move out of poverty. Liberals would support food stamps and welfare for the poor.

Radicals generally would support governmental redistribution programs and certainly would oppose efforts to take economic benefits away from poor people. However, they would argue that redistribution programs have a very limited effect in eliminating poverty. Governmental programs have reduced poverty, but given the source of unequal incomes in private ownership of productive resources and the fundamental individualism of capitalism, the system cannot tolerate the amount of redistribution that would be necessary to eliminate poverty. Only massive redistribution of income to poor people or a radical restructuring of the institutions and goals of the economic system could significantly reduce the incidence of poverty in the United States.

The analyses of current economic problems are distinctive based on different ideologies and theories. And these differences are reflected in the variety of proposed solutions. One of the fascinating aspects of modern economics is the controversy that surrounds our understanding of and efforts to deal with these problems. Conservative, liberal, and radical economics have all contributed to that analysis.

6. Which set of economic ideas do you think is dominant in the United States today?

7. Paul Sweezy, a U.S. Marxian economist, has written, "It seems to me that from a scientific point of view the question of choosing between approaches can be answered quite simply. Which more accurately reflects the fundamental characteristics of social reality which is under analysis?" Critically evaluate each of the different perspectives with respect to that statement. How are your answers affected by your own beliefs?

8. What is the difference between theory and ideology?

Conclusion

There are many different fields within economics, the social science that focuses on building an understanding of how the economy—production, distribution, and consumption of goods of services—works. Economists do many different things, not the least of which is disagree with each other while at the same time working together to build economic theory. One observation that they would probably all agree on is the tremendous growth in a global economy, to which we turn in the next chapter.

Review Questions

1. What is economics? Is that what you thought economics is (or should be)?
2. What is the goal of economic theory? What is the test of an economic theory?
3. Why do economists disagree?
4. What is a paradigm? In your life have you ever replaced one paradigm with another?
5. What are the main differences among conservative, liberal, and radical economists?
6. Paradigms can offer contending explanations of the same reality. Sometimes the contention can reflect intense political, social, and economic struggles. Develop some examples of new paradigms for which the people suggesting them have been subjected to neglect, harassment, ridicule, or even punishment.
7. How might conservative, liberal and radical economists respond to an issue like global climate change?

CHAPTER TWO

Exploring the Emerging Global Economy

■ Introduction

Although we have come to take it for granted, virtually everything we do is directly or indirectly involved with the international economy. To understand how this economy affects your life, just look around. Take five minutes and list things that surround you in your room—shoes, clothes, stereo, furniture, lamps, radio, TV, computer, DVD player.

Even a quick listing likely shows how truly interdependent the global economy has become. This trend is expected to accelerate in the coming years. As we will see throughout this book, the process of technological change and innovation is bringing the world closer and closer together every day.

This chapter will introduce a few fundamental concepts and explore the dynamics of the global economy, which we will develop in greater detail in later chapters. Without these concepts and this perspective, it would be hard to understand much of your daily life. Indeed, the changes taking place right now are creating a new global economy that will determine not only how you live, but also the kind of work you will be doing after you graduate. Most experts suggest that you will have not one but several distinct careers in the future, each largely shaped by the new global economy.

The chapter also explores some forces that have shaped the global economy. The global economy emerged in the post–World War II period, from 1944 to the mid-1970s, but it has undergone a fundamental transformation since then. Much of this change has been driven by technological developments. Technological advances have altered industries and careers, generating new jobs and making others obsolete. At the same time, growing resource use has created tensions among policy makers, producers, and environmentalists.

1. Where were the items in your room made? What about the coffee, tea, juice, or fruit you had for breakfast? How about lunch and dinner? Did you ride a bike or drive a car powered by petroleum today? Where do you work? Your parents? How much of this work is dependent on the international sector? Do you or your parents have investments or a pension fund with investments in international funds? Where do those funds originate? Now make a list of all of the countries that are a part of your daily life. Impressive, isn't it?

Globalization: Making a Big World Smaller

If you are a college student between the ages of eighteen and twenty-five, the world has changed significantly since you were born. The decades of the 1980s and 1990s brought transitions in the political, economic, technological, and environmental arenas. Some of these changes continue to reshape our work and nonwork lives, much as the early Industrial Revolution did during the mid-1800s. This revolution is fueling increased globalization.

Globalization has made a big world smaller. Globalization affects trade, finance, production, communications, and technological change. When we look at a world map (see Figure 2.1), we need to think about how this global community of people and nations is being systematically drawn closer together. At Distributed Service Systems, a small full-service computer company located in Reading, Pennsylvania, a technical consultant sits at a terminal and solves assembly line production problems at Carpenter Technology steel plants in India, China, Mexico, and Taiwan. At the same time, a major U.S. global man-

FIGURE 2.1 The World

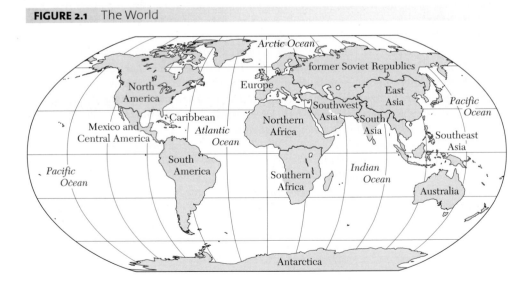

ufacturer in Green Bay, Wisconsin, has a small staff of foreign currency traders working twenty-four hours a day to manage the firm's global financial needs and resources.

Since 1980, world **exports** (goods leaving a country) have increased by over 200 percent, and U.S. **imports** (goods coming into the country) have increased more than five-fold. In 1960, total U.S. trade equaled 9 percent of **gross domestic product (GDP)**, and Gross National Product (GNP), both of which measure the annual output of goods and services; in 2004, it amounted to 26 percent. Nations have found it cheaper and more efficient to trade more with each other than to produce all their products at home.

The World Economy

The global economy has been growing at a rapid rate and has been undergoing a profound transformation during the past two decades. The world's population surpassed the six billion mark as we entered the twenty-first century. Demographers project that four out of five new births in the next twenty years will take place in the developing countries of the world, not the richest industrial countries. As can be seen in Table 2.1, China and India each has a population of one billion or higher and together represent approximately one-third of the people on the planet. However, the wealth of these countries—measured by their gross national income—is not in proportion to the size of their populations. In 2005 China's GNI was $2.3 trillion and India's was $793 billion, while the GNIs of the much less-populated European Union, the United States, and Japan registered $9.9 trillion, $13.0 trillion, and $5.0 trillion, respectively.

From Table 2.2, it is apparent that nations with larger GNIs and smaller populations have a higher GNI per person. In 2005 Japan's GNI per person was $38,980, whereas China's was $1,740 and India's $720. In addition, in 2001, 46.7 percent of China's populations earned less than $2 per day, as did 80 percent of India's population in 2000.

TABLE 2.1   Population and GNI for Selected Countries

Country	Population (2005)	GNI (2002)
China	1.3 billion	$ 2.3 trillion
India	1.1 billion	793.0 billion
European Union	310.6 million	9.9 trillion
United States	300.0 million	13.0 trillion
Indonesia	220.6 million	282.2 billion
Brazil	186.4 million	664.1 billion
Russia*	143.2 million	613.1 billion
Japan	127.9 million	4.9 trillion
South Africa	45.1 million	224.1 billion

Source: Data from World Bank, Data Profile Tables, 2006, www.worldbank.org.

*Russian Federation

TABLE 2.2 Economic Trends in "Emerging 9" (E-9) Nations

Country	GNI/Capita (2005)	Population Earning < $2/day (year)
United States	$45,740	—
Japan	38,980	—
Germany	34,580	—
South Africa	4,960	34.1% (2000)
Russia*	4,460	12.1% (2000)
Brazil	3,460	21.2% (2003)
China	1,740	46.7% (2001)
Indonesia	1,280	46.7% (2002)
India	720	79.9% (1999–2000)

Source: Data from World Bank, Data Profile Tables (GNP/capita), 2006; World Bank, World Development Index, 2006.

*Russian Federation

Nevertheless, over the past two decades some of these countries with lower per capita GNI and large numbers of very poor people have recorded some of the most impressive annual economic growth rates. As can be seen in Figure 2.2, in 2004, among developing and emerging nations, China was the fastest-growing country at 10 percent, followed by Argentina and Turkey, both at 9 percent.

The dynamics of globalization and economic growth during the past three decades have been driven in part by the rapid growth of the international trade in goods and services. Between 1995 and 2000, world export growth, merchandise production and global GNP growth were significant. All three growth indicators declined in 2002, however, as the U.S. economic recession had worldwide implications. Europe and the Western Hemisphere struggled the most during this period, whereas Asia, Japan, and the East Asian Tigers continued to boom with export growth in the 8–10 percent range.

According to the World Trade Organization, the extra-EU countries led exports in world merchandise trade for 2004, and the United States was the leading importer. Extra-EU exported goods valued at $1,203.8 billion represented almost 20 percent of world goods exports. The United States imported goods worth $1,525.5 billion, or 21.8 percent of world goods imports. (See Tables 2.3 and Table 2.4.)

Global Investment Trends

Finance and investment have gone global as well. To finance trade among so many different nations, a foreign exchange market has emerged with daily transactions of more than $2.0 trillion. During the late 1980s, global flows of foreign direct investment rose 29 percent annually—approximately three times the growth in world trade. Global expansion is driven partly by the search for new markets, but it is also driven by diversifying risk and searching for profits all

FIGURE 2.2 GDP Growth in Selected Countries

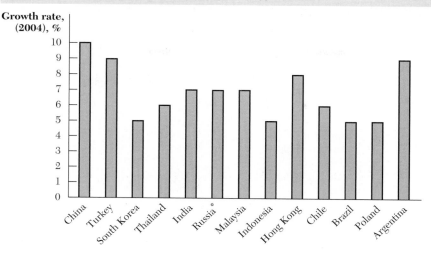

Source: Data from World Bank, Data Profile Tables, 2004; The CIA World Factbook, 2005, www.cia.gov.V

*Russian Federation

over the world. By one estimate, roughly 40 percent of revenues of large investment houses are now made outside the United States. Big firms can borrow money in London or in Tokyo as easily as they can in New York. Electronic banking lets companies shift money from country to country with unprecedented ease. It also lets you withdraw money from a bank machine in Buenos Aires or Santiago with the same bank card used at your local bank. In Buenos Aires, you must decide if you want pesos or dollars from the bank machine.

2. There are advantages and disadvantages to the rapid movement of capital (money) in the new world of global finance. What do you suppose some of these may be?

In the 1950s and 1960s, many big companies had headquarters around the world, often with separate production facilities. Today, however, these firms find the source of their comparative advantage in being able to manage information and knowledge, linking their facilities and making strategic decisions about what to produce where. Production can be quickly moved from Detroit to Singapore to take advantage not only of lower wages but also movements in exchange rates.

Globalization has been facilitated by dramatic changes in communication. Managers in a plant in Mexico can access the same databases in Louisville,

TABLE 2.3 Leading Exporters

Rank	Exporters	Value ($ billions)	Share (%)	Annual Percentage Change
1	Extra-EU	1203.8	18.1	21
2	United States	818.8	8.9	13
3	China	593.3	6.5	35
4	Japan	565.8	8.4	3
5	Canada	316.5	3.5	16
6	Hong Kong, China	265.5	2.9	16
	domestic exports	20.0	0.2	2
	re-exports	245.6	2.7	17
7	Republic of Korea	253.8	2.8	31
8	Mexico	189.1	2.1	14
9	Russian Federation	183.5	2.0	35
10	Taipei, Chinese	182.4	2.0	21
11	Singapore	178.6	2.0	25
	domestic exports	98.6	1.1	34
	re-exports	81.0	0.9	24

Source: Data from World Trade Organization, 2005 International Trade Statistics. © 2005 WTO. Used with permission.

Kentucky, as a domestic manager does from a plant in California. Paper documents fly through fax machines, electronic communications via the Internet and e-mail take seconds instead of weeks, and advances in satellite communications make teleconferencing cheaper and more efficient than business trips.

TABLE 2.4 Leading Importers

Rank	Importers	Value ($ billions)	Share (%)	Annual Percentage Change
1	United States	1525.1	16.1	17
2	Extra-EU	1203.8	18.1	21
3	China	561.2	5.9	36
4	Japan	454.5	4.8	19
5	Canada	279.8	2.9	14
6	Hong Kong, China	272.9	2.9	17
	(retained imports)*	27.3	0.3	13
7	Republic of Korea	224.5	2.4	26
8	Mexico	206.4	2.2	16
9	Taipei, Chinese	168.4	1.8	32
10	Singapore	163.9	1.7	28
	(retained imports)*	82.8	0.9	30

Source: Data from World Trade Organization, 2005 International Trade Statistics. © 2005 WTO. Used with permission.
*"Retained imports" represent imported goods that are retained in the country rather than re-exported to other countries.

FIGURE 2.3   Ford Escort, the First World Car

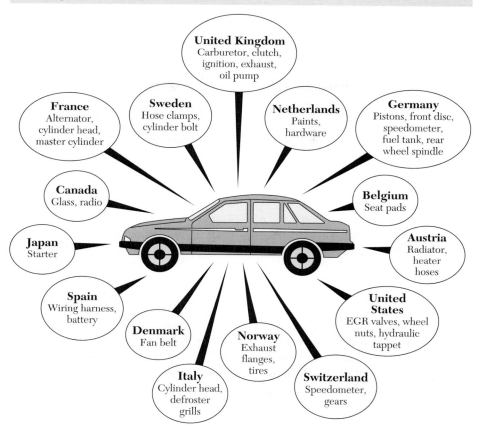

Source: World Development Report, 1990; U.S. Automobile Industry, 1980 (Washington, DC: U.S. Government Printing Office, p. 57).

Globalization has made the world a bigger playing field, including many more players, yet with a smaller, more tightly knit international production system.

Globalization has also transformed the economic environment of individual consumers and employees. It has changed the products you buy. The orange you ate for breakfast was as likely to be from Brazil as Florida. The Ford Escort was one of the first genuine world cars in that it was built with parts from dozens of countries, such as the ones identified in Figure 2.3. Imagine the kind of organization, communication, management, transportation, labor, and technology required to accomplish such a project. As a result, globalization has changed the kind of work you do. The U.S. worker today is more likely to be involved in information systems than assembly line production. And globalization opens up new opportunities for investment. Why limit yourself to lower returns at home if the rewards abroad are great? Many savings, retirement, and pension funds are being invested in foreign countries.

Globalization even reaches beyond the economy to culture. It has in some cases promoted cultural homogeneity (Will Smith plays well in Rio) but also introduces new trends.

Globalization's Winners and Losers

Globalization is not good news for everyone. Some have gained in the global economy, but others have lost. If you were born in one of the great U.S. steel-producing cities such as Youngstown, Ohio, you might have seen the city experience an economic depression in the mid- to late-1980s as many of the steel mills closed, thousands of workers lost their jobs, and the economic base of many communities died. This raised many questions. Why did the steel mills close or relocate? Where did they go? Why did they go?

These are complicated questions to answer. From the end of World War II (1945) to the early 1960s, the United States was the most powerful economic player in the world. The United States had the most advanced technologies, the most educated workforce, and access to inexpensive raw materials (especially oil) and markets. By the early 1970s, this had all begun to change. Western Europe (especially West Germany), Japan, and many so-called newly industrialized countries (NICs) such as Mexico, Brazil, Taiwan, South Korea, and Malaysia began to seriously compete with the United States. These countries adopted and developed competitive technologies and new organizational and management approaches, giving them a decisive advantage over production in the United States. In addition, wage rates in the NICs ranged from $0.60 to $1.00 per hour, making it nearly impossible for the advanced industrial countries to compete with wage rates (including benefits) of $12 to $36 per hour. Today we see jobs in information technology moving to India just as jobs in the steel industry moved abroad two decades before.

Revolutionary technological changes in production, transportation, communications, and information systems enabled firms to produce and market a good or service anywhere in the world. With these advanced systems in place, the cost of labor became one of the most critical competitive variables. Developing countries have relatively low labor costs and few labor unions.

In the late 1980s, U.S. steelmakers were forced to confront nearly a decade of slow growth and the low demand for steel resulting from a highly valued U.S. dollar driving U.S. steel prices above the prices of foreign competitors. Steel mills in Ohio and Pennsylvania relocated to Mexico, Brazil, and South Korea, implementing new technology and using low-wage labor to produce the same, if not better, products. And, in 2004 we saw banks, insurance companies, and retailers move computer programming and call centers to Bangladore, taking advantage of much lower wages through outsourcing these jobs.

This is but one example of the globalization of production. Most U.S. firms have had to become more and more global. These corporations in the sectors of manufacturing, transportation, communications, finance, and banking utilize computer and information systems to expand their operations all over the globe. They find themselves competing head-to-head with giants from every other country. In the 1990s, the United States, Japan, and a unified Germany dominated the global economy, while the collapse of the former Soviet Union along with the transition to market economies in Eastern Europe, Asia, and Latin America symbolized a great transformation that—despite several crises and interruptions—is still under way.

Making sense of this global economic revolution involves understanding some of the basic concepts of international trade and finance. Why do nations trade? How is trade financed? What are the institutional rules that guide trade and financial transactions between countries? Why does it make sense to produce the same product around the world? What are the costs of globalized production? Let's see how economists answer these questions.

Why Nations Trade

International trade has a long and illustrious history. As far back as classical antiquity, nations have traded. The major reason for this is that both parties gain from the process. Another reason is that nations are increasingly interdependent. No nation can be truly self-sufficient without great expense or sacrifice. The United States, for example, is one of the most self-sufficient countries in the world, yet it depends on imports for virtually all of its bauxite, diamonds, tin, coffee, nickel, manganese, rubber, tungsten, bananas, gold, platinum, and chromium, to name but a few commodities. The last two—crucial in the production of jet engines and many other industrial processes—are nonexistent in the United States and come almost exclusively from South Africa.

Every nation needs imports, albeit some more than others. To pay for those imports, it needs to export goods. All nations therefore need international trade. Indeed, it is now virtually impossible to buy anything in the United States that is not produced at least partially abroad. For example, about the only part of an IBM computer that is made in the United States is the outer case. Congresswoman Louise Slaughter (D., New York) once asked the Xerox Corporation to supply her with a copying machine that was completely produced in the United States. Xerox couldn't. Similarly, although VCR technology was invented in the United States, it has never been possible to purchase even one videocassette recorder made in the United States; all are made abroad, as are virtually all color television sets. Automobiles, once produced in Detroit, are now an amalgamation of parts produced around the world.

3. Can you think of some other imported products and resources that the United States depends on? List them.

The Theory of Comparative Advantage

In one sense, international trade is very simple: one nation—given its natural resource endowment, level of technology, and level of development of its labor force—specializes in whatever it can produce relatively most efficiently and trades that product to another nation for whatever the other nation can do relatively best. Trading with others presumably leaves both parties better off than they would be otherwise. This reasoning, called the **theory of comparative advantage**, was first developed by English economist David Ricardo in the early 1800s. This venerable theory basically posits that every country gains by "putting its best foot forward," specializing in the goods it can produce relatively most efficiently and trading them to other countries for what they can produce relatively more efficiently.

This principle is easier to understand on a personal level. Consider actor Harrison Ford (a.k.a. Han Solo, Indiana Jones, etc.), who is also a highly skilled carpenter. Indeed, he earned his living at carpentry before turning to acting. While Ford may be a better carpenter than most he could hire to do repair work around his house, it would be very expensive for him to do his own repairs, because he would have to give up income he earns as a movie star—approximately $25 million per film. Economists use the term **opportunity cost** to express what someone gives up by making a choice. In this case, the opportunity cost of doing carpentry work is very high for Harrison Ford because he can earn so much money as a movie star. Meanwhile, the opportunity cost for Ford's carpenter, who has no other occupation, is very low; she gives up very little by choosing to do carpentry work. According to the theory of comparative advantage, Ford would specialize in acting and hire a carpenter because he has a comparative advantage in acting, while the carpenter has a comparative advantage in carpentry.

By the same reasoning, one nation can benefit from trading internationally even if it is more efficient (that is, it can "do better carpentry") in the production of all products than the nation with which it is trading. The United States might be more efficient than Mexico at producing both textiles and computers, but because the United States has limited resources, the opportunity cost of producing textiles is very high. If the United States chooses to devote resources to producing textiles, it will have fewer resources with which to produce computers (which generate relatively higher profits). Since Mexico can produce textiles with its resources, the United States is better off specializing in the production of computers and importing textiles from Mexico. This allows both countries to produce what they do relatively best (i.e., to produce the good with the lowest opportunity cost). In this way, international trade pays off even if one nation has an advantage in cost efficiency over another in all goods. This, Ricardo argued, will always be true so long as each nation has different resource endowments. We will delve more deeply into the theory of comparative advantage in Chapter 20.

Free Trade versus Protectionism

When we consider trade issues, the debate about the pros and cons of free trade often occupies the stage. Free trade occurs when there are no obstacles to the free flow of goods and services between countries. This means the absence of **quotas** (physical limits) or **tariffs** (taxes) on imports or exports. While most economic theory suggests that free trade is desirable and over time produces positive economic gains for individual nations as well as the larger global trading community, in the short run this is not always the case. Nor is it clear that, in practice, the benefits of free trade come without serious economic cost and consequence for particular sectors of the economy, regions of a country, and workers.

As nations strive to keep income in their country, they may engage in **protectionism,** which means putting up barriers to imports. It seems logical that if your objective is to maximize exports and limit imports to protect domestic jobs, then one simple way to do it is to put a tariff or a tax on imports or to limit by law the quantity of imports allowed to enter the country by imposing a quota on them. Trade restrictions such as tariffs and quotas have the effect of increasing production in domestic industries by protecting them from foreign competition, which saves jobs at home. However, imposing trade restrictions also raises prices on imported goods and allows industries protected by tariffs to sell their products domestically for a higher price than they could if they had to face foreign competition.

Those who favor free trade (a group that includes the majority of economists) argue that international trade increases the overall level of income and consumption possibilities. Opponents argue that free trade comes at too high a cost, especially in terms of jobs lost to foreign competition. Others, as we shall see in Chapter 20, argue that what is needed is *fair* trade, on the assumption that for free trade to occur, countries need to be guaranteed full access to each other's markets.

Financing International Trade

On March 14, 2007, 1 U.S. dollar could be exchanged for 1.11 Canadian dollars, 539.0 Chilean pesos, 44.2 Indian rupees, .75 Euros, 116 Japanese yen, or 11.2 Mexican pesos. These and other exchange rates tend to change over time. For example, in June 1990 the dollar could be exchanged for 128 Japanese yen, whereas a month earlier, the dollar was worth 153 yen. In December 1999, a dollar could be exchanged for only 103 yen. What makes one currency worth a certain amount when measured in terms of the other? In other words, what determines the rate of exchange of a currency? And how do currency exchange rates affect international trade?

When nations engage in international trade, they do not generally trade goods for goods directly; international trade requires a system of paying for transactions. Nations must agree on what is acceptable to use as a medium of exchange and a unit of account for international transactions. Since every nation has its own currency, there has to be some way to determine the value at which currencies exchange for one another. This, among other things, is the role of international finance.

Exchange Rates

The foreign **exchange rate** is the rate at which one country's currency exchanges for another country's currency. These rates of exchange fluctuate daily depending on economic circumstances within, and transactions between, countries. These shifts in exchange rates affect us in direct ways.

We don't think about it very often, but exchange rates come to your attention a little more dramatically if you are on a vacation or business trip in a foreign country. One day you cash a $10 traveler's check in Japan and get, say, 1,000 yen for it—about enough to get into a movie. The next day, the value of the dollar falls, and you get only 800 yen for your $10. Since prices have not changed in Japan, you have to come up with more dollars to see another movie.

Exchange rate fluctuations like that happen all the time. What causes them? Within a country, when we purchase goods or services, only one currency is involved, so the process is fairly simple. You hand over the money to someone, who sells you what you want. The price you pay is, generally speaking, determined by the amount of the product available at the time and by consumers' demand for it. But when you buy a product made in another country, a more complicated exchange process is triggered. If, for example, you buy a Japanese automobile, you pay for it in dollars, and that's all you have to think about. However, the Japanese auto manufacturer can't pay its bills in dollars; it needs yen. Somewhere along the line, your dollars have to be changed (converted) into yen so the Japanese auto manufacturer can be paid in local currency.

This exchange takes place in the foreign exchange market, which is why foreign money is called foreign exchange. The number of yen a dollar will buy depends on a number of factors, but most involve how many yen Americans want compared to how many dollars the Japanese demand. In 1999, the United States wanted (imported) $87 billion more of Japanese products than the Japanese wanted (imported) of ours. This was reflected in a weakening of the dollar and a strengthening of the yen during the last six months of the year.

The weakening of the dollar relative to the yen (or depreciation of the dollar) driven by an excess demand by U.S. consumers for Japanese goods should, however, eventually help to balance trade. As the dollar weakens and buys fewer yen, more dollars are needed to purchase Japanese electronics and cars. As Japanese imports become more expensive in the United States, consumers should respond by reducing their demand for them, taking pressure off the yen and bolstering the dollar. The United States both loses and gains in this process. It pays higher prices for the Hondas and the Sonys, but since Japanese goods are becoming more expensive, U.S. consumers should begin switching to lower-priced domestically produced goods. Then more jobs will be created in the United States. For Japan it's the opposite—lower prices for U.S. blue jeans or airplanes come at the cost of fewer jobs in Japan as Japanese consumers substitute lower priced U.S. goods for more expensive Japanese goods.

As we have seen, the price of one country's goods in relation to another's depends on the rate of exchange between their currencies. If exchange rates are allowed to fluctuate freely according to market supply and demand, then they simply reflect each nation's demand for another's products—its exportable goods and services. This is because the demand for foreign currencies (foreign exchange) is in part a derived demand, derived from the demand for imports and exports. Thus, whenever two countries are trading, two markets are involved: the product market and the foreign exchange market. While this complicates the analysis, the key to understanding exchange systems is to recognize that the demand for foreign exchange is derived from the nation's demand for goods and services, financial instruments such as stocks and bonds, and purchases of physical assets like production facilities. We will explore exchange rates further in Chapter 21.

Technological Change and Competitiveness

The process of economic growth and economic development, including globalization, owes its rapid pace to modern computer and information technology. Technology is thus one of the most important factors contributing to and underlying the globalization of economic activity.

Since the 1800s, economic activity has been driven by a set of changing new technologies. Steam power, cotton textiles, and iron defined the 1800–1850 period. Railways and steel shaped the period from 1850 to 1900. The first half of the twentieth century was marked by transformations in electricity, chemicals, and automobiles. Electronics, synthetic materials, and petrochemicals dominated the 1950s, and at present we are watching the integration of information and computer technology. These stages have been driven by the actions of entrepreneurs and innovators. We have seen technological revolutions in the fields of transportation, communications, information, electronics, and manufacturing. In today's rapidly changing global economy, the information revolution driven by the computer is bringing about changes and competitive pressures that are literally changing the lives of everyone on the planet.

Indeed, changes brought about by the development of the Internet and other forms of information and communications technologies gave rise to the term New Economy. While this term is used and defined in a number of ways, the 2001 *Economic Report of the President* defined the New Economy "by the extraordinary gains in performance—including rapid productivity growth, rising incomes, low unemployment, and moderate inflation—that have resulted from [a] combination of mutually reinforcing advances in technologies, business practices, and economic policies." Throughout the text you will find references to the New Economy and its rise over the past decade and a half.

Energy and the Environment

Globalization of production has increased demand for the world's energy resources. It has also intensified the impact of local demand on the environment worldwide. As developing nations hope to increase growth and developed nations hope to improve on current living standards, more production facilities are established, increasing pollution and resource use while destroying natural habitats.

Energy

Everything that we do requires energy. You cannot lift your finger without expending energy. From an economic perspective, the energy sources of greatest interest are fossil fuels such as petroleum used to generate electricity and provide transportation. Aside from the cost of labor, the availability and price of petroleum are among the most critical determinants of the availability and cost of the vast majority of the goods and services produced in the world.

Until the early 1970s, citizens of industrial countries took for granted that their affluence and material standard of living were based on easily available and affordable (but nonrenewable) fossil fuels, especially petroleum. The OPEC-generated oil crises of the 1970s made people more aware of the fact that petroleum is nonrenewable, the product of a unique historic geologic process. The remaining petroleum reserves are primarily concentrated in the Middle East. Higher oil prices in 2000 and 2001 and 2004 and 2006 brought increased attention to oil production and refining as rolling blackouts plagued Californians in 2000 and 2001, truck drivers in Europe protested with traffic blockades in 2001, and SUV sales in the United States plummeted in 2006.

The United States currently consumes about eighteen million barrels (each barrel contains forty-two gallons) of petroleum a day and depends on foreign imports for more than 60 percent of this amount. This amount represents 1,029 gallons per person annually in the United States, compared to 700 gallons per person in Japan and 481 gallons per person in Great Britain. Since 1991, after Operation Desert Storm (when the United States and European countries carried out a major military action against Iraq to protect Kuwait and oil interests in the Middle East), petroleum conservation in the United States has decreased, domestic oil production has declined, and demand has increased. Many experts predict that by 2010 the United States will be importing even more of its daily petroleum needs, of which two-thirds flows to the transportation sector. Given projected rates of economic growth and global consumption, the world will one day—around the year 2075, say most experts—come close to running out of petroleum.

The fastest growth in energy demand is in the developing countries. Throughout the developing world, there is a phenomenal increase in the demand for not only petroleum but electricity, produced principally by coal or nuclear power.

Energy use has enormous consequences in terms of economics, trade, capital flows, politics, international relations, and the environment. All nations therefore must be thoughtful about their energy resources (supplies, demand, cost) and their use of energy. As we continue into the new century, the search will be on for ways to conserve and enhance the efficiency of energy, develop alternative renewable energy from the sun, and generate viable substitutes for nonrenewable fossil fuels like petroleum.

The Environment

Since the late 1960s, the industrial countries have been keenly aware of the progressive degradation of the Earth's physical environment resulting from the kind of economic growth they have experienced since the 1940s. This economic growth has been characterized by rapid urbanization and industrialization on a global scale. It has been propelled by the availability of cheap energy, especially petroleum. The automobile industry has driven much of this growth.

From the 1940s to the present, industrialization has primarily involved large-scale, energy-intensive industrial and agricultural production, modes of transportation, and development of synthetics, especially chemicals. These practices have increased the material wealth of industrialized nations but generated some negative consequences for the environment:

- Air pollution
- Water pollution
- Diminished soil quality
- Deterioration of the Earth's ozone layer
- Warming of the Earth caused largely by the burning of fossil fuels
- Extinction of species and the resulting loss of biological diversity
- Rapid depletion of nonrenewable resources
- Unsustainable rates of grazing, fishing, burning, and use of many of the Earth's nonrenewable and renewable resources

These issues are controversial and experts disagree profoundly, but it is vital for responsible global citizens to be aware of these issues, to understand them, and to understand how they relate to the global economy. Most of these issues were on the agenda of the International Earth Summit held in Brazil in 1992, while issues related to global climate change were the focus of the international summit held in Kyoto, Japan, in 1997.

4. Do you consider yourself an environmentalist? Explain.

While environmental issues and problems seem at times overwhelming, many organizations and firms are acting to promote sustainable modes of production and life in various parts of the world. A rapid proliferation of non-governmental organizations are educating people about these problems and trying to develop practical solutions. There is an undercurrent of optimism as global awareness is rising and the technical/scientific community is using its knowledge and technology to understand and solve these problems. Many multinational corporations are committing themselves to the goals of sustainable development and the process of greening, or adopting environmentally responsible production processes and programs.

Nevertheless, solving environmental problems is difficult. The world's population is growing at a rate of ninety million people a year. There are already more than six billion people on the planet, and the income per person is very uneven. About 80 percent of the new growth in population will occur in developing nations that are already poor and in some cases plagued by high levels of absolute poverty. Many of these developing countries are struggling with repaying large external debts their governments accumulated in the 1980s.

■ Conclusion

The new global economy is a complex entity. Modern production, communications, information systems, transportation, electronics, and finance technologies are ushering the global community into a new era. The new era will offer many opportunities and challenges for manufacturing workers, service employees, scientists, engineers, physicians, corporate managers, financial managers, environmentalists, economists, and educators. Innovation and risk taking will be the order of the day as opportunities are seized and difficult problems solved. At the same time, the new global economy will require a redefinition of the role of the nation-state in the international arena. Many of the world's challenges—especially the environmental and natural resource issues— will require corporations and countries to transcend narrow self-interest to promote the collective well-being of the global community.

Review Questions

1. Make a list of all of the goods and services you consume or use in an average day that are from outside of the United States. How dependent is your lifestyle on international trade?

2. Take a major daily newspaper, like the *New York Times,* and list all the articles that have a title, topic, or theme directly related to the international economy (trade or finance). Summarize in a paragraph the essence of each article. How many did you find? What were the major topics?

3. What is the process of globalization? What is causing it to take place at such an accelerated pace?

4. Why do nations engage in international trade? How does the theory of comparative advantage contribute to an understanding of international trade? Can you think of any possible flaws in this simple theory?

5. What are the arguments that support the theory of free trade? What are the arguments that support protectionism? Which of these are you more inclined to support? Why?

6. What is an exchange rate? How is it determined? Why is it important?

7. Look on the Internet for data on the exchange rate of the U.S. dollar in terms of the Japanese yen from 1990 to 2007. Make a table of the data, and then plot the data on a graph showing the movement of the annual exchange rate over this period of time. What do you think has caused the exchange rate to fluctuate in the manner that it has?

8. If the Japanese yen is weak relative to the U.S. dollar, what do you think the impact is on business performance in Japan?

9. How has the dynamic of technological change transformed the global economy? Give some examples.

10. Why is energy an important component of the global economy? What is the current level of petroleum consumption in the world? In the United States? How dependent is the United States on imported oil? Where does U.S. imported oil come from? How much does the United States spend on imported oil?

THINKING CRITICALLY

Economic Paradigms and Globalization: What Are Sweatshops For?

In Chapters 1 and 2, we described economics as a social science focusing on production, distribution, and consumption of goods and services while at the same time dealing with human beings and institutions. Today's global economy is characterized by rapid and at times wrenching changes, driven by competition, new technologies, and a continuing search for cheaper resources and markets.

The competitive pressures on multinational corporations in the context of the computer and information technology revolution has pushed firms to all corners of the globe, where they set up production operations to take advantage of cheaper resources (including cheaper labor) and growing markets. All of the recent technological advances have made this geographical shift in capital easier and faster. This process of rapid globalization has produced mixed results and an ongoing debate about its winners and losers.

Critics of globalization focus on human rights issues, particularly the exploitation of labor and the environment. They point out that firms from the industrial countries have either set up operations or used manufacturing firms in Asia, Latin America, and Africa to take advantage of cheap labor, cheap resources, and the absence of government regulations and unions, as well as to capitalize on growing local markets for their products. Reports suggest that it is common to find workers subjected to physical and sexual abuse in factories that ignore basic health and safety conditions, as shown in the table. Wages are exploitative, and workers lack benefits or rights. This image is of a sweatshop or factory characteristic of nineteenth-century England during the Industrial Revolution.

The use of Third World sweatshops by U.S. firms became a national political issue as the United States pushed for the North American Free Trade Agreement (NAFTA) with Mexico and Canada in the late 1980s and early 1990s. After NAFTA was ratified, the issue continued to attract public attention—particularly on college campuses, when well-known companies whose products were popular with students were exposed as employers of sweatshop labor to produce sweatshirts and sneakers. The Nike Corporation was targeted as an example of one of the most visible firms using cheap foreign labor to produce its products. In 1996, the Nikomas Gemilang factory in Serang, fifty miles west of Jakarta, Indonesia, made 1.2 million pairs of Nike sneakers each month. This factory paid a $2.23 daily wage for work performed in a typically abysmal environment. The publicity from this and other cases set into motion a global movement against such production facilities and a response on the part of corporations to either improve the situation or somehow get away from the public eye.

For the first time, a dozen companies that belong to the Fair Labor Assn. (www. fairlabor. org) have made public labor audits of the overseas factories that produce their products.

Sweatshop Report Card

Company	Factory and Product	Audit Findings
Adidas	Vietnam/1,014 workers *bags and accessories*	Workers forced to do overtime—they recently called the police, who fined the factory. Arbitrary firings and widespread sexual harassment allegations. Toilet visits limited.
Levi Strauss	Thailand/3,050 workers *woven shirts*	Child labor, dirty toilets, improperly stored chemical tanks, no drinking water in dining facility. Excessive overtime—sixty-five-hour work weeks, working seven straight days.
Liz Claiborne	China/1,080 workers *knitted garments*	Workers fined for breaking rules like no talking. Blocked exits, no toilet paper or towels, no sick leave. No pay stubs, excessive overtime, seven straight days' work.

Source: Data from Sweatshop Report Card, *BusinessWeek*, 6/23/03, p. 100.

The effort of the World Trade Organization in the 1990s and early 2000s to promote free trade and accelerate the movement of goods, services, and capital across the globe ran squarely into the growing number of critics of globalization. Organizations such as the National Labor Committee based in New York, the Global Alliance in Baltimore, the Fair Labor Association in Washington, DC, and the United Students Against Sweatshops on campuses around the United States are involved in attempting to monitor and report on the activities of multinationals including Wal-Mart, Reebok, Nike, Liz Claiborne, Mattel, and the Gap. Many of these corporations have taken the initiative to establish formal programs dealing with corporate responsibility and the sweatshop controversy specifically. More than forty colleges have joined together to deny companies using sweatshop labor the right to produce products displaying their respective college logos.

We can use the knowledge of economics developed in the first two chapters to examine the global sweatshop controversy. Economics is a social science, and as Joan Robinson wrote in *Freedom and Necessity* (see Chapter 1), "The function of social science is quite different from that of the natural sciences—it is to provide society with an organ of self-consciousness. Every interconnected group of human beings has to have an ideology—that is, a conception of what is the proper way to behave and the permissible pattern of relationships in family, economic, and political life." E. K. Hunt noted (see Chapter 1) that an ideology represents a set of "ideas and beliefs that tend to justify morally a society's social and economic relationships." By examining the use of sweatshops in the production process at Nike, we can begin to appreciate, use, and apply the three competing paradigms in economics—conservative, liberal, and radical.

The following article by Tim Weiner, "Low-Wage Costa Ricans Make Baseballs for Millionaires," reprinted from the January 25, 2004, issue of the *New York Times*, notes that despite continuing information about abusive labor practices, they seem to continue. Use information in this article, on Web sites, and from Chapters 1 and 2 to complete the exercises that follow the article.

Low-Wage Costa Ricans Make Baseballs for Millionaires
Tim Weiner

TURRIALBA, Costa Rica, Jan. 22—The game of baseball is a pure product of America. The ball itself is another matter.

Every baseball used in the major leagues is made here, millions of them. They are handcrafted with the precision of a machine by the men and women of Turrialba and the towns in the green hills beyond.

The baseball workers typically make about $2,750 a year. A baseball player in the United States makes, on average, about $2,377,000, the Players Association says.

"It is hard work, and sometimes it messes up your hands, warps your fingers and hurts your shoulders," said Overly Monge, 37. Temperatures inside the factory can rise to 90 to 95 degrees, he said, and when they do, "we suffocate."

He makes $55 a week after 13 years at the baseball factory, barely above Costa Rica's minimum wage. After he pays for the necessities of life, he has about $2 a day left over for himself, his wife and daughter. His salary, adjusted for inflation, is about the same as when he started.

But that's life, he said with a shrug. Hard work, but far better than no work at all. Many of the coffee and sugar cane plantations around here have collapsed, done in by the forces of globalization. There is only one other factory in Turrialba, population 30,000. Without baseballs, Mr. Monge said, life here "would be more like Nicaragua," the poor neighbor to the north.

The baseball workers arrive at 6 a.m. and work until 5 p.m. Peak production pressures have pushed the day deep into the night. Each can make four balls an hour, painstakingly hand-sewing 108 perfect stitches along the seams. They are paid by the ball—on average about 30 cents apiece. Rawlings Sporting Goods, which runs the factory, sells the balls for $14.99 at retail in the United States.

"After I make the first two or three balls each week, they have already paid my salary," Mr. Monge said. "Imagine that."

Warny Goméz, 33, worked for four years at Rawlings, put himself through college and became a primary school teacher. "People here have no choice but to work there," he said. "There are almost no other jobs."

"There's tremendous pressure to produce," he added. "The balls have to be exactly alike, totally perfect, and for this work people are paid $50 or $60 a week. A machine can't make them—it has to be done by hand. But they demand the precision and speed of a machine."

Rawlings workers past and present say that while their real wages have not risen over the years, workplace safety has improved—particularly since a new manager,

Ken West, arrived four months ago. Previous bosses, they say, screamed at them, pressured them to go faster. Mr. West, an affable 62-year-old Missourian, is not that kind of boss.

Rawlings, founded in 1887, has had an exclusive contract to supply the major leagues with baseballs since 1977. Mr. West says the Costa Rica plant makes about 2.2 million balls a year and sells about 1.8 million of them to the majors. Officials at K2 Inc., the sporting goods company that acquired Rawlings last year, say the wholesale price the majors pay for those balls is a trade secret. Industry analysts say Rawlings sells about $35 million worth of baseballs a year, about one-third of the world market.

Rawlings came to Costa Rica 16 years ago, from Haiti, where workers made $15 to $25 a week. It moved after a 1986 coup deposed the dictator Jean-Claude Duvalier.

"About the time the coup was going on in Haiti, they could see some problems coming," Mr. West said. Rawlings sought "a neutral country that has a good work force."

Rawlings was awarded a 54,000-square-foot free-trade zone by Costa Rica. It pays no taxes. It imports duty-free the makings of millions of baseballs—cores from the Muscle Shoals Rubber Company in Batesville, Miss.; yarn from D&T Spinning in Ludlow, Vt.; cowhide from Tennessee Tanning in Tullahoma, Tenn.

Its operations are a harbinger of a pending free-trade accord between Costa Rica and the United States; negotiations on that agreement, expected to bring more such ventures to Costa Rica, are in their final stages.

"Free trade is excellent for the United States, because they consume so much," Mr. Monge, the Rawlings worker, said. "For other nations, it's more complicated."

As the sole source for major league baseballs, and the biggest employer by far in Turrialba, Rawlings seems to have things sewn up. Mr. West sees no social or economic tensions at the plant. He says his work force is more like a team or a family.

"These people are so good—they're just very good at it," he said. "I am just so impressed by the people."

"The best thing's the pay," he said.

"We're a good place to work." The work itself, he said, is "not demanding." As for repetitive-stress injuries, like carpal tunnel syndrome, "we just do not have that problem."

However, Dr. Carlos Guerrero, who worked at the Rawlings plant as a company doctor in 1998, and at the national health insurance clinic in Turrialba from 1991 to 1997, said a third of Rawlings workers developed carpal tunnel syndrome in those years. (The syndrome, which causes pain and numbness in the hands, is common among assembly-line workers, typists and computer operators worldwide.) He said perhaps 90 percent of Rawlings workers experienced pain from their exacting work, from minor cuts to disabling aches.

Officials at Major League Baseball headquarters in New York referred questions about the plant to Rawlings. The head of baseball's Players Association, Donald Fehr, said workplace injuries at the plant had not been brought to his attention. Dudley W. Mendenhall, a senior vice president of K2, also said he was unaware of any workplace injuries at the plant.

Few baseball players are aware of where the ball comes from, said Charles Kernaghan, the executive director of the National Labor Committee, an international workers' rights group based in New York. "But if the players would actually stand up, it would have enormous consequences" for the baseball workers, including better pay, he said.

Some past employees say they had to quit after developing repetitive stress injuries, and they have the medical records to prove it.

"The work deforms your fingers and arms," said Maribel Alezondo Brenes, 36, who worked seven years at the plant—until her doctor told her to stop sewing baseballs.

Soledad Castillo, 46, cannot make a fist, or touch her right palm with her middle finger after nine years at Rawlings. Disputing Mr. West's contention that workers are not injured by their labor, she said, "If he ever worked a day sewing, he'd know it's hard."

Despite their injuries, the two women say they liked the camaraderie and the atmosphere at the Rawlings plant. "I can't complain about the work environment," Ms. Alezondo said. "The ventilation improved over the years," even if the pay did not. There was time to make small talk and good friends.

Still, when she talks about the difference in wages between baseball workers and baseball players, it takes her breath away.

"We sacrifice a lot so they can play," she said. "It's an injustice that we kill ourselves to make these balls perfect, and with one home run, they're gone."

Source: "Low-Wage Costa Ricans Make Baseballs for Millionaires" by Tim Weiner, *New York Times*, 1/24/04. Copyright © 2004 New York Times Co. Inc. Used with permission.

Exercises

Answer the following questions.

1. Do you believe that using low-wage labor in developing countries to produce goods for U.S. multinational corporations such as Nike represents the "exploitation of labor"? Explain.

2. Do you believe that the working conditions in foreign factories violate the "human rights" of workers? Explain.

3. How would the three economic paradigms that you have studied explain modern sweatshops in this period of globalization? Which do you think offers the best explanation? Explain the reasons for your answer.

4. Should there be an international labor code of conduct for multinational corporations? Explain.

5. Does your college deny the use of its logo to companies employing sweatshop labor?

6. What are the positive and negative aspects of the Rawlings operation in Costa Rica? What would you suggest ought to be done, if anything, to improve the situation?

Part Two

Economic History and the Development of Modern Economic Thought

Modern economic thinking has been influenced by many economists, among them Adam Smith, Thomas Malthus, David Ricardo, J. B. Say, John Stuart Mill, Alfred Marshall, John Maynard Keynes, Joan Robinson, Thorstein Veblen, and Karl Marx. Many of the economists who contributed to the growing body of economic knowledge were British. Britain's emergence as one of the first capitalist powers, through the spread of its colonial empire and the coming of the Industrial Revolution, accounts for this influence. We can trace many of our theories and ideas about the economy back to these early economists.

This book cannot examine all of the ideas of all of the economists who have made significant contributions to the history of modern economic thought; in this part, we will focus on the development of a few selected and persistent ways of thinking about an economy. Your own understanding of the economy may become clearer as you agree or disagree with some of the most important ideas formulated by past economists.

By examining some of the ideas of these economists as they developed and the historical context in which they emerged, we can gain insights into economic concepts and changing economic institutions, ideas, and theories. Some of this will help us directly in understanding our current economic situation, and it will give us perspective on how the thoughts of past economists have influenced the development of economic systems as well as our understanding of the economy today.

CHAPTER THREE

The Evolution of Economic Systems

◼ Introduction

The first premise of all human history is, of course, the existence of living human individuals. Thus, the first fact to be established is the physical organization of these individuals and their consequent relation to the rest of nature. . . .

. . . The writing of history must always set out from these natural bases and their modification in the course of history through the action of men.

Men can be distinguished from animals by consciousness, by religion or anything else you like. They themselves begin to distinguish themselves from animals as soon as they begin to produce their means of subsistence, a step which is conditioned by their physical organization. By producing their means of subsistence men are indirectly producing their actual material life.

The way in which men produce their means of subsistence depends first of all on the nature of the actual means of subsistence they find in existence and have to reproduce. This mode of production must not be considered simply as being the reproduction of the physical existence of the individuals. Rather it is a definite form of activity of these individuals, a definite form of expressing their life, a definite *mode of life* on their part. As individuals express their life, so they are. What they are, *therefore*, coincides with their production, both with *what* they produce and with *how* they produce. The nature of individuals thus depends on the material conditions determining their production.

—Karl Marx, *The German Ideology* (1845–1846)

1. What does Marx mean by "the nature of the actual means of subsistence"? What is its relationship to the productive activity of human beings?

Every society is faced with the problem of providing for the day-to-day survival of its people. Production of goods and services on a systematic basis is necessary for the continuance and development of any society or nation. Institutions, traditions, rules, methods, and laws are developed to determine what goods and services will be produced, how they will be produced, and how they will be distributed among the people. According to Marx, the ways in which people organize themselves for the production and distribution of goods and services—the **economic system**—constitutes "the mode of life" of any society.

Individuals and organizations engage in economic activity for particular reasons and according to accepted procedures. This activity is a central and necessary aspect of all human life and societies. It provides us with food, shelter, clothing, and the other necessities of life. The production and distribution of goods and services transforms nature into human uses for survival and sustenance. People's actions in this process determine, to a large extent, their daily contacts and relationships with other people. The results of economic activity—what gets produced and how it gets produced—organized through an economic system, condition the nature, history, and development of a society and its people. Understanding the economic system, then, is fundamental to understanding that society.

To "know" the United States, it is necessary to acknowledge the importance of private production and consumption in providing for our day-to-day survival. Consequently, we would want to examine the roles of specialization, division of labor, and markets in the operation of our economic system. It is also important to recognize changes in institutions, productive methods, and material conditions over time. Corporations and labor unions emerged and developed. Technology and the standard of living advanced steadily. Mass production led to the assembly line and automation. Government accepted more direct responsibility for the health of the economy. In other words, the economic system evolved.

Economic Development

Over time, all economic systems change. **Economic development** represents progressive changes in a society's ability to meet its economic tasks of production and distribution.

Economic development contains two key elements. One concerns the total amount of goods and services that are produced and available for consumption, and the other concerns institutions. Economic development occurs when a society is able to increase its total output; it experiences economic growth through the generation and usage of its economic **surplus** (more output than necessary for subsistence consumption). Very often a society's ability to produce such growth is a function of the second element of economic development. This concerns the changes in the economic institutions, relationships, and production methods of the society. If the society experiences changes in its economic institutions, relationships, and methods that make it better prepared to produce a growing volume of goods and services for its people, then development will occur. The discovery of new resources will encourage economic development, as will technological improvements in the methods of production. The spread of education and attitudes toward work may facilitate a society's ability to produce goods and services. Economic development is obviously of crucial importance to any society and its continued survival.

The present U.S. economic system, its institutions, and its conditions developed out of previous methods of production and distribution. The historical background lies largely, but not exclusively, in U.S. and European experience. For example, the U.S. market system has its roots in the emergence of trade in the Middle Ages in Europe; the modern corporation has its roots in the development of earlier European and U.S. business enterprises. Yet the foundations of the U.S. labor force have been and are worldwide. An understanding of this background will provide some useful perspective on the current economic system in the United States and the global economy.

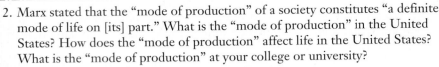

2. Marx stated that the "mode of production" of a society constitutes "a definite mode of life on [its] part." What is the "mode of production" in the United States? How does the "mode of production" affect life in the United States? What is the "mode of production" at your college or university?

3. Marx continues, "The nature of individuals thus depends on the material conditions determining their production." What are these material conditions to which Marx refers? In what ways are people in the United States affected by "the material conditions" of production?

From Feudalism to Capitalism

From time to time, economic change is so wrenching that major transformations occur and completely new economic systems emerge, with new institutions, rules, methods, and laws. Such was the transition from feudalism to capitalism in Western Europe from the twelfth to eighteenth centuries. The change occurred over several centuries but accelerated in the later periods. In the following discussion, we will concentrate on the highlights of this transition to illustrate economic change and to show the historical roots of modern capitalism.

As we have said, all societies must organize themselves for production, distribution, and consumption. If we are clear on what these economic activities are, we will be able to focus on the major differences among economic systems. **Production** refers to the activity that takes the **factors of production** (resources) and transforms them into goods and services. The factors of production are land, labor, and capital. **Land** includes raw materials and the land where productive activity takes place (i.e., farmland or the land on which a factory or office is located). **Labor** is the physical and mental effort of people that is necessary for all production. **Capital** includes the technology, buildings, machinery, and equipment that are used in production, as well as the financial resources necessary to organizing production. **Consumption** is the using up of produced goods and services. **Distribution** refers to the manner in which goods and services are apportioned among the people of a society. As we will see, feudalism accomplished all of these with institutions and methods much different from those of capitalism.

4. All societies must be able to organize themselves for production, distribution, and consumption. What other economic goals should a society have? List at least five.

Precursors of Feudalism

The ancient empires of Egypt, Greece, and Rome were the precursors of modern Western societies. They were largely agricultural societies that struggled to produce enough food for continued subsistence. *Tradition* and *custom* were primarily responsible for organizing production and distribution. Things were done the way they always had been done. Children tended to follow in the footsteps of their parents. Slaves remained slaves. Peasants were agricultural producers tied to the land for generation after generation. The priests, kings, emperors, pharaohs, and lords continued in the role of the elite upper class removed from production. As economist Robert Heilbroner describes them in *The Making of Economic Society*, these societies had "a mode of social organization in which both production and distribution were based on procedures devised in the distant past, rigidified by a long process of historic trial and error, and maintained by heavy sanctions of law, custom, and belief."

Because these societies were unable to produce much more than was needed for subsistence, they could not support a large nonfarming population. Throughout history, the ability to produce an agricultural and economic surplus has been a source of growth and power. The existence of an agricultural surplus allows for a geographically separate urban population. Cities did exist in Egypt, Greece, and Rome, but they were not extensive enough to allow for a significant amount of nonagricultural production. Instead, the cities of ancient times were relatively parasitic and lived off the surplus of the rural area. What surplus the cities were able to produce themselves resulted from trade with other cities and from the institution of slavery, with its ability to exploit unpaid labor. With a largely rural population tied to tradition and an urban economy based on the unstable slave system, the ancient empires were economically stagnant—they were unable to amass economic surplus and to grow. Because of this base of internal weakness, each of these ancient empires eventually crumbled. They were replaced by feudalism, which continued through the Middle Ages.

Before we examine feudalism, it is worthwhile to pause and consider an additional aspect of economic surplus. If a society can produce more than it needs for consumption, it can use this excess to support an urban population that can pursue nonagricultural production, and it can devote resources to increasing further production. The surplus can be used to further a division of tasks within an economic system and thus to spur economic growth.

By forgoing current consumption, a society can use resources to increase its ability to produce goods and services in the future. A simple example would be using excess grain to feed oxen (instead of eating it) so that more grain could be produced in the future. Another example would be transporting food to an urban area where (fed) artisans would fashion simple tools for agricultural production.

Although the surplus can thus be a source of growth, how a society uses its surplus and who controls its use tell us a lot about that society. Egypt, Greece, and Rome did succeed in producing surplus, but very little was used in a direct attempt to further economic production. Religious and military elites controlled the surplus of these societies and used them to build temples, pyramids, sphinxes, magnificent roads, aqueducts, and buildings that are still with us today. Little of the surplus, however, went to the slaves, peasants, or artisans who were the producers of consumable goods and services, nor was the surplus directed toward improving the productive potential of these sectors of the economic systems. As a result, these societies were not able to generate significant economic growth.

5. What does the United States do with its economic surplus? Who determines how it is used?

Feudalism

The economic system that dominated Western Europe throughout the Middle Ages was **feudalism.** What exactly was feudalism? What were its major institutions, methods, and customs? The following selection by economic historian E. K. Hunt, from his book *Property and Prophets*, provides us with a concise description of feudalism.

Feudalism
E. K. Hunt

The decline of the western part of the old Roman Empire left Europe without the laws and protection the empire had provided. The vacuum was filled by the creation of a feudal hierarchy. In this hierarchy, the serf, or peasant, was protected by the lord of the manor, who, in turn, owed allegiance to and was protected by a higher overlord. And so the system went, ending eventually with the king. The strong protected the weak, but they did so at a high price. In return for payments of money, food, labor, or military allegiance, overlords granted the fief, or feudum—a hereditary right to use land—to their vassals. At the bottom was the serf, a peasant who tilled the land. The vast majority of the population raised crops for food or clothing or tended sheep for wool and clothing.

Custom and tradition are the key to understanding medieval relationships. In place of laws as we know them today, the *custom of the manor* governed. There was no strong central authority in the Middle Ages that could have enforced a system of laws. The entire medieval organization was based on a system of mutual obligations and services up and down the hierarchy. Possession or use of the land obligated one to certain customary services or payments in return for protection. The lord was as obligated to protect the serf as the serf was to turn over a portion of his crop or to perform extensive labor for the lord. . . .

The basic economic institution of medieval rural life was the manor, which contained within it two separate and distinct classes: noblemen, or lords of the manors, and serfs (from the Latin word *servus*, "slave"). Serfs were not really slaves. Unlike a slave, who was simply property to be bought and sold at will, the serf could not be parted from either his family or his land. If his lord transferred possession of the manor to another nobleman, the serf simply had another lord. In varying degrees, however, obligations were placed upon the serfs that were sometimes very onerous and from which there was often no escape. Usually, they were far from being "free."

The lord lived off the labor of the serfs who farmed his fields and paid taxes in kind and money according to the custom of the manor. Similarly, the lord gave protection, supervision, and administration of justice according to the custom of the manor. It must be added that although the system did rest on reciprocal obligations, the concentration of economic and political power in the hands of the lord led to a system in which, by any standard, the serf was exploited in the extreme.

The Catholic Church was by far the largest owner of land during the Middle Ages. . . . This was also an age during which the religious teaching of the church had a very strong and pervasive influence throughout Western Europe. These factors combined to make the church the closest thing to a strong central government throughout this period.

Thus the manor might be secular or religious . . . but the essential relationships between lord and serfs were not significantly affected by this distinction. There is little evidence that serfs were treated any less harshly by religious lords than by secular ones. The religious lords and the secular nobility were the joint ruling classes; they controlled the land and the power that went with it. In return for very onerous appropriations of the serf's labor, produce, and money, the nobility provided military protection and the church provided spiritual aid.

In addition to manors, medieval Europe had many towns, which were important centers of manufacturing. Manufactured goods were sold to manors and, sometimes, traded in long-distance commerce. The dominant economic institutions in the towns were the guilds—craft, professional, and trade associations that had existed as far back as the Roman Empire. If anyone wanted to produce or sell any good or service, he had to join a guild.

The guilds were as involved with social and religious questions as with economic ones. They regulated their members' conduct in all their activities: personal, social, religious, and economic. Although the guilds did regulate very carefully the production and sale of commodities, they were less concerned with making profits than with saving their members' souls. Salvation demanded that the individual lead an orderly life based on church teachings and custom. Thus the guilds exerted a powerful influence as conservators of the status quo in the medieval towns.

Source: E. K. Hunt. *Property and Prophets,* 3rd edition. Abridged from pp. 5–7, © 1972, 1975, 2003, M.E. Sharpe, Inc., E. K. Hunt. Reprinted by permission of E. K. Hunt.

6. What were the dominant institutions of feudalism? What classes existed in feudal society?

7. How does the feudal "custom of the manor" differ from our modern system of contracts?

8. What did the "religious lords and secular nobility" do with the economic surplus that they controlled?

The Breakdown of Feudalism

As feudalism developed, several new economic activities and trends emerged that eventually created the preconditions for a new economic order. Most notable were changes in technology, urbanization, medieval merchants, the Crusades and exploration, creation of the nation-state, breakdown of the guilds, the rise of Protestantism and individualism, and the decline of the manor and the rise of private property. These factors and others, as sources of change over centuries in Western Europe, eventually led to the destruction of feudal institutions and relationships. These were replaced by a new set of institutions and relationships that we have come to label capitalism.

Changes in Technology.   In about the eleventh century the three-field crop rotation system replaced the two-field system. The widespread introduction of this revolutionary new system allowed for a much more productive use of agricultural land. In this system, all parcels of land would lie fallow every third year, preventing the land from becoming depleted by constant planting. This simple change increased the agricultural surplus and encouraged the use of more grain in supporting field animals. Agricultural production increased even further with greater use of oxen and horses, and later, with consolidation of agricultural lands. In addition, transportation of agricultural goods was facilitated by more horses and improvements in wagon technology.

Urbanization.   The increasing agricultural surplus supported an expanding and more urbanized population. Larger urban centers fostered specialization in economic production; the early medieval towns and cities began to concentrate on trade and manufacturing. This specialization led to further increases in production and stimulated trading among the cities and between the cities and the countryside.

Medieval Merchants.   Given different specializations of agricultural and manufacturing production in different areas throughout Western Europe, individual merchants during the tenth to fourteenth centuries began traveling from place to place, buying, selling, and trading goods. These transient merchants exposed self-sufficient manors to the variety of products from the rest of Europe and Asia and created interdependencies that whittled away at the traditional patterns of feudal life. This very trade further encouraged the development of regional and urban-rural specialization—a source of increasing economic surplus. It also laid the roots for the later sophistication of European

In the middle ages, lords and vassals lived in a futile system.

That's "feudal" system.

Just when I thought this junk was beginning to make sense.

commerce. Traveling merchants were replaced by permanent markets in commercial cities by the fifteenth century.

The Crusades and Exploration.   Between the eleventh and thirteenth centuries, the Crusades brought Europeans into contact with a civilization much more concerned with trading and moneymaking. It also exposed them to the wealth of Asia and its goods. This exposure encouraged an effort to expand the trading periphery of Europe. The nations of Europe began to explore Africa and Asia. These explorations ultimately led to the discovery of the New World. The example of moneymaking was not lost either. Merchants financed and profited from the Crusades, while European nations used their newfound exploring capability to establish colonies and reap from them raw materials and precious metals. These new forms of economic surplus financed further development and created fledgling capitalist institutions. In fact, the inflow of gold and silver produced such rapid growth that a great price inflation occurred during the sixteenth century in Europe.

Creation of the Nation-State.   An additional factor that broke down feudalism and, in fact, supported exploration was the creation of the nation-state. The self-sufficient and decentralized nature of feudalism began to hamper trade as manors attempted to levy tariffs and tolls on merchants. However, as centralization of political power became the goal of certain nobles and lords, these forces were joined by the commercial merchants in the cities. This coalition of economic and political power ensured the emergence of nation-states. By the sixteenth century these newly unified nations within Europe were encouraging trade within and among their countries and exploration across the Atlantic and the Mediterranean. The new nation-states possessed the economic, political, and military power that formed the basis for a new economic order and increased economic growth.

Breakdown of the Guilds.   The replacement of the guilds by the *putting-out system* contributed to the creation of a laboring class of people and to the extension of the market for labor service. Under the feudal guild system of production, independent craftspeople had used their own tools and shops to produce their products and then sold the products to merchants. Production and sales were overseen by the guilds. As trade expanded and the production of manufactured goods increased, the putting-out system began in the sixteenth century to replace the guilds. In this arrangement, a merchant-capitalist gained control of the tools, raw materials, and workplace and would hire, for wages, skilled individuals to produce the final product. Eventually this system led to the establishment of centralized industrial factories.

Two major elements of this new system differentiated it from the feudal guild system. First, production was controlled by the capitalist—the owner of tools, buildings, and other resources involved in production (i.e., the capital). This person would also arrange for the sale of products. The goal was monetary profit. The guild no longer influenced the production and sale of the goods. Second, this new system created a labor force that depended on the capitalist for work. The craftspeople no longer owned capital; they had only their skills and labor power to sell to the capitalist.

As the putting-out system developed further, markets for goods and resources determined profits for capitalists. These market relationships, rather than the custom and tradition of feudal relations, governed decisions about who would work and for what wages, and how the work would be performed. Industrial production was organized on a capitalist, rather than feudal, basis.

The Rise of Protestantism and Individualism.   Another factor contributing to the decline of feudalism concerned a change in the philosophy of much of the European population as well as a decline in the power of one of feudalism's most powerful institutions, the Catholic Church. The Catholic Church emphasized in its teachings a concern with afterlife and deemphasized material life. In fact, the Church argued against lending money for interest (usury) and profit making; if people were poor, that was their station in this life (it was God's will). This philosophy elevated the role of the Church in the society and economic system and downplayed the importance of the individual. The rise of the Protestant challenge to Catholicism and King Henry VIII's confiscation of Catholic Church lands and installation of the Anglican Church in England weakened the controlling role of the Catholic Church in feudal society.

In addition, Protestantism offered a philosophy more directed toward individual salvation. Calvinism, in fact, provided a justification of profit making as demonstrating service to God in one's "calling." Working hard, earning profits, and plowing those profits back into the business constituted circumstantial evidence that one was among God's chosen. This new religious idea and the Protestant churches as institutions, along with an increased emphasis on political freedom and liberty, supported the creation of a new *individualism*. This spirit, in turn, prompted much of the behavior necessary to the establishment of capitalist institutions.

Decline of the Manor.   One of the most significant trends in the transition from feudalism to capitalism occurred on the manor. Increasingly, the feudal obligations between lords and serfs became monetized. As trade expanded, the need for money caused feudal lords to sell their crops for cash and to put their serfs on money payments for work. In turn, some serfs began to pay rents to the lords for the use of land.

The *enclosure movement* from the thirteenth through the eighteenth centuries sealed the fate of the manorial system. As monetization and trade progressed, lords began to use their manors for cash generation. Common pastureland on the manors, as well as the king's common land, both traditionally accessible to all, were "enclosed" for grazing sheep. The sheep, in turn, were the source of wool to supply the increasing demand throughout Europe for woolen cloth. The effects and methods of this process were widespread. David McNally describes the change in *Political Economy and the Rise of Capitalism:*

> From the late sixteenth century onwards, sections of the gentry took advantage of the weakened status of the village community to launch a sustained offensive against the rights of the small tenants. . . . And, most important, they undertook to enclose and reorganize lands—a path which tended to raise the productivity of the land by 50 percent on average. . . . [M]odern research suggests that by 1700 three-quarters of all enclosure had already taken place. As a result of this multi-faceted offensive, rents doubled during the half-century from 1590 to 1640.
>
> The landlords' offensive often involved a shift to large-scale capitalist farming in the form of pasturage as well as new crops and rotation patterns which brought more land into productive use year in and year out.

While the enclosures contributed to growing output, trade, and incomes for some, the process also made it increasingly impossible for serfs/tenants to support themselves. In essence, they were forced off the land in search of work for wages. Most gravitated toward the cities.

The combination of the enclosure movements and the putting-out system created a new class of individuals who controlled the productive land and resources of Western Europe and whose goal was profit. In both the countryside and the city, this centralization of control and ownership resulted in greater economic production. In addition, the changes created a new class of landless, propertyless individuals—people no longer tied to their hereditary lands or their crafts. This was a new kind of labor force: a "free" labor force in which work was not a guarantee and the individual was free to seek work for wages determined by emerging market forces. The members of this labor force responded to the forces of change by attempting to sell their only resource, their labor power, at the best possible wage. They formed the emerging urban working class.

9. From the preceding material, list the feudal relations and institutions that were destroyed by the centuries of change in Western Europe between 1100 and 1800.
10. List the new relationships and institutions that were emerging to form capitalism.

11. What similarities and/or differences do you see between the enclosure movement in Europe and the modern replacement of family farms in the United States by agribusiness corporations?

The Development of Property in England

Britain is an island (comprising England, Wales, and Scotland) with a total area less than that of Pennsylvania and New York. The Beaker people occupied early Britain; they were followed by the Celts in 800 B.C. The Romans, led by Julius Caesar, arrived in 55 B.C. and departed about A.D. 410. Angles, Saxons, and Jutes arrived in the fifth century, followed by the Vikings in 865.

In 1066, William the Conqueror, with the approval of the pope, invaded England. With his Norman followers, he slew the recently crowned King Harold at the Battle of Hastings, burned houses, and destroyed crops and cattle. William and the Normans confiscated all the land, and William became the chief lord. He redistributed land titles to his favorite Norman subjects, including the Church. About 1085–1086, William ordered a detailed survey of every piece of land in England; it was to include information about the rights by which the land was held. This survey is the *Domesday Book*. William planned to use this information for tax purposes.

Almost two centuries later, in 1215, the barons (landholders), who felt threatened by the Crown, compelled King John to sign the Magna Carta, which

Property rights were established following the Norman Conquest of Britain by the building of a castle such as this one in York. Its vantage point, overlooking two rivers, assured the property holders that no invaders were sneaking up on them.
(Photograph by Tom Riddell)

would ensure the barons' rights from the encroaching authority of the king. This was a rebellion of feudal lords. The peasants and artisans were not rebelling, and the Magna Carta neither improved nor protected their rights.

A few centuries later, Henry VIII (1491–1547) established the Church of England. He closed the Catholic monasteries and abbeys, took all of the Church land, and appointed his own church officers. As British historian Maurice Keen notes in *The Outlaws of Medieval Legend*, "After that the way was clear for the biggest event in our agrarian history—the distribution of all monastery lands to the Tudor millionaires. These landowners—merchants now rather than barons or earls—built themselves . . . superb mansions."

12. In what ways might these events have helped shape the kind of economic system that developed in Britain?

13. What is a property right? What determines a property right?

Thus, private property emerged in England over the course of several centuries. Its roots lie in conquest by foreign armies under the leadership of individuals who became the medieval nobility. Later on, land was appropriated by kings and distributed to vassals, barons, and the Church. This process was enforced by a combination of military power and monarchical or religious legal authority and was often sanctioned by the Church. As we saw above, the enclosure movement in the later Middle Ages accelerated this formal transfer of land to private owners.

The Significance of Property

Through conquest, appropriation, and legislative act, land in England came to be privately owned. This was one of the bases for the private ownership of productive resources—one of the foundations of capitalism as an economic system. Under private ownership of property, an individual (or a group of individuals, as in a modern corporation) owns and controls a piece of land (or a factory, machine, or product). That ownership allows the owner to use the property, rent it to someone else, or even sell it. The decision about what to do with it rests with its owner.

If we assume that individuals are out to maximize their own self-interest, the property will be used in its most productive or profitable way. The property owner determines a use for the property based on his or her motivations, but also based on the operation of markets—for the property itself, either sold or rented, or for the outputs that it can produce. In other words, the property can be used to maximize the economic return to the owner. The owner has a right to the use and control of that property. And the existence of markets allows owners to seek out the most productive and profitable use for their property.

One necessary implication of property and property rights is that both must be defined within a particular society. Property implies possession and control. It has been, and can still be, determined by force and conquest. Property can be appropriated, willingly or unwillingly. In modern capitalist societies, we have legal documents that convey ownership—deeds, registrations, wills, and stock certificates. In addition, there are legislative, administrative, and judicial dimensions to the definition of property and property rights. Land is surveyed, counties record deeds of land and home ownership, communities pass zoning laws that regulate the use of property, and courts adjudicate disputes among property owners and enforce contracts. Property is an institution that is central to the functioning of markets in a capitalist economy, but it is also an institution that gets its status from the social and political processes of the society.

Those without Property—The Peasants

During the early Middle Ages, the serfs on feudal manors seem to have accepted their lot in life. Their lives had security and certainty, if also hard work and poverty. What complaining there was seems to have been confined to individual peasants or manors. In the later centuries of the Middle Ages, however, as feudal institutions began to change and be replaced by emergent capitalist institutions, the peasants began actively and widely to oppose their rulers.

Beginning in the late fourteenth century and continuing through the sixteenth century, peasant revolts sprang up all over Western Europe. In most cases, the peasants were resisting change and attempting to secure their legal places in the feudal order. They opposed increasing mechanization of agricultural work, the consolidation of plots, the enclosure movement, the seizure of lands, and many of the other changes that signaled the rise of the landed gentry—and the demise of the peasants' rights to land and protection. All of these rebellions were brutally put down by the well-armed nobility. The peasants were leaderless, unorganized, and poorly armed. Their actions did, however, reflect a deep sense of outrage at the costs they bore as a result of fundamental changes in the economic, political, and social order of their day. Out of this history came the legends of Robin Hood and other outlaws of the Middle Ages.

During this period, British people in rural England were totally dependent on the productivity of the land. Those who lived in villages used common land to raise their crops, keep their bees, graze their livestock, and gather their firewood. Without access to land, they would have been without any means to sustain their lives. Over an extended period of time, a series of parliamentary acts converted many of the commons into private property. Whole villages were deserted; people who were independent when they could use the common lands became either vagrant or dependent on employment by those who owned the land.

Private Property and the Rise of Capitalism

The formation of truly private property, one of the fundamental prerequisites of capitalism, can be traced to the early history of England. As feudalism faded at the end of the Middle Ages, the notion of property in England was defined in legal terms. Laws conferred or acknowledged the right of ownership and protected the owner's control over the use of property. From the owner's perspective, such property rights and legal protection allowed for maximum earnings from the land and ensured their dominant position in society. From the perspective of the peasants, control of land was torn from them out of their own adversity and weakness through conquest and legal manipulation. This ensured their position at the bottom of society, forcing them into vagrancy or a dependence on wage labor for income. Out of frustration, peasants revolted against the emergence of private property throughout the late Middle Ages.

14. What were the economic roots of the peasant rebellions?
15. What would you predict happened to the distribution of income in England as a result of these changes in property ownership?

Critics of the Institution of Private Property

Socialists and other reform-minded economists blamed the poverty and poor conditions experienced by landless peasants and the working class on the system of private property upon which capitalism was based. Capitalists, these economists wrote, use the productive resources they own for their own benefit, exploiting workers in the process. Workers have no choice but to accept low wages and poor working conditions because they do not own property and therefore must work for someone else in order to survive. Pierre Joseph Proudhon (1809–1865), a French economist, forcefully argued against private property in his essay "What Is Property?" (1840):

> If I were asked to answer the following question: *What is slavery?* and I should answer in one word, *It is murder,* my meaning would be understood at once. No extended argument would be required to show that the power to take from a man his thought, his will, his personality, is a power of life and death; and that to enslave a man is to kill him. Why, then, to this other question: *What is property?* may I not likewise answer, *It is robbery,* without the certainty of being misunderstood; the second proposition being no other than a transformation of the first?
>
> Reader, calm yourself: I am no agent of discord, no firebrand of sedition. I anticipate history by a few days; I disclose a truth whose development we may try in vain to arrest; I write the preamble of our future constitution. This proposition which seems to you blasphemous—*property is robbery*—would, if our prejudices allowed us to consider it, be recognized as the lightning-rod to shield us from the coming thunderbolt; but too many interests stand in the way! . . . Alas! philosophy will not change the course of events; destiny will fulfill itself regardless of prophecy. Besides, must not justice be done and our education be finished?
>
> The proprietor, the robber, the hero, the sovereign—for all these titles are synonymous—imposes his will as law, and suffers neither contradiction nor control; that is, he pretends to be the legislative and executive power at once. Accordingly, the substitution of the scientific and true law for the royal will be accomplished only by a terrible struggle; and this constant substitution is, after property, the most potent element in history, the most prolific source of political disturbances. Examples are too numerous and too striking to require enumeration.

Here, Proudhon identifies the holders of private property (business owners, or capitalists) as dictators who have unchecked power over the laborers who work for them. To Proudhon, this power made the relationship between capitalist and worker akin to slavery and gave the capitalist the power to rob workers of a fair price for their labor.

16. *"What is property? . . . It is robbery."* True or false? What does Proudhon mean by this? What historical developments in the emergence of private property would support this claim?

Proudhon is careful to differentiate **property** from **possessions**. He has no quarrel with people owning *personal* possessions—homes, farms, tools, livestock, furniture, or any of the things we might own and use. He protests the ownership of *impersonal* property that is not used by the owner except to collect rents on land and interest and profits on capital that are produced by others. The difference between property and possessions is an important distinction for many socialist authors. Here is Proudhon's statement about the difference:

> Individual possession is the condition of social life; five thousand years of property demonstrate it. Property is the suicide of society. Possession is a right; property is against right. Suppress property while maintaining possession, and, by this simple modification of the principle you will revolutionize law, government, economy, and institutions; you will drive evil from the face of the earth.

17. To demonstrate your understanding of Proudhon's definition, list five currently familiar examples of "possessions" and five of "property."

Despite the protest by Proudhon and others, the march towards capitalism continued.

Emergent Capitalism

By the late fifteenth and early sixteenth centuries in England, France, Spain, Belgium, and Holland, modern nation-states involving a coalition of monarchs and merchant capitalists had effectively eliminated the decentralized power of the feudal system. In its place emerged a new type of economic system, the key elements of which formed the historical roots of **capitalism.** Profits became the primary motivation for productive activity. The resources necessary for production and distribution—the raw materials, tools, shops, factories, machinery—were owned by a new class of capitalists. Capitalists used their ownership of capital to organize production, sell goods, and earn profits. The profits, in turn, could be used to enrich the capitalists and to develop more capital. More capital led to more output, more profits, and so on in an accumulation of economic growth.

The sources of this early **capital accumulation process** and the emergence of capitalism were rooted in the increase in trade, exploration (along with colonialism and slavery), the enclosure movement, and the putting-out system. The new class of capitalists developed as the leading force in the economic system, and a new labor force, dependent on wages for income, changed the character of society, as well as the distribution of income. Like feudalism, capitalism would also change and develop, although even today it retains its basic elements of private ownership, profit making, and markets. The earliest form that capitalism took was called mercantilism.

Mercantilism

To build and consolidate their political, economic, and military power, the new nation-states adopted a policy of **mercantilism.** Underlying that policy was the assumption that the foundation of a nation's power and prestige was trading. The object of trading was to accumulate and retain gold and silver bullion, which could be used to finance further trade or to enhance the nation's political and military power. This concern led to exploration to discover and hoard more precious metals. It also led to policies designed to maximize the flow of money into the nation and minimize the flow of money out.

Consequently, under mercantilism, the king designated monopolies in the trade of specific products to minimize the prices of imports and maximize the prices of exports. The state also controlled importing and exporting, levied tariffs on imports, subsidized exports, and controlled shipping extensively. The state thus took a large degree of responsibility in geographic expansion and in controlling economic activity. At first, this sponsorship aided some nascent capitalists, but the state's overriding control over the economy eventually began to burden increasing numbers of individualistic and profit-motivated businesspeople.

Like feudalism before it, mercantilism created a series of internal contradictions that gradually undermined the system. The controlled nature of the economy proved to be a constraint for new capitalist businesses, which wanted more trade and greater access to markets. They began to pressure for change and for a new economic philosophy in which free markets reigned and the king and the monopolists no longer held sway. As we will see in the next chapter, this philosophy, called classical liberalism, was championed by the great economist and philosopher Adam Smith.

 Conclusion

In this chapter, we began with a description of what an economic system is and showed how economic systems change over time. In particular, we have explored the historical development of economic systems from antiquity to emergent capitalism. In the remaining chapters of Part 2, we will examine how economic thought has changed as well over the years.

Review Questions

1. Discuss the distinguishing characteristics of ancient economic systems.

2. What must an economic system accomplish? Why?

3. Why is surplus a source of economic growth?

4. Explain the transition from feudalism to capitalism, and identify the main differences between the two systems.

5. Of the factors that caused feudalism to decline, which do you think was most important? Why?

6. Under mercantilism, how was the economy organized?

7. Why was the institution of private property important to the economic development of capitalism? Why were some economists critical of private ownership of land and productive resources (the means of production)?

8. What is the importance of markets to a capitalist economic system?

9. Reread the passage by Karl Marx at the beginning of the chapter. Paraphrase his point in the last paragraph. Do you agree with his argument? Why or why not?

10. "The results of economic activity—what gets produced and how it gets produced—organized through an economic system, condition the nature, history and development of a society and its people." Give examples from human history. Give examples from your own experience.

11. "Economic development is obviously of crucial importance to any society and its continued survival." Why is this obvious? What would happen to a society if it didn't experience economic development? What are the advantages of economic development? Do you think that economic development has advantages for you? What are they?

CHAPTER FOUR

Adam Smith, Classical Liberalism, and the Division of Labor

▪ Introduction

*I*n the eighteenth and nineteenth centuries mercantilist restrictions gave rise to an opposition that ultimately prevailed and drastically reduced the amount of direct state interference in economic affairs. The movement to end mercantilism was spearheaded by a new philosophical and economic body of thought—**classical liberalism.**

Adam Smith was one of the first thinkers to develop a comprehensive description and analysis of this emerging economic system. Property and property rights contributed to the formation of new methods of production, including the division of labor, with specialization of tasks, which promoted an explosive expansion of output. The rise of capitalism also resulted in new ways of distributing income.

Those articulating classical liberal ideas were primarily academics who wanted to transfer control of their national economies from the mercantilism of aristocratic ruling classes that regulated all aspects of production and trade, to an unregulated market system that was thought to be self-regulating. They called this system (from the Physiocrats in France) **laissez-faire,** *meaning "let it happen," or "let it be." J. B. Say, a French economist, popularized Smith's work, particularly the idea of self-regulating markets.*

The Rise of Classical Liberalism and the Industrial Revolution

In 1776, the Scottish philosopher Adam Smith published *The Wealth of Nations*, in which he argued forcefully that mercantilist policies interfered with the ability of private individuals and markets to produce maximum social welfare. Smith maintained that, although everyone was basically out to maximize his or her own welfare, private competition in production and consumption would ensure the best possible outcome for all. Therefore Smith argued that the state should not be overly involved in economic activity, and that beyond providing for law and order, national defense, and some public goods like highways, the state should take a laissez-faire attitude toward the economic system. Individuals would guide production and consumption. The emerging capitalist class in Western Europe seized on this philosophy and used it eventually to legislate an end to most mercantilist restrictions on trade and other economic activity.

Left to their own devices and the profit motive, English capitalists took early advantage of the technological advances of the Industrial Revolution. The development and introduction of more sophisticated machinery in textiles, transportation, iron production, and other industries led to a phenomenal increase in the productive capacity of the English economic system. The Industrial Revolution, as well as the entrepreneurs who financed and led it, spread throughout Western Europe and to North America.

However, the increase in production was not the only outcome of the Industrial Revolution and emergent capitalism. The factory became the symbol of a new manufacturing society, alongside continuing agricultural and community life. In the factory, working conditions were often unsafe and oppressive. Child labor was a fact of early industrial life. Men, women, and children depended almost totally on factory work for their livelihood. Families flocked to the cities in search of work. Outside the factories, people were crammed into the adjacent slums. Friedrich Engels, in *The Condition of the Working Class in England in 1844*, quotes a government commissioner's description of a Glasgow slum, the "wynds":

> The wynds . . . house a fluctuating population between 15,000 and 30,000 persons. This district is composed of many narrow streets and square courts and in the middle of each court there is a dunghill. Although the outward appearance of these places was revolting, I was nevertheless quite unprepared for the filth and misery that were to be found inside. In some bedrooms we visited at night we found a whole mass of humanity stretched on the floor. There were often 15 to 20 men and women huddled together, some being clothed and others naked. There was hardly any furniture there and the only thing which gave these holes the appearance of a dwelling was fire burning on the hearth. Thieving and prostitution are the main sources of income of these people.

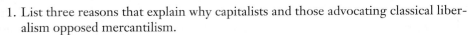
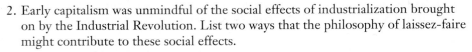

1. List three reasons that explain why capitalists and those advocating classical liberalism opposed mercantilism.

2. Early capitalism was unmindful of the social effects of industrialization brought on by the Industrial Revolution. List two ways that the philosophy of laissez-faire might contribute to these social effects.

The emergence of capitalism and a free market for labor encouraged, as well as fed on, the Industrial Revolution. These forces produced rapid economic growth and the factory system, as well as urban slums and adverse working conditions. Central to these changes was the spread of markets for goods and services throughout Western Europe and the world. With the diminution of the roles of tradition, custom, and the state in the economic affairs of Western Europeans, capitalism relied increasingly on *markets* to organize production and distribution. As factors of production, land, labor, and capital all became commodities that were bought and sold on markets for prices. This required the emergence of a market system in which producers made calculations based on prices of resources and products and directed attention toward the accumulation of profits.

Economic activity was thus directed through the operation of these markets and the determination of prices in them. The treatment of land, labor, and capital as commodities contrasted with the feudal system, wherein land and labor were part of the social organization of communities (feudal manors and guilds) and were regulated by social custom, tradition, and institutions. With the emergence of capitalism, land and labor became subject to the market for their occupation and use. In this way, as historian Karl Polanyi argues in *The Great Transformation*, capitalism required the subordination of social considerations to the economic dictates of the private market system. Production and distribution were organized, for the society, through markets.

3. Explain the significance of markets in capitalism.

Adam Smith and the Division of Labor

Much of our current thinking about specialization and the **division of labor** has been influenced by the writings of Adam Smith (1723–1790). The **division of labor** involves separating different parts of the production process of any good or service. Instead of one person making each computer, teams of workers make the casings, the chips, the boards, the connections, and the final assembly. **Specialization** results from workers' focusing on and developing expertise in one aspect of the entire process of producing computers. Smith was a Scottish scholar, primarily a moral philosopher, but also the father of modern economics. His writing reflected changes he saw taking place, such as the introduction of modern productive methods, including the assembly line, which were derived from the early development of capitalism during the Industrial Revolution.

The year 1776 is significant because Adam Smith's great book *An Inquiry into the Nature and Causes of the Wealth of Nations* was published. It was the first comprehensive treatise about economics. However, there had been many books and essays about economic matters before Adam Smith, and he used some of these ideas in his book. In his text, Smith created a fairly complete picture of the way an economy behaves and why it behaved as it did in 1776. His observations coincided with the acceleration of the Industrial Revolution and the increasing importance of both domestic and international markets to British capitalists. In *The Wealth of Nations*, Smith also argued for the replacement of mercantilism with competitive markets.

Smith begins *The Wealth of Nations* with this classic description "Of the Division of Labour" in the context of emerging capitalist production:

> The greatest improvement in the productive powers of labour, and the greater part of the skill, dexterity, and judgment with which it is any where directed, or applied, seem to have been the effects of the division of labour.
> To take an example from a very trifling manufacturer: but one in which the division of labour has been very often taken notice of, the trade of the pinmaker; a

Adam Smith (1723–1790).
(Bettmann/Corbis)

workman not educated to this business (which the division of labour has rendered a distinct trade), not acquainted with the use of the machinery employed in it (to the invention of which the same division of labour has probably given occasion), could scarce, perhaps, with his utmost industry, make one pin in a day, and certainly could not make twenty. But in the way in which this business is now carried on, not only the whole work is a peculiar trade, but it is divided into a number of branches, of which the greater part are likewise peculiar trades. One man draws out the wire, another straights it, a third cuts it, a fourth points it, a fifth grinds it at the top for receiving the head; to make the head requires two or three distinct operations; to put it on, is a peculiar business, to whiten the pins is another; it is even a trade by itself to put them into the paper; and the important business of making a pin is, in this manner, divided into about eighteen distinct operations, which, in some manufactories, are all performed by distinct hands, though in others the same man will sometimes perform two or three of them. I have seen a small manufactory of this kind where ten men only were employed, and where some of them consequently performed two or three distinct operations. But though they were very poor, and therefore but indifferently accommodated with the necessary machinery, they could, when they exerted themselves, make among them about twelve pounds of pins in a day. There are in a pound upwards of four thousand pins of a middling size. Those ten persons, therefore, could make among them upwards of forty-eight thousand pins in a day. Each person, therefore, making a tenth part of forty-eight thousand pins, might be considered as making four thousand eight hundred pins in a day.

4. In what ways might Adam Smith's perceptions have been influenced by the historical time when he wrote this part of the book?

5. Explain the importance of such specialization in Smith's pin factory. Who gains from such specialization?

With this description of the division of labor, Adam Smith highlighted the role of specialization in significantly increasing productive potential. He attributed this great increase in productivity to three factors:

1. "The improvement of the dexterity of the workman necessarily increases the quantity of work he can perform; and the division of labor, by reducing every man's business to some one simple operation, and by making this operation the sole employment of his life, necessarily increases very much the dexterity of the workman."

2. The worker would gain time that used to be lost in moving from one type of work to another.

3. Labor would be made more productive by the application of machinery that would facilitate the division of labor.

Thus, specialization and the application of new technologies during the Industrial Revolution of the late eighteenth and early nineteenth centuries contributed to rapidly expanding output.

An important result of this increase in output accompanying the division of labor was that each worker "has a great quantity of his own work to dispose of beyond what he himself has occasion for." Since every worker is in the same position, **exchange** will take place. Smith puts it this way: "He supplies them abundantly with what they have occasion for, and they accommodate him as amply with what he has occasion for, and a general plenty diffuses itself through all the different ranks of the society." Through the division of labor, economic output will increase, and the existence of exchange will facilitate and further encourage this growth in output. The extension of **markets** (where goods and services are exchanged) throughout the world, the technological revolution, and the division of labor mutually reinforced one another.

6. "And the division of labor, by reducing every man's business to some one simple operation, and by making this operation the sole employment of his life, necessarily increases very much the dexterity of the workman."
   a. Imagine having a job where one simple operation made the sole employment of your life. Do you think that your dexterity might improve?
   b. Do you think that people working on an assembly line would agree with your answer?

Smith traced the emergence of the division of labor in production to the fact that people do exchange goods and services: "It is the necessary, though very slow and gradual, consequence of a propensity in human nature which has in view no such extensive utility: *the propensity to truck, barter, and exchange* one thing for another" [italics added]. Because people have a tendency to exchange, they will begin to specialize in producing what they do best and to trade with others for the other things that they need. Through this process, the division of labor proceeds and economic output increases. Historically, the rapidly spreading and more sophisticated markets in Western Europe tremendously accelerated the development of the division of labor.

Adam Smith further argued that all of this great economic progress derived from the seeking of self-interest by individuals. Individuals enter markets for exchange to benefit themselves. But out of this quest for self-gain, a general good develops in the form of increasing prosperity for all:

> But man has almost constant occasion for the help of his brethren, and it is in vain for him to expect it from their benevolence only. He will be more likely to prevail if he can interest their self-love in his favour, and shew them that it is for their own advantage to do for him what he requires of them. Whoever offers to another a bargain of any kind, proposes to do this. Give me that which I want, and you shall have this which you want, is the meaning of every such offer; and it is in this manner that we obtain from one another the far greater part of those good offices which we stand in need of. It is not from the benevolence of the butcher, the brewer, or the baker, that we expect our dinner, but from their regard to their own interest. We address ourselves, not to their humanity but to their self-love, and never talk to them of our own necessities but of their advantages.

General prosperity and economic growth—the wealth of the nation—result from the pursuit of self-interest organized through the division of labor and markets. This is the essence of what Smith calls the **invisible hand,** the force whereby the operation of markets—unfettered by mercantilist regulations—produces general welfare for all, where resources are allocated efficiently.

7. Adam Smith thought the division of labor derived from people's "propensity to truck, barter, and exchange one thing for another." Can you think of examples where this holds true today? Are there other factors that might enter into the division of labor today?

8. "But man has almost constant occasion for the help of his brethren, and it is in vain for him to expect it from their benevolence only. He will be more likely to prevail if he can interest their self-love in his favour, and shew them that it is for their own advantage to do for him what he requires of them."

   a. What does Smith assume about the nature of people's behavior? How did Smith arrive at this conclusion?

   b. If it is an accurate assumption about present behavior, do people have any choice about behaving in any other way?

Side Effects of the Division of Labor

Adam Smith focused on the relation of the division of labor, specialization, exchange, and markets to the wealth of nations. He also showed sensitivity to some side effects of the division of labor. The first of these is a problem that we still experience today: the alienation and boredom of manual labor, the assembly line, and office work. These result from the division of labor and specialization within the workplace, motivated by the capitalist's search for profits and the need to manage labor. Smith wrote about this problem bluntly and graphically in this passage from *The Wealth of Nations:*

> In the progress of the division of labour, the employment of the far greater part of those who live by labour, that is, of the great body of the people, comes to be confined to a few very simple operations, frequently to one or two. But the understandings of the greater part of men are necessarily formed by their ordinary employments. The man whose whole life is spent in performing a few simple operations, of which the effects too are, perhaps, always the same, or very nearly the same, has no occasion to exert his understanding, or to exercise his invention in finding out expedients for removing difficulties which never occur. He naturally loses, therefore, the habit of such exertion, and generally becomes as stupid and ignorant as it is possible for a human creature to become. The torpor of his mind renders him not only incapable of relishing or bearing a part in any rational conversation, but of conceiving any generous, noble, or tender sentiment, and consequently of forming any just judgment concerning many even of the ordinary duties of private life.
>
> His dexterity at his own particular trade seems, in this manner, to be acquired at the expense of his intellectual, social, and martial virtues. But in every improved and civilized society this is the state into which the labouring poor, that is, the great body of the people, must necessarily fall, unless government takes some pains to prevent it.

An additional consequence of this tendency is that the guidance of society must fall to the few, the elite, who are not stupefied by the repetitiveness of their labors. In fact, the division of labor under capitalism not only increased efficiency, it also promoted the control of the capitalist over the work process and the workers. This can also be seen in the emergence of the putting-out system and later the factory system (see Chapter 3). This process effectively splits society into classes—the educated elite and the "great body of the people"—which also have different claims on the income generated by production.

9. Does specialization normally result in workers who are "as stupid and ignorant as it is possible for a human creature to become"? How was this statement of Smith's conditioned by historical time? Do you agree with Smith's conclusion? Why or why not?

The Distribution of Income

Economic production creates value—goods and services for exchange on markets. Once this value has been produced, income determines how it will be divided among the people. Early economists, such as Adam Smith, who were beginning to think of economics as a social science, defined and classified income receivers as they appeared at that time. They classified the receivers of the shares of output into the following categories: (1) **laborers,** (2) **landowners,** and (3) **owners of capital.** Smith also named the shares of income that each receives: labor receives **wages,** landowners receive **rent,** and owners of capital receive **profits.**

Each of these shares is received in money, but the money is only a claim for the real goods and services. It would have no value without those goods and services to claim as the money holder's share. Thus, income distribution determines the distribution of products.

> 10. Another way of thinking about money in relation to claims on the shares of production is to imagine each dollar in the hands of the income receivers (labor, landowners, and capital owners) as a draft on people's labor. Are there (or will there be) dollar drafts on your labor? Can you refuse to be drafted? Who might be exempt from the dollar draft? If drafted, when do you have to perform your service?

Adam Smith recognized that this division of the national product into shares must bring about some harsh conflicts among the three groups of share receivers:

> Envy, malice, or resentment, are the only passions which can prompt one man to injure another in his person or reputation. . . . Men may live together in society with some tolerable degree of security, though there is no civil magistrate to protect them from the injustice of those passions. But avarice and ambition in the rich, in the poor the hatred of labour and the love of present ease and enjoyment, are the passions which prompt to invade property, passions much more steady in their operation, and much more universal in their influence. Wherever there is great property, there is great inequality. For one very rich man, there must be at least five hundred poor, and the affluence of the few supposes the indigence of the many. The affluence of the rich excites the indignation of the poor, who are often both driven by want, and prompted by envy, to invade his possessions. It is only under the shelter of the civil magistrate that the owner of that valuable property, which is acquired by the labour of many years, or perhaps of many successive generations, can sleep a single night in security. The acquisition of valuable and extensive property, therefore, necessarily requires the establishment of civil government.

The shares of the national product, then, are distributed unequally, primarily because of the unequal distribution of private property (land and capital). While this may lead to conflicts among the different groups of share receivers because each wants to maximize its own share, the government protects private property and, hence, its share of the output.

> 11. "The acquisition of valuable and extensive property, therefore, necessarily requires the establishment of civil government." Is Smith noting that the purpose of government is to protect the rich from the poor? What is the purpose of government?

In addition to the role played by the state, the operation of markets also resolves the conflict over the division of national output. Each group is out to maximize its position, its own share of production. However, all economic transactions take place in markets for goods and services and, as a result, are regulated by the operation of competition. A worker will not work for a lower wage if he or she can get a higher wage from another employer. A person will not buy a product at a price greater than that of another seller. Smith explains this in the following passage on the "invisible hand":

> Every individual is continually exerting himself to find out the most advantageous employment for whatever capital he can command. It is his own advantage, indeed, and not that of the society, which he has in view. But the study of his own advantage naturally, or rather necessarily leads him to prefer that employment which is most advantageous to the society.
>
> But the annual revenue of every society is always precisely equal to the exchangeable value of the whole annual produce of its industry, or rather is precisely the same thing with that exchangeable value. As every individual, therefore, endeavours as much as he can both to employ his capital in the support of domestic industry, and so to direct that industry that its produce may be of the greatest value; every individual necessarily labours to render the annual revenue of the society as great as he can. He generally, indeed, neither intends to promote the public interest, nor knows how much he is promoting it. By preferring the support of domestic to that of foreign industry, he intends only his own security; and by directing that industry in such a manner as its produce may be of the greatest value, he intends only his own gain, and he is in this, as in many other cases, led by *an invisible hand* to promote an end which was no part of his intention. Nor is it always the worse for the society that it was no part of it. By pursuing his own interest he frequently promotes that of the society more effectually than when he really intends to promote it.

Despite the apparent conflict and the motivation of self-gain, the operation of the economic system produces the greatest good for the greatest number. According to Smith, social good results, even though "society . . . was no part" of directing the activity. Rather, it results from everyone's seeking his or her own advantage.

12. What does Smith mean when he says, "He is in this, as in many other cases, led by *an invisible hand*"? What is an "invisible hand"?
13. Smith says, "But the study of his own advantage naturally, or rather necessarily leads him to prefer that employment which is most advantageous to the society." Can you think of any counterexamples?

The Flow of Economic Activity

As we have seen from Smith's analysis above, three factors of production (land, labor, and capital) are combined to create the national product. Each controller of the three productive factors—landlords, laborers, and capitalists—receives a

FIGURE 4.1   The Flow of Economic Activity

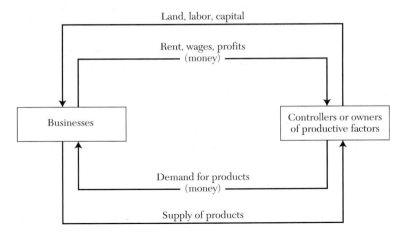

share of the total product transformed conveniently into money and uses it to claim output. Thus, the controllers of the factors of production receive claims on shares for everything they supply in the production process, and these claims become the demand for part of the total product. Demand for the product is therefore created in the process of supplying the product. Figure 4.1 illustrates this flow of economic activity.

J. B. Say and Say's Law

Smith's ideas were widely discussed and popularized by the French economist Jean Baptiste Say (1767–1832). Say argued that removing exacting mercantile control of markets would produce rapid economic progress. The Physiocrats had earlier called for laissez-faire. As laissez-faire ideas were adopted, growth did take place, but it was accompanied by poverty and recurring swings in economic activity (business cycles). During these cycles, a period of rapid economic growth would be followed by a decline in spending, a glut of goods and services, and a recession. Say's 1803 *Treatise on Political Economy* stated the idea, which became known as **Say's law.**

> It is worthwhile to remark that a product is no sooner created, than it, from that instant, affords a market for other products to the full extent of its own value. When the producer has put the finishing hand to his product, he is most anxious to sell it immediately, lest its value should vanish in his hands. Nor is he less anxious to dispose of the money he may get for it; for the value of money is also perishable. But the only way of getting rid of money is in the purchase of some product or other. Thus, the mere circumstance of the creation of one product immediately opens a vent for other products.

Say assured economists that if markets were left free, there could only be temporary and minor problems of unemployment. He believed this was true because he thought that production (supply) would always create its own demand: The income generated from producing goods and services would always be sufficient to buy the goods and services produced. For example, suppose that in order to supply a product, a local business owner pays out $50,000 in wages to workers in exchange for their labor, $20,000 in rent to the landlord, and keeps $30,000 for herself as profits. The community now has a total of $100,000 in income. What will people do with this money? According to the flow of economic activity (see Figure 4.1), they will spend it on various products. When consumers spend money on products, the money is returned to businesses. Thus, the act of supplying products creates the income that is used to purchase products. Supply (of products) creates demand (for other products). This doctrine was widely accepted by most economists throughout the nineteenth century.

J. B. Say and Gluts

A few economists were concerned about unemployment resulting from more production than people might demand. What if some wrong products are produced, and they are not all purchased? Won't there be unemployment because of insufficient demand in those industries? What if there is more production generally than the people are able to purchase? Economists called this situation a **glut** in the market. Throughout the early history of capitalism, there were recurring gluts that led to economic crises, or recessions. During recessions, businesses could not sell all of the goods they produced, factories lay idle, and unemployment, accompanied by poverty and misery, soared.

Thomas Robert Malthus (1766–1834), a British economist, was one of the few economists concerned about these gluts. In his *Principles of Political Economy* (1820), Malthus observed that while laborers usually spent all of their wages on necessities to maintain their families, capitalists spent only some of their profits and saved the rest. Although Say believed that all money saved would be returned to the economy as purchases of capital goods such as machinery and equipment (investment), Malthus disagreed. Malthus thought that as capitalism progressed, capitalists would earn greater and greater profits while wages would fall. With falling wages, laborers would be less able to purchase the products they produced. But if capitalists' profits were invested in ever greater amounts, then—given the decline in labor incomes—production would increase unsustainably, leading to a glut. As firms decreased output in response to a glut, a recession and higher levels of unemployment would follow.

14. If a recession is caused by too little demand, how might a government go about ending a recession?

Say and others countered the underconsumption argument set forth by Malthus by claiming that whenever a glut of any particular product emerged, markets would immediately adjust through price changes and the reallocation of resources. If one product was overproduced, its price would fall, and resources would go elsewhere. Activity would shift to those products "most in request." In addition, if capitalists earned greater profits and saved more money (as Malthus feared), this would simply mean greater pools of money for them to use for purchases of additional capital goods (investment). Say believed that any additional savings would be followed in short order by additional capital goods purchases, which would sustain demand in the market. Consequently, gluts would soon be eliminated through the operation of the market system. This reasoning supported the idea of laissez-faire, because no government intervention was needed to solve the problem of gluts.

Laissez-Faire

J. B. Say won the argument with Thomas Malthus in the realm of economic theory. There were significant reasons for this victory, in spite of the prevalence of repeated gluts, unemployment, poverty, and economic depressions in capitalist nations.

Economists and business owners (capitalists) were convinced that a self-adjusting economy, free from government controls, was the best system for generating profits and growth. This was Smith's concept of an "invisible hand" directing a free economy to prosperity. The idea of laissez-faire was similar to this "invisible hand." Capitalists wanted to run their own affairs without—well, almost without—government interference.

The idea of laissez-faire is to permit market forces *under competitive conditions* to operate unhindered. Economists said that if the market were permitted to work on its own, it would be most efficient and most advantageous to society. People would demand the products they wanted as they spent their income. This would determine which products would be produced. Competition would ensure that products were produced for the lowest price possible. Doesn't that seem better than having a powerful individual or group of people decide which products will be produced?

Laissez-faire, said the economists, has additional benefits: All of the owners of the factors of production will be directed into the most efficient use of the factors of production by the market. It will be to their greatest advantage to produce the products for which there is a demand in the marketplace. If the owners of the productive factors use them to produce only what they themselves want, no one will purchase the products. There will be smaller shares of national income given to those productive-factor owners who don't follow market demand.

Therefore, the theory went, let the market be; *laissez-faire*; don't interfere with it. It is controlled by an "invisible hand." It will regulate itself. Furthermore, markets will eliminate any gluts and unemployment. Let it be.

All of this is based on the assumption that people will work for their own self-interest. Adam Smith had already asserted the validity of this assumption.

In fact, one of the great ironies of the concept of laissez-faire is that it requires the government to define and enforce its primary institution—private property. Karl Polanyi, in his history of the emergence of capitalism and laissez-faire, *The Great Transformation,* emphasizes the willful creation of a new economic order:

> There was nothing natural about laissez-faire; free markets could never come into being merely by allowing things to take their course. Just as cotton manufacturers—the leading free trade industry—were created by the help of protective tariffs, export bounties, and indirect wage subsidies, laissez-faire itself was enforced by the state.

15. Evaluate the strengths and limits of laissez-faire.

16. What are your assumptions about people's behavior? Are they consistently selfish? Are they consistently altruistic (meaning their actions are based on regard for others)? Which are you? Were we born selfish or altruistic? Are we educated to be selfish or altruistic? If so, by whom or what?

17. Would Adam Smith think it is more patriotic to be selfish or altruistic? Why?

As mercantilist policies were abandoned and laissez-faire policies were adopted in England, the Industrial Revolution and the emergence of capitalist institutions proceeded. During this period, business sought freedom from intrusive state control, and prospered.

Adam Smith argued that it would be better to transfer control of the economy from the self-interest of the ruling class to individual self-interest as expressed in the marketplace. His preference for nontraditional direction led him to perceive the market as an impartial control of resource allocation and income distribution. He hoped the market was impartial, but was it? Smith was aware of the difficulties in his solution. He knew about the ability of combinations of employers to overwhelm the bargaining power of workers, but he continued to support markets free from mercantilist government controls —laissez-faire.

What he may not have fully perceived was that the transfer of market controls from the self-interest of the ruling class to the self-interest of those who had the control of the largest quantities of productive resources was not necessarily the ideal solution for a sick economy. But it may have been an improvement in 1776, when compared with the abuses of mercantilism. Smith thought it would be when he wrote in *The Wealth of Nations* about the allocation of capital by an individual:

> What is the species of domestic industry which his capital can employ, and of which the produce is likely to be of the greatest value, every individual, it is evident, can, in his local situation, judge much better than any statesman or lawgiver can do for him. The statesman, who should attempt to direct private people in what manner they ought to employ their capitals, would not only load himself with a most unnecessary attention, but assume an authority which could safely be trusted, not only to no single person, but to no council or senate whatever, and which would nowhere be so dangerous as in the hands of a man who had folly and presumption enough to fancy himself fit to exercise it.

■ Conclusion

Property, markets, exchange, division of labor, and specialization emerged in the development of capitalism. Along with these institutions and aspects of changing economic activity, economic theory began to develop to describe, explain, and promote capitalism. In addition to economists contributing to the development of capitalism there were others critical of the lowered standard of living of workers and of contradictions within the capitalist system. These economists were either ignored or viewed as dangerous radicals by the dominant school of economists in the universities and the ruling classes. In this chapter, we have examined the argument for laissez-faire capitalism. In the next chapter, we will explore in more detail Karl Marx's critiques of the development and operation of laissez-faire capitalism.

Review Questions

1. Much of the argument for laissez-faire was based on assumptions about the economy, including Say's law, the assumption that the economy would always be sufficiently competitive, and the notion that consumers were always selfish, rational, and calculating. Under what circumstances might these assumptions fail? What are the implications for the economy if these assumptions do not hold?

2. Proudhon and other economists argued that laissez-faire meant freedom for the capitalist but bondage for workers. Smith, Say, and other advocates of laissez-faire argued that unregulated capitalism meant freedom for all. Are there circumstances under which Proudhon's view is likely to be more accurate? Are there circumstances when Smith's view is likely to be more apt? Explain.

3. Under mercantilism, in addition to assigning trade monopolies to selected merchants and companies, king's extracted taxes from imports and exports to enrich the royal coffers, funding military and other expenditures. Adam Smith opposed such government intervention in the mercantilist era. What were his objections to mercantilism? What roles did Adam Smith envision for government in the economy?

4. Smith argued that unregulated (laissez-faire) capitalism would lead to substantial increases in income for all. Explain exactly how this was supposed to come about.

5. Smith believed that laissez-faire capitalism would be self-regulating via the invisible hand. Develop an example that illustrates these principles. Using your example, evaluate Smith's argument.

6. Reading Smith in the early twenty-first century, do you find that there are topics that are still applicable to today's economy? If so, which still apply? Do there seem to be areas in which his insight seems faulty? If so, what are those?

7. Have there been times recently when there has been a general glut of goods or services? Has there been a glut of one kind of good? What has been the result? Explain.

8. What reasons can you think of that would cast doubt on Say's law that supply always creates its own demand?

CHAPTER FIVE

Karl Marx and the Socialist Critique of Capitalism

▮ Introduction

As capitalism developed in Western Europe and the United States, a critique of some of its results began to emerge. The conditions of some members of the economy were improving with laissez-faire, but the fate of others was extreme poverty. Why weren't conditions for the poor improving as well? As markets and private property emerged in Western Europe, most people became dependent on wage labor for income. Work was not always available, and many peasants ended up in urban areas, where they inhabited emerging slums and, if possible, worked in the developing factories. Living and working conditions were extremely poor. And with so many competing for jobs, wages were very low. The growing working class during the Industrial Revolution paid the social cost of industrialization in the cities and the factories of Western Europe.

Extreme poverty and poor working conditions led to general strikes with all workers striking at the same time, revolutions, and political education activities working toward evolutionary change. John Stuart Mill (1806–1873), in his Principles of Political Economy, envisioned a different kind of economy from the one of which he was writing in England in 1848:

> The form of association, however, which if mankind continue to improve, must be expected in the end to predominate, is not that which can exist between a capitalist as chief, and workpeople without a voice in the management, but the association of the labourers themselves on terms of equality, collectively owning the capital with which they carry on their operations, and working under managers elected and removable by themselves.

The socialist critique of nineteenth-century capitalism was developed further in a piece also published in 1848. In this year, Karl Marx (1818–1883) and Friedrich Engels (1820–1895) wrote The Communist Manifesto for the Communist League, an association of working people in Germany. In the Manifesto, Marx and Engels argued forcefully that the capitalist system itself was the source of the poverty and instability experienced by the growing working class. They urged workers to organize themselves for their own protection and to fight for socialism.

In the Manifesto, Capital, *and subsequent works, Marx produced one of the first systematic analyses and critiques of capitalism. Marx's analysis provides a comprehensive and consistent framework for understanding, evaluating, and criticizing the structure and development of capitalism. For that reason alone, it is important to summarize Marx's system of thought concerning capitalism. In addition, Marxian economics has contributed to the development of economic thought, and Marxism as a political movement promoting socialism and communism has been widespread in the modern era.*

With the fall of the Soviet Union and other communist states in the late 1980s and early 1990s, it might be tempting to think that Marxism is no longer relevant to the modern world. However, the ideas of Marx are alive and well in the social democracies of Europe and in labor movements and intellectual circles around the world. In fact, in a 1999 BBC poll, Marx was voted the "greatest thinker of the millennium." It is important to understand that Marx's primary contributions to the field of economics were his analysis and critique of the evolution of capitalist economies and his description of the problems that invariably result from laissez-faire capitalism. As John Cassidy, economics writer for the New Yorker, *has stated:*

> *Marx was a student of capitalism, and that is how he should be judged. Many of the contradictions that he saw in Victorian capitalism and that were subsequently addressed by reformist governments have begun reappearing in new guises, like mutant viruses. . . . [H]e wrote riveting passages about globalization, inequality, political corruption, monopolization, technical progress, the decline of high culture, and the enervating nature of modern existence—issues that economists are now confronting anew, sometimes without realizing that they are walking in Marx's footsteps.*
>
> —*John Cassidy, "The Return of Karl Marx"* (New Yorker, *October 20–27, 1997*)

This chapter provides a brief introduction to Marxian analysis, along with a discussion of the relevance of Marx's ideas to our understanding of contemporary society.

Karl Marx: Political Economist and Revolutionary

Marx was born in 1818 in Trier, Germany. His father was a successful lawyer, and Marx began his college career in legal studies. However, he soon switched to philosophy, in which he earned a Ph.D. at the age of twenty-three. Having already become a radical in his student days, he was unable to secure a teaching position. Instead he became the editor of the *Rheinische Zeitung* in Cologne. However, this journal was suppressed by the Prussian government in 1843, and Marx, with his new wife, Jenny von Westphalen, moved to Paris, where Marx was active in left-wing journalism and in the workers' movement. It was there that he met Friedrich Engels and began to study political economy and capitalism.

Over the latter half of the 1840s, Marx's radicalism continually got him in trouble with governments. In 1845, he was expelled from France and moved to Brussels. There he wrote *The German Ideology* and *The Communist Manifesto* with Engels. In 1848 and 1849, several workers' revolutions occurred in Europe, and Belgium sent Marx packing. He first went to Paris and then to Germany. He was soon kicked out of Germany and then out of France again. Finally, in 1849, his family settled in London, where he remained for the rest of his life.

In London, Marx devoted himself to studying political economy and writing. His years there were spent in constant poverty, but he received substantial support from his friend Engels, who had a family interest in a manufacturing firm in Manchester. Marx developed into one of the most profound and widely known critics of capitalism in mid-nineteenth-century Europe. His work had two basic elements: one was his study and writing, and the other was his political activism. He was a correspondent for the *New York Daily Tribune* and published numerous books, the most famous of which is *Capital*. His political activism was as a socialist and communist in the workers' movement. He helped organize the International Working Men's Association—the First International—and was active in workers' struggles throughout the rest of his life.

Marx wrote during the early stages of industrial capitalism. This was a time when it was not uncommon to find child laborers chained to machines and workers regularly losing limbs or even their lives in factories. Most workers lived in desperate poverty. It was in this environment that he developed his critique of laissez-faire capitalism.

Marx's General System of Thought

Marx's political activism and his analysis of capitalism were both based on his general theory of social development. This system amounted to a theory of history and of social change. As he put it in *The Communist Manifesto*, "The history of all hitherto existing society is the history of class struggles." This expressed his "materialist conception of history," which emphasized the role of the economic aspects of life in social development. This conception is central to Marx's system of thought and his analysis of capitalism, and we will explore it briefly here.

Dialectics

Marx's general system was based on two philosophical notions: dialectics and materialism. Marx borrowed dialectics from the German philosopher Hegel (1770–1831). **Dialectics** is the study of the contradictions within the essence of things. It emphasizes the idea that all things change and that all things contain not only themselves but their opposites. A rock is a rock, but it is also, at the same time, "not a rock" because it can become a million grains of sand. Consequently, development becomes the struggle of opposites—things becoming other things. Capitalists cannot be capitalists without their opposites, the workers (and vice versa), and capitalists and workers will develop as they interact with and influence each other. Out of this struggle of opposites comes change in which both elements, capitalists and workers, and the thing itself, capitalism, are transformed into something else. The source of change is internal to the social system. Ultimately, Marx thought that the contradictions and conflicts inherent in capitalism would tear it apart, eventually causing it to develop into **socialism** (social ownership and social goals of production influenced by a strong state), and then into **communism** (communal control of the economy and a weak state).

By emphasizing change, contradiction, and the struggle of opposites, dialectics constitutes a challenge to formal logic that concentrates on things as they are and their interrelationships. Marx wrote the following in his preface to *Capital* (1867):

> Dialectic . . . in its rational form is a scandal and abomination to bourgeoisdom and its doctrinaire professors, because it includes in its comprehension affirmative recognition of the existing state of things, at the same time, also, the recognition of the negation of that state, of its inevitable breaking up; because it regards every historically developed social form as in fluid movement, and therefore, takes into account its transient nature not less than its momentary existence; because it lets nothing impose upon it, and is in its essence critical and revolutionary.

To Marx, one of the main flaws in the theories of orthodox economists was the notion that the economy tended toward stable equilibrium, whereas Marx saw constant change and recurring crises. Marx believed that the key to economics was studying how the economy evolves over time, and Marx sought to discover the "Laws of Motion" that governed the evolution of capitalism via his use of dialectics.

1. Develop your own example that emphasizes the dialectical nature of some thing or process.
2. Why is the dialectic "critical and revolutionary"?

Materialism

The other philosophical notion underlying Marxian economics, **materialism,** concerns the principle that what is basic to the real life of human beings is their activity in the world. Survival is the primary human imperative, and in order to survive, people must work within the existing economic system. We must use our intelligence and energy, along with the materials and resources available to us, to produce (or earn) enough to ensure our survival. To Marx, materialism concerns understanding the world by focusing on real people and their day-to-day activities—especially those concerned with production for continued survival. And, since for most people work determines the structure of our lives, the work process impinges upon all other aspects of life.

According to the materialist approach, to know the world we must study things and their development. In addition, we must study the interrelationships of things: "Things come into being, change and pass out of being, not as separate individual units, but in essential relation and interconnection, so that they cannot be understood each separately and by itself but only in their relation and interconnection." To know the United States, we must study its productive process and how that relates to its laws, beliefs, social classes, patterns of consumption, and so on. Additionally, we must study the history of how all these elements have changed over time and developed.

Materialism contrasts with the notion that change takes place through the development of ideas. For Marx, the source of change rests, ultimately, in actual productive activity.

3. How else could we "know" our world other than through its material aspects?

The Materialist Conception of History: Historical Materialism

From these two philosophical bases, Marx developed his theory of history—the materialist conception of history, or **historical materialism.** All theory requires abstraction and oversimplification, and Marx's system of generalizations about social development is no exception. Historical materialism states that productive activity is fundamental to human beings and to their societies. Consequently, the organization of production, the economic structure, forms the basis of all societies. All other social institutions and ideas are derived from the economic structure of the society. If the economic structure changes, all other aspects of the society will also change.

Marx formalized his analysis in the following way. The economic structure, or base, is the **mode of production** and consists of the forces of production and the relations of production. The **forces of production** include all the things necessary to produce goods and services: tools, machines, factories, means of transportation, raw materials, human labor, science, technology, skills, and knowledge. Over time, obviously, the forces of production change. The **relations of production** are determined by the relationships among people in the

productive process. When the forces of production are organized in a certain way, different classes of people will be defined by their relationship to each other in production. The relations of production, therefore, will be determined by patterns of ownership of productive resources, the nature of property relations, and the division of labor. These will determine a class structure of society. A certain mode of production, then, consists of specific forces of production and specific relations of production (that is, a specific **class structure**).

In addition, the mode of production is accompanied by the **superstructure** of society, which consists of the society's ideas, institutions, and ideologies, including laws, politics, culture, ethics, religion, morals, aesthetics, art, philosophy, and so on. The purpose of the superstructure is to support the economic base of society. For example, feudalism organized production with certain methods and institutions, and it had its own class structure and superstructure.

Within this framework is Marx's theory of historical change. Oversimplifying somewhat, when the forces of production change, the relations of production—social classes—also will change. This brings about a new mode of production that will, in turn, develop its own specific superstructure. It is in this context that class struggle takes place. Different classes have different interests and visions and thus will do battle over the organization of production and, hence, society. The "old" classes will fight to preserve the old mode of production, and the new will fight for change. One of the most fundamental aspects of this materialist conception of history is that people, by acting on the forces of production, create their own history and social change. Marx sums up his historical materialism in this passage from the *Critique of Political Economy* (1859):

> In the social production which men carry on they enter into definite relations that are indispensable and independent of their will; these relations of production correspond to a definite stage of development of their material powers of production. The sum total of these relations of production constitutes the economic structure of society—the real foundation on which rise legal and political superstructures and to which correspond definite forms of social consciousness. The mode of production in material life determines the general character of the social, political, and spiritual processes of life. It is not the consciousness of men that determines their existence, but, on the contrary, their social existence determines their consciousness. At a certain stage of their development, the material forces of production in society come into conflict with the existing relations of production, or—what is but a legal expression for the same thing—with the property relations within which they had been at work before. From forms of development of the forces of production these relations turn into their fetters. Then comes the period of social revolution. With the change of economic foundation the entire immense superstructure is more or less rapidly transformed. In considering such transformations the distinction should always be made between the material transformation of the economic conditions or production which can be determined with the precision of natural science, and the legal, political, religious, aesthetic, or philosophic—in short, ideological forms in which men become conscious of this conflict and fight it out.

4. Apply the "materialist conception of history" (historical materialism) to the transition from feudalism to capitalism (see Chapter 3).

5. "It is not the consciousness of men that determines their existence, but, on the contrary, their social existence determines their consciousness." What does this mean? And how does it mean that human beings create their own history?

6. Can Marx's theory of historical materialism be used to explain the recent changes in the Soviet Union and Eastern Europe? How so?

Marx's model of social change thus focuses on the relationships and contradictions among the forces of production, social classes, and the general institutions and ideologies of society. This complex process, according to Marx, determines the development of societies. In that process, the forces of production are of initial importance, but class struggle and ideology in turn become extremely influential.

The Marxian Analysis of Capitalism

From this view of social change and history, Marx proceeded to develop his analysis and critique of capitalism. His conclusion was a condemnation of capitalism and its results, as well as a scientific appraisal of its likely future development and eventual replacement by socialism. Here we will summarize Marx's theory of capitalist development.

Capitalism advances the methods of production, including factories, transportation, and technology, and as it expands, has access to greater supplies of raw materials. Accompanying this mode of production are its own relations of production. Basically, according to Marx, with the advance of the division of labor and private property, there were two main social classes in capitalism. They were defined by their relationship to each other in the productive process. First of all, there were the capitalists, or the bourgeoisie, who owned the means of production, controlled productive activity, and earned profits from the sale of produced goods in markets. Second, there were the workers, the proletariat, who had nothing to sell in markets but their own labor power and, as a result, had to work for wages to survive. The history of capitalism, then, can be seen as the history of the struggle between these two classes.

Marx condemned capitalism because it reduced social relations to impersonal market relations, or the "cash nexus." As he and Engels argued in *The Communist Manifesto* (1848):

It has pitilessly torn asunder the motley feudal ties that bound man to his "natural superiors," and has left remaining no other nexus between man and man than naked self-interest, than callous "cash payment." It has drowned the most heavenly ecstasies of religious fervor, of chivalrous enthusiasm, of philistine sentimentalism, in the icy water of egotistical calculation. It has resolved personal worth into exchange value, and in place of the numberless indefeasible chartered freedoms, has set up that single, unconscionable freedom—Free Trade. In one word, for exploitation, veiled by religious and political illusions, it has substituted naked, shameless, direct, brutal exploitation.

Within the "cash nexus" that Marx described, workers and capitalists would struggle over wages, the length of the working day, the intensity of work, and working conditions. Additionally, since workers were forced to work for capitalists for wages, and since the capitalists controlled production, capitalism produced **alienation.** Most workers were engaged in mind-numbing, repetitive tasks involving no creativity, which served to sever any connection they might have had to the product that they were producing. In one of Marx's early critical works, *The Economic and Philosophic Manuscripts of 1844*, he described alienation as a consequence of this type of capitalist production. The production of goods was external to the workers; they had no control over their labor or what they produced. Consequently, workers were alienated in their work. They felt dispossessed, and their work was, in essence, forced labor. Alienation, thus, was one more contributor to labor's dissatisfaction with capitalism.

 7. Did Marx deplore the "cash nexus" because it destroyed feudal relationships?

From his early condemnation of capitalism, Marx went on to develop a detailed and lengthy analysis of capitalism in such works as *Wage Labour and Capital* (1849), *The Grundrisse* (1859), *Theories of Surplus Value* (1863), and *Capital* (1867).

Marx accepted the **labor theory of value** as it was developed by Adam Smith and others but turned it to his own purposes. For Marx it became a way of demonstrating the opposition of capitalists and workers and the exploitation of labor in capitalism. Marx contended that the value of all goods and services is a function of the labor that went into them (including both direct labor and the indirect labor embodied in raw materials and capital goods). Workers, in turn, are paid by capitalists to produce goods and services. However, since the capitalists control the productive process and the final output, they will earn **surplus value.** To make a profit, capitalists must pay laborers less than the value of the products the laborers produce. When you graduate from college, you will be hired for a job because the firm that hires you believes you will generate more in revenue for the firm than you will cost in wages (including benefits). The difference between the revenue you generate for the company and the wage you receive is called surplus value. Marx viewed the extraction of surplus value as exploitative. Labor accounts for the value of goods and services, but it receives in return only a portion of that value, since it does not own productive assets or control the production process.

Because of the existence of a mass of unemployed workers (the *industrial reserve army* of the unemployed), the wages of laborers will always hover around "subsistence"—the value of goods and services necessary for continued survival and the reproduction of the working class. Workers can produce enough value in only part of the working day to cover their subsistence needs. The rest of the day they labor to produce surplus value for the capitalist. The more labor that capitalists can get out of the labor power they purchase from workers, the greater the surplus value for the capitalist. Thus, there is an inherent **class conflict** between capitalists and workers. Workers prefer to work fewer hours, with more freedom and flexibility, and for more money. Capitalists prefer workers to work longer, harder, and for less money. To improve the level of profits, capitalists may try to increase the pace and intensity of work, increase supervision over work, or introduce new technology. Workers often resist these trends, sometimes violently. The wage rate hovers around subsistence, but it also varies with the struggle between capital and labor over the level of wages.

Since capitalists derive surplus value and profits from production, and since they operate in a competitive environment in which other capitalists also attempt to earn profits from the same type of activity, they are forced to accumulate capital. **Capital accumulation** is the driving force of capitalism. Profit is used to purchase additional capital goods and thereby increase production. This capital accumulation results in additional profits, which, in turn, will be reinvested in more capital. Capitalists, if they want to stay in business, have no choice about this. If they do not reinvest their profits in new and better forms of capital, they will be driven out of business by their competitors. Marx also emphasized the role of technological development in stimulating capital accumulation.

With a greater stock of capital, which technological improvements make increasingly productive, capitalists must constantly seek out new markets for products. As Marx observed in *The Communist Manifesto,* "The need of a constantly expanding market for its products chases the bourgeoisie over the whole surface of the globe. It must nestle everywhere, settle everywhere, establish connections everywhere." Similarly, capitalists pursue new markets by attempting to turn anything they can into a way to sell commodities. To choose an obvious example, under capitalism religious holidays such as Christmas and Hanukkah have become major vehicles for businesses to increase sales. Advertisers try to connect caring and loving others with the purchase of commodities. If we care for someone, we are urged to buy a more expensive gift!

8. Has the institution of marriage been commodified? If so, how? What are some other holidays or human institutions that have become commodified?

The process of capital accumulation forms the basis of Marx's understanding of **capitalist instability.** Capital accumulation produces economic growth, but it does so in cycles, with periods of prosperity followed by depression. When production is expanding, capitalists buy more machines, raw materials, and other forms of capital. This also requires them to hire more workers. Doing so depletes the reserve army of the unemployed and begins to drive up wages, which tends to reduce profits. Consequently, capitalists introduce new methods of production that save on the use of labor; more capital-intensive production allows them to produce more with less labor (substitution of capital for labor).

In addition, workers lose jobs and the wage goes down as the reserve army is replenished.

This course of action is not without its own contradictions. With more workers out of jobs and with lower wages, capitalists have more difficulty selling what is produced. This tends to reduce capitalists' profits. In addition, with more capital-intensive methods of production, the capitalists reduce relatively the source of profits in production, surplus value generated by labor. This also tends to produce a declining rate of profits. With profits reduced, capital accumulation slows down. All of these effects would combine to produce depressions in economic activity as goods went unsold, profits decreased, workers lost jobs, and capital accumulation slowed. In true dialectical fashion, the expansion, out of its own internal workings, turns into its opposite, a depression. With wage rates depressed, though, capitalists eventually rehire workers because the workers can once again produce surplus value and profits for the capitalists. And out of the depression comes an expansion of economic activity. Capitalism, Marx argued, grew in starts and spurts. The great mass of the people under capitalism, the working class, depends on this unstable process for its livelihood and subsistence.

In addition to this cyclical instability, Marx thought that there were long-run tendencies that would exacerbate the opposition between the capitalist class and the working class. Because of competition, **industrial concentration** tended to occur as capitalists bought out each other or went bankrupt during depressions. The strong survived and came to dominate certain industries. As this occurred, the capitalist class became relatively smaller, as well as relatively more wealthy. Meanwhile, the working class became relatively larger and relatively poorer, as it remained near "subsistence." Marx called this the **immiserization** of the proletariat. And all the while, the capitalist class retained control and the workers were powerless. As a result of continuing instability and these secular tendencies, which reinforce the class structure of capitalist society, the workers would organize for their own class interests. Ultimately, Marx argued, the working-class organizations would overthrow the capitalist system.

The political requirement for workers in the socialist and communist movement was described by Marx and Engels as follows at the end of *The Communist Manifesto:*

> In short, the Communists everywhere support every revolutionary movement against the existing social and political order of things.
>
> In all these movements they bring to the front, as the leading question in each, the property question, no matter what its degree of development at the time.
>
> Finally, they labour everywhere for the union and agreement of the democratic parties of all countries.
>
> The Communists disdain to conceal their views and aims. They openly declare that their ends can be attained only by the forcible overthrow of all existing social conditions. Let the ruling class tremble at a Communistic revolution. The proletarians have nothing to lose but their chains. They have a world to win.

However, this social revolution would not be easy. As Marx emphasized from his general system of social development, capitalism supports itself with its superstructure. The institutions, ideologies, and beliefs of the society defend capitalist economic institutions and social relations. Perhaps most important in this connection is the state. The state, according to Marxian analysis, serves as the "executive committee of the ruling class." The state protects private property and property rights and thereby the class structure of the system. It is in the camp of the capitalists and will actively oppose the workers' movement with all the resources at its command.

9. Evaluate Marx's analysis of capitalism. Does it describe economic reality and the historical development of capitalism? Does it help you understand how capitalism works?
10. Why do you suppose Marx kept getting kicked out of European countries?

Social Revolution

Marx argued that workers would be exploited, alienated, and condemned to subsistence standards of living under capitalism. He further argued that in their association at work and in their communities, they would be able to analyze objectively their reality and the reasons for this oppression. Consequently, they would organize themselves and transform the whole capitalist system. (Indeed, Marx spent much of his time in political activity with workers.) In *Capital*, he describes the process of **social revolution** as follows:

> Along with the constantly diminishing number of magnates of capital, who usurp and monopolize all advantages of this process of transformation, grows the mass of misery, oppression, slavery, degradation, exploitation; but with this too grows the revolt of the working class, a class always increasing in numbers, and disciplined, united, organized by the very mechanism of the process of capitalist production itself. The monopoly of capital becomes a fetter upon the mode of production, which has sprung up and flourished along with, and under it. Centralization of the means of production and socialization of labour at last reach a point where they become incompatible with their capitalist integument. This integument is burst asunder. The knell of capitalist private property sounds. The expropriators are expropriated.

Once the death knell of capitalism sounded, what would the socialists, communists, and workers create? What would they do? Although Marx never wrote extensively on this question, a hint at the answer is contained in *The Communist Manifesto*:

> The distinguishing feature of Communism is not the abolition of property generally, but the abolition of bourgeois property. But modern bourgeois private property is the final and most complete expression of the system of producing and appropriating products, that is based on class antagonisms, on the exploitation of the many by the few.

In this sense, the theory of the Communists may be summed up in the single sentence: Abolition of private property.

We Communists have been reproached with the desire of abolishing the right of personally acquiring property as the fruit of a man's own labour, which property is alleged to be the groundwork of all personal freedom, activity and independence.

Hard-won, self-acquired, self-earned property! Do you mean the property of the petty artisan and of the small peasant, a form of property that preceded the bourgeois form? There is no need to abolish that: the development of industry has to a great extent already destroyed it, and is still destroying it daily.

Or do you mean modern bourgeois private property?

The proletariat will use its political supremacy to wrest, by degrees, all capital from the bourgeoisie, to centralise all instruments of production in the hands of the State, *i.e.*, of the proletariat organized as the ruling class; and to increase the total of productive forces as rapidly as possible. . . .

These measures will of course be different in different countries.

Nevertheless in the most advanced countries, the following will be . . . generally applicable.

1. Abolition of property in land and application of all rents of land to public purposes.
2. A heavy progressive or graduated income tax.
3. Abolition of all rights of inheritance.
4. Confiscation of the property of all emigrants and rebels.
5. Centralisation of credit in the hands of the State, by means of a national bank with State capital and an exclusive monopoly.
6. Centralisation of the means of communication and transport in the hands of the State.
7. Extension of factories and instruments of production owned by the State; the bringing into cultivation of wastelands, and the improvement of the soil generally in accordance with a common plan.
8. Equal liability of all to labour. Establishment of industrial armies, especially for agriculture.
9. Combination of agriculture and manufacturing industries; gradual abolition of the distinction between town and country, by a more equable distribution of the population over the country.
10. Free education for all children in public schools. Abolition of children's factory labour in its present form. Combination of education with industrial production, &c., &c.

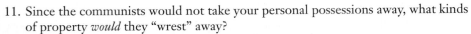

11. Since the communists would not take your personal possessions away, what kinds of property *would* they "wrest" away?
12. In Marx and Engels's ten-point program, which measures are accepted in the United States? Which are partially accepted? Which are rejected?

Hayek and the Road to Serfdom

Writing in the mid-1800s, Marx saw laissez-faire capitalism as a grave threat to human society. Instead, Marx advocated control of the economy by workers and the communist party. By the 1930s, with Hitler running the German economy under a fascist system and Stalin running the Soviet economy via command-style communism, the idea of centralized state control was getting a bad reputation. It was in this context that Austrian economist Friedrich Hayek wrote his important book, *The Road to Serfdom*. Hayek saw state power as dangerous and coercive. In contrast, he argued that "the system of private property is the most important guarantee of freedom. It is only because the control of the means of production is divided among many people acting independently that we as individuals can decide what to do with ourselves." Hayek insisted that central planners could never duplicate the efficient allocation of resources and generation of information that takes place under the market system. To Hayek, the greatest threat to the economy was state intervention, and any expansion of the role of the state beyond the functions of defense and the provision of welfare and basic social services was a threat to liberty.

As we will see in the next chapter, most economists adopted a position in between those of Marx and Hayek. They accepted the need for government intervention to regulate the worst excesses of capitalism, but they also accepted the market system as an efficient method of allocating resources. Such economists believed in a **mixed economy,** in which some economic decisions were made by government officials and others were made by market mechanisms. The economist who persuaded the world that this was the best approach to managing the economy was John Maynard Keynes.

An Assessment of Marxism

Marx died more than a century ago, in 1883. What can we say today about the relevance of his analysis of social change and capitalism? Most Americans either reject Marxism or never really study it. The rejection is often based on the fact that several of Marx's predictions have not transpired: the overthrow of advanced capitalism by socialism; the separation of society into only two classes, capitalists and workers; and the creation of a unified and political working class. In addition, Marxism is often associated with the repressive Soviet Union, and socialism as Marx described it has never really been put in place. Socialism and Marxism also offer a direct challenge to two of the basic economic foundations of U.S. society: private ownership of productive property and economic freedom for capital.

On the other hand, Marxian analysis is used by many economists in the United States and the rest of the world to understand economic events. Some aspects of Marxism offer continuing assistance in explaining the structure and development of capitalism. There remain conflicts between workers and capitalists over workplace health and safety, other working conditions, wages and fringe benefits, and the length of the workweek, not to mention downsizing and relocation. This conflict is built into the different interests that they have in the very structure of the economic system. Capitalists seek profits, and workers' demands often limit profits. Although the historical expansion of the middle class has mediated this structure, there are opposing class interests in the operation of the economy, and the classes do struggle over real economic issues in workplaces, bargaining, and public policy. Furthermore, while these struggles have not led to the collapse of capitalism, they have brought about significant changes in its institutions and operation. Marx's analysis of exploitation, surplus value, and class relations can help us to understand this dynamic of U.S. capitalism.

One of the most long-lived aspects of Marxian economic analysis is its theory of the process of capital accumulation. In this treatment, Marx explained capitalism's tendencies toward business cycles, economic concentration, and market expansion. By focusing on the importance of profits and the centrality of capital accumulation, Marx developed a framework that is still useful in understanding recessions and expansions, merger waves, and U.S. penetration of world markets.

Another strength of Marxian analysis is its integration of the micro and macro aspects of economic activity. At the microeconomic level, profits flow from the organization and control of the capitalist mode of production. The process of capital accumulation and the production of surplus value, in turn, provide the framework within which macroeconomic crises are engendered under capitalism.

The fact that Marx was able to anticipate much of how capitalism would evolve in the century after his death demonstrates the strength of Marx's analytical framework. As Marx predicted in *The Communist Manifesto*, globalization, commodification, and the economic concentration of capital have proceeded apace. Where unregulated, capitalists tend to pursue the cheapest labor and least environmental regulations in order to increase profits. The conflicts between capitalists and laborers have waxed and waned. This evidence in support of Marx's insights ensures that his ideas will be studied for many years to come.

Nevertheless, Marx's system retains some limitations and weaknesses. The labor theory of value used by Smith and Marx was supplanted by the development of economic theory that finds value reflected in the supply and demand for products and their resulting prices. Marx did not anticipate the tremendous increase in the average standard of living in the United States (and Western Europe) as governments, sometimes under pressure from labor unions, reformed capitalism. As the economy grew, a good portion of the increasing surplus was in fact apportioned to the middle class and some segments of the working class (although this varies depending on economic conditions and the strength of the working class). The social revolution in advanced capitalist countries anticipated by Marx required more than his prediction: It also necessitated political organization by the working class in the real world. (To his credit, although it is often not included in discussions of Marx, he did recognize this political fact; much of his life was spent in active political organizing among the working class.) Even though there have been communist and socialist parties in the West and in the United States, they have never been strong enough to organize a transition to socialism. Of course, they have not been unopposed. And throughout Western Europe, the social democracy movement reformed capitalism to take into account social issues, rather than eliminating capitalism. Socialism, instead, has emerged where capitalism has been weaker and where societies have not succeeded in dealing with inequality, often in the developing world.

Marx himself would probably be disappointed with the divergence of his ideal of socialism and its reality in much of the present world (particularly wherever it has taken antidemocratic forms). Even so, his ideas have influenced the development and progress of socialism and the pursuit of social goals in China, Cuba, and North Korea, and in countries that once espoused socialism, including the former Soviet Union, Vietnam, Mozambique, and former Yugoslavia (see Chapter 23). And Marxism as a method of analysis still continues to influence the transitions in the post–Cold War world.

Conclusion

In this chapter, we focused on the ideas of Karl Marx and his critique of capitalism. Marx acknowledged that capitalism was a dynamic system that generated rapid economic growth, but he also noted the inequality, poverty, and horrible working conditions that accompanied it in the mid-1800s. In the next chapter, we turn to the ideas of John Maynard Keynes and the rise of the mixed economy as the primary method by which human societies organize their economies today. We also trace the development of the U.S. economy and its evolution into a mixed economy.

Review Questions

1. The dialectic method consists of identifying the forces within the economy that are in conflict and studying those conflicts to understand the evolution of the economy. What are some of the major sources of conflict in the modern global economy? How do you see the global economy changing as a result of these conflicts?

2. The microcomputer revolution and the rise of telecommunications has dramatically altered the modern world. It has changed how we work, what our lives are like, and the class structures of countries around the world. Using the insights from Marx's method of historical materialism, analyze these changes. What were the major changes in the mode of production? How have the relations of production and the superstructure changed as a result?

3. Why do people in the United States tend to reject Marxism?

4. Why is it that some newly independent countries in the world have Marxian governments (i.e., politicians and leaders who rely on Marxian analysis)?

5. What do you think is the weakest part of the Marxian argument?

6. What do you think is the strongest part of the Marxian argument?

7. What is the purpose of Marxian economics?

8. Marx's theories originated more than 100 years ago. Was labor exploited then? Is it now? Why or why not?

9. Using Marx's concept of surplus value, explain why white-collar workers in the United States today are working longer and longer hours.

10. Are most jobs today alienating in nature? What circumstances seem to create alienating work? Is it possible to create workplaces in which alienation is minimized?

11. Marx predicted that capitalist society would become increasingly commercialized and that more and more areas of human society and culture would become vehicles to sell products and increase profits. Is this an accurate prediction? Explain and give examples to support your answer.

12. Marx was very critical of capitalism during its dark age of the mid-1800s. How do you think he would feel about capitalism today?

CHAPTER SIX

The Rise and Fall of Laissez-Faire in the U.S. Economy

![] Introduction

Despite the conditions of the poor and the socialist and Marxian critiques, laissez-faire capitalism flourished in nineteenth-century England and throughout Western Europe. From 1837 to 1901, Queen Victoria reigned, giving her name to the Victorian Age. This age witnessed increasing commercial dominance over formal and informal institutions that affected social values and behavior. Railway expansion and the telegraph revolutionized transportation and communication, thereby quickening the pace of life. People began to illuminate their homes with electricity. The first cars were on the roads in the United States. The Carnegies, Vanderbilts, and Rockefellers were accumulating their enormous wealth. Coal and oil displaced animals and water power as sources of energy. As a result of these developments, production in the British and the U.S. economies boomed.

However, some economists attempted to call attention to continuing unemployment problems and suggested various ideas for responding to the problems. These economists were either ignored or viewed as dangerous radicals by the dominant school of economists in the universities and the ruling classes. By 1926, John Maynard Keynes was convinced that laissez-faire was no longer an appropriate way of thinking about unemployment. Others had noticed this much earlier, but it was Keynes's contribution in the context of the Great Depression that ultimately signaled the fall of laissez-faire.

The Flowering of Laissez-Faire

As the pace quickened, production increased and more people attempted to succeed in business. A few individuals began to wonder about where all of this movement might lead. Among them was the English essayist John Ruskin (1819–1900), one of the great thinkers and writers in the Victorian Age, whose works about art, architecture, and political economy have continuing relevance

Brantwood, the elegant home of John Ruskin.
(Photograph by Tom Riddell)

today. In an 1864 essay named "Traffic," he questions the "ideal of human life" and describes the worshippers of the "Goddess of Getting-on":

> Your ideal of human life then is, I think, that it should be passed in a pleasant undulating world, with iron and coal everywhere underneath it. On each pleasant bank of this world is to be a beautiful mansion, with two wings; and stables, and coach-houses; a moderately-sized park; a large garden and hothouses; and pleasant carriage drives through the shrubberies. In this mansion are to live the favoured votaries of the Goddess; the English gentleman, with his gracious wife, and his beautiful family; he is always able to have the boudoir and the jewels for the wife, and the beautiful ball dresses for the daughters, and hunters for the sons, and a shooting in the Highlands for himself. At the bottom of the bank is to be the mill; not less than a quarter of a mile long, with one steam engine at each end, and two in the middle and a chimney three hundred feet high. In this mill are to be in constant employment from eight hundred to a thousand workers, who never drink, never strike, always go to church on Sunday, and always express themselves in respectful language.

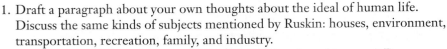

1. Draft a paragraph about your own thoughts about the ideal of human life. Discuss the same kinds of subjects mentioned by Ruskin: houses, environment, transportation, recreation, family, and industry.
2. Ruskin wrote, "There is no wealth but life." What does this mean? Do you agree? Explain.

At the time Ruskin was writing, the majority of people in England lived in poor housing, were paid low wages, and experienced regular periods of unemployment, and their surroundings could best be described as urban squalor. So the Victorian Age was not only a time of general economic growth but also a time of continuing economic disparity. The implications of that disparity offered a potential threat to the existing social, political, and economic order. In *The Victorian Frame of Mind*, historian Walter E. Houghton explains this characteristic of the period:

> To think it strange that the great age of optimism was also an age of anxiety is to overlook the ambivalent reaction which the main social and intellectual tendencies of the period provoked. Expanding business, scientific development, the growth of democracy, and the decline of Christianity were sources of distress as well as of satisfaction. . . .
>
> For all its solid and imposing strength, Victorian society, particularly in the period before 1850, was shot through, from top to bottom, with the dread of some wild outbreak of the masses that would overthrow the established order and confiscate private property.

3. Are wealthy people in the United States today worried about revolution? Why or why not? Are revolutions taking place elsewhere?

The Development of Capitalism in the United States

As capitalism was forming in Europe, many of its institutions and relationships were transplanted to the American colonies. When the colonists eventually removed the yoke of English political and economic control during the American Revolution, they cleared the way for the formation and development of the United States' own form of capitalism. However, they retained their debt to Western civilization, thought, and institutions. This lineage was important to the establishment of emerging capitalist attitudes and institutions in the colonies and their continuance after the Revolution.

Most of the colonists were Protestants who emphasized individualism and hard work. Private ownership of rural and urban production was the dominant form of economic organization. International and domestic trade flourished with the goal of private gain and profit. Markets developed and guided production. In the early years of the new nation, the government utilized mercantilist policies of controlling international trade to foster economic development and to protect the emergence of the United States as a Western nation-state.

Sources of U.S. Development

Throughout its first hundred years as a nation, the United States was primarily an agricultural economy. Through the mid-1870s, agricultural output accounted for more than half of total U.S. production, but by the mid-1880s the value of manufactured goods surpassed the value of agricultural goods. At the same time, the nonagricultural portion of the labor force began to outnumber those who worked on farms. (Later, about 1920, the nation's urban population surpassed the rural population.) Despite the country's being primarily rural and agricultural, the development of industry began early in the nineteenth century. Industrial production accelerated during the middle years of the nineteenth century, stimulated in part by the demands of the Civil War. By the turn of the century, the United States was the world's leading producer of both manufactured and agricultural goods.

What accounted for this tremendous economic achievement? One important source of U.S. economic development, which is often neglected, was the role of the government. In the formative years of the nation, the government played a crucial role in the construction of a federal system in which economic trade flowed freely from one state to another. Indeed, this concern with encouraging trade within the United States was one of the primary reasons behind the construction and ratification of the Constitution. In addition, the government passed tariffs to protect infant industries, established a national currency, and created a legal framework that governed economic transactions. In the nineteenth century, federal, state, and local governments financed and encouraged the development of different forms of transportation that facilitated trade within the expanding nation.

Another source of growth was the vast supply of land and resources available to the United States. The country expanded westward throughout the eighteenth century. This expansion was made possible by conquering one after another of the Native American tribes, by the purchase of land from France and Russia, and by military conquest over Mexico and several European countries that still controlled land in North America. Through what was called Manifest Destiny, the United States eventually controlled the middle part of the North American continent from coast to coast. This expanding geographical territory supplied space for expansion and raw materials for increasing agricultural and industrial production. It also supplied an expanding volume of cotton and wheat exports for sale to Europe. This international market encouraged further agricultural production and made possible imports that facilitated industrial production. At the end of the nineteenth and the beginning of the twentieth centuries, the United States joined Western European countries in the process of expansion beyond their borders. As the United States pursued Manifest Destiny beyond the North American continent into the Pacific, Asia, and Latin America, U.S. imperialism provided raw materials, markets, and investments that fueled further economic expansion.

Technology played a crucial role in the growth and development of the U.S. economy. The adoption of European methods of manufacturing textiles spurred the use of factory production, and the Industrial Revolution in the United States eventually led to the American manufacturing system—relying on interchangeable parts and later the mass assembly line. In agriculture, tractors and combines spurred a tremendous increase in agricultural production.

The American people themselves, both the original colonists and the later immigrants, proved to be an important source of growth and development. Strongly individualistic and dedicated to hard work, they took risks, organized productive activities, educated themselves, invented, worked, and conquered. The United States became a thriving and growing economy through a primarily private economic system based on the efforts of individuals and groups of individuals tied together through an expanding system of national markets for goods and services.

Coincident with all of these sources of growth, many institutions emerged to stimulate development. The banking system, retail and wholesale organizations, and the transportation system facilitated the expansion of economic activity with improved organization and lower costs. Related to the development of these sectors of the economy was the emergence of one of the foremost institutions of U.S. capitalism and economic production, the corporation. A legal combination of individuals, the corporation was a successful device for amassing resources for production. And in several leading industries—oil, the railroads, banking, steel, automobiles, and so on—large corporations led the advance of U.S. growth. In a sense, the history of the corporation and its development is the history of modern U.S. capitalism.

By the middle of the twentieth century, the United States was the dominant economic, political, and military country in the world. It was the most advanced nation in terms of manufacturing and agricultural techniques and production. It had the highest standard of living, on the average, for its almost 200 million citizens. And its people still valued individual economic and political freedom. For the most part, its development had been a success story.

The Situation in the United States and Veblen's Critique

Throughout its history, however, there have also been some negative aspects of U.S. economic development. The conquest and exploitation of the Native American Indians must be counted as—and remain as—a scar in U.S. history. The annexation of much of Mexico is another. Slavery throughout the colonial period and until the Civil War relied on the inhuman subjugation and exploitation of human beings as sources of increased production. As both economic and political power became more concentrated, scandals of political and economic corruption have been rife throughout U.S. history. Private economic power has led to political corruption such as the Crédit Mobilier affair of the 1870s, the Teapot Dome scandal of the 1920s, the savings and loan crisis of the 1980s (see Chapter 17), and the technology bubble of the late 1990s, as well as recent instances of illegal corporate campaign contributions in the United States and bribery abroad.

The latter part of the nineteenth century was marked by the industrialization of the U.S. economy, but it also witnessed the abuses of the "robber barons," entrepreneurs who were generally successful as well as ruthless in their business practices. In the process of consolidating the leading industries of the economy, promoting technological developments, building giant corporations, and amassing great personal fortunes, such men as Jay Gould, Andrew Carnegie, J. P. Morgan, and John D. Rockefeller bilked their partners, eliminated their competitors, underpaid their workers, and/or overcharged many of their customers.

By the beginning of the twentieth century, the United States was the world's leading producer of both agricultural and manufactured goods. U.S. capitalism and markets spread across the North American continent and began to reach out to the rest of the world. Economic output increased dramatically—but this success was not unchallenged. Poverty persisted, a militant labor movement emerged along with a growing working class, periodic financial crises and depressions disrupted the path of growth, and there were continuing problems associated with Native American tribes and the end of slavery. The development of the U.S. economic system was full of successes *and* difficulties.

Thorstein Veblen (1857–1929) was one of the first economists to develop a comprehensive critique of American capitalism. He wrote during a period marked by continuing industrialization and growth, but also by increasing business concentration and recurrent economic depressions. One of his first books, *The Theory of the Leisure Class* (1899), noted the rise of a new class of people in U.S. society, accompanying the economic progress of the Industrial Revolution. These propertied people were privileged to engage in "conspicuous consumption" as testimony to their success. Veblen, in a sarcastic but penetrating style, offered numerous examples of the new leisure class seeking status through the purchase of houses, clothing, and other goods. His tone and insight about "pecuniary emulation" also called attention to the fact that, as in Europe, the industrialization process did not enrich everyone, although it did subject the entire society to the influences of heightened materialism.

In later works, most notably *The Theory of Business Enterprise* (1904) and *Absentee Ownership* (1923), Veblen identified some trends that characterized U.S. economic experience with laissez-faire capitalism. These trends were part and parcel of the American economic success, but they also suggested some future difficulties. Veblen saw a distinction between business and industry. In *Absentee Ownership*, he wrote, "The industrial arts are a matter of tangible performance directed to work that is designed to be of material use to man. . . . [The] arts of business are arts of bargaining, effrontery, salesmanship, make-believe, and are directed to the gain of the business man at the cost of the community, at large and in detail."

This distinction was important to his interpretation of the primary trends in U.S. economic development: a tendency toward business concentration, rapid technological advance, and a constant difficulty with depression. Monopoly resulted from the business instinct to eliminate competition as one of the most effective ways to secure profits. But technological progress also was caused by the business drive for profits. The problem arose because technology constantly pushed the ability of the industrial arts to produce more, but monopoly held back production to get higher prices and profits. The consequence, according to Veblen, was a constant tendency toward depression. The depressions of the 1870s and 1890s in the United States provided real evidence that Say's law should be suspect, and that Veblen's concern with explaining the frequency of high levels of unemployment, if not exactly correct, was at least worth pursuing.

Veblen was an **institutionalist**. The institutionalists were critical of the orthodox school of economics. They argued that the focus of such economists was too narrow and that their method was too abstract. The orthodox economists paid too little attention to the influence of other factors affecting economic behavior. Specifically, the institutionalists, and Veblen as one of their leading figures, argued that analysis of economic events must take account of history, institutions, the pursuit of power, and the complexity of human motivation.

Veblen was particularly critical of the prevailing theory of markets, which used supply and demand (see Chapter 8) to predict prices and quantities. These models were based on restrictive assumptions about human behavior. Consumers in general were assumed to be independent, rational, calculating, and self-interested in their pursuit of personal pleasure (hedonistic). These models were also based on the assumption that markets were stable and tended toward equilibrium unless external factors caused a change, in which case the market would simply move to a new equilibrium. The following passage from Veblen's *The Place of Science in Modern Civilization* (1919) demonstrates the institutionalist critique of the orthodox theory of markets and its assumptions about consumer behavior:

> The psychological and anthropological preconceptions of economists have been those which were accepted by the psychological and social sciences some generations ago. The hedonistic conception of man is that of a lightning calculator of pleasures and pains, who oscillates like a homogeneous globule of desire of happiness under the impulse of stimuli that shift him about the area, but leave him intact. He has neither antecedent nor consequent. He is an isolated, definitive human datum, in stable equilibrium except for the buffets of the impinging forces that displace him in one direction or another. Self-imposed in elemental space, he spins symmetrically about his own spiritual axis until the parallelogram of forces bears down upon him, whereupon he follows the line of the resultant. When the force of the impact is spent, he comes to rest, a self-contained globule of desire as before.

4. Do you consider yourself a "self-contained globule of desire"? Are you subject to "buffets of impinging forces"?

Instead of viewing human beings as isolated individuals making rational, informed decisions about what to buy, Veblen preferred a different view of how people make decisions. He believed that peer pressure (or in his words, pecuniary emulation) and advertising influence people's desires, and that cultural institutions, rather than individuals' independent choices, shape their preferences. Veblen identified the wasteful and unproductive side of capitalism, where businesses could make money by forming monopolies and manipulating consumers with advertising instead of producing good products at low prices. These observations led him to oppose laissez-faire and advocate a greater role for government in the economy. Veblen's call was echoed by John Maynard Keynes.

The Great Depression and the Keynesian Critique of Laissez-Faire

British economist John Maynard Keynes (1883–1946) followed the classical tradition, but in the early 1920s he began to write about his departure from the classical ideas held by most economists. Throughout the late nineteenth and early twentieth centuries, the United States suffered repeated depressions in economic activity. Periods of prosperity and boom were regularly followed by

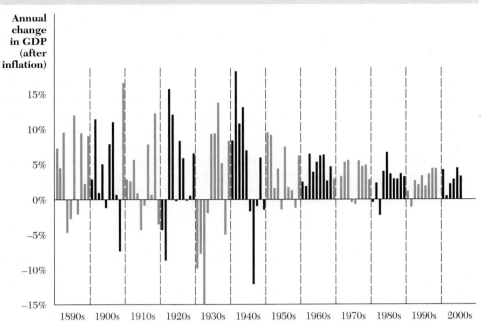

Source: David Wyss, DRI/McGraw-Hill, for the *New York Times*, March 17, 1996; *Economic Report of the President*, 2006, p. 283.

periods of depression and bust. Figure 6.1 graphically depicts this pattern. In the midst of these depressions, unemployment and economic hardship for many people increased dramatically and tragically. The worst depression occurred in the 1930s, when the decrease in economic activity spread around the world. In 1933, almost one-third of the workforce in the United States was without employment. The Great Depression in the U.S. was deep and lasted throughout the 1930s. It was also a worldwide depression and its effects were experienced earlier by Britain. In 1929, Keynes was advising the British government to spend freely on public works programs to promote employment. A bit later, President Franklin Roosevelt, confronted by millions of families without any income because laissez-faire capitalism was unable to provide employment in the 1930s, increased the influence of government in the U.S. economy.

In the 1920s, Keynes wrote an essay, "The End of Laissez-Faire," in which he challenged the notion that the search for private interests always led to the greater good for the society as a whole. In particular, he was convinced that capitalism did not automatically produce full employment. He rejected Say's law because his research indicated that there were times when supply did not create enough demand. For example, toward the end of periods of economic expansion, it was often the case that profitable investment opportunities dried up and capital flowed into increasingly risky areas. Inevitably, some investments failed, and these failures undermined consumer and business confidence in the economy, causing declines in consumer spending and in businesses' purchases of capital goods. Because of this lowered confidence, the pool of savings increased and spending declined. More money was now available in the financial sector, but no one wanted to spend or invest while the economy was in decline. Thus, Keynes noted, there could be regular gluts in the economy: An increase in savings might not be matched by an increase in investment if confidence in the economy was low. In response, Keynes believed the state needed to assume responsibility for the overall health of capitalist economies with increases in spending to offset the declines in consumer and investor spending that occurs in recessions. Capitalism might be stronger, he argued, if some decisions were left in private hands; but some others, which were social in nature, ought to be the responsibility of the state.

Keynes thus began to explore the idea that laissez-faire did not always result in the greatest social good. He argued, in fact, that the state should take an active part in certain economic matters, such as maintaining full employment. This emerging argument and the Great Depression of the 1930s signaled the end of laissez-faire. Keynes, while accepting capitalism as an economic system, rejected the classical notion of laissez-faire. His primary argument in reaching this conclusion was that the laissez-faire capitalist economic system could easily permit chronic unemployment and instability. Beginning in the 1930s, and continuing through the rest of the twentieth century, developed countries used Keynes's ideas to establish a mixed economy, which meant smoothing out the rough edges of markets with increasing amounts of government intervention. Governments added welfare and unemployment programs to assist the poor, social security programs to support the elderly, stabilization policies to reduce hardships in recessions, and regulations to improve market outcomes in the areas of health, safety, and the environment. In capitalist economies, the mixed economy became the norm, and economic debates no longer focused on whether or not the government should intervene in the economy, but how much the government should intervene, and in what areas. In Part 4 we will examine in more detail the Keynesian body of thought on instability and the "proper" role for the state in the economy.

5. What would Adam Smith think about Keynes's argument? Why?
6. Based on your conception of the U.S. economic system, list its five most important attributes. Are these positive or negative attributes? Are they results of the system? Or are they fundamental characteristics of it?

The Great Depression and the "escape" from it with the increased production and employment brought about by World War II engendered one of the more recent alterations of capitalism in the United States. Given the historical instability of capitalism's growth process, the federal government since the

1930s has taken a more direct responsibility for the overall health of the economy. It has attempted to prevent extremes in the cycles of boom and bust. Some would call this mixed capitalism; others might call it state capitalism. Still others, noting the role of the state and the role of large corporations in the economy, call it monopoly capitalism. And the addition of the economic role of the state constitutes one more major change in the continuing development of U.S. capitalism.

 7. What is your name, or label, for our economic system? Why do you call it that?

Joseph Schumpeter, Laissez-Faire, and Creative Destruction

Another prominent economist of the twentieth century, Joseph A. Schumpeter (1883–1950), had great faith in laissez-faire capitalism and opposed government intervention to end recessions, unlike Keynes. Despite the human suffering recessions produced, Schumpeter thought that they were a healthy phase of the business cycle that set the stage for the next expansion. Most economists disagreed, and economists and government officials from the 1930s to the present have widely supported Keynesian stabilization policy.

In addition to disagreeing with Keynes, Schumpeter criticized the static nature of orthodox economics. Schumpeter remarked in *Capitalism, Socialism, and Democracy* (1942), "capitalism . . . [is] an evolutionary process." Schumpeter believed that economists should focus on evolutionary change, and in particular on the process of **creative destruction** in their analysis:

> The opening up of new markets, foreign or domestic, and the organizational development from the craft shop and factory to such concerns as U.S. Steel illustrate the same process of industrial mutation . . . that incessantly revolutionizes the economic structure from within, incessantly destroying the old one, incessantly creating a new one. This process of Creative Destruction is the essential fact about capitalism.

Schumpeter chided orthodox economists for limiting their studies to "how capitalism administers existing structures, whereas the relevant problem is how it creates and destroys them." For example, Schumpeter thought that when orthodox economists focused on price competition and the entry and exit of similar businesses, they missed key elements of capitalist competition:

> In the case of retail trade the competition that matters arises not from additional shops of the same type, but from the department store, the chain store, the mail-order house and the supermarket which are bound to destroy those pyramids sooner or later. Now a theoretical construction which neglects this essential element of the case neglects all that is most typically capitalist about it; even if correct in logic as well as in fact, it is like *Hamlet* without the Danish prince.

Even the process of creative destruction could evolve, according to Schumpeter. In studying the evolution of big corporations in the United States, Schumpeter became convinced that we should not assume that capitalism would always be dynamic and creative. As managers and bureaucrats took over big corporations from the inventors and entrepreneurs that founded them, businesses frequently ceased to be innovative and in fact sometimes hindered innovation. For this reason, Schumpeter thought we might see the end of capitalism—not because of revolution, but because it would eventually cease to function effectively and would have to be replaced with socialism.

In his evolutionary analysis, Schumpeter praised Karl Marx for the scope and depth of his analysis. In particular, as he stated in his *History of Economic Analysis* (1954), he was impressed with how Marx "welded into a single homogeneous whole all branches of sociology *and* economics—a venture that might well dazzle the modern discipline. . . ." However, to Schumpeter, Marx's true claim to greatness as an economist stemmed from the fact that he developed "the only genuinely evolutionary economic theory" of his time.

8. How is the Internet revolution involved in the process of creative destruction (i.e., creating new products and opportunities while destroying existing ones)?

The Post–World War II Experience

Following the demobilization of the economy after World War II, the United States experienced a quarter century of almost unprecedented economic growth and prosperity. During this time, there were periodic recessions, but the average standard of living increased at a rate of about 3 percent per year.

There were several bases for this era of prosperity. One was that the country emerged from the war as the world's leading military, economic, and political power, with its production base fully intact. From this position, it became the leader in establishing a new international economic trading and financial system that stimulated U.S. and Western economies. Following the Great Depression and the war, the federal government, partly based on Keynesian economics (see Part 4), assumed increased responsibility for the general health of the economy and for maintaining prosperity. Building on the labor legislation of the New Deal, which granted labor unions the right to organize and collectively bargain, and the labor peace of that period, big business and organized labor adopted a system of labor relations that minimized conflict and disruptions in production. Corporations themselves became larger and aggressively pursued profit-making possibilities at home and abroad. The result of these and other conditions was vigorous economic growth and the world's highest standard of living.

However, beginning in the late 1960s and early 1970s, some of the bases for the postwar prosperity began to break down, and specific events undermined the overall health of the U.S. economy. Consequently, at the beginning of the 1980s, the economy was plagued with stagflation—high unemployment (stagnation) and relatively high inflation—an energy crisis, and a general economic malaise.

The causes of this "crisis" in the economy were many, and they will be explored to some extent in the remainder of this book. But it is useful to mention a few of them briefly here. The United States lost some of its power in the world, partly as a result of its failure in Vietnam, but also because of the increased power of other countries, including Germany, France, Japan, and the Soviet Union. The United States encountered more effective competition in world markets. Third World countries assumed increased independence, nationalizing some U.S. corporations and adopting independent economic policies. Along these lines, the nations of the Organization of Petroleum Exporting Countries (OPEC) forced the United States to come to grips with expensive and scarce energy resources. The commitment to avoid depressions through the use of governmental economic policies had given the economy an inflationary (as opposed to a deflationary) bias. The relationship between big business and big labor also contributed to an inflationary spiral, with prices and wages moving ever upward. Inflationary expectations further fueled inflation. And there were many other problems as well, including declining productivity, a tax revolt, deregulation, racial and sexual discrimination, and continued poverty.

The Last Decades of the Twentieth Century

In evaluating the operation of the U.S. economy over more recent decades, economists can refer to many standard economic measures—such as the unemployment rate, the rate of inflation, gross domestic product, investment spending, and productivity—that are routinely compiled by government and other economists. By measuring economic activity over time, economists can develop a sense of how the economy is performing. Table 6.1 lists some important economic variables for the United States and shows how they changed over the last half of the twentieth century and into the early twenty-first century.

As Table 6.1 indicates, the U.S. economy performed much less successfully in the 1970s than it did in the 1950s and 1960s. The unemployment rate and the rate of inflation were both higher, on average, than in the previous two decades. Average weekly earnings, after taking inflation into account, actually decreased during the 1970s. The rate of increase in total output per labor hour and the rate of increase in real total output both decreased. The economy was growing at a slower rate, although the rate of profit for corporations was higher than it had been in both the 1950s and the 1960s. In addition, net investment, one of the most important sources of economic growth, was declining as a percentage of total output.

As the United States entered the 1980s, its economic system continued to be plagued with high unemployment and inflation and low rates of economic growth. From 1979 to 1981, real output grew by less than 2 percent per year. The unemployment rate was above 7 percent. Consumer prices were increasing at a rate of 12 to 13 percent a year. The real average weekly earnings for nonagricultural workers in 1980 were less than they had been in 1963. Interest rates were at historic highs. In 1981, the rate that banks charged their best corporate customers for loans was close to 20 percent. The federal deficit was beginning to increase and reached the $50 billion range in 1980 and 1981. And the value of the dollar in international exchange was at its lowest levels for the entire post–World War II period.

These various economic difficulties became a primary concern of economists and the centerpiece of Ronald Reagan's 1980 presidential campaign. The

TABLE 6.1   Selected Measures of Economic Performance, 1950s–2005

	1950s	1960s	1970s	1980s	1990s	2000–2005
Unemployment rate (annual average, percent)	4.5	4.8	6.2	7.3	5.3	5.2
Rate of inflation (annual average increase in consumer prices, percent)	2.0	2.4	7.1	5.5	2.9	2.7
Average weekly earnings (annual increase, in constant dollars, percent)	2.5	1.4	−0.3	−1.0	0.4	0.1
Output per labor hour (annual average increase, percent)	2.6	2.8	1.9	1.0	1.9	3.1
Real output (annual average increase, percent)	4.0	4.3	3.2	2.8	3.0	2.08
Ratio of profit, after taxes (corporate profits as a percent of stockholders' equity, annual average)	11.3	11.1	12.8	12.2	11.9	10.1 (01 only)

Source: *Economic Report of the President*, various years.

"Reagan Revolution" used the analysis of monetarist and supply-side economics to explain the slowdown in the economy and to develop a package of economic policies that came to be known as "Reaganomics." Very simply, Reagan argued that the country's economic difficulties were a result of too little economic growth. The source of the problem, he contended, was the excessive role of the government in the economy. There was too much regulation of business and too much government spending on social programs, taxes on corporations and individuals were too high, and the increase in the money supply was too rapid. All of this resulted in too much demand for output and not enough production to meet that demand—hence, slow growth and inflation. The solution was to increase the incentives and the rewards for the private sector. This would unleash corporations and individuals, and the nation would witness a massive surge in work and investment. The economy would grow more rapidly, providing economic prosperity with price stability once again.

The policies that President Reagan initiated and Congress passed included a three-year package of cuts in individual and corporate income taxes, reductions in federal spending on a variety of social programs, deregulation in a variety of industries and business practices, and large increases in military spending to restore U.S. power in the world. While the Reagan administration implemented these policies, the Federal Reserve tightened the money supply, as described in Chapter 17.

The immediate result of tighter money and cutbacks in federal spending was a severe recession in the early 1980s. Real output actually declined in 1982, and the unemployment rate rose above 10 percent. In 1983, however, the economy began to recover. Real output increased steadily throughout the mid-1980s, and the unemployment rate began to decline very slowly. Along with the recession, the rate of inflation dropped precipitously to just below 4 percent, but workers' average wages also continued to fall. With the recovery, the rate of growth in productivity (output per hour) began to increase, as did investment spending. As a result of the recession, the tax cuts, and the massive increase in military spending, however, the federal deficit mushroomed to annual levels of close to $200 billion. All of these measurements suggest that there was some improvement in the economy but that significant problems remained at the end of the 1980s.

Table 6.1 provides some information on the overall performance of the U.S. economy during the 1980s. Real output continued to grow at a slower rate than in the 1950s and 1960s, at an average of 2.8 percent annually, although the economy grew continuously from 1982 without recession. The rate of productivity growth was less than half of what it was in the two decades immediately following World War II. With slower economic growth, the average unemployment rate actually increased during the 1980s, while the rate of inflation decreased somewhat. Average weekly earnings, adjusted for inflation, continued decreasing and by 1989 were no higher than they were in the early 1960s. Corporate profits, on the other hand, were as healthy as in the 1970s. Meanwhile, the rate of net investment decreased, suggesting continued slow growth in the economy. (Investment is a key determinant of economic growth. It represents spending on capital formation by businesses and expands the ability to produce.) Reaganomics and tight monetary policy by the Federal Reserve certainly led to a reduction in inflation, but they did not produce rampant economic growth, investment, and prosperity. The success, however, was enough to form a basis for George H. W. Bush's winning 1988 presidential campaign.

A number of persistent and emerging problems accompanied these general economic trends. The federal budget deficit was reduced moderately by legislation (the Gramm-Rudman-Hollings Deficit Reduction Act of 1985), but remained in excess of $150 billion in the early 1990s, given Bush's reluctance to raise taxes and congressional resistance to reducing spending on federal social programs. The massive cost of bailing out the many savings and loan institutions that failed during this period compounded the difficulty of deficit reduction. The trade deficit showed some improvement as U.S. exports grew faster than U.S. imports during the late 1980s. But the U.S. economy was increasingly challenged in domestic and global markets by Japanese and European firms. The distribution of income in the United States became more unequal during the 1980s as a result of the 1981 tax cuts, restraints on government social spending programs, and the patterns of growth in the economy. Homelessness became a national concern. At the same time, U.S. military spending was 50 percent higher in real terms than it was at the beginning of the decade. Global environmental problems received increasing public attention. The end of the Cold War held out the promise of reordered priorities.

In the early 1990s, there was a mild recession, just enough to cement George Bush's loss to Bill Clinton in the presidential election. As Table 6.1 shows, the economic news during Clinton's presidency indicates improvement. The unemployment rate declined by 2 percentage points. The rate of inflation fell to half of what it was in the 1980s. Average weekly earnings showed small gains, reversing the trend of the previous two decades. The increase in output per labor hour was the largest since the 1950s and 1960s, while the growth rate for real output reversed its long slowdown. Net investment soared in the late 1990s and government deficits changed to surpluses. The 1990s represented stable growth, high employment, and low levels of inflation.

By early 2000, as George W. Bush was inaugurated president of the United States, growth slowed; unemployment began to rise and the technology bubble that had developed in the stock market burst. The terror attacks of September 11, 2001, left the nation's economy troubled and uncertain about the future. U.S. troops entered Afghanistan in October 2001 and the establishment of a Department of Homeland Security reflected the growing concern with terrorist attacks in the United States. At the same time that U.S. attention turned to terrorism, corporate scandals at energy and telecommunications giants Enron and World Com, and the related collapse of the accounting firm Arthur Anderson, only increased public uncertainty about the economy.

In mid-March 2003, U.S. military forces led a coalition into war with Iraq. Funding needed to support these military actions increased government expenditures. Spending in Afghanistan and Iraq exceeded forecasts and funds needed to rebuild both countries continued to escalate. In four years, budgeted surpluses turned into large and continuing deficits and despite increased military spending and large tax cuts, unemployment rates continued their increase, even with accelerating levels of economic growth brought about by this fiscal stimulus. Investment remained sluggish. As the dollar continued to decrease with respect to most currencies, trade deficits remained high. Many of these conditions remain despite substantial increases in economic growth between 2003 and 2006. Trade deficits continued to mount, as did the budget deficit.

Still, the U.S. economy has come a long way in its 230-year history. It has largely been a history of successful development—not, however, without negative aspects and events. The United States has the world's largest and most industrialized economy. Some questions still face the U.S. economy: Can the expansion be sustained? Can inflation continue to be contained with often recurring news about oil price increases? Can trade deficits be reduced? Can budget deficits be controlled? Can the current rate of productivity growth continue?

Conclusion

In Part 2, we have reviewed the development of economic systems, focusing on capitalism. We have, at the same time, summarized the development of modern economic thought, examining capitalist proponents and its critics. In this chapter we have examined the historical development of capitalism in the United States and how it has changed over time. The ideas of Keynes were influential in assessing solutions for an economy mired in depression. In Parts 3 and 4, we turn to the development of the modern economic theory about how capitalism and markets work—first, in terms of microeconomics, then macroeconomics.

Review Questions

1. List the strengths of laissez-faire capitalism both in theory and in practice.

2. List major shortcomings in the operation of laissez-faire capitalism.

3. How did Keynes reshape the way economists thought about the economy?

4. In what sense can the ideas of John Maynard Keynes be considered a synthesis of the ideas of Smith and Marx?

5. What were the major forces behind the economic success of the United States?

6. What are some current problems facing the U.S. economy?

7. What are the ways in which the ideas of Smith, Marx, and Keynes are incorporated into the structure of the U.S. economy?

THINKING CRITICALLY

Technological Innovation, the New Economy, and the Future

The ideas of Adam Smith and Karl Marx and the intellectual legacy of Joseph Schumpeter continue with us in more ways than we might imagine as we progress into the twenty-first century. Each economist discussed issues of economic growth and conditions necessary for expanding national income. (Also, while we are not focusing on their specific contributions here, Thorstein Veblen and John Maynard Keynes had very important ideas related to technology, technological change, business cycles, and the future of capitalism.) That focus on growth is especially relevant today, with technological change driving the long economic expansion in the United States, lasting from 1991 into 2000. The value of investments traded in the U.S. and global financial markets rose rapidly for those years. The expansion of information and communications technology has also provided the stimulus for capitalism's spread across the globe, as many countries attempt some variation of capitalist development.

The changes amount to more than growth, however. U.S. and global capitalism seem to have entered into a new and different phase made possible by advances in computer and microchip technology and the growth of the semiconductor industry. Satellite technology and the development of fiber optics accelerated a telecommunications revolution. Advances in biotechnology through the human genome project have forever changed the way we approach medical challenges. All the while, the Internet and software developments introduced new ways for consumers and businesses to make purchases. Technology-inspired change transformed all areas of business, from financial operations to marketing, accounting, public relations, advertising, and management practices and strategies.

As every sector of the economy has integrated communications and information technology, productivity (output per worker) grew. The services sector of the economy also has expanded. And all of this has taken place on a global scale. During the mid-to-late 1990s, stock prices soared as investors poured dollars into high-tech stocks and as industry giants—including AOL and Time Warner, Citibank and Travelers—launched a wave of mergers and buyouts. The wealth generated by this wildly rising stock market, including riches gained (and later lost) in the Internet sector, fueled economic growth through the 1990s and transformed many traditional business methods and markets.

While the early economists discussed in these past chapters didn't write about the most recent revolutions in technology, Adam Smith, Karl Marx, and Joseph Schumpeter did introduce important ideas about technological change, innovation, business cycles, economic growth, and the future of capitalism—items that help explain our present-day economy.

Adam Smith and Economic Growth

Adam Smith, whose work we discussed in Chapter 4, didn't foresee the Industrial Revolution that encompassed England as he was teaching about and writing *The Wealth of Nations*. His view of technology nevertheless played a central role in the ongoing development of capitalism. Responding to the free interplay of the forces of supply and demand, Smith confidently noted that the market system would self-adjust through the "invisible hand." The pressure of competition would force capitalists to reinvest profits in new production methods so they would produce better goods more efficiently, helping them retain and capture additional customers and gain a greater share of the market. Capitalists depended on the innovators and the risk takers developing these new processes and the underlying technology to make them more efficient. This constant search for new, more efficient production methods supported Smith's argument that capitalism would advance in periods of growth spurts that would over time improve the progress of society and the well-being of the members of society. (We do, after all, have more pins!) The role for invention was clearly implied in Smith's market system.

Karl Marx, Technical Change, and the Quest for Markets

From our earlier discussion in Chapter 5, we have seen how Karl Marx's analysis of historical change and his capitalist critique incorporated ideas about technology, technological change, business cycles, and the future of capitalism. To Marx, changes in technology would transform the relations of production and eventually the superstructure, ultimately altering society itself. These changes were apparent in the transitions from the early communal societies to the slave societies of Greece and Rome, to the feudal societies of Europe, and finally to the emergence of capitalism in Europe. Indeed, Marx anticipated that capitalism itself would be transformed to a higher stage of development which he defined as socialism, or the first communism.

Marx's theory of capitalist crisis suggested that the capitalist's quest for surplus value would eventually lead to the substitution of capital for labor in the production process to reduce the cost of production. As capitalists invented more and more productive technologies while driving wages down, the result would be a crisis of overproduction. Laborers would no longer be able to purchase all that capitalists produced.

Joseph Schumpeter and Creative Destruction of Technology

In Chapter 6 we noted that Joseph Schumpeter focused on the importance of technical change for the growth process. During the late 1990s and early 2000, Schumpeter's ideas were retrieved from economic history texts and recognized as increasingly relevant in explaining the changes brought about by revolutionary transformations in information and communication technologies. His theories of creative destruction, innovation, and entrepreneurship are today intrinsically associated with the underlying dynamics of capitalism.

Read the following article and answer the questions that follow. "Catch the Wave" is from a special report, "Innovation in Industry Survey," published by *The Economist* on February 20, 1999.

Catch the Wave

Think of innovation as "x" in the economic-growth equation—a factor that clearly matters but no-one is quite sure how much. Annual forecasts of gross domestic product (GDP) are no help. They are just statistical measures, laden with guesswork and opinion. They represent the forecaster's view about the difference between an economy's output and its total productive capacity on the one hand, and the state of the country's consumer confidence, stock building and export prospects in the months ahead on the other hand. If that seems tricky, try forecasting economic growth for a number of years into the future. Nobody has done this successfully, because it requires insight into how productivity can be expected to change in the years ahead—among many other things.

From Adam Smith to Karl Marx, economists have struggled to understand productivity growth. But it was not until after the second world war that the beginnings of an explanation emerged. The theory now generally accepted stems from work done on the so-called "production function" by Robert Solow at the Massachusetts Institute of Technology in 1956. This says, reasonably enough, that the output of an economy depends on its inputs—in short, capital and labour. Double the inputs and you get twice the output. To the basic theory, economists have added a rider to account for embarrassing quirks such as the law of diminishing returns. In the revised version, if you add more and more capital to a given labour force, or an increasing number of workers to a fixed amount of capital, the result will be successively smaller increases in output.

So far, so good. But although the production function, like Newtonian mechanics, may be broadly right, it is nowhere near right enough to make meaningful long-term predictions. The problem is that, as in Isaac Newton's view of the physical universe, the theory assumes an idealised world—in this case, a heavenly paradise in which perfect competition reigns.

Unfortunately, the real world works rather differently. For instance, if the law of diminishing returns operates as it is supposed to, why have returns on investment in America, Europe and Japan been higher in the second half of the 20th century than in the first half? Why, for that matter, has the gap between the world's rich and poor countries widened rather than narrowed? The theory says that where the stock of capital is rising faster than the work force—as has clearly been true in the industrial countries since the second world war—the return on each additional unit of capital should fall over time. Instead, it has risen over the decades rather than fallen, so something is amiss.

For want of a better explanation, that "something" is now reckoned to be technological progress plus other forms of new knowledge—in short, innovation. In this scheme of things, innovation accounts for any growth that cannot be explained by increases in capital and labour. And although the return on investment may decline as more capital is added to the economy, any deceleration in growth is more than offset by the leveraging effects of innovation. This explains why rates of return have stayed high in rich countries, and why poorer countries have not caught up.

There the economists tend to leave the argument, as if technological progress—along with other new knowledge—were simply to be taken for granted, free as air. However, experience shows that technological know-how, manufacturing experience and market research are not free; they have to be acquired at considerable cost. And once acquired, such proprietary knowledge tends to be hoarded as trade secrets or hedged in by patents and other intellectual-property rights. To ignore such quibbles must be justified if innovation contributed only marginally to economic growth. Yet, maddeningly, this residual, intangible and largely ignored factor seems to account for more than half of all growth. Thus, if this reading is correct, it is innovation—more than the application of capital or labour—that makes the world go round.

Godfather of Innovation

All attempts to understand the effects of technological progress on economic growth pay homage to Joseph Schumpeter, an Austrian economist best remembered for his views on the "creative destruction" associated with industrial cycles 50–60 years long. Arguably the most radical economist of the 20th century, Schumpeter was the first to challenge classical economics as it sought (and still seeks) to optimise existing resources within a stable environment—treating any disruption as an external force on a par with plagues, politics and the weather. Into this intellectual drawing room, Schumpeter introduced the raucous entrepreneur and his rumbustious behaviour. As Schumpeter saw it, a normal, healthy economy was not one in equilibrium, but one that was constantly being "disrupted" by technological innovation.

Others had noticed "long waves" of economic activity before him, notably a Russian economist, Nikolai Kondratieff, who drew attention to them in 1925, using data on prices, wages and interest rates as well as industrial production and consumption drawn from France, Britain and the United States. But it was Schumpeter, the economic radical, who studied them in depth.

In his view, each of these long business cycles was unique, driven by entirely different clusters of industries (see Figures II.1A & B). Typically, a long upswing in a cycle started when a new set of innovations came into general use—as happened with water power, textiles and iron in the late 18th century; steam, rail and steel in the mid-19th century; and electricity, chemicals and the internal combustion engine at the turn of the 20th century. In turn, each upswing stimulated investment and an expansion of the economy. These long booms eventually petered out as the technologies matured and returns to investors declined with the dwindling number of opportunities. After a period of much slower expansion came the inevitable decline—only to be followed by a wave of fresh innovations which destroyed the old way of doing things and created the conditions for a new upswing. The entrepreneur's role, as Schumpeter saw it, was to act as a ferment in this process of creative destruction, allowing the economy to renew itself and bound onwards and upwards again.

FIGURE II.1A Schumpeter's Waves

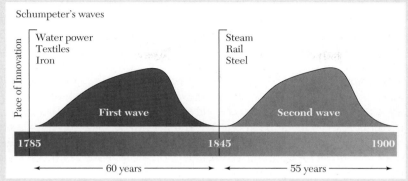

Schumpeter's waves

Pace of Innovation

Water power
Textiles
Iron

Steam
Rail
Steel

First wave

Second wave

1785   1845   1900

←———— 60 years ————→   ←———— 55 years ————→

By the time Schumpeter died in 1950, the third cycle of his "successive industrial revolutions" had already run its course. The fourth, powered by oil, electronics, aviation and mass production, is now rapidly winding down, if it has not gone already. All the evidence suggests that a fifth industrial revolution—based on semiconductors, fibre optics, genetics and software—is not only well under way but even approaching maturity. This may explain why America shrugged off its lethargy in the early 1990s and started bounding ahead again, leaving behind countries too preoccupied with preserving their fourth-wave industries. If so, then Schumpeter's long economic waves are shortening, from 50–60 years to around 30–40 years.

There is good reason why they should. It was only during the third wave, in the early part of the 20th century, that governments and companies began to search for new technologies in a systematic manner. One of the oldest, Bell Laboratories at Murray Hill in New Jersey, was founded in 1925. Rather than leave the emergence of "new-wave" technologies to chance, all the major industrial countries nowadays have armies of skilled R&D workers sifting the data in pursuit of blockbuster technologies

FIGURE II.1B Schumpeter's Waves

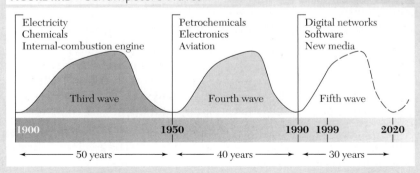

Electricity
Chemicals
Internal-combustion engine

Petrochemicals
Electronics
Aviation

Digital networks
Software
New media

Third wave

Fourth wave

Fifth wave

1900   1950   1990 1999   2020

←———— 50 years ————→   ←——— 40 years ———→   ←— 30 years —→

capable of carving out wholly new markets. The tools they use—computer analysers, gene sequencers, text parsers, patent searchers, citation mappers—are getting better all the time, speeding up the process. The productivity of industrial laboratories today is twice what it was a couple of decades ago.

So the fifth industrial revolution that started in America in the late 1980s may last no more than 25–30 years. If, as seems likely, we are already a decade into this new industrial cycle, it may now be almost too late for the dilatory to catch up. The rapid-upswing part of the cycle—in which successful participants enjoy fat margins, set standards, kill off weaker rivals and establish themselves as main players—looks as though it has already run two-thirds of its course, with only another five or six years left to go. Catching the wave at this late stage will depend on governments' willingness to free up their technical and financial resources, invest in the infrastructure required and let their fourth-wave relics go. Failing that, latecomers can expect only crumbs from the table before the party comes to an end—and a new wave of technologies begins, once again, to wash everything aside.

Source: "Catch the Wave" from *Innovation in Industry Survey* issued by *The Economist*, February 20, 1999. Copyright 1999 The Economist, Ltd., Distributed by *The New York Times* Special Features.

Exercises

Answer the questions that follow.

1. What is the relationship between the process of "creative destruction" and human progress according to Schumpeter?

2. Compare and contrast Schumpeter's core ideas with those of Smith and Marx. Outline key arguments in a debate that the three economic legends might have with one another.

3. What are three ways in which Schumpeter's ideas are relevant for the economy given advances in information and communication technologies? Find support for these three applications in a newspaper article, news or business magazine, or online article. Outline the main factors supporting Schumpeter's theories.

4. If Schumpeter's theory of successive industrial revolutions is correct, where are we now on a historical chart of cycles? Given the sharp economic down turn in 2000 and 2001 and the overexpansion of telecommunications technology expenditures, does Schumpeter's wave analysis still hold? Do you think Marx would agree or disagree with this interpretation?

5. Are we letting our "fourth wave" relics go? Are there recent government policies that would help us evaluate our commitment to the advance or destruction of the fourth wave? Identify and explain those policies.

Part Three

Microeconomics

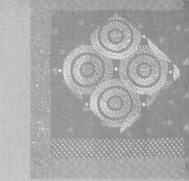

Now that we are about to begin studying modern economic theory, we might pause to ask ourselves what economic theory should do. Ideally, it should have explanatory value to help us understand how economic forces work, predictive power to help us understand what might happen in the future, and relevance to help us solve the economic problems we face. Keep these criteria in mind as you study economic theory in Parts 3, 4, and 5.

Markets have emerged in the Western world as a method of organizing society's production. Markets exist for all of the factors of production and for final consumption goods. Through the information transmitted by markets, producers decide what factors of production to use, and consumers decide what to consume. The information appears in the form of prices. On the basis of these decisions by various economic agents in the society, resources will be used in certain ways to produce certain goods and services. From their participation in production, people will earn certain incomes and will spend them, which will determine how goods are distributed in the society.

Early economists developed theories and concepts to explain these economic activities. The early development of economic thought provided a foundation for modern microeconomics. **Microeconomics** is concerned with describing how the economic system operates to allocate resources, determine incomes, and organize production. Consequently, it focuses on the decision makers—firms, consumers, the government—that determine how resources will be used.

Microeconomics is fundamentally concerned with a major problem facing all contemporary economies: that not enough resources are available to satisfy all the desires of all the economic agents. **Scarcity** is a crucial economic fact of life. Given scarcity, microeconomics also concentrates on how the market system allocates resources by valuing them. Therefore it examines the operation of markets and price determination. Finally, microeconomics is concerned with evaluating how well society allocates and rations its scarce resources. Ideally, society should use resources efficiently. **Efficiency** means the minimal use of scarce resources to achieve the mix of output most highly valued by society.

This section on microeconomics also includes a number of models of economic behavior. Economists use models to focus their analysis on key economic relationships. In a world of boundless complexity, it is literally impossible for economists to consider every factor that might affect the economy. Therefore, economists tend to focus on the most important economic factors and relationships. To do this, they make assumptions that limit the number of variables considered in the relationship being studied, or they may hold variables constant for the time period in question. These assumptions used in economic models can help us to explore key economic relationships in depth. However, if there are circumstances in which the assumptions behind a model do not hold true, inaccurate analyses and predictions may result.

In this part of the book, you will learn to use and apply some basic microeconomic models. These models are used to examine particular economic issues, and we will evaluate the underlying assumptions in some cases to assist in our evaluation of the usefulness of the results.

CHAPTER SEVEN

Scarcity: "You Can't Always Get What You Want"

![] Introduction

Most of us remember the high gas prices of 2007. Few, however, remember an earlier period of even higher gas prices. In the 1970s, the United States experienced an energy crisis. Prices for oil, natural gas, and gasoline increased dramatically. Shortages of petroleum-related products developed and, at times, were serious, driving prices up and forcing long lines at gas stations and even shutdowns of factories and schools. Some observers predicted the shortages would become even more serious.

In 1975, the National Academy of Sciences issued a report warning of future shortages of important resources for advanced industrial societies. The report noted that the United States would continue to depend on oil imports for the next half century and that even the Middle East's oil reserves might be depleted. Other resources in possible short supply included asbestos, tin, copper, helium, and mercury. The academy went on to urge conservation coupled with efforts to increase supplies, substitution, and recycling:

> Because of the limits to natural resources as well as to means for alleviating these limits, it is recommended that the federal government proclaim and deliberately pursue a national policy of conservation of material, energy and environmental resources, informing the public and the private sectors fully about the needs and techniques for reducing energy consumption, the development of substitute materials, increasing the durability and maintainability of products, and reclamation and recycling.

While some reduction in energy use occurred after this crisis in the 1970s, few of the other recommendations were pursued as oil prices fell back to lower levels.

In annual reports on worldwide energy, land, water, and environmental management, the Worldwatch Institute continually warns that the world cannot sustain the rate at which it is using up its resources. Every year, billions of tons of topsoil are *depleted, the world population grows, forests are decimated in the Third World, and there is only small progress in the use of renewable energy and recycling.*

In the twenty-first century, resource problems continue to plague the global community. Resource shortages pose potential threats to energy-dependent economies, insufficient agricultural production threatens some countries with mass starvation, and soil depletion, overfishing, and deforestation endanger normally replenishable resources. Moreover, the environmental complications of these economic activities pose their own hazards, from oil spills to urban slums to global warming. These are profound challenges to human societies in the new millennium.

Because there are constraints on the availability of resources, individuals, communities, and societies must make choices about the best uses of the resources available to them. Economists have developed concepts to highlight the consequences of these choices, and they have focused on understanding how societies allocate scarce resources.

1. Why are there shortages? What factors play a role in creating shortages?
2. What sorts of actions could be taken to alleviate projected shortages?

Scarcity: A Fundamental Economic Fact of Modern Life

Scarcity is one of the fundamental economic facts of modern life. **Scarcity** refers to the limitations on the resources used in production. All societies must develop methods and institutions to produce goods and services and to distribute them to people for consumption. However difficult that task, it is further complicated by the overriding reality of scarce resources and seemingly unlimited human wants and needs. Human societies, and the individual people within them, have certain physical needs for short- and long-run survival. Food, shelter, and clothing must be provided. With the desire to live beyond subsistence and to experience a richer life, the wants of a society are subject to constant expansion.

But the physical and mental resources that can be used to provide for material needs are not subject to constant expansion. This constraint is especially true if we concentrate on the short run—the present and immediate future. The mental capabilities of humans are at a certain stage of development. Physical resources are at a fixed level. There are just so many people who can labor. There is just so much wheat, corn, coal, gas, bauxite, copper, and so forth. With more time, of course, science, technology, and exploration can expand the available resources, but we might also begin to run short of some key resources. In the long run, the problem of scarcity governs the decisions that must be made; society must concern itself with using its resources in the best way possible to meet its needs.

3. Are human wants and needs unlimited? Why or why not? What determines human wants and needs?
4. If wants are not unlimited, does scarcity still exist?

The microeconomic problem for society is to allocate the available resources in the best way possible to meet as many of the needs and wants of its people as it can. This is **efficiency.** A society will be better off if it uses its resources efficiently. This is an incredibly complicated task. How much of our resources should be used to develop nuclear energy? Should we devote more or less to exploring the possibilities of solar energy or growing corn for ethanol production? Should more resources go to housing or to transportation? Should we build automobiles for private transportation or trains for public transportation?

Because of scarcity, we must make choices. In addition to deciding how to organize for production and distribution, a society must develop mechanisms and institutions for making economic decisions—decisions about how best to use the resources that are available. How can we make sure that resources are allocated in the best way possible? Efficiency in the allocation of resources is an important economic objective. Different societies resolve and have resolved this task in different ways—for example, by tradition, by command, and by markets. (Besides efficiency, of course, a society may favor other economic goals, such as economic growth and equitable income distribution.)

In the current U.S. economic system, many of these decisions are made through markets. Cars are produced because people demand them and are willing to buy them for the prices charged by producers. The prices reflect the costs to the producers for the resources that are used in production. Based on price information, income, and individual tastes and preferences, people decide what to spend money on. We will examine the workings of markets in Chapters 8 to 11 to see how they allocate resources.

Resource allocation also includes public choices about the use of resources. For example, every society desires to protect itself from foreign enemies. Some countries do this by establishing a military force; the threat of physical reaction is intended to forestall aggressive actions by others. In the event of attack or hostile action, the country can use military force to protect the society's interests and possessions. The construction of military force, however, requires the use of resources, which are then unavailable for other uses. This trade-off in the use of resources is what economists call **opportunity cost**—that is, the cost of the resources that is devoted to the production of one category of goods or services and therefore cannot be used in another activity. The opportunity cost of using resources to produce guns, tanks, planes, and other military goods and services is that those resources cannot be used for other purposes. Different societies have made different choices about the size of their military establishments, and thus over the use of their scarce resources.

As in this example, microeconomics is largely concerned with the allocation of resources in society. Are resources being used efficiently? What are the opportunity costs of alternative uses of resources?

The Production Possibilities Curve

Economic choices, necessitated by scarcity, have opportunity costs. This fact applies to public choices about how to use tax revenues: Should we build more highways? Should we overhaul the railroad system? Should we expand space exploration? It also applies to analyzing the results of decisions usually made in the private sector: Should we produce more big cars? Or more little cars? Should we produce cigarettes? Or Power Bars? Or more housing? For these and other uses of resources, choices must be made. Choosing to use resources in a specific way means that they cannot be used for other purposes.

5. What is the opportunity cost of not using resources for a particular purpose? For example, what's the opportunity cost of going to work after graduating from high school?

To illustrate this economic principle—that because the resources needed to produce goods and services are scarce, a society cannot have all of the goods and services it desires—economists have developed a model called the **production possibilities curve.** The basic production possibilities model makes the following assumptions:

- The economy is experiencing full employment of all its resources.
- The supplies of the factors of production are fixed at one point in time.
- Technology is constant (again, at one point in time).

We will apply this model to the public choice between producing military and civilian goods. This requires one further assumption: The economy produces consumer goods and military goods (or "butter" and "guns"), and the resources can be used to produce both types of goods (although some resources will be better than others at producing one type of goods). With our resources (and our assumptions), we can make only limited amounts of both types of goods, so we must choose how much of each type of good to produce. Since our resources are fully employed and limited, we can produce more of one type of good only by producing less of the other. That is, if we decide to produce more military goods, we can do it only by taking resources away from the production of civilian goods and thus produce fewer consumer goods. The opportunity cost of producing more military goods is that we will have fewer civilian goods, and vice versa.

Figure 7.1 shows the resulting production possibilities curve (PPC). If we produce only military goods (point *A* on the PPC, where we are using all our resources for military goods), we can have 50 units of military goods but no civilian goods. At the other extreme (point *D*), if we produce only civilian goods, we can have 100 units of them but no military goods. Or we can produce at point *B* or point *C*, with some military goods and some civilian goods. We have available a whole range of different *combinations* of military goods and civilian goods. The locus of all those possible combinations gives us the production possibilities curve.

At a given moment in time, if a society chooses to have more of one type of good, it must sacrifice some of the other type of good. If a society is currently at

FIGURE 7.1   Production Possibilities Curve

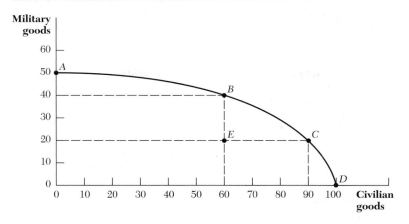

point *C* and decides to produce 20 additional units of military goods (moving to point *B*), the society will have fewer resources to devote to the production of civilian goods. It will have to reduce the production of civilian goods from 90 units to 60 units. Thus, the opportunity cost of increasing the production of military goods from 20 units to 40 units (the movement from point *C* to point *B*) is the 30 units of civilian goods that the society must give up in the process.

The production possibilities curve is shaped the way it is (concave to the origin) because resources are not completely adaptable to other uses. In other words, some resources are *specialized*. For example, beginning at point *A*, where society is producing only military goods, sacrificing 10 units of military goods will increase the output of civilian goods by 60 units, a substantial increase. This occurs because the resources best suited for producing civilian goods (including pacifists and farmland) are being shifted into production of civilian goods. As the society moves from point *B* to point *C*, it gives up 20 units of military goods for 30 units of civilian goods. Eventually, if society moves from point *C* to point *D*, it gives up 20 units of military goods for only 10 units of civilian goods. This happens because some resources, such as generals and missile factories, are very well suited for the production of military goods but less effective at producing civilian goods. As more and more resources are transferred to producing civilian goods, the *addition* to civilian goods will decline because some resources are specialized and are not easily converted from one use to another. To reflect this phenomenon, the slope of the PPC gets steeper and steeper.

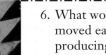

6. What would the PPC look like if resources were not specialized and could be moved easily from one use to another with no loss in efficiency (as in the case of producing more green shirts and fewer blue shirts)?

At any point on the PPC, society is using all of its scarce resources efficiently. If a society were to leave some of its resources unused, or if it were to use its resources inefficiently, then that society would be at a point *inside* the production possibilities curve, such as point *E* in Figure 7.1. A society can attain any point on (or inside) its production possibilities curve with its existing resources and technology. To reach a point beyond the PPC, a society must increase its available resources or increase its efficiency with improvements in its technology.

Economic Growth and the Production Possibilities Curve

Economic growth can occur from technological innovations or decisions to produce greater amounts of **capital goods.** (Economists call the addition of capital goods *investment.*) Capital goods consist of the productive equipment needed to manufacture products. Typical capital goods are machinery, equipment, and infrastructure. Many people consider education to be a capital good (human capital) because it increases productivity, as we will see later in this chapter. Capital goods enhance a society's productive capacity, shifting the PPC out and allowing a society to produce more of all of the goods it desires. Capital goods differ from *consumer goods*, such as food, clothing, and CDs, which are enjoyed by consumers but not used to produce other goods.

Capital goods can be quite important in determining how fast an economy grows. In 1970, the United States was able to produce 2.5 times as many goods per person as Japan was. But in that same year, the Japanese spent more than twice as much per capita on capital goods. In fact, Japan's total capital investment in the 1970s was greater than that made by the much wealthier United States. The result was dramatic economic growth in Japan and mediocre economic growth in the United States. By 1988, Japan was able to produce the same amount of goods per person as the United States because of economic growth generated in large part by Japanese investment in capital goods. The production possibilities curves in Figure 7.2 show that, because Japan devoted a greater amount of resources to capital goods, its economy experienced a greater level of growth in productive capacity, measured on these PPCs as the trade-off between capital and consumer goods. In 1988, Japan's capacity to produce capital goods and consumer goods equaled that of the United States.

One of the reasons that Japan was able to devote a greater share of its resources to capital goods than the United States was that the peace agreement following World War II did not allow the Japanese to maintain a large military. Meanwhile, the United States (and the Soviet Union) was spending vast amounts of money on the Cold War. Military goods, like consumer goods, provide benefits but do not by themselves increase the productive capacity of the economy. As we will see in the next section, devoting so many of a society's scarce resources to military goods may incur significant opportunity costs.

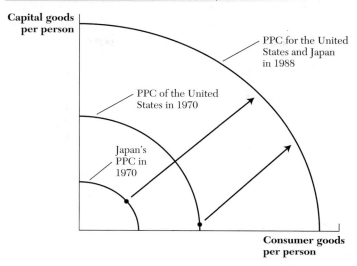

FIGURE 7.2 Growth in a PPC from Capital Goods Production

Capital goods per person

PPC for the United States and Japan in 1988

PPC of the United States in 1970

Japan's PPC in 1970

Consumer goods per person

7. Beginning in 1988 and continuing through the early 2000s, the Japanese economy experienced a number of economic setbacks leading to much slower growth rates for the country, with one result being a reduction in spending on capital goods (less investment) and another being slower growth rates in income. During the mid-to-late 1990s, the U.S. economy grew at historically high rates with firms expanding capital goods purchases and incomes also increasing rapidly.

Using the outermost PPC in Figure 7.2, how can we show the changes in the spending on capital goods and consumer goods in the United States and Japan since 1990? What would the new PPCs for the United States and Japan that result from the changes in capital goods purchases look like? Explain.

Military versus Civilian Priorities

A controversial example of the problem of scarcity in recent years has been the debate about national priorities. Perhaps the sharpest focus of this debate has been on military spending versus spending on civilian priorities. Proponents of military spending want more resources for producing military goods. They argue that more is needed because of the potential military capabilities of the nation's enemies and because they believe military power is the best way to assure national security, including protection from terrorist threats. Critics argue that too many resources are devoted to defense, that military spending deprives the nation of the use of resources for domestic purposes (e.g., education and health care), and that diplomacy is a better way to solve international disputes.

The arguments on both sides have become more sophisticated and complex over the years, but at the heart of the matter is an economic choice about how best to use scarce resources. This public issue, though, is not simply an economic question. It is also concerned with philosophy (what is the best way to resolve conflicts? what is social justice? what is security?) and with international and domestic politics.

8. What is national security? What determines whether a nation is secure?

Since World War II, the United States has devoted a substantial portion of its resources every year to military spending. Before the 1940s, with the exception of U.S. involvement in World War I, only about 1 percent of the nation's annual production of goods and services (measured by gross domestic product, or GDP) was devoted to armed forces. In the massive Allied war effort from 1941 to 1945, however, military production dominated the economy. In the period since then, the annual military budget has fluctuated between about 3 and 9 percent of GDP. The 2006 U.S. military budget of $536 billion represented 20 percent of federal government spending and 4.1 percent of the nation's GDP. If military-related spending—such as foreign military aid, homeland security, the cost of the wars in Iraq and Afghanistan, and military retirement pay and veterans' benefits—is included, those numbers would more than double. Worldwide military spending in 2005 was $1,118 billion (48 percent of which was U.S. spending, excluding expenditures on the wars in Iraq and Afghanistan). This amounted to about 2.5 percent of global GDP. As Figure 7.3 shows, the United States spends almost 10 times more than the United Kingdom, which has the next largest military budget, and over 22 times more than the states that the U.S. government identifies as security risks. Yet, as the events of September 11, 2001, demonstrated, our massive military budget has not kept us safe from terrorist attacks.

What does all this money buy? About 35 percent of the annual military budget pays for the personnel costs of past and present service people and civilian workers for the Pentagon. About 40 percent of it purchases military supplies, equipment, and weapons: uniforms, food, planes, petroleum, ammunition, nuclear warheads, and so forth. The remainder provides for the general support costs (e.g., construction and maintenance) of the entire military establishment.

The history of this post-1940 shift in the military policy of the United States is rooted in the two world wars, the Cold War, and subsequent "hot" wars and military interventions. For World Wars I and II, the United States mobilized private production and military forces for the war efforts. U.S. peacetime military forces, its standing army and navy, were relatively modest and concerned primarily with defending the borders of the United States. After World War II,

FIGURE 7.3 Global Military Spending, 2005 (billions of $)

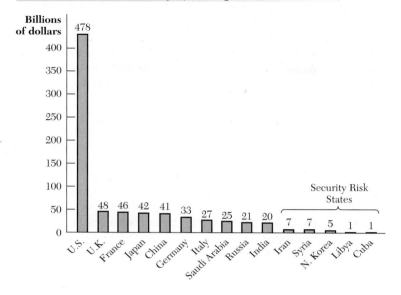

Source: Data from "Recent Trends in Military Expenditure" SIPRI—The Stockholm International Peace Research Institute, www. sipri. org.

however, the United States decided to maintain very large and worldwide military forces. The arguments were that these forces were necessary to *prevent* aggression and that in the post–World War II period the Soviet Union represented a threat to U.S. interests and world peace. The U.S. arsenal consisted of the personnel in the Army, Navy, Air Force, and Marines and sophisticated conventional and nuclear weapons.

From time to time, a perception of an increased Soviet threat or an active military engagement led to increases in military spending. For example, the Korean (1950–1954) and Vietnam (1964–1975) wars led to increased budgets to finance U.S. participation in the conflicts. In the 1980s and 1990s, U.S. military forces were involved in invasions of Grenada and Panama and in the (Persian) Gulf War. In 2001, U.S.-led forces invaded Afghanistan as part of the war on terror, and in 2003 it invaded Iraq. Both led to an increase in military spending.

As noted above, we can use the concept of opportunity cost to analyze the allocation of resources to military goods and civilian goods. For example, during his first term in office, President Ronald Reagan persuaded Congress to increase spending on national defense by $100 billion to counter a perceived threat from the Soviet Union. This increased military spending was accompanied by decreases in spending on social programs (including food stamps, job training, welfare, and education). Thus the opportunity cost of increased military spending on the Cold War in the early 1980s was the cuts in social programs.

Similarly, the 2006 U.S. military budget of $536 billion was more than $230 billion larger than in 2001. Instead of paying for this increase with higher taxes or spending cuts in other areas, President George W. Bush and Congress chose to borrow the money. Yet this too has opportunity costs: The direct costs are the interest payments the government (and taxpayers) must pay on the money borrowed and the stream of payments on these debts in the future, causing U.S. citizens to sacrifice future consumption to pay for current military expenditures and generating an intergenerational transfer of debt.

What are the arguments for and against military use of the scarce material and labor resources of the United States? President Bush and his supporters have argued that the United States must maintain overwhelming military superiority to prevent nuclear war and to be able to attack preemptively states that support terrorism. Moreover, they argue, larger military power will prevent political instability and will enable the United States to protect its vital interests in the Persian Gulf and other regions of the world. Their position is that the rest of the world must perceive that the United States is strong and willing to use its military force; in this way, the United States can contribute to international stability and world peace.

The opponents of this view argue that the United States currently has the capability to blow up the world and deter would-be rogue state attackers. They argue that the United States has more than adequate forces for simple deterrence, and our massive military did not save us from terrorist attacks. In terms of foreign policy, they argue that military power is not the most powerful weapon in promoting peace or U.S. interests in the rest of the world. Rather, diplomacy and economic development would be more useful in creating a more peaceful global environment and reducing anti-U.S. sentiments. Finally, they suggest that a country's national security is determined at least as much by internal health as by military might. Consequently, spending more money on the military and, as a result, denying resources for domestic priorities may actually undermine national security. While the United States is first in military spending, this comes with a substantial opportunity cost, since we are also first among developed countries in poverty and infant mortality.

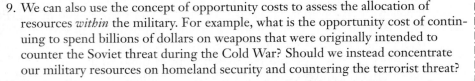

9. We can also use the concept of opportunity costs to assess the allocation of resources *within* the military. For example, what is the opportunity cost of continuing to spend billions of dollars on weapons that were originally intended to counter the Soviet threat during the Cold War? Should we instead concentrate our military resources on homeland security and countering the terrorist threat?

10. What are the opportunity costs of increased military spending? What are the possible opportunity costs of not increasing military spending?

11. What is your opinion in this general debate concerning the use of our society's scarce resources? Focus your response on the economic ramifications of the various choices.

12. The Congressional Budget Office has estimated that the federal government could increase its spending on the nation's deteriorating infrastructure—highways, bridges, water and sewer systems, and so forth—by $10 billion a year. Would you support reducing the military budget to do so? Why or why not? Could the federal government spend more on both military and infrastructural programs? Explain.

Applying the Concept of Choice to Personal Decisions

As is implicit in all of the foregoing discussion, decisions about using society's resources require that we compare the costs and the benefits of different uses of resources. Included in the costs are the opportunities forgone by not using resources for alternatives. This balancing of costs versus benefits also occurs in the economic decisions made by individuals, such as choices about work versus leisure, type of work, consumption, and so on.

Consumers weigh the benefits of buying a particular good (say, a home theater system) against its cost (that is, its price). They can also compare the benefits of purchasing a home theater system against the opportunity costs of not buying other goods (things they could have bought for the same price as the home theater system, such as a new flat screen computer and printer). On the basis of such judgments, consumers decide what goods to purchase in markets. (Furthermore, producers take consumers' decisions into account, and resources are allocated through markets to the production of particular goods and services.)

An example of a personal choice about resources is deciding whether to go to college. In making such a decision, an individual must weigh the benefits of going to college against the costs and opportunity costs of doing so. College costs money—for room and board, tuition, travel, books, and so on—and that money cannot be used for anything else. If you are in college, most of you are not working, getting experience, or earning income from a full-time job. On the other hand, a college education will develop your abilities (your human capital), can enrich your later life, and may qualify you for various types of employment. Your years of college also are a privileged period of time and space for growing and maturing in your experiences (curricular and extracurricular) and developing a philosophy of life.

A college education usually prepares people for white-collar, professional, higher-paying jobs. People with college educations, on the average, earn more than nongraduates. The earnings gap between college and high school graduates is substantial. In 2004, college graduates earned on the average over 107 percent more in annual income. Over their lifetimes, college graduates earn about $1 million more than high school graduates. Typically, the unemployment rate of college graduates is less than half that of high school graduates. Such factors can influence an individual's choice about going to college.

13. What are the benefits of going to college?

14. What are the costs (and opportunity costs) of going to college?

15. Did you make the right decision about going to college? Why or why not?

 ## Conclusion

Scarcity requires choices in both public and private matters. This fundamental economic fact requires societies and individuals to develop institutions and procedures for making hard decisions. Individuals rarely have enough income to buy everything they might want. Governments do not have enough tax money to do everything that their constituents would like them to do. In addition, decisions may result in benefits to someone or some group, while others suffer losses. Decision makers must weigh these costs and benefits in reaching decisions that maximize the use of scarce resources.

One of the most important institutions for facilitating such decisions in a private economy is the market. Markets determine prices for goods and resources. With this information, economic agents can compare alternative courses of action. Producers can decide what to produce and what resources to use. Consumers can decide what goods to purchase. In the next chapter, we will examine the economic theory of markets—how they operate and how prices are determined.

Review Questions

1. From your own experiences, do you think scarcity is really a problem for the United States? Is scarcity a problem in Ethiopia?

2. What is the difference between wants and needs?

3. Are wants and needs really unlimited? If they are, why?

4. How does the concept of opportunity cost help societies and individuals to make choices?

5. Why do economic choices have to be made?

6. Describe examples from your own life when the concepts of scarcity and opportunity cost have influenced your decisions.

7. Why don't the advances of science, technology, and exploration eliminate the problem of scarcity?

8. At the beginning of World War II, why could the United States increase its military output without sacrificing the production of civilian goods and services? Answer using a production possibilities curve.

9. The following table shows production possibilities for Brazil for consumption goods and capital goods:

Consumption Goods	Capital Goods
0	200
50	175
100	145
150	105
200	55
250	0

Graph the production possibilities curve. What are the opportunity costs of increasing the production of consumption goods by successive units of 50? Why might a country want to increase its production of capital goods?

10. Use the graph below, containing a PPC for the small, isolated country of Bucknellica, to answer the following questions.
    a. What is the opportunity cost of moving from point B to point C?
    b. What is the opportunity cost of moving from point C to point B?
    c. What factors could cause the Bucknellican economy to be able to achieve point F?
    d. What are some factors that might cause the Bucknellican economy to operate at point E?
    e. Compute the opportunity cost of one unit of computers for each region of the PPC (A–B, B–C and C–D). (Hint: In the region from A–B, 4 units of computers are equal in terms of resource use to 10 units of beer, so 1 unit of computers is equal to 10/4 or 2.5 units of beer.) Why does the opportunity cost of a unit of computers change as we move from A to D? Explain.
    f. In terms of economic growth, is there a reason to prefer point D over point A? Explain.

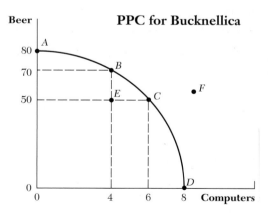

CHAPTER EIGHT

The Theory of Markets

Introduction

Markets guide decisions about resource allocation—that is, how society decides to use its scarce resources. How exactly do markets accomplish this? This chapter will develop the economic analysis of markets to provide some insight into the relationship between markets and resource allocation.

As we saw in Part 2, markets emerged as one of the most fundamental institutions of capitalism. **Markets** are the institutions through which buyers and sellers exchange goods and services. They replaced tradition and feudal authority as the principal organizers of economic activity. Markets exist in capitalism for all consumer goods and productive resources.

Usually, goods and services are exchanged for money. All goods and services, then, must have prices that reflect their values and that govern their exchange. These prices end up guiding production and resource allocation. Producers and consumers use prices as basic information in deciding which resources to use and which products to purchase. Consequently, to see how markets allocate scarce resources, it is essential to understand how markets determine prices.

THE BIG PICTURE

Supply and Demand

The next few chapters introduce more complex economic models that focus on markets and how they work. The Big Picture segments provide an intuitive overview of the models that follow. In this chapter, we develop a model of supply and demand which illustrates how markets work based on the two major groups that participate in any market exchange of a good or service: those who supply the item and those who demand (or purchase) it. Although the graphs depicting supply and demand relationships may seem complex, examining the logic behind the graphs and the models can help in understanding how markets work, and specifically, how prices and quantities in markets respond to the forces of supply and demand.

As an example, consider the market for corn between 2005 and 2006. In September of 2005, corn sold in the U.S. market for $1.72 per bushel (P = $1.72). But higher oil prices and continued instability in the Middle East in the early 2000s had led to to the use of more corn-based ethanol as a fuel substitute for gasoline. In late 2005 new ethanol plants began to come on line. Since these plants used corn to produce ethanol, they purchased more corn. Because of these increased purchases, the demand for corn increased dramatically. This caused the new demand (D) for corn (Figure 8.BP.1) to outstrip supply (S), creating a shortage of corn in the corn market.

FIGURE 8.BP.1   The Corn Market Responds to an Increase in Demand

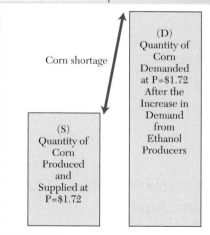

Corn shortage

(D)
Quantity of Corn Demanded at P=$1.72 After the Increase in Demand from Ethanol Producers

(S)
Quantity of Corn Produced and Supplied at P=$1.72

Corn farmers responded predictably to this situation. They reasoned that in the corn market, when more people want your corn (at the current price) than you can possibly supply, then you can increase revenues (a) charge a higher price and (b) produce as much of this "hot" commodity as you can in the given time frame. As a result of this reasoning, (a) corn prices rose and (b) corn production (the quantity supplied) increased. As corn prices rose, some people who wished to purchase corn at the old price of $1.72, scaled back on that desire when corn prices rose to higher levels. The market for corn finally stabilized in November 2006 at a price of $2.76 per bushel. At this price, a larger quantity of corn was produced and sold and the demand for corn (D1) equaled the supply of corn (S1) at this price (see Figure 8.BP.2).

FIGURE 8.BP.2   The Corn Market Responds to an Increase in Demand

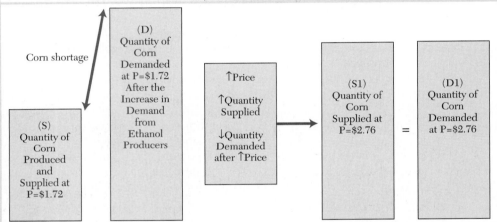

In markets where supply exceeds demand (a surplus), the opposite series of events occurs: The excess supply causes producers to (a) reduce prices and (b) lower the quantity produced in that time frame. The market stabilizes at a lower price with smaller quantities produced and sold. Thus, prices and quantities in markets respond to changes in demand as well as to changes in supply. Below, we develop a model of supply and demand to help us understand the intricacies of these changes in markets.

Markets and Price Determination: Supply-and-Demand Analysis

To highlight the economic analysis of markets, we will use as an example the market for college education in the United States. In Chapter 7, we referred to the decision about going to college as an example of a personal choice about the use of scarce resources. How much does it cost? What else could one do with

Examining snowboards in a sporting equipment store—a market in action. Markets exist whenever and wherever commodities are exchanged by buyers and sellers.

(© David Young-Wolff/PhotoEdit)

the money? Why should (or shouldn't) one go to college? What does one sacrifice by going to college for four years? Does it make more sense to enter the labor force right after high school? What are the benefits of a college education?

Obviously, one crucial element in making such an important decision is the dollar cost of going to college. In the following analysis, we will isolate the factors that determine the price of a college education. The analysis will help us to gain some insights into and understanding of how this market operates—how its price is determined and what implications there are for resource allocation. We will develop a method of analysis, the *theory of supply and demand*, that should assist us in understanding the general functioning of markets in a capitalist economy.

1. During the 1970s, the cost of a year at college for tuition, room and board, and fees almost doubled. However, the rise in costs was slightly less than the overall rate of inflation for the same period. In the 1980s, the costs for a year of college more than doubled, increasing much faster than the rate of inflation. During the 1990s, the costs for college nearly doubled again, while prices in general only increased by about 34 percent. And, from 2000–2007, costs for college increased about 29 percent more than prices in general. Why do you think the price of a college education has been continually increasing? What do you think accounts for the fact that since 1980 college costs have increased much more than the prices of most other goods and services? What can be done about this problem? Why is it a "problem"?

To conduct our supply-and-demand analysis, as in all economic theory, we will have to make some assumptions to simplify our model of the market.

Despite these simplifying assumptions, our theory will provide us with some tools for understanding the functioning of real markets in the economy. It should also help us understand why market prices change over time. And it might help us develop some possible solutions to economic problems.

We will begin with a fundamental assumption of microeconomics: that economic agents are rational, calculating, and motivated by self-interest. We assume that consumers are rational with respect to their purchases and that they try to maximize their own welfare through consumption, given their available spending power (that, through calculations and trial and error, consumers seek to maximize their satisfaction). Generally, we assume that producers calculate costs and revenues and try to maximize their profits from production.

To analyze the market for a college education, we need some additional assumptions and qualifications. First, we will assume that there is, in some sense, a homogeneous product. In other words, we will concentrate on *a* college education as a good that is exchanged in a market of buyers and sellers, assuming away any differences among particular colleges or between private and public universities. Obviously, these differences do exist and account for price differences, but we want to simplify and concentrate on *one* price for a college education. Once we have developed a model of supply and demand, we should be able to use it to account for cost differences at different institutions. We will also assume away the admissions problem (the product is not necessarily available to any buyer who might wish to purchase it), the financial aid dimension (not everyone pays the same price), and the graduation problem (actually getting the product—the diploma—in hand is not merely a matter of paying the costs to the cashier). Finally, although the producer of this product is generally not a profit-making institution, colleges and universities must take their costs and revenues into account, utilize scarce resources efficiently, and charge prices that reflect their costs (minus contributions from alumni, corporations, governments, and other benefactors).

Higher education is a large market in the United States. By the year 2004, this "industry" spent more than $315 billion annually. Almost 15 million students are enrolled as undergraduates in more than 2,300 four-year institutions and more than 1,800 two-year schools. About 56 percent of the students are women, and about 30 percent are minorities.

U.S. higher education also has a very large comparative advantage in the global economy. The U.S. higher education system is the best in the world, and it attracts students from all areas of the globe. Almost 600,000 international students are enrolled in U.S. institutions (about 240,000 as undergraduates), while 180,000 U.S. students study abroad. Of the international students in the United States, 58 percent come from Asia, 13 percent from Europe, 12 percent from Latin America, 6 percent from Africa, and 6 percent from the Middle East.

To see how the market price for a college education is determined, we will begin by examining each side of this market in isolation from the other. For the buyer's side of the market, we will focus on *demand*; for the seller's side of the market, we will focus on *supply*. Then we will put supply and demand together.

Demand

The buyer's side of the market involves the demand for the product. **Demand** is the amount of a particular good or service buyers want, given its price. More specifically, it represents the amounts of a particular good or service buyers are willing and able to purchase at various possible prices.

What determines the demand for any product? Many factors influence the demand for a college education. The essential factor behind the demand for any product obviously is that it is useful to the buyer; it satisfies some want or desire or need. Beyond this, we can list some other influences on the demand for a product: tastes and preferences, income, prices of related goods, number of demanders, and expectations of future prices, among other factors.

Tastes and Preferences.

Consumers' tastes and preferences guide their demand for different goods. Tastes and preferences are influenced by social, political, and cultural forces, as well as by the physical, psychological, and mental requirements of daily survival in the world. Over time, in any given society, tastes and preferences will change and will, in turn, influence changing patterns of consumer demand for different goods and services. Tastes and preferences also differ among different countries.

Throughout the modern history of the United States, a college education has been a valued product. Presumably, it helps prepare people for coping with the world, broadens people's horizons and perspectives, prepares people for professional positions in society, and paves the way for further education. It also helps people gain entry to certain sectors of the labor force.

In recent years, the demand for a college education has been continually increasing (in 1960, there were 6 million students in higher education, less than half as many as today). The primary reason for the increase is that people perceive a college degree to be necessary for obtaining specific types of employment. Indeed, the realities of the labor market suggest that a college education is extremely valuable in this regard. Economists have estimated that the annual rate of return on a college education is about 13 percent (significantly in excess of the return on most financial investments). Consumers' tastes and preferences thus influence the demand for a college education. Throughout the 1960s, the percentage of high school graduates who went on to college steadily increased. In the 1970s, the percentage leveled off, but since 1980 it has increased steadily. In 2003, 64 percent of high school graduates enrolled in college (compared with only 49 percent in 1980 and 45 percent in 1960).

2. Why do you suppose that tastes and preferences changed to cause a leveling off in the percentage of high school graduates who went to college? *Did* tastes and preferences change? Did they change again in the 1980s, 1990s, and 2000s? Why?

Income.   Demand depends not only on the desire to buy, but also on how much consumers have to spend. Spending power, in turn, depends largely on income. And who consumes what products depends on the distribution of income in the society.

Since we have assumed that consumers try to maximize their satisfaction and that they derive it from goods because the goods are useful, we conclude that with more money, consumers will purchase larger quantities of goods and services. During the 1960s, the United States experienced one of its longest periods of prosperity. The real income of the average family increased throughout this period. This increasing income certainly provided the resources for an increasing percentage of U.S. youth to attend college. In the 1970s, however, the increase in average real incomes began to slow down. This probably accounts in part for some of the leveling off in college attendance in the 1970s. When incomes increased in the late 1990s, the demand for college educations also went up. But with the recession of 2001, demand declined somewhat.

Prices of Related Goods.   The demand for a college education may be sensitive to (and influenced by) the prices of related products. Consumers are very sensitive to the prices of goods they consider to be *substitutes*—goods that satisfy the same need. For example, some substitutes for Coke are Pepsi, other soft drinks, fruit juices, and water; substitutes for plane transportation include train and automobile transportation to the same destination. In the case of the demand for a college education, if some nonprofessional training schools lowered their prices, the demand for college educations might fall, as some people substituted that educational experience for college.

Other goods may be *complementary*. Such goods go together or are consumed together. Examples of complements include computers and computer software, stereo components and CDs, and movies and popcorn. For would-be lawyers, college and law school are complements. An increase in the price of law school might dissuade some of these people from going to college.

Number of Demanders.   The total demand for a product is affected by the number of people who desire to consume it. During the 1960s and 1970s, the number of college-age people in the United States was steadily expanding. In the 1960s, with an increasing percentage of youths attending college, the total number of "demanders" in the market increased dramatically. Recently, the increase in the numbers has been less dramatic, although nontraditional students are now increasing their attendance in college.

The number of eighteen-year-olds in the population actually declined by about 25 percent between 1979 and 1994. This had serious implications for the market for a college education in the United States. A number of colleges and universities developed vigorous efforts to recruit nontraditional populations and international students to make up for this reduction in the number of traditional demanders. Some private colleges began to accept part-time students. Many of these factors have had an effect: Students older than twenty-five now make up more than one-third of the almost 15 million undergraduates enrolled in higher education, and about 40 percent of all students are part-time students. The number of eighteen-year-olds has been increasing slowly since 1995, which is having an impact on the composition of current higher-education enrollments.

Expectations of Future Prices.

If consumers expect the price of a product to change, this tends to affect their demand for that product. For example, if high school graduates expect that the price of attending college will continue to increase in the future, this may cause many of them to enroll right away rather than wait, or they may decide not to go at all.

Notice that, as in the first sentence of this section, economists frequently use the words *tend to.* Their conclusions are often tentative because they are usually based on assumptions and expectations of normal behavior on the part of most economic agents and variables the economists are examining. But not everyone acts the same way! In your own thinking, try to replicate this word usage; the conclusions of economists are not carved in stone and should not be accepted as gospel. Economic theory deals with assumptions and tendencies; if "this" happens, probably "that" will happen.

Miscellaneous Factors.

Other factors also may influence consumers' demands for products. One of these is government policies. In the 1960s the federal government and several state governments significantly increased their support of higher education in the United States. Increased interest in higher education's benefits to the country probably by itself influenced the demand for a college education. In addition, the government support made it easier for more high school graduates to attend college. By significantly expanding public universities and community colleges throughout the country, it also opened up the college experience to people who historically had not had access to higher education in the United States. On the other hand, federal and state budget restraints since 1980 reduced levels of assistance and increased students' reliance on loans and work to finance higher education. These factors make the pursuit of higher education more difficult for many people in the society.

3. What other factor(s) would influence the number of students enrolling in college? (Consider only the demand side of the market.)

Ceteris Paribus and the Demand Curve

If you answered the previous question, "the *price* of a college education," you are on your way to becoming an economist. Economists attempt to isolate the effect of price on the quantity demanded for a product. In analyzing the demand for a product, they acknowledge that all of the factors just described do influence demand. But sometimes simplification helps analysis. Therefore, economists concentrate on the relationship between price and the quantity demanded of a good. To do this, they assume that at one moment of time, all of the other factors are given; then only price will affect the quantity demanded. The other factors (the determinants of demand) are considered to be in a *ceteris paribus* category—a Latin phrase meaning "all other things being equal." *Demand is concerned with the relationship between price and quantity demanded, holding all other things constant.*

So let's make that rather large assumption and see what happens. What *is* the effect of price on the quantity demanded of a college education? At one moment in time, assuming (again) that there is some average type of college education, there is only one annual price for this product. For 2006–2007, the College Board estimated that the average cost for tuition, room and board, books, and required fees at four-year private universities was $30,367. For public schools, the average cost was $12,796. Since there were more students in public institutions, we will assume that $16,000 was about the average cost for the nation as a whole for a year of college.

We can hypothesize about what would happen to the quantity demanded if the price were higher or lower. In fact, we would expect that *if* the price were lower, people would consume more—the quantity demanded would increase—and that *if* the price were higher, people would consume less—the quantity demanded would decrease. This is true for almost all goods and services: If the price is lowered, the quantity demanded will increase, and if the price is increased, the quantity demanded will decrease. In other words, price and quantity demanded are inversely related. When the price changes, there is a *change in the quantity demanded*—in the opposite direction.

We can state this relationship mathematically as well. A demand equation, generally, would show that the quantity of college education demanded, Q_d, is a function of the price of a college education, P_c, given all of the *ceteris paribus* conditions:

$$Q_d = f(P_c), \text{ ceteris paribus.}$$

To work with numbers, we can construct a hypothetical **demand schedule** (Table 8.1) showing different possible prices and the quantities demanded at those prices at one moment in time. Let's hypothesize about the national market for college educations for a year (again assuming that there is some average education). If the price were $16,000 (about the national average cost in 2007), then about 15 million people would be enrolled in the nation's colleges and universities as students. If, however, the price went up to $18,000 per year, then the quantity demanded would fall to 13 million. Table 8.1 shows several other possibilities as well.

TABLE 8.1   Demand Schedule for College Education

P_c (Cost per Year, Tuition, Room and Board, and Fees)	Q_d (Number of Students, in Millions)
$22,000	9
20,000	11
18,000	13
16,000	15
14,000	17

FIGURE 8.1 Demand Curve

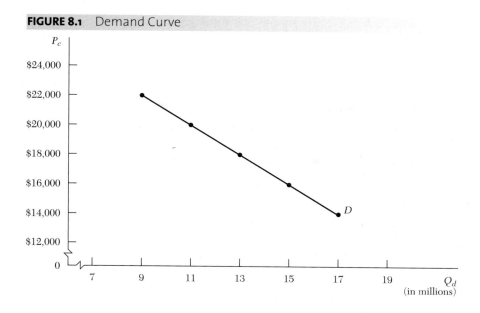

We can also graph the relationship between price and quantity demanded. We call this a **demand curve.** The vertical scale measures price, and the horizontal scale measures quantity demanded. Any point on the graph represents a certain price–quantity demanded combination. Let's take the information from the demand schedule in Table 8.1 and transfer it to the graph. At a price of $14,000, the quantity demanded is 17 million; at $16,000, it is 15 million; and so on. Each combination corresponds to a point in Figure 8.1.

If we connect all the price–quantity demanded points, we get a demand curve for a college education during one year in the United States. It shows, hypothetically, all of the possible prices for a college education and the respective quantities demanded. It has a negative slope, reflecting the inverse relationship between price and quantity demanded. At lower prices, the quantity demanded is greater; at higher prices, the quantity demanded is lower. (For convenience, we normally draw demand curves as straight lines.)

The graphs of demand curves and supply curves are very important tools in economics. Make sure you understand how Figure 8.1 was constructed and what it shows.

The demand curve illustrates the buyers' side of the market. Let's turn our attention to the sellers' side of the market and consider it in isolation. After that, we will put the two sides of the market together in our model and get a market price for a college education.

Supply

Now we will focus on the sellers' side of the market. This side involves **supply**— the amounts of a good that will be offered for sale at different possible prices.

What influences the supply of a product? What factors determine the number of students that colleges and universities can allow to enroll? Obviously, the price that these institutions can charge students has a lot to do with it. But for the moment, let's discuss other influences. These include resource prices, technology, prices of related goods, sellers' expectations, and the number of sellers in the market.

Resource Prices. The costs of producing goods and services weigh heavily on the ability of sellers to supply the market. Thus, resource prices help determine the supply of any product offered for sale. In the supply of college educations, if the salaries of professors and other staff increase, the supply tends to shrink or college educations become more expensive. With the rapid inflation of the late 1960s, 1970s, and early 1980s and the moderate price increases from 1985 to 2007, the labor resource costs of running universities have skyrocketed as employees have demanded commensurate increases in their incomes. Even though dollar labor costs have increased at colleges, in real terms faculty incomes dropped 20 percent during the 1970s due to inflation. This prompted many faculties to form labor unions; there are more than 200 at four-year colleges and almost 400 at two-year colleges. Physical plant workers, cafeteria personnel, and office workers are often in unions on campuses around the country. Increasing costs for food, equipment, maintenance, paper, computers, construction, and energy also have increased total expenses significantly. As a result, the cost of supplying a college education has risen.

Technology. The techniques of production influence supply. If computers and television sets were used to teach students, to grade their work, and to write letters of recommendation for them, colleges and universities would probably be able to greatly increase the numbers of students to whom they could supply a college education. Other ways of changing the techniques of production involve the use of large lecture classes, sometimes even with video lectures, or computer-assisted learning. (Of course, these might make the process of getting an education a bit less attractive. But that is a *demand* factor.) For the time being, however, the technology of education still relies heavily on human beings and, in some places, on relatively small classes.

Prices of Related Goods. The ability of suppliers to supply any product to the market will also be affected by the prices of other products. If a college or a university could earn a better return on operating as a summer camp or research institute than offering summer sessions, then maybe it would decide to supply that product instead. Similarly, a college could display paintings and other artwork on its hallway walls, or it could sell wall space to corporate advertisers. Science faculty could use their labs to do research for companies instead of for teaching students.

Sellers' Expectations. Sellers' expectations about the future will condition their supply of a product to the market. If colleges and universities expect lower enrollments in the future, they might be inclined to try to offer fewer students the chance to go to college now (that is, begin to decrease the supply of the

Today's college students expect computer labs, wired dorm rooms, and network facilities, all of which increase the cost of providing a college education.
(The Terry Wild Studio)

product now). They might do this to prepare themselves for the foreseen lean days ahead. Given the likelihood of continuing high energy prices, some older dormitories might need to be retired, thus reducing the number of spaces available at some schools.

Numbers of Sellers in the Market.   If the number of sellers in the market decreased, it would tend to decrease the supply of the product. And if the number of sellers increased, it would tend to increase the supply. In the late 1970s and early 1980s, a number of colleges and universities in the United States closed their doors. In 1981 there were 3,253 institutions of higher learning in the United States; in 1983 there were 3,111. Since then, the numbers have begun to increase, reaching nearly 4,200 in 2002.

4. Of the five factors described as influencing supply, which, in your opinion, is the most influential in determining the supply of a product? Why?
5. What sorts of factors influence sellers' expectations about their markets?

Ceteris Paribus and the Supply Curve

As we did for the demand curve, we will hold the nonprice influences on supply constant when we create a supply curve. They constitute the *ceteris paribus* conditions for supply. As a result, we will concentrate on the effect of price on the quantity supplied of a product. At one moment in time, we assume that all of the *ceteris paribus* factors (the determinants of supply) are given and consider in isolation the effect of price. *Supply is concerned with the relationship between price and quantity supplied, all other things constant.*

At one moment, there is only one price in existence. But we can hypothesize different possible prices and examine the effects on quantity supplied. If the price were higher, we would expect sellers to increase the quantity supplied. If sellers were offered a lower price, we would expect them to reduce the quantity supplied. For supply, price and quantity supplied are directly related. When the price changes, there is a *change in quantity supplied* in the same direction.

We can state this as an equation as well. With all other determinants of supply held constant, the quantity supplied of a college education, Q_s, is a function of the price offered for a college education, P_c:

$$Q_s = f(P_c), \textit{ ceteris paribus.}$$

As for demand, we can construct a hypothetical **supply schedule** (Table 8.2), showing different possible prices and the quantities that would be supplied at those prices. Table 8.2 hypothesizes about the total national supply of a college education. *If* the price were only $14,000, then colleges and universities would offer places for only 13 million students. *If* the price were $22,000, then colleges and universities would be willing to offer places to 21 million students. The table includes other possibilities as well.

Again, we can show the supply relationship graphically. We measure price on the vertical scale and quantity supplied on the horizontal scale. Each point in Figure 8.2 represents a certain price–quantity supplied combination. If we connect the five combinations from the schedule in Table 8.2, we get a supply curve for a college education. It shows, hypothetically, all the possible prices for a college education and the respective quantities supplied. It has a positive slope, showing the direct relationship between price and quantity supplied; at higher prices, greater quantities will be supplied, and at lower prices, lower quantities will be supplied. (For convenience, we usually draw supply curves as straight lines.)

The supply curve illustrates the sellers' side of the market. The demand curve shows the buyers' side. Let's see what happens when we put them together to look at both sides of the market.

The Market and the Equilibrium Price

Putting the supply and demand schedules together, as listed in Table 8.3 and graphed in Figure 8.3, gives us a hypothetical picture of the market. When we

TABLE 8.2 Supply Schedule for College Education

P_c (Cost per Year)	Q_s (Number of Students, in Millions)
$22,000	21
20,000	19
18,000	17
16,000	15
14,000	13

FIGURE 8.2   Supply Curve

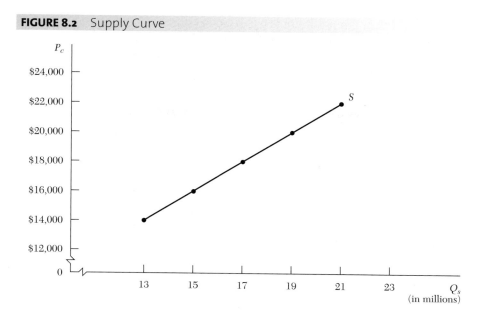

put supply and demand together, the supply and the demand for the product determine a market price. It is an **equilibrium price.** Equilibrium connotes a situation in which the tendency is toward a certain state; once that state is achieved, it will be maintained, in the absence of outside disturbances.

In our example, a price of $16,000 is the equilibrium price. At this price, the desires of buyers and sellers are consistent. Buyers want to buy 15 million places at colleges and universities, and sellers are willing to offer 15 million places. The quantity demanded equals the quantity supplied. Stated mathematically, at $P_c = \$16,000$, $Q_s = Q_d$. On the graph in Figure 8.3, the equilibrium price and quantity exchanged are the point at which the supply and demand curves intersect.

At any other price, Q_s does not equal Q_d, and the price will tend to change because buyers' and sellers' desires are not consistent. For example, at $P_c = \$20,000$, $Q_s = 19$ million and $Q_d = 11$ million. If the price were $20,000, there would be an oversupply, or a **surplus.** That is, 19 million places would be available, but only 11 million students would want to go to college at that price.

TABLE 8.3   The Supply Schedule Combined with the Demand Schedule

P_c ($)	Q_d (in Millions)	Q_s (in Millions)
22,000	9	21
20,000	11	19
18,000	13	17
16,000	15	15
14,000	17	13

FIGURE 8.3   Market and Equilibrium Price

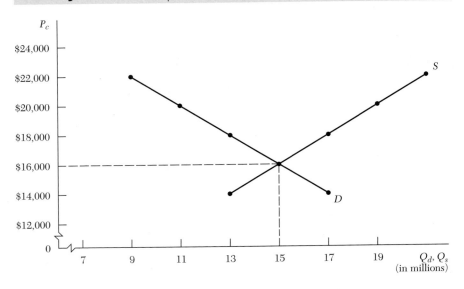

Sellers would lower their prices to eliminate the excess supply. This has a twofold effect. It reduces the quantity supplied and increases the quantity demanded. We can see this by examining what happens at a price of $18,000. At this price, the quantities supplied and demanded have moved closer together, but Q_s still exceeds Q_d (17 million > 13 million). Suppliers will then lower prices again. This process will continue until $Q_s = Q_d$. This occurs at a price of $16,000. Thus, as shown in Figure 8.4, price changes will eliminate a surplus in the market until the equilibrium price is reached.

In the same way, if the price were below $16,000, there would be a tendency to move toward the $16,000 price. At a price of $14,000, $Q_d = 17$ million and $Q_s = 13$ million. In this case, the quantity demanded exceeds the quantity supplied (17 million > 13 million), and a **shortage** of places at college exists. Purchasers, facing a shortage, begin to bid up the price. Again, this has a twofold effect. It increases the quantity supplied but decreases the quantity demanded. This will continue until the desires of buyers and sellers are consistent at one price where $Q_s = Q_d$ (see Figure 8.5).

Supply-and-demand analysis has shown us how markets determine equilibrium prices. There is a tendency to establish, to move toward, the equilibrium price. And once buyers' and sellers' desires are consistent (when the quantity supplied equals the quantity demanded) and there are no outside disturbances, that price will tend to be maintained.

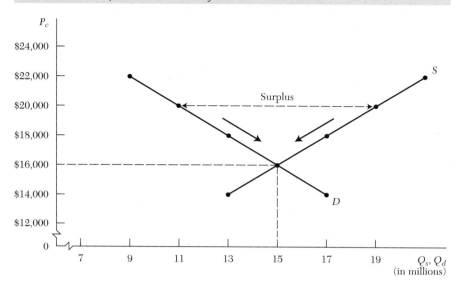

FIGURE 8.4   Surplus Eliminated by Price Decreases

6. Why do sellers lower price when there is a surplus?
7. Why do buyers bid up the price when there is a shortage?

A Tinge of Reality: It's Not a *Ceteris Paribus* World

Our supply-and-demand model so far has included the rather strict and static assumptions involved in our *ceteris paribus* conditions on both sides of the market. However, one of the most useful aspects of this model is that we can use it to accommodate changes in the *ceteris paribus* conditions. In a changing world over time, these other determinants of supply and demand do change. A couple of examples will suffice to illustrate the richness of this approach and the ability of the supply-and-demand model to explain changes in market conditions and prices.

Changes in Demand.   First, let's take a change in the demand conditions. We will call this a **change in demand**, and it will cause the whole demand curve to shift. Recall the various determinants of demand (or *ceteris paribus* conditions)—such as tastes and preferences, income, prices of related goods, number of demanders, and expectations about prices—and consider the complexity of factors that are behind a demand curve. Any of the determinants could change, or all of them could change. They could move in the same direction (causing an increase or a decrease in demand), or they could influence demand in opposite directions.

FIGURE 8.5 Shortage Eliminated by Price Increases

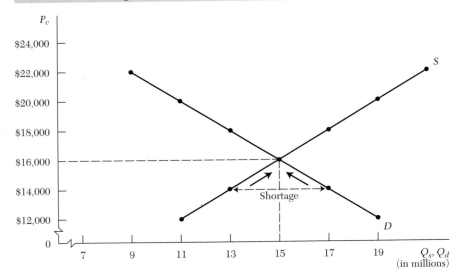

Let's examine just one possibility. Assume that in today's economy, for what-ever reasons, a college degree is perceived as being more attractive to students. This represents a change in tastes and preferences. What will it do to demand? What effect will it have on the market for a college education?

First of all, it will cause a shift in the demand curve. It causes an increase in demand; the demand curve will shift to the right. At every possible price, the quantity demanded will have increased, and we thus get a new demand curve. This is shown in Figure 8.6 as a shift in the demand curve from D_1 to D_2.

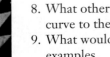

8. What other changes in demand might cause an increase in demand, a shift of the curve to the right?
9. What would cause a shift back to the left, a decrease in demand? Give some examples.

FIGURE 8.6 Change in Demand

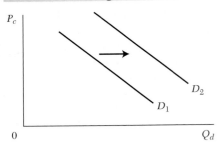

FIGURE 8.7 Effect on Market of Change in Demand

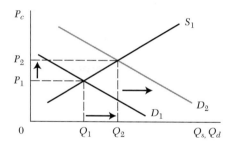

What happens in the market? Here we must look at supply and demand together, as shown in Figure 8.7. With the new demand curve, D_2, we get a new equilibrium price, P_2, and a new equilibrium quantity exchanged, Q_2, where $Q_s = Q_d$. With an increase in demand, we get a new higher price in the market. Also, the amount exchanged by buyers and sellers has increased in our example (from Q_1 to Q_2). This analysis suggests that one place to look for an explanation of increasing prices in a market is in the dynamic changes in the determinants of demand. The market price of a college education tended to increase from the late 1980s to 2007. Because enrollment (the quantity) also increased, we can conclude that the demand for the product increased. A possible cause was a change in the public's tastes and preferences. A word of caution, however, is in order. Tastes and preferences were not the only determinants of demand that changed during this period of time. For example, the increased number of international students also contributed to the shift in demand. Furthermore, the determinants of supply also were changing. We can conclude, though, that the change in preferences was partly responsible for the increase in demand and the increase in price.

Changes in Supply. The supply-and-demand model can also reflect a **change in supply.** Here we allow the determinants of supply to change. Remember the determinants of supply (the *ceteris paribus* conditions)—resource prices, technology, prices of related goods, sellers' expectations, and the number of sellers. Any or all could change, in the same direction or in opposite directions.

Suppose that in 2007 the prices of the resources used in providing college educations increased. As a result, there would be a change in supply. Suppliers would tend to require higher prices for every different quantity supplied (or they would be willing to offer lower quantities supplied at every possible price). There would be a decrease in supply; the supply curve would shift to the left. The supply curve for a college education shifts from S_1 to S_2, as shown in Figure 8.8.

FIGURE 8.8 Change in Supply

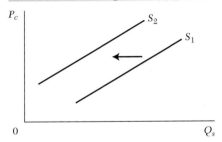

10. What other factors might cause the supply curve to shift to the left?
11. What factors might cause the supply curve to shift to the right?

What will this do in the market? Assume that demand conditions are unaltered. Figure 8.9 puts supply and demand together. (We assume that D_1 remains unchanged.) With the new supply curve, S_2, we get a new equilibrium price, P_2, and a new equilibrium quantity exchanged, Q_2, where $Q_s = Q_d$. With this decrease in supply, we get a new higher market price and a lower quantity exchanged.

Again, this analysis may help us to explain price increases by examining what happens to the determinants of supply. If forces are creating decreases in supply for a particular product, that will help to explain the emergence of higher prices for it.

12. What happens if we combine our examples, an increase in demand and a decrease in supply? Show this result in your own graphical illustration.

FIGURE 8.9 Effect on Market of Change of Supply

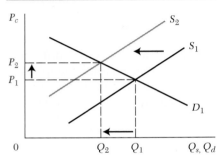

FIGURE 8.10 Effects of a Decrease in Demand

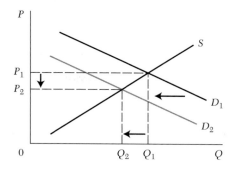

A Word of Caution

One aspect of learning economics is identifying and defining economic concepts—and doing so precisely. This involves using words carefully. In some sense, it is like learning a foreign language. Some words that economists use have very specific meanings for particular concepts.

What happens on a demand curve if the price of the product changes? We get a *change in the quantity demanded.* If the price increases, the quantity demanded decreases. And if the price decreases, the quantity demanded increases. This represents a movement along a particular demand curve. What happens if one of the determinants of demand changes? We get a *change in demand.* If income increases, the whole demand curve shifts out to the right for most goods. Whenever there is a change in demand, the whole demand curve shifts.

For supply, a change in price causes a *change in the quantity supplied,* which is a movement along a supply curve. A change in one of the determinants of supply causes a *change in supply,* which causes the whole supply curve to shift.

A higher price causes a decrease in quantity demanded and an increase in quantity supplied. If the income of households decreases, the demand for most goods would decrease (there would be a change in demand). What would happen to the equilibrium price, then, if the supply curve stays the same? Right—price would decrease. And then what happens to quantity demanded and quantity supplied? Right—smaller quantities are demanded and supplied at the new equilibrium. Figure 8.10 shows this result graphically.

Applying Supply and Demand

Let's put these principles about supply and demand into practice by examining two applications that have drawn coverage from the news media. First, we'll look at the interaction between supply and demand when gasoline prices rose in 2004. Then we'll consider how supply and demand have influenced the price of the dollar in international currency markets.

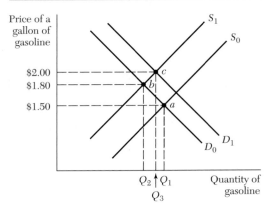

FIGURE 8.11 The U.S. Market for Gasoline

Gasoline Prices

In April 2004, the Organization of Petroleum Exporting Countries (OPEC) moved to reduce their production of oil by 4 percent. In addition, OPEC sold more oil than usual to China (rapid economic growth in China increased their need for oil) and shipped less oil to the United States. Meanwhile, terrorist attacks in Iraq and Saudi Arabia interrupted oil supplies further. The result was a decrease in the supply of gasoline to the United States. Figure 8.11 shows this change as the shift in the supply of oil from S_0 to S_1. As a result, the equilibrium price of gas rose from $1.50 per gallon to $1.80 per gallon, and the equilibrium quantity of gas fell from Q_1 to Q_2, moving the equilibrium from point a to point b.

While OPEC was reducing the supply of oil, the U.S. recovery strengthened and U.S. consumers continued to purchase larger cars, pickup trucks, and sport utility vehicles with low fuel efficiency and that use much greater quantities of gasoline. Thus, consumer demand for gasoline was increasing during this period. This is shown in Figure 8.11 as the shift in demand from D_0 to D_1. The increase in demand resulted in an additional increase in the equilibrium price from $1.80 to $2.00 per gallon and an increase in the equilibrium quantity of gas from Q_2 to Q_3. The equilibrium moves from point b to point c. The outcome was a dramatic increase in the average price of a gallon of gasoline from about $1.50 per gallon in 2003 to about $2.00 per gallon in 2004.

13. What has happened to the price of gasoline recently? How can you use supply and demand analysis to explain any price changes?

Price Controls. As gas prices rise, it is sometimes tempting for governments to impose **price controls** to keep prices low for consumers. Specifically, the government could have imposed a **price ceiling,** a legally set maximum price, on

FIGURE 8.12   The Market for Gasoline with a Price Ceiling

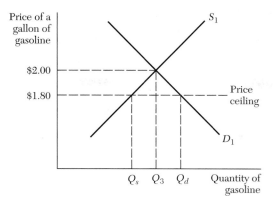

gasoline below the new equilibrium price of $2.00. However, as Figure 8.12 shows, lowering the price to $1.80 per gallon would reduce the quantity of gas supplied from Q_3 to Q_s, while also causing an increase in the quantity of gas demanded from Q_3 to Q_d, resulting in a shortage. This would mean that not everyone who wanted to buy gas at a price of $1.80 per gallon would be able to do so, and it would probably lead to long lines at gas stations (and even black markets) as people try to get scarce supplies of gasoline. This is, in fact, exactly what happened when price ceilings were imposed on gasoline and other goods in the 1970s. Many consumers would benefit from lower-priced gasoline (those who could find it), but many others would not be able to purchase as much gasoline as they wanted.

14. Using supply-and-demand analysis, can you think of some other ways that the government could lower the price of gas for consumers without creating a short-age?
15. Burning gasoline contributes to smog and global warming. If our goal were to reduce the quantity of gasoline purchased (instead of keeping its price as low as possible) to reduce pollution, what policies might work?

Supply and Demand and the Value of the Dollar

Another everyday application of the supply-and-demand model is the determi-nation of the value of the dollar, or the exchange rate. Since the early 1970s, the international financial system has operated on the basis of flexible exchange rates for currencies (see Chapter 21). This means there is an international market with buyers and sellers for all of the different currencies in the world. The prices of currencies are determined in these markets. Currencies are used for international economic activities. For example, people in the United States might want to buy products from Japan or invest in Japanese financial markets;

FIGURE 8.13 Japanese Yen per Dollar, 2000–2007

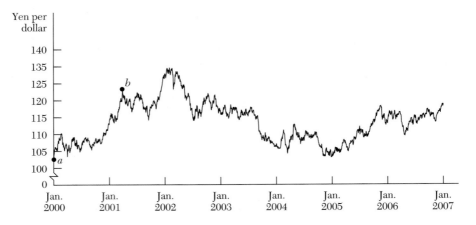

to do so, they have to exchange (supply) dollars for yen. Or people in Japan might want to buy U.S. goods, invest in the U.S. stock market, or purchase U.S. government treasury bonds; to do so, they have to exchange yen for dollars (they would be purchasing, or demanding, dollars). There are exchange markets because people all over the world want to buy goods and services, make bank deposits, travel, or invest in other countries. In addition, sometimes people want to protect the value of their assets by holding them in a currency with an increasing value (and conversely getting out of currencies with declining values).

As a result of changing supply and demand conditions in the foreign-exchange markets, the value of currencies is constantly changing. Figure 8.13 shows the number of Japanese yen that could be purchased for one U.S. dollar from 2000 to 2007. As you can see, the value changes frequently. These changes result from the changes in the determinants of exchange rates. Table 8.4 summarizes how changes in the determinants of exchange rates cause shifts in the supply and demand for dollars.

We can use supply-and-demand analysis to explain the increase in the value (price) of the dollar in yen from January 2000 to April 2001. On January 3, 2000, 1 dollar was worth 102 Japanese yen (point a in Figure 8.13). However, the Japanese economy was mired in an economic slump at the time, while the U.S. economy was booming. As a result, Japanese investors decided to purchase greater amounts of U.S. stocks, bonds, and real estate. Before they could do this, they had to use their Japanese yen to purchase U.S. dollars, increasing the demand for U.S. dollars. As shown in Figure 8.14, the increase in the demand for U.S. dollars shifts the demand curve from D_0 to D_1, causing the price of the U.S. dollar to increase (appreciate) from 102 yen to 127 yen (the value the dollar reached on April 2, 2001; point b in Figure 8.13). The quantity of dollars exchanged increases from Q_1 to Q_2.

TABLE 8.4 Shifts in the Supply and Demand for a Currency (such as U.S. Dollars)

Change in Determinants of Supply and Demand	Change in Supply and Demand	Change in Price of Dollars (Exchange Rate)
Decrease in U.S. demand for foreign goods, services, and assets	*Supply of dollars decreases:* U.S. buyers spend less on foreign items, so they exchange fewer dollars for foreign currency.	*Price of dollars increases:* Decrease in the supply of dollars in foreign exchange markets causes the dollar to appreciate.
Increase in U.S. demand for foreign goods, services, and assets	*Supply of dollars increases:* U.S. buyers spend more on foreign items, so they exchange more dollars for foreign currency.	*Price of dollars decreases:* Increase in the supply of dollars in foreign exchange markets causes the dollar to depreciate.
Decrease in foreign demand for U.S. goods, services, and assets	*Demand for dollars decreases:* Foreign buyers spend less on U.S. items, so they exchange less of their currency for dollars.	*Price of dollars decreases:* Decrease in the demand for dollars in foreign exchange markets causes the dollar to depreciate.
Increase in foreign demand for U.S. goods, services, and assets	*Demand for dollars increases:* Foreign buyers spend more on U.S. items, so they exchange more of their currency for dollars.	*Price of dollars increases:* Increase in the demand for dollars in foreign exchange markets causes the dollar to appreciate.

FIGURE 8.14 The Foreign Exchange Market for U.S. Dollars

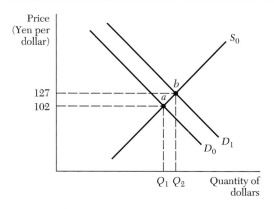

16. Would Japanese importers be in favor of an increase in the value of the dollar? Why or why not?
17. What other factors of demand, the *ceteris paribus* conditions, could cause an increase in the demand for dollars?
18. What might happen, on either side of the market, to bring about a decrease in the value of the dollar? Do some research to uncover the factors behind the decrease in the value of the dollar from 2002 to 2004.

Elasticity

Thus far, we have concentrated on the relationship between prices and quantities supplied and demanded. But if a price changes, *how much* does the quantity demanded change? If the price goes up, *how much* does the quantity supplied increase?

The sensitivity of the demand for (or supply of) a product to changes in its price is called **price elasticity.** This concept is concerned with the relationship between the quantity demanded or supplied and the price of a particular good or service.

Price Elasticity of Demand

All other things held constant, if the price of a college education goes up, the quantity demanded will go down. But how much will the quantity demanded be reduced in comparison with the price increase? The **price elasticity of demand** is a measurement of the sensitivity of changes in quantity demanded to changes in price. It measures the responsiveness of the amount demanded to price changes. (Note that we are using terminology associated with movements along a single demand curve. With all the determinants of demand fixed at one point in time, we focus on the impact of a price change on the quantity demanded.)

The following equation measures the price elasticity of demand:

$$E_d = \frac{\text{percentage change in quantity demanded}}{\text{percentage change in price}} = \frac{\Delta Q_d / Q_d}{\Delta P / P}.$$

The percentage change in price is associated with a certain percentage change in the quantity demanded. In calculating elasticity, we ignore the direction of change of each variable and concentrate on the relative relationship between the percentage changes (that is, we take the absolute value of E_d).

If the percentage change in quantity demanded is larger than the percentage change in price, then $E_d > 1$, and we say that the demand for the good is *elastic* with respect to price. Demand is elastic when the quantity demanded is very responsive to changes in price. If the price of digital cameras is reduced by 20 percent and the quantity demanded increases by 30 percent, then $E_d = 1.5$. In this case, the demand for the cameras is elastic, or relatively sensitive to price changes.

On the other hand, if the price of milk (or beer) increases by 10 percent but the quantity demanded decreases by only 5 percent, then elasticity is 0.5. In this case, we say that the demand for milk (or beer) is *inelastic*, since the percentage change in quantity demanded is less than the percentage change in price ($E_d < 1$). Demand is inelastic when quantity demanded is not very responsive to changes in price.

For example, let's assume a computer store reduced the price of a personal computer model and printer from $2,500 to $2,000. The number of units it sold in a six-month period increased from 100 to 160. We can record these amounts in a table

Price	Quantity Sold
$2,500	100
2,000	160

What is the elasticity of demand? The price decreased by $500, or 20 percent:

$$\frac{\Delta P}{P} = \frac{2,500 - 2,000}{2,500} = \frac{500}{2,500} = 20\%.$$

The quantity demanded increased by 60 units, or 60 percent:

$$\frac{\Delta Q_d}{Q_d} = \frac{160 - 100}{100} = \frac{60}{100} = 60\%.$$

We can use those percentages to find the elasticity of demand:*

---

*Notice that there is another way we could have calculated the elasticity. We used the original price and quantity as the denominator in our calculations of the percentage changes in quantity and price. If we used the new price and quantity, we'd get the following results:

percentage change in price = 500/2,000 = 25%
percentage change in quantity demanded = 60/160 = 37.5%

$$\text{elasticity of demand} = \frac{37.5}{25} = 1.5$$

There is a way to resolve this difference in the calculated elasticity of demand by taking the average of the old and the new prices and quantities. This is called the midpoints formula:

$$E_d = \frac{\Delta Q/[(Q_1 + Q_2)/2]}{\Delta P/[(P_1 + P_2)/2]} = \frac{60/130}{500/2,250} = \frac{46.2\%}{22.2\%} = 2.08.$$

The important point, though, is that the elasticity of demand measures the *relative* change in quantity demanded due to the *relative* change in price, to see how sensitive quantity demanded is to price changes.

FIGURE 8.15 Elasticity along a Demand Curve

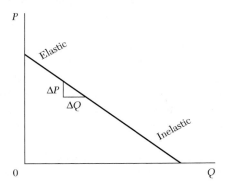

$$E_d = \frac{\text{percentage change in quantity demanded}}{\text{percentage change in price}}$$

$$= \frac{60}{20} = 3.$$

Consequently, the demand for computers is fairly sensitive to price changes; the relative change in quantity demanded is much larger than the relative change in the price.

Elasticity Graphically. On the upper portion of the typical linear demand curve shown in Figure 8.15, the price elasticity of demand is elastic. On the lower portion, it is inelastic. Elasticity changes along the demand curve.

The elasticity of a demand curve does not equal its slope. The slope of the demand curve is the change in the price over the change in the quantity demanded between any two points (the height over the base, the rise over the run, etc.). The slope equals $\Delta P/\Delta Q$. To highlight the difference, we can rearrange the formula for elasticity as follows:

$$\frac{\text{percentage } \Delta \text{ in quantity demanded}}{\text{percentage } \Delta \text{ in price}} = \frac{\Delta Q/Q}{\Delta P/P} = \frac{\Delta Q}{\Delta P} \times \frac{P}{Q}.$$

This obviously makes elasticity unequal to the slope of the demand curve.

On the left portion of the demand curve, any percentage change in quantity demanded will be relatively large (since quantity is at low levels), and the percentage change in price will be relatively small. Consequently, elasticity will be greater than 1. On the right portion, percentage changes in quantity will be relatively small, and percentage changes in price will be relatively large. Therefore, elasticity will be less than 1. Moving along the demand curve to the right will reduce elasticity or increase inelasticity.

The Determinants of Elasticity.
What determines elasticity, or how sensitive to changes in its price is the demand for a product? Can you think of goods you demand regardless of price? Are there other goods to whose prices you are very sensitive?

Generally, whenever there are substitutes for a good, your demand tends to be elastic. The more substitutes, the more elastic the demand. For example, if the price of green beans increases, most people will substitute other green vegetables. When the price goes up, people will reduce their consumption of green beans by relatively more—that is, we expect the price elasticity of demand for green beans to be greater than 1. On the other hand, if you heat your house with only oil and oil prices increase, you may decrease your use of oil, but not by much. The relative increase in price will outweigh the relative decline in the amount demanded; demand is relatively inelastic because there are no convenient substitutes for oil to run your furnace.

Another example that indicates the importance of substitutes in determining elasticity is the difference between the price elasticity of the demand for a product such as gasoline versus the price elasticity of the demand for one service station's brand of gas (e.g., Exxon). Gas stations with many competitors face price elasticities as high as 6. If one station raises its prices even a few pennies per gallon, consumers will take their business down the street to a gas station where prices are cheaper. (With a price elasticity of 6, a 10 percent increase in price would result in a 60 percent decrease in the quantity demanded!) But consumers as a group use almost the same amount of gas every week, no matter what the price is; we need gasoline for our cars, and there are no close substitutes. In fact, the price elasticity of demand for all brands of gasoline is about 0.2, which is very inelastic.

Goods that are necessities tend to have inelastic demands. For example, in a household with young children, the demand for milk is likely to be relatively inelastic. In fact, the price elasticity of the demand for food is between 0.1 and 0.5. As a student, you have a relatively inelastic demand for books. For these items, the demand is not very sensitive to price changes. The demand for luxuries, however, tends to be elastic. You, and others, are likely to be very sensitive to price changes for CDs, stereos, cameras, expensive clothes, automobiles, and so forth.

For the most part, the relative importance of an item in a household's budget also influences elasticity. High-priced items tend to have elastic demands, and the demand for low-priced items is often inelastic because consumers are less concerned about the price.

Finally, time influences elasticity. The more time consumers have to adjust to price changes for goods and services, the more elastic their demand for certain products is likely to be. For example, people in the United States adjusted their usage of energy as a result of higher oil and gas prices in the 1970s. Cars became smaller and more fuel efficient, people burned more wood as a source of heat, bicycles were used more for transportation, and solar energy was developed. However, with the decline in energy prices in the 1980s and 1990s, these trends reversed, and Americans began driving bigger and bigger cars and using more gas and oil. The steady increase in gas prices from 2002 to 2006 did not cause a significant, immediate decrease in demand. Since the short-run price elasticity of the demand for gasoline is only 0.2, a 20 percent increase in price will decrease the quantity demanded by only 4 percent. But the long-run price elasticity of the demand for gasoline is about 0.8, so we can expect a much larger decrease in the demand for gasoline in the future if gas prices continue to stay high. (With a price elasticity of 0.8, a 20 percent increase in price would result in a 16 percent decrease in the quantity demanded.) If U.S. gas prices rise above a certain point and remain high, the next time consumers need to replace a car, they will be much more likely to choose a fuel-efficient one or to consider other modes of transportation such as bicycles, buses, or trains. (We should note that despite the recent increases, U.S. energy prices are among the lowest in the world. In Europe, a gallon of gas costs over $6.00.)

 19. Can you list three ways Europeans have adapted to higher gas prices?

Elasticity and Revenue. Elasticity also holds implications for a firm's revenues or a household's expenditures when the price of a product changes. If the demand for a firm's product is elastic and its price decreases, then the percentage change in quantity demanded in the market will be relatively larger than the price change. The firm's revenues would then increase. (The firm's revenues equal the quantity sold times the price of the product. If the relative increase in quantity exceeds the relative decline in price, then revenues go up.) If a household's demand for a product is inelastic and its price increases, it will decrease its purchases by a relatively lower amount. Consequently, its total expenditures—quantity times price—will increase. Table 8.5 summarizes the possibilities (TR stands for total revenue and equals $P \times Q$). When demand is elastic, the quantity change is relatively larger. When the demand is inelastic, the price change is relatively larger.

It is extremely important for firms to consider price elasticity when deciding what price to charge for their product and how much of that product they should produce. In 2001, the U.S. government released a study stating that the use of growth-promoting drugs on hogs actually resulted in lower hog farm rev-

TABLE 8.5 Elasticity (E_d) and Total Revenue (TR)

Inelastic Demand ($E_d < 1$)	Elastic Demand ($E_d > 1$)
$\% \Delta$ in $Q_d < \% \Delta$ in P	$\% \Delta$ in $Q_d > \% \Delta$ in P
$\uparrow P$ results in a smaller $\downarrow Q_d$, TR$\uparrow$	$\uparrow P$ results in a larger $\downarrow Q_d$, TR$\downarrow$
$\downarrow P$ results in a smaller $\uparrow Q_d$, TR$\downarrow$	$\downarrow P$ results in a larger $\uparrow Q_d$, TR$\uparrow$

Note: Elasticity = $E_d = (\% \Delta$ in $Q_d)/(\% \Delta$ in $P)$; Total Revenue = TR = $P \times Q$.

enues. The increased production caused the price of hogs to fall from $34.80 to $34.02. This resulted in a decrease in total revenue for hog farmers, since the percentage decrease in the price of hogs exceeded the percentage increase in the quantity of hogs purchased. Hog producers face an inelastic demand curve; in fact, the price elasticity of the demand for hogs is estimated to be about 0.4.

Price Elasticity of Supply

We can also identify the **price elasticity of supply,** or the sensitivity of amounts supplied to price changes:

$$E_s = \frac{\text{percentage change in quantity supplied}}{\text{percentage change in price}}.$$

If the elasticity of supply, E_s, is less than 1, the supply of the product is inelastic—that is, the amount supplied is not very sensitive to price changes. If the elasticity of supply, E_s, is greater than 1, then the amount of the good supplied is sensitive to price changes.

Several factors can influence the elasticity of supply. If storage is not possible, then supply will be insensitive to price changes. If you have ten bunches of bananas in your store and the price goes up by 50 percent tomorrow, there is not much you can do to increase the amount of bananas that you have for sale. If you can put an item in inventory, the amount that you have available for sale will be sensitive to price. If the price of pencils goes down, for example, you can store them and reduce the amount you have out for sale. If the price goes up, you can increase the amount you have for sale by taking the pencils out of your inventory. The length of the production process matters as well. The longer the production period, the lower the elasticity of supply. Occasionally a new toy or game is popular (e.g., at holiday season) in the United States. In the short run, the supply is inelastic; consequently, there is a shortage. What happens to price? It rises. With higher prices, in the longer run, the supply becomes more elastic. If it is possible to substitute resources in production, then supply is likely to be more elastic. For example, in the fast-food industry, there are numerous sources of unskilled labor and many sources of hamburger meat, buns, and so forth. Consequently, the supply of fast food is likely to be relatively sensitive to price changes.

Income Elasticity

We can also identify the **income elasticity of demand.** This measures how much the demand for a product changes when income changes. It is expressed by the following equation:

$$E_y = \frac{\text{percentage change in quantity demanded}}{\text{percentage change in income}}.$$

When income changes, we know that one of the determinants of demand has changed. Consequently, the entire demand curve will shift. For most goods, if income increases, the demand curve shifts out to the right. The income elasticity of demand, in essence, measures the relative change in the demand curve.

For most goods, the income elasticity is positive, meaning that increases in income result in greater demand for the good. Only *inferior goods* have a negative income elasticity of demand. For example, you might decrease your consumption of cheap meats if your income increased. For some goods, we increase our consumption by only a little bit when our incomes go up. Food products in general fit into this category. The relative increase in the quantity demanded of food will be less than the relative increase in income. For goods like these, the income elasticity of demand is relatively low. For other goods, we increase our consumption a great deal when our incomes go up. The relative change in quantity demanded is larger than the percentage change in income, and the income elasticity of demand is greater than 1. The demand for "luxuries" is elastic with respect to income.

20. Do you think that the price elasticity of demand for a college education is greater or less than 1? Why?
21. For what kinds of goods and services will quantity demanded be relatively insensitive to price changes (i.e., inelastic)? Give some examples.
22. For what kinds of goods and services is the quantity demanded relatively sensitive to price changes (i.e., elastic)? Give some examples.
23. List some goods for which your income elasticity of demand is greater than 1.

Conclusion

In this chapter we have developed a theoretical model of markets to explain how markets determine prices. We have focused on demand and supply, how they are determined, and how they interact in markets. In the next chapter, we will explore the theoretical implications that this has for resource allocation.

Review Questions

1. Use supply-and-demand analysis to explain why your school's tuition and overall charges have been continually increasing the past few years. Address demand factors first and supply factors second, and then put them together.

2. Some colleges have started to announce efforts to cut prices or to limit their price increases. Why would they do this?

3. How are tastes and preferences for goods and services determined in the United States?

4. Markets and prices for different products are interrelated. Why? Can you give some examples?

5. Examine recent issues of newspapers to see how prices of certain products are changing. Use supply-and-demand analysis to explain these changes.

6. *How* do prices influence resource allocation? Use examples.

7. Assume that the price elasticity of demand for gasoline in the United States is 0.3. If the president wanted to reduce gasoline consumption in the United States by 30 percent, by how much would prices have to be increased?

8. Draw a graph that shows how each of the following events will affect the demand, supply, equilibrium price, and equilibrium quantity of compact discs. *Note:* Be sure to identify whether or not the demand and supply curves *shift*, or whether you are moving along the demand and supply curves. Assume that the average price of a CD is $20 and that 100,000 CDs are sold each week.

   a. The price of DVD audio discs decreases (DVD audio discs can be played in DVD players so the music can be heard in five-speaker surround sound).

   b. The Supreme Court declares sharing music files over the Internet legal and the government is no longer able to prevent music file sharing.

   c. The technology used to manufacture CDs improves, decreasing the cost of producing a CD.

   d. An economic boom causes wages for workers to increase in all sectors of the economy, so CD consumers have more money but CD producers have to pay more to workers.

   e. Use of iTunes becomes widespread.

CHAPTER NINE

Perfect Competition and Efficiency

◼ Introduction

To build a model of a perfectly competitive firm, it is necessary to make some assumptions. Microeconomics assumes that in demanding goods, consumers attempt to maximize their satisfaction. Furthermore, we assume that in supplying goods, firms are concerned with profit maximization. In Chapter 8 we saw how supply and demand for a good determine a market price, given certain conditions (i.e., a supply curve and a demand curve). If either the demand curve or the supply curve shifts, or if both shift, we tend to get a new equilibrium price and quantity in that market.

THE BIG PICTURE

Perfectly Competitive Markets

The goal of this chapter is to present the theory of perfectly competitive markets, and to develop a microeconomic model of a perfectly competitive firm. Before we delve into that theory, however, to understand the "big picture" we need to briefly explore how these markets tend to work in practice and why economists tend to prefer outcomes from competitive markets.

Perfectly competitive markets feature many firms producing identical products. This means that no one firm can charge a higher price than competing firms, so prices tend to stay lower than they would with less or no competition. In this environment, firms can make only a modest profit (what economists call a *normal* profit). Because it is difficult to raise prices in the face of so much competition, firms strive to minimize the costs of production. Thus, competitive markets tend to lead to lower prices, smaller levels of profits, and efficient resource allocation (resources allocated to their most productive, least-cost use). Consumers therefore get the products they want at the lowest possible price. As we will see in Chapter 10, noncompetitive markets do not achieve these results.

This chapter uses supply-and-demand analysis and develops some new tools to examine the decisions that individual firms make about what rate of output to produce—taking into account information from the market for their product and from the markets for the resources they use. We will develop a model of the firm in a competitive market. This model will demonstrate how profit maximization and competition theoretically produce Adam Smith's "invisible hand." That is, we will discover how competitive markets operate to allocate resources efficiently *(to meet the most important demands of the society with the minimum amount of resources).*

Profit Maximization and the Competitive Firm

In this section we will examine a particular market, concentrating our attention on the firm (developing a theory of the firm). This is a theoretical market, so we will state some definitions and make some assumptions about the behavior of the buyers and sellers in the market. As an example we will use a local market for pizza.

The **consumer** is the economic unit that demands goods and/or services because they serve some purpose and give the consumer some satisfaction. Consumers in this example include all of the people in the local area who are interested in purchasing and consuming a pizza.

The **firm** is the economic unit that brings goods to the market. It takes raw materials and other resources and transforms them into final consumer goods. Its motivation, or goal, is to maximize its profits. In our example, the firm would be any company that produces and sells pizzas to the general public. This would include small and large restaurants, convenience stores, health food stores, grocery stores, cafeterias, and all other sellers of pizzas.

If we put the firms and the consumers (the sellers and buyers) together, we have a market for pizza. We will assume that this is a competitive market, that is, one characterized by **perfect competition.** We define a perfectly competitive market as one having the following characteristics:

◆ The product is homogeneous.
◆ There are a large number of buyers and sellers in the market.
◆ No *one* buyer or seller can influence the price of the product. (A seller can't raise his or her price, because buyers can go to a competitor and buy.)
◆ There is free entry into the market. (Anyone can be a buyer or seller. There are no constraints on entry.)
◆ There is no need for advertising (since every seller has the same product and charges the same price).

◆ Firms have all the information they need on resource prices, markets, and technology to make rational, profit-generating decisions.

In a perfectly competitive market, there is a market equilibrium price. Can you illustrate this market graphically?

1. Are any of these theoretical characteristics absent from the actual market for pizza in your community? Why?

Let's return to the firm. The firm's objective is to maximize its profits. Profits equal the revenues the firm earns by selling its products minus the costs it incurs to produce those products:

$$\text{profit} = \text{TR} - \text{TC},$$

where TR equals total revenue and TC equals total cost. **Total revenue** is equal to the quantity sold (Q) times the price of the product (P).

$$\text{TR} = P \times Q.$$

The firm obtains revenues by selling its product. The greater the number of pizzas the firm sells, the more money it receives. In producing pizza and bringing it to market, the firm also has certain costs—labor, raw materials, depreciation, rent, interest payments on loans, and the firm's opportunity cost. **Total cost** is the sum of all the costs of purchasing the necessary resources for production.

As in Chapter 7, we define the firm's *opportunity cost* as the amount of money the firm could earn by using its facilities and its resources to produce and sell something else profitably (such as hamburgers, subs, ice cream, etc.). The opportunity cost would be the "next best use" of its resources. The firm has some expectation of a "normal profit" from doing business, and therefore must earn at least its opportunity cost (a normal profit) to stay in the business of making pizza. Anything above that is **economic profit.**

If the firm's revenues are just sufficient to cover all of its costs for raw materials, labor, and so on, *and* its opportunity cost, then the firm will earn no economic profits. For example, if the firm's revenues were $100,000, its opportunity

TR > TC	Economic profit	The firm's revenues exceed all costs, including opportunity costs.
TR = TC	Normal profit	The firm's revenues equal its costs, including opportunity costs.
TR < TC	Economic loss	The firm's revenues do not cover all of its costs, including opportunity costs.

cost $20,000, and the costs of all other resources $80,000, it would earn zero economic profits. Its opportunity costs would be covered by the $20,000 of "normal" profits. If revenues exceed costs, then there will be economic profits; that is, the firm will earn a return over and above its opportunity cost. This gives us the following possibilities for the firm:

Profits, revenues, and costs for the firm will vary with the amount of pizza produced and sold. For a firm in a competitive market, the price is determined by the market and will not vary with the number of units that the firm sells (see the third characteristic of a competitive market in the list given earlier). Costs, on the other hand, do vary with output, as we will see in the next section.

2. A small firm's "normal profit" is $75,000 for one year. All of its other costs are $200,000. The firm's revenue in one year is $300,000. What are its economic profits?

Specialization, Diminishing Returns, and Short-run Costs

To study a typical firm's short-run costs, we will construct a hypothetical example for the costs of a small pizzeria. We will then apply these same concepts to an entire competitive market.

Economists define the **short run** as the period in which some resources are fixed and others are variable, whereas in the **long run** all resources are variable. Firms can adjust some (variable) inputs such as labor and materials easily and quickly in the short run, but other (fixed) inputs can be adjusted only with difficulty and time—that is, in the long run. Fixed inputs cannot be changed in the short run in order to increase output. For example, to expand the size of its operations significantly, a pizzeria would need more land, a larger building, more pizza ovens, and more delivery vehicles. These inputs take time to purchase, build, and install, a process that cannot be done at a moment's notice. But on a monthly basis, the firm can change some other inputs quite easily. If our firm wants to increase its output of pizzas, it can hire another laborer or pay existing workers to work more hours, and it can purchase more cheese, sauce, and flour to make pizzas. Thus, labor and materials are considered to be variable inputs, since they can be adjusted easily in the short run. Land and capital (including buildings, machinery, and equipment) are considered fixed inputs because they cannot be adjusted in the short run.

With fixed and variable inputs, our firm also has some costs that are fixed and some costs that are variable. Therefore, in the short run, a firm's total costs (TC) are found by adding together total fixed costs (TFC) and total variable costs (TVC):

$$TC = TFC + TVC.$$

Fixed Costs

The **total fixed costs** are the total costs of the fixed inputs—things like rent, capital costs (payments on machinery purchased on credit or the opportunity cost of that machinery), and property taxes that the firm must pay regardless of how much it produces. Our pizzeria's fixed inputs are land and capital (the building, machinery, and equipment needed to produce pizzas, including pizza ovens, a cash register, tables and chairs, and a truck to deliver pizzas). Since fixed costs are, just that, fixed, they do not go up or down as the firm produces more. Thus, total fixed costs do not change.

In contrast, **average fixed cost,** which is equal to total fixed costs divided by quantity, declines as more is produced:

$$AFC = TFC/Q.$$

For example, assume our pizzeria has fixed costs each day of $50. If it produces only one pizza ($Q = 1$), the average fixed costs would be $50/1 = $50. It would have to sell that pizza for more than $50 to make a profit. (Don't forget, in addition to fixed costs, it would have to pay for variable costs such as labor, cheese, sauce, and flour.) However, if the firm produces ten pizzas, then its average fixed costs fall to $50/10 = $5 per pizza. If the firm produces fifty pizzas, then the average fixed cost is $50/50 = $1. This gives us an average fixed cost curve that looks like the one in Figure 9.1. The more the firm produces, the lower its average fixed cost.

Variable Costs

But our firm has more than just fixed costs to contend with. As we noted above, in addition to its fixed inputs such as land and capital, our firm must purchase variable inputs to produce its pizzas. Variable inputs would include labor and the materials necessary to produce pizzas. We will focus our analysis on labor, because it is the most important variable input. Without labor, no pizzas would get made.

Variable (labor) costs are subject to two basic economic laws: the **law of specialization** and the **law of diminishing returns.** The law of specialization refers to the fact that when laborers specialize in one particular task, they gain in skill and dexterity, and they spend less time switching jobs, which improves their efficiency. However, in the short run, when land and capital are fixed, the process of

FIGURE 9.1   Average Fixed Cost

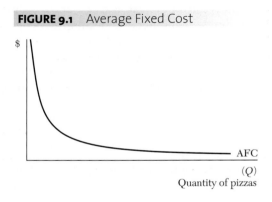

specialization is limited by the size of the firm. Only a certain number of specialized tasks can be done in a small pizzeria. Once the specialized jobs are filled, increasing the output of pizzas becomes increasingly difficult. This is when the law of diminishing returns sets in. According to the law of diminishing returns, in the production of any commodity, as more units of a variable factor of production are added to a fixed quantity of other factors of production, the amount that each additional unit of the variable factor adds to the total product will eventually begin to diminish. In other words, after the specialized jobs are filled, adding more and more labor while keeping other inputs fixed will result in smaller and smaller increases in output. Each laborer gets less efficient after specialization is exhausted.*

To illustrate these fundamental processes of specialization and diminishing returns, suppose our pizzeria has the following fixed inputs: a small dining room with six tables and twenty-four chairs, one cash register, a small kitchen with two pizza ovens, and one truck to deliver pizzas. Suppose also that our firm has enough cheese, sauce, and flour to make as many pizzas as it wants (consider these to be fixed inputs as well for the time being). What will happen as the firm hires laborers at the going wage rate of $8 per hour?

Table 9.1 illustrates how the law of specialization and the law of diminishing returns affects the firm's short-run costs. If our firm hires no laborers, then no pizzas will be produced. It will lose a lot of money, since it must still pay its fixed costs. If our firm hires one laborer for one hour, then that one laborer will have to make the pizzas, cook the pizzas, and deliver them to customers. If our one employee works hard, she can make and deliver six pizzas in an hour. Our one laborer ($L = 1$) has produced six pizzas ($Q = 6$) in an hour at a cost of $8 (the wage rate for one hour of work). This worker's **marginal product of labor** (MPL), the increase in output from hiring an additional laborer for an hour, is six pizzas. The **marginal cost** (MC) of a pizza is the increase in cost from producing another pizza, which is equal to the change in **total variable cost** (TVC) divided by the change in quantity:

$$MC = \Delta TVC/\Delta Q.$$

Firms are very concerned with marginal cost because once they know what each unit of output (each pizza) costs, they know what price they need to charge to make a profit on it. In this case, the change in total variable costs was $8 (the cost of hiring one employee for an hour), and the increase in the output of pizzas was six (the number of pizzas increased from zero to six). Thus, the marginal cost of each pizza when one laborer is working for an hour is equal to $8/6 = $1.33. Total variable cost is the cost of all variable inputs. Since we are employing one worker for one hour, our current total variable costs are $8.

---

*It is important to note that the law of diminishing returns can apply to any variable input (not just labor), when all other inputs are held fixed. For example, if our pizzeria added more and more delivery trucks while keeping all other inputs the same, what would happen to output? Would adding a second delivery truck increase output per hour? What about a tenth delivery truck? (With the number of laborers constant, would there be anyone to drive it?)

TABLE 9.1 Marginal Cost and Average Variable Cost of a Pizza

Number of Laborers (L)	Quantity of Pizzas (Q)	Marginal Product of Labor $\left(MPL = \dfrac{\Delta Q}{\Delta L}\right)$	Total Variable (Labor) Cost $(TVC = W \times L)$	Marginal Cost of a Pizza $\left(MC = \dfrac{\Delta TVC}{\Delta Q}\right)$	Average Variable Cost of a Pizza $\left(AVC = \dfrac{TVC}{Q}\right)$
0	0	–	$ 0.00	–	–
1	6	6	8.00	$1.33	$1.33
2	14	8	16.00	1.00	1.14
3	24	10	24.00	0.80	1.00
4	32	8	32.00	1.00	1.00
5	38	6	40.00	1.33	1.05
6	42	4	48.00	2.00	1.14
7	44	2	56.00	4.00	1.27
8	45	1	64.00	8.00	1.42
9	45	0	72.00	–	1.60
10	44	–1	80.00	–	1.82

Now suppose our pizzeria hires a second laborer to work alongside the first one for one hour. The laborers can now specialize in certain tasks. One laborer can concentrate on making the pizzas, and the other can take telephone orders and deliver the pizzas. The two employees together can produce fourteen pizzas in an hour, more than double what one employee could produce on her own, because of specialization. The marginal product of the second laborer is 8, because the output of pizzas increased by eight when the second laborer was hired. The marginal cost of a pizza has fallen, due to specialization:

$$MC = \Delta TVC/\Delta Q = \$8/8 = \$1.$$

Each pizza is now cheaper to produce because of the efficiency gains from specialization.

Hiring a third laborer will increase specialization (and efficiency) even further. Now one employee can make the pizzas, one person can take the orders and run the cash register, and one employee can deliver pizzas (in the process getting to know the town very well, which will improve delivery time). The output of pizzas increases to twenty-four per hour, and the marginal product of the third laborer is 10, because the output of pizzas increased from fourteen to twenty-four. The marginal cost of a pizza has fallen even further, to $8/10 = \$0.80$ (the \$8 increase in variable cost divided by 10, the increase in quantity).

However, now that the most important specialized tasks are taken, the law of diminishing returns sets in. Hiring additional laborers will increase the output of pizzas, *but not by as much*. Adding a fourth laborer will increase the output of pizzas to thirty-two, so the marginal product of labor declines back to 8, and the

FIGURE 9.2 Marginal Cost and Average Variable Cost

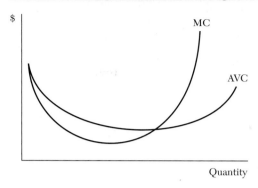

marginal cost of a pizza increases to $1.00. If the firm continues to hire laborers beyond this point, the marginal product of labor declines even further. Eventually, workers start getting in each other's way, and they spend more time standing around and talking than working. The marginal product of the ninth laborer is 0; with a fixed size of operations (land and capital), there is nothing productive for a ninth laborer to do. Adding laborers beyond this would actually *decrease* output. Having too many workers in the small kitchen would prevent work from getting done.

Specialization and diminishing returns determine the shape of the firm's marginal cost and average variable cost curves. As you can see from Table 9.1, as workers get more productive and the marginal product of labor increases, the marginal cost of a pizza declines. When diminishing returns set in and the marginal product of labor declines, the marginal cost of a pizza increases.

The shape of the marginal cost curve determines the shape of the average variable cost curve. Average variable cost (AVC) is equal to total variable cost (TVC) divided by quantity (Q):

$$AVC = TVC/Q.$$

At first, average variable cost is equal to marginal cost; the cost of the first pizza is also equal to the average cost of that pizza. Then, as the marginal cost of each pizza falls below the average variable cost, it pulls the average variable cost of each pizza down as the quantity of pizzas increases. This happens in Table 9.1 as the quantity of pizzas increases from zero to twenty-four; MC < AVC, and AVC falls as quantity rises. When the marginal cost of each pizza exceeds the average variable cost of a pizza, each additional pizza costs more than the average, and this pulls the average cost up. In Table 9.1, this occurs after a quantity of thirty-two pizzas. At a quantity of thirty-two pizzas, MC = AVC. After that point, MC > AVC, and AVC increases as more pizzas are produced.

Together, the law of specialization and the law of diminishing returns give us the marginal cost and average variable cost curves depicted in Figure 9.2. The curves decline at first because specialization improves efficiency and lowers costs. Subsequently, the law of diminishing returns kicks in and the curves increase because efficiency declines, resulting in higher costs.

Average Cost

Now we're ready to construct the firm's **average cost** curve. Recall that total costs are equal to total fixed costs plus total variable costs (TC = TFC + TVC). Similarly, average cost (AC) is equal to average fixed cost (AFC) plus average variable cost (AVC):

$$AC = AFC + AVC.$$

If we take the average fixed cost curve from Figure 9.1 and add it to the average variable cost curve in Figure 9.2, we get our firm's average cost curve, which is shown in Figure 9.3. Note that on the graph we do not need to show the average fixed cost curve. It can always be found by taking the difference between AC and AVC (AC – AVC = AFC). As you can see, the AC curve gets closer and closer to the AVC curve as quantity increases. This is because the difference between the AC curve and the AVC curve is average fixed cost (AFC), and as shown in Figure 9.1, AFC gets smaller and smaller as quantity increases.

The short-run average cost curve has a U shape because the average fixed cost curve declines, the average variable cost curve declines at first due to specialization, and the average variable cost curve increases eventually due to the law of diminishing returns. In Figure 9.3, AC falls quickly from a quantity of zero to a quantity of Q_1 because as quantity increases, both of its components (AFC and AVC) are falling. From Q_1 to Q_2, AC decreases slightly as quantity increases. This is because average fixed cost is falling faster than average variable cost is

FIGURE 9.3   Average Cost Curve

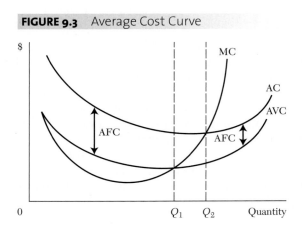

rising (the average variable cost curve increases after). After AC rises because average variable cost is increasing faster than average fixed cost is falling.

Notice also that the minimum average cost occurs where the average cost curve intersects the marginal cost curve at quantity Q_2. The same process applies here as the one that applies to the average variable cost curve: When MC < AC, each unit costs less than the average, and the average falls as quantity increases. When MC > AC, each unit costs more than the average, so AC increases as quantity increases.

The point where average cost is at a minimum has significance for society as a whole. The level of output that minimizes the average cost of output is the *most efficient rate of output.* It means that society is minimizing the cost of using its resources with respect to the production of a good. In Figure 9.3, Q_2 represents an *optimum level of output,* because it minimizes the per-unit cost of producing that good. Raising or lowering output would increase average cost.

Now that we've analyzed the cost side of the firm, we need to study the revenue side in order to determine how much the firm should produce in any situation.

The Firm's Revenues

Total revenue (TR), you'll recall, equals the price of the product (P) multiplied by the quantity of the product sold (Q): TR $= P \times Q$. We can also define average revenue and marginal revenue for the firm. **Average revenue** (AR) is revenue per unit, which is equal to price:

$$AR = TR/Q = (P \times Q)/Q = P.$$

Marginal revenue is the change in total revenue from producing and selling an additional unit of output:

$$MR = (\text{change in TR})/(\text{change in } Q) = \Delta TR/\Delta Q.$$

FIGURE 9.4 Marginal Revenue Curve

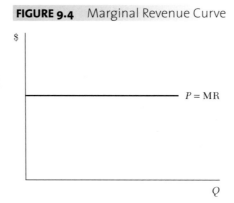

For a firm in a perfectly competitive market, the price is determined in the market by the forces of supply and demand. The firm is so small a part of the market that it has no influence on the price. Thus, as far as the firm is concerned, the price is fixed, and the firm will earn the same amount of money for each unit sold. For the firm in a perfectly competitive market, MR = P. If we were to draw this line on a graph, it would simply be a horizontal line that does not change as quantity changes, as displayed in Figure 9.4.

Profit Maximization

We are now ready to put the cost information and the revenue information together to describe how a typical firm decides to maximize profits in a perfectly competitive market. The firm's objective is maximum profits (or minimum losses if the business climate is poor). What level of output should the firm produce to get the maximum level of profits? The answer is that the firm should produce as long as marginal revenue is greater than or equal to marginal cost. Therefore, *the profit-maximizing quantity will occur where marginal revenue is equal to marginal cost* (MR = MC).

The logic behind the profit maximization rule is quite simple. Every unit that generates more in revenue than it costs will improve the standing of the firm. For example, in Figure 9.5, the firm should produce all units up to Q_e because each unit adds more to the firm's revenue than it costs the firm to produce. If the firm were to stop at Q_1, then it would lose the revenue from the sale of the units between Q_1 and Q_e. However, the fir7m should not increase production beyond Q_e. At Q_2, the firm is producing units that cost more to make than they generate in revenue, which would hurt the firm's bottom line. The profit-maximizing quantity always occurs where marginal revenue is equal to marginal cost.

FIGURE 9.5   Marginal Revenue, Marginal Cost, and Profit Maximization

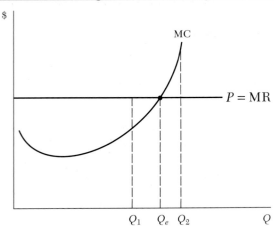

Although the quantity Q_e in Figure 9.5 represents the profit-maximizing or loss-minimizing level of output—the best the firm can possibly do—we don't know how much the firm is making or losing until we add in the other cost information for the firm. Specifically, we need to know the firm's average cost at quantity Q_e. Recall that the firm earns a normal profit when total revenue (TR) equals total cost (TC). Since $TR = P \times Q$ and $TC = AC \times Q$, we can solve for P when $TR = TC$:

$$P \times Q = AC \times Q$$
$$P = AC.$$

The firm earns a normal profit when the price of its product equals its average cost (including the cost of all inputs plus opportunity costs). Similarly, the firm earns an economic profit when $P > AC$, and it experiences an economic loss when $P < AC$.

3. Why do total costs and total variable costs increase at a *decreasing* rate at relatively low levels of output?

An Example of Profit Maximization in the Short Run

Let's use another simple example of a small firm engaged in the production of pizzas to explore how firms maximize profits. The pizzeria is run by a group of individuals, leases a building outside of Chicago, and owns all of the furniture and equipment in its restaurant. It has borrowed money from BankChicago to finance its business. In this sense, then, it has a certain size of operation for its short-run production expectations. Within this fixed size of operations, it can expand its output of pizzas by using more variable resources—that is, more raw materials and more labor. These variable resources can use the fixed size of operations more or less intensively to produce more or less output. (In the long run, as we will see shortly, all of the resources that the firm uses in production can be expanded or contracted. That is, the firm can change the size of its operation.)

Fixed and Variable Costs. As we saw above, in the short run, the firm incurs both fixed and variable costs. Total fixed costs are the costs that the firm must pay for the fixed resources of production involved in the firm's particular short-run size of operations. These costs do not vary with the rate of output that the firm produces. The firm has a monthly mortgage payment that it gives to the bank to repay the loan it used to purchase its equipment for producing pizzas. The owners of the firm also have an opportunity cost for their participation in the firm's activities. In other words, the owners will get salaries based on what they could earn in some other activity. If these salaries weren't paid, the owners would seek some other jobs in which they could earn their opportunity cost (e.g., as managers of a different restaurant). All of these costs are fixed costs; they are incurred by the firm regardless of the level of output in

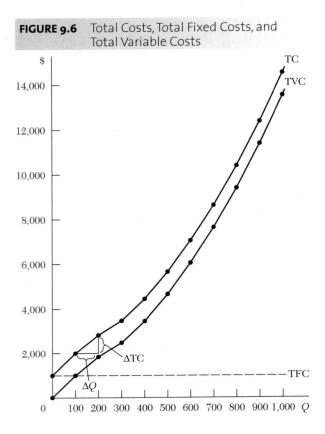

FIGURE 9.6 Total Costs, Total Fixed Costs, and Total Variable Costs

any particular month. Even if output is zero in the short run, fixed costs are still positive.

Let's assume that the monthly fixed costs of this pizzeria are $1,000. Figure 9.6 illustrates total fixed costs (TFC), with costs measured on the vertical axis and output measured on the horizontal axis. It shows that as output (measured on the horizontal axis) increases, total fixed costs remain constant.

This firm's total variable costs are the expenses for using varying amounts of raw materials and labor to expand output within a fixed-size plant (in the short run). To get greater amounts of output, the firm uses more and more variable resources; consequently, total variable costs increase as output increases. However, given the law of specialization, we know that at first, relatively few added resources will achieve expanded output, and that later, given the law of diminishing returns, the firm will have to add greater amounts of resources to get equivalent additions to output. Therefore, total variable costs will normally increase first at a decreasing rate, then at an increasing rate. Figure 9.6 illustrates what happens to total variable costs (TVC), measured on the vertical axis, as output increases. At rates of output below a quantity of 300, total vari-

TABLE 9.2 Pizzeria's Costs at Possible Levels of Output

Level of Output	Total Fixed Costs	Total Variable Costs	Total Costs
0	$1,000	$ 0	$ 1,000
100	1,000	1,000	2,000
200	1,000	1,800	2,800
300	1,000	2,400	3,400
400	1,000	3,400	4,400
500	1,000	4,600	5,600
600	1,000	6,000	7,000
700	1,000	7,600	8,600
800	1,000	9,400	10,400
900	1,000	11,400	12,400
1,000	1,000	13,600	14,600

able costs increase at a decreasing rate, and at rates of output greater than 300, diminishing returns to the use of variable resources set in, and total variable costs increase at an increasing rate. At a rate of output of zero, total variable costs are zero.

If we add total fixed costs and total variable costs together, we again get the total costs (TC) of production:

$$TC = TFC + TVC.$$

Table 9.2 presents different possible levels of output during a one-month period for our pizzeria and the total fixed costs, total variable costs, and total costs of each level of output. Figure 9.6 illustrates total costs. Notice that when output is zero, total costs equal total fixed costs.

Average and Marginal Costs.   We can also use this cost information to derive average and marginal costs. As we saw earlier, these cost measures will prove useful in analyzing the firm's profit maximization decisions. Average cost takes the various total costs of production and averages them over each unit of output. For example, at 100 units of output, total fixed costs are $1,000. The average fixed cost for each unit of output is $10. Recall that for each different level of output, average fixed cost is defined as follows:

$$AFC = \frac{TFC}{Q}.$$

In the same way, average variable cost is

$$AVC = \frac{TVC}{Q},$$

and average cost is

$$AC = \frac{TC}{Q}.$$

Since TC = TFC + TVC, then AC = AFC + AVC.

Marginal cost, again, is the additional cost of producing one additional unit of output. It indicates the amount of change in total costs as a result of additional output:

$$MC = \frac{\text{change in TC}}{\text{change in } Q} \text{ or } \frac{\Delta TC}{\Delta Q}.$$

Since fixed costs do not change with the level of output, marginal costs can also be defined as the change in total variable costs as output changes. For example, when the firm moves from producing 100 units of output to 200 units of output, total costs increase from $2,000 to $2,800 (and total variable costs increase from $1,000 to $1,800). Consequently,

$$MC = \frac{2,800 - 2,000}{200 - 100} = \frac{800}{100} = 8.$$

The marginal cost of producing 100 more pizzas (expanding to 200 from 100) is $800, or $8 for each unit. In essence, marginal cost equals the slope of the total costs (or total variable costs) curve in Figure 9.6. Since total costs first increase at a decreasing rate and then begin increasing at an increasing rate, MC will first decrease and then begin increasing.

As shown in Table 9.3, we can use the information in Table 9.2 to derive data on average fixed costs, average variable costs, average costs, and marginal costs.

TABLE 9.3 Pizzeria's Average and Marginal Costs

Output	$AFC = \dfrac{TFC}{Q}$	$AVC = \dfrac{TVC}{Q}$	$AC = \dfrac{TC}{Q}$	$MC = \dfrac{\Delta TC}{\Delta Q}$
0	—	—	—	—
100	$10.0	$10.0	$20.0	$10
200	5.0	9.0	14.0	8
300	3.3	8.0	11.3	6
400	2.5	8.5	11.0	10
500	2.0	9.2	11.2	12
600	1.7	10.0	11.7	14
700	1.4	10.9	12.3	16
800	1.2	11.7	12.9	18
900	1.1	12.7	13.8	20
1,000	1.0	14.6	15.6	22

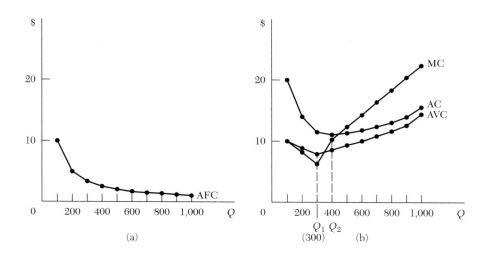

(a)

(b)

Figure 9.7 graphs the resulting data. AFC, AVC, AC, and MC all vary with the rate of output. In each case, costs are measured in per-unit or marginal terms. The horizontal axis always measures output, and the vertical axis measures average or marginal costs. Average fixed cost in Figure 9.7(a) constantly decreases, since it is total fixed cost divided by increasing rates of output. Average variable cost, shown in Figure 9.7(b), is generally U-shaped, reflecting the laws of specialization and diminishing returns. Over a range of output, AVC decreases at first, reaches a minimum at Q_1, and then begins to increase for greater levels of output. At first, when there are increasing returns to the use of variable resources, the per-unit cost of production decreases as output increases. The per-unit amount of resources needed to produce increasing amounts of output decreases. However, beyond Q_1, AVC begins to increase as each unit of output requires the use of increasing amounts of variable resources. This, again, is the result of diminishing returns to the use of variable resources.

Average cost, shown in Figure 9.7(b), is also U-shaped because of the laws of specialization and diminishing returns. Since AC is the sum of AFC and AVC, and AFC is positive and constantly decreasing, AC is above AVC, but the difference between them is constantly decreasing. AC reaches a minimum at the rate of output of Q_2. This is a slightly higher rate of output than Q_1. AVC is increasing, but because AFC is constantly decreasing, it takes a higher level of output for AC to begin increasing (where the effects of increasing AVC begin to outweigh the effects of decreasing AFC).

In Figure 9.7(b), marginal cost is also U-shaped due to the laws of special-ization and diminishing returns. Since marginal costs register the *additional* costs of producing greater rates of output, rather than the per-unit costs, marginal costs will more dramatically illustrate the effects first of increasing returns and then of decreasing returns to the use of variable resources.

4. Explain how the law of diminishing returns causes the MC curve to be increasing beyond some rate of output.
5. Why is marginal cost equal to the slope of the total cost curve? What *is* the slope of the total cost curve?
6. If the Los Angeles Dodgers have a team batting average of .275 (that is, on the average they get 275 hits every 1,000 times they come to bat) and they acquire a new outfielder whose batting average is .298, what happens to the team batting average? What if they trade away two players with averages of .260 and .274 for one player with an average of .278? Relate these examples to MC and AC.
7. Explain why the minimum point on the AC curve represents an optimum rate of output.

Price and Profit.   Recall that, for a firm in a perfectly competitive market, the price is determined in the market by the forces of supply and demand. The firm gets the price of the product for every unit that it sells, so $P = MR = AR$. If the price of a pizza is $12, then the firm's revenues per unit are $12, and its marginal revenues also are $12. Figure 9.8(a) illustrates total revenues, and Figure 9.8(b) shows price and marginal revenue. These graphs show what happens to revenues, measured on the vertical axis, as output expands.

FIGURE 9.8   Total Revenues (a) and Marginal Revenue (b)

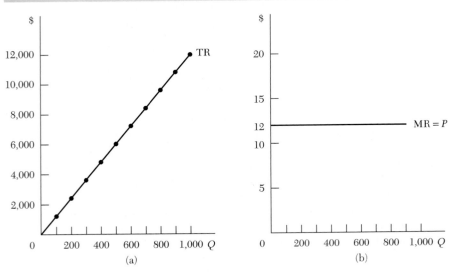

TABLE 9.4 Data for a Firm's Profit Maximization Decision

Output	TC	AC	MC	MR TR	(and P)	Profit (or Loss)
0	$ 1,000	–	–	0	–	$–1,000
100	2,000	$20.0	$10	$ 1,200	$12	–800
200	2,800	14.0	8	2,400	12	–400
300	3,400	11.3	6	3,600	12	200
400	4,400	11.0	10	4,800	12	400
500	5,600	11.2	12	6,000	12	400
600	7,000	11.7	14	7,200	12	200
700	8,600	12.3	16	8,400	12	–200
800	10,400	12.9	18	9,600	12	–800
900	12,400	13.8	20	10,800	12	–1,600
1,000	14,600	15.6	22	12,000	12	–2,600

We are now ready to put the cost information and the revenue information together to describe the profit maximization decision of the pizzeria. Table 9.4 and Figure 9.9 provide information and an illustration of the firm's profit maximization decision. Recall that we have assumed that the firm's objective is to maximize its profits, that in the short run it has a fixed-size of operations (restaurant), that it has access to certain production techniques and technical knowledge, and that it can buy resources in markets for certain prices. What level of output could the firm produce to get the maximum level of profits? The answer is that the pizzeria will produce that rate of output at which the difference between TR and TC is greatest. This also happens to be the rate of output at which MC and MR are equal. *When the marginal cost of producing one more unit of output is equal to the marginal revenue from selling one more unit, the firm maximizes its profits.* This occurs at a quantity of 500 in Figure 9.9.

Table 9.4 and Figure 9.9 demonstrate why profits (or TR – TC) are maximized when MC = MR at 500 units of output. (In this numerical example, because we are increasing output in increments of 100, the marginal cost figure is actually an *average* of the marginal cost of producing each added 100 pizzas. As a result, profits are maximized at both 400 and 500 units of output. The firm could pick either rate of output and maximize its profits—at $400. But since MR > MC at 400 units of output, the firm will expand to 500.) At higher rates of output, marginal costs are larger than marginal revenues, and profits decrease. At lower rates of output, marginal revenues exceed marginal costs, and the firm can increase its profits by producing and selling larger levels of output.

Notice that at a quantity of 500 in Figure 9.9, the price of a pizza is greater than the average cost of producing each unit. That is, for each unit, the revenue that the firm earns exceeds its cost. This is, in fact, profit per unit, since profit = TR – TC:

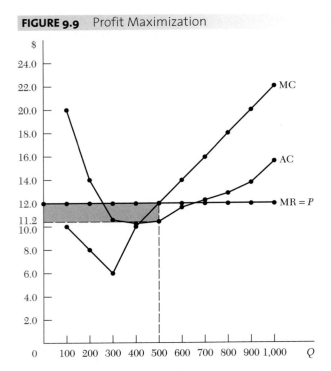

FIGURE 9.9 Profit Maximization

$$\frac{\text{profit}}{Q} = \frac{\text{TR}}{Q} - \frac{\text{TC}}{Q}$$

$$\text{profit per unit} = P - \text{AC}.$$

As long as price exceeds average cost, the firm earns economic profits of $Q(P - \text{AC})$. Total profits are equal to the area of the shaded rectangle in Figure 9.9. If the price is below the average cost, however, the firm experiences losses. Does this conclusion fit the information in Table 9.4?

What we have just shown summarizes one of the most important results of the economic theory of the firm. A firm will maximize its profits when it produces a rate of output at which its marginal revenues equal its marginal costs. This is its equilibrium rate of output. If a firm expands its output to a point at which $\text{MC} > \text{MR}$, its profits decrease. What will it do in response? It will probably reduce its rate of output. The theoretical conclusion would seem to be borne out by what we would expect firms in the real world to do. They will tend to produce that rate of output at which $\text{MC} = \text{MR}$.

Figure 9.10 shows examples of a firm earning an economic profit, earning a normal profit, and incurring an economic loss. In each case, the equilibrium (profit-maximizing or loss-minimizing) level of output is found at the quantity where $\text{MR} = \text{MC}$. The profit or loss per unit is measured by the area between

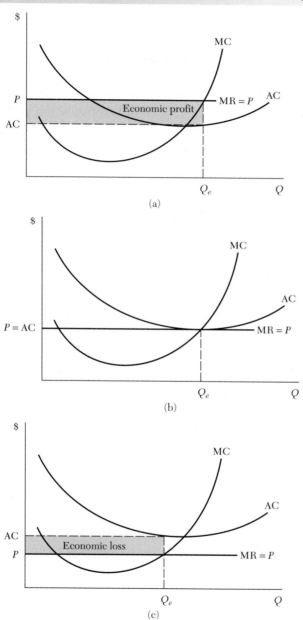

the price (or marginal revenue) curve and the average cost curve for the quantity produced. In Figure 9.10(a), $P > AC$, and the shaded area represents an economic profit. In Figure 9.10(b), $P = AC$, and the firm earns a normal profit. The graph has no shaded area for profit or loss, because a normal profit is already included in the costs of production. In Figure 9.10(c), $P < AC$, and the firm earns an economic loss equal to the shaded area.

8. For our pizzeria, what happens to its profits if it reduces output from 500 to 300? What is the relationship between P and AC at this rate of output? What is the relationship between MC and MR?

9. For Figure 9.9, explain why profits increase if the firm moves from a quantity of 700 to lower levels of output.

10. Construct an AC curve with its own MC curve. What would the firm do if the price of its product passed through the point at which $MC = AC$? What level of output would it produce? What would its profits be? Would this firm be earning its opportunity costs?

11. From Table 9.4, if the firm produces 800 units of output, what are its profits? What is the relationship between P and AC? Between MR and MC?

The Firm in the Long Run

In the long run, the firm always has more options than in the short run. It can alter the size of its plant. It can change the technology it uses to produce its good or service. For pizza firms, if the market for the product expands or the firm thinks that it will, it can seek a larger facility to buy or rent, borrow more money so that it can purchase more machinery and equipment, hire more workers, take on partners to expand the size of its operation, or relocate its operations. In the long run, the firm can vary all of its production resources; there are no fixed resources.

The long run is no specific period of time; rather, it is that time frame in which people make decisions based on the future. If a pizza firm expects its market to expand in the future, it will adjust for the long run. Or if it expects the market to begin to contract, it can make a different long-run adjustment. In addition, in the long run, firms can enter or leave the industry. The decision to enter or leave is a long-run investment decision for individuals and firms.

In essence, the firm can pick an infinite number of different possible short-run plant sizes in the long run. At any moment in time, the firm is in the short run; it has a fixed-size plant with fixed resources, and it has a corresponding short-run average cost curve. Given the long-run option of different possible plant sizes, the firm will obviously pick the plant size that minimizes the average cost of producing every different possible level of output. For example, in Figure 9.11, there are three different short-run average cost curves representing different possible plant sizes for different ranges of output. AC_1 repre-

(© Michael Newman/Photo Edit)

sents the first size plant, AC_2 the second size plant, and AC_3 the third size plant. For Q_1, AC_1 minimizes the average cost of production. So if the firm wanted to produce Q_1, it would pick plant size 1. But if the firm wanted to produce Q_2, it would pick plant size 2, since this minimizes the average cost of that rate of output. Similarly, if it wanted to produce an even larger rate of output, say Q_3 it would pick plant size 3. Notice that this represents a long-run decision. The firm makes a choice of a plant size (or scale of operations) based on

FIGURE 9.11   Deriving Long-run Average Costs

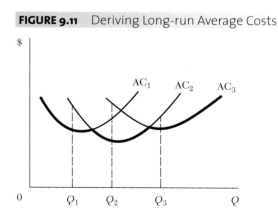

FIGURE 9.12 Typical Long-run Average Cost Curve

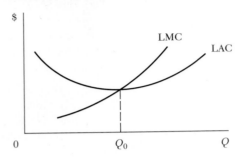

its expectations of or experiences with the market. The decision requires time to make arrangements for physical facilities, new and larger equipment, borrowing, and so forth. The firm generates its long-run average cost curve by picking the plant size that minimizes the cost of producing every possible rate of output. It is the heavy line in Figure 9.11.

When we assume that there is an infinite number of possible plant sizes for the firm to choose from, the firm's typical long-run AC curve looks like the one in Figure 9.12. It is U-shaped just like the short-run AC curve (and has its own long-run marginal cost curve, LMC), but for different reasons. The short-run curve was U-shaped because of the laws of specialization and diminishing returns, which assumed that a firm increased output by applying variable resources to fixed resources. In the long run, however, there are no fixed resources; a firm expands output by using more of all resources. If that is the case, then why would long-run average costs (LAC) decrease over a range of output, reach a minimum at Q_0, and then begin to increase?

Economists attribute the shape of the LAC curve to economies and diseconomies of scale. As the firm adjusts its plant size, it alters the scale of its operations. At first, as the firm expands at relatively low levels of output, by building a larger plant, it can take greater advantage of specialization, division of labor, and more advanced technology. (If the pizzeria we analyzed earlier had a much larger kitchen, there would be many more specialized jobs.) The result is lower average costs. The firm experiences **economies of scale:** long-run average costs decrease as output increases. However, beyond some rate of output (Q_0 in Figure 9.12), the firm encounters difficulties in organizing the now larger operation. Coordination and communication make efficient production more difficult. Average costs begin to increase; it costs more to produce each unit of output. **Diseconomies of scale** have set in. As in the short run, the long-run marginal cost curve (LMC) in Figure 9.12 is below LAC while LAC is decreasing and above it while it is increasing.

The shape of the long-run average cost curve defines an optimum plant size. At the rate of output at which LAC is at a minimum, the firm picks the plant size that produces the rate of output at lowest average cost. The firm expands output and plant size throughout the range of economies of scale. At higher rates of output, LAC begins to increase because of diseconomies of scale. At Q_0, the firm produces a rate of output that minimizes the per-unit cost of production.

In fact, in the long run, in competitive industries, firms tend to produce a rate of output that minimizes long-run average costs. Competition forces them to do so.

12. If a firm experienced economies of scale over some range of output and then LAC was constant, what would its LAC curve look like? Does it seem reasonable to you that a firm could keep expanding and not encounter diseconomies of scale? If this happened, what would the optimum size plant be?

13. In Figure 9.12, Q_0 represents the optimum rate of output and the optimum plant size. Does the firm earn its opportunity costs if it gets a price equal to this level of average costs?

Competitive Markets in the Long Run

In this section, using the model that we developed for the individual firm, we will formulate a general model of the behavior of a competitive market. The analysis focuses on the long-run equilibrium for the firms in the industry and for the entire industry. Although we have concentrated on a single example, the model of a competitive market is intended to be generalizable to all competitive markets or to an entire economy that is competitive. We will also interpret the results of the long-run equilibrium for competitive markets.

In Figure 9.13, with a price of P_1, the firm will produce Q_1, since it is at this rate of output that MR = MC. The price is determined in the competitive market for the firm's product. This price is constant, and the firm has no effect on it. Hence, P = MR, and the firm can produce as much as it wants at that price. The firm, of course, will produce Q_1, since that is where its profits are

FIGURE 9.13 The Firm in the Long Run

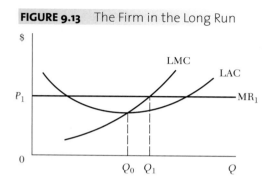

FIGURE 9.14   The Effect of Entry in the Long Run

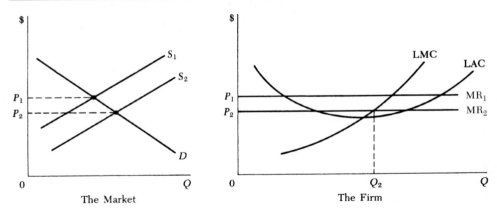

maximized. At Q_1 price exceeds AC, so we know that the firm is earning economic profits.

But in the long run, if resources can earn above their opportunity costs, new firms will enter the industry in pursuit of economic profits. In other words, the existence of economic profits provides an incentive for other firms to enter the industry. If economic profits can be made, given the price in the market for pizza and the average costs of production, new firms will enter that market and begin to produce and market their own products.

As new firms enter the market, however, the market supply curve shifts out to the right. There is an increase in supply because one of the determinants of supply has changed. This increase in supply, assuming the demand does not change, produces a lower price for pizza, say P_2 (see Figure 9.14). At P_2, the firm will pick a new rate of output, Q_2, at which MR = MC. But P still exceeds AC, firms will continue to make economic profits (albeit smaller than before), and other new firms will enter the market. This further increases market supply and drives down the price of the product.

This process will continue until economic profits no longer exist to provide an incentive for new firms to enter the industry. This occurs at a price of P_3 in Figure 9.15. At this price, the firm picks Q_3, since that is where MR = MC. At this rate of output P = AC, so there are no economic profits. The firm is in equilibrium because it is producing the rate of output that maximizes its profits—even though this means zero economic profits. But the firm does earn what we called at the beginning of this chapter, normal profits—that is, it covers all of its opportunity costs. The firm collects enough revenues to pay opportunity costs to all of its variable and fixed resources, including a return to the owners of the business equivalent to their opportunity costs. The firm earns as much from its involvement in this activity as it could earn doing anything else. If a firm cannot earn normal profits in the long run, it will exit the market.

FIGURE 9.15 Long-run Equilibrium in Competition

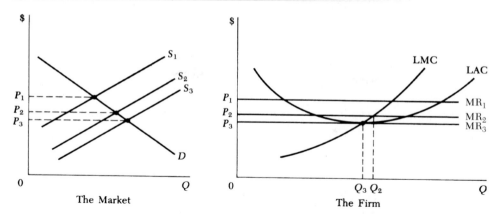

The Market

The Firm

Competition and Efficiency

The existence of economic profits encourages new firms to enter the industry until economic profits are eliminated. Firms choose a rate of output that maximizes their profits, which in long-run equilibrium equals zero economic profits, or normal profits. The industry is in equilibrium because there is no incentive for firms to enter or exit the industry. What are the consequences of this result in terms of a society's use of its scarce resources?

Efficiency in production occurs when the per-unit cost of production is minimized. The firm produces at the rate of output that minimizes AC. This means that the amount of resources used to produce each unit of output is minimized. Given resource scarcity, this is an attractive result of the operation of competitive markets. But note how this has happened. Because of competition and free entry, the firm has been forced to produce at the level of output that minimizes average cost! Competition, through the forces that we have analyzed, tends over time to result in efficient production. Firms tend to produce at the optimum level of output, minimizing the per-unit cost of production. So competition tends to produce efficiency.

What assumptions have we made? We assumed that demand was constant and that the cost curves did not change. With these simplifying assumptions, our analysis showed the tendency toward efficiency. Obviously, changes in the real world would make our analysis a bit more complicated, but the essential conclusion remains: Competitive markets tend to result in efficiency in the use of scarce resources.

14. Explain and show in an illustration what happens in our competitive market when the market price goes below P_3 in Figure 9.15. What happens to profits? What do the firms in the industry do? What happens to market supply? To market price? What is the new equilibrium?

15. Do you think that the model of long-run equilibrium—wherein profits attract entry, prices fluctuate, exit of firms is possible, and there is a tendency toward efficiency in production—applies to the example we have been using, the market for pizza? Why or why not? Can you think of some other markets that have demonstrated some of these same characteristics in recent years?

16. In the personal computer market, IBM (now Lenovo) and Apple, the two firms that dominated the market in the 1980s, have faced increasing competition from other PC producers. What has happened to the price of a PC over the past twenty years? What factors explain the price trend?

Another type of efficiency results from long-run equilibrium in competitive markets: **efficiency in resource allocation.** At the long-run equilibrium in Figure 9.15, P_3 equals minimum AC. But P_3 also equals MC at the equilibrium rate of output, Q_3. This is an important result. The price of a product measures the amount of money that people are just willing to spend to purchase one more unit of that good. In other words, the price provides a measure of the marginal benefit that people derive from purchasing a unit of the good or service. The MC of the good (shown by the LMC curve) measures the cost to society of getting additional units of the good. To get one more unit, resources must be paid their opportunity costs. A rate of output that equalizes the marginal cost to society of getting one more unit of a good with the marginal benefit that people get from consuming one more unit maximizes social welfare (with respect to the production of that good). It also implies that resources have been allocated efficiently, given the opportunity costs of resources and given consumers' valuations of goods as shown by their prices.

To demonstrate this, let's consider different rates of output in Figure 9.15. First, take any rate of output lower than Q_3. At all rates of output lower than Q_3, the price of the product exceeds LMC. As output expands, the marginal benefit from getting one more unit of the good is larger than the marginal cost to society of producing it. Expanding output, then, makes a positive contribution to the society's welfare. The additional benefit exceeds the additional cost, so social welfare increases. More resources should be allocated to producing the good.

On the other hand, any rate of output greater than Q_3 results in MC exceeding P. The additional cost of producing one more unit is larger than the extra benefit from getting one more unit for consumers. Consequently, at rates of output above Q_3, social welfare decreases. To increase social welfare requires reducing the rate of output and allocating fewer resources to its production. Therefore, social welfare is maximized at a rate of output of Q_3 at which $P = MC$. This represents efficiency in resource allocation.

The long-run equilibrium tendency of competitive markets is to produce exactly this result! Competitive markets tend to produce efficiency in resource allocation.

Zero economic profits, production at lowest AC, and efficiency in resource allocation are all theoretical results of competitive markets. These results are brought about by the pursuit of profit by firms within the market and by the force of competition itself—the free entry and exit of firms to and from the market and in competition with one another for consumers.

Notice that we have again been using the phrase *tends to* in our analysis of the long-run equilibrium for a competitive market. We have been constructing a model of competition, a theory about how competitive markets work. Given the assumptions that we have made and the concepts that we have defined, we have determined the equilibrium result for competition. This does not mean that such equilibrium exists all the time for every competitive market, or that there won't ever be any economic profits in competitive markets. What it does suggest, though, is that without disturbances (given our assumptions), there are some general tendencies in the operation of competition. The system tends toward equilibrium. And even if it is disturbed—for example, by a change in consumers' incomes or tastes and preferences, by a change in resource prices, or by technological advances—the model that we have developed will allow us to follow through the effects to determine what the new equilibrium will be. In fact, competition encourages adaptability and responsiveness to changes in consumers' behavior.

The "Invisible Hand" and Consumer Sovereignty

What does all this have to do with the "invisible hand" and consumer sovereignty? Remember, Adam Smith's notion of the invisible hand was that the market tends to promote social welfare. **Consumer sovereignty** means that the market follows the "dictates" of consumers, in terms of their tastes and preferences.

Markets and prices indicate to potential producers where profits can be made in the economy. If producers can produce a product at a lower average cost than the price at which they can sell it, then they can earn an economic profit. In addition, producers will attempt to maximize their profits. We can see immediately, then, that producers will probably try to lower their costs, because that increases their profits. Consumers also benefit from this because the price of the product will eventually be lowered due to the cost reduction.

The price reduction following a cost reduction may not be intuitively obvious, so let's examine this theoretical conclusion in more detail. Suppose we have a pizza producer with an MC and MR graph that looks like Figure 9.16. MC_1 represents the firm's costs, and MR is determined by the market price for pizza. This firm then discovers a new and cheaper method of making pizza. As a result, MC falls from MC_1 to MC_2 (each successive unit can now be brought to market for a lower marginal cost).

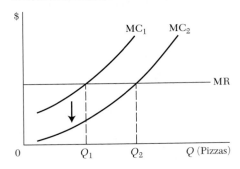

FIGURE 9.16 Change in Costs

With the change in costs, the firm makes a new decision about the level of output to produce. Originally, profits were maximized at Q_1; with the new marginal cost curve, the profit-maximizing level of production increases to Q_2. (Since average costs also decrease, the firm also will make larger economic profits, since price is still the same and the firm is now producing more.) At first, the price stays the same; the firm is so small in relation to the market that the additional amount brought to market is not noticeable and has no effect on market price. However, the firm does have larger economic profits (the AC curve would also shift down).

Eventually, other participants in the market notice the improvement this firm made and the extra profits it is earning as a result. These other suppliers begin to use the same or similar cost-reducing methods of production. In addition, the lure of economic profits (a return to the firm over and above opportunity costs) may induce some new firms to enter the market as sellers. (Again, a characteristic of a competitive market is free entry.) What does this do to market supply? It increases it; more pizza will be brought to market. Graphically, in Figure 9.17, we get a new supply curve, S_2; more pizzas are brought to market at each possible price.

Consequently (note we have assumed that D stays the same), the market price will decrease from P_1 to P_2. The cost reduction ended up also reducing the market price! This was brought about through the market and by competition. The market showed that profits could be made, and competition allowed new firms to enter the market. (Note that each producer's profits are lowered to a normal profit because of the price decrease, although each producer will still bring to market the amount that maximizes its profits. Show this using MR, MC, and AC curves.)

Although each producer (firm) is out to maximize its own profits, the market and competition have brought about a situation in which there is an incentive to lower costs and whereby prices are reduced when costs are. Consumers benefit as a result; they get their product for a lower price. The "invisible hand" lives (at least theoretically)! (Go back to Chapter 4 and review what Adam Smith had to say about the "invisible hand.")

In addition, the market responds to consumers' demands. This response is referred to as consumer sovereignty. For example, let's assume that consumers

FIGURE 9.17 Change in Market Supply

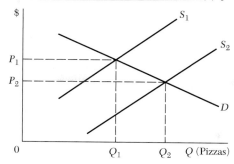

decide to eat out more and, as a result, more and more consumers want pizzas. This change in tastes and preferences (and the increase in the number of consumers in the market) tends to increase the demand for pizza. What effect do these changes have on the market price for pizza? Figure 9.18 shows that the price of pizza tends to increase. What assumption have we made in this illustration? (And is this a realistic assumption? What has happened in recent years in the pizza market on both sides of the market?)

With this increased price, the profits of pizza producers should increase, and they will produce increasing amounts of pizza. Consequently, the desires of consumers show up in the market and indicate to producers what to do with respect to production. If consumers want more pizza, the market price will indicate that, and the producers will respond by producing more. This is consumer sovereignty. By extension, this process also has implications for resource use in the economy. When production of any good or service is expanded or contracted, the use of resources for that purpose will also increase or decrease.

17. Using Figure 9.18, if a reduction in resource costs allowed a pizzeria to lower its long-run average costs, show what the new long-run equilibrium would be for the firm and for the industry.

FIGURE 9.18 Change in Demand

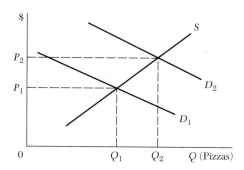

Conclusion

The competitive market model has some attractive results. Firms earn normal profits. There is a tendency toward an equilibrium at which entry and exit cease. The firms in the market produce a rate of output that minimizes average costs; there is efficiency in production. Output takes place at a rate that maximizes social welfare; when P = MC, there is efficiency in resource allocation. If products are homogeneous, then there is no need to allocate resources to advertising. Competitive markets are adaptable. Whenever costs change, or supply and demand conditions change, firms register these changes and take them into account in making decisions in pursuit of maximizing their own profits. Since technological change can lower the firm's costs, the firm always has an incentive to try to lower costs, because profits will increase (at least for a while). Competitive markets register the desires of consumers, and those desires guide production and the allocation of resources. The "invisible hand" will bring about cost and price reductions for consumers.

The competitive market system also links the interdependence of all economic agents in the whole economy. Markets for resources and products provide prices that people use as information in all of the decisions they make about what work they will do, what goods and services they will consume, what business activities they will pursue, and what resources firms will use. As a result of all of these decisions linked by the operation of markets, the scarce resources of society are allocated to meet the needs of people in that society. The competitive market system thus operates to solve the questions of what to produce, how to produce it, and how to distribute it. All of this occurs because of the existence of markets and of competition. Competition and markets guide resource allocation.

If every market were competitive (remember our definition of what that means), then the whole economy would be characterized by efficiency, the operation of invisible hand, and consumer sovereignty in the long run. Stated differently, the competitive market model in theory produces efficiency and consumer sovereignty. As a result, there is little need for the government to be involved in the economy. If the competitive markets are allowed to operate freely and individuals are allowed to follow their maximizing opportunities, the best economic results are achieved. The competitive model, then, justifies a policy of laissez-faire.

Unfortunately, however, the model of competitive markets is not the same thing as the real economy. The theoretical results of the model of competition we have developed are certainly attractive. In fact, this theory is the basis of the argument that the capitalist system is the best economic system possible. It can be seen in innumerable advertisements from corporate America as well as the ideas of chambers of commerce and the National Association of Manufacturers. Many politicians use the argument to support these pro-business policies in their request for voter support and contributions. But the real world doesn't always duplicate theory, and the results of the model cannot uncritically or without qualification be ascribed to the real world.

It is important to recognize the various ways in which the operation of the real economy departs from the model of competitive markets. Most markets are not, in fact, competitive. For example, large chains such as Domino's and Pizza Hut frequently dominate local pizza markets. Corporations and labor unions, for example, have market power, can influence prices, and have been able to limit the effects of competition. Sometimes markets do not work at all; no one can make profits putting up street signs, for example. The calculation of profits by the firm does not take into account the external costs of production (such as pollution), an omission that can interfere with efficient resource allocation. The operation of resource markets can result in an unequal distribution of income. All of these results of the operation of the real economy limit the extent to which it produces the attractive results of the theoretical model of competition.

In the next four chapters, we will develop some economic theory that analyzes these problems in the operation of the real market system. We will also explore the response of public policy to the existence of these problems connected with the operation of the economy.

Review Questions

1. How accurate is this competitive model with respect to the current U.S. economy? Are its conclusions generally applicable to our economy? Why or why not?

2. Why are profits maximized when MR = MC? Can you explain this logically?

3. Do you think firms really do try to maximize their profits? Do they have other goals? Which are most important?

4. Give some examples of the law of diminishing returns in production. Specify which resources are variable and which ones are fixed.

5. Explain why economic profits cease to exist in competition in the long run (as a tendency). What is the implication of this? Why do firms stay in a market in which there are no economic profits?

6. In Table 9.4, show what happens if the price of pizza increases to $18. Fill in new TR, MR, and Profit columns. What rate of output will the firm choose? Why?

7. Illustrate (with cost and revenue curves) a firm making economic profits in the long run. Show the corresponding market-determined price.
    a. Assume (show) an increase in demand for the product (e.g., rugs imported from India). What happens to market price? What adjustments do the firms in the industry make?
    b. How will long-run equilibrium develop? Illustrate long-run equilibrium for the firm and the industry.

8. a. Complete the table on page 188.
   b. How does the information in the table show the basic economic processes of a) specialization and b) diminishing returns?
   c. From the information in the table, plot a graph including AC, AVC, MC, and the firm's demand curve (the Price column). Show the equilibrium (profit maximizing) level of output and the firm's profit or loss on the graph.
      Note: You find a firm's profit maximizing (or loss minimizing) level of output by comparing marginal revenue (price) and marginal cost. A firm should produce a unit as long as marginal revenue is greater than or equal to marginal cost (i.e., a firm should produce every unit that makes the firm more money than it costs the firm). Also, assume that the firm must sell in

whole units (e.g., the firm cannot produce at a quantity of 6.5; it must choose either 6 or 7).

d. Suppose the market price falls to $130. Using the table below, with new Price and TR columns, find the firm's new profit maximizing (or loss minimizing) output (compare Price and Marginal Cost to find the profit maximizing quantity) and compute the firm's new level of profit or loss (compute total revenue and total cost using $110 as the price and using the new profit max-imizing quantity). Assume that the firm must produce whole units.

Output (Q)	TVC	TFC	TC	AVC	AC	MC	MR = P	TR	TR–TC (Profit or Loss)
0	0	330					160		
1	100	330					160		
2	150	330					160		
3	180	330					160		
4	260	330					160		
5	380	330					160		
6	540	330					160		
7	764	330					160		
8	1,060	330					160		
9	1,464	330					160		

CHAPTER TEN

Noncompetitive Markets and Inefficiency

▪ Introduction

*A*ccording to neoclassical theory, competitive markets tend to produce consumer sovereignty, provide for the operation of the "invisible hand," and lead to economic efficiency. However, if markets are not competitive—that is, if they do not have all of the characteristics of competition—these results are less likely. In fact, in noncompetitive markets there is likely to be some amount of producer sovereignty, "monopoly" profits (i.e., economic profits not eliminated by competition), and inefficiency. In this chapter, we will define some other models of market structure and examine their results.

Models of Noncompetitive Market Structures

The competitive market model gives us a standard by which to judge *real* economic markets and other models of market structures. Chapter 9 defined a competitive market and examined its workings and results. In what follows, we will examine some other market structures. With these additional models, we will have a more complete theoretical system for understanding the behavior of firms in the economy and for evaluating their performance.

Before we examine monopoly, oligopoly, and monopolistic competition, we must emphasize that the competitive model is a *model* and that it roughly describes about 10 percent or so of the total private economic activity in the United States. The best examples of competitive markets are those for raw agricultural products—which are homogeneous, are not advertised, have large numbers of buyers and sellers, and can be entered by almost anyone. In the rest of the economy, there are firms and markets from which some or all of these characteristics are missing. The industry may include very few firms, and they may have the market power to control their prices. Products may be differentiated rather

THE BIG PICTURE

Imperfect Competition

Economists focus on four different market structures that characterize most firms and industries. In the last chapter, we studied perfect competition. In this chapter, we study the other three market structures: Monopoly, Oligopoly, and Monopolistic Competition. These market structures are all characterized as imperfectly competitive. Figure 10.BP.1 compares all four market structures according to the key characteristics that define them and highlights the key differences between them.

Monopolistically competitive markets are very competitive and easy to enter (and exit). Firms tend to be small, and because of the high degree of competition,

FIGURE 10.BP.1 Market Structures and Their Characteristics

Type of Market	Perfect Competition	Monopolistic Competition	Oligopoly	Monopoly
Ability to influence price	None	Some	Often	Always
Number of sellers	Many	Many	Few	One
Product differentiation	None	Some	None or Some	Unique product
Barriers to entry	None	Few	Substantial	Prohibitive
Can a firm earn long-run economic profit?	No	No	Yes	Yes
Do firms produce at minimum ATC?	Yes	No	No	No
Examples	Agriculture, baby-sitting, wooden pallets, concrete	Retail trade such as gasoline stations, restaurants, haircutting establishments	Steel, Automobiles, soft drinks, cereal, potato chips, gum	Campus bookstore, local utiliy company, Microsoft Windows (almost)

firms have limited control over their prices. Monopolistically Competitive markets also differ from Perfectly Competitive markets because each monopolistically competitive firm produces products that are slightly different from those produced by their competitors. For example, restaurants compete with each other for diners, but each restaurant has a unique cuisine and location. Product differentiation gives firms an incentive to advertise to attract consumers based on quality differences and to differentiate their product further by brand identification.

Oligopolistic markets differ from markets that are Perfectly Competitive or Monopolistically Competitive because of substantial barriers to entry. For example, in order to enter the automobile manufacturing industry, a firm must have a huge amount of financial capital to invest, access to a vast array of cutting edge technology, a large sales network, and access to a large market of consumers. In such an industry, it is more efficient for a firm to be large, and it is extremely difficult for a new firm to enter the market. Oligopolistic industries tend to be dominated by a few large firms, and oligopolistic firms often advertise heavily to differentiate themselves from competitors.

Monopolies are markets controlled by only one firm. Barriers to entry prevent competitors from entering. Monopolists thus control an entire market, and they are usually able to raise prices and may resist pressures to innovate due to their market domination. For these reasons, governments usually choose to regulate monopolies to prevent abuses. We will begin our more detailed examination of noncompetitive markets by examining monopolies.

than homogeneous. Advertising occurs beyond the simple level of informing consumers about products. And entry into markets isn't always "free" or easy.

The existence and emergence of noncompetitive market structures should not be too surprising. As we demonstrated in Chapter 9, the long-run tendency of competition is to eliminate economic profits. One effective way for a firm to ensure long-run economic profits is to limit the effects of competition, which may involve the elimination of competition.

Monopoly

A **monopoly** market structure is one in which there is only one seller of a good or service. The firm is the entire industry. Some monopolies have developed because of the large initial investment required, and only one firm occupies the market. Some monopolies have been established and protected by governments. Many monopolies are legalized because of the confusion that competition would create. At the same time, their prices are usually regulated by public authority. The characteristics of monopoly markets include the following:

◆ There is one seller of a good or service in a particular market.
◆ The product is unique, and there are no close substitutes; buyers must buy the good or service from the monopolist.

- The monopoly has **market power,** meaning it can exercise control over the price of the good or service, since it supplies the total quantity. (In contrast, for the competitive firm, price is determined by the market; the competitor has no influence on the price of its product.)
- Monopolies usually exist because there are absolute **barriers to entry** into the market; no other firm can supply the product because of legal, technological, or geographical factors limiting provision of the good or service.
- The monopoly may or may not advertise.

Examples of legal monopolies are local gas, electric, telephone, cable, and water companies. Professional sports teams in the United States have regional monopolies. As a result of a contract with the National Science Foundation, Network Solutions, Inc., had a virtual monopoly on the business of assigning Internet addresses. F. M. Scherer, an industrial economist, has estimated that about 6 to 7 percent of private economic output originates in monopolies.

The theoretical results of monopoly markets are that producers tend to restrict output and charge higher prices than they could if there were competition in the market for that monopoly's product. As a result, monopoly markets are less beneficial to consumers, who would prefer to have more of the product at a lower price. Monopolies also interfere with efficient resource allocation. Monopoly power allows a firm to remain immune from competition and to retain monopoly profits. (For these reasons, most monopolies in the United States are regulated.) Monopoly, thus, is less desirable than competition.

Short-run Equilibrium for the Monopolist

We can demonstrate that monopolies generate an outcome less efficient than competitive markets using a theoretical model of a monopolist operating in the short run. The monopolist faces the entire demand curve for a product, since there are no competitors. Thus, to sell more, the monopolist must lower price. Or if the monopolist raises prices, less will be demanded. As a result, the monopolist's marginal revenue curve will be below the demand curve. Since price must be lowered to sell more, the marginal addition to revenue will always be below the price. This is demonstrated in Table 10.1 and illustrated in Figure 10.1.* This information shows the revenue situation for a typical monopoly firm, with a downward-sloping demand curve and a marginal revenue curve below it. If we assume that the monopoly buys its resources in competitive markets, its MC and AC curves will look like the ones we derived in Chapter 9.

With the cost and revenue data in Table 10.1, we can determine the monopoly firm's profit-maximizing level of output. The same profit maximization rule

---

*Note: In order to simplify the presentation of this material, we are assuming in this chapter that firms sell their product in whole units and that quantity sold is not divisible (i.e., firms cannot produce and sell one-half a unit; they must sell a whole unit). Technically, if the demand curve is a continuous function and output is divisible, then the demand curve and marginal revenue curve would intersect at a quantity of 0 (at the Y axis) instead of at a quantity of 1.

TABLE 10.1 Monopoly Revenue and Cost

Output (Q)	Price (P)	Total Revenue (TR = P × Q)	Marginal Revenue ($MR = \frac{\Delta TR}{\Delta Q}$)	Total Cost (TC)	Marginal Cost ($MC = \frac{\Delta TC}{\Delta Q}$)	Average Cost ($AC = \frac{TC}{Q}$)
0	—	$0	—	$5	—	—
1	$10	10	$10	9	$4	$9.00
2	8	16	6	10	1	5.00
3	6	18	2	12	2	4.00
4	4	16	−2	16	4	4.00
5	2	10	−6	25	9	5.00
6	0	0	−10	39	14	6.50

still holds true: The monopolist should produce as long as marginal revenue is greater than or equal to marginal cost, and the equilibrium level of output will always occur where marginal revenue equals marginal cost (MR = MC). In Table 10.1, the profit-maximizing (equilibrium) level of output occurs at a quantity of 3 where MR = MC = $2 and where MR is less than P. At a quantity of 3, P = $6 and AC = $4. This means the firm is earning an average economic profit of $2 per unit over 3 units of output, for a total economic profit of $6.

The same information can be plotted on a graph. Figure 10.2 shows the demand, marginal revenue, average cost, and marginal cost curves for the monopolist from Table 10.1. Notice that the equilibrium level of output occurs at a quantity of 3, where MR = MC. At a quantity of 3, on the demand curve, we get the price of $6. On the AC curve at a quantity of 3, we get an average cost of $4. The difference between price and average cost is the average economic profit

FIGURE 10.1 Monopoly Demand and Marginal Revenue

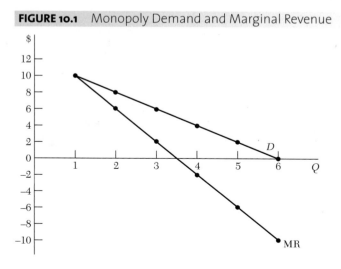

FIGURE 10.2 Monopoly Demand, Marginal Revenue, Average Cost, and Marginal Cost

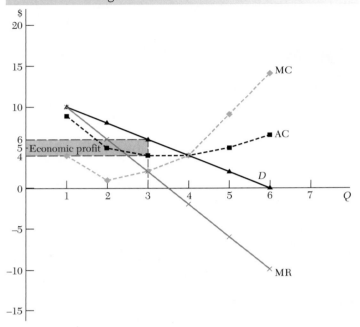

of $2. When we multiply this by the quantity of 3, we get total economic profits of $6, which is the area labeled "Economic profit" on the graph.

Figure 10.3 illustrates a typical equilibrium result for a monopoly firm. What level of output will the monopoly choose to produce? It will produce Q_m, where MC = MR, because that level of output maximizes its profits. It will charge a price of P_m for that amount of output, because that is the price consumers are

FIGURE 10.3 Equilibrium for the Monopoly Firm

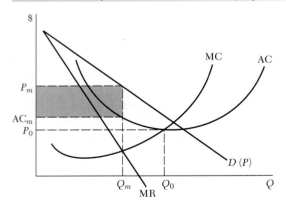

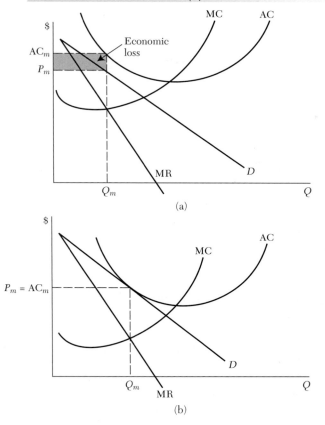

willing to pay for that quantity. The monopoly is earning economic profits equal to the shaded area in Figure 10.3, since P is well above AC. And the monopoly is producing at a rate of output that does not minimize average costs. (Q_0 is where AC is at a minimum, and P_0 is the minimum AC.)

This illustrates the short-run equilibrium for a monopoly. In this case, the monopolist earns economic profits. However, there is no assurance that even monopolies will always earn profits. If costs are too high or there is no demand for the monopolist's product, a monopoly could suffer economic losses. For example, there was no major-league baseball team in Washington, D.C., because in the past several teams had failed there.

Figure 10.4 shows the alternatives to earning economic profit. In Figure 10.4(a), the monopolist incurs an economic loss. The loss-minimizing level of output still occurs where MR = MC. But the price is less than average cost, so the firm is experiencing economic losses. If its profitability does not improve, this firm will eventually go out of business. Figure 10.4(b) shows a monopolist earning a normal profit. The profit-maximizing quantity is where MR = MC,

FIGURE 10.5 Long-Run Equilibrium for the Monopolist

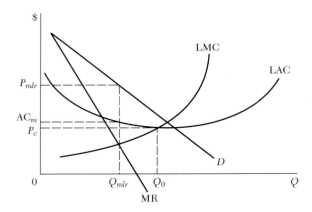

and at this quantity, price is equal to average cost ($P = $ AC). The price of the product is just covering all of the costs of production, including the opportunity costs, earning the firm a normal profit.

Long-run Equilibrium for the Monopolist

What happens in a monopoly in the long run? Figure 10.5 shows the long-run cost and revenue curves for a monopolist (assuming economies and diseconomies of scale). In the long run, the monopolist has the option of building different-sized plants, and over time the demand curve for the product could change. Given the cost and revenue curves in Figure 10.5, the monopolist produces at Q_{mlr}, the rate of output at which LMC = MR, and charges a price of P_{mlr} (from the demand curve). P is above AC, so the monopolist earns economic profits. The monopolist is in long-run equilibrium. But in a pure monopoly, even with economic profits, there is no entry into the market; this firm has a monopoly. Therefore, Figure 10.5 shows the long-run equilibrium result for a typical monopoly market. As long as cost and demand conditions remain the same, the monopoly firm produces Q_{mlr}. charges a price of P_{mlr}. and earns economic profits.

Monopoly and Inefficiency

What conclusions can we draw about the theoretical results of monopoly? Economic profits may exist, but because of the monopoly, no entry occurs to seek those extra returns above opportunity costs. The monopolist will not produce at a rate of output that minimizes average cost (Q_0); nothing forces the monopolist to produce at the most efficient rate of output. In monopoly, then, there tends to be **inefficiency in production** (at least from the perspective of the society, since output is not at minimum average cost). The monopoly firm pro-

FIGURE 10.6   Monopoly—Output Restriction and High Price

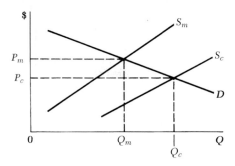

duces the rate of output that maximizes its profits—that is its goal. Moreover, at that rate of output, price exceeds marginal cost. Society values an additional unit of the good or service more than the cost to produce an additional unit. From a social perspective, then, it would be preferable if more resources were allocated to increased production of the commodity. Monopoly thus tends to result in **inefficiency in resource allocation** (since price does not equal marginal cost). Because monopolies usually get economic profits, some resources earn more than their opportunity cost. Finally, some monopolists may engage in advertising, which, although some may be informative or entertaining, requires the use of scarce resources. Consequently, we can see that the long-run equilibrium result of monopoly is significantly inferior to the long-run result of competition. The pursuit of profit, in this case, does not maximize social welfare.

We can also examine the theoretical results of monopoly by focusing on the market, shown in Figure 10.6. *If* there were competition in the market, new firms would enter, market supply would increase to S_c, and market price would decrease to P_c. (P_c in Figure 10.6 corresponds to P_c in Figure 10.5, the minimum long-run average cost.) Thus, monopoly restricts output, since $Q_m < Q_c$. And monopoly charges higher prices, since $P_m > P_c$. Finally, monopolies earn monopoly profits.

An important conclusion that can be drawn from the monopoly model is that the existence of market power (ability to control supply and price) tends to prevent consumer sovereignty, the attainment of economic efficiency, and the operation of the "invisible hand." The monopoly benefits at the expense of society. This says nothing at all about the further problem of the relationship of economic power to political power. Monopolies, through their economic power and resources, may come to wield undue political power. As a result, monopolies may also tend to disrupt democracy. In the words of Henry Simons, an economist who taught at the University of Chicago, "Political liberty can survive only within the effectively competitive economic system. Thus, the great enemy of democracy is monopoly." Any economic unit tending toward monopoly power, consequently, tends toward these same results.

As a result of these adverse effects of monopoly, the public sector has frequently been involved in regulating the operations and/or prices of monopolies. Many times, the public regulation is in return for governmental granting of a legal monopoly, as is the case with local water service. The usual goal of the public oversight is to increase monopoly output, lower monopoly prices, or reduce monopoly profits. In these cases, due to economies of scale, it is more efficient to have only one firm supply the product (the firm is called a *natural monopoly*). But the firm must be regulated to prevent it from charging too high a price and producing too low a quantity. (In Chapter 13, we will explore the regulation of monopoly in more detail.)

Occasionally the profit motive itself can limit the existence of a continuing monopoly. For example, a monopoly might produce a good or service for which a close substitute could be developed. Or the monopolist might have some technical advantage that can be duplicated. The very existence of monopoly profits gives other firms an incentive to try to "break" the monopoly. For example, Xerox developed the technique and the machinery for instant photocopying. Given the lucrative results from the monopoly on the technique, other firms developed substitutes and entered the market. Similarly, Apple once had a virtual monopoly on personal computers, but that was "broken" by IBM and numerous IBM-clone producers. The extent to which other firms challenge a monopoly may reduce the adverse theoretical consequences of monopoly.

1. What is so bad about monopolies? What can we do if they exist? What are some possible benefits of monopolies?
2. Analyze Henry Simons's comment above. Do you agree or disagree? Why?
3. Local phone companies often have a monopoly but advertise. Why?
4. In Figure 10.3, explain what would happen to the firm's profits if it produced at Q_0.
5. "Some resources [in monopoly] earn more than their opportunity costs." Can you think of any examples?

Disrupting Regulated Monopolies

An agreement with the National Science Foundation (NSF) originally granted Network Solutions, Inc., of Herndon, Virginia, a monopoly in assigning "domains," or addresses, for electronic mail and Web pages on the World Wide Web. The firm maintained a registry of addresses on the Internet, including those ending in .com for commercial enterprises, .edu for educational institutions, .gov for governmental entities, and .org for nonprofit organizations. Beginning in 1995, Network Solutions (later absorbed by VeriSign) was allowed to charge fees for registering and renewing addresses. The fees were regulated at first by the NSF, but Network Solutions earned substantial economic profits from

1996 to 1999. In 1999, the Department of Commerce and the Internet Corporation for Assigned Names and Numbers (ICANN) opened the market to other firms. Competition in the market for registering domain names caused the price of registering an address to drop from $9 to $6 within a year, and to $5 by 2004. In the process, Network Solutions' profits declined as well.

This example is part of a trend toward introducing competition to markets that were previously regulated monopolies. Long-distance phone service originating in the United States, for example, used to be a monopoly of AT&T, which owned all of the long-distance transmission lines for phone calls. Changes in technology—fiber optics and satellite transmission—have made it possible to open this market to more competition. Hence, consumers have many options for long-distance telephone service—witness the TV ads and the telephone soliciting campaigns. Do you think that the end of AT&T's monopoly has been good for consumers?

Several states, including Massachusetts, California, and Pennsylvania, are permitting similar experiments in the provision of electricity and natural gas. Traditionally, electric and gas utilities have been monopolies, usually regulated by state utility commissions. The state grants firms exclusive rights to sell electricity and gas, delivered by electric and gas distribution systems, and regulates their prices. The experiments involve letting consumers choose who their supplier will be from among several firms authorized by the state to supply electricity and gas. These firms all use the same distribution system, so there is no duplication of gas transmission pipes or electric lines all over the countryside, but they can offer different prices and services. In 2000–2001, an energy crisis in California caused rolling blackouts and soaring electric bills. Deregulation in California (as well as several other states) was accompanied by the manipulation of prices by a few large firms (including Enron) and an unstable supply of electricity, rather than low prices, substantial competition, and efficiency. While public utility deregulation was more successful in other states such as Pennsylvania, where prices for some customers fell slightly, it has yet to lower prices significantly even in states where deregulation has worked fairly well.

Monopolistic Competition and Oligopoly

The other two major models of market structure that economists have developed to approximate economic reality are monopolistic competition and oligopoly. Around 80 percent of private economic production comes from firms with monopolistic competition or oligopoly elements. In *Economics and the Public Purpose*, Harvard economist John Kenneth Galbraith estimates that about 50 percent of private production originates in industries that are competitive or monopolistically competitive, and the remainder comes from firms that are monopolies or oligopolies.

Monopolistic Competition

The model of **monopolistic competition,** developed in the 1930s by E. H. Chamberlin and Joan Robinson, is used to describe industries that are close to competitive but have some elements of monopoly. Monopolistic competition has the following major characteristics:

◆ There are large numbers of buyers and sellers in the market. The firms are all relatively small with respect to the total size of the industry.

◆ The products are *differentiated*, or distinguished from competitors' offerings by quality and design differences, advertising, and psychological appeal. The products are close substitutes for one another, but each firm tries to create a "monopoly" for its product. A strong stimulus for this behavior is the tendency toward the elimination of profits in competitive industries with homogeneous products.

◆ Firms have limited control over the prices of their products. Although the firms are small in relation to the market, they sell a differentiated product. Some consumers are loyal to the unique brands of individual firms, even though there are close substitutes. This "monopoly" element gives firms some control over prices.

◆ Entry into the market is relatively easy, although the costs of differentiation (e.g., for advertising) can be large. Since firms are small, relatively small initial investments make entry feasible.

◆ Unlike perfect competition, monopolistic competition has an abundance of advertising. The products are not homogeneous, and advertising exists to persuade consumers about the differences. (In 2004, U.S. businesses spent about $264 billion on advertising.)

Some examples of monopolistically competitive industries are retail sales in urban communities, fast-food establishments in any particular area, personal computer and printer stores, processed chicken for retail sales, and clothing.

6. Review the characteristics of monopolistic competition. Does the market for a college education in the United States demonstrate any of these characteristics? Why might this market move toward monopolistic competition?

Short-run Equilibrium.   To develop the model of what happens in this type of market structure, let's begin by examining the firm's output and pricing decision in the short run. The objective of a firm in monopolistic competition is the same as that of any other firm, so this decision will be a function of the firm's cost and revenue conditions.

Because the firm has some control over the price it charges for its differentiated product, it will face a downward-sloping demand curve. It can raise its price and not lose all of its sales, which is what would happen in perfect competition because consumers would just go to the firm's competitors if it raises its prices. In monopolistic competition, some consumers will remain loyal to the firm's product and continue to purchase it even though the price has gone up and there are close substitutes. Even so, when the firm raises its price, it will experience a decrease in its sales because there are substitutes. The firm can also lower its price and expect to get a significant increase in its sales because its loyal customers will consume more and because it may also attract business from its competitors (and because the demand for its product is elastic). In other words, the demand curve for a monopolistic competitor is downward sloping and relatively elastic. Because the demand curve is downward sloping, the firm's marginal revenue curve is also downward sloping and below the demand curve. Figure 10.7 shows typical demand and marginal revenue curves for a firm in monopolistic competition.

Since monopolistically competitive firms buy their resources in the same markets as do all other firms, their cost curves will be the same. The typical short-run average cost and marginal cost curves, reflecting the law of diminishing returns, are shown in Figure 10.8. Figure 10.8 gives us the information we need to describe the output and price decision of the monopolistic competitor in the short run. Given these cost and demand conditions, the firm produces at Q_{mc}, since that is the rate of output at which MC = MR. The firm will charge a price of P_{mc}, since the market will be willing to pay that price for the amount produced and offered for sale. The firm is earning economic profits because P_{mc} is greater than AC_{mc}. This is the firm's short-run equilibrium position.

Long-run Equilibrium.   What happens in the long run in a monopolistically competitive industry if a firm is earning economic profits? In Figure 10.9(a), with demand curve D_1, the firm is earning economic profits. It can charge a

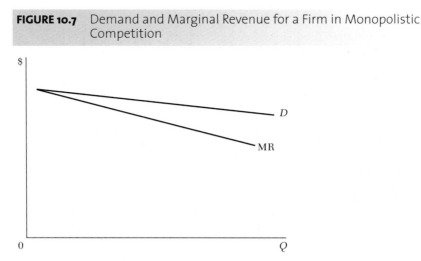

FIGURE 10.7   Demand and Marginal Revenue for a Firm in Monopolistic Competition

FIGURE 10.8 Short-run Equilibrium for a Firm in Monopolistic Competition

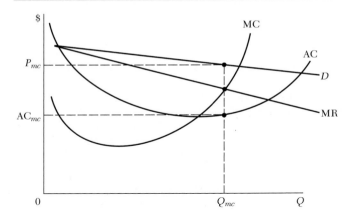

price greater than its average costs ($P > $ AC). In Figure 10.9(b), with demand curve D_1, the firm will produce quantity Q_1 where MR_1 is equal to long-run marginal cost (LMC). Since entry is relatively easy, other firms will enter the market in search of returns above opportunity costs. The entry of new firms means new competitors, and this will tend to reduce the sales of every firm already in the industry. This will have the effect of shifting every firm's individual demand curve to the left. After entry occurs, the demand curve in Figure 10.9(a) shifts from D_1 to D_2. In Figure 10.9(b), when the demand curve shifts from D_1 to D_2, the MR curve also shifts from MR_1 to MR_2 (when the price falls for each quantity, the marginal revenue for each quantity also falls). With a new MR curve, we have a new profit-maximizing equilibrium. The new equilibrium quantity is Q_2, which is directly below where MR_2 is equal to LMC. The firm now charges a lower price, P_2, because of the additional competition it faces.

Even after the demand curve has shifted from D_1 to D_2 however, the firm is still earning some economic profits (P_2 is still above the LAC curve). Since economic profits still exist, even more firms will enter, causing the demand curve in Figure 10.9(a) to shift from D_2 to D_3. Notice that D_3 is tangent to LAC. In Figure 10.9(c), with the new demand curve D_3, the firm produces Q_3, charges a price of P_3, and earns a normal profit ($P_3 = LAC_3$). Since the firm no longer earns economic profits, new firms will stop entering the market, and the market will be in equilibrium. *The firm* also is in equilibrium, earning zero economic profits.

Monopolistic Competition and Efficiency.   What are the implications of this long-run equilibrium result for monopolistic competition? $P = $ AC, so there are no economic profits. However, P does not equal minimum average cost (at Q_0). The long-run equilibrium in monopolistic competition therefore does not result in efficiency of production. In addition, P exceeds MC, which

FIGURE 10.9   Long-run Equilibrium in Monopolistic Competition

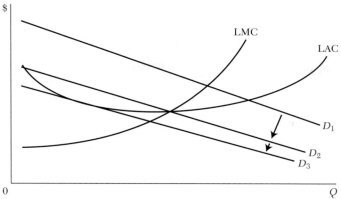

(a) Entry of firms causes demand to decrease.

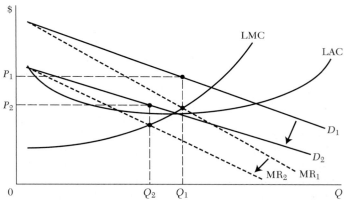

(b) Decrease in demand causes a decrease in the quantity produced and a decrease in price.

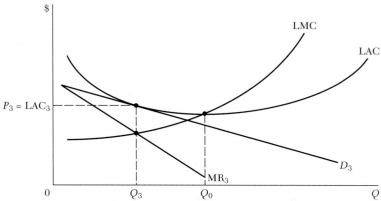

(c) Another decrease in demand causes another decrease in quantity and price until the firm reaches long-run equilibrium.

means that there is inefficiency in resource allocation. From the perspective of social welfare, monopolistic competition results in an underallocation of resources to the production of its goods and services. Since one of the primary characteristics of this market structure is product differentiation, resources also are used in the advertising and promotion of one product over another. From the perspective of the society's use of resources, this represents a waste. Compared with the model of competition, then, monopolistic competition falls short of maximizing social welfare.

On the other hand, the functioning of monopolistically competitive markets has some positive attributes. Relatively free entry by firms when economic profits exist promotes adaptability; resources are reallocated in response to market conditions. Entry also puts downward pressure on prices, as it does in competitive markets. Product differentiation contributes to one of the wonders of the U.S. economy—variety and choice. When efforts to differentiate products lead to quality improvements, consumers benefit, and firms must be sensitive to consumers' desires. There is also a possibility, however, that product differentiation may not lead to real improvements or that too much choice will only confuse consumers' informed decisions. Finally, in monopolistic competition, entry and limited competition do force firms to produce as efficiently as possible. If firms do not match the costs of other firms, they are in danger of being eliminated from the market by economic losses.

Given the tendency of monopolistic competition to eliminate economic profits in the long run, occasionally the firms in such an industry will engage in efforts to prevent the disappearance of long-run economic profits. A favorite tactic is to stay ahead of the effects of entry by continued differentiation and advertising. By improving the quality, design, or even advertising of a product, a firm may be able to continue earning economic profits in the long run. In addition, monopolistically competitive firms might be able to get legislative protection that controls the entry of firms into the industry. For example, beauty parlors and barber shops must have licenses from the state in order to operate. The licensing requirement restricts entry into the market, and it preserves some economic profits for existing firms.

7. In Figure 10.9(c), show and explain what would happen if the demand for the firm's product (and its close substitutes) decreased (e.g., from a change in consumers' tastes and preferences).

8. In Figure 10.9(c), show and explain what would happen if the costs of production decreased as a result of a technological breakthrough.

9. For the long-run equilibrium result of monopolistic competition, show the effect of an improvement in quality, design, or advertising on the part of one firm attempting to maintain long-run economic profits.

10. Why is the market for processed chicken sold in grocery stores an example of monopolistic competition?

Monopolistic Competition in Fast Foods

It used to offer hamburgers, french fries, milk shakes, and soft drinks—and that was it. Now you can get all of that plus breakfasts, chicken nuggets, salad bars, stuffed potatoes, and more—including occasional "new" products. The fast-food industry in the United States is a good example of a monopolistically competitive industry.

Although McDonald's, Burger King, and Wendy's account for about two-thirds of the national hamburger fast-food market, the market is broader than that. The fast-food market consists of hamburger, pizza, chicken, taco, sandwich, and other establishments. And, while McDonald's and other big players dominate the national markets for fast foods, area markets experience stiffer competition, with local and regional firms competing for customers' stomachs and dollars. Also, the fast-food firms must compete in the broader category of commercial dining, a $491 billion industry in 2007.

The market itself has expanded tremendously in the post–World War II period, with mobility and changing lifestyles. The late Ray Kroc took over two hamburger stands run by the McDonald brothers in 1955, and McDonald's hasn't stopped expanding since then. There are now more than 31,000 McDonald's establishments—less than half in the United States and the rest all over the world. Burger King has more than 11,000 outlets.

What characteristics of monopolistic competition are demonstrated by the fast-food industry? Regional markets have a large number of competitors, and entry is relatively easy. You don't have to rival the size or sophistication of McDonald's in order to start a hamburger or pizza joint. The rate of failure also is high, with thousands of restaurants going bankrupt every year. There is obvious and substantial product differentiation. Pizza is not chicken, and hamburgers are not salad. Some hamburgers are frozen, and some aren't. Some are fried, while others are grilled. French fries are notoriously nonstandardized. You can't get a hot dog everywhere. Pizza comes in many styles and qualities. The decors of different places distinguish them from one another. Quality is an issue among the various choices. And, recently, the fast-food industry has become concerned about its junk-food image. Some firms have begun to offer more nutritional and low-fat food

Lunch in a familiar setting.
(© Mary Kate Denny/PhotoEdit)

items. Finally, since McDonald's first started advertising in 1966, television advertising has become a necessary aspect of the competition for the national fast-food industry. The name of the game is diversification, differentiation, aggressive advertising and marketing, and broad appeal.

Oligopoly

An **oligopoly** is an industry dominated by a few large firms. They are not like small competitive firms, but they are also not monopolists. There is great variety in oligopolistic industries, so economists have developed a number of different models of oligopoly to describe their behavior and results. Oligopoly has the following major characteristics:

- A few firms produce most of the output in an industry. These firms are thus usually large with respect to the market, and dominate its activities. Examples include automobiles, computers, steel, aluminum, cigarettes, and chewing gum. In some cases, there may be fewer than ten firms in the entire industry. In others, there may be hundreds of companies, but four or five firms dominate.

- The product of an oligopoly may be homogeneous or differentiated. If it is a consumer good, it is usually differentiated to gain consumers' attention and loyalty (e.g., automobiles). And, if it is a raw material sold to other firms, it is usually homogeneous (e.g., steel, copper, or aluminum).

- There may be technological reasons for domination of an industry by a few firms. Large-scale operations may enjoy lower costs. Economies of scale may allow only a few firms to constitute the entire industry, given the size of the market. Firms may also have grown large due to mergers. As a result, entry into such markets is difficult. Because of the substantial initial investment, a firm must be large to enter.

- The firms in an oligopolistic industry are *interdependent*; their pricing and output decisions affect the other firms in the industry. Each firm must pay close attention to the actions of its rivals. This creates a constant possibility for **price wars** (progressive price cutting to increase sales) among oligopolists or collusion to avoid those price wars. It can also lead to price leadership or a reluctance to alter price. Despite this interdependence, oligopoly firms do have some control over their prices.

- Oligopolies usually have a significant amount of nonprice competition, such as product differentiation and advertising.

Because oligopoly firms are independent, it is difficult to develop one model of what happens in an oligopolistic industry. Depending on how rivals react to price and output decisions, a variety of models are possible, including price wars, collusion, stable prices, and price leadership. We will briefly develop some of these models.

FIGURE 10.10 Oligopoly Pricing and Output with Economies of Scale

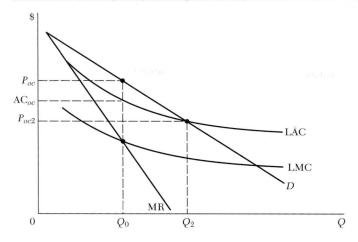

Figure 10.10 illustrates a general possibility for an oligopolist. Because the firm has some control over the price of its product, it has a downward-sloping demand curve and a marginal revenue curve that lies below it. Many oligopolies experience economies of scale. The long-run average cost curve in Figure 10.10 reflects economies of scale; the LAC curve declines over the entire market for this firm's product. The firm does not encounter diseconomies of scale, so there is no limit to the firm's expansion. Given these demand and cost conditions, the firm will pick Q_0 as the rate of output that maximizes its profits (since that is where LMC = MR). The price will come from the firm's demand curve, at P_{oc}. At this price-output combination, the firm earns economic profits, because P is above AC. Since entry is very difficult in oligopoly, these long-run profits are relatively secure.

Price Wars. In oligopoly, however, there is always a possibility of price cutting by rivals. Other firms might try to steal away customers by lowering their prices; this action could spark retaliation. Theoretically, firms could lower prices all the way down to P_{oc2} before encountering losses. As prices decreased, the oligopolists' profits would shrink.

Collusion. In response to a threat of price wars and the possibility of losing all of their economic profits, oligopolists might collude to avoid price competition among themselves. **Collusion,** or agreements to avoid competition and/or to set prices, is illegal in the United States. However, light bulb manufacturers, paperboard companies, and others have been found guilty of price fixing. And oligopolists might avoid price wars through indirect ways of setting prices, such as trade associations, industry meetings, governmental standardization of technical materials, or informal tacit agreements. Given the

FIGURE 10.11 A Cartel to Ensure Oligopoly Profits

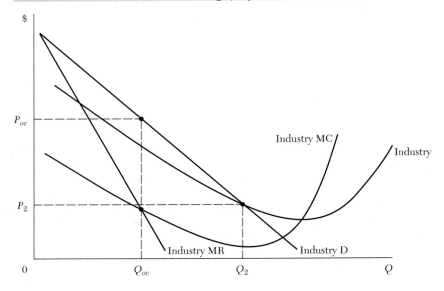

illustration in Figure 10.10, the firms could simply attempt to set prices as close to P_{oc} as possible. This would maximize their economic profits.

In some international markets, **cartels** are legal and may set prices for their products. A cartel is an organization of producers designed to limit or eliminate competition among its members. One example of a cartel is the Organization of Petroleum Exporting Countries. OPEC consists of eleven oil-producing countries that operate government-owned petroleum industries and sell oil in international markets. OPEC functions as a cartel that sets production quotas and prices for its members. The intention of the cartel is to control the world's supply of oil, avoid price wars among the members, and, consequently, maximize members' joint profits. The members of OPEC in the 1970s and early 1980s dominated the international oil market, and they used this position and their cooperation to control the international price of oil. Later, with the development of more non-OPEC oil sources (e.g., Mexico and Great Britain), OPEC's ability to maintain high prices diminished for a time. But as we have seen, oil prices increased again from 2000–2004 and in 2007, primarily because OPEC countries agreed to reduce production.

In essence, a cartel can accomplish a result similar to that of monopoly. For example, Figure 10.11 shows the combined cost and revenue conditions for a cartel as a whole. The cartel decides to produce a combined output of Q_{oc} and to charge a price of P_{oc}. As is the case in monopoly, output is restricted, and the price is higher than it would be if there were competition. Economic profits exist for the cartel as a whole. The members of the cartel then agree among themselves how to split up the production goal and profits based on their different cost functions, reserves, and negotiating skills. In a market without collusion, the price could fall as low as P_2 if firms were actively competing with each other.

Whether collusion is formal, as in a cartel, or informal, its members often have difficulty maintaining it, even though the reward for doing so is the avoidance of price wars and the accumulation of continued long-run economic profits. If the cartel consists of a large number of countries or firms, it has more difficulty reaching and maintaining agreement on production quotas and price levels. If the products of the cartel are differentiated (e.g., by quality of oil), the cartel has more difficulty establishing consistent price schedules for the varieties of the commodity. If the members of a cartel have different cost conditions in their productive operations, they will have more difficulty agreeing on price levels. Those with relatively high costs will want higher prices, or they will experience lower profits. In the same way, the size of the firm or country in the market will influence its bargaining power in the cartel—that is, different members will have different negotiating power when it comes to setting production quotas and prices. Additionally, an external force, e.g., the United States, might attempt to disrupt the unity among cartel members through its pursuit of foreign policy objectives.

The characteristic of cartels that most demonstrates their fragility is their tendency toward price breaks. Given the controlled price of the cartel, which will always be higher than the price that might prevail without the cartel, there is a temptation for an individual member to offer lower prices to attract its rivals' customers. If it can get away with secret price breaks, it can increase its sales and profits. The problem is that once one member does so, others are likely to do the same, and then the cartel is faced with a price war and reduced profits for all its members. The other difficulty with cartels in the United States is that they are illegal. For all these reasons, collusive behavior and its ultimate form—the cartel—are difficult to establish and maintain.

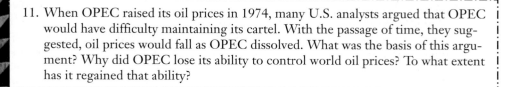

11. When OPEC raised its oil prices in 1974, many U.S. analysts argued that OPEC would have difficulty maintaining its cartel. With the passage of time, they suggested, oil prices would fall as OPEC dissolved. What was the basis of this argument? Why did OPEC lose its ability to control world oil prices? To what extent has it regained that ability?

Game Theory

Economists call the study of the strategic behavior of competing, interdependent firms (e.g., oligopolies) game theory. To illustrate, let's construct a model of the behavior of OPEC countries just discussed. First, we will simplify our analysis so that we consider the actions of only two countries, Saudi Arabia and Kuwait, and two strategies, cutting oil production or increasing oil production. Assume for now that Saudi Arabia and Kuwait

FIGURE 10.12   Sample Payoff Matrix

		Kuwait's Strategies	
		Cut Production	**Increase Production**
Saudi Arabia's Strategies	**Cut Production**	Kuwait earns $200 billion. Saudi Arabia earns $200 billion.	Kuwait earns $300 billion. Saudi Arabia earns $50 billion.
	Increase Production	Kuwait earns $50 billion. Saudi Arabia earns $300 billion.	Kuwait earns $100 billion. Saudi Arabia earns $100 billion.

produce all of the oil output of OPEC. If Saudi Arabia and Kuwait collude and cut production (remember, collusion is the primary purpose of forming a cartel), the world price of oil will increase dramatically, and both countries will make substantial economic profits on their oil, say, $200 billion each.

But suppose Kuwait needs extra oil revenues in order to finance a war with Iraq (exactly what happened in the 1990s). To gain additional oil revenues, Kuwait will have to increase production beyond the amount it agreed to produce. In other words Kuwait will have to renege on its agreement with Saudi Arabia. If Kuwait reneges on the agreement with Saudi Arabia, it can sell more oil at a slightly lower price and reap tremendous benefits. Countries all over the world will want to purchase Kuwaiti oil because it is virtually identical to Saudi oil but costs less. As a result, Kuwait will substantially increase its economic profits from $200 billion to $300 billion. Meanwhile, with Kuwait cutting prices, Saudi Arabia's oil will be more expensive, and few customers will buy Saudi oil. Saudi Arabia's economic profits from oil production therefore decline from $200 billion to $50 billion.

Will Saudi Arabia allow this situation to continue? Of course not. As soon as Saudi Arabia finds out that Kuwait is reneging on the OPEC agreement, it too will increase output and lower price. So both countries end up

producing a greater quantity of oil at a lower price, which lowers the economic profits for both countries. (With an inelastic demand for oil, the price falls more than the quantity sold increases.) Both countries end up earning economic profits of $100 billion after the increase in production.

The same thing would happen if Saudi Arabia reneged on the agreement and produced more oil instead of Kuwait. In the short term, Saudi Arabia would earn $300 billion after reneging, and Kuwait would earn only $50 billion in economic profits. But in the long term, Kuwait would also increase production and lower prices. Again we end up with both countries earning $100 billion.

We can illustrate this example with the payoff matrix in Figure 10.12. The payoff matrix demonstrates that, if both countries cut production, they both earn $200 billion in profits, which is the largest amount of combined profits possible of any of the four possibilities. If either country reneges on the agreement to cut production, then the country that increases production will earn more economic profits while the other country earns less. But if both countries ultimately end up increasing production, they both end up earning less than they would have if they maintained their collusive agreement and kept production levels low.

How do Saudi Arabia, Kuwait, and other OPEC countries behave in the real world? As we have seen, in the 1970s, they stuck to their production cuts and made vast economic profits. In the 1980s, countries reneged on production agreements, and new competitors entered the oil market, causing oil prices to plummet. But from 1999 to 2007, OPEC again agreed to keep production levels low, and oil prices increased. Maintaining a collusive agreement is difficult, especially where the number of competitors is large. The fewer the competitors, the easier collusion is, but even then, collusion can be unstable.

Price Stability.   Another tactic that oligopolistic industries use to avoid price wars involves simply keeping prices stable. If all of the firms in the industry maintain their prices over some period of time, they will avoid the tendency of interdependent firms to engage in self-destructive price competition.

Price Leadership.   When oligopolists do change their prices occasionally, they may use one other tactic they have developed to avoid price wars. It is called **price leadership**—the practice of a single firm in an industry announcing a price change, which most if not all of the other firms follow. In some industries, the same firm is consistently the leader. In other industries, the leader may change; it may be one of the giants in the field, or it could be one of the smaller firms. The leader of changes in the prime rate, the rate that banks charge their best borrowers, is not always one of the big New York City banks. In addition to this form of price leadership, uniformity in prices that avoids the danger of price wars can also be achieved through the sharing of information in informal contacts (at lunch, golfing, etc.) among the members of firms in an industry or through more formal meetings in conferences and trade associations. The primary goal is the same, though: the protection of oligopoly profits.

Outcomes of Oligopoly.   What are the theoretical results of oligopoly? There is no one model of oligopoly, as we have seen. But, in general, difficulty in entering the market protects oligopolies from the results of competition. Oligopolies have market power over their output and prices, they tend to earn oligopoly profits, and they are somewhat insulated from the dictates of market forces. The force of competition does not require them to produce at the most efficient rate of output. And because they, like other noncompetitive firms, face a downward-sloping demand curve, P will always exceed MC; consequently, oligopolies result in inefficiency in resource allocation. Oligopolies that sell differentiated products also engage in advertising and use scarce resources to convince consumers that their products are better than those of their rivals. Because oligopolies do not face the competition of new entrants into their markets and have market power, some critics suggest that such firms can resist technological change. For example, it might be possible for an automobile company to introduce production and product improvements that would benefit consumers, but because the firm has money tied up in current production techniques and product lines, it puts off introducing changes.

Large oligopolistic firms have enormous resources at their command. They have economic power over plant location, the pace of investment spending in the economy, and the advance of technology. This concentrated economic power can also be translated into concentrated political power, which can pose some difficulties for the operation of democratic institutions.

On the other hand, the defenders of oligopoly and large firms have argued that the pursuit of profit by such firms has spurred technological advancement and economies of scale in many oligopolistic industries. The history of some of the dominant heavy industries in the United States offers proof that economic concentration has accompanied increased output and efficiency. The steel and automobile industries pioneered large factories and the assembly line. The aircraft industry stimulated other industries and transportation in the post–World War II period. More recently, photocopying and computers have revolutionized information processing. With their economic profits, large firms can also afford to establish research and development labs to discover new processes and products. Finally, the persistence of large corporations may lend a certain stability to the operation of the entire economy. Without the rapid entry and exit of competitive markets, oligopolists can plan for the long run and serve the society.

12. Can you think of examples of firms in oligopolistic industries that have not been very sensitive to the wishes of U.S. consumers in recent years? Do you think the increase of global competition, even among very large firms, minimizes the market power of oligopolies (i.e., forces them to be more attentive to change and the preferences of consumers)?

13. Do you think large corporations tend to provide a certain dynamism to the economy, or do you think they obstruct progress?

Movie Rental Oligopoly

At the local level, most communities have a host of movie rental stores, with a good bit of competition among them in terms of inventory, pricing, membership fees, parking convenience, etc. However, the national market has one clear, emerging giant, Blockbuster. Will Blockbuster, with its vast supply of recent titles, global distribution system, and healthy complement of older movies, drive out the smaller, local video stores? Will local firms be able to find their own niche in the market and discover methods of staying in business? Or will TV cable companies saturate the public's demand for movies with direct provision of numerous movie channels, as well as access to video libraries? Will consumers increasingly rent movies through the mail or download them over the Internet? What difference will these trends make for consumers?

The Importance of Noncompetitive Markets in the U.S. Economy

The models of noncompetitive market structures are helpful in building a theory of how the U.S. economy operates, because product differentiation and economic concentration are present throughout the real economy. The following data on economic concentration demonstrate the pervasiveness and importance of concentrated markets in the United States.

For the last century, about a third of U.S. manufacturing industries have been dominated by oligopolies, while most of the rest are classified as monopolistic competition. Tables 10.2 and 10.3 show the concentration ratios in various U.S. manufacturing industries. The **concentration ratio** is the percentage of total sales in an industry that is accounted for by a specific number of firms. Usually, if the ratio is above 50 percent for the four largest firms in an industry, we say that the industry is an oligopoly. By this standard, all the industries in Table 10.2 are oligopolistic. If one firm had 100 percent of a national market, it would be a monopoly. If the eight largest firms had less than 10 percent of industry sales and there were many other firms in the industry, we would say that the market was close to being competitive. Table 10.3 lists some markets with relatively low concentration ratios; these have some of the characteristics of

TABLE 10.2   Share of Value of Shipments Accounted for by the Largest Companies in Selected High-concentration Manufacturing Industries, 2002

Industry	Four Largest Firms	Eight Largest Firms	Twenty Largest Firms	Total Number of Firms
Cane sugar refining	99%	100%	100%	13
Cigarettes	95	99	100	15
Household laundry equipment	93	100	100	13
Breweries	91	94	96	349
Aircraft	81	94	98	184
Men's and boys' trousers, slacks, and jeans	80	87	94	92
Breakfast cereal	78	91	99	45
Tires	77	93	98	112
Automobiles	76	94	99	164
Computers (electronic)	76	89	95	465
Pens and mechanical pencils	74	81	92	87
Cookies and crackers	67	79	91	296
Women's handbags and purses	67	86	93	99
Dry pasta (spaghetti, etc.)	65	80	88	185
Dog and cat food	64	81	93	176
Creamery butter	58	80	99	33
Semiconductors and related devices	57	64	78	904
Explosives	54	78	93	57
Coffee and tea	51	63	82	258

Source: U.S. Census Bureau, 2002 Economic Census.

TABLE 10.3 Share of Value of Shipments Accounted for by the Largest Companies in Selected Low-concentration Manufacturing Industries, 2002

Industry	Four Largest Firms	Eight Largest Firms	Twenty Largest Firms	Total Number of Firms
Ice cream and frozen desserts	48	64	82	364
Audio and video equipment	43	59	78	544
Milk (fluid)	43	54	69	315
Bread and bakery products	39	50	60	9,515
Men's and boys' shirts (except work shirts)	38	53	73	180
Cheese	35	50	73	366
Sporting and athletic goods	23	32	46	2,157
Women's and girls' dresses	22	32	49	525
Jewelry (except costume)	22	31	45	1,923
Women's and girls' blouses and shirts	21	33	57	352
Furniture and related products	11	18	29	21,523
Ready-mix concrete	11	17	28	2,614
Wood containers and pallets	7	10	17	2,792
Signs	5	9	16	6,125

Source: U.S. Census Bureau, 2002 Economic Census.

monopolistic competition. The only manufacturing industries that approach the characteristics of perfect competition in Table 10.3 are signs and wood containers and pallets. In these industries, the product is virtually homogeneous, there are many competitors, and there is easy entry. These two tables demonstrate the importance of concentration in the U.S. economy. Most of the leading sectors of the U.S. economy are heavily concentrated—hence the relevance of models of noncompetitive market structures.

Table 10.4 shows measures of economic concentration in nonmanufacturing industries, including retail trade, information, finance and insurance, health care and social assistance, and accommodation and food services. As you study this table, notice the wide variations in concentration ratios. Some industries are concentrated, while others are not. For example, warehouse clubs and supercenters are heavily concentrated, while the market for florists approaches perfect competition; credit-card issuing is an oligopolistic market, while commercial banking is closer to monopolistic competition; hospitals are oligopolies, while doctors' offices are competitive; and coffee shops are somewhat concentrated, while bars and restaurants are not. We have already explored some of the conditions (such as costs of entry) that may influence the degree of concentration. In the next section, we will consider additional factors.

14. Examine Tables 10.2, 10.3, and 10.4. Are you surprised by the high or low concentration ratios of any industries in these tables? Do the industries exhibit the characteristics of monopolistic competition and/or oligopoly? Explain.

TABLE 10.4 Concentration Ratios for Selected Nonmanufacturing Industries

	Four Largest Firms	Eight Largest Firms	Twenty Largest Firms
Retail Trade			
Warehouse clubs and supercenters	92.1%	99.7%	100.0%
Athletic footwear stores	70.8	79.3	84.6
Department stores	66.4	88.8	99.4
Supermarkets and grocery stores	32.5	45.6	57.3
Clothing stores	28.0	37.8	52.0
Convenience stores	15.5	18.4	21.6
Gasoline stations	8.2	14.7	25.2
Florists	1.7	2.4	3.9
Information			
Cable programming	63.9%	77.7%	91.9%
Cellular and wireless telecommunications	63.4	83.9	91.9
News syndicates	57.7	70.0	83.7
Television broadcasting	50.2	60.9	76.0
Finance and Insurance			
Credit-card issuing	75.8%	87.0%	96.6%
Investment banking and securities dealing	41.3	66.6	83.4
Commercial banking	29.5	41.9	56.3
Insurance agencies and brokerages	9.9	13.4	18.2
Health Care and Social Assistance			
HMO medical centers	90.5%	97.8%	100.0%
General medical and surgical hospitals	71.8	83.7	92.2
Offices of physicians	3.4	4.3	6.2
Child day-care services	2.5	4.4	8.8
Accommodation and Food Services			
Coffee shops	–	66.2%	68.5%
Full-service restaurants	8.6	11.0	15.5
Drinking places (alcoholic beverages)	2.2	2.9	4.2

Source: U.S. Census Bureau, 2002 Economic Census.

15. Can you offer explanations for why some of the industries in Table 10.2 (and 10.4) are oligopolies, and why some of the industries in Table 10.3 (and 10.4) are less concentrated?

Sources of Concentration in the Economy

Several factors have contributed to increasing concentration and centralization in the economy over the last century. First, legislation and government policy have promoted both competition and monopoly. Governments have granted legal monopolies. In addition, the government has provided support and assistance to several industries with a high degree of concentration—for example, railroads, airlines, defense, and automobiles. On the other hand, antitrust legislation and some regulatory legislation are designed to promote competition. The goal is to control the adverse results of market power by splitting up companies, preventing mergers, prosecuting price setting and other noncompetitive activities, and regulating monopolies. These laws are based on economic arguments; our theory has demonstrated that competitive markets tend to produce efficiency and consumer sovereignty, and that noncompetitive markets, with market power and economic concentration, do not operate as well. One could argue over how well the antitrust laws have been enforced and whether they have prevented the accumulation of economic power by many industries and large firms.

16. Articulate why the government ought to promote competition and prevent extreme economic concentration and market power.

Business policies and practices, including trusts, pools, holding companies, and mergers, also have tended to create monopolies and oligopolies. If competition tends to eliminate economic profits, then one way to ensure long-run profits is to eliminate competition. Many firms have amassed substantial economic power in their markets and in the economy at large. The elimination of cutthroat competition through bankruptcy, mergers, and so on has decreased the number of competitors in many industries. The auto industry comprised more than 100 companies in the late 1920s. Several merger waves in U.S. economic history have produced increased economic concentration. Corporate America experienced a wave of "unfriendly" mergers in the 1980s, in which a company was merged with another against its will. The merger continues to be a strategy of firms to increase market share and economic power.

Technology has developed in some industries to the extent that large-scale operations are necessary for efficiency. This trend promotes large firms and oligopoly. Technology allows some firms to take advantage of economies of scale and outpace their competitors, which then fall by the wayside. An argument in favor of oligopoly, in fact, is that a firm in this market can use some of its oligopoly profits to finance research to further advance technology (and presumably its own oligopoly power!).

Capitalism's economic freedom of enterprise is permissive of the growth of private corporations. With a motive of profit making and a laissez-faire attitude by government, the creation of economic power has been tolerated (and even lauded by some) in U.S. economic history.

 ## Conclusion

Whatever the reasons for noncompetitive markets, we can still conclude that they are theoretically inferior to competitive markets in terms of consumers' and society's preferences. Resources are allocated throughout the noncompetitive sectors of the U.S. economy, but noncompetitive markets and prices do not produce the ideals of the "invisible hand," consumer sovereignty, and efficiency, as do competitive markets (theoretically). (Adam Smith, where are you, and what would you think?)

In the next chapter, we will shift our attention to the operation of resource markets and examine the factors that influence resource prices. One important result of resource markets is that they determine the incomes of resource owners. We will also take a look at the distribution of income in the United States.

Review Questions

1. What are the theoretically adverse results of monopoly markets?

2. What benefits might be derived from oligopoly to offset its inefficiencies and higher prices? Can you give some examples?

3. Why do you think the automobile industry is not competitive, according to our model of competition? What evidence can you cite to show its noncompetitiveness and inefficiency?

4. Why is local water service usually a monopoly? What would happen if it weren't?

5. What would happen to the marijuana "industry" if it were legalized in the United States? What kind of market is it now?

6. If you were the adviser for an OPEC country that had relatively low levels of petroleum reserves, would you advise the setting of high or low prices? Why? What if you were advising a country with extensive reserves?

7. In 2006, the movie *Cars* premiered. It was accompanied by a new line of toys. What kind of market is this? Can you think of other examples of this kind of phenomenon?

8. In each of the cases below, match the industry with the market structure (Perfect Competition, Monopoly, Monopolistic Competition, and Oligopoly) that best fits the industry's characteristics. Explain your answer.

   1. Textbooks for your courses that are not available online
   2. Informal baby-sitting services provided by teenagers
   3. Personal computer manufacturing
   4. Legal services (Lawyers)

9. The table on page 218 shows cost and revenue data for a Monopoly. Complete the table. Determine the profit maximizing level of output, and compute economic profit or loss at this level of output.

10. Draw a graph of a Monopolistically Competitive firm earning an economic profit. Include demand, marginal revenue, average total cost, and marginal cost on your graph, and show the profit maximizing price and quantity. Assuming that the cost curves are long-run cost curves, show what will happen to the firm in the long run. Explain carefully.

11. Explain why oligopolists have an incentive to collude or form a cartel. Also, explain why oligopolists in a collusive arrangement might have an incentive to renege on such an agreement.

Q	P	TR	MR	TC	MC
0	56			80	
1	54			100	
2	52			112	
3	50			120	
4	48			126	
5	46			134	
6	44			146	
7	42			164	
8	40			190	
9	38			226	
10	36			274	

CHAPTER ELEVEN

Resource Markets and the Distribution of Income

▣ Introduction

*I*n the last two chapters, we developed models of competitive and noncompetitive markets for produced goods and services. As we mentioned previously, there are also markets for the resources used by firms in production. (It's a bit more complicated than that, since some firms produce raw materials used by other firms as factors of production.) The basic resources of the society are mental and/or physical labor; land and its raw materials, and capital.

Resource markets are important for two primary reasons. First of all, resource prices determine costs for firms. Second, since individuals own resources, the operation of resource markets forms the basis of the distribution of income in the society.

In this chapter, we will explore the operation and significance of resource markets—including the determination of resource prices and the allocation of resources throughout the economy. We will also examine the distribution of income in the United States and attempt to explain why it is relatively unequal.

THE BIG PICTURE

Resource Markets

Resource markets differ from markets for consumer goods in several key ways.

- First, the demand for resources comes from firms producing goods and services, and the supply of resources comes from households. This is different from consumer goods markets where the demand for consumer goods comes from households and the supply of consumer goods comes from firms. In resource markets, consumers supply labor, land or capital, and firms purchase these resources.

- Second, the demand for resources is an indirect or *derived* demand: Firms demand resources only because there is a demand for their goods and services. Thus, changes in the demand for a product also cause changes in the demand for the resources used to produce that product.

- Third, the demand for a resource is affected by the productivity of that resource. If a resource becomes more productive, then it produces more value for the firm, and the firm will want more of it (assuming the firm can sell more units of output).

Briefly, let's explore some of the implications of the characteristics of resource markets, by focusing on the market for labor, a key resource for all firms.

- First, households supply labor and firms demand labor. When laborers decide to work more hours to buy more goods, this increases the supply of labor and puts downward pressure on the price of labor (the wage rate). When firms replace laborers with robots, this reduces the demand for labor and puts downward pressure on wages.

- Second, the demand for labor is tied to the demand for the firm's products. For example, when the automobile market is booming, automobile manufactures hire (demand) more laborers, putting upward pressure on the wages of workers who build automobiles. When the demand for automobiles declines, the opposite occurs: The demand for automobile workers declines and there is downward pressure on wages.

- Third, the demand for labor is directly affected by the productivity of labor. If laborers become more productive (due to better technology, or more skills and education), they increase the firm's output and lower the firm's average variable costs of production. Firms usually respond to such events by increasing the demand for labor because of the increased revenue from the additional productivity, which then causes upward pressure on wages.

Thus, in resource markets, the supply of a resource from households, the demand for the firm's products, and the productivity of the resource are major factors in determining the price of the resource and the quantity of the resource purchased in markets. We explore resource markets in more detail below.

The Economics of Resource Markets

There are markets for all resources because they are productive; they are used to produce goods and services sold in markets. The demand for resources is thus a **derived demand,** meaning these resources are demanded for the production of the final product.

In the following discussion, for the sake of simplicity, we will concentrate on one resource to illustrate the general operation of resource markets. While we could develop models of the markets for raw materials, land, and capital, we will present a model of the market for unskilled labor as an example. It is one of the broadest of labor markets. The number of people who could work in a McDonald's restaurant or do unskilled work in a factory is about equal to the size of the labor force in the United States—now more than 142 million people. And there are many businesses that hire unskilled workers.

Like all markets, this one has a demand side and a supply side. Figure 11.1 illustrates the market for unskilled labor. On the supply side of the market, there is a positive relationship between wages offered and the amount of unskilled labor supplied by workers. The higher the wage, the greater the amount of labor supplied. On the demand side, there is an inverse relationship between wages and the amount of unskilled labor demanded by employers. The higher the wage, the lower the amount of unskilled labor that employers will want to use.

This market, with large numbers of suppliers and demanders, will determine an equilibrium wage (W_e) and quantity (Q_e) for unskilled workers. That wage influences a firm's potential costs and its decisions about how much of this resource to use (compared with other resources). The wage also determines the decisions that workers make about offering their labor to employers (or not) and influences their incomes.

In a general way, this model applies to other resource markets. To see how resource markets work, let's explore both sides of this market in a little more depth.

FIGURE 11.1 The Market for Unskilled Labor

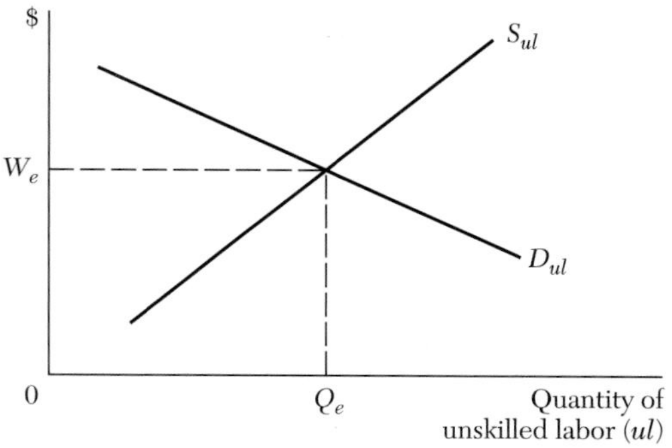

Demand for a Resource

The demand for any resource is derived from consumers' demands for goods and services and from producers' "demands" for profitable enterprise. But we can be much more specific about the nature of the firm's demand for a resource.

Remember, the firm's objective is to maximize profits, the difference between total revenues and total costs. Whenever a firm uses a resource, the firm's costs and revenues are both affected. If a firm uses one unit of a resource, how much will its costs increase? If a McDonald's restaurant hires one more unskilled worker to be a cook, its costs will go up by the worker's wage times the number of hours worked. The firm's costs increase by the price of the resource, and that price is determined in a market. The added cost of the resource, or its **marginal factor cost** (MFC), equals its price:

$$MFC = \text{price of one additional unit of the resource.}$$

In this case, we find the marginal factor cost of unskilled labor:

$$MFC_{ul} = P_{ul}$$

where P_{ul} is the price or wage of unskilled labor. Since the market is competitive (i.e., there are many laborers competing for jobs), the firm will be able to use as much unskilled labor as it wants at that price.

The second effect of using more of a resource is that it adds to the firm's revenues if demand is elastic. Why? Because using more resources adds to the firm's output, and that output presumably gets sold in a product market. In fact, the addition to the firm's revenues, which we will call the **marginal revenue product** (MRP) of unskilled labor, equals the **marginal physical product** of unskilled labor (MPP_{ul}) times the marginal revenue of the product (MR_x):

$$MRP_{ul} = MPP_{ul} \times MR_x$$

The marginal physical product is the extra output from adding one more unit of a variable resource. For unskilled labor, MPP_{ul} is the additional output from adding one additional worker to the production process (with other factors held constant). Table 11.1 shows the marginal physical product in terms of the

TABLE 11.1 Marginal Physical Product and Marginal Revenue Product of Unskilled Labor

Number of Workers	Total Output of Big Macs	Marginal Physical Product of Unskilled Labor	Price of Big Macs	Marginal Revenue Product of Unskilled Labor
1	20	–	$2	–
2	27	7	2	$14
3	34	7	2	14
4	40	6	2	12
5	45	5	2	10
6	49	4	2	8
7	51	2	2	4

FIGURE 11.2   The Firm's Use of a Resource

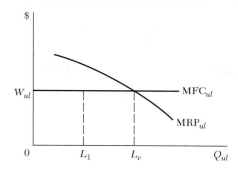

number of Big Macs produced in one hour as McDonald's hires additional cooks. For example, the MPP of the sixth worker is three Big Macs. Notice that the output from this variable resource follows the law of diminishing returns.

What happens to the extra output in the example? It will be sold for the market price of Big Macs. If we assume, for ease of analysis, that McDonald's is in a competitive market, then the marginal revenue of a Big Mac equals the price of a Big Mac (that is, they are both constant). For this example, we will assume that the price of a Big Mac is $2. The firm's additional revenue from hiring one more unit of unskilled labor—the marginal revenue product of unskilled labor, MRP_{ul}—comes from the extra output produced and then sold. In Table 11.1, MRP_{ul} is found by multiplying the marginal physical product of unskilled labor by the price (marginal revenue) of a Big Mac.

Given that using more of the resource has a marginal effect on the firm's costs and revenues, it should not surprise you that a firm maximizes its profits by choosing the amount of a resource for which the marginal contribution to the firm's revenues equals the marginal contribution to the firm's costs:

$$MFC_{ul} = MRP_{ul}.$$

This is illustrated in Figure 11.2. Since MPP_{ul} is decreasing because of the law of diminishing returns and MR_x is constant if the firm sells its product in a competitive market, MRP_{ul} decreases as we add more unskilled labor (along the horizontal axis). MFC_{ul} is equal to the prevailing wage in the market for unskilled labor.

To maximize profits, this firm would use L_e of unskilled labor, since that is where $MFC_{ul} = MRP_{ul}$. If the firm uses less unskilled labor, the firm's revenues from using one more worker exceed the extra cost of using an additional unit (e.g., at L_1). Therefore, expanding the use of the resource would add to the firm's profits. At levels above L_e, the cost of adding the resource exceeds what it adds to the firm's revenues. If the firm uses unskilled labor beyond L_e, the firm's profits will decrease. (Notice that we are assuming the demand for the product is constant; this is reflected in the marginal revenue the firm receives for selling additional units of output.)

1. Assume that the current wage for unskilled workers is $8 an hour and that the price of a Big Mac is $2. Given the information in Table 11.1, how many workers would McDonald's hire? Why?

Profit maximization leads a firm to choose a specific amount of a resource to use in its productive activities. In addition, the marginal revenue product curve in Figure 11.2 represents the firm's demand curve for this resource. Remember, a demand curve shows the amounts of a good or service that will be demanded at different possible prices. If the price of unskilled labor were lower, with everything else the same, the firm would hire additional workers; if the price were higher, the firm would hire fewer workers. The MRP_{ul} curve, then, gives us the firm's demand for unskilled labor.

The firm's demand for a resource is thus determined by the productivity of the resource, the importance of that resource in producing the good, and the price of the good itself.

2. Using Figure 11.2, explain why a firm would hire fewer workers if the price of the resource were higher.

3. Show what would happen to the demand for unskilled labor if there was an increase in the demand for Big Macs.

Supply of a Resource

As we pointed out earlier in this chapter, in general the amount supplied of a resource increases as its price increases. If the wage for unskilled work increased, for example, we would expect the amount of unskilled labor offered to increase. From the workers' perspective, the wage for labor indicates the opportunity cost of time. An increase in a wage or a salary makes time more valuable and, in most cases, encourages people to work more. From the perspective of an employer, the wage indicates the opportunity cost for the resource; it is what the firm must pay to get that resource to work for it. In a similar manner, buildings and land earn rent, raw materials have prices, capital or money earns interest, and professional workers get salaries.

The sensitivity of a resource to the price offered for its productive services varies over time. That is, the elasticity of supply of a resource can differ in the short run and long run. In the short run, the amount of a resource supplied depends on the mobility of the resource to different possible uses. For example, for unskilled workers, raising the wage at McDonald's could lead to a significant increase in the number of people willing to work there. (Remember, a supply curve is a hypothetical construction; it shows the amounts supplied at different possible prices.) Many individuals are available to work for the relatively low wages in fast foods and would be attracted by a higher wage. This means that the supply of unskilled labor is relatively elastic. On the other hand, if wages increased for computer programmers, some time is necessary for the quantity of programmers supplied in the United States to increase, because of the training necessary. For computer programmers, then, the supply is somewhat inelastic in the short run. For buildings and machinery, supply is relatively inelastic in the short run because time is required to construct them or to free existing ones for other uses.

In the short run, the supply of a resource can be elastic or inelastic, depending on the type of resource. Price increases (or decreases) will produce large or small responses in the quantity supplied, depending on the nature and qualities of the resource.

In the long run, the supply of most resources is more elastic. The long-run supply of any resource depends on decisions about the development of resources, which are in turn determined by expected rates of return. People decide to go to college depending on the expected payoff from graduating. That decision consequently influences the supply of professional employees. Decisions about graduate, law, or medical school involve the same calculation, which eventually affects the supply of PhDs, lawyers, and doctors.

These factors determine the supply curves for resources. And, as we suggested at the beginning of this chapter, the supply-and-demand conditions for resources, taken together, produce resource prices. Markets for resources establish resource prices.

What other factors influence resource prices? Legislation may affect the wage paid to certain types of workers, as in the case of the minimum wage. Licensing requirements affect the supply of hair stylists, real estate agents, and many professional workers. Unions can control the supply of certain types of workers through apprenticeship programs, seniority systems, and membership dues. Cartels and trade associations can influence some resource prices. Finally, the general state of the economy and the level of unemployment profoundly affect wages and salaries. The higher the level of unemployment, in general, the lower the wages of unskilled and semiskilled workers.

4. Why would higher rates of unemployment put downward pressure on wages?

5. Wages in Alaska are relatively high. Why would the elasticity of supply for labor partially explain this?

The Economics of the Minimum Wage

Our assumption that the wage for unskilled labor is determined by the supply and demand for that resource (see Figure 11.1) is a slight oversimplification. In fact, whenever interstate commerce is involved, employers must pay workers at least the minimum wage. This wage is mandated by congressional legislation, and it has progressively increased throughout the post–World War II period. During the 1980s it was constant at $3.35 an hour. In 1990, it increased to $3.80, and in 1991 it increased to $4.20. By early 1996, the minimum wage had

TABLE 11.2   The Real Value of the Minimum Wage, 1950–2006

Year	Minimum Wage in Current Dollars	Price Level (2006 = 1.00)	Minimum Wage in 2006 Dollars
1950	$0.75	0.12	$6.27
1960	$1.00	0.15	$6.81
1968	$1.60	0.17	$9.27
1970	$1.60	0.19	$8.31
1980	$3.10	0.41	$7.58
1990	$3.80	0.65	$5.86
2000	$5.15	0.85	$6.03
2006	$5.15	1.00	$5.15

Source: Authors' calculations from Bureau of Labor Statistics data.

increased a nickel, to $4.25, and it increased to $5.15 in mid-1996. In early 2007 Congress passed legislation that increased the minimum wage to $7.25 over the following two years. (States may set their own minimum wage higher than this level.)

The fact that the minimum wage has increased seems to indicate that unskilled workers are earning more money today than they did in the past. However, when we consider the value of the minimum wage in real terms, or its actual purchasing power after inflation is taken into account, we see something quite different. The minimum wage in *real* terms is found by dividing the minimum wage rate in any year by the price level in that year. As Table 11.2 and Figure 11.3 show, in 1968 the minimum wage was only $1.60 per hour, but

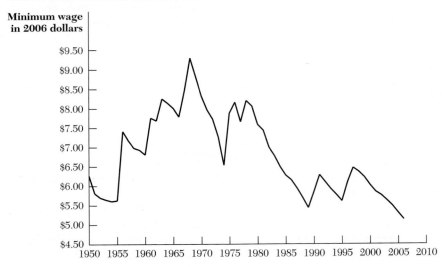

FIGURE 11.3   Minimum Wage in 2006 Dollars, 1950–2006

FIGURE 11.4 Effect of Minimum-
Wage Laws on
Unskilled-labor Market

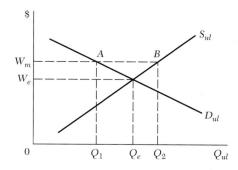

prices were also much lower in 1968 than they are today. In fact, $1.60 an hour in 1968 would buy as many goods as $9.27 an hour in 2006. From the data we can see that the minimum wage in real terms (2006 dollars) has fallen considerably from its peak of $9.27 an hour in 1968 to $5.15 an hour in 2006, a decline of almost 45 percent. At $5.15 an hour, a full-time worker would earn only $10,300 before taxes, which is well below the poverty line for a two-person family.

The intent of legislating a minimum wage is to require employers to pay a wage higher than the rate determined by the market for unskilled labor. It is meant to support the incomes of people who work in low-wage jobs, and it was motivated by a concern for fairness. The people who hold low-wage jobs usually have little experience or few skills. In other words, their marginal productivities are relatively low. Also, the products they produce may have low market values. Dishwashers get low wages; doctors, lawyers, and engineers earn much more. In addition, with any amount of unemployment, there is ample supply of unskilled workers.

These factors produce a market that can be illustrated with the supply and demand curves shown in Figure 11.4. The equilibrium wage would be at W_e, but legislation mandates a wage above that, at W_m.

What are the results of the minimum wage? At W_m, employers hire Q_1 of unskilled workers. But Q_2 workers are willing to work at W_m. Hence, there is a surplus of unskilled workers—unemployment of unskilled workers equal to AB. Those who have jobs have higher incomes than they would have at a wage of W_e. But Figure 11.4 shows that the minimum wage has increased unemployment among unskilled workers.

Some economists and politicians have argued that lowering the minimum wage would decrease unemployment. The Reagan administration several times suggested a lower minimum wage for teenage workers. Along with the increase in the minimum wage in 1990, Congress created a "training wage" for teenage workers for six months of initial employment. The basis of the argument lies in

Figure 11.4. If the wage were reduced to W_e, there would be an increase in the amount of unskilled labor demanded and a decrease in the amount of unskilled labor supplied. At Q_e, an equilibrium amount would be supplied and demanded—no unemployment in this market! Employers would tend to use more unskilled workers.

But several critical questions can be raised about this analysis. Seven of every ten workers earning a minimum wage are over twenty years of age. For households with a minimum-wage worker, these wages are a major source of income, representing on average 58 percent of the families' weekly income. Sixty percent of all women laborers work in minimum-wage jobs. Employers might replace older, higher-paid workers with younger, lower-paid workers, which would only shift the incidence of unemployment and would not necessarily reduce the overall amount of unemployment. And what about the difference between Q_2 and Q_e in terms of the amount of unskilled labor supplied? One effect of lowering the minimum wage would be that some teenagers would prefer to spend their summers doing something other than working for a "subminimum wage." Does that mean they are not unemployed?

In reality, raising the minimum wage usually does not create unemployment. To some extent, it may seem to exacerbate unemployment because it could reduce the amount of unskilled labor demanded and increase the amount supplied. But the reasons for unemployment among low-wage, inexperienced, and unskilled workers have more to do with the overall level of economic activity than with the minimum wage.

A number of recent studies indicate that moderate increases in the minimum wage have had *no effect* on the rate of unemployment. The implication is that firms already minimize the number of laborers they need to produce their good or service. Once the minimum wage is increased, firms must continue to hire the same number of unskilled workers in order to supply sufficient quantities to their customers. In other words, the demand curve for unskilled labor is extremely inelastic.

Increases in the minimum wage tend to result in greater worker productivity because workers are more satisfied with their jobs and less likely to change jobs (which reduces training costs and means that more experienced workers stay at their jobs). This offsets somewhat the increase in firms' costs associated with a higher minimum wage, although firms also might increase prices slightly due to higher wage costs.

Because the minimum wage in the late 1990s and early 2000s was very low (in terms of purchasing power) and moderate increases in the minimum wage have had no significant impact on unemployment levels, some economists and activists have called for a "living wage" to be paid to all employees. Paying a living wage would mean setting wages high enough that one full-time worker could support a family. The City of Baltimore passed the nation's first living-wage ordinance, increasing the minimum wage in Baltimore to $7.70 an hour by 1999, enough to support a single parent with one child above the poverty line. Since then, 140 cities and towns have enacted living wage laws, many establishing wage rates of more than $10 an hour. However, some economists oppose minimum-wage ordinances because, while small increases in the minimum wage may not affect employment significantly, large increases in the minimum wage could have a much greater effect on employment.

6. What are some arguments for increasing the minimum wage? What are some arguments against raising the minimum wage? Which arguments do you find most compelling?

7. Redraw the graph in Figure 11.4 with a steeper (more inelastic) demand curve and a steeper (more inelastic) supply curve. How do these changes in the graph affect the arguments for and against a minimum wage?

The Distribution of Income

In Chapter 4, we examined the division of income among the different factors of production in a private, market economy: Labor gets wages, landowners get rent, and owners of capital get profits. Adam Smith concluded that any conflict over the distribution of income would be resolved, to the benefit of all, by the operation of the competitive market system. However, there are some other ways of looking at income distribution. A society may decide that the way markets distribute income is undesirable.

In a market system, the distribution of income tends to be fairly unequal. Why? As we have suggested, income is derived from the participation of resources in productive activity. Income is paid to the factors of production for their involvement in the production process. The incomes that individuals earn therefore depend on the resources they own and the prices they command in resource markets. Some individuals have only their unskilled labor power to sell; consequently, they tend to have low incomes. People who possess professional skills, work experience, or capital resources will have higher incomes.

The Size Distribution of Income

What is the actual distribution of income in the United States? A convenient and instructive method of examining the distribution of income is to group people in families and then rank them by income. The result is called the size distribution of income. Table 11.3 shows the size distribution of income for the United States in 2005. It covers all before-tax income—including governmental transfer payments such as Social Security and veterans' benefits, unemployment compensation, and welfare—for the 77.4 million American families. When all of the families are ranked by income from the highest to the lowest, we take each successive 20 percent (15.5 million) of the families, add up all of their incomes, and take that income as a percentage of total income. For example, the poorest 20 percent of the families received 4.0 percent of total family income in 2005, the middle 20 percent got 15.3 percent of total income, and the

TABLE 11.3   Size Distribution of Family Income in the United States, 2005

Grouping	Percentage of Total Income	Income Range ($)
Poorest 20%	4.0	0–25,616
Second poorest 20%	9.6	25,617–45,021
Middle 20%	15.3	45,022–68,304
Second richest 20%	22.9	68,305–103,100
Richest 20%	48.1	Above 103,100
Top 5%	21.1	Above 184,500

Source: U.S. Census Bureau, Table F-1, F-2 (www.census.gov).

top 20 percent got 48.1 percent. If income were distributed equally, each 20 percent would get 20 percent of total income.

Table 11.3 also shows the ranges of income for each successive 20 percent. For example, families with incomes of $25,616 or less found themselves in the poorest 20 percent. If a family's income was $70,000 in 2005, the family was in the fourth quintile. To get into the top 5 percent of annual family income required at least $184,501.

These statistics indicate a relatively unequal distribution of income. The 15.5 million families at the bottom of the income ladder got only 4.0 percent of total family income, while the same number of families at the top got 48.1 percent. The top 5 percent (the 3.9 million families with incomes over $184,500) receives twenty-one times as much income on average as the poorest 20 percent.

Increasing Inequality in the United States.   One of the most discussed trends in the United States recently has been increasing income inequality. As shown in Table 11.4, the share of national income going to the bottom 80 percent of U.S. families has decreased since 1980. Figure 11.5 illustrates that, since 1973, the incomes of the richest 20 percent of U.S. families have grown at a far faster rate than those of any other quintile. The incomes of the poorest 20 percent of U.S. families have barely increased.

Economists believe that a number of factors may be behind these trends. Globalization and the ability of U.S. firms to move their operations overseas has undermined the position of workers in the United States, who must now compete with workers around the world for jobs. Meanwhile, globalization has opened up unprecedented opportunities for those with skills and capital. Improvements in technology, especially computers, increase the demand for skilled workers who can use that technology, but new technologies often replace unskilled workers. The decline of unions in the United States (which we will study in Chapter 12) also may have played a role, since historically unions have represented the interests of less-skilled workers. Furthermore, as we will study in Chapter 13, the government has been scaling back programs that benefit poorer U.S. citizens while at the same time reducing taxes on the wealthiest citizens.

Many conservative economists are not troubled by increasing economic inequality. They generally believe that people are paid according to their productivity, and higher wages for those at the top are deserved because these

TABLE 11.4   Changes in the U.S. Distribution of Income Since 1950

Year	Poorest 20%	2nd Poorest 20%	Middle 20%	2nd Richest 20%	Richest 20%	Richest 5%
1950	4.5	12.0	17.4	23.4	42.7	17.3
1960	4.8	12.2	17.8	24.0	41.3	15.9
1970	5.4	12.2	17.6	23.8	40.9	15.6
1980	5.3	11.6	17.6	24.4	41.1	14.6
1990	4.6	10.8	16.6	23.8	44.3	17.4
1995	4.4	10.1	15.8	23.2	46.5	20.0
2000	4.3	9.8	15.4	22.7	47.7	21.1
2005	4.0	9.6	15.3	22.9	48.1	21.1

Source: U.S. Census Bureau, Table F-2 (www.census.gov).

people contribute more to the economy than those at the bottom. Also, they argue that increases in income for the wealthy do not harm people at the bottom, who are not worse off than they used to be. (For the bottom 80 percent, incomes have increased since 1973, albeit by much smaller amounts.) Most liberal economists disagree, arguing instead that inequality leads to a host of problems, including crime and the erosion of civil society. As one European official quipped during the economic summit of the G8 (The Group of Eight nations, including Canada, France, Germany, Italy, Japan, Russia, the United Kingdom, and the United States) in Denver in 1997, "Americans keep telling us how successful their system is—then they remind us not to stray too far from our hotel at night." Radical economists dispute the notion that wages are paid according to productivity. They believe that wages for the working class are determined by the degree of working-class power in the economy, and that globalization, technology, and the decline of unions have undermined workers' power while enhancing the power of capitalists. Both liberal and radical economists see economic inequality as a major problem facing the United States at the beginning of the twenty-first century.

International Size Distribution of Income.   No society has a totally equal distribution of income. However, the degree of inequality varies among the nations. Table 11.5 shows that many of the Western and Northern European countries have distributions of income that are significantly less unequal than that in the United States. At the other extreme, many poor countries in Latin America, Africa, and Asia have very unequal income distributions.

Measuring the Degree of Inequality.   A **Lorenz curve** illustrates the degree of inequality in the distribution of income. Figure 11.6 shows a Lorenz curve based on the distribution of income in the United States in 2005. The horizontal axis measures each 20 percent of the families, and the vertical axis measures their cumulative shares of total income. In 2005, the bottom 20 percent got 4.0 percent of total income, the lowest 40 percent got 13.6 percent, and so on. If income were distributed equally, we would get a straight Lorenz curve at a 45° angle. Instead we get the curved line in Figure 11.6.

FIGURE 11.5   Real family income growth by quintile, 1947–2005

1947–1973

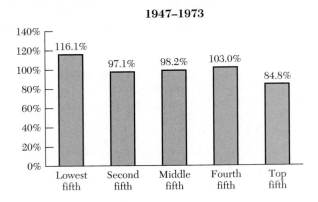

1973–2000

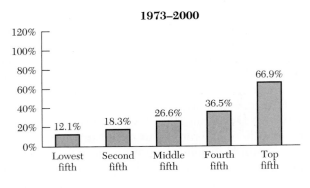

2000–2005

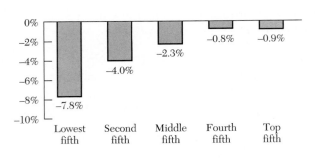

Source: Reprinted from *The State of Working America 2006/2007*. An Economic Policy Institute book. © 2007 ILR Press, an imprint of Cornell University. Used by permission of the publisher.

To measure the degree of inequality, we can compare the area between the straight line and the Lorenz curve (area A) to the area below the 45° line (area A plus area B). The technical name for this ratio is the **Gini coefficient.** The lower this ratio, the lower the degree of inequality; the higher the ratio, the greater the

TABLE 11.5   Income Distribution of Selected Developed and Developing Nations

	Year	Gini Coefficient	Poorest 20%	2nd-Poorest 20%	Middle 20%	2nd-Richest 20%	Richest 20%	Richest 10%
Namibia	1993	0.743	1.4	3.0	5.4	11.5	78.7	64.5
Brazil	2003	0.580	2.6	6.2	10.7	18.4	62.1	45.8
South Africa	2000	0.578	3.5	6.3	10.0	18.0	62.2	44.7
Mexico	2002	0.495	4.3	8.3	12.6	19.7	55.1	39.4
China	2001	0.447	4.7	9.0	14.2	22.1	50.0	33.1
United States	**2000**	**0.408**	**5.4**	**10.7**	**15.7**	**22.4**	**45.8**	**29.9**
United Kingdom	1999	0.360	6.1	11.4	16.0	22.5	44.0	28.5
France	1995	0.327	7.2	12.6	17.2	22.8	40.2	25.1
Canada	2000	0.326	7.2	12.7	17.2	23.0	39.9	24.8
India	2000	0.325	8.9	12.3	16.0	21.2	43.3	28.5
South Korea	1998	0.316	7.9	13.6	18.0	23.1	37.5	22.5
Netherlands	1999	0.309	7.6	13.2	17.2	23.3	38.7	22.9
Germany	2000	0.283	8.5	13.7	17.8	23.1	36.9	22.1
Czech Republic	1996	0.254	10.3	14.5	17.7	21.7	35.9	22.4
Sweden	2000	0.250	9.1	14.0	17.6	22.7	36.6	22.2
Japan	1993	0.249	10.6	14.2	17.6	22.0	35.7	21.7
Denmark	1997	0.247	8.3	14.7	18.2	22.9	35.8	21.3

Source: Data from *World Development Indicators*, 2006 by World Bank.

degree of inequality. In 1970, the Gini coefficient for the distribution of family income in the United States was 0.353 and in 2005, it was 0.440. Figure 11.7 shows that as income inequality in the United States increased from 1970 to 2005, the Lorenz curve shifted out away from the line of perfect equality.

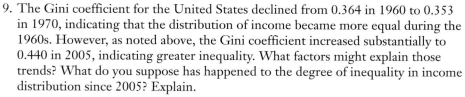

8. List five beneficial effects that might occur from a more equal income distribution. List five negative effects.

9. The Gini coefficient for the United States declined from 0.364 in 1960 to 0.353 in 1970, indicating that the distribution of income became more equal during the 1960s. However, as noted above, the Gini coefficient increased substantially to 0.440 in 2005, indicating greater inequality. What factors might explain those trends? What do you suppose has happened to the degree of inequality in income distribution since 2005? Explain.

Why is income distributed so unequally in the United States? Fundamentally, it is a function of the ownership of resources and the prices of those resources. Individuals possess different labor and nonlabor resources, and different resources get different prices. Furthermore, the private market system relies on those very differences to allocate and motivate resources.

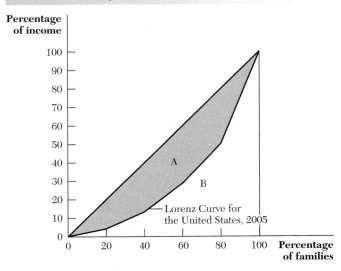

FIGURE 11.6 Lorenz Curve and Gini Coefficient Computation

The Influence of Property

The U.S. economy is basically a capitalist system with private property as one of its most fundamental characteristics. The ownership of land, money, and capital resources is even more unequally distributed than income. Wealth statistics for the United States show that the poorest families have very little in financial and personal assets.

Table 11.6 indicates that the distribution of net worth (assets minus liabilities) in the United States is more unequal than the distribution of income. The median net worth of families in 2004 totaled $93,100, with the median for white families at $140,700 and the median for "nonwhite" and Hispanic families at $24,800. Table 11.7 shows the shares of different forms of personal wealth—corporate stocks and other financial assets—owned by the bottom 80 percent, the wealthiest 20 percent, and the wealthiest 5 percent of all families. For example, the wealthiest 5 percent of families held 59 percent of all net worth, 65 percent of all stock, 32 percent of housing equity, and 72 percent of other (non-stock) financial assets, such as business equity. Other financial assets, including individual checking account deposits, automobiles, and owner-occupied primary residences, are more evenly distributed among the population. Also, as Figure 11.8 shows, the share of household wealth going to the top 1 percent of U.S. families increased steadily from 1976 through 1998, before declining with the recession of 2001.

The unequal distribution of wealth contributes to the unequal distribution of income in the United States. Households with the highest 20 percent of income earn close to 70 percent of the income from owning and renting property.

FIGURE 11.7   U.S. Lorenz Curve, 1970 and 2005

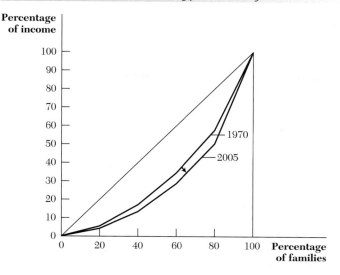

Households in the lowest quintile of the income distribution earn only about 1 percent of the property income generated.

10. Do you or your family members own any income-producing wealth?

The Influence of Labor Incomes

Approximately 60 percent of personal income in the United States comes from wages and salaries. This percentage is higher for families in the middle of the income distribution. Like property income, income from mental and physical labor is unequally distributed. There are a variety of reasons for the differences in wages and salaries that individuals receive for their contributions to eco-

TABLE 11.6   Distribution of Financial Wealth in the United States, 2004

Family Income	Median Net Worth
Poorest 20%	$7,500
2nd-poorest 20%	34,300
Middle 20%	71,600
2nd-richest 20%	160,000
Richest 20%	617,600
Richest 10%	924,100

Source: Federal Reserve, *Survey of Consumer Finances.*

TABLE 11.7 Distribution of Personal Wealth

Asset	Percent of Total Assets Held by Families		
	Bottom 80%	**Wealthiest 20%**	**Wealthiest 5%**
Total net worth	15.3	84.7	59.0
Stocks	9.4	90.6	65.3
Other financial assets	9.1	90.9	72.2
Housing equity	34.6	65.4	32.4

Source: Reprinted from *The State of Working America 2006/2007.* An Economic Policy Institute book. © 2007 ILR Press, an imprint of Cornell University. Used by permission of the publisher.

nomic activity. The labor that people perform is not homogeneous, and there are differences in the jobs that people hold.

The capabilities, training, and intelligence of individuals have a great deal to do with their respective incomes. Consequently, the distribution of these attributes contributes to an unequal distribution of income. Some people are more productive in certain tasks than others are. For example, someone with physical strength probably can lift and stack more bales of hay in an hour than someone with less strength; someone with mathematical aptitude can balance a firm's books more quickly and accurately than someone without such aptitude. Some people, because of their concentration and motivation, produce more than other people in specific activities over a given period of time. In general, the greater an individual's productivity or contribution to economic output, the higher her or his wages will be.

Different people also have different skills. A large number of people are available for jobs that require minimal skills (e.g., clerks, sales personnel, custodians). As a result, they usually command low wages in labor markets. Others, who make up a smaller segment of the population, have professional skills (doctors, lawyers, economists) or possess unique qualities (athletes, entertainers) that earn them higher incomes. The more specialized the skill or the longer the period of training or education necessary to develop a skill, the higher the wages of people with those skills tend to be. For example, people with college educations, on the average, earn about 50 percent more per year than people with high school diplomas.

Age and experience also contribute to the unequal distribution of income. People who are older and have accumulated work experience tend to be paid more than younger, less experienced workers. An English professor who has taught for twenty years in a university earns more than a colleague who has taught for only two years.

Individuals also have different attitudes and preferences about work and income. Some people have a strong preference for work over leisure. Some people have very strong desires to earn high incomes. In fact, capitalism relies on monetary incentives for productive activity, so it has developed a hierarchy of

FIGURE 11.8 Top 1% Share of Household Wealth, 1922–2004

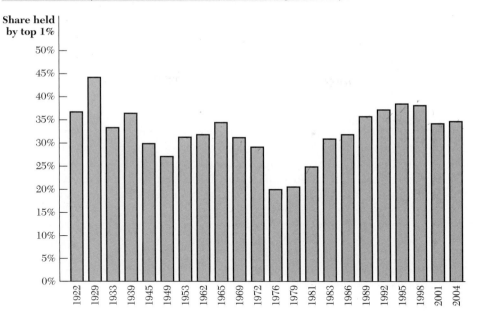

Source: Data from Edward Wolff, reported in Lawrence Mishel, Jared Bernstein, and Sylvia Allegretto, *The State of Working America*, various years. Copyright © 2007 by Cornell University. Used by permission of the publisher.

jobs with different levels of pay. People are motivated to work hard in order to move up the job ladder and to get higher incomes.

Racial and gender differences also have an impact on the unequal distribution of income. As we shall see in some detail in the next section, white males in the United States tend to earn higher incomes than nonwhite males, and males tend to earn more than females.

In addition, differences in the kinds of jobs that people perform contribute to inequality in income distribution. The type of work performed and the conditions surrounding it influence compensation. Dangerous or unpleasant work (e.g., coal mining or garbage collection) is often rewarded with premium wages. Some people, on the other hand, may be willing to give up higher wages in return for significant control over the work that they do. Teachers or people who work for small businesses tend to be paid less than people whose work is more directly controlled by supervisors or institutional demands. The organizational structure of employment also influences wages and salaries. People who work for large corporations tend to earn more. Workers who are members of labor unions usually have higher wages than nonunion workers (see Chapter 12). Finally, the location of a job may influence an individual's remuneration. Someone who works in Idaho tends to be paid less than a person who works in Los Angeles with exactly the same job, skills, and experience.

Many factors account for the differences in the wages and salaries people earn for the work that they do, and these factors help to explain the inequality of income distribution in the United States. Most of the explanations just given imply that market forces play an important role in determining the different wages and salaries individuals receive in our society. The necessity of a medical education, for example, limits the supply of doctors and hence tends to increase their incomes. The widespread demand of moviegoers and video purchasers for films starring Will Smith, Denzel Washington, Brad Pitt, or Cameron Diaz accounts for their astronomical incomes.

On the other hand, many nonmarket conditions also influence people's wages and salaries. In the United States, women do most of the work related to household management and child care, and their work is often unpaid. People's class backgrounds have an impact on the development of their skills and attitudes toward work. Luck—being in the right place at the right time—can influence the jobs and incomes people have.

Income from wages and salaries is somewhat more equally distributed among households than overall income. However, labor incomes tend to be positively related to property income; that is, those with high labor incomes are also likely to have property income. This further contributes to the unequal distribution of income.

11. Why does class background play an important role in determining one's career and salary?

Transfer Income

As we noted earlier, in measuring income distribution, we calculate household income before taxes and include governmental transfer payments such as Social Security and veterans' benefits, unemployment compensation, and welfare payments. While property income is positively related to wage and salary income, transfer income largely goes to those at the lower end of the income distribution spectrum.

Some transfer payments are non-means-tested government programs, including such programs as Social Security, unemployment compensation, and some veterans' benefits. Other programs, including Temporary Assistance for Needy Families (TANF), Supplemental Security Income (SSI), and some veterans' benefits are means-tested, so recipients must meet minimum income and/or other requirements before the transfer is awarded. While the means-tested transfer payments are allocated to low-income individuals and families, Social Security—by far the largest transfer program—is not.

How much do transfer payments influence income distribution in the United States? Table 11.8 shows the impact on income distribution in 2004. The first column shows the distribution of income before any government taxes, trans-

TABLE 11.8 Percentage of Aggregate Income Received by Income Quintiles, 2001

Quintile	Market Income	Post-Social Insurance Income	Disposable Income
Lowest 20%	1.5	3.3	4.7
Second 20%	7.4	8.6	10.3
Third 20%	14.1	14.5	16.1
Fourth 20%	23.6	23.0	24.0
Highest 20%	53.4	50.6	44.9

Source: U.S. Census Bureau, *The Effects of Government Taxes and Transfers on Income and Poverty: 2004*

fers, or social insurance programs are included. Column 2 shows what the distribution looks like after including transfer payments such as Social Security. Column 3 shows the effect of including all taxes as well as noncash transfers such as food stamps and subsidized housing.

Without means- and non-means-tested transfer income, income is distributed even more unequally. Without taxes and transfers, the highest 20 percent of income earners would receive about 53.4 percent of the income, and the lowest 20 percent would receive 1.5 percent of the income. If we add back the non-means-tested transfers, the largest of which is Social Security, income distribution approaches the actual 2004 levels. This shows that non-means-tested transfers are a significant contribution to households in lower income brackets. Ultimately, tax and transfer programs do indeed change the distribution of income; in 2004, they accounted for an 8.5 percent decrease in the percentage of income received by those in the highest quintile and a 6.1 percent increase in the percentage received by the lowest two quintiles.

In the mid-1990s, many of the means-tested transfer programs came under attack in an attempt to significantly alter the U.S. welfare system. While we see that means-tested transfer programs do contribute income to families in the lower quintiles, they tend to be less significant contributions than non-means-tested programs. Means-tested transfers are often received by women who head low-income households where children are present.

The Influence of Race and Gender

Another characteristic of income inequality in the United States is that blacks earn lower incomes than whites and that women often earn lower incomes than men. The existence of racism and sexism in our society contributes to income inequality in a number of ways. Racism and sexism are systems of social, political, cultural, ideological, and economic domination, whereby one group has less power and control over decisions and resources than another group. Instances of both racism and sexism are manifested in numerous noneconomic ways in the day-to-day life of our society. In addition, racial minorities and

TABLE 11.9   Occupations by Gender and Race in the United States, 1983 and 2005

Occupation	% Female 1983	% Female 2005	% Black 1983	% Black 2005
Engineers	5.8	13.8	2.7	5.1
Lawyers	15.3	30.2	2.6	4.7
Physicians	15.8	32.3	3.2	5.3
College Teachers	36.3	44.4	4.4	6.7
All Occupations	**43.7**	**46.4**	**9.3**	**10.8**
High School Teachers	51.8	56.8	7.2	7.3
Textile Workers	82.1	77.4	18.7	13.8
Elementary School Teachers	83.3	82.2	11.1	9.6
Cashiers	84.4	75.9	10.1	15.5
Health Service Aides	89.2	88.7	23.5	32.5
Nurses	95.8	92.3	6.7	10.0
Secretaries	99.0	97.3	5.8	9.2

Source: *Statistical Abstract of the United States, 2007.*

women in the United States are systematically less well off in economic terms than white males.

The racial and ethnic composition of the U.S. population is quite diverse and will change dramatically in the near future. Approximately 80 percent of all Americans are white, while 13 percent are black, 5 percent are Asian or Native American, and 14 percent are of Hispanic origin (and may be of any race). Blacks, Native Americans, and those of Hispanic origin are more likely to be unemployed than whites. In 2005, the unemployment rate for all white persons over sixteen was 4.4 percent; for blacks, it was 10.0 percent; and for Hispanics, it was 6.0 percent. Members of racial minority populations in the United States are less likely to work in professional and white-collar occupations than whites and are more likely to work in the lower-paying blue-collar and service sector jobs. More than 63 percent of whites work in professional white-collar jobs, compared with only 52 percent of blacks and 38 percent of Hispanics. Correspondingly, blacks and Hispanics are much more likely to be in lower-paying blue-collar or service sector jobs. Table 11.9 illustrates that, in 2005, blacks represented 10.8 percent of the workforce in the United States but accounted for only 4.7 percent of lawyers and 5.3 percent of physicians. Hispanics, who represented 13.1 percent of all workers, made up only 3.5 percent of lawyers and 5.2 percent of physicians. Table 11.9 shows that blacks are more heavily concentrated in occupations such as health service aide or textile worker, which tend to be low-paying jobs. The data in Table 11.9 also show that some progress has occurred since 1983. For example, black representation in some professional white-collar jobs increased. But despite these increases, there is still substantial segregation along racial lines (and along gender lines, as we

TABLE 11.10 Median African-American Family Income
as a Percent of White Family Income

Year	Percentage
1955	55.0
1960	55.0
1965	55.0
1970	61.0
1975	61.5
1980	58.0
1985	58.0
1990	58.0
1995	60.9
2000	64.2
2004	62.3

Source: U.S. Census Bureau, Historical Income Tables, Table F-5.

discuss below), with black workers overrepresented in low-wage service and blue-collar jobs.

As a consequence of these factors as well as outright racial discrimination, nonwhites in the United States, on the average, earn less than whites do. The data in Table 11.10 compare the median income of black families with that of white families for various years from 1955 to 2004. The median income of black families has consistently been significantly below that of white families. Some of the decline from 1975 to 1995 reflected an increase in black families headed by women, and some of it reflected the impact of the recessions of the early 1980s and 1990s. The boom from 1995 to 2000 helped to raise black incomes significantly, to 64 percent of white family incomes. However, the recession and sluggish growth of the early 2000s caused median black family incomes to fall relative to that of white families. In 2001, the median income of

TABLE 11.11 Median Female Worker Income as a Percent of
Median Male Worker Income

Year	Percentage
1960	60.7
1970	59.4
1980	60.2
1990	71.6
2000	73.3
2005	77.0

Source: U.S. Census Bureau, Historical Income Tables, Table P-38.

(© 2004 by Nicole Hollander.)

Hispanic families was 62 percent of the median income of white families, virtually the same as for black families.

The incidence of poverty also differs among racial groups. In 2004, the federal government classified 10.8 percent of whites in the United States as being in poverty. The figure for blacks was 24.7 percent; for Asians, 9.8 percent; and for Hispanics, 21.9 percent.

These data suggest that racial factors have an important impact on the unequal distribution of income in the United States. In a 1982 report to President Reagan, the U.S. Commission on Civil Rights concluded that, despite a generation of civil rights and affirmative-action legislation, discrimination persists "virtually everywhere, at every age level, at every educational level, at every skill level." This statement continues to reflect the reality of poverty data today.

Similarly, women are concentrated in low-paying jobs, tend to work for low-paying concerns, and are "systematically underpaid." A study in 1981, prepared for the Equal Employment Opportunity Commission by the National Research Council (a branch of the National Academy of Sciences) and focusing on the economic position of women, found that "despite the tremendous changes that have occurred in the labor market over the past 20 years, there has been no change in the relative earnings of men and women." When that study was published two decades ago (as the cartoon illustrates), women workers earned sixty cents for every dollar earned by a male worker. Today women earn more—moving the ratio of women's earnings to 77 cents for each dollar earned by male workers. Table 11.11 presents information on the incomes of year-round, full-time female workers compared with the incomes of year-round, full-time male workers from 1960 to 2005. According to Aaron Bernstein ("Women's Pay: Why the Gap Remains a Chasm," *Business Week*, June 14, 2004, p. 58), numerous studies indicate that outright discrimination against women probably accounts for about 10 percentage points of the pay gap. The rest has to do with other factors such as occupational segregation, described below.

The gap between what full-time, year-round male and female workers earn becomes more dramatic when we consider lifetime earnings. According to a 2004 study by economists Stephen J. Rose and Heidi I. Hartmann, "When you look at how much the typical woman actually earns over much of her career, the true figure is more like 44% of what the average man makes" (*ibid.*). The lower long-term income for women stems from the fact that many women take time off from work or work part-time because of family responsibilities. Taking a single year off from work reduces a woman's earnings by an average of 32 percent. Similarly, the hourly wages of part-time jobs average 47 percent less than the hourly wages of full-time jobs, and women more often fill these part-time jobs. As Bernstein (*ibid.*) observes, "speedier progress probably won't happen without more employers making work sites family-friendly and revamping jobs to accommodate women and men as they seek to balance work and family demands."

Over the past four decades, the participation of women in the paid labor force increased substantially. In 1960, about 40 percent of women over sixteen were in the labor force (working for wages or looking for paid work). By 1980, women's labor force participation rate was up to 52 percent. In 2000, it had increased further, to about 60 percent where it remained through 2005.

Men and women remain segregated into different occupations, and usually women are concentrated in the lower-paying occupations. To eliminate occupational segregation in the workplace, 55 percent of the nation's working men and women would have to switch jobs. Almost half of the nation's working women are in occupations that are at least 70 percent female, and one-fifth of working women are in occupations that are at least 90 percent female. As Table 11.9 indicates, women make up 46 percent of the workforce, but in 2005, women constituted 89 percent of health service aides, 92 percent of nurses, 97 percent of secretaries, 82 percent of elementary teachers, and 76 percent of cashiers. Men constituted 86 percent of engineers, 76 percent of CEOs, 68 percent of doctors, 70 percent of lawyers, 56 percent of college teachers—and 85 percent of tenured economists at Ph.D.–granting institutions. For many jobs that require equal educational levels and comparable skills, women are systematically paid less than men. The influence of occupation-linked gender differences and sex discrimination thus also contributes to inequality in the distribution of income in the United States.

12. Why do economic differences based on race and gender persist in the United States?

13. In recent years, the civil rights and women's movements have challenged racism and sexism. These struggles have led to legislation regarding equal opportunity and affirmative-action programs, as well as to some court cases. In a case in Colorado in the late 1970s, a group of nurses sued the city and county of Denver for sex discrimination. Tree trimmers, sign painters, and repairmen were all paid more than nurses. U.S. District Judge Fred Winner decided against the nurses' claim and concluded, "This is a case pregnant with the possibility of disrupting the entire economic system of the United States of America. . . . I'm not going to restructure the entire economy of the U.S." What was Winner worried about? In a 2004 class action lawsuit, Wal-Mart was accused of sex discrimination. Does the operation of the U.S. economy still require that women be paid less than men (even for comparable work)? Why or why not?

TABLE 11.12 Percentage of Children under Nineteen below the Poverty Line

Year	All Races	White	African American
1970	14.9	10.5	41.5
1980	17.9	13.4	42.1
1990	19.9	15.1	44.2
2000	15.6	12.4	30.9
2005	17.1	13.9	33.2

Source: U.S. Census Bureau, Historical Poverty Tables, Table 3.

Income Distribution and Child Poverty

Despite the high levels of income on average, substantial numbers of children in the United States still live in poverty. In 2005, some 12.3 million children under the age of eighteen, were poor. This represents 17.1 percent of all children. Table 11.12 shows the distribution of child poverty among white and African American children under eighteen. The risk of an African American child living in poverty is more than two times that of a white child.

Child poverty is dramatically higher in the United States than in other industrial nations. Figure 11.9 shows the results of a UNICEF study published in 2005, showing that the percentage of poor young people in the United States was the highest of all industrialized nations. The researchers could not fully determine the causes but attributed the possible causes to several factors, includ-

FIGURE 11.9 Child Poverty in Selected Industrialized Countries, 2005

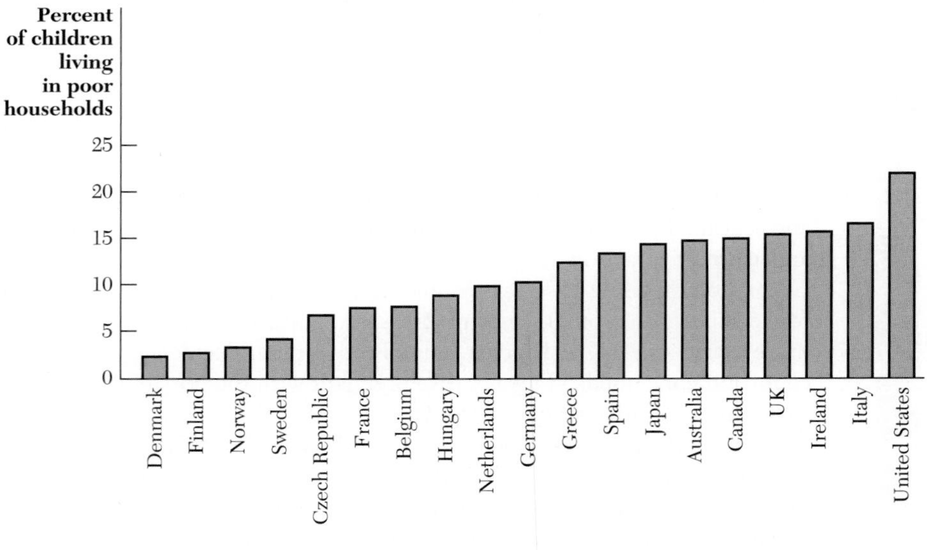

Source: **UNICEF**, *Child Poverty in Rich Countries 2005*.

ing the widest gap between the rich and poor among all of the other countries studied.

The past few decades have seen rapid growth in the number of children in poverty who live in homes where a single female is the head of the household. In 1960, 20 percent of all families below the poverty line were headed by women with no husband present. By 1986, this figure had increased to 46 percent. In 2004, 28.4 percent of all female-headed families with related children were living in poverty (37.6 percent for African American families with female heads). The lower incomes received by women have a detrimental effect on these families. Just over half of all poor children live in female-headed households. Single female heads of households in poverty are almost five times as likely as other women to experience unemployment and involuntary part-time work (working less than full time because full-time work is unavailable), and they are almost nine times as likely to have low earnings.

14. What impact does the federal government have on the distribution of income? How does it affect the distribution of income?

Conclusion

In this chapter we have briefly considered the operation of resource markets and the distribution of income in the United States. Resource markets, through the forces of supply and demand, determine the costs of production for firms and the incomes of households. Many factors account for the relatively unequal distribution of income in the United States. People own different resources, the jobs they do are different, and race and gender both influence wages and salaries. Unequal income distribution in turn affects the well-being of families and of the children who live in them.

Review Questions

1. Why is the market for unskilled labor relatively competitive?

2. What influences a firm's demand for a particular resource?

3. A firm tends to use the amount of a resource at which its MRP equals its MFC. Explain why.

4. In the September 17, 1984, issue of *Business Week*, there was an article titled, "The U.S. May Finally Have Too Many Lawyers." Using the economic analysis of resource markets, explain how a surplus of lawyers could happen.

5. Money is a resource; it can be used to finance capital projects. What influences the demand for credit? What influences the supply of credit? What is the price of credit?

6. Polls have reported that a significant majority of people in the United States believe that star athletes, entertainers, and corporate executives are overpaid. In 2005, Tiger Woods earned $87 million (most coming from appearance fees and

endorsements) for playing golf and Maria Sharapova earned $18 million for playing tennis. Tom Cruise had a total income of $67 million in 2005, and Oprah Winfrey earned $225 million. Richard Fairbank, CEO of Capital One, earned $249 million in the same year in salary, bonuses, and stock options, and the average CEO of a large company earned more than $11 million. What drives these high salaries? What are the economic effects?

7. Do you think the federal government should develop explicit policies to redistribute income to reduce the inequality of income distribution? Why or why not?

8. What are the sources of inequality in the distribution of income? Which ones might be reformed to reduce income inequality? What political and/or systemic limits are there on the redistribution of income?

CHAPTER TWELVE

Corporations and Labor Unions

▪ Introduction

Now that we have examined the economic theory of competitive and noncompetitive market structures and explored the results of different types of firms, it is worthwhile to examine firms as they are encountered in the United States today. The corporation, as a productive unit in the U.S. economic system, has become a dominant institution. In Chapter 10 we saw statistics that showed the impact of the largest U.S. industrial corporations on several economic categories—manufacturing employment, manufacturing assets, and so on. U.S. corporations stand out for consideration in any discussion of production and resource allocation in the United States. Therefore, this chapter concentrates on U.S. corporations, describing what they are and the economic power they have and analyzing what that power implies.

In Chapter 11, we surveyed the operation of resource markets. We suggested that in addition to the forces of supply and demand, labor unions have an impact on labor markets. Labor unions serve as important institutions in the structure of the U.S. economy. The chapter concludes with a brief examination of the history and the effects of labor unions in the economy and how each of these relate to the behavior of corporations.

Kinds of Firms

There are more than 27 million businesses in the United States, and two-thirds are small businesses. Each year about 1 million new firms are started—many of which fail. Profit-driven businesses fit into one of three major classifications: (1) sole proprietorships, (2) partnerships, or (3) corporations.

A sole proprietorship has a single owner, who has the right to all profits and who bears the unlimited liability for the firm's debts. This kind of business is simple and easy to organize. The owner is in complete control but must be responsible for

247

FIGURE 12.1   Number and Sales of Each Type of Firm

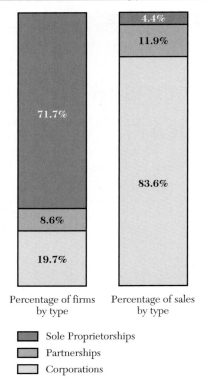

Source: U.S. Census Bureau, *Statistical Abstract of the United States*, 2007.

investing the capital necessary to establish the business. In 2003, sole proprietor-ships represented 72 percent of all firms in the U.S. economy, yet because they are generally small, they represent only 4.4 percent of all business sales.

A partnership has two or more owners, who share the firm's profits and who bear unlimited liability for the firm's debts. It is often easier to raise the financial resources required to go into business. Partnerships are common in the fields of law, medicine, and accounting. This is the least common form of business orga-nization, making up only 8.6 percent of all firms and accounting for around 12 percent of all business sales.

Figure 12.1 shows the types of business organization in terms of their number and sales.

The Corporation

A corporation is a legal entity that engages in the provision of goods and ser-vices for the public. Corporations have legal authority to enter into contracts with other parties. The characteristic of corporations that distinguishes them from other productive units—such as partnerships or proprietorships—is that the individuals who own the corporations, the stockholders, have limited liability. Stockholders are liable to the corporation's creditors only to the extent of the value of their stock. They cannot be sued by creditors. This differs from other forms of business, in which the individuals who operate the business are personally liable to creditors.

This gives the corporation a great advantage in amassing financial resources to underwrite production. Issues of corporate stock can raise capital, and this capital base can be used to raise further capital through bank loans and so forth. Corporations have used this ability to form large productive operations—large plants, nationwide production and distribution facilities, and even worldwide networks. The technological advances of the Industrial Revolution spurred the development of larger and larger corporations, and modern technology continues to do the same. Through these legal advantages and historical developments, many U.S. corporations have grown to be quite large in terms of assets, profits, employees, and economic (and political) power.

How many corporations are there in the United States? And just how large have they grown? In 2003, there were more than 5 million corporations in the United States; they constituted 20 percent of businesses but had 84 percent of all business receipts. So corporations handle the vast majority of business transactions in the United States and most of the profits in the economy.

Which corporations are the biggest, in terms of receipts? The largest firms, less than 1 percent of the corporations in the United States, earned more than two-thirds of corporate receipts. Some U.S. corporations have grown very large indeed and dominate certain sectors of the economy. So what? The question is a good one, and the answers to it will differ among those of us in the United States who are affected by corporations. Some will argue that the large size and dominance of corporations are necessary to organize production, provide employment, and produce goods and services efficiently. Others might use economic arguments, pointing out that almost all large corporations are in concentrated industries and are thus theoretically likely to be deficient because of their economic power. (If the economy were perfectly competitive, there would be many more companies, and none would be so dominant.) Others might be less theoretical and say that corporations are only out to make a buck, have too much economic power, and sometimes do things to the detriment of society.

1. How do you feel about corporations?
2. Why do you think corporations can become so big?

The Role of Profits in the Corporate System

In 1974, the chairman of General Motors, Richard C. Gerstenberg, argued in *The New York Times*, "There is no conflict between corporate profits and social progress. Not one of our grand national goals can be accomplished unless business prospers. Profits fuel the growth of our nation, and our future depends on the profitability of free enterprise." Many would argue that he is correct. We depend on corporate success and profitability for jobs, products, economic growth, technological change, innovation, research and development, and so on. Corporations are in business to earn profits, and in the process of doing so, they provide jobs, investment, goods and services, and economic growth. If they are profitable, they pay taxes that help to finance social programs, and they often contribute to civic and educational endeavors.

However, over the years, a set of counterarguments has informed public sentiments about corporations and led to public opinion polls that at times have concluded that corporate profits are too high. The following list of complaints of corporate wrongdoing and questionable behavior is long and not exhaustive: pollution for decades without cost to the corporation; exploitation of workers (minorities, women, children, illegal immigrants, etc.); three-martini lunches charged off as business expenses; corporate bribery of foreign officials; illegal corporate political campaign contributions; high oil company profits in the midst of gas shortages and rolling blackouts in California homes and industries; food additives that destroy our health; disproportionate economic and political power; misleading advertising; and so on—all to make a buck.

Corporations have tended to respond to these criticisms defensively. Gerstenberg charged, "Most [Americans] are ill-equipped to recognize the economics in these issues, much less to recommend the economic remedies. This lack of public understanding," he suggested, "seriously threatens the continuation of our competitive private enterprise system."

Early in the 1980s, *The Wall Street Journal* and the Gallup Organization polled about eight hundred chief executives of small, medium, and large companies on their perceptions of the public's opinion of business. Almost two-thirds of the executives from medium and large businesses thought the public's opinion was unfavorable, whereas only 36 percent of the small-business executives thought so. "The public thinks when business reports a profit, it goes right into our pockets. They have to be told the truth," said one business leader.

Businesspeople had plenty of ideas about how to improve the image of business in the country. Small-business leaders suggested the importance of product quality and ethical standards. Many of the executives of the large companies emphasized communication and education, based on the conclusion that the low regard for business comes from a lack of knowledge. Suggested remedies ranged from getting the "media and press on the side of business," increasing corporate involvement in community issues, teaching more courses about free enterprise in high schools and colleges, and making advertising better. "We need to start in the elementary schools, with teachers and students both," said one respondent. An energy executive said, "We need to make people realize that it is business and not the government that provides over 100 million jobs in this country." And a transportation company official added, "We need to make it clear that business profits are not just arbitrarily squirreled away, but reinvested for the benefit of the company, its workers and the public. If we can get this across, we may be able to change the adverse to at least normal."

3. Do you have a positive, negative, neutral, indifferent, or balanced view of the corporation's role in the U.S. economy? Explain.

U.S. Corporations Go Global

No treatment of the modern U.S. corporation would be complete without reference to one of the dominant corporate trends in the post–World War II period—the increasing multinationalization of U.S. corporations. We explore this issue in more detail in Part 5 on international economics. The multinational corporation was introduced in Chapter 2.

Multinational corporations have productive facilities, offices, and operations in more than one country. Some U.S. multinational companies date back to the end of the nineteenth century. At that time, international activities of most companies involved trade. In the post–World War II period, U.S. corporations began increasingly to invest in productive facilities in other parts of the world. At first, foreign direct investment was directed toward getting around tariff barriers and other impediments to U.S. exports. Much of this investment took place in Western Europe and Canada. In addition, multinationalization could also cut transportation costs for international markets, take advantage of various tax incentives offered by many countries, and cut production costs with cheaper foreign labor. In the 1950s and 1960s, much of this investment by U.S. corporations took place in the underdeveloped countries of Latin America, Asia, and Africa.

In the 1970s the pace of U.S. multinational investment in the rest of the world slowed down somewhat for a variety of reasons. The dollar lost value during the 1970s, making foreign investment more expensive for U.S. corporations. Many developing nations had become more critical about unconditional multinational investment in their countries. Political instability and the expropriation of corporate assets in some developing countries also led to a deterioration of the investment climate, as perceived by U.S. multinationals.

The primary motivation for multinationalization, as with virtually all corporate activity, has always been profitability—from cutting transportation and labor costs to access to raw materials and foreign markets. As the potential profitability of foreign investment was reduced or threatened, U.S. corporations slowed down their overseas expansion. In the 1980s this trend was reversed, and U.S. multinational investments began to increase again. In 2005, the book value of U.S. direct investment in foreign countries was $3,524 billion. The income from these and other foreign investments amounted to more than $228 billion in 2005.

The existence and operation of U.S. multinationals raise a multitude of issues. In some sense, multinational facilities are of crucial importance to the corporations in their search for profits. In 2002, about 17 percent of the profits of U.S. corporations came from their overseas operations. As far back as 1976, about one-third of U.S. imports came from majority-owned U.S. corporations in foreign countries. Without these international activities, many U.S. corporations would be less profitable than they are.

On the other hand, multinational corporate activities place constraints on the development of U.S. foreign policy. For example, multinationals tend to operate in countries that limit organized labor unions, and often these countries are dictatorial and oppressive in other ways as well. Consequently, U.S. foreign policy may support these regimes and oppose national independence movements as it "protects" U.S. investments. Similarly, policies of the United States toward the Middle East have always been at least partly formed by its importance to U.S. oil companies. In both recent wars with Iraq (1990 and 2003–2007), the U.S. military went to great lengths to safeguard oil stocks in the region.

The relationship between multinationals and Third World countries has created a debate about the effects of these corporations on economic development. Some argue that the multinationals bring jobs and technology and stimulate growth. Others suggest that they cause economic dependence and unequal growth where some individuals prosper while others are exploited and remain mired in poverty. They further argue that corporations take advantage of cheap labor and raw materials but export their profits.

There is no question that wages are a primary motivation for corporations to become global producers in developing countries. When labor is $.07 an hour in Burma, $.25 an hour in China, and $.60 an hour in Mexico, a company that must pay its U.S. labor anywhere from $6 to $35 an hour will seriously consider moving production abroad.

The incentive to relocate production operations in foreign locations (outsource production) is incredible at these low wage rates. Geography is less important when corporations have the advantage of mobile capital resources; easily transferred technology, communications, transportation, computer information and production system technologies; and access to raw materials and other markets. For many larger corporations, becoming a global entity is an imperative to remain competitive. Smaller companies are also discovering opportunities for growth and expansion abroad.

A particularly controversial domestic consequence of U.S. multinationals is the movement of productive facilities out of the Northeast and the Midwest, as well as other parts of the country. Corporations often choose to close down old factories and to relocate new facilities in other parts of the United States or the world. This is a fundamental aspect of the free enterprise system. Capital is mobile, and corporations make decisions about what to do with their capital based on profitability. "Capital flight" may occur in the search for lower taxes, lower wages, less regulation and unionization, or closer proximity to expanding markets. Unfortunately, along with these "run-away shops" go the jobs and, in some cases, the economic health of local communities. Labor unions and communities often react to threats of corporate capital flight with wage and tax concessions, because when corporations close down operations, people lose their jobs, communities lose income and business, and governments lose tax revenues. Occasionally, workers or communities succeed in taking over the legal ownership and operation of corporate facilities rather than letting them leave.

TABLE 12.1 Sales, Profits, Assets, and Market Value of the Largest U.S. Corporations, 2006

Company	Industry	Sales (billions)	Profits (billions)	Assets (billions)	Market Value (billions)
ExxonMobil	Oil & gas	$328.2	$36.1	$208.3	$362.5
Wal-Mart Stores	Retailing	312.4	11.2	138.2	188.9
General Motors	Cars	192.6	−10.6	475.3	11.5
Chevron	Oil & gas	184.9	14.1	124.8	126.8
Ford Motor	Cars	178.1	2.3	276.0	15.2
ConocoPhillips	Oil & gas	162.4	13.6	107.0	84.0
General Electric	Conglomerates	149.7	16.4	673.3	348.5
Citigroup	Banking	120.3	24.6	1494.0	230.9
American Intl. Group	Insurance	107.0	11.9	843.4	172.2
IBM	Technology	91.1	8.0	105.8	126.7

Source: Data from Reprinted by permission of Forbes Magazine. © 2007 Forbes, Inc. Available at www.Forbes.com.

4. What effect does capital flight have on workers and communities? What might Adam Smith say about this?
5. In the late 1980s Congress passed legislation that requires notification of shutdowns. Additional legislation has been proposed to grant assistance to workers who want to restart businesses. Does this seem like a good idea to you? How might U.S. multinationals react to these proposals?

Global trade has helped some U.S. corporations grow to enormous size. Table 12.1 shows the sales, profits, assets, and employees of the ten largest U.S. companies, ranked by sales revenue. The largest two—Exxon Mobil and Wal-Mart—are also the two largest companies in the world. General Motors, the third largest U.S. company in sales, is the fifth-largest company in the world. With sales of $328.2 billion, Exxon Mobil has more income than most countries in the world, including Norway, South Africa, Finland, Greece, and Israel.

Free Enterprise versus Regulation

A perennial issue surrounding corporate power is the relationship between corporations and the federal government. Corporate officials and their supporters constantly complain of governmental regulation and interference with business, such as occupational health and safety legislation and environmental protection legislation. They argue that restrictions on business hamper their initiative and independence in bringing goods to U.S. consumers. Sometimes they even imply that continued regulation will reduce their profits and hence their corporations. These officials see corporations and government as adversaries. Others argue that if regulation and other governmental controls over business increase the costs of business, corporations then simply pass on these costs to consumers. Those skeptical that unregulated corporations always perform in the public interest counter that while corporations do create jobs and contribute to economic growth, they must be regulated carefully to prevent abuses. Critics believe that only with sufficient laws preserving competition, protecting laborers and the environment, and preventing corporate meddling in politics do corporations actually serve the public interest. Without such safeguards, these economists believe that corporations would often act to further their own interests for greater profits, often to the detriment of society as a whole.

Beyond these perspectives, a more fundamental criticism often voiced by corporate critics is that government regulations protect corporations from competition—government is seen as an ally of business. The government has provided direct assistance in the form of loans to troubled corporations, such as the bailouts of Lockheed and Chrysler in the 1970s and 1980s. Similarly, the Fed helped to orchestrate the private sector bailout of Long-Term Capital Management in 1998. This symbiotic relationship has its roots in common goals shared by business and government, such as economic growth, profits, employment, technological advance, and defense. Furthermore, corporations have substantial political power in the government through lobbying, direct campaign contributions, and corporate representatives in all branches of the government. In this view, government usually sides with business interests, usually at the expense of less powerful groups.

A series of corporate scandals in the early 2000s highlighted the debate over government regulation of corporations. In the Enron–Arthur Andersen scandal, investigators discovered that upper managers at Enron used questionable accounting maneuvers to pad earnings, misleading investors in order to boost the company's stock price. The artificially inflated stock price would then allow executives to cash in their stock options at a higher price. Meanwhile, Enron's auditor, the accounting firm Arthur Andersen, overlooked Enron's accounting schemes so as to maintain its lucrative consulting contract with Enron. Subsequently, accounting manipulations were discovered at General Electric, American International Group (AIG), WorldCom, and a host of other large corporations. Another set of scandals surrounding Wall Street research analysts surfaced around the same time. Analysts at Morgan Stanley and Merrill Lynch were found to have pushed dubious stocks on unsuspecting clients for the benefit of the investment bank that employed them.

These scandals shook confidence in U.S. financial markets and prompted calls for renewed regulation of corporations and markets. The U.S. government responded with a modest new regulation, the Sarbanes-Oxley Act of 2002, which requires CEOs to certify the accuracy of their books and mandates that outside auditors concur with the CEO's assessment. While some corporate officials complained that this was overregulation, many corporate critics saw it as a cosmetic reform that did not address fundamental problems in corporate board rooms. Similarly, the National Association of Securities Dealers (NASD) responded to the corrupt practices of research analysts by fining those found guilty of research malpractice and barring them from working within the financial industry. Yet the NASD did not require that research be divorced from investment banking to prevent future conflicts of interest from arising. Thus, the response of regulators to the corporate scandals of the early 2000s had been a modest tightening of controls. Substantial changes in the structures or incentives that existed prior to the scandals have not materialized, and the potential for future abuses due to conflicts of interest still exists.

6. What are the pros and cons of government regulation of corporations? Are any regulatory debates making headlines now? What are the issues? How do you think conservative, liberal, and radical economists would respond to the issues?

The Corporate Climate Today

Today, U.S. multinational firms are leaders in global competitiveness. Faced with the new global competition that began in the 1970s with the economic emergence of Japan and West Germany, and newly emerging industrial countries (NICs) including Mexico, Brazil, Taiwan, Singapore, Malaysia, South Korea, and Hong Kong, U.S. global corporations charted a strategy for increasing their competitiveness. This strategy involved the following actions:

◆ Moving some operations overseas
◆ Reducing the wage level and the amount of labor used
◆ Increasing the use and quality of technology
◆ Reorganizing the structure and management of the corporation
◆ Devoting more resources to the training and education of the labor force
◆ Becoming more flexible and lean

The past decade has been a time of rapid change for global corporations, including the controversial process of downsizing or restructuring. The management revolution that took place forced global firms to reexamine every aspect of their behavior.

Global firms accepted the challenge of focusing on total quality management and continuous improvement. They placed the goals of customer satisfaction and value-added production at the top of their performance objectives. Global competition gave them little choice. These firms also accepted the challenge of entering into new relationships with other firms, many of which had been their traditional rivals. It is common today for firms to form alliances in activities ranging from research and development to the full production of a good or service.

Of all of the forces driving the competitive character of the global economy, none has been as significant as the information system revolution. The use of computer technology in all activities of the firm—design, production, finance, accounting, services, information, sales, and planning—has changed everything. Rapid advances in computer technology and software have pushed the firm into the virtual world of the Internet.

Many firms successfully adapted to the changing global reality, but others did not. Each firm had to find ways to become more efficient and productive, and it needed a stable and healthy domestic economic context to support its efforts.

The combination of the management revolution (e.g., downsizing, globalization, better implementation of computer technologies), deregulation (including free trade agreements) on the part of governments, and the Internet created a boom from 1990 to 2000 that was very profitable for most U.S. companies and the U.S. stock market. Another merger wave swept the country from 1998 to 2000. Many of these were "megamergers" with purchase prices exceeding $1 billion. In 2000 alone, there were 208 megamergers. Most of these mergers were accompanied by downsizing as merged firms sought to eliminate redundant positions.

While technology companies fueled much of the boom, the inability of most Internet companies to become profitable led to a crash in the value of technology stocks in 2000–2001. Other stocks followed suit as corporate scandals, high energy prices, and high interest rates slowed the economy, ending the boom in early 2001. Looking back on the boom, we see a dramatic economic expansion that generated healthy economic growth, rapid and large gains in stock prices, swelling corporate profits, and a government budget surplus for the first time in decades. Still, there was a downside. The U.S. trade deficit was larger, and downsizing had become a regular occurrence in corporate America. Although workers' productivity per hour increased by 18 percent from 1989 to 1998, workers' average hourly wages increased by only 3 percent over the same period. Despite unemployment rates below 5 percent from 1997 through 2001, many workers were afraid to ask for higher wages because they feared downsizing and firms moving operations overseas.

The recession of 2000–2001 was followed by a period of economic growth, but the recovery did not create the number of jobs that usually accompanies an economic expansion and workers' wages did not increase. From the official end of the recession in November of 2001 until early 2004, the U.S. economy lost 2.2 million jobs, the first time since the Great Depression that an economic "recovery" saw such sustained job losses. During this period, the U.S. continued to lose manufacturing jobs, but job losses also occurred in other areas. Facilitated by inexpensive bandwidth and the Internet, U.S. corporations outsourced millions of jobs in traditional white-collar employments, including engineering, design, accounting, law, insurance, health, and financial analysis. Numbers of young workers left the labor force in response. From 2004–2007, job creation improved and wages finally began to increase. But it was also clear that job displacement from technological advances and outsourcing would continue to occur. Some politicians and labor advocates reacted to these events by renewing demands for greater protections for labor and labor unions in global markets.

Labor Unions in the United States

The role of labor in corporate decision making and growth is crucial. We have noted the influence of labor unions on wage rates and on the decisions that firms make about plant location. In the remainder of this chapter, we will briefly explore the history of labor unions in the United States and the effects they have on the economy.

In 2005, labor unions and employee associations represented just less than 16 million workers, or 13 percent of the approximately 125 million people in the public and private sectors of the labor force. There are more than 200 labor unions across the United States, representing industrial workers, secretaries, teachers, and many other employees. Some of the largest and most powerful unions are well known—for example, the United Auto Workers, the Teamsters, and the United Steel Workers. Others are less well known but are of growing importance, such as the United Food and Commercial Workers; the American Federation of State, County, and Municipal Employees; the Service Employees International Union; the United Farmworkers; and the Union of Needletrades, Industrial, and Textile Employees.

Labor unions were formed and exist to promote the interests of their members and other workers. Early unions attempted to do the following:

- Get better pay and benefits for their members.
- Provide job security for their members.
- Improve the health and safety of their members.
- Provide for legitimate representation of their members in the decision-making process of the firms for which they work.

Today, however, unions are often blamed for higher costs, for fewer domestic jobs, and for disrupting economic and community life with strikes and other acts of conflict. How has the impact of labor unions changed over time?

The History of U.S. Labor Unions

Labor unions emerged as a response to the lack of bargaining power that individual workers in a capitalist economy had with their employers over wages, benefits, the control of work, and working conditions. The employer owned the factory and offered employment paying the lowest wages possible. If there was a large pool of unemployed people, an individual employee would not be very successful in demanding higher wages or better working conditions.

In response to this structural reality of capital–labor relations, employees formed associations. Only through such unity could they have the power to protect their interests. In the early part of the nineteenth century, courts held such worker organizations to be illegal restraints of trade, so labor unions were legally powerless to bargain with employers or to strike—to refuse to work. However, in 1842 the Supreme Court ruled that attempts to organize workers into labor unions were not criminal conspiracies. After this ruling, labor unions began to have a national presence. It was also during this period that the economy became increasingly industrialized—a precondition for effective labor organization.

Following the Civil War, the National Labor Union attempted to build a social and political movement around a loose federation of trade unions. However, the craft unions left the organization because they were more interested in union recognition by employers, bargaining with employers over wages, and increasing their wages. In the 1870s and the 1880s, the Knights of Labor attempted to unite all workers against monopolies and to promote the interests

Child labor in a Carolina cotton mill, 1908.
(© Lewis Hine/Bettmann/Corbis)

of working people. The Knights of Labor organized some successful nationwide strikes against the railroads, but the organization was eventually disbanded because of a lack of internal cohesiveness and as a result of Jay Gould's use of strikebreakers in the 1886 railroad strike.

The modern labor movement can be traced back to the formation of the American Federation of Labor in 1886. The American Federation of Labor (AFL), under the leadership of Samuel Gompers, organized in the crafts, accepted capitalism as an economic system, and focused on obtaining higher wages, better working conditions, and shorter hours through collective bargaining, trade agreements, and strikes. The AFL was a confederation of craft unions, each powerful in its own area, that united in conventions and cooperated in strikes, picketing, and boycotts. The AFL believed firmly in the union shop, requiring all employees in a factory or shop to belong to the union (and this requirement was included in labor contracts with employers). The AFL also supported the strike as the ultimate weapon of organized labor in disputes with employers.

The AFL shunned direct political activity and also avoided organizing the emerging industrial sectors of the U.S. economy in the late nineteenth and early twentieth centuries. Many of these industrial workers were unskilled, and many were immigrants. Other labor organizers throughout the 1920s and 1930s actively began industrial organizing and eventually formed the Committee for

FIGURE 12.2 The Decline in Nonfarm Unionization, 1948–2006

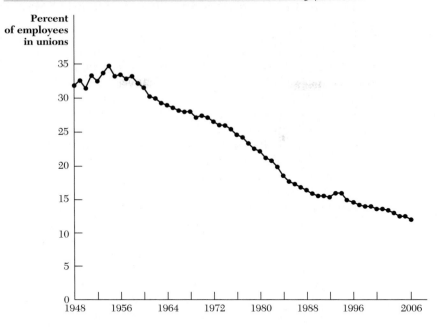

Source: U.S. Bureau of Labor Statistics.

Industrial Organization (CIO). In the 1930s, these forces were successful in forming labor organizations that won the right to represent and collectively bargain for the automobile and steel workers. Also in the 1930s, the **Wagner Act** was passed. This important piece of labor legislation gave all labor unions the legal right to organize and to collectively bargain for their members with employers. Since 1935, labor relations have been overseen by the National Labor Relations Board, which has the authority to spell out the rules of labor organizing for both employers and labor unions.

Since World War II, industrywide contracts have been negotiated by industry representatives and national labor unions in some cases. In other cases, large corporations and large labor unions have reached settlements that establish a pattern for the rest of an industry. During this period there also was a tremendous increase in public employees' unions for police, firefighters, teachers, and so forth. The Taft-Hartley Act, in 1947, allowed states to pass "right-to-work" laws that forbid union shops. Most of the right-to-work states are in the South. The act also allowed the president to order a ninety-day injunction against any strike deemed to threaten "national security" The 1950s saw the merger of the AFL and CIO as a national labor organization—the AFL-CIO—to support workers' interests.

Figure 12.2 shows the size of the organized labor force in the United States. There has been a clear decline in union membership since 1958. Some analysts suggest that the 1980–1992 drop was a result of the Reagan administration's critical stance toward unions. In 1981, President Ronald Reagan fired federal air traffic controllers who went on strike over working conditions. The hostility toward labor unions was also apparent in a National Labor Relations Board that was less hospitable to labor union organizers' disputes with employers. Higher unemployment rates than in the 1960s and 1970s made it more difficult for labor unions to organize, because people were worried simply about getting and holding jobs. Also, much of the job loss since 1980 was in industries with heavy union membership. With reduced output and employment in auto and steel, for example, labor unions lost members. While the service sector has been expanding, it has traditionally had fewer workers organized into labor unions. As globalization has proceeded, employers increasingly threaten workers with moving overseas if they demand higher wages or threaten to strike. This, too, has weakened unions recently.

Labor organization in this country has often been characterized by conflict and occasionally by violence. Capital owners and corporations have always had the power of ownership, and labor has had the power of numbers, unity, and strikes. There have been clear and opposing interests over such issues as the rights of employees to form labor unions, the level of wages, the length of the working day, and working conditions. The interests have clashed, and tempers have flared. Labor organizers were often branded as revolutionaries and Communists. Police have often been used to break strikes, and working people have often responded violently. To some extent the conflict is inherent in the structure of the economy, with private ownership and workers both dependent on labor for their incomes. However, one of the great achievements of modern labor legislation has been to mute this conflict and reduce it to legal and institutional forms that are much less likely to break out into violence.

7. Do any members of your family belong to labor unions? What are their opinions of their unions? What do you think of labor unions? Would you want to be in one? Why or why not?

The Economic Effects of Labor Unions

Labor unions are an important force in the economy and in U.S. society. They affect wages, working conditions, and the lives of union members. They also affect business decisions about location, numbers of employees, and so on. Unions affect communities through civic work, political action, and sometimes strikes. In the following discussion, we concentrate on two of the most significant effects of labor unions on economic conditions: wages and workplace environment.

First of all, what is the general effect of labor unions on wages and employment? Here it will be useful to refer to the supply-and-demand model for a labor market, as shown in Figure 12.3. Assume that there is an organized workforce negotiating with an employer over a new contract. The workers are will-

FIGURE 12.3 The Effect of Unions on Wages and Unemployment

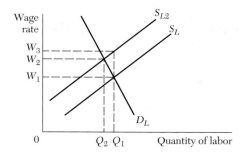

ing to supply their labor power for wages. The higher the wage, the greater the quantity of labor power they will tend to supply, as shown in the supply curve, S_L. The employer has a demand for labor; the higher the wage, the lower the quantity of labor the employer will demand, which is shown in the demand curve, D_L. At the point where the two curves, S_L and D_L intersect are the equilibrium wage rate and the equilibrium quantity of labor that will be supplied and demanded.

The labor union is presumably interested in obtaining higher wages for its workers and achieves this goal with the threat of its ultimate weapon, the strike. The workers can shift their supply curve for labor upward to get higher wages. What this means is that it will take a higher wage rate to get union workers to supply the same amount of labor. For example, union workers will only be willing to supply a quantity of labor power of Q_1 if they are offered a wage of W_3. If the employer is unwilling to meet this request for higher wages, the workers may go on strike. Shifting the supply curve upward, to S_{L2}, increases the equilibrium wage rate. It also tends to reduce the equilibrium quantity if the demand curve for labor does not change. Consequently, we can conclude that labor unions tend to increase wages for their members. It has been historically true that labor union members do get higher wages and higher wage increases than nonunion workers (see Figure 12.5 later in this chapter).

8. Data indicate that union workers generally are more productive than nonunion workers. What would this difference do to the demand for labor in Figure 12.3?

On the other hand, the rapid transformation of the global economy has brought increased competitive pressures on U.S.-based companies and concurrent pressures on labor unions to retain their members and successfully represent their interests. Since the early 1970s, U.S. workers have received a smaller share of national income, and their real wages have declined by an average of 8

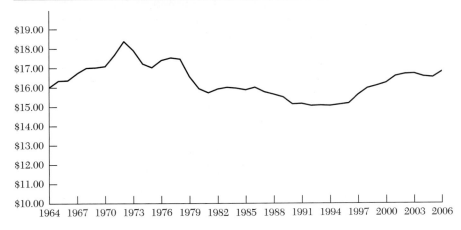

FIGURE 12.4 Average Real Hourly Earnings, 1964–2006 (in 2006 dollars)

Source: Authors' calculations using U.S. Bureau of Labor Statistics data.

percent. Figure 12.4 shows the average real hourly earnings for production and nonsupervisory workers in the private sector. Real wages fell from 1972 to 1997, in contrast with the period from 1947 to 1972, when workers' real wages increased by an average of 79 percent. The modern trends of globalization, downsizing, outsourcing, and declining union representation have been associated with a significant worsening of workers' position in the economy.

When we compare real hourly compensation (wages plus benefits) for manufacturing workers in the United States with the compensation of their counterparts overseas, we see that the United States falls in the middle in terms of compensation when compared with other developed countries, as shown in Table 12.2. U.S. manufacturing compensation tends to fall below those countries with strong unions and powerful labor-oriented political parties such as Norway, Germany and Denmark. But U.S. workers fare better than those in some developed countries, including Japan and Italy. Workers in newly industrialized countries such as Korea and developing countries such as Mexico earn significantly less hourly compensation, which contributes to the trend of U.S. corporations moving manufacturing operations to places like Korea and Mexico.

U.S. workers, however, fare less well than their international counterparts in developed countries with respect to working hours and vacation days. While full-time U.S. workers are guaranteed two weeks of paid vacation per year, many European governments mandate five or six weeks of paid vacation. Workweeks in the United States tend to be much longer as well. The result, as shown in Table 12.3, is that U.S. laborers average more hours of work per year than almost all other developed OECD countries. Table 12.3 also shows that Korean and Mexican workers face longer work hours, as is often true in newly industrialized and developing countries.

TABLE 12.2 Average Hourly Compensation of Manufacturing Employees, 2005

Country	Hourly Compensation
Norway	$39.14
Denmark	35.47
Germany	33.00
Netherlands	31.81
Switzerland	30.50
Sweden	28.73
United Kingdom	25.66
Australia	24.91
France	24.63
Canada	23.82
United States	**23.65**
Japan	21.76
Italy	21.05
Korea	13.56
Czech Republic	6.11
Mexico	2.63

Source: U.S. Bureau of Labor Statistics.

Many of these international differences in wages and work hours can be attributed to the relative strength of labor unions in the various countries. Workers in countries where unions are powerful tend to be paid better and to receive better benefits (including more vacation days) than their counterparts in countries with less powerful unions.

TABLE 12.3 Average Annual Hours Worked per Employed Person, 2004

Country	Average Hours Worked
Korea	2,380
Czech Republic	1,986
Mexico	1,848
United States	**1,824**
Australia	1,816
Japan	1,789
Canada	1,751
United Kingdom	1,669
Italy	1,585
Sweden	1,584
Switzerland	1,556
Denmark	1,454
Germany	1,443
France	1,441
Norway	1,363
Netherlands	1,357

Source: Data from *OECD Employment Outlook,* 2006.

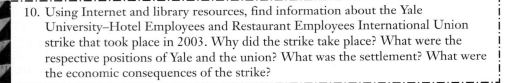

9. What has happened to real wages and to labor compensation as a share of national income in the past few years? What explains these trends? What are some of the consequences of these trends for U.S. labor? The U.S. economy? The global economy?

The second significant effect that labor unions have had on the economy is reforming the institutions and the conditions that surround work in the United States. In negotiations with employers, labor unions have focused on their own members' wages and conditions of employment, but the labor movement has been at the forefront of political efforts to improve the wages and the working conditions for all workers in the country. Legislation at the state and federal level includes workers' compensation, minimum-wage laws, the eight-hour day and overtime, the right of workers to form labor organizations and collectively bargain with employers, improved working conditions, and occupational health and safety regulations. Unions have also supported broad social legislation to improve the lot of working and poor people, including public education, maternity and paternity leave, Social Security, Medicare and Medicaid, environmental protection, civil rights laws, and the government's income-support programs.

10. Using Internet and library resources, find information about the Yale University–Hotel Employees and Restaurant Employees International Union strike that took place in 2003. Why did the strike take place? What were the respective positions of Yale and the union? What was the settlement? What were the economic consequences of the strike?

Over their long history, labor unions have succeeded in gaining legitimacy in our society, winning improved wages and working conditions for members, and promoting general labor and social legislation. In their ongoing efforts to comment on public policy and institutional arrangements affecting working people, labor unions have been increasingly critical of the growing disparity between rank-and-file worker incomes and chief executive officer (CEO) salaries.

In the past two decades, compensation for top management soared relative to average real wages for workers. In 2005, the average salary and bonus for a CEO of an S & P 500 company was $3.3 million. Including gains from long-term compensation, such as stock options, the average CEO's pay was actually $10.9 million. The highest-paid CEO in 2005 was Richard Fairbank of Capital One, who earned a total compensation package of $249.4 million. Lawrence Ellison, CEO of Oracle Corporation, set the record for annual CEO compensation in 2001 when he earned $706.1 million for exercising a large quantity of stock options.

The extent to which CEO pay has skyrocketed is clear when it is compared with the wages that average workers earn. According to *Business Week*, the average CEO made 42 times the average worker's pay in 1980, 84 times in 1990, and an astounding 531 times in 2000. The recession and the corporate scandals of 2000–2001 helped reduce this ratio. Still, CEO pay in the United States was 431 times the average worker's pay in 2004. Japanese CEOs earn about 10 times more than what Japanese workers earn, and German CEOs earn an average of 11 times more than German workers.

11. Do you think that the compensation of the nation's top executives is excessive? Explain your answer.

The Future of Labor Unions

Over the past three decades, organized labor's position in the U.S. economy weakened somewhat. Now, however, many unions are developing new strategies and approaches for this new economic and global context, becoming more aggressive and assertive in terms of seeking new members and performing their historic functions with more diligence. The head of the AFL-CIO, John Sweeney, has made expanding labor union membership one of his top priorities.

Labor-Centered Principles

In his book *Why Unions Matter,* Michael Yates, a professor of economics and labor educator at the University of Pittsburgh at Johnstown, argues that unions bring significant benefit for workers and are the best hope for combating some of the negative trends that have been affecting U.S. workers recently (longer hours, lower wages, downsizing, outsourcing). Yates believes that unions are essential because most workers are powerless on their own:

Let's be honest. Almost every person who works for a living works for someone else. We work in all sorts of jobs, in all types of industries, and under all kinds of conditions. But no matter what the exact circumstances, we do not work for ourselves or for each other, which means that the most fundamental aspects of our work are not controlled by us. Furthermore, our employers try to organize their workplaces so that we cannot exert much control by our own actions. For example, each of us needs to work; we do not labor for the fun of it but to pay our bills and support our families. Yet none of us can guarantee that we will have work on any given day, let alone for an entire working life. If

our employer decides to shut down the business, move it, or introduce labor-saving machinery, none of us acting alone can do anything about it....

If we are honest, we must admit that our employers have real power over us. Some of them may be nice and some of them may be nasty, but none of them will spend money just because it would be good for one of us. They know that as individuals we are less powerful than they are. We have only our ability to work to sell, but they have the jobs. In our economic system, these jobs belong to them and not to us, and they can do with them whatever they want. It is a simple but powerful truth that working people and their employers do not face each other as equals. Their employers have the jobs they need, and workers are replaceable....

A worker standing alone is a worker in trouble. For every Michael Jordan, whose amazing talent gives him tremendous power, there are millions of the rest of us, eminently replaceable. Our only hope is to stand together, and, . . . when we do, we can greatly improve our lots in life. There is no doubt that unions force employers to pay their workers higher wages and

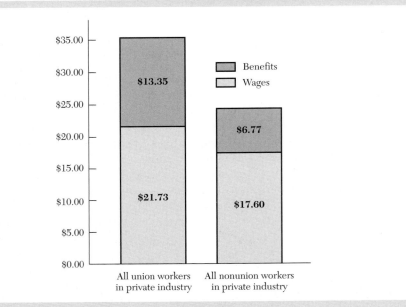

FIGURE 12.5 Union Compensation Advantage, 2006

Benefits
Wages

$13.35
$21.73

$6.77
$17.60

All union workers
in private industry

All nonunion workers
in private industry

Source: U.S. Bureau of Labor Statistics.

to provide them with more and better fringe benefits. And furthermore, unions compel employers to listen to their employees and to respect them as human beings. Employers know these things, and this is why they fight our collective efforts.

Are unions as effective as some economists believe? As Figure 12.5 shows, on average union workers receive $4.13 more per hour in wages and $6.58 more per hour in benefits than nonunion workers. The "union advantage" in total compensation is $10.71 per hour, or 44 percent more than nonunion workers. In addition, union workers are more than twice as likely as nonunion workers to have been employed with their current employer more than ten years, indicating greater job stability. Unions tend to be particularly beneficial for blue-collar workers who have little power in the workplace unless they band together.

Yates concludes his book by calling for a new set of labor-centered principles to advance the interests of working Americans:

This is a more hopeful time for unions and the labor movement than any time in the past thirty years. For labor to be reborn, however, it must become more willing to declare its political independence. As a first step in that direction, organized labor should declare its fundamental principles.... A list of labor-centered principles .... might look like this:

1. **Employment as a right.** Unemployment not only wastes the output that the unemployed could have produced, it also wastes human beings and leads to a large number of social problems from arrest and imprisonment to murder and suicide.

2. **Meaningful work.** Human beings have the unique ability to conceptualize work tasks and then perform them. Yet most jobs utilize only a fraction of human ability. This leads to profound alienation and a hatred of

work. Instead of seeing labor as the fulfillment of our humanity, we see it as a necessary evil to be avoided if at all possible.

3. **Socialization of consumption.** We waste enormous efforts to purchase goods and services that ought to be provided by society. Examples include education at all levels, health care (including care of the aged), child care, transportation, and recreation (parks, libraries, playgrounds, and gyms). It would be far more efficient to share responsibility for such public needs.

4. **Democratic control of production.** We pride ourselves on having a free society, yet nearly all workplaces are run as dictatorships. Shouldn't we have control over the production of the outputs which we depend upon for our survival? Why should the glass factory that dominated my hometown for nearly a century be able to pack up and leave without the will of the people being considered, much less being decisive?

5. **Shorter hours of work.** At the same time that hundreds of millions of people worldwide cannot find enough work, millions of others are working hours comparable to those who worked during the industrial revolution. People are working too much to enjoy life. Why should this be so?

6. **An end to discrimination.** What possible justification can there be for the gross inequalities in jobs, incomes, housing, and wealth that exist between those who are white and male and just about everyone else? No just society can be built on a foundation of racial, ethnic, and gender discrimination.

7. **Wage and income equality.** I can think of no good reason why I should earn four times as much as the men and women who clean the buildings in which I labor and teach. Would I refuse to work if they earned the same as I do? How can it be justified that a CEO makes tens of millions of dollars per year? For what? Does anyone believe that no one would do these jobs for a lot less?

… In grassroots organizing, based as it must be on rank-and-file control, in struggles for the hearts and souls of our national unions, in alliances with organizations and individuals committed to building the kind of society that is within our grasp, in battles with the employers, whose usefulness becomes less apparent each day, a new labor movement and a new social movement might be born.

Source: Michael Yates, *Why Unions Matter* (New York: Monthly Review Press, 1998), various pages.

12. Which (if any) of Yates's labor-centered principles do you support? Why? What impact do you think his suggestions would have on the U.S. economy if they were actually implemented?

Corporations and Labor: The Twenty-first Century

Today, in the early part of the twenty-first century, U.S. corporations have firmly reestablished their economic and financial dominance in the global economy. This transition, which began in the mid-1970s, has left the U.S. economic landscape radically altered. New relationships exist between corporations and government, corporations and labor, and corporations and communities.

FIGURE 12.6   Total U.S. Corporate Profits, 1980–2005

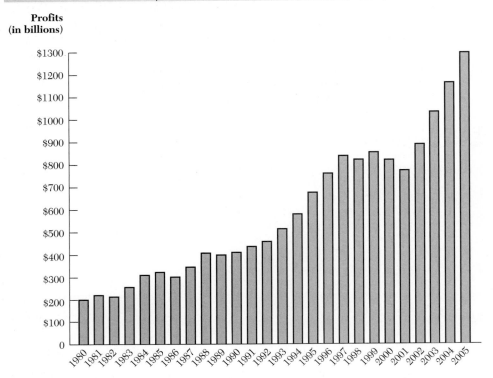

Profits (in billions)

Source: *Economic Report of the President,* 2006
Note: Profit figures include adjustments for inventory valuation and capital consumption.

While the issues and arguments put forward by critics of corporations are just as legitimate today as they were decades ago, for most U.S. citizens and the larger global economic community, the corporation is the dynamic organizational engine that drives the growth and prosperity of the global economy. The sustained economic growth and performance of the U.S. economy from 1992 to 2000, highlighted by the phenomenal growth of the stock market and corporate profits (see Figure 12.6), is largely attributed to the success of multinational corporations in the U.S. economy. With the government's policy of deregulation, corporations can do most of what they believe necessary to grow and compete in world markets. Yet, the speculative Internet stock bubble and the corporate scandals that contributed to the recession and slow growth of the early 2000s are also attributed to large corporations. Many of the job losses that occurred from 2002 to 2004 can be linked directly to corporate outsourcing and downsizing, which helped to reestablish corporate profits at the expense of workers (profits increased by more than 20 percent during this period). And, workers only regained some of their lost ground as the economy grew from 2004 to 2007. Organized labor and community members will continue to criticize such practices and demand social responsibility for corporations. They insist that corporations be held publicly accountable for their decisions and actions that impact domestic politics, the health and safety of individual workers, the economic viability of individual communities, and the natural environment. It is unlikely that these conflicts will ever disappear.

Conclusion

This chapter focuses on two of the most important economic institutions in the United States: corporations and labor unions. Having stepped outside the realm of pure microeconomic theory, we examined the development, behavior, and importance of corporations and labor unions.

Review Questions

1. Why is the corporation a dominant institution in the U.S. economic system?
2. Why do corporations go global? What are some of the implications of this trend?
3. Why are labor unions an important institution in the U.S. economy?
4. Is the relationship between big corporations and big labor unions adversarial or symbiotic?
5. Do you think U.S. CEOs are worth the large compensation they receive?
6. Corporations have gone global. Will labor unions? Why or why not?
7. In your next job, how much control do you think you will have over your wages, hours, and working conditions? Would Yates's proposals for labor-centered principles improve your position in the workplace? Why or why not?
8. What do you think will be the relationship between corporations, labor, and the government in the next century? What do you think it should be?

CHAPTER THIRTEEN

The Economic Role of Government

■ Introduction

*I*n the previous chapters of Part 3, we concentrated on the operation of markets and their role in allocating resources. We also introduced the importance of corporations and labor unions as economic factors in the private sector. But the United States has a **mixed economy**—one in which business firms and markets in the private sector exist alongside economic institutions in the public sector. In fact, all the world's economies are "mixed," with varying levels of public sector involvement.

The **public sector**, in the form of local, state, and federal governmental offices, organizations, and institutions, performs many important economic functions. Think about your local community. What goods and services are provided by governmental units? The list is actually quite long, and the activities are fundamentally important to the day-to-day economic (as well as noneconomic) operation of a community. Public services also provide capabilities for the long-run survival of a society. Postal service, police and fire protection, road construction and maintenance, street signs, sewers, parks and recreation services, a court system, schools, traffic signals, welfare services, and so on are all provided by local, state, and federal governmental units.

In general, the economic role of government in capitalism results from the failure of markets to allocate resources to certain tasks or from a public conclusion that the results of markets are unacceptable. Consequently, governments have taken responsibility for limiting the practice and the results of economic concentration, correcting the inequality of the distribution of market-determined incomes, providing public goods when markets fail to supply them, and regulating activities of the private sector that produce external costs to the rest of society. In this chapter, we will explore each of these aspects of governmental economic activity in more detail.

The Role of Government in the Economy

Most government intervention in the economy can be grouped under two categories: policies to support the functioning of markets and policies to correct situations when the market fails. Before we consider the government's role in the economy in more detail, it is useful to reflect on the conditions that are required for markets to function efficiently. Markets require an economic framework within which private economic activity takes place, and governments provide that framework. Thus, certain government actions in the economy complement, support, and even make possible private sector activity. For example, a market economy requires clearly defined property rights, including intellectual property, to function efficiently. Property rights encourage owners to invest and innovate, sure in the knowledge that they will be the beneficiaries of successful projects. In countries without clear property rights, such as some dictatorships, business owners are reluctant to invest because the proceeds from their investments can be seized without compensation. Governments provide judicial and legal systems to protect property rights so that productive economic activity can proceed under clear rules and laws.

As we will explore in Part 4, markets also need monetary and banking systems to function efficiently. Money reduces transactions costs (the cost of exchanging goods and services) and facilitates exchange by enabling buyers and sellers to express all products and services in terms of a common unit of currency. A stable, safe banking system also facilitates markets by channeling funds from savers to borrowers, thereby increasing investment and economic growth. Federal regulations that safeguard the health and stability of the banking sector are crucial in this process. Similarly, a stable macroeconomic environment also encourages investment and growth. The federal government utilizes its policy tools to further growth and reduce economic instability.

Another important action of government that supports market activity is the provision of infrastructure, which lowers transactions costs and improves the functioning of markets. Transportation and public utilities are critical parts of the U.S. infrastructure. Where it is prohibitively expensive to distribute products, little market activity will occur. Where the public infrastructure is more elaborate, the cost of exchanging products is lower and more exchange is likely to occur. For example, a new major road attracts investment and commerce to communities near the road.

For markets to function efficiently, both buyers and sellers must have accurate information. People need to know with some degree of certainty how much something is worth to make an informed decision, and they need to be protected from deceptive information, including misleading advertising. Government disclosure and production standards, including labeling requirements, make it easier for consumers to compare products and get the information they need to make an informed decision. Similarly, in financial markets government regulations ensure that stock purchasers get accurate information regarding the value of stocks and that insiders are not able to manipulate markets at the expense of others. Thus, in a capitalist economic system, one major function of government is to create a framework conducive to productive market activity.

However, even after an appropriate framework for markets has been established, when there are market failures the government has to intervene further to ensure that the market system functions efficiently. In response to the various failures of the market system, government has developed many different programs. Public regulation of monopolies and antitrust legislation are intended to control economic concentration. The progressive income tax system and income support, job training, equal opportunity, and affirmative-action programs exist for the purpose of reducing economic inequality. The public use of resources to provide such socially desirable goods and services as education, parks, police and fire protection, and roads results from the failure of the private sector to adequately supply them. Zoning laws, pollution controls, environmental protection legislation, restrictions on child labor, occupational health and safety regulations, and food and drug inspections are meant to correct some of the abuses resulting from the operation of private markets. These public activities have all been developed throughout the history of U.S. capitalism, as well as in other economic systems.

Local, state, and federal governments have created taxation and revenue systems to finance their activities. Through raising money, governments can make a claim on the resources of the society by purchasing them in markets.

All these governmental activities are intensely political and controversial. The decisions about which programs to pursue, how much money to spend on them, and how to raise the revenues to finance them involve public discussion and debate, legislative resolution, administrative direction, and judicial oversight. People, organizations, politicians, political parties, and even ideas are joined in the political process to decide what governments will do and how they will do it.

1. What government programs do you consider to be most important? Least important? Are there programs you would like to see added? Cut?

Throughout the history of U.S. capitalism, there has been debate about the economic role of the government. At times the debate has been lively and heated. More than two hundred years ago, Alexander Hamilton and Thomas Jefferson argued about whether the country should be an agrarian or industrial society and about what role the federal government ought to play in promoting one or the other. Before the Civil War, the South and the North disagreed about the imposition of tariffs by the federal government as well as slavery. Later in the nineteenth century, a controversial issue was the role of the government in giving land to the railroads and then in regulating their rates. During the Great Depression, there was vociferous debate about the growing role of the government in regulation, relief, public employment, social spending, labor legislation, and even public ownership.

Since that time, along with the growth of government, the debate has continued. During Ronald Reagan's presidency, the discussion was revitalized with a renewed attack on the general role of the government in the economy. One of Reagan's primary campaign themes was that the government was interfering too much in the private sector and that its size and its rules were preventing economic growth. President Bill Clinton echoed these sentiments when he declared, "The era of big government is over." President George W. Bush expressed similar sentiments during his presidency. However, the attacks of September 11, 2001, sparked calls for the expansion of government to fight terrorism. Only time will tell whether the role of government in the economy will shrink or if its role will increase to meet new challenges.

Going back to the writings of Adam Smith, we can see that there has always been a case for some necessary tasks on the part of the state in support of the operation of the economy. Smith suggested that the government needed to protect private property, enforce contracts, provide for a monetary system, supply a defense capability, and provide some public goods, such as education and transportation. Beyond that, he believed the role of the government should be circumscribed. Note, however, that what Smith has delineated is of fundamental importance to the economy and requires a large and powerful government. Smith said that its powers should be limited—never that it should be weak or small.

Since Smith's time, the general discussion about the role of the government has been partly about the scope of its activities and partly about its limitations within the kind of economic system that we have. To review the debate, it is useful to use the conservative, liberal, and radical perspectives.

Conservatives argue that the state's involvement in the economy limits personal freedoms and that markets, if left alone, will produce economic growth and social welfare. Individuals, pursuing their own interests in business, will provide jobs, technological development, and growth in the economy. Conservatives, consequently, tend to oppose efforts to regulate big corporations, redistribute income, and regulate directly the externalities of the private sector. Such governmental activities interfere with the operation of the "invisible hand." It is largely the conservatives who mount the attacks on the government's role in the economy. (Part of their critique also deals with Keynesian fiscal and monetary policy, which we will discuss in Part 4.)

The liberal position suggests that the operation of the market economy in capitalism tends to produce economic growth and efficiency, along with an emphasis on individual economic freedom. However, liberals acknowledge some of the problems that the development of the economy produces, such as economic concentration, income inequality, and externalities. Consequently, they think it is entirely appropriate for the government to attempt to correct and address some of those problems. They also argue that such government intervention can, in fact, improve the allocation of resources in society. This position has largely won out in public debate concerning the role of government over the past century, although that may be changing.

The radical position begins with the assertion that the government plays a particularly important role in the operation and maintenance of capitalism as an economic system. For example, the state protects private property and the rights of owners to pursue their economic freedom. However, it does not offer the same kind of freedom or protection to poor people. Another way of saying this is that the state's role is constrained by its relationship to capitalism as a particular type of economic system. This point is the basis of the radical critique of liberal policies of government involvement in the economy. There is a limit on the extent of government involvement in the private sector as to redistributing income, regulating externalities, or enforcing antitrust laws. The limit is the requirement of capital accumulation for the growth of capitalism. Without capital accumulation, the economy will stagnate. If state policies interfere with corporate profits or profit expectations, capital accumulation can become endangered. In other words, if state intervention proceeds too far, it may interfere with capital accumulation, and government policies will have to retreat somewhat. Radicals recognize that the political response to the abuses and inequities of capitalism has required and led to governmental programs that address these problems, but ultimately radicals see the government as serving the interests of the wealthy elite.

2. What programs are included in "welfare spending"? Does welfare spending hinder the operation of capitalism? How would you find out if you are right (or if you don't know)? Why does welfare spending take place? What would a conservative say? A liberal? A radical?

3. Which position best describes your attitudes toward government spending in general? Why?

The Growth of Government's Role

The public sector significantly expanded its role in the economy during the twentieth century. Through the political process, governmental institutions make decisions about pursuing particular programs. Table 13.1 presents information on the range of spending programs and the relative priorities of state, local, and federal governments in the United States today. Education is by far the most important category for state and local governments; it accounted for 34 percent of state and local government spending in 2002–2003. In the federal government's budget for fiscal year, 2005 (October 1, 2004, to September 30, 2005), Social Security, national defense, income security, and interest on the debt were the four largest spending categories; they accounted for more than two-thirds of $2.5 trillion in total federal spending.

Table 13.2 presents information on public sector taxes and receipts for various years from 1929 to 2002. The table includes data on the total amount of governmental revenues as well as their percentage share of gross domestic product (GDP), the total value of output for each year. For example, in 1929, total governmental revenues were $11.3 billion, which amounted to 10.9 percent of total output. From even a quick look at this table, we can see that the relative importance of government in the economy has increased significantly over the past 75 years, although government revenues shrank as a percentage of GDP from 2000 to 2004. Revenues in 2004 amounted to more than $3.2 trillion and have increased by almost three-hundredfold since 1929! However, the most useful way to gauge the relative position of any economic variable is to compare it to GDP. Revenues in 2004 were 26.5 percent of GDP. This more than

TABLE 13.1   State and Local and Federal Government Spending

State and Local Government Spending, 2002–2003	
Program	**Spending Level (in billions)**
Education	$ 621.3
Public welfare	310.8
Highways	117.7
All other*	772.1
Total	1,821.9
Federal Budget Outlays, Fiscal Year 2005	
Social Security	$ 523.3
National defense	495.3
Income security	345.8
Medicare	298.6
Health	250.6
Net interest	184.0
Education, training, employment, and social services	97.5
Veterans benefits and services	70.2
Transportation	67.9
Administration of justice	40.0
Natural resources and environment	28.0
General government	17.0
Agriculture	26.6
International affairs	34.6
General science, space and technology	23.7
Community and regional development	26.3
Energy	0.4
Commerce and housing credit	7.6
Offsetting receipts	−65.2
Total	2,472.2

*Includes health and hospitals, police and fire protection, corrections, interest on debt, parks and recreation, sanitation, administration, housing and urban renewal, protective inspection and regulation, and so on.

Source: *Economic Report of the President*, 2006.

twofold increase in government's share since 1929 represents a shift in the role of government in the economy.

From 1929 to 1940, total revenues increased from 10.9 percent to 17.7 percent of output. Most of this increase occurred in the federal sector in response to the Great Depression. The increase in the share of total revenues from 1940 to 1950 from 17.7 to 24.1 percent resulted from the expansion of the federal government and the retrenchment of state and local governments during World War II. From 1950 to 1970, the public sector continued expanding, and revenues increased to almost 28 percent of GDP. During this period, federal revenues increased their share by less than 3 percent while the share of state–local revenues expanded by almost 50 percent. More recently, the relative share of governmental revenues in

TABLE 13.2   Public Sector Taxes and Receipts, from Own Sources

Year	Total Government $ Billions	Total Government Percentage of GDP	State and Local Governments $ Billions	State and Local Governments Percentage of GDP	Federal Government $ Billions	Federal Government Percentage of GDP
1929	11.3	10.9	7.5	7.3	3.8	3.6
1940	17.8	17.7	9.1	9.1	8.7	8.6
1950	69.4	24.1	19.0	6.6	50.4	17.5
1960	134.4	25.5	40.5	7.7	93.9	17.8
1970	286.7	27.6	100.8	9.7	186.0	17.9
1980	798.0	28.6	265.9	9.5	532.1	19.1
1990	1,707.8	29.4	626.4	10.8	1,081.5	18.6
1995	2,212.6	29.9	806.1	10.9	1,406.5	19.0
2000	3,125.9	31.8	1,072.2	10.9	2,053.8	20.9
2004	3,208.2	26.5	1,233.4	10.2	1,974.8	16.3

Source: *Economic Report of the President*, 1990, 1997, 2006.

GDP has stabilized and even begun to decline. Total revenues have fallen below 30 percent of GDP, federal revenues are about 16 percent, and state–local revenues have been about 10 percent of GDP since 1970.

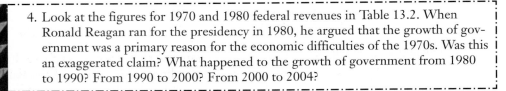

4. Look at the figures for 1970 and 1980 federal revenues in Table 13.2. When Ronald Reagan ran for the presidency in 1980, he argued that the growth of government was a primary reason for the economic difficulties of the 1970s. Was this an exaggerated claim? What happened to the growth of government from 1980 to 1990? From 1990 to 2000? From 2000 to 2004?

For comparative purposes, Table 13.3 shows the relative importance of government in several economically advanced countries. Government taxes and receipts as a percentage of gross domestic product are higher in all these countries, except Japan and Korea, than they are in the United States.

We can also measure the size of the government in terms of what it spends. Table 13.4 contains data on governmental expenditures in the United States from 1929 to 2004. In 1929, all levels of government spent $10.3 billion, which was 9.9 percent of output. By 2004, total governmental spending surpassed $3.6 trillion, or 30.9 percent of GDP. In this period, there has been a threefold increase in the relative importance of the governmental sector in the economy. The relative share of state and local government spending has increased by 80 percent, while the share of the federal government has increased more than seven times. From 1929 to 1940, most of the growth was in the federal sector as a result of New Deal programs to cope with the effects of the Great Depression. From 1940 to 1970, the federal share grew as a result of defense spending and expanding social spending. There was also an expansion of federal grants to

TABLE 13.3   Total Tax and Non-tax Receipts as a Percentage of GDP, 2006*

Country	Taxes as a Percent of GDP
Norway	61.1
Sweden	58.8
Denmark	55.2
France	51.1
Belgium	49.0
Austria	47.8
Netherlands	46.3
Italy	44.9
Germany	43.5
New Zealand	43.4
Greece	42.9
United Kingdom	42.3
Poland	40.6
Canada	40.5
Spain	39.4
Czech Republic	39.2
Australia	36.5
Switzerland	35.7
Ireland	35.6
United States	34.2
Korea	31.9
Japan	31.7

Source: Data from *OECD Economic Outlook*, December 2006.
*includes fees for services and other collections

state and local governments, which contributed to their increasing share. From 1970 to 1980, the share of state and local spending and the share of the federal government increased slightly, reflecting continued growth of social spending in the 1970s. From 1980 to 2004, the share of state and local governments again increased slightly. Despite the efforts of the Reagan team to reduce the federal government's role in the economy, the federal share increased from 18.4 percent in 1980 to 19.7 percent in 1990. This resulted from increased spending on the military, Social Security, and interest payments on the federal debt. From 1990 to 2000, federal spending decreased to 17.1 percent of GDP, mostly as a result of efforts to reduce the federal budget deficit and the growth of GDP in the late 1990s. Between 2000 to 2004, federal spending in the United States increased relative to GDP. Additional spending on homeland security, the military, and an array of pork projects was primarily responsible.

The government spending in Table 13.4 includes transfer payments. **Transfer payments** are governmental programs that transfer spending power to qualified individuals. Examples include veterans' benefits, unemployment compensation, Medicaid, food stamps, Social Security and Medicare benefits, and Temporary Assistance for Needy Families. Consequently, total government spending overestimates the claim of government programs on the society's resources. Currently when the government collects Social Security and Medicare taxes

TABLE 13.4   U.S. Governmental Expenditures

Year	Total Government		State and Local Governments		Federal Government	
	$ Billions	Percentage of GDP	$ Billions	Percentage of GDP	$ Billions	Percentage of GDP
1929	10.3	9.9	7.8	7.5	2.5	2.4
1940	18.5	18.4	9.3	9.3	9.2	9.1
1950	61.4	21.3	22.5	7.8	38.9	13.5
1960	122.9	23.3	40.2	7.6	82.7	15.7
1970	294.8	28.4	113.0	10.9	181.8	17.5
1980	842.8	30.2	329.4	11.8	513.4	18.4
1990	1,872.6	32.3	730.5	12.6	1,142.1	19.7
1995	2,397.6	32.4	978.2	13.2	1,419.4	19.2
2000	2,886.5	29.4	1,269.5	12.9	1,617.1	16.5
2004	3,620.6	30.9	1,587.5	13.5	2,033.0	17.3

Note: Intergovernmental grants are counted by the spending source.

Source: *Economic Report of the President,* 1990, 1997, 2006.

from people's wages and salaries (and from their employers), it pays benefits to people who are retired and eligible for Social Security and Medicare. Today resources are transferred through these programs from one set of people (those working now) to another (those retired). People who pay taxes have their spending power reduced, and people who receive benefits have their spending power increased. The money flows through the Social Security Administration, but the federal government makes no direct claim on resources in this transfer program (except for the costs of administering the program). Much of the growth in federal government expenditures as a percentage of output since 1929 has come as a result of the expansion of federal transfer programs.

This conclusion is reinforced by the fact that governmental purchases of goods and services have declined as a percentage of GDP since 1970. In contrast to transfer payments, governmental purchases of goods and services represent **exhaustive spending.** With this type of spending, governments are making claims on society's resources in the pursuit of their priorities. Exhaustive spending includes the purchase of weapons, pencils, government employees' labor, road construction materials, computers, police and fire vehicles, and so forth. By spending on public programs, governments demand the use of resources. This is different from a governmental program that transfers spending power from one group to another.

From 1929 to 1940, total governmental purchases almost doubled their share of output, with almost all of the growth in spending coming from the federal government. From 1940 to 1960, total purchases increased their share of output from 14.2 percent to 21.2 percent. Most of this growth occurred in the federal government sector, with the lion's share being accounted for by purchases of goods and services for national defense. However, from 1950 to 1960, there was

FIGURE 13.1   Public Sector Employment

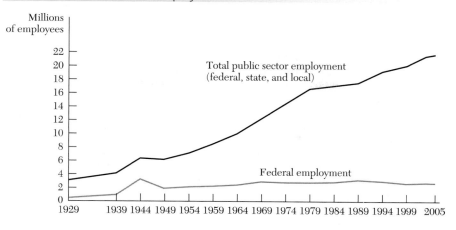

Sources: Advisory Commission on Intergovernmental Relations, *Significant Features of Fiscal Federalism,* 1984 ed., (Washington, D.C., 1985) and the U.S. Census Bureau.

also a significant postwar expansion in state and local spending, especially for roads and schools. Since 1960, the overall level of government purchases has stabilized at about 20 percent of GDP, although it has fallen recently. Government consequently makes a direct claim on about one-fifth of U.S. output every year.

Public sector employment also demonstrates the growth of government in the twentieth century in the United States. Figure 13.1 illustrates the increase in public sector employment since 1929. In 1929, public sector employees were about 6 percent of the total U.S. labor force; by 2005 this figure had increased to 15 percent. In 2005, almost 22 million people were employed by the federal, state, and local governments, with more than 19 million working for local and state governments and 2.7 million civilians employed by the federal government. The vast majority of the growth in public sector employment since 1950 has come in state and local governments. These workers are employed in education, hospitals, law enforcement, highway work, and general governmental administration.

5. Why has the relative importance of government increased over the past fifty years? Why has it decreased since 1990?

Market Failure, Public Goods, and Externalities

In Chapter 9, we demonstrated that competitive markets operate in a manner that produces efficiency in resource allocation and a maximization of social welfare. The theoretical model of perfect competition proves Adam Smith's contention about the operation of the "invisible hand" in a private market economy—it promotes growth, efficiency, and consumer sovereignty. However, some aspects of economic reality interfere with the attractive theoretical results of competitive markets.

We have already examined one instance when markets fail to produce an efficient allocation of resources. In Chapter 10, we showed that whenever there is imperfect competition in a market, there is also inefficiency in resource allocation. In perfect competition, allocative efficiency occurs because firms in the long run produce at the rate of output where $P = MC$. In oligopoly, monopoly, and monopolistic competition, firms tend to produce a rate of output in the long run at which P is greater than MC. Because P indicates the extra benefit that consumers derive from one more unit of a good and MC indicates the extra cost of one more unit of the good, society would prefer to have more of that good produced. That is, there is a restriction of output, or an underallocation of resources to the production of that good. Whenever markets are imperfectly competitive, the operation of markets fails to maximize social welfare.

In Chapter 11, we also learned that the distribution of market-determined incomes might fail to satisfy society's concerns with fairness. Consequently, the public sector might decide to redistribute income through taxing and spending programs.

But there are other instances in which markets fail. Private markets organize the exchanges of goods and services between suppliers and purchasers. These exchanges between willing participants are based on the costs to producers and the benefits to consumers of the relevant commodities. The price indicates how much money someone is willing to give up in order to possess something, and it also registers the amount of money a seller must get to turn that something over to someone else. However, this exchange can miss a proper evaluation of the true social benefits and costs of the production and consumption of some goods and services.

Social benefits or costs that occur outside the sale of a good or service are called **externalities.** For example, when someone buys a pack of cigarettes based on that person's demand for them and the producer's costs, there are external effects outside of this exchange. These externalities include the effects of cigarette smoke on other people and smoking-related medical problems the buyers may develop (which may not have been part of the original demand, regardless of required warnings!). These are *external costs* connected with this one good. In a similar fashion, if someone who lives next to you purchases a CD and plays it so loud that you can hear it, and you like it, then you derive an *external benefit* from that exchange. In both cases, the external results are not taken into account in the transaction between the buyer and the seller of the commodity. Whenever externalities are present the operation of markets does not assure an efficient allocation of resources. Markets also fail to allocate resources efficiently when goods generate benefits for large groups of consumers, including those who do not pay for it. For example, public (commercial-free) radio is listened to by thousands of people, but most people choose not to pay for the service. These **public goods** cannot be allocated in sufficient quantities by the market because too many people choose not to pay for a service that they consume (i.e., they choose to be *free riders*).

In all of these instances of **market failure** (where the market fails to register all of the costs or benefits of a transaction, or to produce an efficient result), the public sector may attempt to improve the allocation of resources. That is, governmental programs to limit the effects of economic concentration and to account for external benefits and costs may improve the allocation of resources and increase social welfare.

6. Identify at least one other example of an external cost of a specific exchange. Also, identify one other example of an external benefit.

7. What external costs might be associated with a cigarette smoker's eventual medical bills? What parties might be affected by these bills besides the smoker?

Public Goods

A commodity is considered a public good when it is difficult or impossible to exclude people from using it, even when they do not pay for it, and when its benefits are not depleted when one additional person uses it. For example, freeways are a public good: Anyone with a car can drive on the freeway; one person driving on the freeway does not prevent another person from using it; and people are allowed to drive on the freeway even if they did not help pay for its construction and maintenance. In contrast, a private good is reserved for use by its owner and it is usually used up after it is consumed. If society relied only on markets to allocate resources to public goods, there would be inefficiency in resource allocation. For example, in some cases, the operation of markets either fails to provide any of a good or underallocates resources to it. Consider street signs. Without street signs, businesses would be unable to deliver products, people could not find each other's homes, and general confusion would reign. But street signs are not provided by markets.

The reason is that private markets require suppliers to be able to charge people for the right to possess or consume a commodity. There is property ownership in a private exchange. Someone who owns a bicycle can prevent other people from using it. With street signs, however, there is no ownership, and people cannot be excluded from using them. Everyone going down the street can use the street signs, whether or not they helped to pay for them. The firm that put up the street sign could not prevent those who did not pay from using it to identify the street, otherwise the sign would no longer serve its purpose. In this case, no private firm would provide street signs in sufficient quantities because there would be no way to force people to pay for using them. Some people might be willing to pay, but others would choose to be free riders. People will not generally pay for something they can get for free. Consequently, communities have used governmental institutions to provide street signs, and citizens are compelled to pay for them through taxation.

The key issue here is that if it is left up to individuals, society is unlikely to get the optimal quantity of public goods, thereby generating a market failure. Consider national defense as another example. National defense is not depleted when one person uses it. When national defense is provided, every person inside the country is protected, even if she or he did not pay for the service. However, a private firm could not profit from providing national defense because it could not exclude nonpayers from benefiting from the service. The annual bill for national defense is about $4,000 per household. If several households on a block decided not to pay for defense one year, the whole block would still be protected by national defense (you cannot protect one house and leave others open to attack). However, if more and more households chose not to pay, national defense would be provided in insufficient quantities, resulting in an inadequate military.

Since public goods cannot be provided efficiently by the private sector, we rely on government. Elected government officials decide on the level of public goods that they think the voters want, and voters select politicians to reflect their demand for public goods.

External Benefits

As with public goods, if external benefits are not taken into account, then private markets tend to underallocate resources to the commodity that generates the external benefits. In general, the purchaser of a good that generates an external benefit will benefit the most from that product, but other individuals will receive residual benefits. Because those residual benefits are not incorporated into the market price, the market will tend to provide some amount of the good, but less than the optimal amount.

For example, consider vaccinations. The person being vaccinated gets the greatest benefit from a vaccination, since she is protected from a disease. But a whole host of other individuals benefit from her vaccination. Her employer benefits because she is less likely to fall ill and miss work. Her family, friends, and co-workers benefit because they are less likely to get an illness from her. But these external benefits that flow to people not purchasing the commodity are not reflected in the market price of the vaccination. The marginal benefit going to the vaccination purchaser (marginal private benefit) is reflected in the market price. The demand curve for the product reflects how much the individual consumer values the product (how much benefit is received for each unit). However, because other people benefit from the product but do not pay for it, the market price of the good does not capture society's true benefit. A demand curve that reflected both the individual's marginal benefit and society's external benefit would be shifted up and to the right, reflecting the fact that the product generates a greater value to society than just to the individual, and indicating that an efficient equilibrium would involve more of the product being produced.

Education is another apt example of a good that generates external benefits. Figure 13.2 shows the demand for education based on the collected individual preferences of people for their own education (D_e) and the supply of education based on the resources necessary and their costs (S_e). The market equilibrium is at P_e and Q_e.

FIGURE 13.2 External Benefits from Education

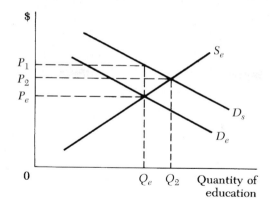

But there are external benefits to education that accrue to the whole society. Literacy, the advance of science and technology, culture, and economic intercourse require and benefit from having an educated population. The total social benefits from education, then, include the private benefits to individuals plus the external benefits to society. In Figure 13.2, D_e shows the private demand for education, the marginal private benefit of additional amounts of education. D_s, however, is a "social demand curve" that includes both the private and the external benefits of education. That is, it shows the marginal social benefit of education:

$$MSB = MPB + MEB,$$

where MSB = marginal social benefit, MPB = marginal private benefit, and MEB = marginal external benefit. The marginal external benefit of education is the difference between D_e and D_s.

If the external benefits are not taken into account, there will be an underallocation of resources to education. At Q_e, the social benefit of education, at P_1, exceeds its marginal cost at P_e (from the supply curve). Society would benefit from increased output of education. In fact, maximal social welfare would occur at Q_2, where the marginal social benefit of additional education equals the marginal cost of education (where the supply and social demand curves intersect). The public sector in the United States, for more than a century, has responded to this situation by providing various forms of assistance to education—the provision of public schools, scholarship assistance, tax exemptions to private educational institutions, funds for teacher training and educational development, and others. In this way, when external benefits are present and markets tend to underallocate resources, public sector provision of the good or service or subsidization can improve social welfare by encouraging increased allocation of resources to the activity. This is called *internalizing* an external benefit. Benefits accruing to those external to the market are brought into the market (internalized) as a result of a pubic sector action. In general, to internalize an external benefit the government tries to increase the quantity of the good that is consumed using revenues taken from those receiving the external benefits. This creates a more efficient allocation of resources.

8. In an interview in the October 1984 *Redbook*, Dr. Benjamin Spock, the famous pediatrician, argued that "the family is the most important thing in life" and that "fathers have just as much responsibility as mothers for caring for their children or deciding who will care for them." Spock went on to suggest that the United States needs more quality day care centers and that there should be subsidies for parents who prefer to stay home with young children. What are the external benefits from good parenting that might justify the use of public resources for child care or home-parenting subsidies? Would you favor such programs? Why or why not?

External Costs

In Chapter 9, we developed the cost curves that the firm faces in making decisions about what level of output to produce (the one that maximizes profits). We also saw how the competitive market encourages firms to produce at the lowest average cost—that is, the rate of output that minimizes the per-unit use of scarce resources. However, this characterization of the competitive firm's behavior poses one large problem.

When firms make decisions about the use of resources and the rate of output, the cost information they take into account concerns their own out-of-pocket, internal costs. But there may be some other costs of production that are external to the firm. These externalities are costs of productive activity that the firm is not forced to bear. For example, in the process of making paper, a paper company may produce air and water pollution. The costs are borne by people who must breathe and smell the befouled air and by the potential downstream users of the dirtied water. These are social costs of production. The firm does not have to pay a price for the use of these resources.

Because these costs do not enter into the firm's calculations, these resources will tend to be overused, and there will be an inefficient use of resources. Therefore, the conclusion that competitive markets tend to produce resource efficiency is true only if there are no externalities in the production process.

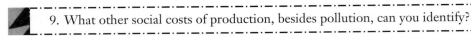
9. What other social costs of production, besides pollution, can you identify?

We can illustrate this point graphically. In Figure 13.3, we assume a constant price, at MR = P (the market is perfectly competitive). MC represents the marginal private costs that face the firm at different levels of output, and MSC represents the marginal social costs of production at different levels of output (including both MC and the social costs that are external to the firm). That is, MSC = MPC + MEC, where MSC = marginal social cost, MPC = marginal

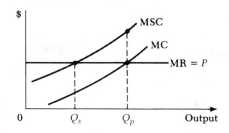

FIGURE 13.3 Marginal Social Costs

private cost, and MEC = marginal external cost. In attempting to maximize its profits, the firm will produce output Q_p. However, from a social perspective, at Q_p, MSC > P, so resources are overallocated to output of this product. Social welfare would be maximized where MSC = P at output Q_s. With social costs taken into consideration, there would be a tendency toward lower rates of output. Alternatively, if the external costs were considered and the firm were to maintain its rate of output at Q_p, the product's price would have to be higher.

The government tries to correct the fact that external costs (such as pollution and toxic waste) created by a firm are passed on to society as a whole. The government usually tries to force a firm to reduce the external costs by installing cleaner technologies or by cleaning up the offending emissions or by-products. Instead of regulations that require firms to reduce emissions, the government could impose an emissions tax, which charges a firm for each unit of pollution. The revenues from the emissions tax could then be used to clean up pollution or to compensate those harmed by the pollution. In both of these cases, the government is attempting to reduce the impact of the external costs on society by shifting the external costs generated in the production process back to the polluting firm. Here again, the government is trying to *internalize* an externality.

10. Would an individual firm be willing to take any or all of the social, external costs of production into account? Why or why not?

The existence of externalities in capitalist production has made it necessary for federal, state, and local governments to intervene by requiring firms to consider externalities. Eliminating such externalities as pollution involves costs, so firms will avoid incurring them—because they reduce profits and because the firm faces competition. Consequently, government control forces firms to take the externalities into account. Areas where governmental regulation has emerged include occupational health and safety, noise pollution, hazardous wastes, strip-mined land reclamation, air and water pollution, and the operation of nuclear power plants and disposal of their wastes. In each of these cases, the government has made private firms accountable for the external costs.

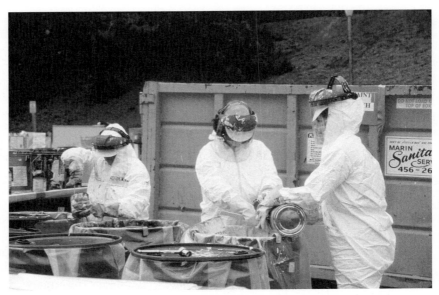

Sanitation workers disposing of hazardous paints and chemicals.
(© Bonnie Kamin/PhotoEdit)

For example, each year industries in the United States generate billions of pounds of hazardous wastes—acids, strong bases, and chlorinated hydrocarbons. In the past, most hazardous wastes found their way to illegal waste dumps, where they pose severe potential health problems for local communities. Douglas Costle, former administrator of the Environmental Protection Agency, noted the dangers in 1980: "These sites with their contents of long-lasting chemicals now represent time capsules releasing their toxic contents into the surface waters, into our groundwaters and seriously degrading our landscapes and our water supply." Some experts have estimated that there are more than 55,000 illegal waste dumps in the United States; the Hooker Chemical Company dump at Love Canal in Niagara Falls, New York, was one of the most widely publicized of these.

Toxic chemicals are linked to higher incidences of cancer among workers and residents of areas where such chemicals were produced. Toxic wastes are considered to be the third largest environmental cause of cancer. The high-tech industry, one of the most rapidly expanding sectors of the U.S. economy, relies heavily on the use of many chemicals (arsenic, strong acids, and solvents) that are poisonous or carcinogenic. Thus, early in the twenty-first century, workers and communities across the United States are faced with a major, continuing environmental hazard in coping with the production, usage, and storage of toxic chemicals and the possible reintroduction of nuclear energy.

As a result of rules established by the Environmental Protection Agency in 1980, companies are responsible for keeping track of their hazardous wastes and ensuring their proper disposal. Firms must take some of the cost into consideration and may not pass all of it along to the public at large. Thus, firms are forced to reduce their external costs, which moves the market closer to a more efficient outcome.

How much of our resources should we devote to dealing with this problem? Environmentalists want increased funding for the cleanup of hazardous waste sites, but the Congress is concerned about spending too much money and over-regulating businesses. Who is responsible for the dangerous waste sites already in existence? Who should have to pay for their cleanup? How long will it take? Who will be liable for the health effects of toxic wastes, which may not appear for more than two decades? The externalities associated with one of the most dynamic and important sectors of our economy in the post–World War II period obviously raise some fundamental economic and political questions.

The Tragedy of the Commons: Property Rights and Atlantic Fishing

In the 1990s, fishing in the North Atlantic Ocean had to be suspended for a number of years by several countries, including the United States, Canada, and members of the European Union, because excessive fishing had depleted these traditional fishing areas. The "overfishing" of the North Atlantic is a recent example of what is commonly referred to as the tragedy of the commons. Shared or "common" resources, such as fish in the ocean, or even air and water, can be used freely by anyone. Each individual is able to take resources from and put wastes into the commons. Common resources tend to be abused over time. In the case of North Atlantic fishing, firms kept increasing the size and sophistication of their operations, catching more and more fish each year. Eventually, fish stocks began to dwindle because of this overfishing, but firms in the North Atlantic fishing trade took no action. Firm owners needed to generate income to live on and pay for production costs. Indeed, many small firms began to fish more intensively as fish stocks dwindled in order to preserve their standard of living, make payments on their boats, and cover other production costs. But as fishing became more intense, fish stocks fell so low that most species could no longer replenish themselves. An external cost was created by these firms as a result of catching more fish at the expense of the common resource (and the other people depending on the common resource). But fishing firms do not pay for the cost imposed on the rest of society because no one owns the common resource (ocean fish).

Ultimately, fishing was temporarily banned in the North Atlantic by the National Marine Fisheries Service to allow fish stocks to replenish. What we have learned from this and other incidents is that markets tend to overuse and abuse common property resources. In order to safeguard the health of such resources, and to ensure that they are available for future generations, the government is forced to manage the resource to reduce external costs.

11. Explain why no one firm would be likely, *on its own*, to reduce the air pollution or to keep track of and clean up the toxic wastes from its production process.

12. In recent years, there has been intense controversy over acid rain. Many residents of Canada and the northeastern United States, as well as scientific studies, blame pollution from coal-burning, electricity-generating plants and other factories in the Midwest for higher acidity in lakes and rivers. The higher acidity, in turn, has threatened the ecology; in fact, many lakes no longer can support fish life. In 2004, the administration of George W. Bush proposed even greater reliance on coal-burning plants to ensure adequate supplies of electricity.
    a. Explain why acid rain is or is not an externality. What should be done about it? By whom? What difference does it make?
    b. The 1990 Clean Air Act required utilities in the Midwest to use more expensive, low-sulfur coal to reduce acid rain. What might the long-term economic effects of this legislation be?

Regulation of Economic Concentration

In Chapters 9 and 10, we demonstrated that the theoretical results of competitive markets are superior to those of all forms of imperfect competition. This conclusion suggests that an appropriate response by the public sector would involve attempting to control the effects of imperfect competition and to encourage competition. The regulation of monopoly prices and antitrust policy are both informed by this approach.

Regulating Monopolies

If a monopoly exists, the government has several options. The government can leave the monopoly alone, with the notion that in the long run monopoly profits will provide an incentive for some competition. The government can take over the operation of the activity itself, as in the case of the postal service. It can break up the monopoly so that it has less economic power, as in the reorganization of AT&T in the 1980s. In many cases, governmental units acknowledge the existence of a monopoly, give it legal sanction, and then regulate its prices.

Why would the government allow a monopoly to exist? In the case of a *natural monopoly*, it is actually more efficient to have one firm in the market, but that firm must be regulated in order to achieve a fair price and an efficient outcome rather than the monopoly profit position.

A natural monopoly exists when one firm can supply the entire market output more efficiently than more than one firm can. To see how this works, consider Figure 13.4, which illustrates the demand and cost conditions for a natural monopolist. This firm is considered to be a natural monopoly because of economies of scale. The demand curve intersects the average cost curve while the average cost curve is still declining, indicating that the more the firm pro-

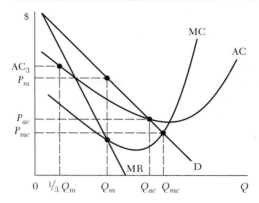

FIGURE 13.4 Price Regulation of a Natural Monopoly

duces for the market, the lower the cost of the product. The larger the firm is, the more efficiently it is able to produce for the market.

As we learned in Chapter 10, with the goal of profit maximization, the monopolist will produce quantity Q_m, where marginal revenue is equal to marginal cost, and charge price P_m. This will result in a substantial economic profit for the firm. However, if the government were to use antitrust policies to generate competition in this market, it would not improve the outcome for consumers given the shape of the average cost curve. For example, suppose the government forced the monopolist to split into three equal-sized firms, each producing one-third of the monopolist's original level of output ($Q_m/3$). In order to earn a normal profit, these three firms would all have to charge at least AC_3, their average cost of production. But the price that they would need to charge is actually *higher* than the price the monopolist would charge! Clearly, that is not an outcome that benefits consumers or society.

Instead, the government can allow the monopolist to be the only supplier in the market, but it can regulate the price the monopolist is allowed to charge. The government can establish a price ceiling (a legally set maximum price) that prevents the monopolist from charging above a certain price. If the goal is to allow the monopolist to earn a fair rate of return, a normal profit, government officials can set the price the monopolist can charge at P_{ac}, where the demand curve intersects the AC curve. Since price is just equal to average cost, the monopolist will earn a normal profit, the price for consumers will be much lower than the price the monopolist would normally charge ($P_{ac} < P_m$), and the quantity consumers purchase is larger as well ($Q_{ac} > Q_m$). This is called *average cost pricing*—forcing the monopolist to set price equal to average cost so that the firm earns a normal profit, consumers benefit, and the market generates efficiency in production (the good is produced for the lowest cost possible given the size of the market).

Another option the government can choose is *marginal cost pricing*—forcing the monopolist to set price equal to marginal cost, in order to generate maximum social welfare and efficiency in resource allocation. Recall in Chapter 9 it was noted that maximum social welfare is achieved when price is equal to marginal cost, because the opportunity cost of the resources used in production is exactly equal to the benefit to consumers from the product. In Figure 13.4, this occurs where the demand curve intersects the marginal cost curve, at price P_{mc} and quantity Q_{mc}. To achieve this outcome, the government could set a price ceiling on the monopolist at P_{mc}. However, while this outcome would be best for consumers, generating the lowest price and the highest quantity of any of the options we are considering here, we see it is not so good for the monopolist. In this example, at Q_{mc}, $P_{mc} <$ AC and the firm earns an economic loss. The firm would have to shut down if it were required to charge P_{mc}, unless the government subsidized the firm enough to offset losses. Marginal cost pricing is only used in the case of goods that generate significant external benefits, such as public transportation and vaccinations, where society has deemed it worthwhile to subsidize the monopolist and to encourage society's consumption of the good in question.

Governmental price regulation therefore can improve the economic results of monopoly. However, the actual process of price regulation is not quite as easy as Figure 13.4 suggests. Governmental regulators need to have information on the monopoly's costs, its capital assets, and the demand for its products. They cannot regulate the quality of the service provided. Other problems involve the relationships between regulators and the regulated.

The Federal Communications Commission's regulation of AT&T's long-distance phone service offers some examples. The FCC began with a decision to provide AT&T with a certain rate of return based on the value of its capital assets. Prices were then set so that the excess of revenues over costs produced the determined rate of return. AT&T then had an incentive to exaggerate its capital base as well as its costs so as to increase its profits. Not only did the FCC need to collect a great deal of information, it needed to keep tabs on AT&T's capital and cost estimates. Given the specialized knowledge required to regulate AT&T's business, the regulators were often people familiar with the industry, perhaps through past involvement in it, so there were potential conflicts of interest. (To some extent, the purpose of opening long-distance phone service to other companies was to reduce the regulatory effort, since prices would be influenced by some competition.)

Despite these potential difficulties, price regulation of utility rates throughout the United States does succeed in limiting monopoly pricing power and in requiring monopolies to submit to some degree of public accountability.

Antitrust and Economic Concentration

Based on the economic theory that competition produces a maximization of social welfare and that imperfect competition, in the form of economic concentration, interferes with an efficient allocation of resources, the U.S. government has developed antitrust policies. In general, **antitrust policy** consists of laws intended to limit monopoly and promote competition. Antitrust policy in the United States has always been controversial.

The first national antitrust legislation was the **Sherman Antitrust Act,** passed by Congress in 1890. Political support for the act was based on a reaction to and antipathy toward large and rapacious corporations at the end of the nineteenth century. Farmers, workers, consumers, and small businesses all were, or felt they were, victimized by the railroad, steel, sugar, and other trusts. The act prohibited combinations in "restraint of trade" and price-fixing. Most national corporations and the trusts themselves, however, were not enthusiastic about the new legislation. In fact, the Sherman Antitrust Act was first applied to labor unions as conspiracies in restraint of trade! Since that time, the act has been used to break up some large companies (e.g., the Standard Oil Company), and it has been supplemented by other legislation aimed at preventing mergers that would limit competition or move industries toward "too much" concentration.

In recent years, the antitrust debate has shifted ground to some extent. During the 1980s and 1990s, two merger waves swept the U.S. economy. Mergers occur when one company purchases the stock of another company. In a **horizontal merger,** companies in the same industry are merged—for example, Exxon Oil's purchase of Mobil Oil in 1998. In a **vertical merger,** the merged companies are in different production stages of a particular product, as in the case of the large oil companies that have merged the production, refining, and distribution systems of petroleum products. A **conglomerate merger** takes place when the merging companies do not have similar or related businesses, as was the case with ITT, which once comprised a large number of previously inde-pendent companies producing many different goods and services. (ITT grew so large that it became too difficult to manage, and it divested one hundred sub-sidiary businesses in the 1980s and 1990s.) Antitrust policy has historically been concerned with mergers because they tend to limit competition and to increase economic concentration—with the possible consequences of higher prices, monopolization, and economic inefficiency. In addition, increased economic concentration has always been accompanied by a fear that individual firms will wield increased economic and political power.

Some economists have charged that the merger waves of the 1980s and 1990s increased corporate borrowing and contributed to higher interest rates. Others are concerned about the implications for the concentration of economic and political power if this trend is not checked. Many economists would like to see the antitrust laws enforced more vigorously, and some would even like to see some of the larger corporations broken up.

On the other hand, some liberal economists and most conservative econo-mists would prefer to follow a policy of "benign neglect" toward merger activi-ty and large corporations. They do not see bigness per se as a problem. Even large firms must be sensitive to the market, they argue; if the demand for a product shifts, the firms will respond. Even large firms have an incentive to innovate, because it might increase their profits. Large firms can take advantage of economies of scale, thereby increasing the efficiency of production. Antitrust enforcement, charge these economists, can limit the ability of U.S. firms to compete with overseas companies, or it can prevent a healthy company from swallowing up an unhealthy one, which might improve the overall operation of the merged entity. Furthermore, antitrust litigation costs corporations, and ultimately consumers, billions of dollars in court and legal fees.

During the 1980s, the Ronald Reagan and George H. W. Bush administrations adopted a policy of very lax enforcement of the antitrust laws. The Bill Clinton and George W. Bush administrations did not adopt a very different stance toward preventing corporate mergers. However, the last two administrations did participate in the largest antitrust lawsuit of the last decade. The U.S. Department of Justice and nineteen states sued Microsoft for monopolizing the market for personal computer operating systems and engaging in anticompetitive behavior.

The Microsoft Monopoly Case

In November 1999, a U.S. district court ruled that Microsoft was a monopoly and had engaged in anticompetitive practices:

◆ The court stated that there were no viable substitutes for Windows in the market for operating systems for Intel-based personal computers and that it would be prohibitively expensive for a new operating system to gain acceptance in the market. (Everyone was used to Windows, and people were used to applications that ran on Windows.) These circumstances created substantial barriers to entry. Also, Microsoft had a dominant, persistent, and increasing share of the relevant market. The combination of dominant market share and prohibitive barriers to entry indicated to the court that Microsoft Windows did have a monopoly on the relevant market.

◆ The court also held that Microsoft wielded its monopoly power by engaging in anticompetitive practices. Specifically, Microsoft's efforts to take over the Internet browser market from Netscape included predatory pricing (giving away its

Internet Explorer browser for free) and unlawful tying (bundling Internet Explorer with Windows so consumers would have no need to purchase Netscape Navigator).

On June 7, 2000, U.S. District Court Judge Thomas Penfield Jackson ruled that Microsoft should be split into two separate companies, one producing the operating system Windows and the other producing all other Microsoft software applications. The objective of this penalty was to separate the operating system from other software applications so Microsoft could not expand its dominance in operating systems into new areas. Microsoft appealed, and in June 2001, the U.S. Court of Appeals threw out the lower court's ruling that Microsoft should be broken up. However, the Court of Appeals supported the lower court in finding that Microsoft was a monopoly and that it had frequently abused its monopoly power. After Microsoft was (again) found guilty of violating U.S. antitrust laws, the company reached a settlement with the Bush administration and U.S. District Court Judge Colleen Kollar-Kotelly. In the settlement, Microsoft agreed to provisions that were designed to increase competition in the software market. PC makers and users would be allowed to remove the icon for Microsoft applications, but not the underlying software, and Microsoft agreed to license its technology to rivals to build products that seamlessly communicate with computers running Windows software. However, few companies purchased these licenses, and the software market in the United States remained uncompetitive despite the settlement.

In 2004, the European Union also found Microsoft guilty of abusing its monopoly power. After Microsoft and the European Commission, which enforces European Union competition law, failed to agree on a settlement, the commission levied penalties designed to prevent the software company from using its monopoly position as leverage in other software markets. Specifically, Microsoft was fined $613 million, ordered to divulge Windows programming codes to competitors, and forced to offer a version of Windows without its media player. Microsoft paid the fine and complied with much of the ruling, but in December 2005 the EU announced that Microsoft did not comply fully. In July 2006 the EU fined Microsoft an additional $ 357.3 million.

As was the case in the United States, the European Commission was responding to Microsoft's use of its monopoly on Windows to dominate most areas of software, including Internet browsers, word processing, servers, and most recently, media players. The commission noted that more than 95 percent of personal computers in the world are powered by Microsoft Windows software, and that Microsoft gradually took over software markets where the dominance of Windows provided an advantage. In contrast, Microsoft was much less successful in markets that have nothing to do with Windows PCs, such as mobile phones. The fact that Microsoft had difficulties competing in non-software markets seemed to indicate to commissioners that its edge in the software market was a product of its monopoly on Windows more than fair competition.

13. Is there a difference between a "bad" merger and a "good" merger? Were the mergers between Exxon and Mobil, Travelers and Citicorp, and Viacom and CBS good or bad? Explain?

14. What are some costs to society of Microsoft's dominance in the market for operating systems? What are some benefits? How might the market for personal computers and software be different in a more competitive environment? Did the antitrust lawsuit against Microsoft produce benefits to consumers? Why or why not?

15. In 1984, a Supreme Court case upheld a law that involved an example of the public (and political) definition of property in Hawaii, where the state took land to reduce economic concentration. In the mid-1960s, eighteen landowners held more than 40 percent of the private land in Hawaii. In writing the majority opinion for the Supreme Court, Justice Sandra Day O'Connor concluded, "Regulating oligopoly and the evils associated with it is a classic example of a state's police powers. We cannot disapprove of Hawaii's exercise of that power. . . . [It is] a comprehensive and rational approach to identifying and correcting market failure." What is the "market failure"? Is it appropriate for the state to correct it?

Poverty and Income Redistribution

In Chapter 11, we examined the size distribution of income in the United States and explored why it is distributed relatively unequally. One aspect of income inequality is the existence of poverty. Poverty can be both an absolute and a relative concept. In an absolute sense, poverty might refer to a society or individuals within it that cannot easily meet the day-to-day requirements for continued survival. For example, street beggars in an underdeveloped country or homeless people in the United States are poor. But poverty can also have a relative meaning. Even the families in the United States with the lowest incomes are probably better off materially than many families were in the latter half of the nineteenth century. Nevertheless, given the standard of living and the operation of markets in the U.S. economy, it is clear that some people and some families are demonstrably much less well off than most and that survival and development are very difficult for them.

The federal government estimates a level of income called the poverty line. For different family sizes and locations in the country, the poverty line is meant to measure the amount of income required to purchase the basic necessities of life—food, clothing, and shelter. For an urban family of four in 2005, the poverty line was $19,971. All urban families of four with incomes less than this for 2005 are classified as being poor. (Only cash income from work or from assistance is counted.) Given this standard, the federal government estimates the number and percentage of people below the poverty line every year. Table 13.5 shows the number of persons below the poverty line and their percentage of the total population for various years from 1960 to 2005.

In the early 1960s, almost 40 million Americans, more than one-fifth of the nation's citizens, were classified as being poor. In 1973, the number and the percentage reached their lowest levels—23 million people and 11.1 percent of the population. Since then, both the number and the percentage in poverty

TABLE 13.5   Persons Below the Poverty Line

Year	Number of Persons (in Millions)	Percentage of Population
1960	39.9	22.2
1970	25.4	12.6
1980	29.3	13.0
1985	33.1	14.0
1990	33.6	13.5
1995	36.4	13.8
2000	31.6	11.3
2001	32.9	11.7
2002	34.6	12.1
2003	35.9	12.5
2004	37.0	12.7
2005	37.0	12.6

Source: U.S. Census Bureau, Historical Poverty Tables, Table 2.

increased until 1983 and decreased moderately through 1990. In part, the general health of the economy in the 1960s and early 1970s as well as the war on poverty accounted for the reduction in the country's poverty population. From 1973 to 1993, slower economic growth and growing income inequality were associated with higher levels of poverty. The number of people in poverty decreased somewhat from 1993 to 2000 as the economy expanded. Poverty increased, however, with the recession of 2001 and in the jobless recovery of the early 2000s.

Over the past forty years, the response of the public sector has also had an impact on the incidence of poverty. The case for income redistribution to correct for the inequality of market-determined incomes is at its strongest when directed toward attempts to limit poverty. Poverty is associated with a host of social and economic problems, including homelessness, crime, low-birth-weight babies, increased illness, family disintegration, and lower productivity. Thus, poverty imposes significant costs on society. At the height of its postwar prosperity in the early 1960s, the United States recognized the extent of the poverty in its midst and developed public policies to try to eradicate it. A former Catholic lay worker, Michael Harrington, wrote *The Other America*, identifying the extent and incidence of poverty in the country; another Catholic, John F. Kennedy, took up the political challenge of persuading the country to develop federal programs to give relief and promise to its poor.

In 1980, the National Advisory Council on Economic Opportunity in its twelfth annual report on poverty concluded that the progress in reducing the ranks of the poor between the mid-1960s and 1980 almost totally resulted from federal income assistance and antipoverty programs. During the 1970s, the report noted, the number of poor people stayed fairly constant, at about 25 million, and the growth of the economy did not contribute much to the access of poor people as a whole to adequate jobs and earnings. And, while the total number of poor remained stable, the composition of the poverty population became increasingly concentrated among women, the very young, and minorities. The council also predicted that if federal programs for the poor were cut back, the poverty rate would increase.

That prediction was borne out. As part of its overall economic program, the Reagan administration cut back on the growth of many federal programs directed toward the poor, including cash transfer programs such as Aid to Families with Dependent Children and noncash programs such as food stamps, housing assistance, Medicaid, and school lunch subsidies. As a result of these cutbacks and the worst recession (1981–1983) since the Great Depression, the poverty rate increased. In 1983, more than 35 million people were classified as poor—15.3 percent of the U.S. population. In the decades since 1983, poverty levels have fallen during boom times and increased during recessions. Since 1995, the government has steadily reduced the amount of money it spends on cash assistance, food assistance, and housing, while increasing spending on education, child care assistance, and other services. This has been part of the major overhaul of federal antipoverty programs that has been termed welfare reform.

The major programs the U.S. government uses to fight poverty include food assistance (food stamps, the women, infants and children special supplemental nutrition program), health care assistance (Medicare, Medicaid), housing assistance, and cash assistance (the earned income tax credit and welfare). Welfare was one of the most potent weapons in reducing poverty in the 1960s and 1970s, but the program has been scaled back and restructured in recent years. Specifically, a major overhaul of the welfare system in 1996 created the Temporary Aid to Needy Families (TANF) program. This new policy imposed strict requirements on welfare recipients, including work requirements and limited lifetime benefits, while shifting money from cash assistance to noncash benefits and services such as child care, education, and job training. Under TANF, the number of people on welfare plunged from 12.2 million in 1996 to 4 million in 2007 and many former welfare recipients were able to find work, causing supporters to view TANF as a major success story. However, poverty levels fell only slightly during the same period, and 40 percent of those who left welfare rolls had no discernible source of income, which helps to explain rising rates of hunger and homelessness. Furthermore, 60 percent of former welfare recipients who did find work were still living in poverty due to the low wages and poor benefits associated with the jobs they were able to find.

16. Do you think the federal government should contribute income to poor families? Noncash assistance such as food stamps? Training programs for disadvantaged youth? Why or why not? Does society have a public responsibility to reduce poverty? What external costs does poverty have? What is the chance that you will be poor in the future?

17. In 2001, the Census Bureau reported that 32.3 percent of all citizens received at least one form of federal assistance ranging from Social Security to unemployment compensation. Further, 20 percent of households received benefits based on need, such as Medicaid, food stamps, public housing, or Temporary Assistance for Needy Families. Why is the impact of the federal government on people's incomes and economic status so widespread? Is it too widespread?

The Limits of Government's Role

In this chapter, we have focused on the role of government in the economy and the economic arguments that can be and have been made to justify government intervention. During the twentieth century, the liberal view of the state largely won the debate and informed public choices about antitrust policy, the provision of public goods, the regulation of externalities in the private sector, and income redistribution programs. However, some criticisms can be made of government's economic role, and its ability to pursue its objectives efficiently has some inherent limitations. These views served as the rationale for the declining size of government from 1990 to 2007.

As conservatives point out, governmental programs often limit the pursuit of individual freedom in a democratic society. Public provision of goods and services, taxation to finance governmental activities, and regulation all require compulsion. Children must go to school, property owners must pay taxes, factories must clean up their pollution, and so on. Political decisions in a democracy by nature place some limitations on individuals in the interests of the general welfare. The trade-off, which is often only implicit, is a collective good for individual sacrifice. In return for paying taxes, we get schools, parks, national defense, roads, welfare, and so on. As individuals, we might not choose all of the things we get, but as members of local, state, and national communities, we participate in the political decision-making process (to a greater or a lesser extent) and must live with the results. Freedom is not an unqualified right. Nevertheless, there is a fervent debate about the appropriate degree of limitation on individual freedom.

To facilitate the legislative process and to administer public programs, public institutions have been created. Office buildings, legislatures, and other public edifices are physical evidence of the public sector, and the bureaucracies they contain are living and continuing proof of its vitality. To accomplish public objectives, bureaucracies are necessary, but their operation can produce some problems. If there is no measurable output sold in markets (as there is in the private sector), there is no way to calculate success in economic terms. Without profits as an indicator, bureaucracies may have difficulty maintaining efficiency. Roads obviously provide an important public service, but how do we know whether construction companies or road crews are performing at top efficiency? In the private sector, the market theoretically weeds out inefficiency. In the public sector, patronage and/or a civil service system might limit the ability of supervisors to fire employees (justly or unjustly). Finally, bureaucracies develop vested interests in their own programs. Consequently, inertia may affect decisions about the allocation of resources to public programs—rather than having the decision based on the maximization of social benefit compared with the social costs incurred in the use of scarce resources.

The decision-making process in the public sector is imperfect. When we suggest that public involvement in the economy might improve the overall allocation of resources or correct some of the problems of the private sector, we are implicitly assuming that the decision-making process is rational. Through reasoned debate, research on the effects of different programs, cost-benefit analysis, a free press, and democratic procedures and institutions, we may approach rationality. However, the practice of democracy may also veer off from the ideal. Voters and the voting process often emphasize the people, personalities, and parties involved rather than an unemotional, reasoned consideration of the issues. Modern media certainly reinforce the tendency toward superficiality. Special interests have the edge in the political process. Their issues are well defined, their numbers are organizable, and they often have access to significant amounts of money. They lobby, advertise, and persuade, and they are effective in influencing the course of legislating and administering public policies.

As we emphasized at the beginning of this chapter, the government's role in the economy is an issue rich with controversy. In addition, the interpretations of its actual operations and institutions are varied, depending in part on the ideological predispositions of the analysts.

Conclusion

Much of the analysis in Part 3 on microeconomics is directly derived from classical and neoclassical economics. In the realm of the market and the firm, the analysis is helpful, although qualified by the historical emergence of noncompetitive market structures and the corporation. We are no longer in the ideal and competitive world of Adam Smith. However, supply-and-demand analysis can still help us understand how markets work to determine prices and allocate resources. And the focus of microeconomics on the firm has caused economists to pay increasing attention to the modern corporation and labor unions. The existence of various market failures, ranging from external costs and benefits to the distribution of income to economic concentration, has also led to the continued development of the role of the public sector in the economy.

In the realm of the operation of the total economy, classical theory has had more severe problems. It contends that the market system will produce growth and full employment. However, this theoretical result conflicts with historical experience. As a result, Keynesian theory emerged to provide an alternative understanding of the macroeconomy. We will explore this theory in Part 4.

Review Questions

1. What is the appropriate role of the government in the economy? What functions should it be responsible for performing?

2. Is it proper for the government to regulate the prices of monopolies? Why or why not?

3. The federal government, in particular, has a number of programs intended to reduce poverty in the United States. Should the government be responsible for this effort? What other possible solutions are there to the problem of poverty? Or is there nothing that can be done about it?

4. Traffic accidents as a result of intoxication are an external cost of the consumption of alcohol. Is this true? Why or why not? If yes, specify what the external costs are. If not, explain. What private and public efforts might contribute to a reduction of this problem?

5. The postal service provides a public good, for example, in the delivery of first-class mail anywhere in the country for the same price. (Before you start thinking of unkind jokes and comments about the post office, consider what has to happen in order for a letter that you put in a box somewhere to get to its recipient, say, all the way across the country.) What is the *external* benefit from postal service? Could the same service be provided by the private sector? Who would object to the private provision of postal service?

6. In March 1990, an Exxon supertanker, the Exxon *Valdez,* crashed into a reef and spewed 11 million gallons of crude oil into Alaska's Prince William Sound.
   a. What were the external costs of this event? Who bore the costs?
   b. Later, fishing firms, tour operators, and the state of Alaska sued Exxon for damages. Why? How could damages be valued?

c. In 1990, a federal grand jury indicted Exxon for violating federal pollution and marine safety laws. What was the purpose of those laws? What steps were taken to make Exxon account for the external costs of this oil spill? What were the effects on Exxon?

7. R. J. Reynolds Tobacco now owns Nabisco foods. Philip Morris Tobacco purchased Kraft Foods and Miller Brewing Company. Why are tobacco firms interested in food companies? What kinds of mergers are these? Do you think antitrust policy should be concerned about such mergers?

8. Many states have laws requiring the use of seat belts in automobiles.
   a. Using concepts from this chapter, what is the logic of these laws?
   b. School buses are not required to have seat belts. Why not? Should they be?

9. In the mid-1990s, welfare reform was summarized by the slogan "workfare, not welfare." From 1996 to 2000, along with a growing economy, millions of welfare recipients moved from welfare to work. Welfare rolls continued to drop between 2000 and 2002, despite the recession and a poor job market. What factors might account for the drop in welfare rolls during an economic slow-down?

THINKING CRITICALLY

Explorations in Microeconomics
—Affirmative Action

The debate over reforming or abolishing the nation's affirmative-action policies is a major topic on college campuses and in workplaces around the country. In the past decades, voters, courts, and politicians in seven states have outlawed the use of racial preferences in college admissions, and many other colleges are scaling back their affirmative-action admissions for fear of lawsuits.

Issues present in the current debate over affirmative action reflect not only different assumptions held by conservatives, liberals, and radicals, but also incorporate many microeconomic concepts we have studied, including opportunity costs, resource markets, cost, revenue, income distribution, poverty and discrimination, equality of opportunity versus equality of condition, and access to markets. Below we explore the affirmative action debate in two key arenas: employment and college admissions.

Source: Field Guide to the U.S. Economy: A Compact and Irreverent Guide to Economic Life in America; Jonathan Teller-Elsberg, Nancy Folbre, James Heintz with the Center for Popular Economics

Affirmative Action in Employment

Initially, affirmative-action policies were aimed at increasing employment opportunities for black workers. Executive orders in 1941 and 1961 barred race discrimination in employment, and in 1967 President Lyndon Johnson signed an executive order extending nondiscrimination to include women. At the same time, Johnson emphasized the need for companies to go further to ensure that women and minorities would be actively recruited, hired, and promoted. In 1972, the Equal Employment Act mandated that federal contractors with more than fifty employees take "affirmative action to ensure that applicants are employed and that employees are treated during employment without regard to their race, color, religion, sex, or national origin." These contractors are to have an affirmative-action plan with timetables and goals to correct any shortcomings, which might include an obvious underrepresentation of women or minorities on the company payroll. As a result of suits brought under Title VII of the Civil Rights Act, courts ordered that employers must take steps to ensure nondiscrimination. Complaints are heard by the Equal Employment Opportunity Commission for private employers and the Department of Justice for state and local governments. In 2005, the EEOC received 75,428 charges from employees in private sector workplaces. Most cases are remedied via administrative resolutions or mediation, and about 0.5 percent are litigated. The EEOC obtained $379.3 million in monetary benefits for victims of employment discrimination in 2005.

These affirmative-action programs—executive orders mandating nondiscrimination and the Equal Employment Act—have been under attack for the last two decades.

The Critics

In a 1994 essay titled "Discrimination and Income Differences," economist June O'Neill noted the mounting concerns about affirmative-action policies:

> Generally speaking, I believe that the civil rights movement of the 1960s played a positive role. During the 1970s, however, antidiscrimination policy took a more militant and, in my opinion, a destructive turn as the policy known as affirmative action took center stage. At the federal level, the policy requires that firms holding federal contracts set numerical hiring goals for women and minorities with the threat of loss of their federal contracts if they fail to meet these targets. The setting of hiring goals requires the estimation of available pools of qualified minorities and women that in practice cannot be done with any precision. In consequence, the original standard of the Civil Rights Act, which made discriminatory behavior by employers illegal, has given way to a new standard based almost entirely on numerical results. A firm that does not have the proper composition of women and minorities can be found in violation, even if it has not engaged in any discriminatory act.
>
> There are several things wrong with this new direction. One is that it is a serious departure from the principle of equal treatment under the law, which requires that a person's race, religion, national origin, or gender should not be the basis for

preferential treatment. Affirmative action is intended to help disadvantaged groups overcome the effects of past oppression. But in violating principles of justice and individual freedom to enforce equality, it employs tactics that become reminiscent of a Maoist "cultural revolution." . . . Moreover, it is not likely to be genuinely helpful. Some who obtain a job through affirmative action may be pleased. But if the job is viewed as undeserved, the process will generate ill will and divisiveness, and perhaps a loss of self-image on the part of the protected minority. Finally, affirmative action has misplaced the emphasis on what is really needed to improve economic status, and in so doing it has given young people the wrong message. In the long run, it is hard work and the acquisition of job skills that ensure success, not jumping ahead in the queue. A better direction for public policy is to provide the resources that are needed to acquire these skills.

> —June Elenoff O'Neill, "Discrimination and Income Differences" in *Race and Gender in the American Economy: Views from across the Spectrum*, Susan F. Feiner, ed. (Upper Saddle River, N.J.: Prentice-Hall, 1994). Reprinted by permission of Prentice-Hall.

The Defenders

Defenders of affirmative action argue that despite very limited federal enforcement of affirmative-action policies, they nonetheless have led to small increases in the number of women and minorities in traditionally white male workplaces. One limited, but successful example of this is found in a 1989 class-action suit filed against the Shoney's restaurant chain for alleged racial discrimination. After settling the suit out of court for $134.5 million, the company initiated a "turnaround" and began to actively pursue workplace diversity. (For more information on the Shoney's case, see *The Wall Street Journal*, April 16, 1996.) In another example, a 1997 EEOC class-action lawsuit against Publix Super Markets alleged discrimination against women in job assignments and promotions. After an investigation supported the allegations, Publix agreed to a settlement that ensured greater promotional opportunities for women, along with $63.5 million in back pay to current and former female employees.

Class action lawsuits have also improved the workplace environment for women and minorities. For example, in 1998, the EEOC resolved two sexual harassment suits involving large classes of female victims. In one lawsuit, Mitsubishi Motor Manufacturing of America was accused of engaging in a pattern of sexual harassment and then retaliating against female employees who spoke out. In response to the lawsuit, Mitsubishi agreed to pay $34 million in monetary relief to more than 300 female employees. In a second lawsuit, the EEOC charged that Astra USA had engaged in a "continuous pattern of sexual harassment of its female employees." In that settlement, Astra agreed to pay nearly $10 million to more than 80 female victims. In both cases, these settlements are credited with significantly improving the workplace environment. It will be interesting to see if the sex discrimination class action lawsuit against Wal-Mart, filed in 2004 and still in process when this book went to press, generates a similar result.

In her 1996 book *In Defense of Affirmative Action*, economist Barbara Bergmann notes that affirmative action seldom comes into question when a black or woman candidate is clearly superior to other job applicants. Nor do critics complain about "casting a wide net" to obtain the best applicant pool (thus also casting the net to white males who would otherwise be excluded). The difficult decisions come on the close calls, when there is no clearly superior candidate, when white male, white female, and minority candidates have comparable skill levels and strengths—but they are clearly *not* alike in what they bring to the workplace. Bergmann makes the following observations about such circumstances:

> Some might say that in those hard cases fairness and justice are best served by putting an immediate end to segregation by giving a chance to a highly acceptable black candidate. Others would say that fairness to the "best" candidate overrides all other considerations, and requires that the employer put off ending the segregation for as long as it takes to find that black candidate who will be judged to be the "best." In deciding which side to come down on in these hard cases, we have to balance the value of bringing segregation to a quick end with the value of avoiding violations of a (perhaps imperfect) merit system. . . .
>
> That violations of the merit system occur regularly for purposes other than bringing race segregation to an end—purposes such as helping a nephew or a friend, or taking on someone who will help the sports team—also needs to be taken into account when thinking about the hard cases. When such violations occur, fairness to the displaced "best" candidate is seldom an issue.
>
> It causes no adverse comment when large and important businesses such as the W. R. Grace Company, the Washington Post Corporation, and the New York Times Company place at their head the son or son-in-law of the majority stockholder or the previous head. No protest is made that the company is acting unfairly to a better-qualified non-relative who might otherwise have gotten the position. Nor is there any complaint, even from the stockholders that the company's performance will be degraded by its failure to find the most qualified person. But if the *New York Times* attempts to ensure that it has blacks among its reporters and editors, then resentments arise. That some departures from choosing the "best" are accepted with no complaint at all, while departures made for the purpose of reducing the exclusion of African Americans or women are complained of bitterly, is something that bears thinking about. . . .
>
> The fact is, of course, that in the labor market white males retain largely intact the highly favored position that they had in 1964, the year employment discrimination by race and sex was made illegal. In 1994, among those working full-time, pay for white non-Hispanic males was 49 percent higher than pay for other labor force participants. Differences in skill levels account for some of this pay difference, but nowhere near all of it. Segregation on the job by race and sex remains a common pattern. Opening access for all to the job enclaves that are now the preserves of white males would take a far more rigorous application of affirmative action techniques than has yet occurred. It would take the introduction of vigorous affirmative action programs into the many workplaces where they have been absent or ignored.
>
> —From *In Defense of Affirmative Action*, by Barbara R. Bergmann. Copyright © 1996 by Basic Books. Reprinted by permission of Basic Books, a member of Perseus Books, LLC.

Many of the concepts discussed in the chapters on microeconomics and earlier chapters apply to the issue of affirmative action. In the following case, Bergmann raises additional questions of affirmative action when viewed through the eyes of an outside observer giving employment advice to the company in

Acme and Affirmative Action

The Acme Company employs 310 machine operators, who operate large machines used in construction, such as bulldozers and cranes. Acme pays them $525 a week, which is good pay for a person without a college education. The personnel manager is concerned that the company has never hired a black in this job. The law says the company has to treat blacks and whites fairly, and he wants to make sure the company is hiring in a fair way.

A machine operator for Acme needs the kind of ability and judgment that an excellent car driver has. The person also needs a sense of responsibility, since careless mistakes could be costly and dangerous. All special training can be given on the job.

Acme had twenty-three vacancies last year, about two a month. Each time there is a vacancy, the employees are asked to spread the word, and an ad is put in the newspapers. Those who apply are given an aptitude test and an interview. The personnel department is then supposed to pick the best applicant.

The company, which is in a city that is half black, got applications last year for the machine operator vacancies from 440 whites and 45 blacks.

Acme's personnel manager reviewed what had happened to the black applicants. He found that they had done about as well as the white applicants on the aptitude test, however, most of the black applicants did not make a good impression on the interviewers. No black had been selected as the best candidate for any of the twenty-three vacancies, although for one of the vacancies a black had been rated third best.

Given this scenario, which of the following actions would you endorse? Briefly explain why.

1. The personnel manager should remind the interviewers to be careful to be fair to blacks. He should tell them that black and white applicants have an equal right to be considered for machine operator jobs.

2. The personnel manager should try to find ways to encourage more black candidates to apply, with a goal of doubling the number of black applicants.

3. The personnel manager should encourage the interviewers to hire at least a few of the blacks who have been judged competent to perform the job.

4. For the next few years, the personnel manager should try to fill at least 10 percent of the vacancies with blacks who have been judged competent to perform the job.

5. To break the pattern of an all-white work force, the personnel manager should ask the interviewers to find competent blacks and hire them for the next five vacancies.

Source: Excerpt from *In Defense of Affirmative Action* by Barbara N. Bergmann. Copyright © 1996 Basic Books. Reprinted by permission of Basic Books, a member of Perseus Books, LLC.

question. Read the case and develop your own recommendations, building on the discussion of affirmative action in employment above.

Affirmative Action on Campus

The issue of affirmative action in employment differs somewhat from affirmative action applied to the college admission process. In addition to remedying inequities due to past discrimination, college affirmative-action programs seek to ensure a diverse student body. But affirmative action on college campuses is similar to workplace affirmative action in that it is a controversial topic that arouses passionate opinions on both sides. In the landmark 1978 Bakke decision, the Supreme Court held that because of past discrimination, a "state has a substantial interest that legitimately may be served by a properly devised admission program involving the competitive consideration of race and ethnic origin." Justice Lewis F. Powell Jr. added that universities had a compelling interest in obtaining a diverse student body. Other justices did not support that argument.

In the past decade, voters, courts, and politicians in several states have outlawed the use of racial preferences in college admissions, and many other colleges are scaling back their affirmative-action admissions for fear of lawsuits. The first of these efforts was Proposition 209, approved by California voters in 1996, which banned affirmative action at all state institutions. Since Proposition 209 was implemented in 1998, enrollment of African American, Hispanic, and Native American students has plummeted at the University of California at Berkeley and other elite state institutions. At Berkeley, between 1997 and 2001, enrollment by African American students fell by 32 percent, enrollment by Hispanic students fell by 23 percent, and enrollment by Native American students fell by 45 percent. Many university officials argue that this decline in diversity interferes with their ability to provide a good education, part of which includes interacting with those from different backgrounds. Nevertheless, foes of affirmative action have celebrated the changes as a much-needed return to a meritocracy.

A major new challenge to affirmative action in admissions came in the form of two lawsuits against the University of Michigan in the late 1990s in which white applicants sued the university for racial discrimination resulting from giving preference to minority candidates. In a landmark decision in 2003, the Supreme Court upheld affirmative-action admissions in principle but threw out an admission policy that was not narrowly tailored. Below we explore the ideas of critics and supporters of college affirmative action programs, and describe the Supreme Court's decision.

The Critics

The critics of affirmative action range from conservatives who decry the government interference in the labor market to those who support government action to end race and gender discrimination but who believe that affirmative action is a flawed policy. Both groups weighed in on the Michigan case.

In early 2003, President George W. Bush issued a statement on the Michigan case, arguing that "the Michigan policies amount to a quota system that unfairly rewards or penalizes prospective students based solely on their race." He called such affirmative-action programs "divisive, unfair and impossible to square with our Constitution." Thus, Bush believes that affirmative-action programs, designed to remedy inequality due to past discrimination, are a form of reverse discrimination.

African American columnist Armstrong Williams opposes affirmative action for different reasons. While acknowledging the problems of racism and discrimination, Williams argues against affirmative action because he sees it as creating a culture of victimhood:

> A shared history of slavery and discrimination has ingrained racial hierarchies into our national identity, divisions that need to be erased. There is, however, a very real danger that we are merely reinforcing the idea that minorities are first and foremost victims.... If the goal of affirmative action is to create a more equitable society, it should be need-based. Instead, affirmative action is designed . . . to reduce people to fixed categories: at many universities, it seems, admissions officers look less at who you are than what you are. As a result, affirmative-action programs rarely help the least among us. Instead, they often benefit the children of the middle- and upper-class black Americans who have been conditioned to feel they are owed something. . . . It is time to stop. We must reach a point where we expect to rise or fall on our own merits.
>
> —Armstrong Williams, "Admissions Policies Like Michigan's Focus Not on Who, But What You Are," *Newsweek*, January 27, 2003, p. 33.

Criticisms like those of Williams gained additional weight with the 2003 publication of a Century Foundation study indicating that 74 percent of students at America's 146 most selective colleges were from the most privileged 25 percent of the U.S. population, and only 3 percent were from the most disadvantaged 25 percent. Blacks and Hispanics were also underrepresented, making up 12 percent of students at selective colleges compared with 28 percent of the country's college-age population. However, the fact that minority students (28 percent of the population, 12 percent of students) are more likely to go to an elite college than students from the poorest families (25 percent of the population, 3 percent of students) may indicate that middle- and upper-income students from minority groups are the principal beneficiaries of college affirmative-action programs and that they may benefit at the expense of more disadvantaged white students.

The Defenders

Defenders of affirmative action include liberals who advocate using government intervention to correct inequality along racial and gender lines as well as advocates of diversity in universities and the workplace. Microsoft, General Motors, a host of other corporations, and the U.S. military supported the

University of Michigan affirmative action programs, filing amicus briefs on behalf of the university. For many institutions, including global multinational corporations, a globalized world demands employees who are comfortable dealing with people from diverse backgrounds. The only way to ensure that college graduates can handle such experiences right out of college is if they encounter them in school. In fact, before deciding to interview students from a particular campus, employers often ask colleges to provide information regarding the diversity and size of the student population to help them determine if the students hail from a sufficiently diverse atmosphere.

In addition to those who see diversity as essential to a well-rounded education, other supports of affirmative action admissions believe that it is necessary to redress inequality of opportunity. Ronald Dworkin, a professor of law and philosophy at New York University Law School, makes such an argument:

> All of us who are not racists—liberals and conservatives alike—have an instinctive tic against explicit racial classifications, which is understandable given our nation's history of racial injustice. But if we really want a more just society, we must be prepared to re-examine this instinct with an important distinction in mind: we must distinguish between policies whose premises deny equal citizenship and those whose premises affirm it.
>
> Of course, no one should be penalized for his or her race, and no race should be thought to have special rights or privileges. Black applicants have no right to preference now because other blacks suffered from injustice in the past. But affirmative action assumes no such right: it has a forward-looking, not backward-looking, justification. The policy promises a better educational environment and a less racially stratified society for everyone. It recognizes that prejudice has poisoned society for all of us, and that fostering opportunities for different races to study and work together is part of an effective, even if slow-working, antidote.
>
> Is affirmative action unfair? Universities are not honor societies rewarding applicants for past achievements. They have a public responsibility to choose students with an eye to the future—students who will contribute to the institution's educational, academic, and social goals. If a university judges that it can offer a better education to everyone if its student body is racially diverse, then its judgment is no more unfair to anyone that its judgment that it can do better with a geographically diverse class or with athletes as well as scholars. It would, of course, be unfair if a university's judgment were corrupted by bias or favoritism, and universities should be required, if challenged, to offer persuasive evidence rebutting any such claim. But no one's rights are infringed when a university makes an honest and uncorrupted decision about how best to meet its academic responsibilities.

> —Ronald Dworkin, "Race and the Uses of Law,"
> *The New York Times*, April 13, 2001, p. A17.

The Supreme Court's Decision

In a 5–4 ruling in June 2003, the Supreme Court upheld the Bakke decision and Justice Powell's view that past discrimination and diversity provided compelling reasons for universities to operate narrowly tailored affirmative-action programs. A university may not use a quota system, but it may consider race or ethnicity as a "plus" factor in a particular applicant's file, while "insuring that each candidate competes with all other qualified applicants." The majority agreed that "student body diversity promotes learning outcomes, and better prepares students for an increasingly diverse workforce and society, and better prepares them as professionals."

However, the Supreme Court struck down one affirmative-action plan that it thought gave too much weight to race, amounting to a quota system that did not consider applicants separately. Furthermore, the Supreme Court anticipated the end of affirmative-action admissions policies, stating, "We expect that 25 years from now, the use of racial preferences will no longer be necessary."

Although the Supreme Court has decided the issue for now, the debate over affirmative action admissions on college campuses is far from over. Several states are considering legislation that would ban affirmative action admissions in their state, following the lead of California and Texas. And conservative groups continue to attack diversity as a legitimate goal for universities to promote. Meanwhile, most universities continue to defend affirmative action admissions and diversity as essential to their educational mission.

Exercises

1. Does affirmative action in college admissions necessarily lower the quality of incoming students? Why or why not?

2. Should children of alumni be given preference in college admissions, as they often are now? Should trumpet players? Football quarterbacks? Explain your answers.

3. Contact the admissions office at your school and find out how they deal with issues of affirmative action and diversity. What methods (if any) do they use to insure a diverse student body? What "plus factors" are given to students from disadvantaged backgrounds? Do you think your school goes too far or not far enough in this area?

4. If you were in charge of admissions, which of the following applicants would you admit to your school: (1) a minority applicant from a substandard inner city school who finished in the top 10 percent of her high school class and has SAT scores of 1000, just below the national average; or (2) a white applicant from a good suburban school in an affluent neighborhood who finished in the top 50 percent of her high school class and has SAT scores of 1050, just above the national average? Justify your decision. Now construct an argument for admitting the applicant you did not choose.

5. In an article in the January 2004 issue of *The American Prospect*, Lisbeth Schorr, a lecturer in social medicine at Harvard University and director of the Harvard University Project on Effective Interventions, noted that it would take just over $110 billion to create true equality of opportunity for minority students. If the

Supreme Court wants to eliminate racial preferences in admissions in 25 years, then she believes certain steps will have to be taken. These include eliminating racial disparities in birth outcomes, school readiness, public school quality, community programs, and health care. Do you think it is reasonable to expect the elimination of affirmative action admissions without such steps being taken? Would such steps be enough, in your view, to provide true equality of opportunity in college admissions?

6. What are the opportunity costs of affirmative-action policies to each of the following groups?
   a. qualified women and minority workers
   b. employers
   c. consumers
   d. other employees of the company
   e. society

7. What are the opportunity costs of not using affirmative-action policies to each of the following groups?
   a. qualified women and minority workers
   b. employers
   c. consumers
   d. other employees of the company
   e. society

8. How might Shoney's cost analysis have been affected by its alleged race discrimination? Its revenue stream?

9. Is Bergmann correct in her assessment that few are concerned when sons of corporate leaders (or even coaches) are hired? Why or why not? Does merit have different meanings in different circumstances? Explain.

10. John Bates Clark, one of the early contributors to microeconomic theory, wrote, "The distribution of the income of society is controlled by a natural law, and . . . this law, if worked without friction, would give to every agent of production the amount of wealth which that agent creates." What does this mean? (Use $MRP = MFC$ to explain your answer.) Does this explain why college-educated women and black men earn lower incomes than college-educated white men?

11. Watch newspapers and other media for current affirmative-action cases. What are the major issues in these cases? Have any gone to trial? Were any settled out of court? What are the circumstances?

Part Four

Macroeconomics

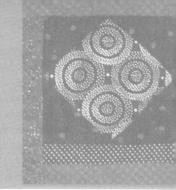

I n Part 3, we examined how microeconomics analyzes the behavior of consumers and firms in the U.S. economic system. We focused on the behavior of markets, the different types of market structures, efficiency, scarcity, the nature of the modern corporation and labor unions, and the role of the government.

We will now supplement this microeconomic theory with macroeconomic theory and policy. **Macroeconomics** is the body of economic theory that attempts to analyze the behavior and performance of the whole economy. It describes and explains the dynamics of the institutional and governmental framework of our economic system by focusing on *the total or aggregate performance* of the economy. We begin our discussion of macroeconomics with an exposition of income-expenditures theory, which explains the performance of the economy in terms of employment, income, output, and price levels. A macroeconomic perspective further requires that we explore the relationship between the monetary system and the economy's aggregate performance. We can then use our understanding of monetary theory and policy and the role of governmental fiscal policy (government spending and taxation) to focus on how best to achieve the major macroeconomic goals of full employment, economic growth, and price stability.

While microeconomics focuses on the decisions of individual actors in the economic system, macroeconomics studies the more aggregate behavior of consumers, businesses, and the government, as well as the market for imports and exports. Although we are shifting to the macroeconomic viewpoint of the aggregate, our examination of the markets for goods and services, money, and even labor will use many of the tools of microeconomics. Such microeconomic concepts and methods as markets, supply, demand, equilibrium, and marginal analysis can help us describe and explain aggregate economic behavior. Thus, while the focus of the discussion will clearly be different, macroeconomic theory relies heavily on microeconomic foundations.

Chapter 14 identifies and describes some of the most important goals and problems of macroeconomics. It also introduces the measuring tools of the National Income and Product Accounts (NIPA). In Chapter 15 we begin to explore the theoretical roots of modern macroeconomics and begin to construct an economic model that is used for analyzing economic activity. We continue to build this model and add to it in Chapters 16 through 19. In some of these chapters we include "Big Picture" sections that illustrate an overview of the part of the model that follows. Figure IV.1 provides a framework of the structures we will develop in The Big Picture sections that are introduced throughout Part IV. Chapter 16 focuses on the role of government in making fiscal policy. Chapter 17 introduces money, financial intermediaries, and monetary policy. Chapter 18 combines elements of monetary theory and aggregate expenditures theory in examining aggregate supply and aggregate demand. Finally, Chapter 19 explores the major macroeconomic problems of unemployment, inflation, and slower economic growth. It also integrates, summarizes, and critically reflects on the past and present efficacy of contemporary macroeconomic policy in the United States.

FIGURE IV.1

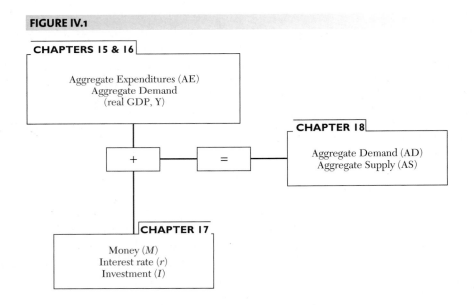

CHAPTER FOURTEEN

Macroeconomics: Issues and Problems

■ Introduction

T his chapter begins our focus on macroeconomics, which examines the economy as a whole. Instead of studying individual parts of the economy, such as firms or labor unions, or concepts such as property and value, we turn our attention to entire sectors that make up our national and international economic system and to aggregate concepts and problems, such as unemployment, inflation, interest rates, taxation, and budget deficits. These topics affect every one of us.

In this chapter, we will examine the goals of macroeconomics, review postwar U.S. macroeconomic trends, develop several tools that will aid our understanding of macroeconomic theory and macroeconomic policy, and define aggregate measures for economic activity in the National Income and Product Accounts. We will begin by considering the importance of macroeconomic theory and some of the ways macroeconomic policy might help to alleviate economic problems.

Macroeconomic Goals

In the early 1950s, the U.S. government accepted as its responsibility three basic macroeconomic goals: (1) economic growth, (2) full employment, and (3) price stability. Government policies should help the economy attain these goals. However, as we will see later, these goals are not necessarily compatible. Despite conflicts among these goals, many would agree that economic growth, full employment, and price stability are rational goals. We want people employed. Stable prices are good for most of us. And economic growth has become synonymous with a higher standard of living and economic progress.

Economic Growth

Simply put, **economic growth** is the increased output of goods and services over time. Not only is growth assumed to be necessary and good, but more growth is assumed to be better than less. Economic growth, after all, creates employment and income.

To measure economic growth, economists have developed sophisticated tools that measure the performance of the economy and its annual rate of real growth. By using a method known as national income accounting (explained later in this chapter), they calculate the **gross domestic product (GDP)**—the total dollar value of all goods and services produced in a given year—and monitor its rate of growth. GDP has grown from $2 trillion in 1978 to $13.3 trillion in 2006. The United States continues to have the world's largest GDP. Once we have measured GDP, we can find the percentage change to calculate its growth rate from year to year. Table 14.1 shows recent and historic average growth rates.

During the 1960s and early 1970s, critics challenged the basic assumptions concerning economic growth, arguing that more growth does not necessarily mean an improved standard of living. Others now charge that the GDP merely quantifies the performance of the economy but does not reflect the qualitative dimension addressed by the question, What is the real societal value or cost of increased GDP growth?

Much of this critique stems from a consideration of the environmental aspects of increasing economic growth. Human health and well-being are endangered by toxic wastes and air and water pollution, while acid rain threatens the quality of our food supply. Issues including the demise of the rain forests, climate change, and population growth have reminded us that these are worldwide concerns. Growing ecological awareness in the context of energy and environmental crises has made us examine our values, attitudes, goals, and economic assumptions more intensely.

The economic growth controversy also focuses on issues of income distribution in the United States. Annual increases in economic growth do not lead to more equitable distribution of the increased output. Empirical data support the claim that despite the tremendous increases in GDP since World War II, the distribution of income in the United States did not change significantly until the 1980s, when it became *less* equal. Despite rapid economic growth in the 1990s and mid-2000s, income distribution continues to become even more unequal.

TABLE 14.1 Average Annual Rates of Growth, Unemployment, and Inflation

	1950s	1960s	1970s	1980s	1990s	2000–2005
Real growth rate[a]	4.0%	4.1%	2.8%	2.7%	5.4%	4.0%
Unemployment	4.4	4.8	6.2	7.3	5.8	5.2
Inflation	2.4	2.0	7.1	6.7	2.9	2.5

[a]In constant dollars.

Source: *Economic Report of the President,* 1984, 1990, 2001, 2006.

Those who advocate economic growth often use the metaphor "a rising tide lifts all boats." Indeed, "all boats" did rise during the period from 1993 to 2006, but the "boats" of the most wealthy in the United States rose the most.

Another concern is that economic growth may be too rapid, causing labor and input shortages, which in turn increase prices. In addition, economic growth has not evolved in a stable pattern. The United States has experienced nine major recessions since World War II. The instability characterized by fluctuations of the business cycle before the 1990s has been a primary feature of the postwar era.

Full Employment

The attainment of high levels of employment has been a goal of the U.S. government since the passage of the Employment Act of 1946 following the Great Depression of the 1930s. Congress reaffirmed that goal in passing the Full Employment and Balanced Growth Act of 1978, which set targets of 3 percent inflation and 4 percent unemployment and directed the president to take steps consistent with these goals. These steps might include creating a more favorable business climate and establishing policies for direct federal expenditures, among others. The country has come closest to full employment mostly during times of war.

Unemployment refers to people who would like to have jobs but don't. The Department of Labor defines people as unemployed when they are older than age sixteen, are actively seeking work, do not have a job, and have made some effort to find work during the past four weeks. The unemployment rate is the percent of people without jobs relative to the total number of people in the labor force (those with jobs or looking for jobs). About 63 percent of the U.S. population is in the labor force, and this base is used for the unemployment estimates. By 2006, almost 189 million of the 300 million people in the United States were in the civilian labor force. Table 14.2 shows unemployment rates for selected groups of workers from 1950 to 2005.

1. Does it surprise you that married men typically have lower unemployment rates than other groups of men (see Table 14.2)? Why or why not?

Economists have defined five basic types of unemployment:

1. **Frictional unemployment** is caused by the temporary mismatching of people with jobs because workers change jobs, employers seek new workers, and new people enter the labor market. All labor markets have frictional unemployment; even during the severe labor shortage of World War II, unemployment persisted at about 2 percent.

2. **Seasonal unemployment,** as the name implies, results from changing seasonal demand and supply for labor. Ski instructors seeking jobs in the summer and farmworkers laid off in the winter contribute to seasonal unemployment.

3. **Structural unemployment** presents a more serious problem. It results from permanent displacement of workers due to shifting product demand or technological changes that require new skills. The shift in demand from natural to synthetic fibers created problems of structural unemployment for places such as Fall River, Massachusetts. The mechanical picking of tomatoes caused many migrant farmworkers to become structurally unemployed. Such unemployment is a function of geography, as well as skill level, and mobility.

4. **Cyclical unemployment** is due to the decreased demand for labor during a downturn in the business cycle. The high unemployment of the 1930s was basically a problem of cyclical unemployment. The high unemployment rates of the early 1990s also were predominately cyclical.

5. **Hidden unemployment** is not included in the official unemployment rate and is probably the hardest concept to define and measure. Growing evidence suggests that many people would like a job if they thought one was available, but many have become so discouraged by their past failures to find employment that they have literally given up trying. Technically, such people are outside the labor force, but as a practical matter, they are unemployed and not offically counted as such. One sign that hidden unemployment exists is the rise in the labor force participation rate (the proportion of the total population seeking jobs) during the early stages of economic recovery. If more people seek jobs as the number of jobs increases, why weren't they part of the labor force when the unemployment rate

TABLE 14.2 Civilian Unemployment Rate by Demographic Characteristics, 1950–2005 (percent)

Year	By Sex and Age				Demographic Characteristic			By Selected Group		
	All Workers	Both Sexes, 16–19	Males, 20 and Over	Females, 20 and Over	White	Black or African American	Hispanic or Latino Ethnicity	Experienced Wage Earners	Married Men (Spouse Present)	Women Who Maintain Families
1950	5.3	12.2	4.7	5.1	4.9	—	—	6.0	4.6	—
1960	5.5	14.7	4.7	5.1	4.9	—	—	5.7	3.7	—
1970	4.9	15.3	3.5	4.8	4.5	—	—	4.8	2.6	5.4
1975	8.5	19.9	6.7	8.0	7.8	14.8	12.2	8.2	5.1	10.0
1980	7.1	17.8	5.9	6.4	6.3	14.3	10.1	6.9	4.2	9.2
1985	7.2	18.6	6.2	6.6	6.2	15.1	10.5	6.8	4.3	10.4
1990	5.6	15.5	5.0	4.9	4.8	11.4	8.2	5.3	3.4	8.2
1995	5.6	17.3	4.8	4.9	4.9	10.4	9.3	5.4	3.3	8.0
2000	4.0	13.0	4.1	3.6	3.5	7.6	5.7	3.9	2.0	5.9
2003	6.0	17.5	5.6	5.1	5.2	10.8	7.7	—	3.8	8.5
2005	5.1	16.6	4.4	4.6	4.4	10.0	6.0	—	2.8	7.8

Source: *Economic Report of the President*, 1990, pp. 338–339; 2003, p. 326; 2006, pp. 332–333.

was higher? In addition, many people work part-time but would prefer to work full-time. These people are counted as being employed.

More than 10 million people (on the average) were unemployed during the recession of 1980 to 1982. (Princeton economist Alan Blinder called them "cannon fodder in the assault on inflation.") Although the number of unemployed fell to 6.5 million in 1989, it quickly rose to 9.4 million in 1992 as the result of the recession that began in 1990. Unemployment rates then trended downward to 4.0 percent in the recovery through 2000. By 2001, the economy was showing signs of recession as economic growth slowed and the unemployment rate increased to 4.7 percent in 2001 and peaked at 6.0 percent in 2003. In late 2003 and 2004, with increases in government spending and tax cuts kicking in to jumpstart the economy, growth had renewed, but joblessness remained stubbornly at 5.6 percent. By February 2007, however, unemployment rates had dropped to 4.5 percent. Unemployment has direct social consequences for unemployed individuals, their families, and communities facing closed factories, unemployment lines, and discouraged workers.

Counting the Unemployed.   Beyond the real costs to those unemployed and to lost output, there are also problems in simply counting and defining the unemployed in our economy. Critics claim that the national measures of unemployment actually understate the real rate of unemployment. They argue that a different definition and measurement technique would reveal a national "underemployment" rate of 9 to 16 percent.

David Gordon, who taught at the New School of Social Research, called attention to the problem of *underemployment* and suggested that it was a more appropriate measure than the traditional notion of unemployment. As a more meaningful statistic, it would give economists better information and be more instructive to policy makers. Gordon defined underemployment as the number of people who fall into any of the following four categories:

1. *Unemployed people*—those who are actively looking for work but unable to find a job

2. *Discouraged workers*—those who are unemployed and want work but have given up in frustration because they believe no jobs are available

3. *Involuntary part-time workers*—those employed part-time who want full-time work but are unable to find it

4. *Underemployed people*—those who are working full-time but earning less than the poverty level of income as specified by the Bureau of Labor Statistics (for an urban family of four, $20,000 per year in 2006, compared to approximately $10,712 per year paid to a person working full-time at the 2005 minimum wage).

We can use these categories to adjust the traditional measure of unemployment. In 2005, the Bureau of Labor Statistics reported just over 4.35 million workers who were involuntary part-time employees. Discouraged workers were estimated at 4.9 million. When combined with the unemployed, these discouraged and involuntary part-time workers generated an "expanded unemployment rate" of 8 percent in 2005.

2. Do you anticipate unemployment in your future? Why or why not? What are your "odds"?

3. Does it make any difference how we count the unemployed? Explain.

Costs of Unemployment and Underemployment. Unemployment is an economic (opportunity) cost. Every 1 percent of the labor force that is unemployed represents several billion dollars of potential GDP.

In addition, unemployment has social and psychological costs—crime, family disintegration, and increasing mental health problems, to name a few. An examination of the nature of unemployment in the United States also reveals an identifiable institutionalized process of discrimination according to race, gender, and age. This became increasingly evident as unprecedented numbers of minorities, women, and teenagers entered the labor force after January 1980. In January 2006, when the Bureau of Labor Statistics reported a national unemployment rate that averaged 5.1 percent, the unemployment rate for black or African Americans averaged 10 percent—and more than 30.0 percent for black teens.

A last consideration related to unemployment involves poverty and welfare. In 2003, the poverty rate for those who did not work was more than 8 times the rate for those who worked (21 percent versus 2.6 percent), and part-time workers were 4.5 times more likely than full-time workers to fall into poverty. For U.S. citizens who are neither employed nor receiving any form of income from unemployment compensation, Social Security, or disability, welfare is the only way to meet survival needs. In addition, there has been an increase in the percent of part-time jobs. While some workers opt for part-time schedules, some 4.7 million workers who hold part-time jobs prefer to work full-time. Part-time jobs are characterized by lower wages, lower skill levels, more limited promotion opportunities, and fewer benefits than full-time jobs.

Price Stability

One thing that many people have in common is an aversion to **inflation,** which is an upward movement in the general price level. Deflation, in contrast, indicates a downward movement of the general price level. Price stability occurs when there is relatively little movement in the general price level.

The price level is measured by some sort of price index, such as the **Consumer Price Index (CPI).** A typical price index measures the average level of prices in one year or period as a percentage of the average price level in some base period. The Consumer Price Index is computed by the Bureau of Labor Statistics (BLS). Each month the BLS surveys markets in some fifty urban areas for the prices of 400 "typical" consumer goods and services. The bureau then computes the CPI by measuring the present cost of this "basket" of items as a percentage of the cost in some base period:

$$CPI = \frac{\text{current cost of basket}}{\text{cost of basket in base year}} \times 100$$

The inflation or deflation rate then measures the percentage change in the price level:

$$\text{current inflation or deflation rate} = \frac{\text{current CPI} - \text{last year's CPI}}{\text{last year's CPI}} \times 100$$

In the 1970s, the U.S. economy experienced frequent periods of inflation. During the 1980s, 1990s, and through 2004, annual rates of price increase remained low overall but began increasing through 2006. Still, price increases have been greater than the overall inflation rate in some selected markets. For example, oil prices have seen large increases and college students have experienced rapid rises in the cost of tuition each year, as well as higher than average prices for textbooks. Between 2000 and mid-2006, potential home buyers were confronted by much higher than average housing prices.

Because rapidly increasing prices often affect our consumption and saving decisions, we tend to have a greater sense of well-being when prices are stable. We don't have to worry (as much) about whether our savings will suffice to send us to college or help maintain our standard of living after we retire. We do know, however, that inflation is not a problem for those who correctly anticipate it and take appropriate precautions. For example, if prices rise by 4 percent and workers are aware of these economic developments, they expect a 4 percent inflation rate. To keep real (inflation-adjusted) wages at the same level, workers will demand at least a 4 percent wage increase. They will also put their savings into assets that will yield at least 4 percent. With these adjustments, workers correctly anticipate inflation and insulate themselves from it. But, if wages rise by only 3 percent with a 5 percent increase in prices, workers' income will lose 2 percent in purchasing power.

Those hurt by inflation include people on fixed incomes, usually the elderly; those working under fixed-cost or fixed-wage contracts; and individuals or institutions who have lent money at an interest rate less than the current rate of inflation. Many contracts now allow for price fluctuations, and many pensions are adjusted for inflation. Financial institutions react to inflationary pressures by charging higher interest rates, or even variable interest rates pegged to bonds that reflect price or inflationary changes. Still, people prefer price stability as a way to avoid the necessity of forecasting correctly and adjusting behavior to that forecast.

During the 1970s, the United States experienced record levels of inflation caused by factors related to demand, supply, and expectations. Owing to the same factors, the 1980s brought an ebbing of inflationary pressures. Several unexpected forces entered into the scenario during the 1970s, all of which heightened the problem of inflation. In 1973, an embargo imposed by the powerful Organization of Petroleum Exporting Countries (OPEC) nations sent energy prices soaring. The reduced supply of oil caused the general price level to rise and output to fall. Shortages and price increases were also felt in the markets for food, metals, and other primary materials.

The 1970s also ushered in a period of increased government regulation. This time, instead of antitrust legislation, the government regulated various aspects of our living and working environments and promoted equal opportunity. While the social benefits of these regulations were widespread, they were also expensive, and these costs initially came on board during the 1970s. Accelerated government expenditures resulting from the Vietnam War added an estimated 3.25 percent to the underlying inflation rate, while the surge in oil prices, first in 1973 and again in 1979, added 4.75 percent. These factors alone explain an inflation rate of 8 percent during the 1970s.

At the beginning of the 1980s, events eased inflationary pressures. Oil prices began to drop as production increased and demand fell. The prices of other raw materials declined as well, due to overproduction in many of the developing nations. Deregulation, or the rollback of government regulations, in a number of industries increased competition and lowered prices. The value of the dollar restrained prices of imported goods, helping to lower inflation in the United States by providing a supply of cheaper imports and by keeping domestic prices in check as U.S. producers struggled to remain price-competitive. Labor made many concessions during the recession of 1980 to 1982, and these "givebacks" kept wages from rising. More importantly, the Federal Reserve cut the growth rate of the money supply to halt the inflationary trends, and lower inflation rates were gained at the cost of high rates of unemployment.

With the Federal Reserve policy continuing to target low inflation rates, the late 1980s through 2004 saw stable prices, averaging growth rates between 2 and 4 percent. This period was accompanied by relatively stable oil and resource prices, slow wage growth, and in the late 1990s, cheap imports. Oil prices began increasing rapidly in 2004 due to concern about Middle East oil supplies and increased oil demand by India and China. The effect of huricane Katrina's disruption of U.S. oil production in late 2005 and the Israel-Lebanon war in 2006 kept oil prices increasing at a robust rate. However, by the end of the year, oil markets calmed and prices fell.

The goal of price stability is sometimes achieved due to good economic policy, good luck, or some combination of the two, particularly when factors outside the realm of domestic economic policy tools are operating.

4. Which of the three macroeconomic goals—growth, full employment, or price stability—is the most important to you? Why?

5. If you could add another goal to this list, what would it be? Explain.

Macroeconomic Tools

To achieve the three macroeconomic goals of growth, full employment, and price stability, economists and government policy makers use economic theory to analyze the economy and to formulate macroeconomic policy. The primary macroeconomic tools are monetary and fiscal policy. Let's briefly define each of these and see how they are used.

The Federal Reserve System manages, coordinates, and controls the monetary system of the U.S. economy. Proper management of this system makes available the quantity of money necessary for desired economic growth at interest rates capable of inducing the desired levels of investment and spending. **Monetary policy** consists of tools that can change the amount of money and credit available in the economy. It is administered by the Federal Reserve System to achieve and promote economic growth, maximum employment, and price stability.

Through **fiscal policy,** the government manipulates its expenditures and taxation to attain the basic macroeconomic objectives. Fiscal policy is administered by the executive and legislative branches of the federal government and is coordinated with monetary policy. (See Chapters 16 and 17 for more on fiscal and monetary policy.)

Fiscal and monetary tools have both been part of contemporary macroeconomic policy as it has developed over the past sixty years. Several important issues and problems are associated with this policy. We shall examine a few of these in the context of the economic history of the post–World War II period, when monetary and fiscal policy became mainstays in a U.S. economy aiming to achieve the goals of growth, high employment, and price stability.

The Rise of Pax Americana: 1946 to the 1960s

Just as the Victorian period in the late nineteenth century was dubbed "Pax Britannia," the period after World War II until the middle to late 1960s has been called "Pax Americana." The world seemed ripe for economic quests and successes by the United States. The three decades that followed, however, saw a reduction in U.S. power in the international economic arena. The U.S. position continued to worsen until conditions taking advantage of economic growth, improvements in levels of employment, stable prices, and deficit reductions arose in the mid-1990s.

By the end of World War II, many important institutions characteristic of the U.S. economy were already in place. Monopolies and large corporations had been present since the turn of the century, and the 1930s brought increasing levels of government intervention in the economy. After the prolonged recession and depression of the 1930s and the wartime economy of the 1940s, the setting was ripe for the United States to push ahead and prosper. The 1950s arrived with abundant potential and opportunity; Europe and Japan lay in ruin, and the United States possessed the only productive industrial capacity not debilitated by the war. These industries were immediately called on in the effort to rebuild Europe and Japan, as well as to meet the increased demands for consumer goods and services that had developed in the United States during the war. In the decade following the war, U.S. economic growth skyrocketed. Real weekly earnings increased at an average of 2.3 percent per year. Productivity increases held steady at 3.2 percent, and real GDP growth was about 4 percent. Unemployment averaged 4 percent. When unemployment rose to 5.5 percent in the recessions of 1949, 1954, 1958, and 1960, inflation slowed to 2 percent.

As the prosperity of the 1950s passed into the 1960s, the government began to actively participate in the growth that had earlier been dominated by the private sector. The new federal interstate highway system was the highlight of federal expenditures of the 1950s. These expenditures continued into the 1960s and were joined by a federal Model Cities program that contributed to the U.S. urban infrastructure. In 1964, Congress passed a tax cut specifically designed to increase income—the first planned policy action of its type. Later in the 1960s, the Great Society program was put into place to reduce poverty. Only now are we realizing the successes of these programs—as well as some of their short-comings. The 1960s also brought the war in Vietnam and a demand for more federal expenditures to finance it.

Also by the 1960s, Japan and the industrial nations of Western Europe had rebuilt their factories, and their economies were strengthened. Increased foreign production challenged U.S. goods in world markets, and U.S. economic growth slowed. In the international sphere, the dollar, which served as the "key currency" in all international transactions, was coming under economic attack as other nations regained their prewar economic positions. This pressure eventually led to a devaluation of the dollar and a new system for determining international exchange rates.

The Decline of Pax Americana: The 1970s to mid-1980s

During the 1970s, U.S. economic growth and strength were challenged from several sides. The oil embargo of 1973, coupled with agricultural shortages, showed the vulnerability of the U.S. economy (and others as well) to supply shocks on a world level. A severe recession in the mid-1970s sent unemployment to 9 percent. As the economy began to recover in 1977 and 1978, inflation skyrocketed to 13.3 percent. In the last half of 1979, the Federal Reserve put in motion a series of credit restraints that sent the economy plummeting into yet another recession. Economic growth slowed, and throughout the decade, growth was due almost entirely to rising employment and not greater productivity. The service sector dominated the employment growth of the seventies, with many dead-end, low-paying jobs providing entry for an expanding labor force.

While the 1970s were marked by record levels of inflation in the United States, the early 1980s witnessed both the highest levels of unemployment since the 1930s and the lowest levels of inflation since the 1960s. In 1981, the economy experienced a recession and modest recovery, then plunged into the deepest recession since the Great Depression. This recession can largely be explained by actions of the Federal Reserve, which was using monetary policy to actively restrict growth in the supply of money between late 1979 and 1982. (Chapter 17 explains these concepts in more detail.)

Monetary ease and historically high government expenditures and tax cuts combined to generate the recovery of 1983 to 1984, which, despite very slow economic growth, persisted until 1989. Unemployment fell as some workers headed back to the factories and many others moved into the service sector. Inflation remained stable at 3 percent, but increases in real weekly earnings averaged only 0.3 percent. The economy, however, had been left with very high real rates of interest, resulting at least partially from large government expenditures and tax cuts creating deficits. Throughout the 1980s, the federal government incurred large and persistent budget deficits. High interest rates hurt the economy by hindering job creation and investment in new plants, equipment, and housing. These high rates of return also attracted foreign money to the United States and kept the value of the dollar high through 1985. This promoted the importation of relatively cheap foreign goods, helping consumers but hurting U.S. producers, who lost out in two ways: Not only were more foreign goods purchased in the United States, but fewer U.S. products were exported to the rest of the world. In the early 1980s, high interest rates also affected debt-plagued developing nations, whose debt payments mounted with each rise in the U.S. interest rate.

6. Why do you think inflation might rise when unemployment is low? Explain.

7. What is debt? How does it arise? Do you worry about going into debt? Why?

The U.S. Economy: The Late 1980s and Early 1990s

During the 1980s, the Federal Reserve continued to increase the money supply, resulting in lower interest rates. During this period of sustained growth and low inflation, a stock market crash in the United States wiped out some $500 billion of wealth, signaling that not all was well with the U.S. economy. By the end of the week of October 19, 1987, nearly $1 trillion of wealth had vanished.*

The repercussions of the crash were felt throughout the world. Quick intervention by the Federal Reserve assured both confidence and sufficient liquidity to underwrite any instability that might spread to the banking and credit industries. Indicators showed the economy to be in reasonable health; the 6 percent unemployment level was the lowest in a decade, prices were stable, and economic growth had been led by a massive consumer spending boom. There were, however, economic as well as structural and institutional problems that prompted the dramatic decline in the New York Stock Exchange on that day, referred to as Black Monday.

---

*Some people call this wealth "paper wealth." It accumulates from the changing value of stock prices.

After the 1987 crash, the underlying U.S. debt, low saving rate, and institutional problems persisted. The economic recovery of the early 1980s continued, with economic growth averaging just over 3.7 percent between 1987 and 1989. In 1989, unemployment reached its lowest point since 1973, when it fell to 5.3 percent. After this, growth stagnated and an economic slowdown continued through 1992.

A Rebirth of Pax Americana: 1992 and Beyond

A buoyant recovery followed the 1989 to 1992 recession and was characterized by increased investment, strong productivity growth, lower levels of unemployment, and steady economic expansion without any signs of inflation. Indeed, the economic growth experienced in the United States between the trough of the recession in 1991 and peak of the upturn in 2000 was the longest economic expansion on record.

Growth between 1992 and 1997 was accompanied by changes in corporate organization including downsizing. While the rate of growth was initially slow, it increased steadily. The president and Congress paid increasing attention to budget and trade deficits and were successful in reducing budget deficits. The income gap between the haves and have-nots continued to widen, with women and children bearing the brunt of the effects of income redistribution. Although an impressive number of jobs were created between 1982 and 1988 and 1992 and 2000, the number of less-educated workers vying for those jobs reduced the real earnings of high school graduates and dropouts alike. Rank-and-file workers experienced an 18 percent decrease in real (inflation-adjusted) wages between 1973 and 1997, while corporate chief executive officers watched their pay increase by an average of 19 percent (66 percent after taxes). Homelessness became a national problem.

Financial crises in Asia, Latin America, and Russia in 1997 and 1998 failed to stem the economic expansion in the United States. Rather, as countries in these areas experienced a deep economic downturn, their falling currencies and lower wages signaled cheaper exports to the United States. The relatively low prices of imports from these areas kept U.S. prices low.

With inflation well under control, investment continued to increase, and economic growth become even more rapid, reaching an extraordinary level of 6 percent in 1999 before falling to more normal and sustainable rates of 4 percent in 2000. Employment remained strong as growth kept unemployment hovering around 4 percent between 1997 and 2001. With rising income, productivity increases, and moderation in public policy, budget deficits turned into surpluses in 1999 and 2000 for the first time since World War II. Internationally, U.S. growth rates were much stronger than those in Europe and Japan.

Still, despite this remarkable period of economic expansion, the U.S. infrastructure—the stock of highways, bridges, and water and sewer lines that had contributed to growth in the 1950s and 1960s—continued to deteriorate. Fewer U.S. workers were covered by health insurance and the number of uninsured children grew. By early 2001, a recession was underway. After a decade of uninterrupted and often accelerating growth, postwar unemployment record lows, and vigorous productivity increases, growth did finally slow and a number of economic "shocks" prolonged the slowdown into 2003. In March 2001, the high-flying stock market, largely propelled by technology and .com stocks, began a quick descent, with most stock measures dropping more than 20 percent, wiping out an estimated $4.7 trillion in "paper" wealth from the change in value of stock prices. The Federal Reserve pumped money into the economy and targeted much lower interest rates designed to stimulate investment and consumer spending. Congress passed a series of tax cuts with the hope of increasing the economic stimulus. In the fall, more economic shocks left the economy reeling. The terror attacks of September 11, 2001, had profound impacts on all aspects of American lives, including the economy. Uncertainty and confusion surrounding the attacks led investors and consumers to be more wary about expenditures. And, while Americans were still trying to deal with the aftereffects of September 11 and plan for the future, a series of corporate scandals led to the failure of several large firms, including Enron (the seventh largest firm in the United States in 2000), and Arthur Andersen, one of the (then) "big five" accounting firms. War in Iraq, declared in March 2003, also had economic consequences.

The lowest mortgage rates in four decades, low interest rates, increases in government spending and tax cuts, resilient consumers, and a buoyant housing market stimulated economic activity. By late 2006, economic growth and productivity returned. But lethargic job creation and discouraged workers, accompanied by growing budget deficits and trade deficits (despite a weaker U.S. dollar), continued to cause concern about the strength and endurance of the recovery. Additionally, health insurance coverage continued to be of concern and income inequality worsened. There is little agreement on how best to solve these problems or which problems should have priority.

Has the focus on macroeconomic national goals been effective in the postwar years? Certainly the United States has approached desired levels of price stability, lower unemployment, and steady economic growth, but at what cost to the economic future of its citizens?

8. What has happened to economic growth since 2007? What has stimulated the rapid or slow growth? Has unemployment increased? Inflation? Why or why not?

9. List five macroeconomic goals you think are important for this millennium. Briefly explain your choices.

National Accounting Measures

As we chart macroeconomic goals through the next few years, it is important to understand what these concepts mean and how we measure them. The scheme of National Income and Product Accounting was developed to put economic growth measures into perspective. These measures give quantifiable definitions to the activities of the major macroeconomic actors (consumers, businesses, governments, and the international sector) and show how they interact to generate production, consumption, and investment.

To help understand the ways in which the economy continues to change over time, economists collect and analyze data that measure economic variables. Economic measurement is usually designed to aid forecasting and explanation of economic events, or it may be used to compare the size or the value of things. When economists speak of the value of the annual output of a nation, they refer to gross domestic product (GDP), published in quarterly reports issued by the Department of Commerce. The media, politicians, and others who regularly comment on economic affairs await the Commerce Department reports in order to assess whether GDP and its accompanying growth rate are up or down. Economists then assess these results and often qualify them—for example, GDP was up 2.5 percent over last quarter, but prices have been increasing by 3 percent at the same time.

In December 1991, the Bureau of Economic Analysis began to emphasize GDP in place of gross national product (GNP). The distinction between the two accounting measures is that GDP includes the income earned by foreign residents and companies in the United States, but not the income earned by U.S. citizens and corporations abroad. The change from GNP to GDP occurred because GDP more closely follows the short-term economic performance of the economy and because most other countries use GDP as their primary accounting measure.

In fact, for the United States, the difference between GNP and GDP has usually been very small. In a typical year, the income earned by foreign-owned businesses and noncitizens in the United States is very close to the income earned by U.S. citizens and companies abroad. Therefore, the differences between GNP and GDP nearly cancel each other out in the United States. However, in small countries with much business activity by foreign companies, the two measures may be significantly different.

Economists and policy makers use GDP and the rest of the National Income and Product Accounts as the basis for many decisions. We therefore will spend some time looking at the components of these accounts.

There are two basic ways of arriving at final figures for the various accounting measures:

1. The *goods- or expenditures-flow approach* focuses on the prices and quantities of goods and services sold.
2. The *income-flow approach* focuses on income paid to those producing goods and services.

These approaches appear in the circular flow diagram in Figure 14.1. We can measure either the top part of the circular flow (the income flow) or the bottom part of the circular flow (the goods or expenditures flow) to arrive at equal measures of national income.

FIGURE 14.1 The Income and Spending Flows

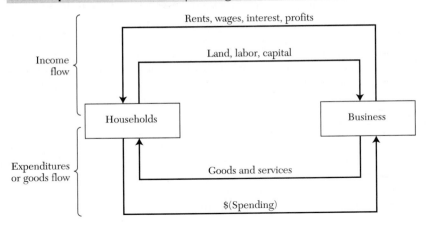

The definitions, relations, and data in Tables 14.3 and 14.4 show the derivation of GDP with the goods-flow approach. GDP consists of the total expenditures of the four sectors that purchase goods and services:

$$GDP = C + I + G + (X - M),$$

where C represents the expenditures made by consumers, I is investment expenditures made by the business community, G is expenditures on goods and services by government, and $(X–M)$ represents net exports, or exports (X) minus imports (M). The income-flow approach entails summing the various forms of income received from the production process.

Potential Problems with the National Income Accounts

The measures in the National Income Accounts are corrected for inflation with the use of a price index. Also, use of a value-added approach in the measurement process avoids possible double-counting. There are, however, criticisms of the accounts that have not been addressed. Particularly troublesome are issues of what is and what is not included in the National Income and Product Accounts. Let us see how some potential problems have been avoided and discuss some that remain.

Real versus Nominal GDP

These definitional relationships ignore many difficult and rather perplexing problems. First, there is the problem of the yardstick, money. This is a very flexible yardstick, since dollars are most often worth more or less as time passes

TABLE 14.3 Relation of Gross Domestic Product, Net National Product, National Income, and Personal Income

The sum of	Billions of Dollars		
	1996	2000	2005
Personal consumption expenditures (C)	5,151.40	6,757.30	8,745.70
Gross private domestic investment (I)	1,117.00	1,832.70	2,105.00
Government consumption expenditures and gross investment (G)	1,406.40	1,743.70	2,362.90
Net exports of goods and services (X–M)	−98.70	−370.70	−726.50
EQUALS: Gross domestic product (GDP)	7,576.10	9,963.10	12,487.10
PLUS: Receipts of factor income from the rest of the world	228.40	370.60	507.60
LESS: Payments of factor income to the rest of the world	237.30	374.90	474.00
EQUALS: Gross national product (GNP)	7,567.20	9,958.70	12,520.80
LESS: Consumption of fixed capital	858.30	1,257.10	1,574.10
EQUALS: Net national product (NNP)	6,708.90	8,701.60	10,946.70
LESS: Indirect business tax and nontax liability	617.90	769.60	–
Business transfer payments	32.20	41.70	–
Statistical discrepancy	−74.60	−87.70	42.80
PLUS: Subsidies less current surplus of government enterprises	17.50	27.90	–
EQUALS: National income (NI)	6,150.90	8,002.00	10,903.90
LESS: Corporate profits with inventory valuation and capital consumption adjustments	654.70	946.20	1,351.90
Net interest	403.30	567.20	498.30
Contributions for social insurance	689.70	705.60	871.20
Wage accruals less disbursements	0.00	0.00	0.00
LESS: Taxes on production (–) M subsides	–	–	848.00
Net Business Transfer Payments	–	–	80.20
Other	–	–	
PLUS: Personal interest income	1,056.70	1,034.30	945.70
Personal dividend income	738.20	396.60	511.70
Government transfer payments to persons	230.60	1,037.10	1,483.70
Business transfer payments to persons	23.00	30.70	41.60
EQUALS: Personal income (PI)	6,451.70	8,281.70	10,248.30
LESS: Personal tax payments	863.80	1,291.90	1,209.70
EQUALS: Disposable personal income (DPI)	5,587.90	6,989.80	9,038.60
LESS: Personal outlays		6,998.30	9,072.10
Personal consumption expenditures (C)	5,151.40	6,757.30	8,743.70
Interest paid by consumers	146.30	212.20	205.90
Personal transfer payments	16.30	28.80	120.70
EQUALS: Personal savings (S)	273.90	−8.50	33.50

Note: Dollars are not constant dollars.
Note: Numbers do not add up to the totals shown because of adjustments or inclusion of minor categories. In 2006, revisions changed the accounting for items shown as dashes (–).
Source: *Survey of Current Business*, April 1997; April 2001, 2004, 2006.

TABLE 14.4   Definitions of Primary Accounts in Table 14.3

The sum of

1. *Personal consumption expenditures (C)* consist of the market value of purchases of goods and services by individuals and nonprofit institutions and the value of food, clothing, housing, and financial services received by them as income in kind.
2. *Gross private domestic investment (I)* consists of acquisitions of newly produced capital goods by private business and nonprofit institutions and of the value of the change in the volume of inventories held by business. It covers all private new dwellings.
3. *Government consumption expenditures and gross investment (G)* consist of government expenditures for compensation of employees, purchases from business, net foreign purchases and contributions, and the gross investment of government enterprises. This measure excludes transfer payments, government interest, and subsidies.
4. *Net exports of goods and services (X–M)* measures the excess of (1) domestic output sold abroad over purchases of foreign output, (2) production abroad credited to U.S-owned resources over production at home credited to foreign-owned resources, and (3) cash gifts and contributions received from abroad over cash gifts and contributions to foreigners.
5. The *residual (r)*—in real GDP only; see item 6—is the amount created by chain-weighted measurement of GDP. (See footnote in the section titled "Real versus Nominal GDP.")

EQUALS

6. *Gross domestic product* (GDP) is the market value of the newly produced goods and services that are not resold in any form during the accounting period (usually one year).

PLUS

7. *Receipts of factor income* from the rest of the world are the moneys received from foreign affiliates of U.S. corporations. The moneys take the form of interest, dividends, and reinvested earnings.

LESS

8. *Payments of factor income* to the rest of the world are the payments to foreign residents of interest, dividends, and reinvested earnings of U.S. affiliates of foreign companies.

EQUALS

9. *Gross national product* (GNP) is the market value of the newly produced goods and services that are not resold in any form during the accounting period (usually one year).

LESS

10. *Capital consumption allowance* is an allowance for capital goods that have been consumed in the process of producing this year's GDP. It consists of depreciation, capital outlays charged to current expense, and accidental damage.

(usually less). To solve the flexibility dilemma, economists use index numbers, meaning they compare a "market basket" of selected goods and services from one accounting period with a similar "basket" from some previous accounting period, or base year.* Thus, they can avoid the perils of price instability by inflating or deflating the dollar value accordingly. For example, if prices increase at a rate of 5 percent during a year, a good that cost $100 at the beginning of the

---

*In January 1996, the Bureau of Economic Analysis (BEA) released new estimates for the national income and product accounts, moving to a system that uses chain weights instead of fixed weights in the adjustment of real GDP, to remove biases caused by the fixed-weight price system of the past. The formula for this adjustment is no longer as simple as the common market basket example using fixed weights. By adopting the chain-weighting system, the BEA hopes to provide more accurate measures of real GDP. For additional information on these changes, see the 1996 *Economic Report of the President*, pp. 48, 50, and 59.

TABLE 14.4 Continued

11. *Net national product (NNP)* is the net creation of new wealth resulting from the productive activity of the economy during the accounting period.
LESS
12. *Indirect business tax* consists primarily of sales and excise taxes, customs duties on imported goods, and business property taxes. These taxes are collected from businesses and are chargeable to their current costs.
EQUALS
13. *National income (NI)* is the total income of factors from participation in the current productive process.
LESS
14. *After-tax corporate profits* with inventory and capital consumption adjustments subtracts federal and state taxes levied on corporate earnings and depreciation allowances from corporate profits.
15. *Net interest* is interest earnings minus interest liabilities and part of national income.
16. Contributions for *social insurance* consist of payments by employees and the self-employed.
PLUS
17. *Personal interest income* includes all interest payments made to persons.
18. *Personal dividend income* includes that part of corporate profits returned to stockholders.
19. *Transfer payments* (government and business) consist of monetary income received by individuals from government and business (other than government interest) for which no services are currently rendered.
EQUALS
20. *Personal income (PI)* is income received by households, as opposed to income earned by households.
LESS
21. *Personal taxes* consist of the taxes levied against individuals, their income, and their property that are not deductible as expenses of business operations.
EQUALS
22. *Disposable personal income (DPI)* is the income remaining to persons after deduction of personal tax and nontax payments to general government.
LESS
23. *Personal consumption expenditures (C)*—this is the same as item 1.
EQUALS
24. *Personal savings (S)* may be in such forms as changes in cash and deposits, security holdings, and private pension, health, welfare, and trust funds.

first year would be priced at $105 at the beginning of the next. Using a price index, this item would be valued at $100 in constant dollars. This device allows us to remove the effects of price changes from GDP, so that we can measure the changes in *real* output and better assess the actual physical volume of production in the two periods.

The GDP deflator is a systematized equation that has been shown to be a reasonable indicator of how much the national product has gained or lost due to recession or inflation. For example, in 1979 GDP went up by 12 percent, but prices went up by 11.3 percent, so real GDP increased by only 0.7 percent. Figure 14.2 shows the variation between real and nominal GDP since 1989.

FIGURE 14.2 GDP in Current and Constant Dollars 1989–2005

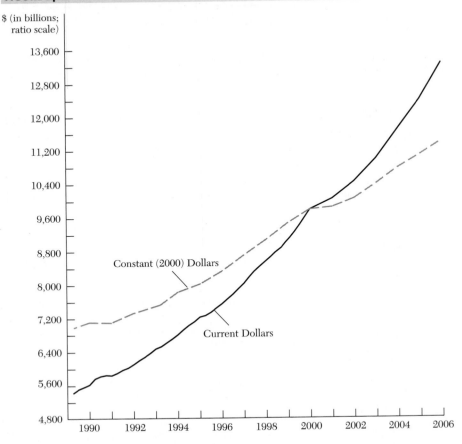

$ (in billions; ratio scale)

Constant (2000) Dollars

Current Dollars

Source: U.S. Department of Commerce, *Economic Indicators*, October 2006, pp. 1–2.

Value-added Accounting

A second problem encountered in the national income accounting framework is the actual counting process. We can either count the final products produced or sum the amount of value added by each stage of the production process. For example, to enter a loaf of bread into the accounting scheme, we could use the final sale price of the loaf of bread, or we could sum the value added to the loaf of bread by the wheat farmer, miller, baker, grocer, and so on. Both methods should yield the same result, but in the final-product method, there is often a chance of double-counting the components of production. Therefore, the value-added approach is preferred.

What Is Counted in GDP?

The significance of the accounts also has been called into question. These accounts are primarily derived from market transactions with known prices and quantities, but some market transactions are excluded. Excluded transactions include capital gains and losses as well as all illegal transactions. (What would the illegal drug market add to the GDP?) Also excluded is the economic activity of the underground economy—individuals who earn but do not report income on services they render or goods they produce, for example, cash paid for babysitting. Barter exchange also is part of the underground economy. The size of the underground economy has been estimated at 5 to 30 percent of GDP. Other industrial nations are estimated to have underground economies comparable to that of the United States.

The accounts also include some imputed values for nonmarket transactions. For example, imputed values are added for owner-occupied homes (room and board services exchanged for). But imagine what would happen to the accounts if we made yet another nonmarket inclusion, the value of unpaid child care provided by parents. If families simply exchanged child care with their neighbors each day and paid one another $50 or more a day (the estimated market worth of child care services), their production would be included in the accounts. These activities are productive; they are services. Currently, however, they are neither measured nor included in the National Income Accounts.

Marilyn Waring, a political economist and former member of the New Zealand Parliament, has suggested in her book *If Women Counted: A New Feminist Economics*, that throughout the world, accounting systems that define productive activity, as well as the economic analysis and teaching that sustain them, automatically exclude the nonmarket activities of women. To this point she quotes retired Harvard economist John Kenneth Galbraith:

> That many women are coming to sense that they are instruments in the economic system is not in doubt. But their feeling finds no support in economic writing and teaching. On the contrary, it is concealed and on the whole with great success, by modern neo-classical economics—the everyday economics of the textbook and classroom. This concealment is neither conspiratorial nor deliberate. It reflects the natural and very strong instincts of economics for what is convenient to influence economic interest—for what I have called the conventional social virtue. It is sufficiently successful that it allows many hundreds of thousands of women to study economics each year without their developing any serious suspicion as to how they will be used.
>
> —Marilyn J. Waring, *If Women Counted*, HarperCollins Publishers, 1989.

10. How will you be used by the economic system? Does it matter? Why?

11. What are "natural" instincts? Do you trust them?

The National Income Accounts are often misrepresented as an indicator of social well-being. In 1995, Clifford Cobb, Ted Halstead, and Jonathan Rowe published an article in the *Atlantic Monthly* entitled "If the GDP Is Up, Why Is

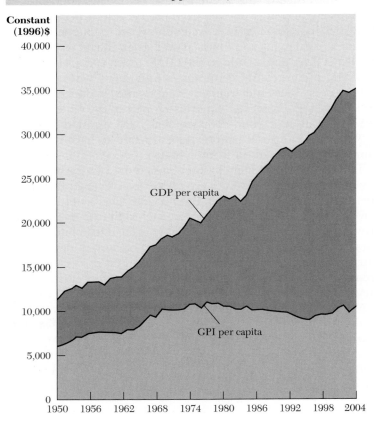

Source: Data from Redefining Progress, *Genuine Progress Report* 2004, p. 4.

America Down?" The article noted that the U.S. economy was performing in textbook fashion, with productivity and employment increasing and inflation remaining at low levels, but people didn't "feel" better. Indeed, President Clinton later called it a malaise. These authors argue for new measures for economic progress that would "change the social and political landscape":

> The GDP is simply a gross measure of market activity, of money changing hands. It makes no distinction whatsoever between the desirable and the undesirable, or costs and gain. On top of that, it looks only at the portion of reality that economists choose to acknowledge—the part involved in monetary transactions. The crucial economic functions performed in the household and volunteer sectors go entirely unrecognized. As a result the GDP not only masks the breakdown of the social structure and the natural habitat upon which the economy—and life itself— ultimately depend; worse, it actually portrays such breakdown as economic gain.

Economic "bads," such as pollution and deaths due to lung cancer attributed to smoking cigarettes, actually increase the GDP. These social costs are not subtracted from, but added to the GDP. As we spend more and more to clean up the environment, the spending *adds* to our national product. As cigarette sales increase, GDP increases. As hospital costs for increased numbers of cases of lung cancer and emphysema occur, GDP increases. GDP, in other words, is not a measure of overall welfare.

The environment think tank, Redefining Progress, has constructed what it calls a genuine progress indicator (GPI). The GPI tries to monitor "sustainability"—or the conflict between sustaining human life and the integrity of nature ... or living satisfactorily without destroying our environment. Thus the GPI monitors human consumption of resources *and* our contentment with our social, personal, and civic life. In other words, the GPI takes some economic "bads" such as environmental degradation into account. Figure 14.3 compares trends in per capita GPI with trends in per capita GDP in the United States since 1950. Although GDP has risen over that period, the level of GPI has barely changed.

12. Can you give other examples in which individual or societal welfare is diminished but GDP is increased?

Social scientists are attempting to construct a qualitative index that measures social welfare. Thus far, the index is quite crude, but it shows that nations with the highest GDP do not necessarily have the highest social welfare ratings, while a few countries with extremely low GDP have *relatively* high standings on the social welfare index.

The United Nations has constructed a Human Development Index (HDI) that measures a set of average human achievements in a single index. These achievements include life expectancy at birth, adult literacy rate, and per capita income. Table 14.5 lists the top twenty countries according to a recent HDI.

13. Why is it important to collect data on all of these different macroeconomic variables?

 ## Conclusion

This brief overview of macroeconomic problems and issues and summary of aggregate economic measurements provides a conceptual framework for describing relationships among important economic variables. While it is clear that recent trends in the U.S. economy have left us with many questions concerning future directions, we need to ask ourselves, To what extent does contemporary macroeconomic theory adequately explain our current economic reality? We will attempt to provide satisfactory answers for this question and develop an understanding of macroeconomic theory and policy in the following chapters. So let us continue this voyage through macroeconomics by first defining aggregate measures and then interpreting the theory in the context of its historical roots.

TABLE 14.5 Top Countries Rated with the UN's Human Development Index

Rank	Country
1	Norway
2	Iceland
3	Australia
4	Luxembourg
5	Canada
6	Sweden
7	Switzerland
8	Ireland
9	Belgium
10	United States
11	Japan
12	Netherlands
13	Finland
14	Denmark
15	United Kingdom
16	France
17	Austria
18	Italy
19	New Zealand
20	Germany

Source: Data from United Nations, *Human Development Report*. Copyright © 2005 The United Nations. Used with permission.

Review Questions

1. Why do you think full employment, economic growth, and price stability were selected as the basic macroeconomic goals in the United States? Can you think of others possible goals? Explain.

2. The three goals are often at odds with one another. Has the relative emphasis of these different goals changed over time? Why?

3. What do you see as some of the costs associated with unemployment? Inflation?

4. Do events elsewhere in the world affect the U.S. economy? Give some examples.

5. Is it possible to establish an effective body of macroeconomic policy using only fiscal tools or only monetary tools? Why or why not?

6. Do policy measures aimed at alleviating one set of economic problems sometimes make others worse? Should a policy action be undertaken to aid one aspect of the macroeconomy to the detriment of another? Explain.

7. Examine a daily newspaper (e.g., *The New York Times*) for a few days, and see how many articles address macroeconomic issues and problems. Make a list of the macroeconomic terms, concepts, and issues that you find.

8. Why should reports of current levels of GDP be received with care?

9. What do the National Income and Product Accounts measure?

10. Increasing numbers of women have entered the paid labor market during the past three decades. What impact would you expect this to have on GDP? Explain.

CHAPTER FIFTEEN

Macroeconomic Theory: Classical and Keynesian Models

◼ Introduction

The tenets of classical macroeconomic theory formed by Adam Smith, David Ricardo, John Stuart Mill, and others, which focused on growth, were carried pretty much intact through the nineteenth century. Economists in the latter part of that era concentrated more on the microeconomic concepts of utility and production than on the total economy. This chapter will provide a guide to our current understanding of the macroeconomy, discuss four major parts of the classical doctrine, illustrate their use, and then examine the Keynesian critique of classical macroeconomic theory and its inability to deal with high unemployment in the depression-plagued world of the 1930s.

In this chapter, we also will start to construct an economic model that is used for analyzing economic activity and forecasting the outcome of policy measures and/or economic shocks. This aggregate demand–aggregate supply model builds on macroeconomic models of income and output, and adds to that the effect of including money (through monetary policy). We first formulate the Keynesian model, which combines with monetary theory to form the underlying foundation for macroeconomic analysis. We will continue to develop and add to the model over the next four chapters. These building blocks are created from the tools, concepts, and definitions developed in these chapters. Additionally, each stage in the development of the aggregate demand–aggregate supply framework will include a descriptive overview, with a Big Picture feature providing an intuitive guide to a specific theory that is more fully developed in the text.

The completed aggregate demand–aggregate supply graphs resemble the market supply and demand graphs we developed in Chapter 8, but this resemblance is where the similarity ends. Information about financial markets, goods and service markets, and economic policy are reflected in an aggregate demand–aggregate supply analysis, which tells us how those markets respond to economic events, including policy decisions. We will be able to assess aggregate output and price levels for the economy when the model is completed.

We begin with Keynes's theory which challenged long-standing economic traditions. Some view the Keynesian contribution as a new paradigm, while others view it as simply a major revision of classical theory. The classical model we discuss in this chapter was never formally set up as such by any of the classical economists. Rather, Keynes drew together the foundations from the writings of the classical economists and constructed the model primarily as a foil against which he could contrast his model in The General Theory of Employment, Interest, and Money.

The Classical Model

THE BIG PICTURE

An Introduction to the Classical Model

If we were to summarize the contributions of various classical and neoclassical economists prior to the Great Depression of the 1930s, they would share the view that a capitalist economy (using an analogy of Cambridge economic historian Mark Blaug) generated its own automatic pilot. If there were disturbances in various markets creating disequilibrium prices, then wages or interest rates would adjust so that equilibrium in markets would once again be attained. For example, if there was not enough saving among the public to generate required levels of investment, the interest rate would be bid up—attracting more saving and lowering investment—and equilibrium would be restored, as we see in Figure 15.BP.1

If there was unemployment, wages would be bid down until employers would be willing to hire those unemployed, thus restoring labor market equilibrium (Figure 15.BP.2).

FIGURE 15.BP.1 Saving and Investment in the Classical Model

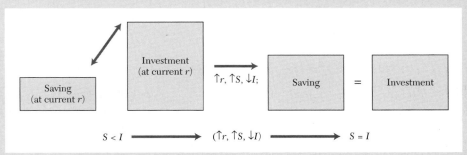

FIGURE 15.BP.2   Labor Market Adjustment in the Classical Model

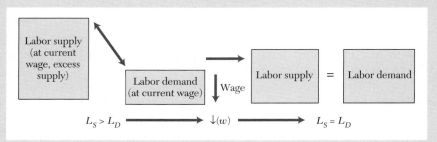

All one needed to do was wait. The automatic pilot takes over, markets adjust, and equilibrium is restored. But the Great Depression, which was felt throughout the world, found capitalism's markets slow to restore equilibrium. Prices fell and gluts occurred. Wages fell and unemployment increased. The economy crashed before the automatic pilot restored order.

We will now discuss four specific elements of the classical model that show how economists analyzed unemployment, inflation, and growth, particularly when the economy suffered during the Great Depression. We will begin by examining the quantity theory of money and the equation of exchange, which was used to show the relationship between money and prices. Next we will briefly examine the goods and labor market, Say's law, and the credit market in the classical model.

The Quantity Theory of Money

A major tenet of classical economic theory is the **quantity theory of money.** Most often this is expressed by the **equation of exchange:**

$$MV = PQ,$$

where M is the money stock in the economy, V is the income velocity of money (the rate of turnover of money), P is the price level, and Q is the level of real national income (real GDP). This equation appears simple enough—perhaps too simple, for when it is examined carefully, it becomes an identity. It is true because it is by definition true. This is because of the definition of velocity—the rate at which money moves through the economy during a given period, or the number of times a piece of money gets spent:

$$V = \frac{PQ}{M}$$

Since national income is a measure of all output (Q) in a country for a year multiplied by the price (P) of each good or service, V is equal, in effect, to national income in a given year divided by the total amount of money available (on the average) during that year.

The classical economists elaborated further on each of the variables in the equation of exchange. They proposed that each of the variables in the equation is affected by both external and internal forces. Q, or national output, is determined primarily by real factors that change slowly over time, such as capital, technology, resource availability, and labor. The quantity of money (M) would not influence these variables in any significant way. The classical economists argued that the income velocity of money (V), on the other hand, is determined by institutional factors that are also independent of any change in the money stock (M). Some of these institutional factors are population density, custom, transportation factors, the state of the art of banking, and wage payments and practices. With Q and V unaffected by changes in the supply of money, the level of prices (P) is directly related to changes in the quantity of money (M).

Since Q and V were defined as relatively constant, this means changes in the quantity of money produce nearly proportional changes in the price level. Thus, if the quantity of money in the economy doubles, the price level is likely to double as well. In terms of output and employment in the economy, money, therefore, does not matter very much; in terms of wages and prices, however, it matters a great deal. The following equations show this:

$$M\overline{V} = P\overline{Q} \qquad \Delta M = \Delta P$$

Assuming that $\overline{V}$ and $\overline{Q}$ are constant at a point in time, any changes in the quantity of money (ΔM) must lead to changes in prices (ΔP).

The classical economists viewed money as neutral in that it satisfies no direct utility or want. It merely reflects real activity in the economy. It serves as a veil behind which the *real* action of economic forces, such as the growth of the national product and employment, are concealed. Yet money was viewed as a lubricant for the economy, keeping it well oiled and enabling it to run smoothly and effectively. In the classical model, money does not affect the level of output. The labor market plays a role in determining output.

The Goods and Labor Markets in Classical Economics

A second part of the classical model centers on the production of goods, or real output. Equilibrium output is determined by the demand for and supply of labor. Increases in the demand for labor increase output (Q), and decreases in the supply of labor decrease output. In the classical system, the level of output is determined by full employment. The equilibrium real wage defines the level of full employment in the labor force. Anyone willing to work at the prevailing equilibrium wage will be employed—the quantity supplied of labor equals the quantity demanded of labor. Anyone unwilling to work at that wage is regarded as not desiring to work, and therefore not classified as unemployed. As long as wages are flexible (both upward and downward) in the classical world, no conflict will arise. Full employment, as they defined it, is the norm. This fully employed labor force will produce an equilibrium level of goods and services (Q) for the economy.

Say's Law

A third part of classical macroeconomic theory is Say's law, named for the French economist Jean Baptiste Say (1767–1832) which is introduced in Chapter 4. In its oversimplified form, the "law" is often expressed as supply creating its own demand. Businesses in the process of producing or supplying goods and services for the market will pay wages or rents to employees, landlords, and others engaged in producing the product. That income may be used to purchase goods supplied by the firm or goods supplied by other firms. The act of production, which supplies goods to the market, at the same time generates income to workers and others, who in turn demand goods and services in the market and spend the dollars they earn on those products. For every dollar of product produced, a dollar of income is created and spent.

Say's law is the basis of the circular flow diagram shown in Figure 14.1, which is important to both the Keynesian and classical models. The crude circular flow of the classical economists shows the flow of goods and the flow of income. The lower part of the loop shows the movement of goods from the business sector of the economy to the household sector in return for income spent (expenditures). The upper loop shows the transfer of land, labor, and capital from households to business for use in the production of goods and services in exchange for rents, wages, and interest (income).

The supply, or output, that "creates its own demand" consists of the goods and services produced by the firms or businesses. The factors of production (land, labor, and capital) receive returns of rents, wages and salaries, and interest and profits for their part in the production process. Over time, with expanding population, higher income levels in the household sector create more demand for goods and services. The household sector then spends this income on the goods and services that have been produced, thereby creating an income stream for the business sector. As a result, the aggregate expenditures on goods and services by the household sector will equal the aggregate supply of those goods and services produced by the business sector. Equilibrium occurs when aggregate income or output equals aggregate expenditures.

The Classical Credit Market

Thus far we have assumed that Say's law means all income received during the production process will be spent on goods supplied by producers. But what if some of that income is saved? The classical model accounts for both saving and investment in its analysis of the credit or loanable funds market. Any income saved by consumers will flow into the business sector as investment,

FIGURE 15.1   The Classical Credit Market

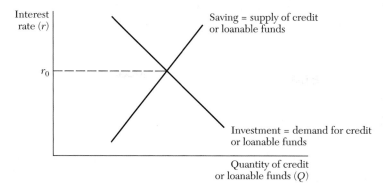

through the credit or loanable funds market. In this market, a flexible interest rate adjusts to yield an equilibrium between saving and investment.

The classical model assumes that both saving (S) and investment (I) are functions of the rate of interest (r): $S = f(r)$, and $I = f(r)$. The supply of credit comes from people who save. Income not spent is saved in the credit market. The classical economists assumed that higher interest rates cause people to save more because of the higher return on any money they save. Therefore, interest rates are directly related to saving. As Figure 15.1 shows, this gives us an upward-sloping curve that represents saving or the supply of credit or loanable funds.

Investment is inversely related to the interest rate. If businesses must borrow funds at high interest rates to finance investments, they will be less willing to borrow and invest. So, at higher interest rates, investment will be low; at lower interest rates, investment will be higher. Investors, like savers, make decisions based on the interest rate. In Figure 15.1 the downward-sloping curve represents investment or the demand for credit or loanable funds. At r_0 the amount saved is motivated by the amount invested; what isn't spent by some is borrowed and spent by others.

Flaws in the Classical Model

Between 1860 and 1929, the U.S. economy generally displayed rapid economic growth. The phases of growth tended to be cyclical, with upswings in economic activity accompanied by downswings, but with an overall upward trend in economic activity averaging about 2 percent per year. We call these recurrent swings in business activity **business cycles.** (See Figure 5.1 for data on U.S. economic performance and cyclical behavior in the economy.) Figure 15.2 shows a hypothetical series of business cycles. Note that periods of growth and peaks are followed by periods of slump and troughs.

FIGURE 15.2 Business Cycles

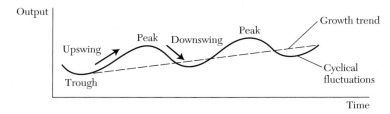

Economists have offered many explanations to account for business cycles. While few classical economists fully explained these fluctuations, economists who followed them offered explanations ranging from increases in sunspot activity to theories suggesting problems in overconsumption and underinvestment, monetary expansion and contraction, and innovation trends. Indeed, compelling arguments have been made for most of these in explaining cycles of growth.

1. If you were to extend Figure 15.2 to include this year, where would the economy be? In an upswing? A downswing? A peak or a trough? Why?

When economic conditions were in the downswing or trough of the cycle, as in the 1930s, classical economic theory explained the resulting levels of unemployment by insisting that those out of work were voluntarily or temporarily unemployed. They believed that businesses could make more employment opportunities by reducing the prevailing wage rate. As wages fell, the amount of labor demanded by businesses would increase. According to classical theory, these unemployed workers would be more than happy to work as long as their wages were above zero. However, during the Great Depression, as wages dropped lower, the number of people out of work actually rose. The classical system failed to explain this.

The Great Depression

The Great Depression lasted for ten years, from 1929 to 1939, and left enduring imprints on millions of Americans. It resulted from many different phenomena that seemed to culminate all at once. Some people who are interested in business cycles believe that short-, medium-, and long-run cycles all reached bottom at the same time. Certainly, more than just the 1929 stock market crash sustained the Great Depression for such a long period. Despite the robustness of the stock market before its fall, several industries in the economy were essentially weak.

Agriculture and manufacturing were perhaps the most important sectors contributing to the duration of the Great Depression. As the United States grew in the first few decades of this century, the number of agricultural workers fell. Hurt by the exploitation of the rail and storage bosses, and burned by their own speculative activities in land, more and more farmers were leaving or selling out to join the urban migration or to become tenants. The number of independent farms dropped by 40 percent during the 1920s. Output, however, was increasing, and the inelastic demand for farm production did little to help farmers. Unlike the other industries, in which greater supplies meant lower prices and increased demand, demand did not increase for the lower-priced agricultural products. In addition, the European export market declined, as European agricultural production was restored following World War I.

In manufacturing, conditions were mixed. Many people in business foresaw a time of weakness, and although sales, prices, and output were at all-time highs, employers cut back their workforces substantially, especially in the mines and mills. Only in the service and construction industries did employment levels hold their own, for these were areas in which men and women could not yet be displaced by technology. Growth increased throughout the 1920s, but workers were no better off than before. Wages and employment levels simply did not increase. Profits, on the other hand, swelled rapidly, as did the concentration of economic power in the hands of a few wealthy individuals. Profits in 1929 were three times those of 1920. But firms were not reinvesting. This was partially because firms had no incentive to invest; supply was already greater than demand.

The weaknesses in these two industries are directly linked to other causes of the depression: the lopsided distribution of income, with 5 percent of the population receiving about 30 percent of all income, and the lack of new investment by the business sector. In addition, the existing banking system was troubled. A series of unexpected and urgent demands by customers on some poorly managed banks created fear among all bank depositors, so that even economically sound banks were subjected to "runs" (when large numbers of depositors withdrew their money) and potential failure. Some 5,000 of the nation's banks failed during the Great Depression. Other factors added to the instability: Several European governments defaulted on U.S. loans, and in the United States, Congress adopted a balanced-budget philosophy that, by increasing taxes and reducing government expenditures, helped to worsen an already bad situation.

From this description, you can see that the U.S. economy had fundamental problems at the time of the stock market crash. From the widespread prosperity of the early 1920s, the late 1920s saw a lack of capital formation, overproduction of goods and services, and an agricultural glut, in addition to international disequilibrium and deep-seated psychological effects of the crash. All these led to prolonged instability, which caused many businesses, organizations, and institutions to collapse and brought havoc to the lives of unemployed workers, the heads of failed businesses, and their families and friends. The depression of the

1930s was a time of severe unemployment and poverty for the men, women, and children who endured it. More than one-third of the nation was unemployed or living in poverty. Conditions were abysmal for all but a few of the well-to-do.

As conditions worsened worldwide, the U.S. Congress passed the Smoot-Hawley Act imposing a 45 percent tariff on a third of U.S. imports. Other nations retaliated with high tariff barriers to protect their domestic industries from U.S. imports. Retaliation led to even higher tariffs and very high prices on all imported goods. World trade slowed dramatically. During this same period there was a severe contraction in the supply of money, which worsened financial conditions. Between 1929 and 1932, in the United States, 85,000 businesses failed, and stock values decreased from $87 billion to $19 billion. Manufacturing and farm income decreased by 50 percent. By 1933, the GDP had declined from $104 billion in 1929 to $56 billion, and unemployment stood firmly at 25 percent, with 12 million people unemployed. Despite the human misery that swept the nation, Secretary of the Treasury Andrew Mellon advised, "Liquidate labor, liquidate stocks, liquidate the farmers, liquidate real estate."

Enter John Maynard Keynes

The most important work of John Maynard Keynes (1883–1946) came at a time when the classical model was most under fire because of its inability to account for continued and worldwide depression with the masses of unemployed in the 1930s. Keynes watched the economic importance of his native Britain continue to wane after World War I, as the rapid growth of the United States and continental Western Europe accelerated. He developed his ideas and critique of the classical model slowly over a long period of time. Much of his writing was highly critical of the British authorities. Keynes was one of the first to recognize the implausibility of the British attachment to the gold standard for international payments and to object to the Versailles Peace Treaty after World War I. (He believed correctly that it would be impossible for Germany to meet the reparations called for by the treaty.)

During the 1930s, the major question being asked in each world capital was what to do about the depression. According to the classical doctrine, the simple remedy was to reduce wages to eliminate the excess supply of workers. But wages were falling, and more unemployment resulted, not less, violating Say's law. Supply was not creating its own demand. The circular flow was not working as it should. Markets were not adjusting to an equilibrium position as laissez-faire predicted. Classical theory and economists who were following these classical tenets were in a quandary.

Keynes focused on unemployment and argued, "The postulates of the classical theory are applicable only to a special case and not the general case … and not … those [conditions] of the economic society in which we actually live." In so doing, he illustrated the futility of the classical scheme, particularly Say's law and the limited circular flow.

Capitalism's Savior

John Maynard Keynes is endlessly fascinating. A product of Eton, Cambridge, and the British Treasury, he was also a member of the Bloomsbury group, that influential collection of writers, artists, and intellectuals in London that included Virginia Woolf and E. M. Forster. A top academic and public policy polemicist, he also ran an insurance company and made a fortune in the markets. The philosopher Bertrand Russell considered Keynes's mind the "sharpest and clearest" he had ever encountered. "When I argued with him," Russell said, "I felt that I took my life in my hands, and I seldom emerged without feeling something of a fool."

But it is as an economic innovator that Keynes is best remembered. Keynes changed how economists study business cycles, price levels, labor markets, and economic growth. His insights have largely kept downturns in the business cycle over the past half century from turning into depressions. "Keynes's lasting achievement is the invention of macro-economics," says Deidre McCloskey, an economic historian at the University of Illinois at Chicago.

Indeed, Keynes can lay claim to playing a crucial role in saving capitalism and, perhaps, civilization during the Great Depression. Despite millions of unemployed workers in the industrial nations, economic orthodoxy demanded that government do nothing or, worse yet, tighten the purse strings. Little wonder that the totalitarian solutions of fascism and communism exerted such pull. U.S. Treasury Secretary Andrew W. Mellon expressed a widespread sentiment among elites when he said in 1930 that the depression would "purge the rottenness out of the system. High costs of living and high living will come down. People will work harder, live a more moral life. Values will be adjusted, and enterprising people will pick up the wrecks from less competent people."

Keynes battled against such harsh counsel. With his landmark 1936 book, *The General*

© Hulton-Deutsch Collection/CORBIS

Theory of Employment, Interest, and Money, he persuaded a generation of thinkers and leaders to abandon a near-theological belief in balanced budgets. He showed how economies could get trapped in recession or depression—and argued that government could break the spiral by borrowing to finance public spending that stimulated consumer activity and restored business confidence. His ideas helped create the golden era of postwar growth, and two institutions he championed in the 1940s still operate on a global scale, the International Monetary Fund and the World Bank.

Keynes is the philosopher-king of the modern mixed economy. It's a sign of his influence that there are no true believers in laissez-faire left. We are all Keynesians now. Governments routinely run deficits during downturns to increase the overall level of demand and, hence, employment. And many economists believe Japan's long stagnation in the 1990s largely reflected timid policymakers unwilling to boldly use the levers of fiscal and monetary policy.

Like Adam Smith and Karl Marx before him, Keynes believed economics wasn't merely about studying the efficient allocation of resources. For him, the good life meant beauty, art, love, morality—the passions that define civilization—and the value of economics lay in its pursuit of the stability and wealth that would allow our passions to flower.

Source: "Capitalism's Savior" by Christopher Farrell, *Business Week,* 4/12/04, p. 20.

THE BIG PICTURE

The Keynesian Model
Part 1: Consumption, Saving, Investment, and Income

During the 1930s, nations mired in the Great Depression suffered massive levels of unemployment; little if any investment; falling prices (deflation); and reduced production. John Maynard Keynes's *The General Theory of Employment, Interest, and Money*, published in 1936, offered a macroeconomic analysis that challenged the time frame for market adjustment and the argument that the economy was best left unregulated. One message of the Keynesian theory is that market forces won't reliably generate full employment in a society. Market forces take too long—and are perhaps too weak—to return an economy to full employment in a timely way. In addition, the economic and social costs are too high to wait for market adjustment in the national and international markets for goods and services.

Several Keynesian assumptions about economic behavior differed from some assumptions of the classical model. For example, Keynes viewed full employment as <u>one</u> *possible equilibrium;* the classical model viewed full employment as *the <u>only</u> equilibrium* possible. Keynes noted that the economy could be in equilibrium when labor was fully employed, when it was underemployed, or even when it was over fully employed.

Equilibrium in Keynes's theory occurred when aggregate expenditures equaled aggregate output or national income—and that could be at full employment or not. Keynes noted that unemployment was part of the normal process of economic expansion and contraction in capitalist economies. Economies based on capitalism to this point displayed a history of expansion when employment increased, followed by economic contraction that left large numbers of people unemployed for substantial periods of time, without any sign of an automatic pilot reversing the trend. But, for Keynes, there was hope that an economy enduring recession and unemployment could be restored to full employment quickly with government borrowing and government spending. Since the economy could be in equilibrium below full employment, there was no reason to think the economy would reach full employment—or adjust on its own. Thus, a *decisive actor* replaced the automatic pilot.

Two building blocks of the Keynesian model are the consumption function; viewing savings and investment adjustment through income, not interest rate changes; and the Keynesian multiplier.

Consumption Income can either be consumed or saved and Keynes viewed both consumption and saving as functions of income, so that as income increased, consumption would increase—but not by as much as the increase in income—with the remaining income saved (Figure 15.BP.3). By examining the relationship between income and consumption expenditures in a country over time, we find that as income rises, consumption also rises, and that there is a fairly stable relation between consumption and income.

FIGURE 15.BP.3   Saving, Consumption, and Income

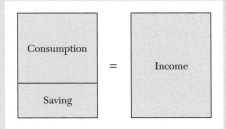

Savings Equals Investment In Keynes's explanation of macroeconomic relationships, just as in the classical system, in equilibrium, saving must equal investment. Keynes argued that consumers most often make spending decisions based on changes in their income, not changes in interest rates in the economy. If we think about what drives our decision, say to purchase a new pair of jeans, it is our income that we consider, not the current interest rate. So, since in the Keynesian model consumption and thus saving are functions of income, it is

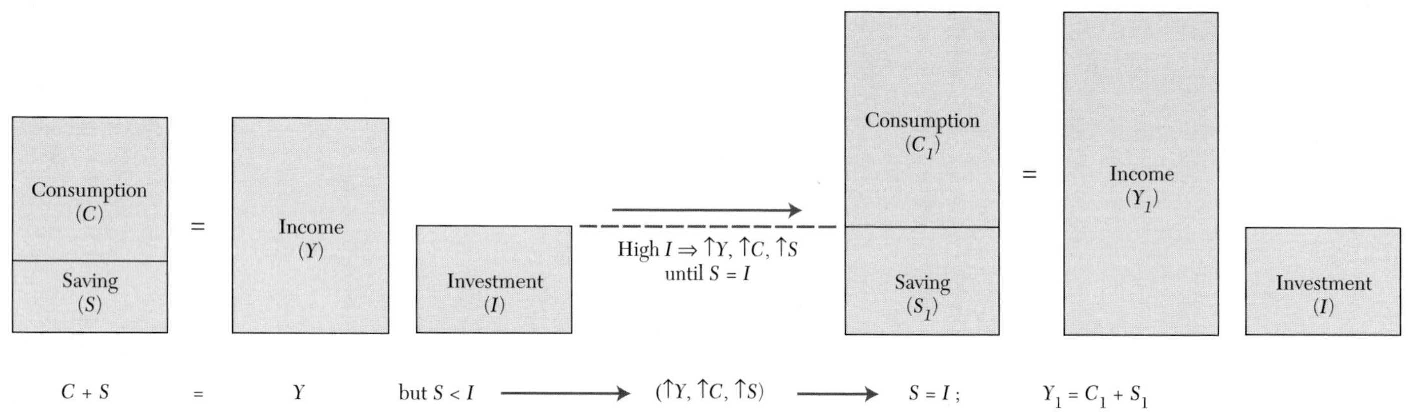

FIGURE 15.BP.4 Saving, Investment, and Income in the Keynesian Model

changes in income that equate savings and investment. For example, if investment is greater than saving, increased investment will generate higher levels of income that will raise both consumption and saving, and the economy reaches equilibrium (Figure 15.BP.4).

The Multiplier (k)   In the circular flow we examined in Chapter 4, we observed that business payments to the factors of production (income in the form of wages, rents, and profits) would be used by households to purchase goods and services produced by businesses (Figure 15.BP.5).

FIGURE 15.BP.5   Simple Circular Flow

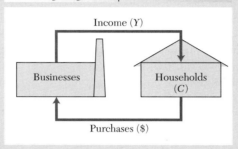

But Keynes pointed out that not all of income households earn will be spent on business-produced goods and services. Some will be saved—a leakage from the circular flow (Figure 15.BP.6).

FIGURE 15.BP.6   Saving Leakage from the Circular Flow

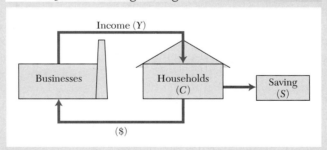

To restore equilibrium to the system, business must *inject* investment expenditures that add new facilities, technology, and tools, as we see in Figure 15.BP.7.

But Keynes sees these investment expenditures as a source of higher income since investment has a multiplier effect on income. In other words, an increase in investment will increase income by much more than the initial investment expenditure.

FIGURE 15.BP.7 Investment Injection into the Circular Flow

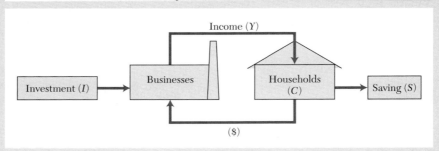

Let's see how that works. First, the initial investment expenditure becomes income in the economy. The expenditure on that investment is received by the seller as income (Figure 15.BP.8).

FIGURE 15.BP.8 Initial Investment Received as Income

When income is received, some will be spent or used for consumption—perhaps on groceries and shoes, and the rest on replacement materials (glass, concrete). The amount spent on consumption adds to the income stream. If consumption (C) averages three-fourths of income, 75 cents of each dollar of income (Y) is spent as consumption and 25 cents is saved. So here C_1 is added to I as part of income. Now the grocer and shoe dealer and concrete supplier have additional income—three-fourths of which will be consumed; one-fourth saved. The three-fourths adds income. The multiplier continues through this respending effect to finally increase income by the multiplier times the change in investment. The multiplier depends on the percent of income that is consumed and saved. For our example, whesn consumers spend three-fourths of their income, the multiplier is 4. An increase in investment spending of $1,000 would result in an increase in income of $4,000. The higher the percentage of expenditure out of each dollar, the higher the multiplier. (If a nation's public spends four-fifths of each dollar of income, the multiplier is 5.) We can see each of these additions to income from the initial $1,000 investment in Figure 15.BP.9.

To see how this works in a possible real-life example, consider a business that invests $100,000 in new computer equipment. This generates $100,000 in income for the computer manufacturer. Using a multiplier of 4 (above), the computer manufacturer will spend three-fourths of the $100,000, or $75,000, on purchases from suppliers, workers, and other goods or services. The suppliers and workers will continue the spending cycle, with three-fourths of $75,000, or $56,250, worth of purchases—perhaps on CDs, groceries, gasoline, amusement parks, and so forth. The spending cycle continues until the total increase

FIGURE 15.BP.9 The Keynesian Multiplier Effect

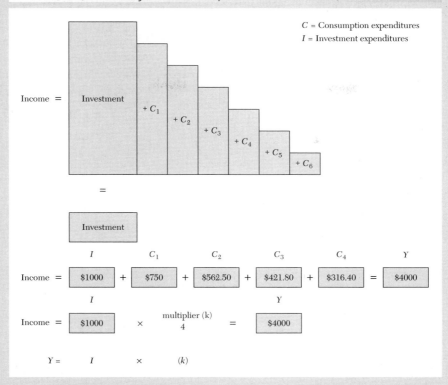

in income generated by the $100,000 investment in computer equipment increases income by $400,000, which equals the multiplier (4) times the initial investment ($100,000). We can see the result of the initial investment expenditure leading to the continuing respending effect in Figure 15.BP.10.

FIGURE 15.BP.10 The Keynesian Multiplier

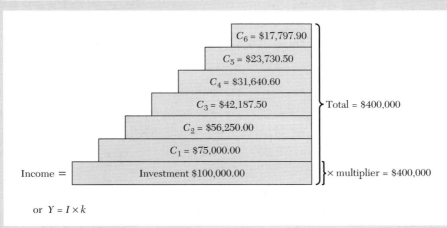

The Keynesian Model: The Details

Keynes defined aggregate expenditures as the sum of consumption expenditures, investment expenditures, government expenditures, and net exports. He and some contemporary economists recognized that there are leakages (transfers of funds out of the income and spending flows) and injections (additions of funds to these flows). Leakages include saving, taxes, and purchases of goods and services in international markets (imports). With each of these leakages, income flows out of domestic economic activity and thus out of the circle in the circular flow diagram of the classical economists. Saving and hoarding remove money from the spending stream and occur when households, deciding that future consumption is better than present consumption, put their money into savings accounts at banks, into the stock market, or under their mattresses. Taxes leave the spending stream of the household and business sectors and are turned over to the government. Imported goods and services from other nations increase the goods and services received by households but reduce the total domestic spending, since these dollars go abroad to pay for the goods and services received.

In contrast to leakages, funds can enter into or be added to domestic economic activity. These injections into the income and spending stream may take the form of government spending, investment, and the sale of goods in international markets (exports). Government spending, like consumer spending, increases the income received by the business sector, since government and consumer purchases are made of business products. Government spending may also go directly to the household sector in the form of wages, transfer payments, or income supplements, which in turn will increase spending as well. **Investment** occurs when the business sector creates new capital in the form of new plants, additions to equipment, and the buildup of inventories, or existing

FIGURE 15.3 The Circular Flow with Leakages (L) and Injections (IN)

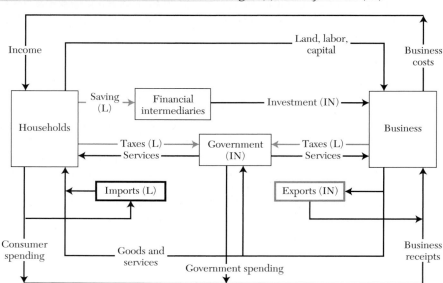

stocks of goods and services. Investment is, in effect, business spending. Exports create an injection into the income stream, since businesses have a new market for their products and receive income. Figure 15.3 illustrates the dynamics of these flows, with leakages indicated as (L) and injections as (IN).

For the economy to be in equilibrium, the injections must equal the leakages. As a result, aggregate expenditures for goods and services in the economy will equal the aggregate output or income. This establishes an equilibrium level of income and output that may or may not be at full employment. According to Keynes, an economy can have an infinite number of equilibrium positions, one of which is at full employment. The equilibrium depends on the level of spending in the economy. The classical economists, however, saw one and only one equilibrium—the one that exists at full employment.

Keynes recommended that governments use spending policies to counter cyclical upswings and downswings. These policies could cure a full range of economic maladies. In a depression, increased government spending would increase the levels of income, employment, and output. To ward off inflation, government spending could be cut and/or taxes increased.

The Keynesian model has remained a prevailing economic paradigm for the past half century. It has not always been successful, and economists have continued to add to and revise its core. Despite the challenges of the 1980s, however, it still solidly forms the basis for much of New Keynesian macroeconomic theory. The late Nobel Prize recepient and monetarist Milton Friedman perhaps stated it best when he said, "We are all Keynesians now."

The Keynesian Economic Model

In the discussion that follows, we will describe the assumptions, methods, and implications of the full Keynesian model, exploring the sources of spending and how they affect aggregate output or GDP in any period.

Consumption

To begin our construction of a simple Keynesian model, we will first examine the assumptions and hypotheses for the consumption function. The importance of consumption on economic activity is fairly straightforward. In 2005, the U.S. population spent 85 percent of personal income on goods and services. Consumption is simply purchasing of goods and services, spending of income for necessities and luxuries. The level of consumption depends on many things, including income, interest rates, price levels, and expectations, along with the other financial assets the consumer might possess. But as one might well expect, consumption is primarily a function of income. In our simplified version of the Keynesian model, we will express consumption as

$$C = f(\text{DPI}),$$

FIGURE 15.4   The Consumption Function

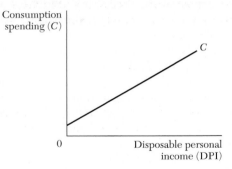

where C is the consumption of individuals over some period of time, DPI is disposable personal income and f is a functional notation (see Table 14.4).* In what Keynes called a "fundamental psychological law," he states, "As a rule and on the average, [people] are disposed to increase their consumption as their income increases." In other words, as your income increases (perhaps after graduation and upon securing a better job), your consumption spending will rise as well—but, says Keynes, not by as much. This relationship can be expressed graphically with consumption (C) measured on the vertical axis and disposable personal income (DPI) on the horizontal axis. Since consumption is an increasing function of disposable income, as DPI increases, C will also increase (see Figure 15.4).

What happens to the income *not* spent on consumption? People save it. *Saving* is any part of income that is not spent on consumption. There is nothing left to do with it. (Burning it isn't rational, and Keynes assumes that we are all rational.) We can express the relationship between income, consumption, and saving as follows:

$$DPI = C + S,$$

where DPI is disposable personal income, C is personal consumption expenditures, and S is personal saving. Saving is a residual of consumption.

Saving occurs when individuals defer present consumption and keep the funds for future use. People save for many different reasons: precaution or fear of what might lie ahead, financial independence, or pride or avarice. In contrast to the classical model, which assumes that saving is a function of the rate of interest, Keynes assumed that consumption expenditures are a priority, and we save whatever funds are left after we make these consumption expenditures.

---

*Studies have shown consumption to be a linear function of income, or $C = a + b$ DPI, where C is the consumption of individuals over time, a is the intercept of the consumption function (or C where DPI $= 0$), b is the slope of the function, and DPI is disposable income (that is, GDP – depreciation – taxes –u ndistributed corporate profits + transfer payments). DPI, then, is income that a household has available for consumption spending. Since a is positive, individuals must consume some amount of food, clothing, and shelter even if they have no income.

No matter how much a high interest rate might make us want to increase our saving, we pay for food, housing, and other necessary consumption expenditures first. Whatever is left can be saved. So in the Keynesian model, saving, like consumption, also is a function of income:

$$S = f(\text{DPI})$$

2. Do you or your family behave as though $S = f(\text{DPI})$ or $S = f(r)$? Which comes first, the mortgage or rent payment, grocery, and clothing expenditures—or saving?

Before we proceed further in the analysis of consumption and saving, it is important to establish a reference position (or helping line) to make it easier to discuss the relation of the level of consumption spending to the level of income. This helping line is a 45° line from the origin of the consumption-income axis (see Figure 15.5). The 45° line represents the locus of equilibrium points where total spending equals total output or disposable personal income (DPI). If firms produce $3.0 trillion worth of goods and services, and spending in the economy equals $3.0 trillion, we will be at point A on the 45° line. Each of these points is on the 45° line, which bisects the origin and represents a level of spending just equal to a corresponding level of disposable personal income (DPI). Here and throughout the Keynesian analysis, we assume that *prices are constant*.

We can now use the relationship between expenditures and income in examining consumption. Since the 45° line bisects the 90° angle, at any point on the 45° line, income (DPI) will equal consumption. For example, at point A, DPI $= C = $3.0 trillion; at point B, DPI $= C = $4.0 trillion. If we superimpose the consumption curve on this 45° line, we can compare the relationship of consumption spending to the actual level of disposable personal income in the economy.

FIGURE 15.5   The 45° Line

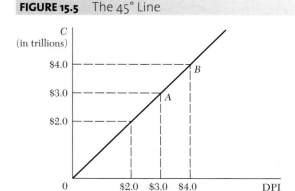

FIGURE 15.6 The Consumption Function and the 45° Line

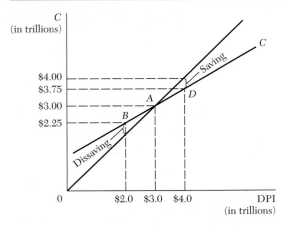

FIGURE 15.7 Your Consumption Function

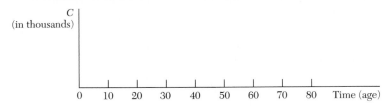

In Figure 15.6, at point A, consumption and disposable personal income are equal, since the consumption curve passes through the 45° line at that point. Saving equals 0 (since $S = \text{DPI} - C$, and 3.0 trillion $- \$3.0$ trillion $= 0$). At point D, however, consumption (C) is less than disposable personal income, indicating that saving occurs. Since disposable personal income is 4.0 trillion and consumption is only 3.75 trillion, 0.25 trillion must be saved. At point B, consumption is greater than disposable personal income; income is 2.0 trillion, but consumption spending is 2.25 trillion. Dissaving is taking place to allow the desired level of consumption. Dissaving consists of borrowing or drawing down other financial assets in order to purchase products for current consumption. Individuals on low fixed incomes frequently dissave, as do young people starting families or households. (Note that even when income is 0, there is some amount of consumption spending.)

3. Do you dissave now? Do you expect to dissave in the next year or two? Draw a curve on the graph in Figure 15.7 indicating what you expect your consumption pattern to look like for the rest of your life. At what periods do you think you might be dissaving?

TABLE 15.1   Data for Hypothetical Consumption Function

DPI (in Trillions)	C (in Trillions)	MPC = ΔC/ΔDPI
$2.0	$2.25	0
3.0	3.00	0.75
4.0	3.75	0.75

FIGURE 15.8   Marginal Propensity to Consume

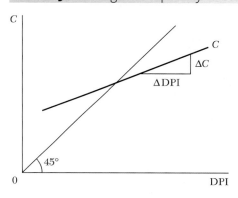

Marginal Propensity to Consume

From the information given thus far, we can determine two ratios: the average propensity to consume (APC) and the **marginal propensity to consume (MPC).** APC is simply C/DPI. MPC is the ratio between the *change* that occurs in consumption with some given change in disposable personal income:

$$MPC = \Delta C / \Delta DPI,$$

where Δ is a symbol for change, C is consumption, and DPI is disposable personal income. In the previous example, if disposable personal income increases from $3.0 trillion to $4.0 trillion, consumption increases from $3.00 trillion to $3.75 trillion. The change in disposable personal income is $4.0 trillion – $3.0 trillion, or $1.0 trillion; the change in consumption is $3.75 trillion – $3.00 trillion, or .75 trillion. The MPC, then, is $\Delta C / \Delta DPI$ = $0.75 trillion/$1.0 trillion, or 0.75 (see Table 15.1). For every additional dollar of disposable personal income, consumers use $0.75 for consumption and save the remaining $0.25 (see Table 15.1 and Figure 15.8).

The relationship MPC = $\Delta C / \Delta DPI$ is also the slope of the consumption function* (see Figure 15.8). Note that the consumption function is a straight

---

*MPC is the slope of the consumption function, or b in C = a + b (DPI).

line only when MPC is constant at all levels of disposable personal income. This will seldom occur in practice, since each individual as well as each income-earning group reacts differently to changes in income. However, to simplify the analysis, in most cases we will assume a constant MPC (and thus a straight-line consumption function).

4. How might your reaction to a change in income be different from that of George W. Bush, Tiger Woods, Julia Roberts, or Oprah Winfrey? From that of a poor person?

Saving

Given that saving is a residual of consumption (DPI $= C + S$, so $S =$ DPI $- C$), we can analyze the saving function as we did the consumption function. Data for a saving function are derived in Table 15.2 and graphed in Figure 15.9.

Marginal Propensity to Save

We can also express the average propensity to save (APS) and the **marginal propensity to save (MPS).** APS is the ratio of saving to disposable personal income, S/DPI. MPS is the ratio of the change in saving to any change in disposable personal income:

$$\text{MPS} = \Delta S / \Delta \text{DPI}$$

TABLE 15.2 Derivation of Saving Function from Consumption Data

DPI (in Trillions)	C (in Trillions)	S = DPI – C (in Trillions)
$2.0	$2.25	–$0.25
3.0	3.00	0.00
4.0	3.75	0.25

FIGURE 15.9 The Saving Function

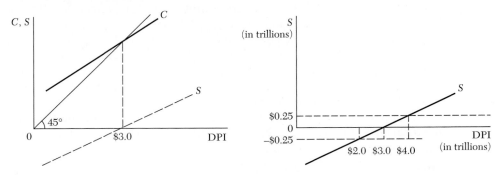

TABLE 15.3 Data for Hypothetical Saving Example

DPI	S (in Trillions)	MPS = ΔS/ΔDPI
$2.0	−$0.25	
		0.25
3.0	0.00	
		0.25
4.0	0.25	

In Table 15.3, we find MPS using the data for S we derived earlier.

Note that MPS + MPC = 1. This must be true, since the change in C and the change in S must add to the whole of every new dollar of disposable personal income.*

Consumption and Real GDP

We have just seen how consumption (C) changes when disposable personal income (DPI) changes. What causes changes in disposable personal income? Disposable personal income changes whenever real GDP (Y) changes or when there is a change in tax rates. As long as tax rates are constant (which we will assume they are for this analysis), real GDP (Y) is the only influence on disposable personal income. In equations we can write this as follows:

$$\text{DPI} = Y - Tx$$

because we are assuming that

$$Tx = 0, \text{DPI} = Y$$

Consumption therefore depends not only on disposable personal income, but also on real GDP. In the sections that follow, we will add other variables that determine real GDP (Y), including investment expenditures, government expenditures, and net exports.

Investment and the Two-sector Model

The simplest Keynesian model describes the behavior of two sectors in the economy: the household and business sectors. This simple model ignores the

---

*
$$\text{DPI} = C + S$$
$$\Delta\text{DPI} = \Delta C + \Delta S$$
$$\Delta\text{DPI}/\Delta\text{DPI} = \Delta C/\Delta\text{DPI} + \Delta S/\Delta\text{DPI}$$
$$1 = \text{MPC} + \text{MPS}$$

government and foreign sectors. We represent total spending by individuals and businesses as follows:

$$AE = C + I,$$

where AE is income or real GDP, C is consumption, and I is investment. In equilibrium, $Y = AE$; all aggregate expenditures (AE) become someone's income (Y). This relationship is derived from expenditures flow in the circular flow diagram in the National Income Accounts examined in Chapter 14, Figure 14.1. Consumption represents spending by households, and **investment** consists of business spending on additions to plants, equipment, inventories, and newly constructed housing. Inventories may be goods of any type, from raw material inputs to intermediate and finished products. Together, consumption and investment make up the aggregate expenditures for goods and services produced. In the preceding sections, we learned about consumption, but we know little about investment.

In this simple two-sector model, we assume that investment is determined outside the model itself.* For example, if General Motors decides to invest $1,000, it makes the decision without considering the variables included in this model. Expected profits, interest costs, or business confidence might be more important to investment decisions than income and consumption levels. Graphically, then, investment would be constant at all levels of GDP, as shown in Figure 15.10.

In the two-sector model, we know that aggregate expenditures (AE) equal consumption plus investment (AE $= C + I$) and that the resulting GDP (Y) can be spent or saved $(Y = C + S)$. For equilibrium in the macroeconomy, income (Y) and expenditures (AE) must be equal $(Y = AE)$. A level of spending produces a level of income, which, in turn, generates the same level of spending, and so on (as in the circular flow of activity). Putting these two equations together tells us that in the two-sector Keynesian model, the only leakage, saving, must equal the only injection, investment. This describes the equilibrium condition for the model: when aggregate income $(Y = C + S)$ equals aggregate expenditures (AE $= C + I$), then $S = I$.

$$Y = AE$$
$$C + S = C + I$$
$$S = I$$

---

*Investment in a more sophisticated model is a function of changes in income, since as GDP increases, businesses will likely increase their level of investment. Investment decisions also depend on interest rates, expected inflation, expected profits, depreciation, and other factors. Investment fluctuates over time and plays a major role in accounting for business cycles. With a more sophisticated model, our analysis can include investment decisions more typical of businesses. For simplicity, however, we use the less complex model and assume that investment decisions are given and constant.

FIGURE 15.10   The Investment Function

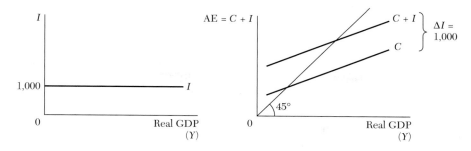

TABLE 15.4   Data for Hypothetical Investment Function

Y	C	S	I_p	I_a
$6.0 T	$5.75 T	$0.25 T	$0.25 T	$0.25 T
6.5	5.50	0.50	0.25	0.50

Several factors are important in the $S = I$ relationship. First, saving and investment are done by two different groups of people for totally different reasons. Second, realized (or actual) saving must equal realized (or actual) investment. There is no guarantee that the dollar amount of investment *planned* by the business sector will be the same as the saving planned in the household sector.

Using the data in Table 15.4, which assumes planned investment spending of $0.25 trillion, we can illustrate this with an example. I_p equals planned investment, and I_a equals actual investment. Figure 15.11 shows that the equilibrium income level in this simple model is at point A, where the $C + I$ line intersects the 45° reference line. This graph is sometimes referred to as the *Keynesian cross*. Here, AE = $C + I$ = $6.0 trillion, C = $5.75 trillion, and I = $0.25 trillion. All higher and lower levels of income are not at equilibrium; planned S does not equal planned I, and planned aggregate expenditures do not equal planned aggregate income. At $Y = $ AE = $6.0 trillion$C + I = C + S$ and aggregate expenditures equal real GDP. Only at the $6.0 trillion equilibrium point does planned investment equal actual investment ($I_p = I_a$).

At disequilibrium position B, C = $6.0 trillion, S = $0.50 trillion, and Y = $6.5 trillion. Here, intended saving is greater than intended investment, since saving is $0.50 trillion and investment is only $0.25 trillion. With I_p at $0.25 trillion, there will be an unplanned increase in inventories; some of the goods produced will not be sold, because consumers desire to increase their saving balances. At Y = $6.50 trillion (GDP), $C + I$ = (only) $6.25 trillion (and $C + S$ = $6.50 trillion). Aggregate output is greater than aggregate expenditures. Total output is $6.50 trillion, but total spending is only $6.25 trillion. Therefore, inventories increase by $0.25 trillion. Since the increase in

FIGURE 15.11   Equilibrium Level of Income

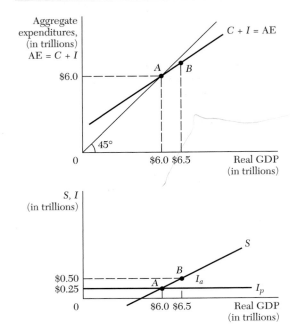

inventories is counted as investment, I_a will increase to $0.50 trillion. Actual saving equals actual investment.

5. In the next time period with an accumulation of inventories, what do you expect the I_p response of business would be? What does this do to the equilibrium level of income where aggregate expenditures equal real GDP and $S = I$?

Since planned S is greater than planned I, however, this is not an equilibrium position. With increased inventories, which were unplanned, producers will cut back production and lay off workers. As output is cut, income will also be reduced. This movement will continue until an equilibrium is reached where aggregate expenditures equal aggregate output or income. This new equilibrium occurs at point A, where $C + S = C + I$, and where planned S of $0.25 trillion equals planned I of $0.25 trillion. This equilibrium may be or may not be at full employment. Unlike the classical model, the Keynesian model may have equilibrium conditions at greater than full, less than full, or full employment.

FIGURE 15.12   An Increase in Investment Spending

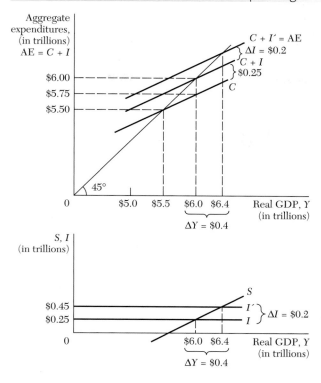

Changes in Investment and the Keynesian Multiplier

Once the economy is in equilibrium, it tends to remain unchanged until some disturbance occurs, such as a change in the level of investment. Suppose investment increases from $0.25 trillion to $0.45 trillion, a change of $0.20 trillion. This change is graphed in Figure 15.12.

How much does income increase as a result of this $0.20 trillion increase in investment? What is the new equilibrium level of income? Here, the **Keynesian multiplier (k)** has its effect. When additional investment enters the model, the equilibrium level of income (Y) increases by some multiple of the change in investment. This multiple (called the Keynesian multiplier) equals $1/(1 - \text{MPC})$ or the ratio between the change in income and the change in investment ($\Delta Y/\Delta I$).

To demonstrate how the multiplier works, consider a nursery that decides to expand by adding a greenhouse costing $200,000. The first round of spending is $200,000, which is added to the income stream. The contractor and workers

TABLE 15.5 Keynesian Respending Effect

Expenditure for Greenhouse $\Delta I = \$200,000$	ΔY	$\Delta C = 0.5\,\Delta Y$	$\Delta S = 0.5\,\Delta Y$
Round 1	$200,000	$100,000	$100,000
Round 2	100,000	50,000	50,000
Round 3	50,000	25,000	25,000
Round 4	25,000	12,500	12,500
Round 5	12,500	6,250	6,250
Round 6	6,250	3,125	3,125
Etc.			
Total*	$400,000	$200,000	$200,000

*The rounds continue until they have generated $200,000[1/(1 − 0.5)] = $200,000 × 2 = $400,000 in new income. The initial increase in spending is multiplied through the economy.

who built the greenhouse now have the $200,000 (as income) and will respend it according to the MPC. If the MPC is 0.5, the contractor and her workers will spend $100,000 and save the remaining $100,000. The $100,000 then enters the income stream (as other people's income); half of that will be spent and half saved in the third round. Table 15.5 illustrates this process.

A Simple Derivation of the Multiplier

The Keynesian multiplier gives us the amount of income (GDP) generated by an increase in spending. We know that at equilibrium in the Keynesian model, $\Delta I = \Delta S$. If both sides of this identity are divided by ΔY, the right side of the equation becomes MPS:

$$\frac{\Delta I}{\Delta Y} = \frac{\Delta S}{\Delta Y} = \text{MPS} = \frac{1}{\text{the multiplier}}.$$

To get the multiplier (k), we invert the equation:

$$k = \frac{\Delta Y}{\Delta I} = \frac{\Delta Y}{\Delta S} = \frac{1}{\text{MPS}}.$$

Since MPC + MPS = 1, we can restate this in terms of MPC:

$$\frac{\Delta Y}{\Delta I} = \frac{1}{1 - \text{MPC}} = k.$$

Example: Given MPC = 0.75,

$$k = \frac{\Delta Y}{\Delta I} = \frac{1}{1 - 0.75} = \frac{1}{0.25} = 4.$$

In this example, for each ΔI, real GDP (Y) will increase by 4 times ΔI.

In the example of a nursery adding a greenhouse, the MPS of 0.5 yields a multiplier of 2. Thus, the $200,000 increase in investment will generate $400,000 of new income. In Figure 15.12, an increase in I of $0.2 trillion will produce a new equilibrium level of (representing a "multiplied" increase in Y of $0.4 trillion).

6. What is the new level of consumption in Figure 15.12 at $Y = \$6.4$ trillion? What is the level of saving?

The Three-sector Model

To add a bit more realism, we can add the government sector to the simple two-sector Keynesian model. *Government expenditures* (G) are purchases of goods and services by the government during a given period. Like investment, we will assume in this extension of our simple model that government spending is determined outside of the Keynesian model. For example, Congress decides to spend $G = G_0$. This means there is a given level of government spending for goods and services at all levels of income, as shown in Figure 15.13.

Once we add government spending to the model, aggregate expenditures become AE $= C + I + G$, as shown in Figure 15.14. Now, in our three-sector model, we have

FIGURE 15.13   The Government Spending Function

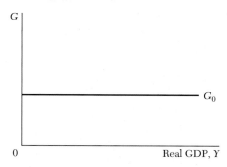

FIGURE 15.14   The Keynesian Model with C, I, and G Spending

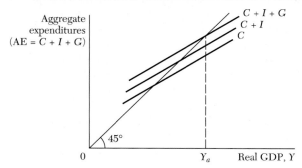

$$AE = C + I + G,$$

where aggregate expenditures (AE) equal the sum of consumption (C), investment (I), and government expenditures (G). In our three-sector model, real GDP (Y) will equal the sum of consumption (C), saving (S), and—now that we have introduced the government—taxes (Tx):

$$Y = C + S + Tx$$

Given our definition of disposable personal income (DPI), we can also state this as

$$Y = DPI + Tx$$

In equilibrium, $Y = AE$, so the two sides of our three-sector model are equal:

$$C + S + Tx = C + I + G$$

To simplify, we subtract C from both sides of the equation, in equilibrium (when $Y = AE$):

$$S + Tx = I + G$$

The 45° line again represents equilibrium points where aggregate spending equals aggregate output or income. Expenditures for goods and services are now made by consumers, investors, *and* the government, creating the aggregate expenditures graph for the three-sector economy. The equilibrium level of income is Y_a where $AE = Y = C + I + G$. At any other level, $Y \neq C + I + G$.

Government expenditures include expenditures by state and local governments as well as by the federal government. Currently, about 17.5 percent of the GDP is made up of purchases by the government. The government buys a wide range of goods and services, from paper to computers to B1 bombers. The government makes such purchases to support its normal operations or as part of programs designed to stimulate the economy when the business cycle is declining, as Keynes suggested in his *General Theory*. Transfer payments from the government are not included as part of these government purchases. (We will examine the effect of transfers in Chapter 16.)

The size of G may change. Indeed, the government may make decisions that will affect the level of income in the economy. These expenditures are often aimed at *directly* changing the level of income—perhaps from a level not at full employment to a new equilibrium level at full employment. Government expenditures for goods and services are subject to the Keynesian multiplier just as investments are. Government spending becomes income that enters the spending flow as recipients consume and save at increased levels by their MPC and MPS. Any increase in G will increase Y by an amount equal to $\Delta G/(1 - MPC)$.

We can analyze the results of government spending by looking at a purchase of a new defense system at a total cost of \$0.5 trillion. Figure 15.15 shows that aggregate expenditures have increased from the equilibrium position at \$8 tril-

FIGURE 15.15 Effects of Increased Government Spending on the Equilibrium Level of Income

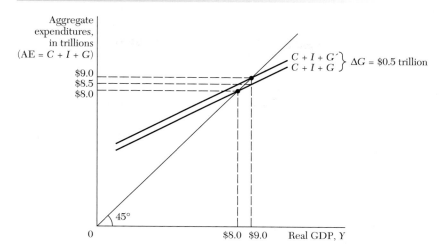

lion (where AE = $C + I + G$). If the marginal propensity to consume remains at 0.5, the multiplier is 2. The increase in income that results from the purchase of the defense system is $k \times \Delta G = 2 \times \$0.5$ trillion = $1.0 trillion. The new equilibrium level of income is therefore $9 trillion ($8 trillion + $1 trillion).

An increase in government allocations for research for the space program and NASA will boost the economies of Huntsville, Alabama; Houston, Texas; and Cape Canaveral, Florida, as well as increasing the enrollments in aerospace engineering courses. Cuts in government expenditures reverse the Keynesian multiplier effect. A decrease in defense spending, such as military base closures, will have the effect of contracting the economies of Alameda, California, and Charleston, South Carolina. Entire communities will be affected by the decreasing income and increasing unemployment levels.

7. What kinds of government spending programs would stimulate growth in your area? What are a few government spending programs that would help us all?

The Four-sector Model

Thus far, we have extended our economic model by adding *injections* of investment expenditures and government purchases of goods and services into the spending flow and observing how the Keynesian multiplier affects each of them. There is, of course, one more injection into the spending stream, and that comes from the foreign sector through foreign trade. Whenever U.S. goods and services are exported to other nations, dollars flow into the U.S. economy in payment for these exported goods. These dollars then enter the spending stream as injections. On the other hand, imports take money out of the income flow, since goods and services come into the country in return for dollars that flow out of the U.S. income stream and into the income stream of the exporting nation.

In dealing with both of these flows, we will use the quantity *net exports*, which is simply $X - M$, where X represents exports and M accounts for goods and services imported into the nation. If $X - M$ is positive, then money is flowing into the U.S. income stream. If $X - M$ is negative, then money is flowing out of the U.S. income stream as imported goods and services flow in. A positive net export figure ($X - M > 0$) will mean additional income, as Y expands. If net exports are negative ($X - M < 0$), Y will fall.

We can express this four-sector model as an equation:

$$AE = C + I + G + (X - M)$$

Now aggregate expenditures (AE) equals the sum of consumption (C), investment (I), government expenditures (G), and net exports ($X - M$). Real GDP (Y) is still equal to the sum of consumption (C), saving (S), and taxes (Tx):

$$Y = C + S + Tx$$

As noted previously, we can also say that real GDP equals disposable personal income (DPI) plus taxes: $Y = \text{DPI} + Tx$. In equilibrium, $Y = AE$, so the sum of their components is equal:

$$C + S + Tx = C + I + G + (X - M)$$

We can simplify by subtracting C (consumption) and M (imports) from both sides of the equation. Thus, in equilibrium (when $Y = AE$),

$$S + Tx + M = I + G + X$$

The equilibrium level of income is at the point where the total for expanded aggregate expenditures intersects the 45° line. When imports to the United States exceed exports, more goods and services are coming into the country and more income (money) is going out of the country. Net exports are negative. The equilibrium level of income will be lower.

Domestic and foreign economic policies may directly affect import or export expenditures or both. We will direct our attention to some of these policy effects in Chapter 16.

THE BIG PICTURE

Chapter 15 Wrap-up

Thus far The Big Picture has looked only at two sectors in the economy: consumers, through their consumption expenditures (C), and businesses through investment expenditures (I). And we discovered how investment expenditures work through the Keynesian multiplier (k) to increase income (real GDP) by more than the initial investment expenditure.

We must now complete our examination of aggregate expenditures (AE)—which to this point includes only investment (I) and consumption (C) expenditures. To complete the model we must also add government expenditures (G) and the expenditures of the international sector, which we defined in Chapter 14 as net exports ($X - M$).

Thus, if we put the features of the Keynesian model together using the building blocks we've explained above, we see that equilibrium in this model is where aggregate expenditures (AE) is equal to aggregate output or real GDP (Y) (see Figure 15.BP.11).

FIGURE 15.BP.11 The Keynesian Model—Four Sectors

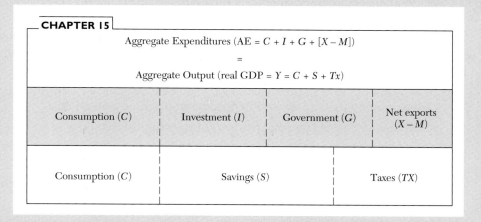

Conclusion

We have examined the impact of the Keynesian multiplier on several sectors of the economy and noted that income (output) expands by the value of the multiplier times the value of the injection. Prices do not change in the Keynesian model as a result of changes in aggregate expenditures. In this chapter we have examined only how changes in injections affect income. The next chapter will explore the effect of changes in leakages, including saving and transfers, and Chapter 18 will explore the complications that arise from price changes. We have made many assumptions about investment and spending decisions; the economy is somewhat more complex than our model. Nevertheless, the model helps us begin to understand how the macroeconomy functions.

The Keynesian model gives us a theoretical framework within which to analyze how the aggregate economy operates and to examine the sorts of macroeconomic problems one might expect to encounter and how we might develop stabilization policies to try to correct them. If real GDP exceeds aggregate expenditures, we can expect a lower level of national income. Conversely, if aggregate expenditures exceed real GDP, we would expect an expansion of economic activity and a higher equilibrium level of national income. An equilibrium level is where real GDP (Y) equals aggregate expenditures (AE = C + I + G + [X − M]).

Review Questions

1. What phenomena caused the Great Depression? Why did it continue for so long? Why did it affect so many sectors of the economy?

2. What did your grandparents and their families do during the Great Depression? How were they affected by the economic conditions of the time?

3. Why would the classical economists distinguish between real factors and monetary ones as influences of the variables in the equation of exchange? What is the implication of prices increasing as the quantity of money increases?

4. Why might Keynes's theory be called a "depression theory"? Can you make a few arguments as to why it might command a more general use?

5. What were Keynes's major criticisms of the classical theory?

6. What are leakages? Why are they called leakages? How do leakages differ from injections?

7. Why must leakages equal injections in the Keynesian world for an equilibrium level of income to exist?

8. In the Keynesian circular flow diagram (Figure 15.3), do leakages and injections ever leave the economy permanently? How are they fed back into the economy?

9. If depressions become self-fulfilling prophecy, can inflationary periods also be self-fulfilling? What would you expect the Keynesian prescription to be in such a case?

FIGURE 15.16 A Problem on the Keynesian Model

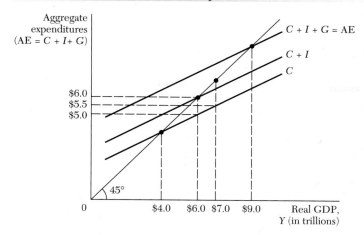

The intersection of income or output (Y_y) and aggregate expenditures (Y_e)=$900.

Use the information in Figure 15.16 to answer Questions 10–17.

10. Explain in words why the equilibrium would be $4 trillion if there were no saving, investment, or government spending. What would be the level of output at this income level?

11. Why would the consumption function (if extended) intersect the spending axis at a positive value? What does this mean? Is it realistic?

12. The slope of the consumption function tells us that as real GDP increases, consumption (increases/decreases) but at a (slower/faster) rate. Is this realistic?

13. What assumptions are required to draw an investment function parallel to the consumption function? How realistic are these assumptions? What is the amount of desired investment in Figure 15.16?

14. Assuming no government expenditures, what is the level of saving at $Y = $6 trillion? What is the level of desired investment at $Y = $6 trillion? Why is $Y = $6 trillion an equilibrium level (with $C = I$)?

15. What would be the level of saving if the real GDP (Y) were at $7 trillion? What is the level of desired investment at this level? What forces are at work at a real GDP of $7 trillion? What will be the equilibrium level of real GDP?

16. What is the MPC in Figure 15.16?

17. Assume that real GDP is $6 trillion but real GDP of $9 trillion is needed to generate enough jobs for full employment. What level of government spending will be necessary to achieve full employment?

18. Why is there a multiplier effect for injections into the U.S. economy? What determines the multiplier?

19. How do net exports affect real GDP? Can real GDP be reduced by net exports? How?

CHAPTER SIXTEEN

Fiscal Policy: Government Spending and Taxation

■ Introduction

F or the past fifty years, the federal government has been officially committed to maintaining employment, price stability, and output. The **Employment Act of 1946** states,

> The Congress hereby declares that it is the continuing policy and responsibility of the Federal Government to use all practicable means consistent with its needs and obligations and other essential considerations of national policy, with assistance and cooperation of industry, agriculture, labor, and state and local governments, to coordinate and utilize all its plans, functions, and resources for the purpose of creating and maintaining, in a manner calculated to foster and promote free competitive enterprise and the general welfare, conditions under which there will be afforded useful employment opportunities, including self-employment, for those able, willing, and seeking to work and to promote maximum employment, production, and purchasing power.

Within the framework of these economic objectives, the government establishes and implements its **fiscal policy**—actions of taxation or government spending that are designed to change the level of income.

According to Keynesian theory, when poverty, unemployment, or inflation rises, the government has tools to try to fix each problem. The existence of unemployment and poverty suggests a need for government spending and/or transfers. These may take the form of unemployment and welfare benefits, food stamps, Medicaid, or a variety of other payments, or they may be purchases of goods and services. Other possible remedies are increases in employment opportunities and decreased tax levels. The government may try to stimulate employment by directly adding programs that put people back to work—for example, through a series of tax credits or advantages for those firms increasing employment and investment. To combat inflation, fiscal policy requires spending reductions and/or tax increases. Cutbacks of all types and tax increases restrict household and business spending. Fiscal policy can also be used to *affect aggregate supply; for example, a tax cut might be designed to lower business costs, increasing supply.*

While normally we think of the federal government as the major purchasing, borrowing, and taxing authority, state and local governments are very active in the process as well. In some cases, however, state and local governments exacerbate economic problems (pursuing procyclical *rather than* countercyclical *measures—for example, spending during times of economic expansion rather than during times of contraction).*

Fiscal policy is also subject to the constraints of the political process. At the federal level, the president receives advice on fiscal policy from the Council of Economic Advisors (CEA) and the National Economic Council created in the 1990s to coordinate policy making. Some of the advice is accepted and successfully makes its way through the bureaucratic channels, but other advice does not. In addition, the president receives advice from the Office of Management and Budget. Meanwhile, in addition to its own committees, Congress has the Joint Economic Committee and Congressional Budget Office to assist in legislative decisions on government spending and taxation. Policy studies in all these bodies are constantly ongoing. Often the dynamics of these public offices, plus the host of private organizations engaged in economic research, lead to a profusion of mixed analysis and advice. Since each advisory body has its own priorities and operates under its own assumptions about economic growth, policy recommendations vary widely.

This chapter will explore how each type of fiscal action works. Some fiscal policies may directly affect the level of imports and/or exports as well as the domestic economy. We will explore these implications and deal with the shortcomings and advantages of using fiscal policy to address economic problems. We will also explore the budget process of fiscal policy's major player, the federal government. The discussion of the federal budget includes the impact of federal debt on the economy, balanced budgets, and the difference between structural and cyclical budget deficits.

Fiscal Policy

The tools of fiscal policy may be selected to resolve a particular problem, or they may occur automatically with a given change in economic conditions. The former uses constitute **discretionary fiscal policy.** The automatic, nondiscretionary forms of fiscal policy are called **built-in stabilizers.** Examples of built-in stabilizers include the progressive income tax system, unemployment insurance, and all other compensatory programs that come into effect when income levels are low and that are shut off when income levels are high. As economic activity decreases during a recession, income is lost. This threatens additional decreases in economic activity. However, as unemployment increases, unemployment compensation *automatically* increases income and spending to slow a cumulative decrease in economic activity. Additionally, during a recession, people find themselves in lower tax brackets, which reduces the tax bite on individuals as their incomes fall.

1. If income is increasing at a highly inflationary rate, how do progressive income taxes help to stabilize the economy automatically?

THE BIG PICTURE

Fiscal Policy

When government officials pass a bill that increases public spending on the interstate highway system or to repair the nation's infrastructure, once undertaken, these projects work like expenditures on investment. As we saw in Chapter 15, an increase in investment spending worked through the multiplier through respending. Fiscal policy also works through the multiplier to increase income in the economy by more than the initial policy expenditure. In our example, if Congress approved a $10 billion expenditure on the highway system, we would find that the initial $10 billion spent would increase national income through the multiplier. This first $10 billion could be spent to employ designers, engineers, and asphalt firms and to purchase concrete and orange safety barrels. (We will follow the same analogy we developed in the Big Picture in Chapter 15, with consumers spending three-fourths of new income and saving the remaining one-fourth.) After this first round of spending, the designers, engineers, firm owners, concrete makers, and so forth would spend three-fourths of the $10 billion (or $7.5 billion) on supplies, labor, and other goods and services. Next, laborers, suppliers, and others will spend three-fourths of this new $7.5 billion (or $5.63 billion) of income on groceries, clothing, entertainment, and other goods and services. And the process continues until the initial $10 billion expenditure on highways results in $40 billion in income in the economy.

Instead of authorizing expenditure increases or cuts (which work in reverse), policy makers might consider a tax policy. This would involve tax cuts (to increase income) or tax increases (to decrease income). Tax policies also have a multiplier effect, but the tax multiplier is not as large as the investment and government expenditures multiplier since some portion of the income received from a change in tax policy is saved. Because there is no initial one-time expenditure, the effect is to reduce the multiplier by 1. In our earlier example, the expenditure multiplier was 4, and this tax multiplier would be 3 (or 4 − 1). The effect on the economy of reducing taxes by $10 billion to increase income would cause total income to increase by $30 billion, or by $10 billion less than by increasing highway expenditures by $10 billion. Figure 16.BP.1 illustrates the difference in the two outcomes.

FIGURE 16.BP.1 The Effect of Expenditure and Tax Policies on Income

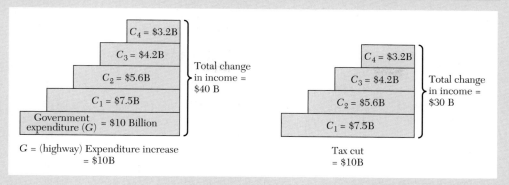

Government Spending

The government often adopts a fiscal policy position when politicians and public opinion consider employment levels to be inadequate—for example, if the full-employment level of income is thought to be at $5.7 trillion and income is currently $5.1 trillion. In this situation, a substantial amount of unemployment is likely, and the government can opt for fiscal action that will increase employment and boost the level of income by $0.6 trillion ($5.7 trillion – $5.1 trillion).* In its arsenal of policies are spending, taxing authority, and the ability to issue transfer payments (income supplements such as Social Security and welfare paid to individuals). Since transfer payments are not for current productive services, they are not included in the yearly national product accounts but enter the income-spending flow as part of the personal income tally.

Government spending on goods and services such as military operations, the space program, and public buildings will have the largest expansionary impact on income in the economy, since the full amount of spending enters the economy in the first round. In the case of transfer payments and tax reductions, some of the impact in the first round is "leaked" into savings. Table 16.1 provides an example of the difference.

In the example, the equations show the amount of government spending or tax reductions necessary to increase the level of income by $0.6 trillion (or $600 billion), assuming MPC in the economy is 2/3. The first set of equations addresses government spending. With an MPC of 2/3, we can use the formula

---

*Conversely, we could establish an example in which inflation was the primary problem, with income being above the full employment level. For example, income could be at $5.7 trillion, with the full employment level at $5.1 trillion. In that case, the policy measures would be the opposite of those we discuss in the following sections.

TABLE 16.1 Multiplier Effect of Government Expenditures and Tax Cuts

Spending Sequence	$\Delta G =$ **$200 billion**		$\Delta Tx =$ **$300 billion**	
Round 1 (direct expenditure: $\Delta G = \Delta Y$)			(indirect expenditure $\Delta Tx \times$ MPC $= \Delta Y$)	
	$\Delta G = \Delta Y = \$200$ B		$\Delta Y = \$300$ B $\times \frac{2}{3} = \$200$ B	
Round 2 ($\Delta Y \times$ MPC)	$\$200$ B $\times \frac{2}{3} = \$133$ B		$\$200$ B $\times \frac{2}{3} = \$133$ B	
Round 3	133 B $\times \frac{2}{3} = \$90$ B		$\$133$ B $\times \frac{2}{3} = \$90$ B	
Round 4	90 B $\times \frac{2}{3} = \$60$ B		90 B $\times \frac{2}{3} = \$60$ B	
Round 5	60 B $\times \frac{2}{3} = \$40$ B		60 B $\times \frac{2}{3} = \$40$ B	
Round 6	40 B $\times \frac{2}{3} = \$27$ B		40 B $\times \frac{2}{3} = \$27$ B	
Round 7	27 B $\times \frac{2}{3} = \$18$ B		27 B $\times \frac{2}{3} = \$18$ B	
Round 8	18 B $\times \frac{2}{3} = \$12$ B		18 B $\times \frac{2}{3} = \$12$ B	
Round 9	12 B $\times \frac{2}{3} = \$8$ B		12 B $\times \frac{2}{3} = \$8$ B	
etc.	Total	$600 B	Total	$600 B

$k = 1/(1 - \text{MPC})$ to determine that the multiplier is 3.* Knowing the multiplier ($k = 3$) and the desired level of income ($\Delta Y = \$600$ billion), we have enough information to determine the necessary amount of government spending (ΔG):

$$\Delta Y = k \times \Delta G$$
$$\Delta G = \Delta Y/k = \$600 \text{ billion}/3 = \$200 \text{ billion}$$

Our policy recommendation, then, is that the government build a (big) dam at a price of $200 billion to increase income by $600 billion to the full employment income level of $5.7 trillion. This is illustrated in Figure 16.1.

Although the example shows that the needed increase in income is $600 billion, policy decisions certainly are not made by such quick calculations. Partisan politics and economic philosophies play a crucial role in these decisions. We might recommend the construction of a dam, but each of the 435 representatives and 100 senators has his or her own plan, which often involves a particular congressional district or state. This and the following examples describe technical economic "solutions" to extremely complex economic, political, and social problems—what theoretically needs to happen to achieve economic goals.

2. Clip a recent newspaper article on some federal, state, or local economic issue. What, besides the economics of the problem or policy, does the article address?

$$^{*}k = \frac{1}{1 - \text{MPC}} = \frac{1}{1 - \frac{2}{3}} = \frac{1}{\frac{1}{3}} = 3$$

FIGURE 16.1   Effect of Increased Government Spending

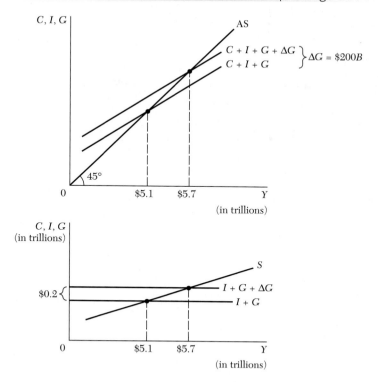

3. In the example you found, are the various positions based on ideology, economic theory, or rhetoric?

Tax Policy and Income Effects

If the government decides it wants to accomplish the desired income increase of $600 billion through a cut in taxes, it must decide how much of a tax reduction is needed to generate new increases in income equal to the $600 billion. Since tax cuts are initiated through a different channel for their progression within the economy, we must address the behavior of leakages, rather than the effects of injections on spending flows. The crucial difference between the effect of leakages and that of injections occurs during the first round of spending.

Instead of $200 billion being directly spent on a dam, the $200 billion in tax cuts goes into the pockets and bank accounts of the taxpayers. According to the marginal propensities given, taxpayers will save part of the $200 billion and spend the remainder. With an MPC of 2/3, the first action is to consume 2/3 of $200 billion, or $133 billion, and save $67 billion. Thus, only $133 billion *initially* enters the total income stream, instead of the $200 billion that would enter in the case of government spending.

The *tax multiplier* is therefore less than the spending multiplier—in fact, 1 less*:

$$k - 1 = k_{tx}$$
$$k_{tx} = -MPC/(1 - MPC)$$

(Note the negative sign for the tax multiplier, since a tax *cut* will increase income.) Using our previous example, to get a $600 billion increase in income with a tax multiplier of 2 (because 3 − 1 = 2), the following decrease in taxes must occur:

$$\Delta Y = -k_{tx} \times \Delta Tx$$
$$\$600 \text{ billion} = -2 \times \Delta Tx$$
$$\Delta Tx = -\$300 \text{ billion}$$

In other words, as detailed in Table 16.1, taxes must be reduced by $300 billion to increase income by $600 billion. (The impact of a tax cut on equilibrium income is outlined at the end of the chapter.)

Transfer Payments

The logic behind the macroeconomic effects of changes in transfer payments is essentially the same as those of tax cuts. Transfer payments, however, redistribute income, while tax cuts may not. Looking at the impact of transfer payments on the economy, we find that the income of households will increase. In our example, the change in spending during the first round will be two-thirds of $300 billion, since part of the transfer will be consumed and the remainder will be saved. The **transfer multiplier,** like the tax multiplier, is $k - 1 = k_{tr}$ (note that the transfer multiplier is positive, since an increase in transfers will increase income). Transfer expenditures worth $300 billion would be necessary to raise income by $600 billion.

4. If Social Security transfers were to increase by $4 billion and if MPC were 0.9, how much of an impact would this transfer package have on the economy?

The government, of course, might choose one or any combination of tax, spending, or transfer alternatives. It also might decide to pass legislation to

---

*This can be derived as follows:
$$-k_{tx} = [1/(1 - MPC)] - 1$$
$$= \frac{1}{(1 - MPC)} - \frac{(1 - MPC)}{(1 - MPC)} = \frac{MPC}{(1 - MPC)}$$
$$k_{tx} = -MPC/(1 - MPC).$$

encourage new consumer or investment spending. Tax credits and incentives have been used in recent years to stimulate certain industries that might be suffering more than others. During a housing slump in 1974, Congress gave a 5 percent income tax credit to purchasers of newly constructed homes. The measure was designed to pick up a depressed housing industry, as well as to stimulate economic activity in general. More recently, unemployment benefits were extended during the 1990–1993 and 2001 recessions so that those who were unable to find jobs during the normal benefit period could receive an additional six weeks of benefits.

Problems with Fiscal Policy

With these "mechanical" fiscal fixes firmly in mind, it is well to remember that problems are likely to arise in the determination of fiscal policy. The political machinery involved in fiscal decisions is often slow, the product of many lags. Additionally, policies of state and local governments offer their own brand of fiscal effects, which more often than not are ill-timed for national objectives because of interest costs, spending capacity, and political considerations.

Lags and Lumps in Fiscal Measures

From the discussion thus far, it seems that full employment in the economy requires only a mighty snap of the government purse strings. Several rather sticky problems emerge in the deployment of these strings, however. One problem encountered early on is the time it takes simply to recognize that a problem exists—in other words, a *recognition lag*. Another is trying to estimate MPC and thus the multiplier effect that each expenditure might have on the economy. Additionally, government spending tends to be lumpy. Projects are normally large and are generally confined to a reasonably small geographical area. Constructing a flood wall in Lewisburg, Pennsylvania, will probably not help alleviate unemployment in Dubuque or Detroit.

Legislation also tends to move slowly through Congress. By the time funds are allocated, new and different problems might emerge. During this time, higher resource prices might increase the inflation rate, and the expenditure of government funds would only add to the problem of rising prices. The enactment of tax policies takes time. For example, the 1964 tax cut was proposed in 1963 and approved after more than a year of hearings. This particular tax cut was an example of Keynesian economics well thought out and proposed, but legislative reluctance delayed the cut for over twelve months. Oftentimes a conflict between the president and the Congress leads to bitter policy debates. We refer to the undue passage of time before a proposed policy measure is signed into law as the *legislative lag*.

Execution presents another delay in transferring the legislation into action. Tax policies tend to be faster and more efficient after passage, but spending packages may be hung up in a bidding and allocation process for months. This has been called the *implementation lag*.

Finally, once the legislation for government spending or tax cuts is enacted and executed, time passes before the policy becomes effective. Results from empirical econometric models show that this *reaction lag* can be as long as a year or more before even part of the policy has affected GDP.

Procyclical Tax and Spending Policy

In the introduction to this chapter, we mentioned that policies of state and local governments have their own fiscal effects. These governments are active in spending and taxing as well as in issuing transfers. Often, however, they use their tools at the "wrong" time in the business cycle. Federal fiscal policy is usually designed to counter inflationary and recessionary trends in economic activity. Yet local government spending often occurs when fiscal "good times" prevail. Voters more readily approve bond issues for schools, libraries, or parks during boom periods, so these construction projects add to the boom. In the same vein, when times are hard, state and local governments often have difficulty financing new spending projects that might stimulate the economy, thus reinforcing a recession.

5. What does Keynesian theory tell you about this kind of spending? What would be the economic effects?
6. Is there any salvation to the procyclical spending of state and local governments? (What happens when bond issues to finance libraries and schools are passed?)

Fiscal Policy in an Open Economy

Thus far, we have examined the effects of fiscal policy in our three-sector closed economy of domestic households, businesses, and government. Since international economic activity plays an increasingly important role in U.S. transactions, we need to examine how the foreign sector or net exports (as we are representing the foreign sector) responds to fiscal policy. We can examine two specific effects on net exports: responses to changes in interest rates and responses to changes in currency value. Both affect national income.

Fiscal policy, such as an increase in government expenditures or a tax cut financed by an increase in government borrowing, may cause interest rates to rise in the short run as the government increases its demand for credit. Higher interest rates on government bonds will make U.S. government securities more attractive to both domestic and foreign investors than foreign security offerings with lower interest rates. An increase in the demand for U.S. bonds by foreign investors will create an increased demand for dollars by foreign individuals and institutions and a decrease in the supply of dollars offered by U.S. investors in foreign security markets. As we learned in Chapter 8, this will cause the value of the dollar to increase with respect to other currencies. Each dollar will purchase a larger volume of foreign goods, so imports should increase. On the other hand, U.S. products (exports) will cost more to those desiring U.S. goods, so the demand for U.S. exports should fall because of their relatively higher prices on international markets.

When we account for this effect of fiscal policy actions in an open economy, we see that it acts in opposition to the initial fiscal policy designed to increase levels of income and output. With imports rising and exports falling, net exports $(X - M)$ will fall. In our aggregate expenditure analysis, where $Y = C + I + G + (X - M)$, the increase in G may, through a higher interest rate, cause an appreciation of the U.S. dollar and thus a decrease in net exports. The expenditures multiplier therefore will be less effective in the presence of an international market. In contrast, tax cuts financed by lowered government surpluses rather than by increased government borrowing should stimulate consumption spending. Some of this increased consumption will be spent on imported goods and services, but overall, income (Y) should rise.

A second effect of fiscal policy in an open economy is the effect of output on exchange rates. Here, however, the effects on imports and exports are offsetting, so the total effect is assumed to be zero. As increased government expenditures or tax cuts increase income, those who receive this additional income will be inclined to increase their expenditures on goods and services. Some of this increased demand will be for international products. The demand for imports should increase as incomes rise. This increased demand for imports will yield a greater supply of dollars in the currency markets as U.S. customers exchange dollars for imported goods. The increased supply of U.S. dollars will have the effect of decreasing or depreciating the value of the dollar in the international market. A lower-valued dollar will increase the demand for U.S. exports and decrease the demand for imports in the United States. In this case, fiscal policy in an open economy most likely has a neutral effect. An initial increase in import demand will be followed by a rise in exports and a fall in imports as the dollar depreciates in value, so the original fiscal policy stimulus maintains its effectiveness.

The Federal Budget

The federal government's fiscal policy is directly related to the federal budget. During the 1980s, 1990s, and after 2002, the public and politicians objected to the size of the federal government, the size of the budget deficit, and its effects. As illustrated in Figure 16.2, the level of the federal budget deficit increased dramatically in the 1980s, with annual deficits of more than $150 billion and the total accumulated debt of around $1 trillion in 1980 increasing to more than $5 trillion by 1997. Then, between 1998 and 2000, federal surpluses halted the growing debt. After 2002, federal budget deficits sharply increased until faster economic growth and higher tax receipts reduced the deficit level in 2005 and 2006.

In the United States, a few deficit watchers have always been alarmed at prospects of deficits and their implications, but when large deficits were projected to continue throughout the 1990s, deficit reduction became an important political and economic issue.

FIGURE 16.2   The Federal Budget Surplus or Deficit, 1935–2006

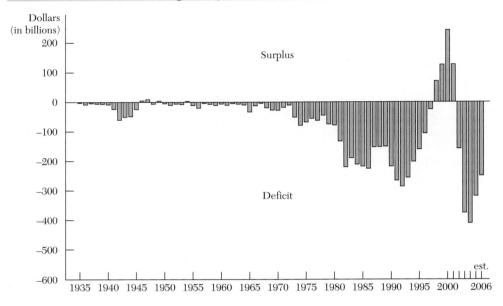

Source: *Economic Report of the President,* CBO, 2006.

The Federal Budget and the Economy

Just as the budget of a family or business determines the direction, priorities, and obligations of that unit, the federal budget determines the direction, priorities, and obligations assumed by the nation. The federal budget consists of expenditures (such as direct purchases of goods and services) and receipts (such as taxes). Elements of fiscal policy are directly reflected in the annual federal budget, which not only indicates a president's view about fiscal and social policy, but also reflects electoral policies and the process of government. The budget that the president proposes and Congress passes, in what is now a yearlong process, reflects what the government will do and what priorities it will set. As is the case with household budgets, receipts are balanced against expenditures. If receipts are greater than expenditures, a surplus results; if expenditures exceed receipts, there is a deficit.

The most obvious source of federal government revenue is tax receipts. Individual income taxes provided 43 percent of the roughly $2.0 trillion collected in 2005. As shown in Figure 16.3, the importance of individual income taxes has grown since the 1940s. Social Security taxes now provide the next largest single receipt, having increased from only 11 percent in 1950 to 37 percent in 2005.

FIGURE 16.3 Tax Type as a Percentage of Government Revenue, 1940–2005

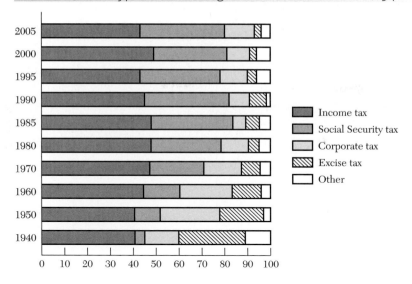

Source: *Economic Report of the President,* 2006, p. 378.

Corporate income taxes provided a substantial portion of federal receipts during the 1950s and 1960s, but as a result of the Reagan tax cut package of 1981, the corporate share of the total tax burden shrank to 6.2 percent in 1983. The Economic Recovery Tax Act, as it was called, cut personal income tax rates by 23 percent over three years. The measure also accelerated the rate at which businesses could take depreciation deductions, and gave other deductions and additional loopholes to individuals and businesses alike. The much-heralded Tax Reform Act of 1986 reduced corporate tax rates, eliminated the investment tax credit (which had saved corporations billions in taxes), and made depreciation allowances stricter. The corporate share of taxes increased to 11.4 percent in 1988 and in 2005 corporate taxes contributed 13 percent to total revenues.

The other side of the federal government's budget is expenditures. Table 16.2 shows federal expenditures both as the proportion of the budget going to selected areas and as a percentage of GDP for selected years. Military expenditures, while not changing dramatically as a percentage of the federal budget, increased dramatically as a percentage of GDP during the 1980s. In 1988 total defense expenditures were $290 billion, or 6.0 percent of GDP. Thanks to the end of the Cold War and the breakup of the former Soviet Union, U.S. defense expenditures were $294 billion, or roughly 3 percent of GDP by 2000. However, the Iraq war has brought additional military expenditures, and substantial increases have occurred in Social Security and Medicare expenditures. At the same time, interest payments on the federal debt have declined as a percent of GDP, thanks to lower interest rates.

TABLE 16.2 Government Expenditures as a Percentage of Budget Outlays and GDP, 1975–2005 (Selected Categories)

Expenditure	1975 % Budget Outlay	1975 % GDP	1980 % Budget Outlay	1980 % GDP	1985 % Budget Outlay	1985 % GDP	1990 % Budget Outlay	1990 % GDP	1995 % Budget Outlay	1995 % GDP	2000 % Budget Outlay	2000 % GDP	2005 % Budget Outlay	2005 % GDP
National defense	26.5	5.3	23.2	4.8	26.7	6.0	23.9	5.2	18.0	3.7	16.4	2.8	20.0	4.0
Education/health	13.2	2.6	9.2	1.9	6.6	1.5	7.7	1.7	11.2	2.3	11.9	2.1	14.2	2.8
Social Security (includes Medicare)			26.1	5.4	26.9	6.1	27.7	6.0	29.8	6.8	33.9	6.0	20.0	3.96
Medicare	—	—	—	—	—	—	—	—	—	—		6.0	12.1	2.4
Income security	33.3	6.7	15.0	3.1	13.5	3.0	11.8	2.6	14.5	3.0	13.8	2.4	14.0	2.7
Net interest	9.5	1.9	9.1	1.9	13.7	3.1	14.7	3.2	15.3	3.2	12.8	2.2	7.4	1.4
Agriculture	0.5	0.1	0.8	0.2	2.7	0.6	0.9	0.2	0.6	0.1	2.2	0.4	1.1	0.2
Total budget	20.0		20.7		22.6		21.7		20.9		17.5		19.8	
Surplus/(deficit)	(2.8)		(2.1)		(5.0)		(3.8)		(2.2)		0.8		(4.0)	

Source: *Economic Report of the President*, 1989, pp. 316, 398, 399; February 1996, p. 369; February 2006, p. 380; February 2006, p. 378.

FIGURE 16.4   Federal Spending by Budget Category (FY 2006 Budget)

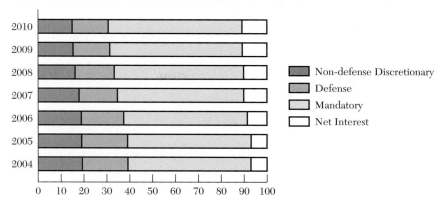

Source: Data from OMB, *Historical Tables, FY 2006 Budget*, February 2005; *Concord Coalition Report*, February 15, 2005.

Most budgeted programs were, in fact, cut as part of the Reagan and Bush programs to enhance the role of the private sector while reducing the role of government. However, since military, agriculture, Social Security, and interest expenditures increased so significantly in the 1980s, Reagan was unable to keep his campaign promise of reducing government's role. Under his administration, expenditures rose to a peace time record of 23.7 percent of GDP in 1983. During the Clinton administration, government expenditures as a percentage of GDP declined to 17.5 percent of GDP. In 2003, the G. W. Bush administration saw government expenditures rise to 19.5 percent of GDP.

By grouping these outlays another way, we can see why policy makers had such a difficult time reducing the deficit. Figure 16.4 shows the discretionary, non defense–discretionary and nondiscretionary spending as a percentage of the total budget using assumptions based on the 2006 fiscal year budget. Discretionary spending is voted on annually. The government automatically spends money on these mandatory programs. The largest of these entitlements are Medicare and Social Security, which grow as increasingly large numbers of the population reach retirement age.

The combination of tax reductions and expenditure increases led to then-record **budget deficits** between 1980 and 1993. Although the federal budget deficit has been larger when measured as a percentage of GDP, deficits comparable to those registered during the 1980s through the mid-1990s have seldom been recorded during a time of peace or economic growth. In early 2007, the U.S. federal debt stood at $9.0 trillion. The United States is the largest debtor nation in the world.

In the early 1990s, in an attempt to deal with large actual and projected deficits, Congress passed the Balanced Budget and Emergency Deficit Control Act (better known as Gramm-Rudman-Hollings), which mandated a balanced budget by 1993 and required automatic spending cuts in military and nonmilitary expenditures if Congress and the president failed to meet annual deficit reduction targets in the federal budget. Those targets were never achieved, in part because of the money spent to bail out failing savings and loan institutions in the late 1980s (see Chapter 17). In 1990, Congress enacted spending cuts and tax increases to cut the deficit. The Budget Enforcement Act limited discretionary spending and ensured that new entitlement programs would not worsen the deficit. Unfortunately, these were enacted at the same time the 1990 recession began, so tax receipts did not rise as they were expected to and government spending increased to offset the higher unemployment levels generated by the recession. In 1993, Congress passed a five-year deficit reduction plan designed to cut spending and increase revenue. Deficits fell from $290 billion in 1992 to $164 billion in 1995. In 1996, a seven-year plan to balance the budget was passed, and, by 1998, thanks in part to a surging economy resulting in increased tax revenues, the government realized its first surplus since the 1960s. Forecasts were mildly optimistic through 2000 but weakened in 2001 with tax reductions curbing receipts and increases in military and homeland security expenditures. Surpluses turned quickly into deficits as tax cuts continued and military expenditures grew. Economic growth rebounded with these fiscal stimuli.

7. Which categories of federal government expenditures have grown most rapidly over the past two decades? Which revenues have seen the greatest growth?
8. What is the forecast for the deficit this year?

Federal Deficits and Surpluses

Deficits in the federal budget give rise to the **national** (or **federal**) **debt.** The national debt is the debt or obligation of the federal government and is the accumulation of annual budget deficits. When expenditures are greater than revenues, the government must borrow the difference to finance its spending. The government finances its deficits by borrowing from the public through the sale of treasury bills and bonds. Treasury bonds are debt issues of the government that guarantee the repayment of the original investment plus a specified rate or amount of interest. The Treasury Department sells them to the public, to government agencies, and to institutional investors. Surpluses cause some to wonder about the future of treasury bond sales. In the remainder of this chapter, we examine concerns related to federal deficits and federal surpluses.

The national debt has been one of the great conversation topics of Americans concerned with its growth and size. The historical record indicates that all forms of debt increased dramatically after World War II. In the 1960s, the total federal debt was $300 billion, and in 2007 it reached $9 trillion. The debt more than tripled during the 1980s, stabilized in the late 1990s, and has expanded since.

We might ask why the debt is so worrisome to citizens, as well as to economists and policy makers. The government could eliminate it quite simply by assessing every man, woman, and child in the country an additional $28,700 (in 2006), their per capita share of the national debt. But more important facets of the debt need to be examined. The federal debt did not overly concern the majority of U.S. economists until the 1980s. To understand why such an issue is being made of the debt, we need to examine how debt that accumulated before the 1980s differs from debt that accumulated during the 1980s and after.

The Budget Deficit through Leakages and Injections. One way to examine the federal deficit in terms of the problems deficits bring to our economy is to analyze aggregate expenditures. In Chapter 15, we noted that in equilibrium, all leakages out of the economy must equal all injections into the economy:

$$\text{injections} = \text{leakages}$$
$$G + I + X = S + Tx + M$$

We can also restate this by subtracting M from both sides of the equation:

$$G + I + (X - M) = S + Tx,$$

where G represents government expenditures, I is investment expenditures, $(X - M)$ is net exports, S is saving, and Tx is taxes. We can rearrange the terms in this equation to show the federal budget deficit or surplus:

$$G - Tx = S - I - (X - M).$$

We know that the deficit or surplus is represented by government expenditures less receipts, or $G - Tx$. If taxes (receipts) are less than government expenditures, there is a deficit.

Reviewing this budget equation clarifies the government's options. If tax receipts are chronically less than government expenditures, the deficit must be offset by one or a combination of factors represented on the right side of the equation just given. The government can fund its expenditures by borrowing savings balances from the private and public sectors. This leaves fewer funds for private investment. Or it can increase borrowing from abroad, thus increasing its obligations to foreign citizens and institutions.

----

*We can also express this in our national accounting framework, since

$$Y = C + I + G + (X - M),$$

where

$$Y = C + S + Tx$$

Now substitute and simplify:

$$C + S + Tx = C + I + G + (X - M)$$
$$S + Tx = I + G + (X - M)$$
$$G - Tx = S - I - (X - M)$$

What's the Problem with Deficits?   Before the 1980s, most of the national debt accumulated during war years, especially during World War II and the Vietnam War. Until early 1982 and begining again in 2001, the debt as a percentage of national income continued to fall. As long as GDP was rising faster than the debt each year, there were only three major concerns:

1. Does the debt compete with other uses of credit?

2. Who pays the interest?

3. Who owns the debt and receives the interest?

The question of alternative financing sources is particularly cause for concern when the economy is operating at close to full employment. The government can increase taxes or borrow. Either action reduces the spending potential of another sector. Tax increases reduce the spending power of consumers and businesses. Borrowing, or enlarging the debt, may force interest rates up because government bond issues will have to be offered at a higher yield to attract enough buyers. Most of these bond issues will be sold to financial intermediaries, corporations, and others, so government spending will tend to take place at the expense of investment (instead of consumption); the financial intermediaries would otherwise lend to corporations for investment purposes rather than buying government bonds. This crowding out of private investment may occur when the economy is expanding. If there were severe levels of unemployment and excess capacity, interest rates would probably not have to rise with the new government bond issues, and businesses would be reluctant to invest anyway, no matter how low the interest rate fell.

Large budget deficits cause concern for future levels of economic growth, which in turn affects wealth and future living standards. While there are many uses for funds made available by businesses and household saving, there is a limit to that saving. National saving consists of private saving and government saving. Government saving is the budget surplus, or the part of its revenues the government does not spend. If the government must borrow from private saving to finance its deficit, it may divert funds from domestic investment. This is a particular problem when savings rates fall markedly. Figure 16.5 shows that the national saving rate fell from around 8.0 percent of GDP in the 1950s through the 1970s to 3 percent in the first half of the 1980s and to 2.4 percent in the last half. The national saving rate rose to 5 percent of GDP in the 1990s, only to fall to 2 percent in 2005. Private saving dropped from 9 percent in the 1950 – 1980 period to 6 percent in the 1980s. Private saving continued to fall through the 1990s, reaching 1 percent in 2004. Government deficits thus consumed many of the resources that had to be parceled out among a variety of credit demands. If interest costs rise, the higher costs can lower the demand for housing and reduce investment. Many economists believe that deficits must remain low if the nation is to achieve long-term prosperity.

The second, more obvious, concern over who owns the debt arises with regard to repayment. It is one thing to pay the interest to ourselves and quite another to owe it to someone else. In 1985, about 11.5 percent of the debt was owned by foreign individuals and governments. By 2007, this figure approached

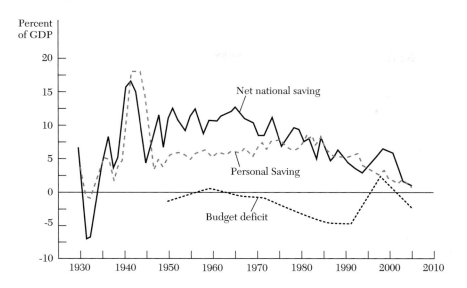

Source: GAO analysis of NIPA data from the Bureau of Economic Analysis (BEA). GAO Report, GAO-06-628T.

25 percent. We will examine the links between borrowing from international sources and the U.S. government debt in Chapter 21.

9. Why did the foreign-held debt increase? Do you think it will continue to do so? Why or why not?

It would be naive to assume that all of us own some of the debt (government bonds) held equally within the U.S. public. Some of us own much more of the debt than others, and the richer we are, the more debt (or bonds) we are likely to own. The poorer among us hold few if any bonds. Institutions and middle- and upper-income individuals use government bonds as a safe and profitable way to hold their savings. Lower-income groups tend not to have substantial savings, since they consume most if not all of their income.

This brings us to the final problem of the interest payments on the debt. In 2005, the debt cost taxpayers more than $183 billion in interest payments. Since the interest payments come from budget receipts, and budget receipts come from taxation, this pattern of interest payments and ownership leads to a redistribution of income in the economy, from bottom to top. Almost everyone pays taxes, some of which are used to pay the interest on the debt. But only individuals who own government bonds receive these interest payments. This is a concern for some economists and politicians.

10. Why is ownership of the debt of some concern to you?
11. What groups benefit from the redistributive effects of the debt?

Historically, the debt has financed wars, higher levels of employment and income, and inflation. In the 1980s, it financed additional military and Social Security expenditures and lower taxes. Some argue that the results are a bargain at $28,700 (in 2006) per person! While many economists believe that deficits are an urgent problem, others believe that part of the debt funds much-needed public investments in education, infrastructure, the military, consumer protection, and other public goods.

Cyclical and Structural Deficits and Surpluses

The Keynesian philosophy toward budgets was that deficits should accumulate during recessions, when additional government expenditures are necessary to boost the economy by stimulating aggregate expenditures, and governments should accumulate surpluses during times of prosperity. The results would be a cyclically balanced budget. Granted, the amounts spent during the recessions might not equal the amounts accumulated during prosperity, but on the whole they would more or less even out. In the United States, however, during the eighty-eight quarters between 1960 and 1981, only four surpluses were recorded. After that, eighteen more years passed until the next surplus, recorded in 1999.

When deficits accumulate as a result of economic downturns, they are called **cyclical deficits,** measured by the economic cost of the recession in terms of added expenditures due to unemployment and lost tax receipts. During the recession of the early 1990s, higher levels of unemployment and lower incomes meant that cyclical factors were acting with structural factors to create a much larger than projected federal budget deficit. Cyclical surpluses occur in economic upturns when strong employment and growth yield higher tax receipts. The surpluses of 1999 and 2000 were cyclical surpluses.

Deficits that accrue during times of prosperity or high employment are called **structural deficits.** They result from the structure of federal receipts and expenditures, regardless of the level of economic activity. Between 1960 and 1980, structural deficits averaged less than 2 percent of GDP until 1983, when they reached 2.9 percent of GDP. With economic growth between 1993 and 1995, the cyclical component of the deficit shrank. In 1995, there was a negative cyclical component, since unemployment was below 5.7 percent (the unemployment rate used to calculate "full employment"). With unemployment levels at or below this level in 2005 and 2006, large federal deficits were primarily structural.

The structure of federal receipts and expenditures can also produce structural surpluses. Structural surpluses would occur if the economy were at full employment when the government accrued surpluses. Some economists argue that structural surpluses are detrimental to the economy. According to this argument, surpluses act as a drag on future economic activity by shifting savings from private to public sources. In the 1960s, this phenomenon was called "fiscal drag." Higher tax returns lowered private saving, possibly lowering consumption and limiting loanable funds for private investments.

12. Are cuts in federal expenditures are possible? Why or why not?
13. Have any tax cuts or tax increases been passed since 2006? Have new or different types of taxes been proposed? What are they?
14. How large was the federal deficit last year? How large is the federal debt?
15. What would be the effect on income of a decrease in government spending of $0.3 trillion and a tax cut of $0.3 trillion? Is this a balanced budget?
16. Economists have called an unemployment rate of 5.7 percent "full employment." Is there recent evidence that this rate should be changed? If so, what evidence?

Conclusion

This chapter has highlighted how fiscal policy works through the tax, transfer, and spending multipliers. For a wide variety of reasons, fiscal policy is not always efficient, but it is most often effective—at least when estimated by Keynesian models. We have also seen the growing concern with structural budget deficits and the desire to balance government receipts against expenditures in periods of economic growth. Chapter 17 will introduce money into the Keynesian model of the economy; this provides yet another set of tools for achieving policy objectives.

Review Questions

1. What fiscal policy recommendations would you make to combat unemployment and recession?

   a. What fiscal measures would you recommend if the economy were in the middle of a prolonged period of inflation?

   b. Would you favor a tax policy over a curb on government spending? Why or why not?

   c. What might be the end result of your policy?

   d. How long do you expect the lags to last before your policy would be enacted?

2. What are the differences between automatic stabilizers and discretionary fiscal policy?

3. Would you ever recommend a balanced budget for the federal government? Why or why not? If so, when?

4. Can federal budget deficits be beneficial to the economy?

5. How might deficits limit the productive potential of the economy?

6. Are structural deficits more cause for concern than cyclical deficits? Explain.

7. If MPC = 0.8, what would be the effect of a $10 million tax cut and a $6 million increase in government purchases?

Note

The body of this chapter dealt only with the effect of injections (government spending, investment, and net exports) on equilibrium income. Now we examine in more detail the effect of leakages or withdrawals in the Keynesian model. We will focus specifically on taxation, although the analysis is similar for other withdrawals, including trans-fers. In the two-sector model, the only leakage we encountered was saving. When saving increases (S to S') and consumption decreases (C to C'), the saving schedule shifts up and to the left, while the consumption schedule shifts down and to the right, and equilibrium income moves to Y_1 in Figure 16.A.

FIGURE 16.A Decrease in Consumption; Increase in Savings

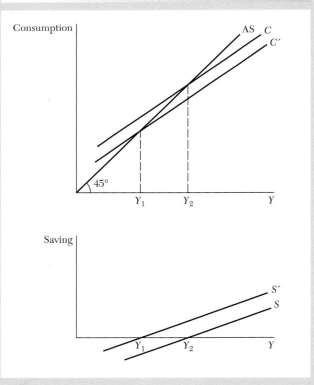

Just as all injections—C, I, G, and $(X - M)$—are components of aggregate expenditures and are graphically represented as part of the aggregate expenditures function, all leakages or withdrawals are represented on an aggregate leakage curve. To illustrate our aggregate leakage curve, we again expand the model from two to three sectors by adding the taxation leakage to the saving schedule. We add the exogenous tax leakage to the savings function, which in this analysis gives the leakage function its slope (MPS), just as the consumption function gives the injection function or aggregate expenditures curve its slope (MPC). The leakage curve represents positive and negative tax and saving changes. (A tax increase would represent a positive leakage; a tax decrease would represent a negative leakage.) An increase in saving or taxes will shift the leakage curve up and to the left. A decrease in saving or taxes will shift the curve down and to the right; thus, at every level of income, leakages are lower.

FIGURE 16.B   Impact of a Tax Cut
(a) Tax decrease of $300 billion is shown as a negative leakage.

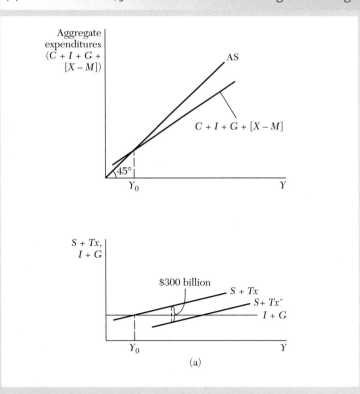

(a)

Returning to the previous example of a $300 billion tax cut, we arrive at the new equilibrium income after a series of three steps (see Figure 16.B). These three steps occur simultaneously but are shown as a series to clearly demonstrate each part of the adjustment process. The steps describe how people respond to a cut in taxes. (Note that this is not a cut in the tax rate.) The cut brings an increase in income, but how is that increase allocated? Our answer conforms to what we learned in Chapter 15. Part of the $300 billion will be consumed, and part will be saved; the MPC and MPS tell us how consumption and saving are allocated. In the first step, Figure 16.B(a), the saving–tax leakage curve shifts down by $300 billion, as taxes are cut by that amount. Second, since income initially rises by the amount of the tax cut, individuals will boost their consumption by MPC times the tax reduction($2/3 \times$ $300 billion = $200 billion). In Figure 16.B(b), we see the effect of this increase in consumption as the aggregate expenditures curve shifts up by $200 billion. At this point, there is an equilibrium level of income in the upper, aggregate

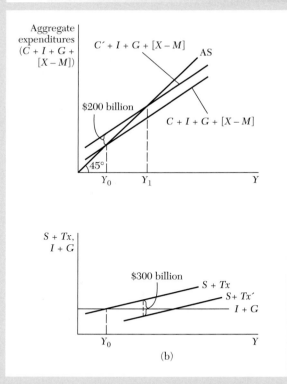

FIGURE 16.B (Continued)
(b) Consumption increases as a result of the addition to income from the tax cut
($\Delta C = 2/3 \times$ $300 billion = $300 billion).

(b)

expenditures graph, but not in the lower, leakage graph. To arrive at equilibrium in both the upper and lower graphs, we must complete the final step. Just as individuals increase consumption by MPC times the tax reduction, they will increase their saving by MPS times the tax reduction (1/3 × $300 billion = $100 billion). Thus, the saving–tax leakage curve shifts up and to the left by $300 billion, as shown in Figure 16.B(c). In the final analysis, income increases from Y_0 to Y_1, or by $600 billion. To arrive at this result more directly, we can multiply the tax multiplier by the change in taxes:

$$-k_{tx} \times \Delta Tx = \Delta Y$$
$$-2 \times -\$300 \text{ billion} = \$300 \text{ billion}$$

FIGURE 16.B (Continued)
c) Saving increases as a result of the addition to income from the tax cut ($\Delta S = 1/3 \times \$300$ billion = $100 billion).

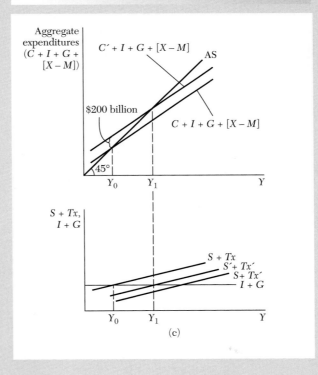

(c)

CHAPTER SEVENTEEN

Financial Markets, Money, and Monetary Policy

 Introduction

Money *is an asset accepted in exchange for the goods and services we want to purchase. The role of money and the operation of the markets for money and other financial instruments are important in economic decision making and policy making, and economists do not always agree on the way money works through the economy or on its potential impact.*

Key players in the market for money and other financial instruments are institutions called **financial intermediaries,** *which hold the funds of savers and make those funds available to borrowers. Financial intermediaries include commercial banks, savings and loan institutions, mutual savings banks, finance companies, credit unions, life insurance companies, mutual funds, and pension funds. They provide financial services demanded by consumers in a changing society. Depository institutions are more directly linked to Federal Reserve Board (Fed) actions than are other financial intermediaries.*

To begin examining money and a group of financial intermediaries accepting deposits of savers, we will first look at the uses of and demands for money. Next, we will examine the money supply, including the ways the Fed can increase and decrease the money supply and the role of money in the Keynesian model. Finally, we examine monetary policy.

The Uses of Money

Money is important to economics because of its uses. Some say that money is as money does. Few individuals hold dollars for the sheer joy of counting or stacking them.

Money is valued for the goods and services that it buys—for its use as a **medium of exchange.** It is commonly accepted in payment for goods and services. Before money was institutionalized, barter economies prevailed; people simply exchanged goods and services. Of course, problems arose when two parties could not agree upon objects to trade or when there was no double coincidence of wants. For example, barter fails if one trader desires shoes and has only nuts to offer in exchange, while the shoemaker wants only leather in exchange for shoes. Larger problems would arise if one had only assets that could not be divided, such as a horse to trade for less valuable objects.

Because it is an accepted medium of exchange, money can also be used as a measuring rod for the value of each good or service—in other words, as a **unit of account.** In our economy, goods are measured by a dollar amount. In shopping we observe that a pound of nuts is priced at $4.69, a pair of shoes at $85.98, and a horse and buggy at $5,753. In Chapter 14, we used money as our unit of account in measuring the National Income Accounts of GDP and NNP. Firms use money to account for the flow of goods and services produced and sold.

Besides its unique role as a medium of exchange and unit of account, money has two functions that it shares with other assets (things of value that are owned). Money may serve as a **store of value.** To be a store of value, an asset must hold its value into the future. Some other assets that serve this function are stocks, bonds, precious metals, gems, and property. Money may also be a **standard of deferred payment.** Standards of deferred payment are assets accepted by others for future payment.

1. What assets would you accept as payment for your work?

Demand for Money

The four uses of money are associated with the three categories of demand for money. The **transactions demand**—the only category recognized by the classical economists—indicates the amount of money balances that individuals desire for transaction (purchasing) purposes. This demand corresponds to money's function as a medium of exchange and is often constant with a given level of income and pattern of consumption expenditures.

People also have a **precautionary demand** for money, or a demand for money to hold to meet unforeseen expenses. John Maynard Keynes wrote about this demand as a separate category in *The General Theory*. We observe this precautionary demand as we try to hedge our risks by saving, perhaps for the proverbial "rainy day" or for some other reason.

2. Divide your demands for money into transactions and precautionary balances. What percentage of your money balances do you hold for each?

The precautionary demand, like the transactions demand, is generally constant; people at certain income levels will tend to save or keep a relatively fixed proportion of their income for precautionary purposes. Figure 17.1 shows a demand curve for the transactions and precautionary balances plotted on a price-quantity axis. (This adds money to the array of goods and services for which there is a demand—and later, of course, a supply.) The quantity of money

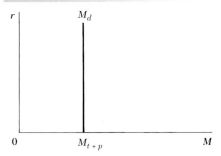

FIGURE 17.1 Precautionary and Transactions Demand for Money

(M) is measured along the horizontal axis, and the price of money, represented by the interest rate (r),* is measured along the vertical axis. The vertical line M_d indicates that at all rates of interest, the precautionary and transactions demand will be constant for a given individual at a given income level.

The third demand for money (or, as he called it, liquidity preference[†]) recognized by Keynes is the **speculative demand.** This demand arises from people's desire to maximize their returns on the funds left over after satisfying their transactions and precautionary demands. The speculative demand for funds is inversely related to the interest rate. If the interest rate is high, people will hold relatively few speculative or liquid balances. Instead, they will exchange these speculative money balances for bonds or other assets. If the interest rate is low, individuals may decide to wait and see what happens to interest rates in the future. If interest rates rise, people want to avoid being locked into low-yielding assets, so they prefer to hold (speculative) cash or money balances. One can plot the speculative demand for money with respect to interest and the quantity of money, since $M_{\text{spec}} = f(r)$, as shown in Figure 17.2.

At extremely high interest rates, the speculative demand for money balances approaches 0, whereas at very low rates of interest, people will desire to hold only money balances. This low-interest range in which the demand for money is perfectly elastic is called the Keynesian **liquidity trap.** Keynes pointed out that at extremely low rates of interest, people believe interest rates can go no lower and can only rise. To buy bonds would be courting disaster, so people hold on to

---

*The price of money is the rate of interest, since a person who buys or borrows money pays for it at the prevailing rate of interest. Although there is a wide array of interest rates in the economy at any one time, depending on such factors as risk and time until the asset matures, we will focus on *an* interest rate, assuming that all of them behave similarly.

[†]Liquidity is the degree of "moneyness." One hundred percent liquid suggests that all of one's assets are in cash and/or demand and checkable deposits. Stocks and bonds and property are assets of somewhat lesser levels of liquidity, since they cannot immediately be converted into cash.

FIGURE 17.2   Speculative Demand for Money

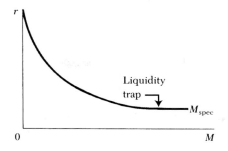

their cash. This liquidity trap area becomes important when discussing various aspects of monetary policy, a topic we will return to later in the chapter.

If we combine all three demands for money, we obtain the total demand for money, which is plotted in Figure 17.3. This demand curve for money, like all demand curves, indicates that the quantity demanded varies inversely with price. As the interest rate rises, people will hold smaller money balances, down to the amount needed to satisfy transactions and precautionary demands.

Changes in the Demand for Money

Like other demand curves, the demand for money may not remain constant over time. Shifts, or changes in demand, are often caused by a change in the level of income. For example, if an individual's income increases from $40,000 a year to $45,000 a year, that person's demand for money will more than likely increase. The reason is that the demand for precautionary and transactions balances increases as income increases. Figure 17.4 shows how changes in income affect the demand for money.

FIGURE 17.3   Total Demand for Money

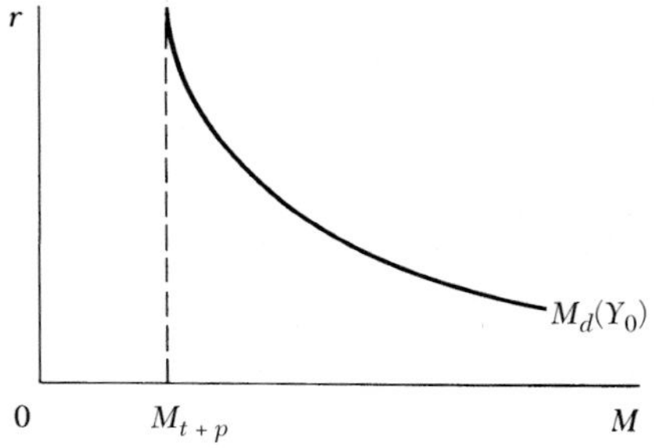

FIGURE 17.4 The Effect of Income Changes on the Demand for Money

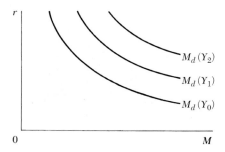

Supply of Money

Unlike the supply of most goods and services, the total supply of money is controlled not by individual firms, but by the Federal Reserve System, more commonly known as the Fed.

The Fed

To mend an ailing national banking system by promoting stability in the banking system, the Federal Reserve Act of 1913 established the **Federal Reserve System** (the **Fed**) as the central bank in the United States. The Fed is an independent agency of the government, established by Congress to centralize control over the banking system and the money supply. Figure 17.5 shows the basic organizational structure of the Federal Reserve System.

Members of the Board of Governors of the Federal Reserve System, appointed to fourteen-year terms by the president with congressional approval, coordinate and regulate monetary policy in the United States. The chair of the Board of Governors acts as spokesperson for the entire system. The Federal Open Market Committee directs Fed sales and purchases of U.S. Treasury bonds, and the other councils advise. The twelve regional Federal Reserve Banks and their twenty-four branches throughout the country oversee operations of the member commercial banks in their districts. Figure 17.6 shows the locations of these regional banks.

The Monetary Control Act of 1980 stipulated that the Federal Reserve can require that *all* banks and depository institutions in the country hold reserves (or a percentage of deposits). The passage of this act gave the Fed control over the reserves placed on money held in commercial banks, savings banks, savings and loan institutions, and credit unions.

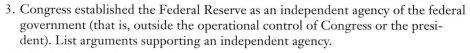

3. Congress established the Federal Reserve as an independent agency of the federal government (that is, outside the operational control of Congress or the president). List arguments supporting an independent agency.

4. Who is the current chair of the Fed?

FIGURE 17.5 Federal Reserve System

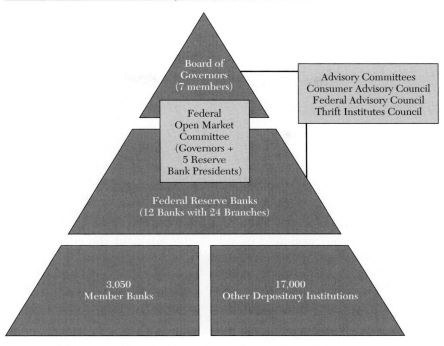

Source: Board of Governors of the Federal Reserve System, *The Federal Reserve Today*, p. 2.

FIGURE 17.6 Boundaries of Federal Reserve Districts and Their Branch Territories

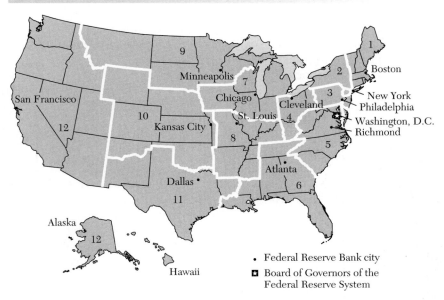

Source: Board of Governors of the Federal Reserve System, http:/ /www. federalreserve. gov/otherfrb.htm.

Regulation of Financial Markets

Operating within the U.S. financial markets are many institutional players, all of them subject to some degree of regulation. Commercial banks are the oldest financial intermediaries. Savings banks and insurance companies emerged in the late nineteenth century, while credit unions, real estate trusts, investment banks, bank holding companies, and finance companies developed in the twentieth century. A number of innovations in existing financial institutions occurred in the 1980s, and changes resulting from new regulation and deregulation legislation continued throughout the 1990s.

There is a long history of financial market regulation in the United States. Financial institutions have seen periods of total control and regulation, as well as periods that might be called banking anarchy. The current period of regulation resulted from controls instituted after the Great Depression, as Congress enacted legislation to avoid the recurrence of widespread banking failures. Investors as well as depositors wanted protection from financial market failures. The federal and state governments responded with laws and regulations designed to assure the safety of the financial system. Federal deposit insurance agencies began insuring a variety of deposits, and agencies began to regulate the activities of financial institutions. However, in the 1980s and in 1999, Congress moved to eliminate at least some of the regulations dating from the 1930s.

Regulation limited the kinds of loans and assets each type of financial institution could issue and possess. As a result, the financial industry was segmented into largely different types of institutions with little competition among them. Commercial banks, for example, specialized in commercial loans to businesses, while savings and loan institutions generated home mortgages. Started by builders in the 1870s, savings banks made money available to people wanting to buy the builders' products.

Perhaps the most onerous of the depression-era regulations was **Regulation Q,** which placed ceilings on the interest rate financial institutions could pay for time and savings deposits. The purpose of interest ceilings was to "restrain excessive price competition," which was thought to be one of the causes of the 1933 banking collapse. The interest ceiling was above the market rate of interest through the mid-1960s, so until then it caused no concern. After 1966, market rates rose above the interest ceiling on several occasions. This effectively prevented financial intermediaries from attracting money and then lending it. Instead of depositing their funds in financial intermediaries, people withdrew their dollars and put them into stocks or other assets to get higher returns. Instead of **financial intermediation,** there was **disintermediation.** To avoid interest ceilings, financial intermediaries began creating new financial instruments, since only time and savings deposit accounts were then subject to Regulation Q. But the Federal Reserve was not to be caught short. While Regulation Q covered only two types of accounts in 1965, twenty-four types were covered by 1979.

Because of these rapid financial innovations, Congress came under pressure to deregulate financial markets. The regulation of the 1930s had limited competition and the ability to work within the market system to bid for funds. By the end of the 1970s, the mood toward regulation had substantially changed as described in the 1984 *Economic Report of the President*:

> In the 1930s, financial instability was attributed to the natural operation of competitive markets, and this view supported a very substantial extension of regulatory controls over financial markets. More recently, however, a renewed respect for the efficiency of competitive markets has developed, as well as increased recognition of the costs of regulation. Regulation tends to spread in unproductive directions and often causes industries to evolve less efficiently than they otherwise would. For these reasons, the promotion of efficiency by furthering competition is also an important regulatory goal. The purpose of regulation should not be to protect poorly managed individual firms from failure, but rather to prevent such failures from shaking the stability of the financial system as a whole. Regulation should be designed to achieve stability of the system, while individual firms are afforded the maximum possible freedom to compete and innovate.

In the early 1980s, financial deregulation significantly changed the rules of the game in the financial markets. Between 1980 and 1984, most interest rates on federally insured deposits were deregulated, allowing banks and thrift institutions (savings and loan institutions, savings banks, and credit unions) to freely determine the rate of interest they paid on most types of deposits. This added both competition and uncertainty to a vast financial system. The deregulatory activity was started by the Monetary Control Act of 1980 and extended by the Garn–St. Germain Depository Institutions Act of 1982. The Monetary Control Act set lower reserve requirements for all nonmember banks, established the Fed as the lender of the last resort for depository institutions, and eliminated Regulation Q. The Garn–St. Germain Act authorized all financial institutions to offer interest-bearing checking accounts and extended the power of regulators to promote mergers for depository institutions that were failing. It also expanded the lending and deposit powers of thrifts. This permitted some new lending and investing powers, including commercial and real estate loans by savings and loan institutions.

Following deregulation, the rate of bank failures and instability increased, and the savings and loan industry nearly collapsed. Continental Illinois, a major U.S. national bank, paved the way for bank failures in the late 1980s and early 1990s. Unable to arrange a merger for this ailing giant, the Federal Deposit Insurance Corporation (FDIC), which insures deposits of most banks, took over operations. Other failing banks and thrifts were either merged with institutions believed to be more stable or liquidated. Many have therefore questioned the wisdom of aspects of this particular financial deregulation.

Two major reforms in bank regulation took place in the 1990s. In 1994, Congress set nationwide standards for banks wishing to expand or operate branches beyond their home state boundaries. Late in 1999 the Gramm-Leach-Bliley Act was passed by Congress allowing commercial banks to engage in investment banking activities in order to compete more effectively with other financial intermediaries. This legislation revoked part of the Glass-Steagall Act of 1933 designed to protect the public from financiers who might fund some investment activities while denying funds to equally worthy activities.

Banking and Thrift Instability, 1980s and 1990s Style

Deregulation posed enormous problems for the nation's commercial banks and savings institutions. Nearly eight times as many banks closed between 1980 and 1990 as closed during the 1970s. Some 1,570 savings institutions closed their doors or merged with other depository institutions during this period. The government's response to the turmoil in the thrift industry cost U.S. taxpayers an estimated $500 billion or more.

A number of thrifts were in financial difficulty prior to deregulation. Initially chartered to provide mortgage funds to the housing market, savings and loan institutions were legally restricted to holding only mortgages as assets. After World War II, amidst a large upswing in purchases of single-family homes, the demand for mortgages rose, and savings institutions prospered despite the long-term, low-interest nature of these mortgages. Thanks to Regulation Q limiting the interest rate that could be paid to depositors, tax benefits to the industry, and federal insurance guarantees to depositors, savings institutions could thrive as long as interest rates remained low. However, interest rates rose markedly in the 1970s, and savings institutions had to pay higher interest rates to attract deposits. Their profits were squeezed, since the long-run returns on the mortgages already in their portfolios remained fixed at low rates, even though new mortgages reflected the higher rates. Furthermore, the institutions faced geographic restrictions on their customer base, so institutions in agriculture and oil-producing states were especially fragile. Energy and agricultural prices plunged in the 1980s, and increasing numbers of firms in the Midwest and Southwest failed, rendering many loans worthless. Deregulation freed these institutions to engage in potentially more lucrative but riskier areas of investment. Thrifts diversified into office buildings, commercial loans, and some direct purchases of franchises. At the same time, federal depository insurance was increased from $40,000 per account to $100,000 per account, so thrifts sought out larger deposits by offering more attractive rates of return. They hoped the new channels of investment open to them would more than offset the higher interest rates they were paying for funds. The risk for bankers (and depositors) was limited, since most deposits were insured.

During this same period, federal budget cuts, combined with a spirit of deregulation, reduced the number of bank examiners hired to oversee these more risky (and sometimes fraudulent) activities. The reduction in regulation and inspection, along with an overextension of risky loans, left many institutions with deposit liabilities in excess of the value of their assets. These ingredients completed a recipe for widespread thrift failure.

With the mounting failures draining federal deposit insurance funds, Congress in 1989 enacted the Financial Institutions Reform, Recovery and Enforcement Act (FIRREA). This law provided funds to merge or liquidate failing thrift institutions and prevent the thrift failures of the eighties from recurring. FIRREA created the Resolution Trust Corporation (RTC) to manage a bailout of the savings and loan industry through the early 1990s. Among its charges, the RTC was to sell houses, apartment buildings, golf resorts, office buildings, and other assets of failed thrifts. Much of the real estate sold at bargain-basement prices, recouping only a small fraction of the monies lost. These massive sales depressed real estate markets and new construction in communities with the highest levels of RTC sales.

FIRREA also eliminated other thrift regulatory agencies and established several new agencies in their place. The law established more stringent capital standards, requiring thrifts to meet the higher capital requirements of banks. Regulators continued to examine bank and thrift capital requirements through the 1990s.

Economists estimated that in the early 1990s, closing or selling insolvent thrifts cost taxpayers some $10 million for each day the S&Ls stayed open.

5. List some of the opportunity costs of the thrift bailout. (What could have been purchased with these amounts?)

6. Some economists argue that markets function more efficiently without regulation. Explain why deregulation of the S&L industry worked so poorly.

Measures of the Money Supply

Besides controlling the amount of credit in the system of depository institutions (which is often referred to as the banking system), the Fed also regulates the money supply. Because a number of financial assets are "used" as money,

Source: TOLES © 1992 *The Buffalo News.* Reprinted with permission of UNIVERSAL PRESS SYNDICATE. All rights reserved.

economists measure the money supply in broader terms than currency used for exchange. They use measures of the money supply called **monetary aggregates,** which include measures for M_1 and M_2. Figure 17.7 details the components of each measure.

The most narrowly defined monetary aggregate includes most of the "money" that we use for our day-to-day transactions and is called M_1. M_1 includes coins and currency plus demand deposits (checking accounts), traveler's checks, and other checkable deposits (including NOW and ATS accounts*) held by the public. In 2005, currency and coins accounted for about 52 percent of M_1 demand deposits for 23 percent, other checkable deposits for 23 percent, and traveler's checks for 0.5 percent. The total money supply measured as M_1 stood at \$1.4 trillion in late 2005. M_1 has historically grown at an annual rate of around 5 or 6 percent. In 1990, the growth rate of M_1 was only 4 percent, but it increased to 14 percent in 1992 as the economy slowed. After 1995, the annual change in M_1 averaged a 2 percent increase.

An expanded monetary aggregate M_2 includes M_1 and adds other short-term accounts that are easily converted into money. M_2 equals M_1 plus short-term time and savings accounts and other interest-bearing accounts, including money market deposit accounts, noninstitutional money market mutual funds, and some other very liquid assets.[†] In 2005, M_2 was \$6.7 trillion—almost five times the value of M_1.

Some economists believe that the use of the M_2 definition better explains consumption and other decisions made in the economy. Other economists, however, believe that the Federal Reserve—when reflecting on policy actions that will result in changes in the money supply—really looks at the availability of credit in the economy rather than any precise M_1 or M_2 definition. For example, if the Fed concludes that credit is too tight, it will take measures to increase credit availability by increasing the money supply.

Although the Fed is responsible for initiating changes in policies to alter the money supply, individual depository institutions allocate the money to the public. To a large extent, their allocation reflects the interest rates in the economy. If interest rates are low, depository institutions are reluctant to lend large quantities of money and risk being locked into low-yielding assets. On the other hand, if interest rates are high, the depository institutions will be more willing to lend money *if it is available to them* (or if the Fed has allocated additional money by implementing policies that increase the money supply). We can illus-

---

*Negotiable order of withdrawal (NOW) accounts are interest-bearing checking accounts. They became legal throughout the United States on November 1, 1980, with an initial maximum interest rate of $5\frac{1}{4}$ percent. NOW accounts may be issued by all depository institutions. ATS accounts are automatic transfer service accounts.

†Money market mutual funds (MMMFs) and money market deposit accounts (MMDAs) are funds issued to savers and backed by holdings of high-quality short-term assets. MMDAs are federally insured bank deposit accounts.

FIGURE 17.7 Components of the Monetary Aggregates, September 2006

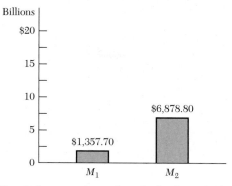

M_1 includes currency, traveler's checks, demand deposits, and other checkable deposits.

M_2 includes M_1, small-denomination time deposits, savings deposits and money market deposit accounts, money market mutual fund shares (noninstitutional), overnight repurchase agreements, and overnight eurodollars.

Source: Board of Governors of the Federal Reserve System, *Federal Reserve Bulletin*, November 2006.

trate this by constructing a money supply curve. The interest rate is on the vertical axis, and the quantity of money is on the horizontal axis, as in Figure 17.8.

When we combine the supply and demand curves for money, the intersection of the two curves signifies equilibrium in the money market, as shown in Figure 17.9. At point E the quantity of money demanded equals the quantity supplied at an interest rate of r_0. In equilibrium, there is no excess demand or supply. If the Fed allows the money supply to increase, then the M_{s0} curve will shift to the

FIGURE 17.8 The Money Supply

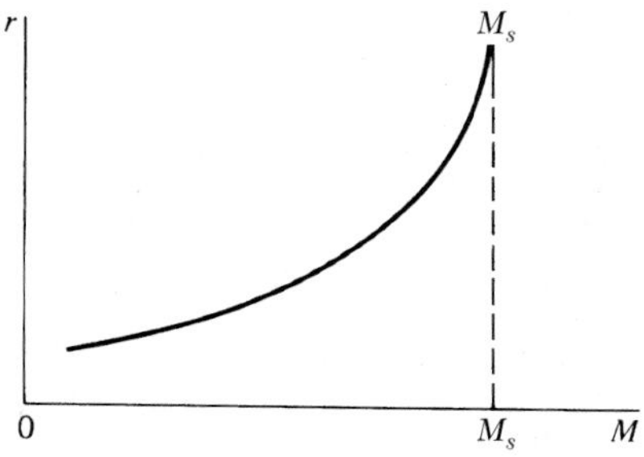

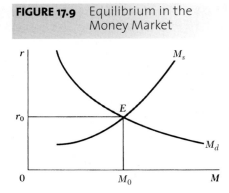

FIGURE 17.9 Equilibrium in the Money Market

right (SM_1), usually resulting in a lower interest rate (r_1), as in Figure 17.10. A decrease in the money supply will shift M_{s0} to the left (M_{s2}) and increase the interest rate (r_2). Later in this chapter, we will look at the tools with which the Fed changes the money supply. First we will examine the process by which commercial banks "create" money and how this money works within the Keynesian model.

Suppliers of Money

All financial intermediaries facilitate the exchange of money, but commercial banks and other depository institutions also have the power to "create" money. They create money on the basis of a **fractional reserve system** of deposit balances. The Fed requires that every depository institution hold reserves, setting aside a certain percentage of its total deposits in its vault or in the nearest Federal Reserve Bank to ensure safety and the ability to meet deposit withdrawals. The **reserve requirement** (the percentage of reserves that must be held) varies according to the asset size of the depository and the type of account. Table 17.1 lists the most recent reserve requirements mandated by the Fed.

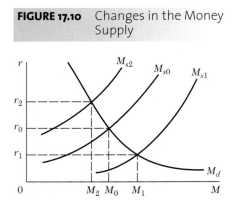

FIGURE 17.10 Changes in the Money Supply

TABLE 17.1 Reserve Requirements of Depository Institutions

Type of Liability	Requirements	
	Reserve Percentage (%) of Liabilities	Effective Date
(Net Transaction Accounts)		
$0 to $8.5 million	0	12/21/06
More than $8.5 million to $45.8 million	3	12/21/06
More than $45.8 million	10	12/21/06
Nonpersonal time deposits	0	12/27/90
Eurocurrency liabilities	0	12/27/90

Source: *Federal Reserve Bulletin*, December 2006.

7. Why isn't there a 100 percent reserve requirement?

An example of the money creation process should help clarify what happens to a deposit in a commercial bank or other depository institution. For simplicity's sake, we shall use a 10 percent reserve requirement for demand deposits and begin with a newly created $1,000 deposit. With this deposit, new deposits in the depository or banking system increase by $1,000, and required reserves increase by $100. This leaves the commercial bank with $1,000 minus $100, or $900. The prudent (profit-maximizing) banker would use the $900 to generate loans and investments of an equal amount.

Perhaps you are in the market for a $900 loan. If our friendly neighborhood banker decides you are creditworthy, you may receive the "extra" $900. If you spend the $900 on new stereo components, there is a good chance that the full $900 will enter the banking system when the Stereo Shack deposits its daily balances. The banking system then has another deposit, this time one of $900. It must hold 10 percent of $900, or $90, as the reserve requirement on the *new* $900 deposit. Total new deposits are now $1,900, and total new required reserves are $190 in the banking system. And what will happen to the $900 minus $90, or $810, left in the bank? Of course, it becomes a potential source for increases in loans and investments. Table 17.2 shows the final result of the initial $1,000 demand deposit.

Rather than carrying this process to its final result, we can more easily find the total amount of money "created" by using the following formula:

$$\Delta R \times 1/r_{dd} = \Delta DD,$$

where ΔR is the original change in reserves, r_{dd} is the reserve requirement on demand deposits, and ΔDD is the total change in demand deposits. We can substitute numbers from our example:

$$\$1,000 \times 1/(1/10) = \Delta DD$$
$$\$1,000 \times 10 = \Delta DD$$
$$\$10,000 = \Delta DD$$

TABLE 17.2 Money Creation: Example

Position of Depository Institution	New Deposits	New Loans and Investments	Required Reserves
Original depository institution	$ 1,000.00	$ 900.00	$ 100.00
2nd depository institution	900.00	810.00	90.00
3rd depository institution	810.00	729.00	81.00
4th depository institution	729.00	656.10	72.90
5th depository institution	656.10	590.49	65.60
6th depository institution	590.49	531.44	59.05
7th depository institution	531.44	478.30	53.14
8th depository institution	478.30	430.47	47.83
9th depository institution	430.47	387.42	43.05
10th depository institution	387.42	348.68	38.74
11th depository institution	348.68	313.81	34.87
12th depository institution	+ 313.81	+ 282.43	31.38
Sum of 12 depository institutions	$ 7,175.71	$ 6,458.14	$ 717.61
Sum of remaining depository institutions	+ 2,824.29	+ 2,541.86	+ 282.39
Total for system as a whole	$10,000.00	$9,000.00	$1,000.00

Note: Totals may not be accurate due to rounding.

From $1,000, with the stroke of a pen, depository institutions can "make" $10,000—representing $9,000 of *new* money.

Before we accept this fountain pen magic, however, we must take note of several conditions. The first is that an individual bank or depository institution acting alone cannot create money. The process must operate throughout the whole system. To more easily understand this, imagine that a single depository institution tried to expand or create money on its own. Based on the $1,000 increase in its reserves with the $1,000 deposit, the institution loaned $9,000. What happens to that depository institution when someone comes to withdraw or use the funds the depository institution has just lent? As you might imagine, many problems can result, one being that the bank cannot maintain its reserve requirement.

 8. What other difficulties might this depository institution run into?

A second point to remember is that the simplified money creation process as described works only if there are no leakages in the system. Leakages can occur in several places. Individuals may decide to place their funds elsewhere, either outside the depository institutions or in hoards. If they do not deposit the funds, then there are no reserves to expand upon. Consumers may place some funds in time accounts. These funds have lower reserve requirements, so the money multiplier is larger. Consequently, such deposits will lead to an even greater expansion of the money supply.

Another leakage may appear within the financial system itself. Bankers and other deposit managers may decide that they can earn greater profits by holding assets other than loans or securities. Perhaps they believe their liquidity is too low and desire to place their remaining funds (or excess reserves) in more short-term assets, such as government bonds. In either case, there is a leakage of funds that do not reenter the demand deposit flow for an indefinite period of time. Indeed, the amount of assets that depository institutions hold in loans or securities is approximately 60 percent of their total portfolio.

Caution should therefore be the byword when examining the money creation process. Nevertheless, the process does suggest that commercial banks and other depository institutions can expand the money supply by "creating" demand deposits. In addition, the simple formula $\Delta R \times r_{dd} = \Delta DD$ approximates the amount of money that the system can create from a new deposit.

9. What happens to the money supply when people take $1,000 out of their depository institution deposits?

The Myth and Mystique of Money

In the following excerpt from "Commercial Banks as Creators of Money," Yale economist James Tobin tries to steal our thunder in explaining the multiple money creation process in a principles text:

Perhaps the greatest moment of triumph for the elementary economics teacher is his [her] exposition of the multiple creation of bank credit and bank deposits. Before the admiring eyes of freshmen [s]he puts to rout the practical banker who is so sure that [s]he "lends only the money depositors entrust to him [her]." The banker is shown to have a worm's-eye view, and his [her] error stands as an introductory object lesson in the fallacy of composition. From the Olympian vantage of the teacher and the textbook it appears that the banker's dictum must be reversed: depositors entrust to bankers whatever amounts the bankers lend. To be sure, this is not true of a single bank; one bank's loan may wind up as another bank's deposit. But it is, as the arithmetic of successive rounds of deposit creation makes clear, true of the banking system as a whole. Whatever their other errors, a long line of financial heretics have been right in speaking of "fountain pen money"— money created by the stroke of the bank president's pen when she approves a loan and credits the proceeds to the borrower's checking account.

In this time-honored exposition two characteristics of commercial banks are intertwined. One is that their liabilities—well, at least their demand deposit liabilities—serve as widely acceptable means of payment. Thus, they count, along with coin and currency in public circulation, as "money." The other is that the preferences of the public normally play no role in determining the total volume of deposits or the total quantity of money. For it is the beginning of wisdom in monetary economics to observe that money is like the "hot potato" of a children's game: one individual may pass it to another, but the group as a whole cannot get rid of it. If the economy and the supply of money are out of adjustment, it is the economy that must do the adjusting. This is as true, evidently, of the money created by bankers' fountain pens as of money created by public printing presses.

The commercial banks possess the widow's cruse [an expression implying unending supply]. And because they possess this key to unlimited expansion, they have to be restrained by reserve requirements.

Excerpt from J. Tobin, "Commercial Banks as Creators of Money," in BANKING AND MONETARY STUDIES, D. Carson, ed. © 1963 Irwin.

THE BIG PICTURE

Money and the Keynesian System

In Chapters 15 and 16 we saw how increases in spending—whether by businesses (as investment) or the government (as expenditures or taxes) worked through the multiplier to increase income by amounts greater than the original spending increases or tax cuts. Similarly, we saw how decreases in investment or government spending or increases in taxes would reduce income by more than the original spending cut or tax increase through the multiplier. In the sections just above we saw how equilibrium in the money market, where the supply of money M_s equals the demand for money M_d is at an interest rate (r). In Figure 17.BP.1 we see that this interest rate is at r_0.

With just one more piece of information we can see how increases in the money supply will—in our Keynesian analysis—impact investment decisions and thus income. Increases in investment as saw in Chapter 15 work through the multiplier to increase income by more than the original investment. (Decreased investment will have the opposite effect on income.)

The key to linking monetary policy and the money supply to investment decisions is the interest rate. In Figure 17.BP.2 we see a demand for investment

FIGURE 17.BP.1 Money Market Equilibrium

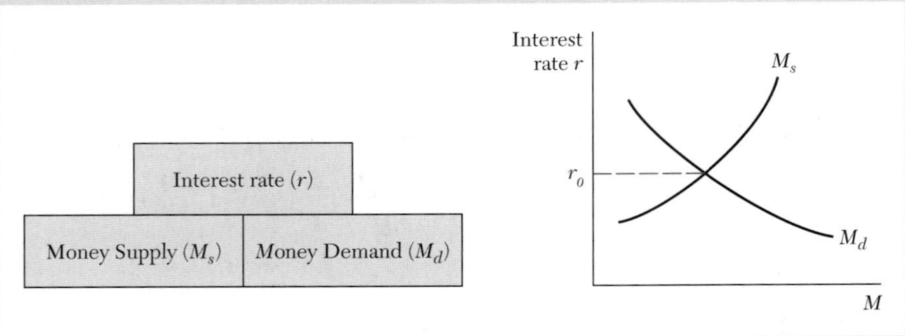

FIGURE 17.BP.2   Investment Demand

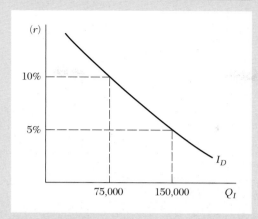

graph, with interest rates (r) on the vertical axis and the quantity of investment (Q_I) on the horizontal axis. This demand curve is downward sloping, illustrating that at high interest rates, the cost of investment funds is high and managers will need to earn very high returns from any investment made—thus the demand for investment is low at high rates of interest. As interest rates fall, investment demand increases as money to fund investment activities becomes cheaper.

When the Federal Reserve increases the money available and interest rates fall, businesses will find investment opportunities more attractive at these lower interest rates. As they undertake these additional investments—these new investment expenditures work through the Keynesian multiplier to increase income—by more than the initial investment expenditure. Thus we have another possible policy aid to expand income.

Figure 17.BP.3 illustrates the effect of this additional investment. In Chapter 15 we traced the process of a business investing $100,000 in new computer

FIGURE 17.BP.3   Money, Interest Rates, Investment and the Keynesian Multiplier

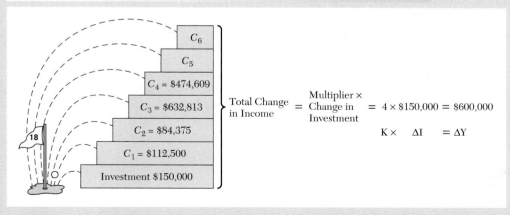

equipment and how this generated income for the computer manufacturer and the respending effect through the multiplier. Now suppose that owners of a golf course decide that lower interest rates make it possible for them to install a watering system that costs $150,000. When interest rates were high, the cost of the system was too high and the returns to making such an investment decision too small. So this additional investment is triggered through lower interest rates. This generates $150,000 in income for the firm manufacturing the automatic watering systems. Using a multiplier of 4 (from Chapter 15), the watering system manufacturer will spend three-fourths of the $150,000, or $112,500 on purchases of components, equipment rental, labor, and other goods or services. Again, the component suppliers and workers will continue the spending cycle, with three-fourths of $112,500 or $84,375 worth of purchases—perhaps on vacations, rent, travel, food, and so on. And the spending cycle continues until the total increase in income generated by the $150,000 investment in watering equipment generates increased income of $600,000, which equals the multiplier (4) time the initial investment ($150,000).

If the Federal Reserve contracts the money supply, interest rates will rise (*cet. par.*) and investment will drop—and thus income will fall.

Money and the Keynesian System: The Details

Money can be an integral part of the Keynesian system. In Chapters 15 and 16, we saw that the gist of the Keynesian system is that changes in consumption, investment, and government spending can effectively be used to expand or lower the level of income in the economy. Money can and most often does work within the Keynesian sphere to allow income changes as well. Changes in the money supply often directly influence both the business and household sectors in their investment and consumption decisions.

An increase in the supply of money will lower the interest rate (see Figure 17.10), just as (*ceteris paribus*) any increase in supply will decrease the price of a product. As Figure 17.10 shows, an increase in M_s from M_{s0} to M_{s1} lowers interest rates from r_0 to r_1. These interest rates and the demand for investment are shown in Figure 17.11. As money becomes "cheaper," investors reconsider their present levels of investment. Low interest rates will encourage businesses to borrow from commercial banks and to spend these funds on new buildings and equipment (i.e., investment); high rates, on the other hand, deter investment decisions. This is expressed graphically in Figure 17.11 as an inverse relationship between the rate of interest (r) and the level of investment (I), or $I = f(r)$. As the interest rate falls from r_0 to r_1, investment (in housing, equipment, or plants) will expand from I_0 to I_1.

Returning to the Keynesian model developed in the last two chapters, we can again examine the effect of an increase in investment. This time, however, the investment increase is stimulated by a reduction in the interest rate, generated by an increase in the money supply (see Figure 17.10). As the money supply increas-

FIGURE 17.11 The Interest-Investment Relationship

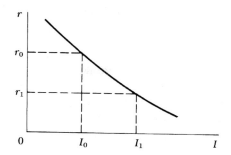

es from M_{s0} to M_{s1} in Figure 17.10, the interest rate decreases from r_0 to r_1. As this occurs, investment increases from I_0 to I_1 (see Figure 17.11). Finally, this increased investment, working through the multiplier, generates a new higher income level, Y_1, as in Figure 17.12. (Remember, $I_1 - I_0 = \Delta I$, $Y_1 - Y_0 = \Delta Y$, and $\Delta Y = k \times \Delta I$.)

10. When the Fed decreases the money supply, what happens to interest rates? The level of investment? The level of income? Employment?

The Liquidity Trap

Keynes relied more on fiscal policy for the stimulation of aggregate expenditures because he expected that during times of depression the economy would operate in the area of the liquidity trap. In this area, no matter how much the money supply increased, the rate of interest would fall no lower. And the business community's grim expectations of the future would discourage any further

FIGURE 17.12 Income Response to a Change in Investment

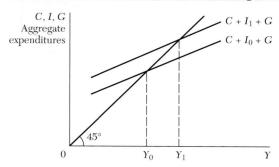

FIGURE 17.13 Money Supply Increase in the Liquidity Trap

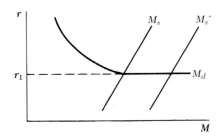

investment activity, even with low rates of interest. As we can see in Figure 17.13, changes in the money supply within the range of the liquidity trap will have no effect on interest rates. And if interest rates are unchanged, the levels of investment and income also will remain the same, yielding no effect on aggregate expenditures. For example, as interest rates in Japan fell to almost zero in 2001, some characterized Japan as experiencing a liquidity trap at that time.

Keynes also believed that business and consumer expectations could change during depressions, thereby thwarting the effect of monetary policy. For these reasons, economists often say that increasing the money stock to increase investment is much like pushing on a string. In *The General Theory*, Keynes expressed substantial doubt about the ability of monetary policy—a policy that changes the money supply—to rescue the economy from a severe depression. Yet, during the past four decades, we have seen the power of monetary policy to affect the levels of aggregate expenditures in the economy. During this period, the Fed has played an active role in determining aggregate expenditures, a practice that has drawn frequent criticism. Still, monetary policy has continued to be an important tool for economic stabilization.

Monetary Policy

Some critics have argued that the Fed is too powerful, too independent, and too business-oriented. Others believe that the money supply is much too important to be left to the discretion of mere mortals. In this section, we shall examine the tools that enable the Federal Reserve to control the supply of money and credit in the economy and outline effects of international markets. After a review of the Greenspan years, we shall examine recent Federal Reserve policy and the interaction between monetary and fiscal policy.

Tools of the Trade

To affect the level of income in the economy, the Fed has at hand several tools. The two primary tools are (1) reserve requirement changes and (2) open-market operations. On occasion—for example, during World War II—the Fed has implemented several selective credit controls on home mortgages and consumer credit. The only credit control that it regularly uses is the margin requirement for stocks, which stipulates the percentages of payment that must be in cash on any security purchase. In March 1980, the Fed responded to President Carter's request for tighter credit to help quell the inflationary trends by announcing new controls on consumer and business credit. It quickly withdrew these controls when evidence showed they were dramatically worsening the recession of 1980. The Fed can also use moral suasion in pursuit of its economic goals; that is, it can attempt to persuade relevant economic actors to engage in or refrain from certain activities. Since 2003, changes in the discount rate have been pegged to the fed funds rate (see below).

Reserve Requirements.

As we saw earlier in Table 17.1, each depository institution must keep a reserve requirement at the Federal Reserve or as cash in vault. The Board of Governors of the Federal Reserve can change the levels of reserves required at any time. In general, the central bank views its ability to change reserve requirements as its most powerful tool and uses this tool with utmost discretion. Since a change in reserve requirements of only 1 percent alters the monetary situation geometrically, changes in reserve requirements have been infrequent since 1935, when this tool became available. In more recent years the Fed has altered the size of liabilities on which reserves are held.

Critics claim that this tool works like an ax rather than a scalpel. An example shows why. Assume the Fed wants to restrict economic activity by reducing the money supply (e.g., to fight inflation). If banking assets are at $400 billion with 10 percent reserve requirements, some $40 billion is being held as reserves. If reserve requirements are increased by 1 percent, to 11 percent, some $44 billion must be held. This takes $4 billion out of the money supply immediately, as loans and investments are called in to increase reserves to the new level. More would be taken out of the system later through multiple deposit contraction—the reverse of the multiple deposit expansion explained previously.

11. In the example just given, what might happen to interest rates? Why?
12. What would happen if reserve requirements were lowered by 1 percent? How much would member banks be required to hold? What would happen to the "extra" money (or excess reserves)?

An increase in reserve requirements can absorb large changes in *excess reserves*, or additional monies held by depository institutions, such as those that occurred during the 1930s when substantial amounts of gold flowed into the country. A reduction in the reserve requirement may offset a large loss in reserves. In either case, a change in reserve requirements announces a change in Fed policy to the public as well as to the banks and other depository institutions. Critics of the Fed suggest that other means are more appropriate for the announcement of policy changes.

Open-Market Operations. The Fed is engaged daily in **open-market operations** through the activities of the Federal Reserve Open Market Committee. Activities in the open market involve purchases and sales of government bonds, bills, and notes at the Federal Reserve Bank of New York. These actions affect the money supply as well as interest rates. To increase the money supply and economic activity (e.g., to combat recession), the Fed actively buys bonds (Treasury issues). Buying bonds takes them out of the hands of the banks and other depository institutions and increases the money supply by exchanging the bonds for money (in the form of a check or cash from the Fed). If, on the other hand, the Fed wants to reduce the money stock, it will step up bond *sales* to commercial banks and other depository institutions, this time increasing the holding of bonds at banks and decreasing their holding of reserves.

As discussed in the box below titled "Interest Rates, Bond Prices, and the Money Supply," the effect on interest rates of these bond sales and purchases is inversely related to the money supply. When bond sales reduce the money stock, interest rates must increase in order to attract businesses as well as households to purchase the bond offerings. Otherwise, investors would place their funds elsewhere. Bond sales, then, encourage interest rates upward as they compete with other assets for the public's cash balances. Once the sales have been made, the interest rate will also rise because of the shortage of money.

Open-market operations are the Fed's most important tool. They take place on a day-to-day basis, and the Fed's Open Market Committee meets regularly to decide how open-market operations should affect the money supply and interest rates.

13. How do bond purchases by the Fed affect interest rates in the economy? Why?

Interest Rates, Bond Prices, and the Money Supply

We can use an example to illustrate how the interest rate is related to the price of bonds and to the purchase of a bond by the Federal Reserve. First, assume you receive a $100 government bond for your birthday. In the fine print on this bond, the U.S. government promises to pay you $100 at the end of ten years. Obviously, the people who gave you the bond did not pay $100 for something that is worth $100 at the end of ten years; they paid less.

To find the price they paid, we can examine a present-value table such as Table 17.3.

The *present value* of your $100 bond payable in ten years is the amount it is worth today; more generally, present value is what a dollar at the end of a specified future year is worth today. Examining the abbreviated present-value table in Table 17.3, we find that the present value depends on the interest rate. At an interest rate of 10 percent, the present value is $38.50; if the interest rate were 15 percent, the price of the bond would be $24.70. As the interest rate rises (from 10 to 15 percent), the price of the $100 bond falls (from $38.50 to $24.70). There is an inverse relation between

TABLE 17.3 Present Value of $100.00

	Interest Rate			
Year	3%	7%	10%	15%
1	97.10	93.50	90.90	87.00
2	94.30	87.30	82.60	75.60
3	91.50	81.60	75.10	65.80
4	88.90	76.30	68.30	57.20
5	86.30	71.30	62.00	49.70
6	83.80	66.66	56.40	43.20
7	81.30	62.30	51.30	37.60
8	78.90	58.20	46.60	32.60
9	76.60	54.40	42.40	28.40
10	74.40	50.80	38.50	24.70

Note: The formula for finding the present value entries in the table is $P = R/(1 + r)^t$. The present value, P, equals the future return, R (in this case, $100), divided by $(1 + \text{rate of interest})^t$, where t is the number of years to maturity. (In our example, $t = 10$ years.)

the rate of return (interest rate) and the price of the bond. In essence, the bondholder earns interest on the bond every year it is held.

When the Federal Reserve purchases bonds (not $100 savings bonds, but $100,000 and larger denominations of U.S. Treasury bonds, notes, and bills) in the open market in order to increase the money supply, the demand for bonds increases, so the price of bonds rises (Figure 17.14). The interest rate is inversely related to price, so the interest rate falls. Thus, as the Fed buys bonds, increasing the money supply, interest rates fall.

FIGURE 17.14 Increased Demand for Bonds

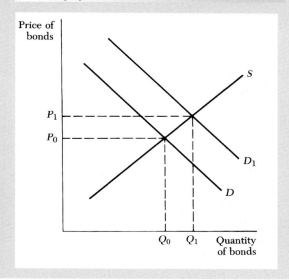

The Discount Rate. The Federal Reserve also establishes the **discount rate**—the rate at which a bank or depository institution can borrow from the Fed. Often, institutions borrow from the Fed to protect their reserve position. They typically present collateral consisting of bonds, which the Fed discounts for short-term borrowing purposes. In 2003 the Fed adopted a policy that "tied" the discount rate to the fed funds rate (see below). If the Fed increases the fed funds target rate, for most banks and other depository institutions the discount rate will be 1 percent greater than the fed funds target. This will insure that funds are available when there might be a shortage of liquidity within the banking system. (This rate is called the primary credit rate.)

In "emergency" situations, the Fed may serve as "the lender of last resort," with the discount rate historically providing liquidity. The Fed stood ready in this capacity immediately after the stock market crash of October 1987. Alan Greenspan, then chairman of the Fed's Board of Governors, issued the following statement on the day following the crash: "The Federal Reserve, consistent with its responsibilities as the nation's central bank, affirmed today its readiness to serve as a source of liquidity to support the economic and financial system." This brief statement seemed to reassure financial markets, particularly as the Fed took necessary actions to ensure adequate liquidity to the financial system. To calm the uncertainty accompanying the terror attacks of September 11, 2001, Greenspan issued a similar statement, again ensuring liquidity.

The Fed Funds Rate. For more than two decades, the interest rate on federal funds (fed funds) instruments has played an important role in Federal Reserve monetary policy. The fed funds instruments are overnight or very short-term loans in which one bank lends another some of its deposits at the Fed. (Typically, these deposits are at the Fed to meet reserve requirements.) If a bank has deposited more money at the Fed than is necessary to meet its reserve requirements, the bank may lend those excess deposits to banks needing additional reserves. The **fed funds rate** is the interest rate that banks charge when they lend these reserves for short periods of time. The Fed can "target" the fed funds rate by using its reserve requirement and open-market operations tools. In recent years, the Federal Reserve Open Market Committee has voted to raise or lower targets for the fed funds rate. The Fed usually uses open-market operations and accompanying changes to the discount rate to meet the fed funds target rate.

Lags in Monetary Policy

As is true with fiscal policy, lags or delays are inherent in monetary actions. Economists have classified these lags into two major types: the *inside lag* and the *outside lag*. The inside lag comprises a *recognition lag* (the time it takes for the Federal Reserve authorities to recognize there is a problem in the economy) and an *action lag* (the time of recognition until the time some policy is implemented). These lags are usually a function of measurement and forecasting.

After the action takes place, there is an outside lag before the impact of the policy (either partial or total) is felt in the economy. The length of impact lags is a subject of dispute among economists and economic models. Monetarists— economists who favor monetary policies over fiscal policies—argue that the impact lag with monetary actions is much shorter than the one estimated by their Keynesian counterparts.

Monetary Policy in an Open Economy

Monetary policy has two types of effects on international markets in an open economy. One is an interest effect, similar to but not the same as that experienced in fiscal policy in an international environment. The second is an effect on prices due to monetary changes.

If the Fed takes some policy action to increase the money supply (to expand the economy), interest rates will fall. In international financial markets, demand for U.S. assets, which yield a return attached to this lower interest rate, will decline. This will decrease the demand for dollars, shifting the dollar demand curve to the left, such as the shift from D_0 to D_1 in Figure 17.15. At the same time, because of the lower interest rates, U.S. investors will seek higher-yielding securities in the international arena. As U.S. citizens trade their dollars or dollar-denominated securities for higher-yielding foreign securities, the supply of dollars in the international market will increase, shifting the dollar supply curve to the right (the shift form S_0 to S_1 in Figure 17.15). These changes in the demand for and supply of dollars in the international financial markets will depreciate the value of the dollar (bid the value of the dollar down with respect to other currencies currently in demand).

This lower-valued dollar will create a demand for U.S. exports, since they are now cheaper to foreign citizens. At the same time, imports into the United

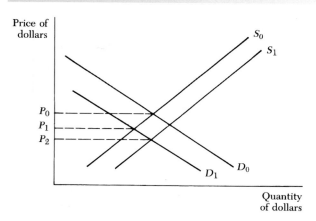

FIGURE 17.15   Demand and Supply of Dollars in the International Market

States will decline, since imports now cost more of the lower-valued dollar. Net exports $(X - M)$ will rise. This increases aggregate expenditures and income, thus reinforcing the monetary expansion also designed to increase aggregate expenditures.

Monetary policy will also produce a long-run price effect in the international financial markets. To the extent to which increases in the money supply lead to increases in domestic prices, foreign exchange markets of U.S. trading partners will be affected. If the increase in the money supply brings about a 5 percent increase in prices of domestic products, this price increase will be felt in both domestic and international markets.

Let's look at the effect of this type of policy on trade between the United States and Japan. A 5 percent increase in the price of U.S. products will decrease the demand for or purchase of U.S. products by the Japanese (assuming an elastic demand for U.S. exports). This will cause a decrease in the demand for dollars, since the Japanese are purchasing fewer U.S. goods. This decrease causes the demand curve for dollars to shift to the left (from D_0 to D_1 in Figure 17.15). At the same time, a 5 percent increase in domestic prices makes Japanese products relatively less expensive in the United States. As U.S. consumers increase their demand for Japanese products, they supply more dollars to the international market, thus shifting the supply curve for dollars to the right, as in Figure 17.15.

Both of these actions serve to lower the value of the dollar and appreciate the value of the yen. From here on out, consumer reactions are reversed. The Japanese will resume purchasing U.S. products. Although prices did increase, the yen appreciation offsets this price increase. Likewise, demand for Japanese products will fall back to previous levels. Despite the price effects produced by monetary policy, after currency adjustments, the level of exports and imports should remain about the same.

14. After income has increased due to monetary expansion, what will be the reaction in international markets?

U.S. monetary policy does not operate on a one-way street with respect to the world economy. Actions of other industrial countries might hinder the functioning of U.S. economic policy as well. The Fed usually succeeds in its bid to reduce short-term interest rates, but the international community may make its task a bit more difficult. In late 1989, for example, the Fed attempted to decrease interest rates but failed. While the Fed was actively working to lower rates, buyers of bonds in the international community were actively purchasing U.S. bonds, believing that U.S. financial markets were preferable to a German market facing reunification.

15. Can you think of ways the Fed might regain control of interest rates?

A Brief History of Monetary Policy

The Fed has powerful tools, and its independence gives it the authority to carry out the monetary policy it views as best. During the 1950s and 1960s, the Fed followed its collective instinct in managing money matters. After economists severely criticized this policy in the mid-1960s, the Fed began to target interest rate levels in adjusting the nation's money supply. This type of policy, despite outcries from monetarists, continued until the fall of 1979. Monetarists believe that control of the nation's money supply is far more important than control of interest rates. In contrast, the Keynesians rely heavily on interest rates to transmit the effects of monetary policy to the economy.

In 1982, amidst low inflation and economic recession, the Fed, under chairman Paul Volcker, began increasing the monetary growth rate and paid more attention to interest rate targets. Low inflation continued and, coupled with economic growth, left the recession of the early 1980s behind. By 1987, when Alan Greenspan assumed the chairmanship of the Fed's Board of Governors, the economic recovery was into its fifth year.

Greenspan's Fed: 1987–2005

Looking for a conservative Republican to replace Paul Volcker as chairman of the Federal Reserve Board of Governors, the Reagan administration in 1987 turned to Alan Greenspan. Greenspan had served as chair of the Council of Economic Advisors beginning in 1974 under President Nixon and continuing through the Ford administration. Known as a meticulous observer and student of statistical data of all economic markets, Greenspan played a more activist role in fine-tuning the economy, carefully watching leading indicators that might suggest greater levels of inflation. Indeed, the first Bush administration criticized his tolerance of higher interest rates at the expense of slower economic growth and argued that the Fed did not do enough to lower interest rates to ward off the recession of the early 1990s.

Fed policy actions during the Greenspan years were often credited for bringing economic stability in the late 1980s and setting the stage for economic growth between 1995 and 1999. As illustrated in Figure 17.16, Greenspan's Fed raised the fed funds and discount rates to reduce inflationary tendencies during the late 1980s. During the recession of 1990–1991, the Fed lowered these rates. The series of prolonged reductions in the fed funds targets and discount rates helped the economy to rebound into a period of prolonged economic growth, which continued into 2001. Fear of inflation began to spread in the mid-1990s, and between 1994 and 2000, the Fed responded by increasing the fed funds targets and discount rates several times. The Fed continued to monitor for potential inflationary activity until early 2001, when it abruptly lowered the discount rate and fed funds targets, hoping to avert a serious economic downturn, and continued lowering the targets until mid-2004, when growth expanded and inflationary pressures returned in the form of higher oil prices. The Fed quickly targeted a higher fed funds rate.

FIGURE 17.16   FOMC Expected Federal Funds Rate and Discount Rate

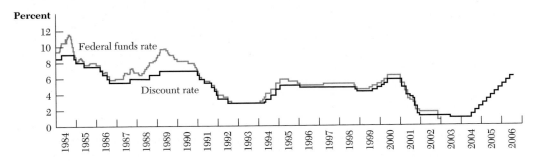

Source: Federal Reserve Bank of St. Louis, March 2007.

16. Why can't the Fed target both the money supply and interest rates?

17. Plot what has happened to the general level of interest rates and to M_1 and M_2 since this book has been published. (This information is published monthly in the *Federal Reserve Bulletin*.) What does the Fed appear to have been targeting?

In the mid-1990s, the press portrayed Greenspan as the "poster boy for the new economy." Economic growth was exploding at a rate of 6.5 percent. The Fed helped the U.S. economy maintain growth in spite of currency crises in Mexico, Asia, Russia, and Latin America, as well as fears of a "Y2K" meltdown of computer systems at the turn of the millennium in the United States and abroad. During this period, a hedge fund called Long Term Capital Management made massive money-losing speculative transactions in financial instruments of the Russian, Asian, and Latin American markets.* The New York Fed helped to avoid panic by orchestrating a bailout of the fund by private companies.

By early 2001, however, many who had sung Greenspan's praises were wondering whether he had lost his touch and reacted too slowly. Greenspan's Fed tried to engineer a "soft landing" for the economy, which would see continuing growth, albeit at a slower rate. The stock market, as described in the next section, declined dramatically and the economy abruptly slowed, with unemployment rising to 6 percent in 2003. Monetary policy kept interest rates low and while business investment lagged, consumer spending continued. Housing construction and mortgage refinancing led some to conclude that a "bubble" might

---

*Hedge funds engage in very speculative trades (or "bets") for wealthy individuals. They remain largely unregulated.

have developed in the housing sector—as housing "wealth" fueled consumption expenditures and consumer borrowing. Economic growth rebounded and late 2004 the Fed initiated policies to target higher interest rates as raw material and oil prices increased inflationary expectations. Through all of this, Greenspan, initially appointed to chair the Fed by President Reagan in 1987, ended his career at the Fed on January 31, 2006, and was succeeded by Ben Bernanke.

Bernanke's Fed

In the fall of 2005, President George W. Bush announced his choice of Ben S. Bernanke to replace Alan Greenspan as Chairman of the Board of Governors of the Fed. The former Princeton University professor has held many Federal Reserve roles and his nomination was easily approved by Congress. Bernanke's Fed continued to target higher fed funds rates through the spring of 2007. Before his appointment, Bernanke favored a program of "inflation targeting," which has been adopted by both the European Central Bank and by the Bank of England. Time will tell if inflation targets become part of U.S. Federal Reserve policy making.

18. Are you convinced that there is a relationship between the money supply and prices? Why or why not?
19. Have inflation rates increased? What is the current inflation rate?
20. Have Federal Reserve policies helped the United States avoid a recession since 2007? Were there two consecutive quarters of negative growth in the economy?

Stock Markets in the Greenspan Era

In early October 1987, the Dow Jones Industrial Average (one measure of U.S. stock market performance) was at 2,700 points. On October 19, 1987, two months after Greenspan was sworn in as chairman of the Federal Reserve Board of Governors, the Dow dropped 508 points, losing $1 trillion in (paper) wealth and 20 percent of its value. By the end of the month, the Dow stood at just 1700.

The Greenspan Fed moved to ensure liquidity of financial intermediaries and reassured the stumbling financial markets with a simple one-line statement reinforcing the Fed's role as a lender of last resort. This was enough to steady markets and begin an era that often characterized Greenspan as legendary—an almost mythical figure who steps in at exactly the right time to reassure the financial system.

Between 1991 and 1996, U.S. productivity boomed, reflecting growth in the high-technology "New Economy" sectors. The Dow Jones Industrial Average and the then-fledgling NASDAQ Composite Index (an index for the NASDAQ, an exchange for smaller, often high-tech companies' stocks) galloped to all-time highs. With the Dow reaching 10,000 points, Greenspan on December 5, 1996, tried to moderate the growth by referring to it as "irrational exuberance."

Nevertheless, money continued to pour into the stock market, which reached a peak on March 10, 1999.

By many accounts, the rapid increases in stock prices during the late 1990s represented a "bubble" in the stock market. Bubbles are nothing new. In the late 1500s and early 1600s, speculation in tulip bulbs drove prices of some bulbs to exorbitant levels. Prices eventually crashed, and many speculators were left penniless. Similarly, as graphed in Figure 17.17, a bubble in the Dow grew and burst between 1924 and 1932, and Japan's Nikkei stock average experienced a bubble between 1982 and 2001. The NASDAQ's bubble also burst. Between the end of 2000 and beginning of 2001, investors in U.S. stock markets lost more than $5.2 trillion of (paper) wealth. Some critics blamed Greenspan for the accompanying slowdown in the economy. We must be careful, however, not to confuse stock market performance with economic performance. The stock market is just one part of the U.S. economy.

Between 2001 and March 2004, the NASDAQ and Dow recovered from their 2001 lows. But, as the Federal Reserve prepared to pare the growth of the money supply and increase interest rates, stock market volatility resumed.

FIGURE 17.17   Stock Market Bubbles

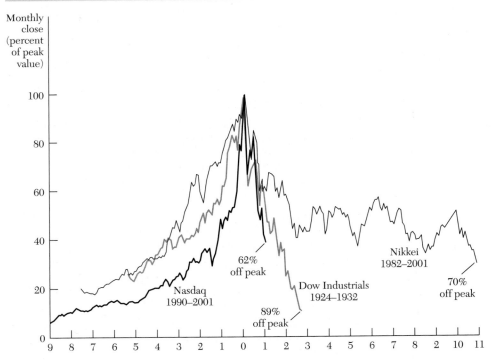

Source: Data from *Investor's Business Daily,* Vol. 17, No. 240, 2001. Copyright © 2001 Investor's Business Daily, Inc. Reprinted with permission.

As interest rates began to rise, concern arose that a "housing bubble" crash might dampen the longer-run future of an economic recovery as consumers face the repayment of high debt levels and potentially lower home values. By the end of 2006, housing prices began to fall and inventories of unsold housing grew significantly. While a down turn was evident at that time, there was no "crash" in the housing market in most areas of the United States. Over the next few years we should know if there is indeed a housing bubble—or just the illusion of a bubble.

The Future of Monetary Policy

Recent changes in both supply and demand factors for money, caused by financial deregulation and innovation, and increased international interdependence have caused concern about the effectiveness of monetary policy. Macroeconomists have debated the effects of these changes on monetary policy. Not only is the institutional framework that facilitates financial transactions changing rapidly, but money itself has been changing with the advent of money market accounts and the rapid movement into Internet transactions. These financial innovations might bring about changes in the responsiveness of expenditures to variations in interest rates and/or the amount of money demanded at various levels of income. John Weinninger, an economist at the Federal Reserve Bank of New York, stated the problem clearly: "If relationships between key variables are changing, then it simply is not practical for policy to focus in some mechanical way on any single variable, whether it be M_1, GDP, interest rates, or even reserves themselves."

During the past years, the Fed has been unable to target effectively, with M_1 exceeding the targets on many occasions. If the predictability and stability of these known relationships continue to deteriorate because of these changes and innovations in the financial sector, monetary policy cannot be as reliable or as predictable as it has been in the past. This will impose additional problems on policy makers as problems of recession and inflation arise.

The effectiveness of monetary policy was questioned during the recession of the early 1990s as well. Economic turnaround was not forthcoming despite lower interest rates in the late 1980s and early 1990, in part because of a credit slowdown or "credit crunch." While the Fed made more money available, financial intermediaries did not lend large sums to businesses and consumers—thus thwarting any chance at economic growth. Borrowers and lenders both apparently shared in responsibility for the credit crunch. Several hypotheses put forward to explain this lack of lending included fallout from the deregulation of the 1980s, hangovers from debt that financed the 1980s, an overinvestment in real estate, and the thrift crisis. Whatever the cause, credit flows slowed. In 1993, low interest rates sent funds into the stock market in search of higher returns.

Furthermore, the role of depository institutions in the economy has shrunk, thus potentially weakening the effectiveness of the Federal Reserve's policies.

TABLE 17.4   Financial Sector Assets

	Year	
	1980	**2000**
Bank and thrifts as % of financial sector assets	49%	21%
Deposits as % of household financial assets	22%	11%
Bank and thrift shares of outstanding credit market debt	43%	22%
Reserve balances with Fed	$27.4B	$7.2B
Reservable deposits		$860.0B
Financial sector assets (potentially reservable)		$35.8T

Source: Data from *FOMC ACCRT*, March 20, 2001, Financial Markets Center, vol. 5, no. 2, p. 8.

Table 17.4 shows this decline between 1980 and 2000 as funds shifted from banks and thrifts to mutual and pension funds. One solution would more closely regulate all financial intermediaries. Former Fed chair Greenspan expressed concern about the declining importance of banks and the growing importance of less-regulated financial institutions: "Public policy should be concerned with the decline in the importance of banking;" "The issues are too important for the future growth of our economy and the welfare of our citizens." As banks have declined in importance, brokerage firms, mutual funds, finance companies, and even hedge funds have grown. During the stock market volatility of 2001 and 2002, firms within these sectors were involved in financial manipulation scandals. Federal and state charges led to discussions of increased regulation, but not Federal Reserve regulation. In a *Wall Street Journal* article "Losing Ground: Banks' Declining Role in the Economy Worries Fed, May Hurt Firms," Kenneth H. Bacon points out that lessening influence could:

◆ Weaken the Fed's ability to influence the economy through monetary policy.
◆ Increase the size and complexity of risks the Fed must get under control in a stock market crash or similar crisis.
◆ Hurt small and medium-sized businesses that depend primarily on banks for loans and financial advice.
◆ Reduce access to traditional banking offices by spurring consolidation among the nation's 8,000 commercial banks.

While this may weaken the impact of monetary policy on the economy, there are additional concerns, including the shifting of risk from the government insuring the public's bank deposits and thrift institutions to riskier and uninsured mutual funds and pension funds funded by defined contributions and undefined benefits. Bacon also noted that

> . . . a paper by Jane D'Arista and Tom Schlesinger contends that all financial institutions should operate under the same regulation, including capital and reserve

requirements and fair-lending standards. At a time when banks say regulation should be relaxed so they can operate more like securities firms, the paper seeks the opposite: the imposition of bank-type regulation over the "parallel" financial system of mutual funds, investment banks and insurers that are performing banking function.

Bacon's July 9, 1993, article observes

. . . when making loans, bankers face capital, documentation and collateralization rules that don't apply to nonbank lenders. In addition, the Fed requires banks to hold noninterest-earning reserves of 10% against checking accounts and other transaction balances. The FDIC imposes at a deposit-insurance premium averaging 24.8 cents (up threefold over four years) on each $100 of domestic deposits. One reason money-market mutual funds can pay depositors higher returns than banks can is that they don't face such expenses.

21. List reasons why economists are concerned that monetary policy is becoming less effective due to the declining importance of banks and other depository institutions directly affected by Federal Reserve actions.
22. Should the public be concerned with the declining importance of banks? Why or why not?
23. What are the opportunity costs of requiring all intermediaries to operate under the same type of regulation?

Still another concern has been the growth of foreign banks in the United States. In 1991, the Foreign Bank Supervision Enhancement Act (FBSEA) strengthened the Fed's control over foreign banks and their branches operating in the United States. The Bank of Credit and Commerce International (BCCI) scandal in 1991 illustrated how foreign-owned banks and their branches could underwrite illegal activities here and abroad. The failure of the British bank Barring and continuing weaknesses in the Japanese banking system underscore these concerns. During the past three decades, the international community has worked to set guidelines for regulating capital and assessing risk with the goal of promoting stability within the international financial system.

Monetary and Fiscal Policy

Models constructed to measure the effectiveness of monetary and fiscal policy yield different results if underlying assumptions used in the models differ. Monetarists emphasize velocity as the mode of transmission, and the Keynesians stress the rate of interest.

Monetarists assume that there can be no effective expansion of fiscal policy unless it is accompanied by an increase in the money supply. Why? The government *must* finance its expenditures with increases in taxes or by debt issue. Either method transfers money from one sector of the economy to another. As government spending proceeds and GDP increases, if the money supply has not grown, consumers and investors will find themselves short of cash and will begin to try to increase their liquidity by selling their financial holdings. This will increase bond sales even further, driving the price of bonds down and the interest rate up. As the interest rate rises, business investors are crowded out of financial markets by the government, so GDP doesn't change. Spending is just transferred from one sector to another.

For Keynesians, however, the reason for government spending is to stimulate an economy in which neither business *nor* households are spending. The government at least gets the process started. Expansionary fiscal policy increases economic activity. This encourages spending by consumers and businesses in the future.

In practice, monetary policy is very effective at slowing the economy but not very effective when used to stimulate economic activity. The presence of an international sector tends to reinforce the income and output effects of monetary policy.

Coordination of Monetary and Fiscal Policy

Monetary and fiscal policy may provide a rather powerful punch when used together to fight inflation or stimulate economic recovery. However, coordinating the two policies may be problematic. Since the Fed determines monetary policy, and fiscal expenditures are in the hands of Congress and the president, policy decisions sometimes offset one another or are not complementary. For example, the Fed reacted to the high inflation rates of 1980 by attempting to reduce the money supply in order to decrease aggregate expenditures. On the other hand, Congress decreased taxes, which increased aggregate expenditures. High interest rates created by the tight money supply tended to counteract the desired investment effects from lower tax rates. The chairman of the Federal Reserve Board now regularly informs Congress of impending Fed action so that there are no surprises, but policies may still offset one another.

Some people have called for a reduction in the Fed's independence in order to achieve greater coordination of monetary and fiscal policies. Critics of this suggestion argue that to have either the legislative or the executive branch of the government control the Fed would make the money supply a political tool—as surely as many fiscal expenditures and taxing decisions already are. They argue that we could expect regular increases in the money supply in election years and decreases after elections. Whatever the solution, an effective economic policy clearly requires that monetary and fiscal policy at least be aimed in the same direction.

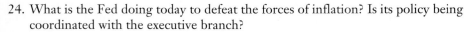

24. What is the Fed doing today to defeat the forces of inflation? Is its policy being coordinated with the executive branch?

25. What kinds of "political mischief" might occur if the monetary authority were controlled by the executive branch?

Conclusion

By examining the institution of money and the institutions that extend and regulate monetary instruments in the economy, we have discovered a rather powerful tools by which the economy has been regulated over the past several decades. This regulation has focused on monetary ease during economic downturns and monetary restraint during periods of inflation. While monetary policy may wave strong economic effects, changing institutions, financial instruments, lags, velocity changes, and internal financing of corporate investment may at times offset or thwart an intended monetary policy action. In the following chapter, we will see how changes in the money supply and demand coupled with fiscal changes affect aggregate expenditures in the economy and the importance of aggregate supply.

Review Questions

1. Explain the differences among the transactions, precautionary, and speculative demands for money. List five factors that influence your demands for money.

2. Why is a barter economy unsuitable for today's world?

3. What is the difference between M_1 and M_2? Is it important to distinguish between them? Does it really matter what the money supply is? Discuss.

4. Suppose you discovered $50,000 of old dollars stuffed in a mattress in your dorm.
   a. What would be the effect of the $50,000 of "new money" on the banking system? Explain.
   b. What would be the effect if you spent the money on a new BMW?
   c. What if you stuffed the money back into the mattress?

5. How do the demands for money relate to Keynesian income and employment theory?

6. Which of the monetary policy tools is used most actively by the Fed? Under what situations would the Fed use another tool?

7. Why do monetarists argue that fiscal policy is ineffective in adjusting the economy?

8. What are some of the factors that inhibit the successful implementation of monetary policy?

9. In what kinds of situations is fiscal policy more effective than monetary policy? In what kinds of situations is monetary policy more effective than fiscal policy?

10. What would be some of the complications of finding the proper mix of monetary and fiscal policy?

11. If the economy were experiencing high unemployment and moderate inflation, what would be the appropriate monetary policy? Why?

CHAPTER EIGHTEEN

Aggregate Demand and Aggregate Supply

THE BIG PICTURE

Introduction

In Chapters 15 through 17, we developed the building blocks of Keynesian macroeconomic theory, including the multiplier, the components of aggregate expenditure, and financial markets. In this chapter we add another building block to our macroeconomic theory: the analysis of prices using a model of aggregate demand (AD) and aggregate supply (AS).

Although Keynes himself pointed out limitations to his theory of aggregate expenditures, the shortcoming of the Keynesian analysis that has most bothered modern economists is the lack of an analysis of prices. In the "real world" economy, since the 1960s, the United States has experienced price changes sometimes larger, sometimes smaller. These changes have occurred not just on certain goods and services, but across the whole economy. In this chapter, we will develop an analysis of aggregate demand and aggregate supply that allows us to illustrate how changes in economic policy or changes in other economic variables affect aggregate prices and output. From this analysis, we will be better able to examine the potential stabilizing effects of policy changes, an issue central to the ongoing debate over stabilization policy.

Aggregate demand is the total quantity of goods and services demanded by households, businesses, government, and the international sector at various prices. The aggregate demand curve illustrates the sum of these sector demands, showing the negative relationship between the aggregate output of goods and services, or real GDP demanded, and the overall price level. **Aggregate supply** is the total quantity of goods and services firms are willing to supply at varying price levels. The aggregate supply curve illustrates the relationship between the aggregate output supplied by all firms and the overall price level. The aggregate demand curve for the economy is downward sloping, while the aggregate supply curve generally illustrates a positive relationship between the price level and GDP, depending mostly on the time frame we choose to examine. Both Figure 18.BP.1 and Figure 18.1 show the relationship between aggregate demand and aggregate supply. Equilibrium is the point where aggregate demand equals aggregate supply.

FIGURE 18.BP.1 Aggregate Demand and Aggregate Supply

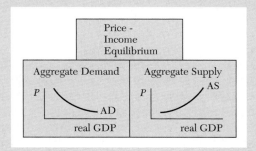

Aggregate Analysis

We will save derivation of the aggregate demand curve for a more advanced course in macroeconomic theory, but we will show logically why the curve is downward sloping and examine economic variables that are reflected by shifts in the aggregate demand curve. Recognizing that in macroeconomic theory, an analysis of supply has historically accompanied one of demand, we will then turn our attention to factors important to aggregate supply. We will also attempt to understand why supply policies are often precarious in their outcome. We will discuss the views of supply-side economists in the 1980s and the results of supply-side policies during the Reagan administration.

Aggregate demand has served as the center of economic theory and policy for the past four and a half decades, and Keynesian solutions have remained at the helm of economic thought and have often been preferred by policy makers. Our analysis of aggregate demand and aggregate supply will allow us to understand the role of economic policy variables as well as of supply shocks and productivity changes on real income and prices.

Aggregate Demand

The aggregate demand curve relates the price level to real output (or real GDP) in the overall economy. It shows how the demand for goods and services varies

FIGURE 18.1 Aggregate Demand and Aggregate Supply

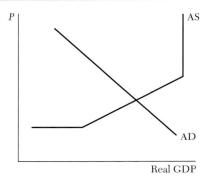

with the price level. This is possible since all points on the aggregate demand curve are equilibrium points in both the money (financial) market and the market for goods and services. Exogenous changes in both the money and goods markets affect the aggregate demand curve and thus prices and real GDP.

Although this particular aggregate demand curve looks like demand curves we saw in Part 3 on microeconomics, it is very different. A price rise is not analogous to a jump in the price of butter that prompts us to switch to margarine or some other substitute. A price increase signals that *all* domestic prices are rising, including the prices of domestically produced substitutes.

Conditions for Goods and Money Market Equilibrium: A Review

Equilibrium positions in the goods market are found at every point on the aggregate demand curve. Recall from Chapter 14 that the components of the goods and services market are

$$C + I + G + (X - M) = \text{aggregate expenditures,}$$

where C is consumption expenditures, I is investment expenditures, G is government expenditures, and $X - M$ is net foreign expenditures (net exports). This market is at equilibrium when aggregate expenditures equal aggregate output of goods and services.

We saw in Chapter 17 that, in the money market, equilibrium is achieved when money supply equals money demand. The aggregate demand curve is derived from equilibrium conditions in both markets. Therefore, at any point on the aggregate demand curve, aggregate expenditures are equal to aggregate output, and money supply equals money demand.

Prices are measured by some weighted price index such as the GDP deflator, and are represented by P on the vertical axis in Figure 18.2. Real income and output changes are represented by real GDP on the horizontal axis. We have

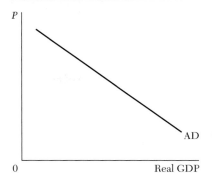

FIGURE 18.2 Aggregate Demand

assumed that the aggregate demand curve is downward sloping, showing an inverse relation between prices and real GDP. While we do not have all the tools necessary to derive this relationship here, we can intuitively show that this relationship is plausible by asking ourselves what happens to aggregate demand when there is a general rise in prices. If we aren't careful, however, we are likely to arrive at an answer that would yield a downward-sloping aggregate demand curve, but for the wrong reasons. Since our experience has been more as consumers rather than as economists, we are likely to conclude that a general rise in prices will decrease the real income of consumers, thus reducing consumption expenditures. Aggregate expenditures for goods and services would decline, leading to a decrease in GDP. But price increases yield additional revenues for producers, which they may share with the household sector through wage increases or higher dividends. If production is unchanged, then income would stay the same, so our assumption about the effect of an increase in the general price level on the goods market is a bit premature.

If, however, we look to the money or financial market, we will arrive at a better answer to our question about the slope of the aggregate demand curve. If there is a rise in prices, and if the Federal Reserve does not increase the growth rate in the money supply, the demand for money will increase, since consumers will need more money to keep their levels of consumption if velocity is constant. (With M constant and P rising, the demand for money increases.) As the demand for money rises, interest rates will rise. (Figure 18.3 shows that in response to an increase in the overall price level, money demand increases from M_{D0} to M_{D1}, and with M_s constant, interest rates rise from r_0 to r_1.) This means that less money is available at every interest rate for investment by the business sector (see Figure 18.4) and for expenditures by consumers. So, with everything else remaining the same, a rise in prices means that the same amount of (nominal) money balances must be used to purchase goods and services at higher prices. Interest rates will be bid up, demand for funds for investment and consumption purposes will fall, and thus aggregate expenditures will fall. This analysis logically gives us the downward-sloping aggregate demand curve and the inverse relation between prices and real GDP. On the graph in Figure 18.5,

FIGURE 18.3 Money Demand with a Price Increase

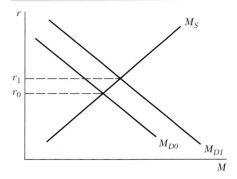

we can see that a price increase from P_0 to P_1 decreases real GDP from GDP_A to GDP_B, a movement from point A to point B on the aggregate demand curve.

Two other relationships explain the inverse relationship between prices and real GDP. As prices rise, the real wealth of people holding money balances declines. Those who are holding money balances cannot purchase the same quantity of goods and services as they did at lower prices, so the demand for goods and services falls, as does real GDP. Secondly, when prices increase in the United States, we can expect net exports $(X - M)$ to decline, since the prices of domestic goods have increased relative to foreign goods. U.S. exports are relatively more expensive, so the international market will demand fewer U.S. exports. Again, price increases will lower GDP—hence the movement from point A to point B in Figure 18.5.

Conversely, a decrease in the price level will raise the aggregate quantity of goods and services demanded. Three reasons account for this: The real interest

FIGURE 18.4 Demand for Investment Funds

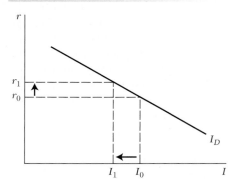

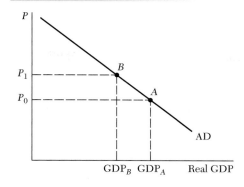

FIGURE 18.5 Movement along the Aggregate Demand Curve

rate falls due to a greater availability of money balances, since the real money supply increases as prices fall. The real wealth of persons holding money balances increases when prices fall. Net exports increase as prices of domestic goods fall relative to prices of foreign goods.

Shifts in the Aggregate Demand Curve

The analysis of aggregate demand allows us to observe how exogenous changes affect aggregate demand and thus the overall price level *and* the level of real GDP. The aggregate demand curve describes the economy in equilibrium in both the market for goods and services and the money market. Any exogenous or induced change that results in a shift in the aggregate expenditures curve or in the demand or supply curve of money will by definition cause a shift in the aggregate demand curve. As we saw in Chapters 15 and 16, with prices remaining constant, increases in government expenditures (G), investment expenditures (I), exogenous consumption expenditures (C), and net exports ($X - M$), as well as tax cuts and an increase in the money supply, will increase income in the goods market and will cause the aggregate demand curve to shift outward to the right. In Figure 18.6, the aggregate demand curve AD_0 shifts to the right to AD_1. At every price level, real GDP is higher on AD_1. Tax cuts or increases in G, C, I, net exports ($X - M$), and the money supply cause the aggregate demand curve to shift to the right, away from the axis, as shown by AD_1 in Figure 18.6. With this shift, at every price level, GDP is higher.

We can now envision the effects of monetary policy and fiscal policy and changes in autonomous spending on price levels as well as on real income and output. Table 18.1 summarizes the effects of policy changes on aggregate demand.

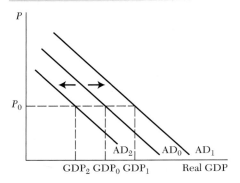

FIGURE 18.6 Shifts in the Aggregate Demand Curve

1. The 2005 federal budget called for further income tax reductions, with the more wealthy receiving greater returns from these cuts. The budget proposal also included increased military spending. Using the preceding analysis of aggregate demand curves, illustrate and explain what these curves predict would happen to aggregate demand.

While we are primarily interested in policy changes that can shift the aggregate demand curve, several non-policy-related factors can cause a shift in the aggregate demand curve. An increase in real wealth will cause an outward shift. When stock market prices rose dramatically in 1999, holders of corporate stock increased their wealth, and their demand for goods and services increased. The increase in housing prices produced the same result. The increased equity in the homes caused homeowners to increase their borrowing and thus increase their demand for goods and services.

Expectations also influence shifts in the aggregate demand curve. If consumers and investors become increasingly optimistic about the economy, aggregate demand may shift to the right. An expectation that the inflation rate will rise will produce the same result, as consumers and investors purchase durable

TABLE 18.1 Effects of Monetary and Fiscal Policy on Aggregate Demand

Effect of Policy	Policy	Effect on Aggregate Demand (AD)
Monetary Policy	Increase in money supply	AD curve shifts to the right.
	Decrease in money supply	AD curve shifts to the left.
Fiscal Policy	Increase in G	AD curve shifts to the right.
	Decrease in Tx	AD curve shifts to the right.
	Decrease in G	AD curve shifts to the left.
	Increase in Tx	AD curve shifts to the left.

goods now while prices are lower than those they predict in the future. On the international front, if real income rises abroad so that foreign citizens have more to spend, we can expect an increased demand for domestic goods and services. Again, the aggregate demand curve will shift to the right. All of these shifts indicate that real GDP is higher at every level of prices, as shown in Figure 18.6.

2. List the conditions unrelated to economic policy that would cause the aggregate demand curve to shift to the left, indicating lower real GDP at all price levels.

Short-run Aggregate Supply

The short-run aggregate supply shows the relationship between the output that is hypothetically supplied by the nation's producers of goods and services in response to changes in the price level. In the short run, producer responses will be restrained by the level of plant or factory capacity available for producing additional output and by the speed at which the prices of inputs or factors of production respond to the increase in the overall price level. Many economists believe that there is a delay between a rise in the general price level and resulting increases in prices for raw materials and labor. We will assume that in the short run, input prices do not change. Our examination of long-run aggregate supply will account for increases in resource prices in response to increases in overall prices.

Producers respond to increases in demand by increasing production, since increases in demand tend to bid output prices up and, with factor costs stable, to increase producer profits. Thus, we must examine the level of plant capacity available in the economy to trace the level of real output (GDP) that can be supplied at various price levels, given increases in demand. Tracing these responses will give us a curve that represents short-run aggregate supply.

If the economy is in a severe recession or depression, plenty of plant capacity will be available for producing additional products. Excess labor and capital will be available for the production process, since by definition, high levels of unemployment and low levels of output mean that greater increases in output (GDP) can be made available without producers incurring large costs. Thus, if the economy were operating at a point such as point A in Figure 18.7, a small increase in demand—to point B—would increase real GDP without an overall price increase or with only a very small increase.

At the other extreme, if the economy is operating near or at full capacity, large quantities of output are already being produced. By definition, at full capacity, no new output can be produced. Producers are literally using every available machine, worker, and plant as much as is possible. At point C in Figure 18.7, an increase in demand—to point D—can only bid up the level of prices. Little or no additional output will be forthcoming.

Most often the economy is operating somewhere between these two extreme possibilities of short-run aggregate supply responses. More normally the economy

FIGURE 18.7   Short-run Aggregate Supply

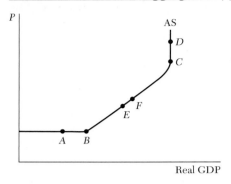

might be at point *E*. At this point, if demand is increased—to point *F*—there will be increased GDP in the form of goods and services, and there will be a modest increase in the overall price level.

The upward slope of the aggregate supply curve is partly due to diminishing returns and partly due to resource and factor costs (particularly fixed wages) rising less rapidly than prices when demand for additional output increases. Moving along the aggregate supply curve illustrates the effect of increased aggregate demand at different levels of output and different price levels. Thus, the aggregate supply curve shows us the price level associated with each level of output, where firms will produce a profit-maximizing output at a fixed wage rate and a given level of productivity.

Causes of Shifts in the Short-run Aggregate Supply Curve

The short-run aggregate supply curve may shift for many reasons, including changes in the labor market, supply shocks, and government policies that affect supply. Positive factors that cut costs, such as technological innovations, will cause the aggregate supply curve to shift to the right. Negative factors, such as rising costs, will cause a shift to the left. Let's examine some conditions that will cause such shifts.

Labor market forces have had and continue to have effects on the aggregate supply curve. Increases and decreases in the labor force are obvious causes of a shift. Over the past four decades, women have entered the U.S. labor force in record numbers. Increases in the labor supply will, of course, increase aggregate supply and shift the curve to the right. Any factor that makes people want to work less—such as attending school, avoiding higher taxes, or pursuing more leisure activities—will cause a shift to the left.

Expectations also cause the short-run aggregate supply curve to shift. If producers expect higher inflation in the future, they will adjust short-run production levels to reflect the expected price hikes. Expected crop failure or surplus will also be reflected in the short-run aggregate supply curve as drought or perhaps freezing weather affects the production level of various crops.

3. If most producers expected prices to rise in the near future, which way would the short-run aggregate supply curve shift? Why? Illustrate with an example.

Most of us are familiar with price changes for domestic and imported resources, another factor affecting the aggregate supply curve. The oil price increases of the 1970s created supply shocks throughout the world, causing a leftward shift in the short-run aggregate supply curve. **Supply shocks** are unexpected events that cause increases in prices. They occur when the cost of producing a wide variety of products increases dramatically, causing the aggregate supply curve to shift to the left and thus push prices upward. During the 1970s, the United States and the world economy experienced a variety of supply shocks, which sent prices soaring. The most noteworthy supply shock occurred in 1973 and 1974, when the powerful OPEC nations placed an embargo (restriction on the import or export of a good) on oil exports. The reduced supply of oil products to many nations of the world severely curtailed production and increased prices, as shown by the shift from AS_0 to AS_1 in Figure 18.8. The price level on AS_1 is raised for each level of real output.

Other, less noteworthy supply shocks have affected the prices and output of many goods and services throughout the world. Price increases of raw materials and/or agricultural products have often been the cause of these shocks. The price increases may be caused by weather—from drought to floods, earthquakes and hurricanes—and by wars, both of which are beyond the control of policy makers. Large, rapid, and perhaps unexpected currency depreciations may also result in dramatic price increases or a supply shock for a nation heavily reliant on imported goods.

FIGURE 18.8   A Supply Shock

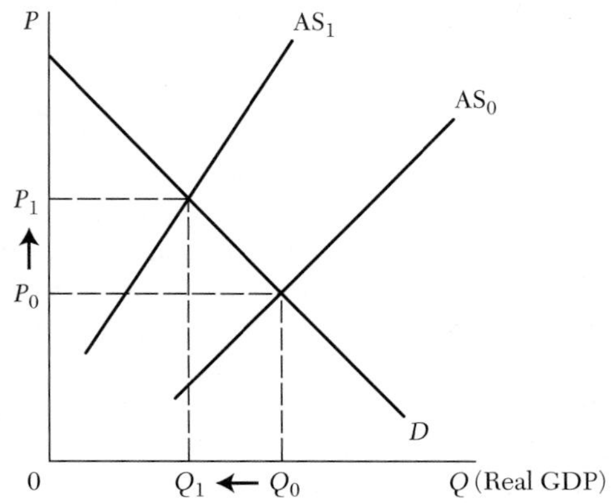

During the 1998–2000 U.S. economic expansion, low prices of imported goods affected the aggregate supply curve. In the late 1990s, many Asian economies, weakened by recession and its accompanying high unemployment, produced and exported goods very cheaply. A strong dollar and weakening Asian currencies ensured that exports to U.S. markets would be priced even lower. These cheap imports pressured U.S. producers to keep prices low so that their products could remain competitive in international markets. The low prices in an increasingly global marketplace served, in effect, as a "reverse supply shock." In contrast, from 2004, through mid 2007 as the U.S. economy grew, price pressures on the supply side were felt in some commodities markets, including copper and oil.

4. List other possible shocks to a nation's aggregate supply.
5. List some other factors that would be the reverse of shocks and would increase the nation's supply.
6. List five ways that the government might increase production of the supply of goods and services to the public (i.e., shift the AS curve to the right).

Long-run Aggregate Supply

Many economists believe that in the long run, the aggregate supply is a vertical line at the full-employment level of output; as new resources and technologies develop, this vertical line shifts to the right. According to this view, in the long run, economic policy will have only price effects unless productivity or technology improves. Before we examine these factors that cause shifts in long-run aggregate supply, we will illustrate how equilibrium is reached using the short- and long-run aggregate supply curves with the aggregate demand curve.

Arriving at Equilibrium

Now that we have introduced the concept of aggregate supply, let's see how changes in aggregate demand will lead first to equilibrium with short-run aggregate supply and then move to an equilibrium on a long-run aggregate supply curve. In our previous analysis in Chapter 14, we assumed that any increase in aggregate expenditures increased real output or real GDP but left prices unchanged. (In Figure 18.9 the entire multiplier effect is seen on the horizontal part of the short-run aggregate supply curve AS.) However, under normal economic conditions, the short-run aggregate supply curve slopes upward. As aggregate demand increases from AD_0 to AD_1, perhaps due to increased government expenditures or decreased taxes, the effect of the expenditure increase is shown as increased real income, GDP, or output; GDP rises from GDP_0 to GDP_1. Moving along the short-run aggregate supply curve AS_0, real GDP increases (from GDP_0 to GDP_1) as do prices (from P_0 to P_1). Equilibrium is

FIGURE 18.9

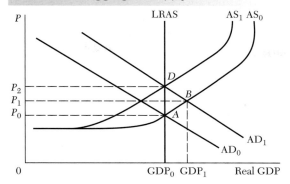

found where $AS_0 = AD_1$ at point B. Equilibrium moves from point A to point B. As the economy reaches its capacity to produce additional goods and services, further increases in aggregate demand push up prices.

Is this a stable equilibrium? No. Firms may be happy with this adjustment, but workers will not be. Prices have increased from P_0 to P_1, so workers' real wages have fallen. Workers will not be satisfied with a reduction in their real wages and will insist on a nominal wage increase during the next round of wage negotiations. Since the short-run aggregate supply curve was derived within the context of a model that assumed nominal wages were set and unchanged, any increase in the nominal wage, which increases producers' costs of production, will cause the short-run aggregate supply curve to shift. Responding to the increase in nominal wages, the short-run aggregate supply curve shifts from AS_0 to AS_1 in Figure 18.9. Now we find our short-run equilibrium position at D, where GDP has fallen from GDP_1 to GDP_0 and P has increased from P_1 to P_2.

If there are no additional exogenous changes, there will be no more tendency for movement in the economy. We can see that the long-run aggregate supply curve (LRAS) is vertical at GDP_0. (If, as we will see later, technology improves in the long run, LRAS would shift to the right, and so would real GDP.)

We examine the short-run aggregate supply curve to see the effect immediately after some fiscal, monetary, or other stimulus to aggregate demand has been introduced, before the economy has time to adjust to these changes in the long run. Firms will adjust their production levels based on the changes in aggregate demand. They will try to increase output to meet the increased demand at a higher price level, since, as we learned in Chapter 8, supply is a function of price. Short-run effects are particularly important to economists who see stabilization policy as important to fine-tuning the economy, and to an

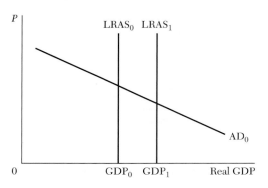

understanding of the economy that we face from day to day. Perhaps Keynes expressed the concerns of those economists interested in the short run best when he remarked, "In the long run, we are all dead."

Shifts in the Long-run Aggregate Supply Curve

Since the long-run aggregate supply curve is not responsive to price changes, it is vertical. Any shift in the long-run aggregate supply curve will reflect a change in the quantity of resources available, a change in the productivity of resources, a change in technology, or perhaps some institutional change that affects resource efficiency or productivity. Each of these will increase or decrease output at all price levels and thus cause the LRAS curve to shift. These factors are mostly insensitive to price changes and are not *immediately* affected by short-term macroeconomic policy.

Productivity

An important source of shifts in the long-run aggregate supply curve comes from increases and decreases in labor **productivity,** or the amount of output produced by a unit of input, in this case, a laborer. Increased productivity shifts the LRAS curve to the right, indicating more output at each price level. The importance of productivity growth is that it allows for noninflationary increases in real GDP, as shown in Figure 18.10.

Productivity is difficult to measure. One problem is the measurement of actual output. As the nation's labor force has shifted from industrial production to service activities, physical output is more difficult to measure. Approximately 18 percent of the nation's nonagricultural workers produce a tangible product. The rest produce services that can be measured in dollars only by examining the

TABLE 18.2 Growth of U.S. Output per Person-Hour Worked, 1973–2005

Period	Average Annual Growth
1973–1980	0.6%
1980–1981	0.7%
1981–1990	0.9%
1990–1995	2.2%
1995–2000	3.1%
2000–2005	3.6%

Source: Bureau of Labor Statistics, 2000, 2006.

number of hours worked. Furthermore, the lack of accounting for quality improvements in manufactured goods has in the past understated U.S. productivity figures. Increases in the numbers of temporary workers paid by temp agencies rather than firms tends to overstate productivity increases.

In the 1970s and 1980s, economists and politicians were concerned with the apparent decline in the growth rate of U.S. productivity. Gains in labor productivity, measured as output per person-hour worked, appear to have been sluggish until the 1990s. While the average annual growth of output per worker was 1.9 percent between 1950 and 1973, Table 18.2 shows it grew 0.6 percent annually between 1973 and 1980, and it averaged less than 1 percent until the 1990s. In contrast, between 1960 and 1973, productivity increased by more than 4 percent annually in Germany and by more than 5 percent in Japan. Since 1979, productivity increases have averaged between 2 and 3 percent in Germany and 3 and 4 percent in Japan (see Figure 18.11).

Recent trends in the United States show productivity gains have slowed after averaging 3.4 percent annually between 1995 and 2005. Productivity normally increases during a recession, so this increase would have been expected in the early 1990s. During the second half of the 1990s, increases in investment spending, particularly in information and communications technology, are believed to have sparked further increases. Historically, productivity increases as labor has more capital to work with, more education, and more training. Despite rapid growth rates in output per worker in Japan and Germany, U.S. workers remain the most productive in the world, with the average worker producing some $28 worth of goods and services per hour and more than $49,000 worth of goods and services annually.

Economists often attribute slowdowns in worker productivity to a slowdown in innovation and technological change. Other culprits that have been cited as contributors to slowdowns in productivity growth include slower growth of private and public investment expenditures, flagging funding for research and development efforts, increased costs of health and safety regulations, and high energy prices during the 1970s. In 2006, slowing productivity rates were partly attributed to cost-cutting options. Aggressive cost-cutting after 2001 sparked productivity

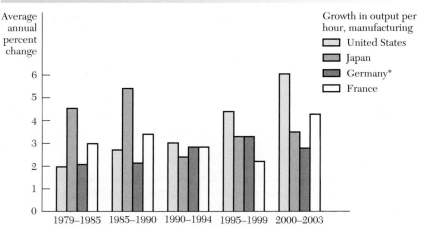

FIGURE 18.11   Output per Manufacturing Employee in Selected Countries

Source: Bureau of Labor Statistics "International Comparisons of Manufacturing Productivity," 1950–2005.

increases, but further cost reductions are limited. A reduction in investment in high tech has also been linked to a slowing of productivity growth.

7. Why would slower growth of investment expenditures contribute to decreases in productivity growth rates? How would increased energy costs contribute?

Labor and capitalists, however, sometimes hold different views of policies to increase productivity. Corporations would suggest tax cuts for business to stimulate capital investment and other incentives for research and development and thus shift the aggregate supply curve to the right, providing lower prices at each level of output. Labor, on the other hand, would argue for training programs and higher wages to improve productivity growth. That approach requires that output increase faster than the costs of training and pay increases.

Princeton economist William Baumol and his associates have argued that while productivity is a concern, it should be viewed in a long-run rather than a short-run context, and that increases in U.S. and U.K. productivity growth over the past decade must be sustained to have a long-run impact, since rising productivity and resulting economic growth can help rising debt levels. In discussing recent trends in productivity in their article "Pause Stirs Concern That Growth in Productivity May Be Flattening," Mark Whitehouse and Tim Aeppel write:

Productivity matters for everyone, because it provides the essential ingredient that makes nations rich. When companies produce more for each hour their employees work, they can pay higher wages or reap bigger profits without having to raise prices. Annual productivity growth of 2 percent would more than double inflation-adjusted wages over 40 years, all else being equal. Add another percentage point in productivity growth, and wages would more than triple.

—The Wall Street Journal, November 3, 2006, p. 1

Productivity, along with increases in the labor force, increases in capital, and changes in technology, has a powerful effect on aggregate supply and on the nation's standard of living. Therefore, now that we have developed the theory of aggregate supply and understand how various factors influence it, we must examine how our theory of supply relates to economic policy.

Aggregate Supply and Economic Growth

Thus far in our examination of macroeconomics we have seen how changes in aggregate demand and in aggregate supply affect real GDP, our primary measure of economic performance. Economic growth, remember, is defined as the change in real GDP from one year to the next and is in part determined by the growth in the labor force (or quantity of labor), by physical and human capital accumulation, and by advances in technology. Politicians and policy makers often discuss plans to increase the economy's growth rate, but even a seemingly slow rate of growth has a profound impact over the long term. Compounded over many years, growth at a rate of just 1 or 2 percent contributes greatly to the size of a nation's economy.

Figure 18.12 shows real growth in the U.S. economy over the past century. Over that period, real GDP per person grew on average at about 2 percent annually. Between 1960 and 1973, GDP growth per person averaged 4.2 percent, but between 1975 and 1985, the growth rate fell to 1.1 percent per year. It then rebounded a bit, averaging 2.1 percent between 1990 and 2004.

Factors that cause changes in medium- and long-term economic growth are the same factors that cause shifts in the long-run aggregate supply curve: changes in labor productivity and discoveries of new technologies or innovations. What is responsible for these? Often, investment (funded from saving) in new capital or public investment in a nation's infrastructure will increase worker productivity. Investment in human capital has historically improved productivity as well. This investment may take the form of public-sector expenditures on education and training or private expenditures on worker training.

New technological innovation may be fostered by investment expenditures on research and development—for instance, Defense Department research and development expenditures that led to the

Internet*—or simply "learning by doing." Once a technical innovation that may improve productivity occurs, investment in capital (perhaps through equipment expenditures) employing this technology or innovation makes it available to the labor force. There is a crucial link between technology, science, and knowledge; advances in one serve as a catalyst for advances in another.

FIGURE 18.12   Economic Growth in the United States, 1895–2005

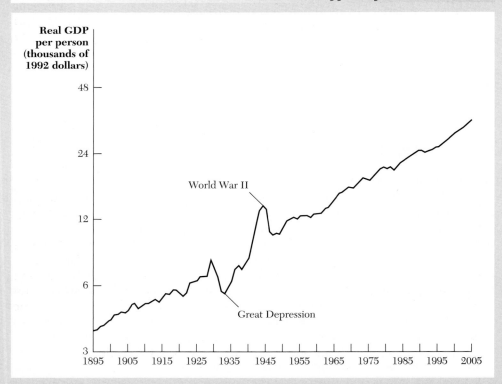

Sources: Data from Christina D. Romer "The Prewar Business Cycle Reconsidered: New Estimates of Gross National Product, 1869–1908," *Journal of Political Economy* Vol. 97 (1989); *National Income and Product Accounts of the United States; Historical Statistics of the United States Colonial Times to 1957* (U.S. Department of Commerce, 1960); *Economic Report of the President*, 1999; Michael Parkin, *Economics*, 5th ed., Addison Wesley, 2005. p. 463; and www.gov/fls/flsgdp.pdf, 2006.

---

*Internet technology is a product of Department of Defense expenditures during the Cold War. The Advanced Research Projects Agency (ARPA), set up by the Eisenhower administration in 1957, began exploring computer communication, and in 1969 ARPAnet linked four research universities. During the 1970s ARPAnet expanded, and other networks were established—again, mostly linking universities. Research reports and articles were read and discussed on e-mail (electronic mail) and electronic discussion groups. In the 1980s, establishment of a communication standard, or protocol, allowed for the development of the Internet.

Supply-side Economic Policy

In 1975, a handful of academic economists, together with politicians and journalists, began to reexamine the problems of the U.S. economy from a different perspective than mainstream Keynesian economics. The focus of the reexamination was on the "supply side." As we have seen previously, the orthodox Keynesian approach to the problems of inflation and unemployment focused on the demand side of the economy. If the economy showed signs of recession or depression, the verdict was that the economy was suffering from insufficient aggregate demand. If there were inflationary trends, then aggregate demand was too robust. Supply-side economists argued that those policies tended to be inflationary; once the government had initiated spending for particular programs, spending was hard to reduce.

Rationale for Supply-side Economics

Neither Keynes nor the classical economists totally ignored the supply side of the market in their economic analysis, but the policies Keynesians designed were predominantly aimed at either shoring up a weak aggregate demand or calming one that was excessive. To them, income or output was a function of aggregate demand.

Proponents of the supply-side approach argued that federal, state, and local governments had stifled production and incentive in the United States with their emphasis on policies leading to increased spending, taxation, and regulation. They argued that higher tax rates (particularly progressive taxes) and increased government regulation reduced incentives, while spending fueled inflation.

Supply-side advocates argued that increased tax rates inhibited production and reduced output as people substituted leisure activities for productive activity and did more work in which they had less skill. This would reduce the time spent in more productive economic activities, which because of higher taxes were less financially rewarding, and lead to an inefficient allocation of economic resources. Further inefficiencies would occur if tax-deductible goods became less desirable than those that were nondeductible. Finally, advocates of a supply-side approach pointed to the declining productivity in the United States and argued that lower corporate tax rates would generate more business investment and thus increase productivity.

This theory also predicted increased saving and perhaps increases in the rate of saving. Supply-side economists argued that lower tax rates would induce more saving in the private sector; the tax reductions would leave people more income from which to consume and save. If the government also reduced its spending, additional investment funds would become available. Greater investment should lead to lower interest rates and economic growth.

In summary, advocates of the supply-side approach to economic policy saw tax rates as extremely important in determining total output in the economy. They believed that decreases in tax rates caused individuals and businesses to substitute such productive activity as work, investment, and specialization for nonproductive activities. This would result in a more efficient allocation of resources. Total economic output would rise with lower tax rates.

8. How do taxes directly affect supply? Illustrate on a graph of aggregate supply and aggregate demand how a tax cut works.

Supply-side Critics

Some economists sympathized with the notions put forth by advocates of the supply-side approach but noted that policies to stimulate supply-side increases take long periods of time before having noticeable effects on the economy. Indeed, they added, some of those policies might increase aggregate demand at the same time.

Another supply-side argument that came under fire was the assertion that lower tax rates would provide incentives for people to work more, since they could "keep" more of their income. Critics of this notion argued instead that higher tax rates had forced some people to work more than they would like to simply to maintain their standard of living. These people already had two jobs or worked overtime to keep the same level of income in the face of high tax rates. It was hard to conceive of them working more, yet easy to envision their working less if the tax rate fell.

Tax cuts for businesses had critics as well. Although in theory the cuts should stimulate investment, the critics questioned whether these funds would in fact be spent on new, productive activities. They cited corporate mergers in the 1980s, such as the purchase of Montgomery Ward by Mobil Oil, and Nabisco by R. J. Reynolds, as examples of corporate spending that created no new jobs or productive output for the nation.

Finally, the supply-side aspects of 1980s economic policies tended to shift the distribution of income. Wealthy individuals benefited far more than middle- and lower-middle-income groups. In absolute-dollar amounts, the benefit to those earning less than $10,000 a year was minimal, if not negative.

The Federal Reserve set the recovery of 1983–1984 in motion by pumping up the growth rate of the money supply in 1982, at the same time Congress increased military spending and enacted tax cuts. This stimulated a *demand-led*, rather than a supply-led, recovery, although business tax cuts did kick in somewhat higher levels of investment as the recovery mounted. The effects of supply-side policies of the early 1980s had decreased economic growth rates while increasing unemployment and budget deficits. Tax incentives to individuals and businesses had unexpected outcomes: decreases in the personal saving rate and investment expenditures as a percentage of national income.

THE BIG PICTURE

And The Big Picture Concluded

In this chapter we have completed the construction of the aggregate supply–aggregate demand model that allows us to analyze and show the effects of prices when economic policies are implemented. While the aggregate demand–aggregate supply graphs resemble the market supply graphs we developed in Chapter 8, this resemblance is where the similarity stops. Information about money markets, goods and services markets, and economic policy is reflected in the aggregate demand–aggregate supply analysis, telling us how those markets respond to economic events, including policy decisions. We can now assess aggregate output and price levels for the economy. Figure 18.BP.2 outlines the path we have taken to develop this model to this point in Part IV.

FIGURE 18.BP.2   Construction of the Aggregate Demand–Aggregate Supply Model

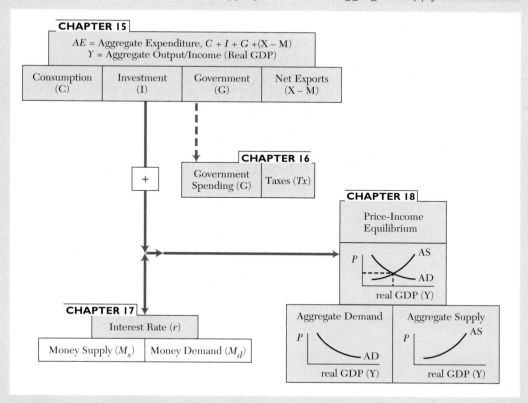

Conclusion

Because price stability is one of the three macroeconomic goals, we need to be aware of price changes that may result from supply shocks—such as oil or energy shortages and productivity changes. With this in mind, we move to Chapter 19, where we examine stabilization policy and the trade-off between inflation and unemployment. This chapter illustrates The Big Picture in action.

Review Questions

1. How is monetary policy related to aggregate demand?

2. What incentives do supply-side policies attempt to improve? Are incentives important in economic analysis?

3. Explain the relationship between supply-side tax policies and "demand-side" policies. Are the two interrelated? Explain.

4. Why is it difficult to increase output and thus expand economic growth through supply-side policies?

5. What was the last supply shock to occur in the United States? Explain its significance.

6. What were some of the reasons for the slowdown in productivity in the late 1970s and early 1980s? Increases in the 1990s?

7. Does it matter whether productivity is viewed in the short or long run? How does one increase productivity?

CHAPTER NINETEEN

Unemployment, Inflation, and Stabilization Policy in a Global Economy

 Introduction

As the United States entered the twenty-first century, it was experiencing the longest period of sustained growth on record. But as the economic slowdown in 2001 was exacerbated by the terror attacks on the World Trade Center and the Pentagon, policy makers began again to reconsider policies concerning unemployment and inflation. During the years of economic growth in the 1960s, some economists declared the business cycle "dead," only to have it roar back in the 1970s and 1980s. From the economic experiences of those decades, economists not only learned about trade-offs, but they also discovered how economic variables might respond to policy.

The previous chapters dealing with macroeconomic theory and policy have touched only slightly on the controversy that surrounds most policy decisions. We have hinted that there is some conflict between the monetarists and the Keynesians about solving these problems and that there might be other contending opinions. Conservatives, liberals, and radicals see different sorts of problems and different sets of solutions. One issue, which we shall focus on in the first part of the chapter, is the trade-off between the macroeconomic goals of unemployment and inflation. An even more troublesome situation happens when inflation and unemployment occur at the same time, resulting in what economists call **stagflation.**

We will begin by examining unemployment and inflation, the trade-off between the two, and the implications for stabilization policy. From there we will outline the views of several competing schools of economic thought to see how (or, in some cases, if) we can effectively use macroeconomic policy to reach societal goals.

The Trade-off: Unemployment and Inflation

Given the economic goals of price stability, full employment, and growth, Keynesian macroeconomic policy prescriptions advise us that increased spending and/or increases in the money supply may be necessary to attain full employment, with price increases as a side effect. On the other hand, if policy makers attempt to curb inflation through monetary and fiscal measures, income will fall—and so will employment. We seem to be between a rock and a hard place. But an even more difficult problem emerges when the economy develops high inflation as well as high unemployment rates.

The Phillips Curve

At one time, economists believed they had a rather simple answer to questions dealing with the trade-off between full employment and price stability. Economist A. W. Phillips studied the British economy for 100-plus years and found a rather stable relationship between increases in the wage rate and the rate of unemployment. High rates of unemployment were associated with low wage increases, and wage increases appeared to be related to the general rate of inflation. In the 1960s, U.S. economists Paul Samuelson and Robert Solow related rates of price increase to rates of unemployment and found that inflation and unemployment were inversely related. High inflation rates were associated with low unemployment rates and vice versa. When plotted, this downward-sloping relationship between the inflation rate and the unemployment rate came to be known as the **Phillips curve.**

If the Phillips curve is valid, then the matter of priorities seems to be rather straightforward. Economists could present a menu of the various trade-offs that were possible—perhaps a 4 percent inflation rate with a 5 percent unemployment rate, or a 2 percent inflation rate with a 6 percent unemployment rate. Through the democratic process, the electorate would establish which combination it desired, and the policy makers would fine-tune the economy to obtain this trade-off. If the economy had 5 percent inflation and 4 percent unemployment but the electorate and policy makers desired 4 and 4.5 percent rates, then economic policy should be ever so slightly more restrictive.

During the 1960s, the United States had one of its longest periods of uninterrupted economic growth, inflation averaged around 2 percent (although it accelerated to over 5 percent by the late 1960s), and the unemployment rate declined from 6.7 percent in 1961 to 3.5 percent in 1969. (Figure 19.1 graphs these rates, which are listed in Table 19.1.) But the 1970s and early 1980s presented a vastly different picture. In 1971, the unemployment rate climbed above 5.9 percent while the inflation rate rose to nearly 5 percent. By 1981, the unemployment rate reached 7.6 percent, and inflation was 10.3 percent. As inflation dropped to between 3 and 4 percent, unemployment peaked at 9.6 percent in 1983 and declined somewhat to 7.5 percent in 1984. The idea of a simple trade-off between inflation and unemployment had broken down. It took increasingly higher levels of unemployment to reduce inflation by increasingly smaller amounts.

Despite the generally inverse relationship between unemployment and price pressures, the trade-off appeared to worsen, leading some economists to suggest that the Phillips curve had shifted. By "connecting the dots" between the annual points plotted between 1960 and 1968 and between 1969 and 1974 on Figure 19.1, we show a shifting Phillips curve. After that time, connecting the dots cre-

FIGURE 19.1 The Phillips Curve and the U.S. Economy, 1960–2005

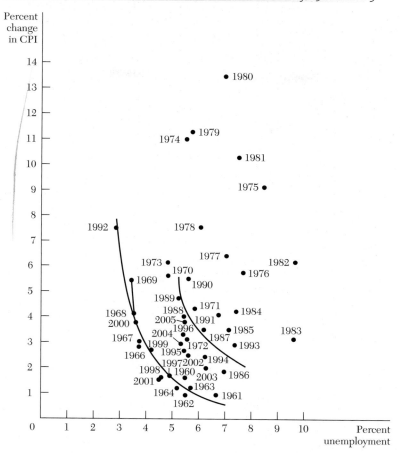

ates an upward and then a downward spiral, indicating a longer upward move-ment in the 1970s and early 1980s, followed by a more recent downward trend in the late 1980s and the 1990s, renewing the idea of a trade-off.

Some economists attributed shifts in the Phillips curve in the 1970s to supply shocks the economy received during those years. These included the very high increases in oil prices caused by the OPEC embargo, increased prices of agri-cultural products, and the increased prices of foreign goods brought about by the fall in the dollar's value in 1973. This period generated critiques of the Phillips curve, with Edmund Phelps and Milton Friedman arguing that infla-tionary expectations might be generating the higher levels of inflation and unemployment.

The 1990s brought the U.S. economy low levels of unemployment and infla-tion, accompanying a record number of months of sustained economic growth. As economic activity slowed in 2001–2003, higher unemployment levels peaked

TABLE 19.1 Inflation and Unemployment in the U.S. Economy, 1950–2005

Year	Inflation Consumer Price Index*	Inflation Year-to-Year Change	Unemployment Rate	Year	Inflation Consumer Price Index*	Inflation Year-to-Year Change	Unemployment Rate
1950	24.1	1.3%	5.3%	1978	65.2	7.6	6.1%
1951	26.0	7.9	3.3	1979	72.6	11.3	5.8
1952	26.5	1.9	3.0	1980	82.4	13.5	7.1
1953	26.7	0.8	2.9	1981	90.9	10.3	7.6
1954	26.9	0.7	5.5	1982	96.5	6.2	9.7
1955	26.8	−0.4	4.4	1983	99.6	3.2	9.6
1956	27.2	1.5	4.1	1984	103.9	4.3	7.5
1957	28.1	3.3	4.3	1985	107.6	3.6	7.2
1958	28.9	2.8	6.8	1986	109.6	1.9	7.0
1959	29.1	0.7	5.5	1987	113.6	3.6	6.2
1960	29.6	1.7	5.5	1988	118.3	4.1	5.5
1961	29.9	1.0	6.7	1989	124.0	4.8	5.3
1962	30.2	1.0	5.5	1990	130.7	5.4	5.5
1963	30.6	1.3	5.7	1991	136.2	4.2	6.7
1964	31.0	1.3	5.2	1992	140.3	3.0	7.4
1965	31.5	1.6	4.5	1993	144.5	3.0	6.8
1966	32.4	2.9	3.8	1994	148.2	2.6	6.1
1967	33.4	3.1	3.8	1995	152.4	2.8	5.6
1968	34.7	3.7	3.6	1996	156.9	3.3	5.4
1969	36.7	5.5	3.5	1997	160.5	1.7	4.9
1970	38.8	5.7	4.9	1998	163.0	1.6	4.5
1971	40.5	4.4	5.9	1999	166.6	2.7	4.2
1972	41.8	3.2	5.6	2000	172.2	3.4	4.0
1973	44.4	6.2	4.9	2001	177.1	1.6	4.7
1974	49.3	11.0	5.6	2002	179.9	2.4	5.8
1975	53.8	9.1	8.5	2003	184.0	1.9	6.0
1976	56.9	5.8	7.7	2004	185.9	2.7	5.5
1977	60.6	6.5%	7.1	2005	195.3	3.4	5.1

*The Consumer Price Index (CPI) measures changes in the "cost of living" (1982 – 1984 = 100). The inflation rate is the percent change in CPI.

Source: *Economic Report of the President*, 2006, pp. 335, 353, 357.

at 6 percent in 2003 while prices remained low. As the recovery gained momentum in 2004, job growth was initially sluggish and inflationary pressures edged prices upward. The economy continued to grow at an accelerated rate through 2005 and early 2006. Growth slowed to modest levels in late 2006 as prices continued to rise. In addition to concerns about levels of employment and price stability, significant concerns about trade deficits and other structural problems remained. In a nation with one of the world's highest standards of living, homelessness persists, and the infant mortality rate remains among the highest of the industrial nations. Continuing increases in poverty levels, especially among the young, are particularly troublesome, as are the growing numbers of workers without health insurance. Even in periods of low inflation and unemployment, these troubling economic issues remained unsolved.

Inflation

We have defined inflation as a rise in the general price level. We can expect price increases to accompany a growing, viable economy, but if these price increases are larger than increases in productivity or real output would dictate, they are inflationary. Table 19.1 indicates what has happened to prices in the past half century, measured as changes in the Consumer Price Index (CPI). These numbers reflect revisions that government economists have made to the way they measure inflation, beginning in 1995. The revisions lowered the level of inflation from earlier years by about 0.68 percentage points per year. The purpose of these changes was to provide a more accurate measure of inflation experienced by consumers. Note the lower rates of inflation in recent years.

1. On the average, how much would something that cost $200 in 1967 cost in 2005? How much have prices increased since you were born?

2. Does any information in the table surprise you? If so, what surprised you? (If not, what met your expectations?)

From our analysis of aggregate demand and aggregate supply in Chapter 18, we can see that any action that shifts the aggregate demand curve to the right or the aggregate supply curve to the left causes price increases and possibly inflation. We can classify the prevailing types of inflation according to the possible cause of each: demand-pull inflation, cost-push inflation, and expectations-generated inflation. These types of inflation can occur simultaneously or independently.

Demand-pull inflation is a rise in the price level attributed to excessive aggregate demand. Aggregate demand can increase for a number of reasons, including increases in autonomous consumption, investment, government spending, net exports, and the money supply or decreases in taxes or saving. We can view this graphically in Figure 19.2, where AS represents the aggregate supply curve, and AD represents aggregate demand. All are plotted with respect to real output (real GDP) and the general price level (P). A rightward shift of the aggregate demand curve from AD_1 to AD_2 increases both prices and real output in the short run as real GDP increases from GDP_0 to GDP_{fn} and prices increase from P_0 to P_1. As income levels increase, the demand for goods and services will rise. Initially, as demand increases, prices are bid up, output increases, and more laborers are hired to produce products. If resources are fully employed and aggregate demand continues to rise, as illustrated by a shift from AD_2 to AD_3, there is no increase in GDP, only an increase in prices. From our analysis in

FIGURE 19.2 Demand-Pull Inflation

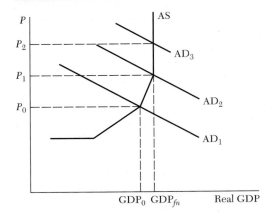

Chapter 18, we know that the higher aggregate demand in the face of limited supply will cause shortages of goods and services and the need for additional labor to increase production. The increased demand for goods and services, raw materials, and labor may even exceed the capacity to generate new output.

A simple remedy for inflation generated by increased aggregate demand is to cut back on spending and the money supply. The same technique can thwart inflationary expectations. Reductions in the growth rate of the money supply are particularly effective (and painful).

Cost-push (or supply) **inflation** puts the responsibility for price increases on rising costs of production. From the analysis of demand and supply in Chapter 8, we found that as production costs increased, the supply curve shifted to the left, leading to higher prices. A few of the cost factors that might cause a shift in the supply function are wages, raw material prices, interest rates, and profits. In Figure 19.3 higher costs bring about increases in price as well as a reduction in output. In the long run, producers will be able to reduce wages because of

FIGURE 19.3 Cost-Push Inflation

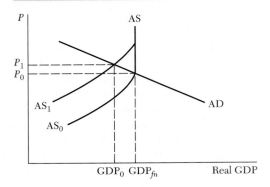

higher levels of unemployment, and output will return to the original level (GDP_{fn}).

Cost increases can come from many places, including increases in raw material prices, labor costs, and higher profits. As market structures have become more concentrated, some large corporations have gained more ability to administer prices for their own benefit—which in most cases means to increase prices and profits. During the 1970s, resource shortages pushed the prices of some goods upward. The lack of supply created a bottleneck in the production process, with limited amounts of raw materials forthcoming, even at higher costs.

Unlike aggregate demand inflation, cost-push or supply inflation has no simple remedy. Resource shortages are difficult to prevent. Cartels that withhold raw materials are hard to bargain with. Controls placed on wages and prices, and other types of incomes policies, do not seem to work very well, when viewed in a historical context. Indeed, controls often lead to contrived shortages, as suppliers hesitate to continue production when they cannot recoup rising costs.

If businesses respond to higher output and profits sparked by an increase in aggregate demand by hiring additional workers, more jobs become available, and unemployment falls. If the current rates of inflation are expected to continue, *expectations-generated inflation* may occur. Workers, trying to restore the purchasing power of their wages, press for increases based on inflationary expectations. Once workers attain higher wages, the aggregate supply will decrease to reflect the increased costs to firms. With these higher costs, profits fall, and firms cut back on output. No real GDP falls back to its original level, but prices are now at a higher level.

While expectations may seem an unlikely candidate for economic analysis, inflationary expectations are at times important in explaining inflation. Each time we expect inflation, we tend to generate inflationary price increases. Yale economist William Nordhaus stated this well:

> Inflation is a highly inertial process. It will go along to whatever rate it has been going at until it is shocked to a different level. . . . From 1973 to 1980 we had 6 to 9 percent inflation built into the wage and price system. It [higher inflation] was built into contracts. It was built into expectations. The recession [1980–1982] beat it down to 5 percent and now we have lower inertial rates.

Inflationary expectations directly affect aggregate supply. As wages increase because workers expect inflation, costs to firms increase. Firms then pass on these increased costs to consumers in the form of higher prices. On the demand side, expectations of higher interest rates generate consumer and business borrowing and expenditures. These activities increase aggregate demand and drive up prices.

When inflationary expectations are low, inflation is easier to moderate with monetary and fiscal policy. In the 1970s, when inflationary expectations were high, the fiscal policies employed were largely ineffective. They resulted in increased unemployment without significantly lower inflation. From the late 1980s through the late 1990s, expectations remained low and thus aided in maintaining stable prices. As the U.S. and industrial economies expanded from

2004 through 2006, inflationary expectations increased as rising oil and commodity prices and consumer demand pushed prices upward.

The Impact of Unemployment and Inflation

Although policy makers and politicians would prefer to have the low inflation *and* low unemployment characteristic of the late 1960s and late 1990s, when unemployment or prices begin to rise, policy makers must respond to those changes. Decisions must be made about which goal, full employment or price stability, is preferable. Economists studying this question have found that higher unemployment and higher inflation affect different groups in different ways.

According to a study by Princeton economist Alan Blinder, former member of the Federal Reserve Board and Council of Economic Advisors, and Northwestern University economist Rebecca Blank, the unemployment rate for teens increases at two times the base rate, and unemployment for the elderly increases at about half the base rate. Blinder and Blank also made the following observations:

> The burden of unemployment is distributed unequally across age, race, and sex groups. In particular, nonwhite and young workers are more severely affected. On the other hand, female and older workers—who are also typically low-wage workers—are not as sensitive to changes in general unemployment levels.

They conclude, "The business cycle is not neutral in spreading the burden of unemployment. Certain workers experience much larger increases in unemployment when the general economy turns down than others." Blank and Blinder also found that whites, males, and the middle-aged receive a larger share of unemployment compensation than do unemployed workers in other categories.*

Inflation particularly hurts creditors and those on fixed incomes, while borrowers in general benefit. The poor seem to be hurt less by inflation than the rich. Prices generally rise for consumers at all income levels, but so do wages and salaries. However, the income from and worth of wealthy people's assets are more readily eroded by inflation.

3. What effect will supply shortages have on the trade-off between inflation and unemployment when unemployment is increasing?

4. How might inflation benefit a person who borrows money? Is this always so?

---

*Rebecca M. Blank and Alan S. Blinder, "Macroeconomics, Income Distribution and Poverty," in Sheldon H. Danziger and Daniel Weinberg, eds., *Fighting Poverty: What Works and What Doesn't* (Cambridge, MA: Harvard University Press, 1986), p. 191.

Stabilization Policy: An International Perspective

Unemployment and inflation concern policy makers throughout the world's industrial and developing nations. The 1990s brought generally low rates of unemployment and inflation in the United States, Germany, and Japan, but several other industrial nations experienced substantially higher unemployment. Table 19.2 shows recent unemployment and inflation rates in some of the nations that actively compete with the United States in international markets.

Many of the European nations listed in the table have chosen more aggressive social programs than those in the United States for dealing with the effects of unemployment. These more generous programs have at least partially resulted in higher taxes. As Figure 13.3 illustrates, the United States, along with Japan and Korea, has a relatively lower tax burden than the other industrialized nations. At the same time, many of these nations have also experienced higher government deficits.

Macroeconomic Solutions: The Alternatives

While the Keynesian aggregate expenditures model we have explored commends the use of monetary and fiscal policy in stabilization efforts, other economic models and theories question the effectiveness of intervention. The dilemma is what to do—not so much about inflation and unemployment but about government budgets, trade deficits, economic and productivity growth rates, and the myriad of other economic problems that surround us in the context of a complex and increasingly interdependent world economy. Traditional Keynesian remedies, declared deficient during the stagflation of the 1970s, returned with renewed vitality to the New Keynesians by the end of the 1980s.

Ever an evolutionary theory, Keynesianism is becoming more eclectic, encompassing some of the better ideas presented by other schools of macroeconomic thought in the 1980s. These include a larger framework on which consumers base their expectations of the future and a reaffirmation that, along

TABLE 19.2 Unemployment and Inflation Rates in Selected Countries, 2004

Country	Unemployment Rate	Change in Consumer Price Index
United States	5.5%	2.0%
Australia	5.5	2.3
Canada	7.2	1.8
France	9.6	2.1
Germany	9.8	1.7
Italy	(NA)	2.2
Japan	4.7	0.0
Sweden	6.3	0.4
United Kingdom	(NA)	3.0

Source: *Statistical Abstract of the United States,* 2006, pp. 872, 881.

with fiscal policy, monetary policy is important to stabilization efforts. As Keynesians returned to the limelight, popular movements of the 1970s and 1980s lost favor. To better understand the status of stabilization policy, we will briefly summarize some of the theories and policies of contending schools of thought and review their standing in the early twenty-first century.

Monetarist Solutions

Monetarists believe that growth rates of money control inflation and business cycle activity. Monetary policy, therefore, is the most effective way to stabilize the economy, although most monetarists prefer a nondiscretionary rule rather than small changes in policy that aim to fine-tune the economy. Monetarists contend that only money matters, since increases in money allow fiscal policy to be effective in the long run. (Actually, it is monetary policy that is effective.) The monetarists focus on the long run and avoid short-run solutions.

Boosted by the failures of Keynesian theory and policy to explain and counter the stagflation of the 1970s, the monetarists entered the 1980s with their theories at the top of the hit parade. But even the 1970s and certainly the following two decades dealt monetarists a cruel blow. Predictions fell by the wayside. Velocity was unstable, as was the demand for money. The money supply proved hard to target. Inflation of the 1970s proved not to be a monetary phenomenon, and inflation predicted in the 1980s failed to materialize. The monetarists fell from favor. Keynesians, however, accepted the need to use monetary policy with fiscal policy to achieve stabilization targets.

Supply-side Solutions

Although supply-siders fell from favor at the end of the 1980s, the election in 2000 of George W. Bush helped them regain some power in policy-making circles. In the 1980s, wishful thinking proved no match for the economy that resulted from supply-side policies. Marginal tax rate policies designed to stimulate investment and incentives brought about increased unemployment, decreased saving and investment, large budget deficits, and increased income and wealth inequality. We discussed supply-side economics at length in Chapter 18 and will not repeat those arguments here. Economists accept the supply-side idea that marginal tax rates can help to increase incentives and investment, but most economists see them having a rather small effect on overall economic activity. Supply-side stabilization policies should not be disregarded, but their stabilization effect is small.

New Classical Solutions

The New Classical or Rational Expectations school of macroeconomic thought gained support and prestige during the 1970s and early 1980s. Its abstract theoretical and mathematical model, based on classical assumptions of pure and perfect competition, appealed to a number of academic economists. New Classical economists argue that firms and workers acquire, assess, and utilize information very quickly and rationally. For example, in our prior discussion of inflation, economists subscribing to the New Classical view would argue that as soon as laborers realized policy makers were trying to stimulate demand, they would adjust their consumption and wage demands, making the "short-run" Phillips curve trade-off even shorter and making the long-run aggregate supply and vertical Phillips curves the only appropriate ones for examining policy actions. Short-run stabilization policy would be useless, since rational people would react immediately and "outguess" the policy. Only policy "surprises" would be effective. Rational individuals would use all information, not just past data about prices or income. Policy makers could introduce or curb inflationary expectations simply by appointing a new Federal Reserve chair known to be easy or tough on inflation. New Classical economists would rely on perfectly competitive markets—ones without collusion, price fixing, or monopoly—to chart the best course for the economy.

When economists examined the evidence from the late 1970s and 1980s, New Classical theories fell short. According to the theories, inflation could be reduced without an increase in unemployment. With the Federal Reserve decreasing the growth rate of the money supply, economic actors should have adjusted their inflationary expectations downward, avoiding high levels of unemployment. But that period showed the short-run Phillips curve to be alive and well, and Rational Expectations remains a theory without an accompanying reality.

Post-Keynesian (Managed Capitalist) Solutions

Post-Keynesians, distrustful of solutions that rely solely on market activity, and the long-run timing of such solutions, and relying heavily on the role of demand in the economy, recommend adoption of an incomes policy to determine an annual noninflationary rise in all types of income. This would involve controls over the rates of increase in personal and business income. Tax incentives would assure compliance. The post-Keynesians believe that government and business should jointly make decisions for long-run public and private investment, and that employment and growth policies are central to a recovery and economic restructuring.

In the 1980s, post-Keynesian alternatives such as wage and price controls faded from sight as means to combat inflation or reduce unemployment. In the postwar era, however, every president until Ronald Reagan at some point flirted with controls or guidelines. Nevertheless, outside of the political machismo derived from controls, there has been little evidence that the particular types of controls instituted have been effective.

Feminist Economists' Solutions

Feminist economists note the failure of present economic models to predict and address real-world concerns of women, children, and men. They seek to go beyond formal economic models based on what they see as oversimplified assumptions about human behavior. For example, feminist economist Nancy Folbre has pointed out that while Adam Smith noted the role that competitive markets play in our lives (see Chapter 4), the expanding role of the market has sometimes come at the cost of care for others. Smith considered this problem but, according to Folbre, "didn't take it seriously, because he optimistically assumed that people were not all that selfish. He considered love of family, duty to others, and loyalty to country the hallmarks of an advanced civilization. The book that launched his career was entitled *The Theory of the Moral Sentiments*. In it he wrote:

> However selfish soever man may be supposed, there are evidently some principles in his nature, which interest him in the fortune of others, and render their happiness necessary to him, though he derives nothing from it, except the pleasure of seeing it.

Folbre, too, considers a more caring macroeconomics, where societal goods other than wealth are factors:

> Extending family values to society as a whole requires looking beyond the redistribution of income to ways of strengthening cultural values of love, obligation, and reciprocity. . . .
>
> We could encourage greater civic participation, offering tax credits and other incentives for the provision of care services that develop long-term relationships between individuals and communities. We could discourage residential and cultural segregation by class and ethnicity. We could defend and enlarge our public spaces. Our educational institutions could encourage the development of caring skills and community involvement. Among other strategies, we might invite young people to repay the money invested in them through national service rather than simply through taxes.
>
> Policies designed to promote care for other people appear unproductive only to those who define economic efficiency in cramped terms, such as increases in GDP. The weakening of family and social solidarity can impose enormous costs, reflected in educational failures, poor health, environmental degradation, high crime rates, and a cultural atmosphere of anxiety and resentment. The care and nurturance of human capabilities has always been difficult and expensive. In the past, a sexual division of labor based upon the subordination of women helped minimize both the difficulties and the expense. Today, however, the costs of providing care need to be explicitly confronted and fairly distributed.
>
> —Nancy Folbre, *The Invisible Heart: Economics and Family Values*,
> New Press, 2001, pp. 229–230.

Feminist perspectives on economics, such as the one seen here, often expand the scope of the traditional meaning of stabilization policy, pushing it beyond indicators such as inflation and unemployment rates.

Radical Solutions

Radical economists argued that the stagflation of the 1970s was symptomatic not only of a failure of Keynesian theory and policy but also of a fundamental breakdown of U.S. capitalism. Radicals viewed U.S. capitalism as experiencing a long-term structural crisis, explained not by factors external to the economy but by the business cycle. A radical critique of Keynesian theory and policy challenges the "theory of the state," with the state as the legitimate arbiter of societal conflicts resulting from interest groups' political behavior and lobbying. Arguing that the state consciously guides the economy and cyclical instability in order to serve the needs of the dominant economic class, Raford Boddy and James Crotty summarize the functional analysis of a recession in the business cycle:

> It is the economic function of the recession to correct the imbalances of the previous expansion and thereby create the preconditions for a new one. By robbing millions of people of their jobs, and threatening the jobs of millions of others, recessions reduce worker demands and end the rise of labor costs. They eventually rebuild profit margins and stabilize prices. During recessions inventories are cut, loans are repaid, corporate liquidity position is reversed. All the statements of Keynesian economists to the contrary notwithstanding, recessions are inevitable in the unplanned economy of the United States because they perform an essential function for which no adequate substitute has thus far been available.
>
> —Raford Boddy and James R. Crotty, "Who Will Plan the Planned Economy?" *The Progressive*, February 1975.

Radicals see increases in concentration and specialization of production by domestic and multinational corporations as expanding both their political and their economic power. An increasingly symbiotic relationship between government and business explains the structural transformation of U.S. capitalism since World War II, prohibits the possibility of genuine democracy in the United States, and clearly depicts an underlying class character of government functions and policies. Radicals view stabilization policies as outside the interests of workers and the democratic process.

Conclusion

We must increasingly adapt our theory and policy within the context of the existing U.S. and world economies, finding solutions that are effective within this context. The U.S. economy is far different from what it was in the post–World War II era. The workforce is changing, and the economic base, which was continually regenerated through economic growth, is no longer industrial. Additionally, policy decisions must reflect the fact that the U.S. economy in this century is greatly dependent on the other nations of the world. As government leaders plan for economic growth in the United States, they must do so within a world context. Today around 10 percent of the products made in the United States are exported to other nations. Exports plus imports made up about 20 percent of the U.S. GDP in 2004, compared with 12.4 percent of GDP in 1970 and less than 10 percent in the 1960s. If the economies of U.S. trading partners are unhealthy, we cannot expect the U.S. economy to remain vigorous.

This chapter completes our discussion of macroeconomics. We have seen that the Keynesian approach to economic policy has carried us a long way from the classical approach. Yet problems still exist, and new approaches may be needed to deal with future problems. Many of these issues are increasing our attention toward macroeco-

nomics and the functioning of specific markets. Before we look further at policy, however, we need to broaden our perspective and see what is happening in international economics. An understanding of the global arena is necessary to appreciate the full complexity of macroeconomic problems.

Review Questions

1. What is the basis for the trade-off or inverse relationship between inflation and unemployment? Why can't there be zero unemployment and zero inflation?

2. Do you think fighting inflation is more important than fighting unemployment? Why or why not?

3. What competing theories explain inflation in the economy?

4. What structural elements in the economy limit the effectiveness of fiscal and monetary policies?

5. How does avoiding a boom avoid a recession? What is the resulting impact on inflation?

6. What are the main schools of thought with respect to macroeconomic stabilization policy? What are the main issues of contention? Does the recent macroeconomic performance of the U.S. economy suport the ideas of one schoool more than another?

THINKING CRITICALLY

Spend me to the Moon

In examining macroeconomic theory and policy, we have seen how and why both monetary and fiscal policies are important to economic growth and stabilization. While at times complicated by the increasing globalization of economic activity and fluctuations beyond U.S. borders, stabilization policies, when employed, have had some success in calming national and international markets. As you might expect, opinions about macroeconomic goals and the policies the government or the Fed should pursue to accomplish them are often linked to belief systems (as we learned in Chapter 1). We understand how monetary and fiscal policy works. We understand the limitations and the strengths of monetary, spending, and taxation policies. But one of the most often-asked questions is, What should U.S. or Fed policy be? In answering this question, conservative, liberal, and radical perspectives play an important role in establishing the dialogue and the parameters of discussion.

Between 1999 and 2000, economists representing every perspective applauded the Fed's use of monetary policy to sustain a buoyant and growing economy (although some believed even higher growth could have been generated with lower interest rates). However, economists from each paradigm criticized the Fed's failure to recognize hints of recession in early 2000 and its tardy response. And, in 2004, many questioned whether or not the Fed once again was slow to recognize inflation expectations. While there is some agreement among economists about the effect that expenditures have on GDP (and on employment and prices) there is little agreement about who should do the spending—businesses, consumers, or the government—or just whose taxes should be cut or increased. There is also disagreement about the priority of economic goals and objectives. Some prefer targeting full employment, while others would rather focus on inflation. Some economists, including Jamie Galbraith at the University of Texas, focus on links among factors, such as how increased income inequality tends to signal economic downturns in the overall context of unemployment and inflation. (For more information about this linkage, visit the Utip Inequality Watch Web site at utip.gov.utexas.edu.)

As the economy slowed in late 2000, with growth and unemployment nudging upward, some economists (including those in the Bush administration) argued that tax cuts were important and necessary for the continued well-being of the economy. While highly critical of the projected effects of the Bush cuts on income distribution, some radicals argued that the initial cuts were not large enough, and that payroll taxes as well as income taxes should be cut to ensure economic growth.

Some supporters of tax cuts have argued that smaller deficits or surpluses encourage more government spending. Some conservatives view politicians as resembling children given extra money on a visit to the local candy store: unable to restrain themselves from spending the surplus. Given half a chance, this argument goes, politicians would spend any excess revenues on new programs or expansion of existing programs. Over past decades, persistent and ongoing deficits have effectively squelched serious public policy discussions about new spending programs—after all, when can nations "afford" to discuss innovative policies focusing on public goods?

Over the years, one group of economists has as a goal continued reduction of structural deficits and paying down the accumulated federal debt. They focus on the short- and long-run effects of lower interest rate costs on the federal budget and the economy. To them, the opportunity cost of a large deficit is high.

Other economists, such as the late Robert Eisner, a past president of the American Economic Association who taught at Northwestern University, have argued that part of the federal deficit amassed from government spending can be seen as a good thing when viewed in the context of public investment expenditures. Eisner argued, "Much of the debt goes to pay for physical assets—roads, buildings, schools, the defense system—which ought to be separated, as is done by corporations, into a capital budget." He further argued that "budget deficits not only do not inhibit real growth but also that deficit spending is what promotes national growth, prosperity and savings."

So what should a macroeconomic policy aimed at long-term growth look like? As you might expect by now, economists (and politicians) are of at least three different minds on this question. One group, favoring tax cuts, argues that by putting funds into the pockets of taxpayers, greater consumer spending will stimulate business investment, innovation, and long-term growth. Yet even among those favoring tax cuts there are disagreements over who exactly should receive the tax advantages. Should the benefit fall to wealthier taxpayers, middle or lower income groups? Certainly tax cuts will stimulate economic activity, but is it the best way to stimulate long-term growth?

Certainly not, argues another group, pointing out that tax cuts and spending used separately or together are fine to reverse cyclical downturns in economic activity—but they note that structural, not cyclical, deficits have left the United States burdened with a large public debt that may slow down long-term growth. Interest payments must be made on the debt and deficits potentially generate higher interest rates from government borrowing in times when monetary authorities are restraining monetary growth. Critical of the advocates of tax cuts, this group argues that the resulting reduced government revenues simply add to structural deficits. Tax cuts may not have expiration dates and may not be changed after the cycle has reversed. (They also remind us that the political leaders in the United States have shown little fiscal or budgetary restraint in curbing expenditures despite the reduction in revenues.) Their argument, then, is that minimizing or eliminating structural deficits and "paying down" or repaying cyclical deficits during economic upswings (or booms) leads to lower interest rates—thus stimulating long-term economic growth.

A final group argues that neither deep tax cuts nor "buying" lower deficits will ensure long-term growth. They argue that government spending in areas such as education, science, and technology inspires innovation producing long-term investment payoffs. Indeed, in his book *The Internet Galaxy*, Manuel Castells writes about ARPANET, the predecessor of the Internet:

> However, to say that ARPANET was not a military oriented project does not mean that its Defense Department origins were inconsequential for the development of the Internet. For all the vision and all the competence these scientists displayed in their project, they could never have commanded the level of resources that was necessary to build a computer network and to design all the appropriate technologies. The Cold War provided a context in which there was strong public and government support to invest in cutting-edge science and technology, particularly after the challenge of the Soviet space program became a threat to U.S. national security.

In excerpts from the article, "Forget Bush and Gore; Our Economy Needs Another Khrushchev," Barry Bluestone, professor of political economy at Northeastern University, continues the debate in the tradition of Professor Eisner—but with a twist. Bluestone argues that the great growth in technology generating the productivity surge in the late 1990s was initiated not by Reagan, Clinton, or Greenspan, but by government expenditures that started during the Cold War era. (The Cold War began at the conclusion of World War II and ended in 1989 with the fall of the Berlin Wall and the collapse of the Soviet Union.) These expenditures resulted in defense projects and a space program, which brought miniaturization, computer technology, Teflon, and the Internet, among other innovations. Bluestone argues that the vast expenditures on research and development necessary to fund such projects can be generated only through the deep pockets of the government. Research and development budgets of individual companies—while large when added together—are simply too shallow and unfocused to yield impressive and prolonged results. He also argues that emphasis on education and training in science and mathematics had an enormous impact on today's economic expansion, and that too little interest in these areas bodes ill for the future. So, argues Bluestone, it is not tax cuts or deficit repayments but investment expenditures in science and technology, that stimulate long-term economic growth.

On the other hand, David Leonhardt provides an outline of some of the "country's big economic problems," in a November 8, 2006, *New York Times* article. While Bluestone points to the "deep pockets" of the government, Leonhardt focuses on areas he sees as needing specific attention and focus of economists, lawmakers, and the general public. With so many major economic problems looming on the horizon, some economists wonder if we should be running budget surpluses to prepare for future outlays.

Exercises

Read the excerpts from the Bluestone's article along with the Leonhardt article, and then answer the following questions.

1. In what ways are Bluestone's arguments similar to Schumpeter's analysis of long waves of economic cycles? How long are the time lags in cycles as predicted by each economist? How would each economist stimulate the economy to

yield such technical advances? List the ways macroeconomic policy can stimulate growth. Are any of these policies consistent with Leonhardt's concerns?

2. Look at recent articles or information about the telecom industry, which after explosive growth and huge investments in capital during the late 1990s faced grave economic difficulties when the tech bubble crashed. Contrast this to the development of the first telephone network by AT&T—a government-protected monopoly. Using information in Chapter 8 about competitive and noncompetitive markets, could different government policies in these two eras have yielded different outcomes? Explain.

3. Could the policies Bluestone recommends be used to stabilize the economy? Explain. Can the concerns highlighted by Leonhardt be dealt with using Bluestone-type recommendations? Explain.

4. Use the Keynesian-cross diagram and the model of aggregate demand and aggregate supply to show the effects on GDP and prices of spending of the sort Bluestone recommends. How would the multiplier effects work?

5. Bluestone believes that an emphasis on math and science education during the Cold War advanced today's developments in science and technology. Are you a science or a mathematics major? Are you planning on enrolling in a number of science and mathematics courses during your undergraduate years? Why or why not? What is currently happening to math and science enrollments? Who is receiving Ph.D.s in the sciences and mathematics? What jobs are available for scientists and mathematicians?

6. Eisner and Bluestone seem to think that if the government accumulates deficits to fund expenditures that advance society, we should simply consider the future return to the private sector (and perhaps resulting surpluses) to be a cost of "doing the public's business." Others, particularly groups such as the Concord Coalition, see deficits as bad at all times. Examine Bluestone's arguments, and take a look at information from the Concord Coalition (www.concord.coalition.com), then assess your own position on deficits.

7. In the debate over government tax and expenditure policies, what underlying assumptions of conservatives, liberals, and radicals inform their positions, as detailed in Bluestone's article?

8. Which of the problems Leonhardt discusses is the most pressing? Explain. Does "solving" one problem exacerbate another? Explain.

Forget Bush and Gore; Our Economy Needs Another Khrushchev

Barry Bluestone

... the conventional wisdom holds that it took three initiatives to restart the American growth machine. The first was Reagan's effort to get government regulation and social spending under control beginning in the 1980s. The second was President Clinton's getting the deficit under control after 1993. And the third was the amazing prowess of Federal Reserve Chairman Alan Greenspan in keeping inflation under control despite strong consumer demand and extraordinarily low unemployment.

In the bad old days, according to this logic, regulations undercut corporate intentions to invest, while public borrowing forced up interest rates to the point that borrowing became too expensive. The threat of inflation dampened enthusiasm for new capital improvements. Consequently, productivity suffered and economic growth slowed.

The annual growth in the nation's real gross domestic product fell from 4.4 percent in the 1960s to 3.2 in the 1970s to 3.0 in the 1980s and finally to only 2.3 percent during the first half of the 1990s. Only *after* Clinton and Congress moved decisively to reduce the federal deficit, and only after Greenspan snuffed out any hint of inflation, could the economy grow again.

That story sounds plausible, and the timing seems exquisite. Yet it's mostly wrong. The best data tracking the U.S. economy reveal that corporations were already investing heavily before the 1990s even though deficits were soaring and we were still worrying about inflation. Moreover, the investments were paying off, the proof being that productivity completely rebounded in the United States' manufacturing sector by the mid-1980s. It was the service sector that was dragging down overall productivity growth, but even in that labor-intensive sector, productivity began to pick up by the early 1990s. So even before we reined in federal deficits and stopped inflation cold, the economy was perched to take off.

Our rapid growth today has its roots in a technological revolution that has been underway for nearly three decades. Since it takes so long for business to move up the "learning curves" of new technologies, and often longer still to diffuse those technologies throughout the economy, there has always been a long lag time between the introduction of innovations and their payoff in the marketplace.

After the introduction of the steam engine in the early nineteenth century, it took nearly two decades for the new technology to yield a growth premium. Only after years of tinkering with that revolutionary technology and teaching a generation of mechanics how to use it did the steam engine provide for a sustained period of economic growth. The same lag pattern occurred between the introduction of the electric motor at the end of the nineteenth century and the realization of long-term growth we witnessed at the beginning of the twentieth century.

The lag phenomenon has recurred with the revolution brought about by the integrated circuit, the computer, and sophisticated software. It took more than two decades for the information-age technology to become sufficiently user-friendly that it could revolutionize production in nearly every goods-producing industry and in the service sector. During the same period, we were educating a work force to operate these marvels. As a result, productivity is now rising at better than 3 percent a year—three times faster than during the early 1990s. Tied to a labor supply growing at 1 percent annually, we have seen better than 4 percent growth for the past five years, every bit as high as we enjoyed during the booming post–World War II era.

Whom do we have to thank for all this? Reagan? Clinton? Greenspan? A more likely candidate is Nikita Khrushchev. Behind the information-age revolution were investments the federal government made beginning decades ago in basic research, education, and training. Khrushchev, the podium-thumping leader of the Soviet empire, challenged the United States to a nuclear arms race and then a space race beginning at the end of the 1950s. We took that challenge.

Massive computing power stuffed into the cramped quarters of missile cones was needed to guide ICBMs and rockets. The government, therefore, paid for the development of the first integrated circuits and microprocessors. Software was needed for the instruction sets for those minicomputers, and the government paid for that as well. The personal computer and all that followed were the direct descendants of those federally sponsored Cold War research projects. Later, it was the Department of Defense's investment in the ARPANET that led to the modern-day Internet.

Without those investments, today's ubiquitous e-commerce would never have come about—or at least it would have been delayed by decades. Moreover, money the federal government poured into science and math education after the launch of Sputnik in 1957 was critical for preparing a generation of scientists and engineers who developed all the new technology.

Alas, Khrushchev is gone, the Cold War is over, and Americans refuse to lavish money on the civilian side to anywhere near the extent we once did on the military. As a result, the federal government has been unwittingly destroying vital elements of the public-private research partnership.

The good news is that the Clinton administration included in the fiscal year 2001 budget a nearly $3-billion increase in research funds—including a $1-billion boost in biomedical research at the National Institutes of Health and a much-larger-than-usual $675-million increase in support for the National Science Foundation. On the education front, the administration called for $450 million more to reduce class size and $1 billion to improve teacher quality. Across a battery of other school programs, the administration would add several billion more in school construction funds and financial aid for college students.

The bad news is, even if the Republican-controlled Congress had approved the entire Clinton budget, this would be but a drop in the bucket. Constrained by the number-one goal of paying down the federal debt as fast as possible, the amount spent on federal research and education has been plummeting, and these new initiatives would do little to reverse that downward trajectory. Back in the mid-1960s, federal spending on research and development was equivalent to 2.15 percent of the gross domestic product. Today, it has fallen to only .8 percent. Over the same period, federal spending on education as a proportion of the GDP has declined by almost half, from 1.07 percent to .56 percent. If *all* of President Clinton's spending plans for education were implemented over the next five years, the share of discretionary spending by the federal government allocated to this vital area would increase from just 5.0 percent to 5.8 percent—and basic research would fare no better. As a percentage of GDP, both education and basic research would continue to decline.

It would be nice to think that the private sector could make up the difference. But increased cost pressures from global competition and the deregulation of such industries as telecommunications have made it more difficult for private firms to set aside funds for basic research. Such investment is highly speculative, the payoffs are distant, and it is often impossible to restrict the benefits to those who paid for the research in the first place. As a result, while private research support is growing, only a small fraction pays for the kind of basic research that powers technological revolutions. And, of course, the private sector finances only a small portion of basic education.

So where is Khrushchev when we need him? We need something like the civilian equivalent of the Cold War to assure us of a continuing stream of technological breakthroughs that can fuel sustained prosperity.

There are many candidates for such government-sponsored research investments. Mounting a fully financed "war on cancer" and other medical scourges is one. Adding to the research on nanotechnology and biotechnology are two more. Certainly we could use more research into alternative fuel supplies and other efforts aimed at the problem of global warming.

On the education front, the federal government could underwrite a program to assure every child in the United States a prekindergarten year of schooling to help them get off on the right foot. Further expansion of federal backing for science and math education could be important as well, especially given the fact that the proportion of college students majoring in science and engineering has not increased since the 1970s.

There is surely enough federal surplus from the booming economy to reduce the federal debt and still invest more in our future. Unfortunately, the tax-cut nostrums of the Republicans and the debt obsession of many Democrats divert our attention from the growing federal-investment deficit that could ultimately condemn the nation to slower growth.

Source: Barry Bluestone, "Forget Bush and Gore; Our Economy Needs Another Khrushchev," *The Chronicle Review*, 1/5/01, pp. 311–312. Copyright © Barry Bluestone. Used with permission.

Election's Over. Now to Tackle The Realities.
David Leonhardt

We could use some fresh economic ideas right now.... [H]ere is a breakdown of the four biggest [issues facing the U.S.]:

THE DEFICIT -- When the latest budget numbers came out this summer and they showed a drop in the estimated deficit, I called some former Bush aides -- Glenn Hubbard, Greg Mankiw, Doug Holtz-Eakin, Andrew Samwick -- to give them a chance to gloat. But not one of them was in the mood.

They all said that the decline was obscuring a much bigger problem: the enormous long-term deficit caused by future Social Security and Medicare payments. "The real big problem is a decades-long generational issue," Mr. Mankiw said. "That basic challenge often gets forgotten when the short-term situation is getting better."

Fortunately, imagining a bipartisan agreement on Social Security isn't all that difficult. Small groups of economists from both parties, including Mr. Samwick, have already negotiated some hypothetical deals.

Republicans might compromise by agreeing to increase the amount of income that is subject to the payroll tax -- now $94,200 -- and by cutting benefits for high earners. "We have a problem," Mr. Hubbard says, "and the most well-off among us ought to bear the biggest burden."

Democrats could then clear the way for an expansion of personal retirement accounts. Even people who hated Mr. Bush's failed plan for personal accounts should be able to agree that more individual savings would be a good thing.

HEALTH CARE -- There are two main problems with American health care today, and they tend to get confused. The first is that far too many people don't have health insurance. If you are not insured through your job, buying a policy is incredibly expensive, because insurers know that the people in the market for a policy are the ones who expect to get sick.

A few states -- like Arkansas, Massachusetts and New Mexico, all with ambitious governors -- are trying to address this problem by pooling together their uninsured residents into one buying group, much as a company spreads its medical costs across sick and healthy workers. It's a great idea.

But it won't solve the second problem: soaring health care costs, which are a much larger part of the long-term deficit than Social Security. Reining in these costs will require cutting back on expensive drugs and procedures that haven't been proved to make a real difference. This issue is about the toughest one around, and I would be surprised if its political moment had yet arrived. We'll probably have to wait for health care spending to go even higher.

GLOBAL WARMING -- Two weeks ago, Sir Nicholas Stern, a top economics official in the British government, released a report that should change the debate over climate change. Sir Nicholas and his staff concluded that without sharp reductions in greenhouse gases, global warming -- and the droughts, hurricanes and floods that it brings -- will probably reduce the world's economic output by at least 5 percent a year. "The benefits of strong and early action far outweigh the economic costs of not acting," the Stern report stated.

In this country, neither political party is serious about the problem. Instead, both have trotted out laundry lists of futuristic alternative-energy programs. No one can know which ones will actually work, and the planet will keep getting hotter in the meantime.

There are only two ways to slow global warming. One is to raise the cost of putting carbon dioxide into the atmosphere, through an energy tax. From Alan Greenspan and Mr. Mankiw on the right to Al Gore and Larry Summers on the left, there is enormous support for this idea, which would do far more to spur research than the current hodgepodge of alternative-energy tax credits.

That said, none of the big advocates of an energy tax are running for office right now. The second idea -- less efficient but perhaps more politically palatable -- relies on regulations like higher mileage standards for vehicles and limits on carbon use by companies. Senator John McCain says he favors such caps. I suspect we'll hear more from him in the next couple of years.

LIVING STANDARDS -- Ben Bernanke, the Federal Reserve chairman, recently noted that sweeping economic changes threatened the livelihoods of many workers, and he warned that rising inequality could set off a political reaction. Henry M. Paulson Jr., Mr. Bush's Treasury secretary, said that "many Americans simply aren't feeling the benefits" of the current expansion. Nancy Pelosi, the Democratic leader in the House, puts it this way, "For the first time in generations, parents worry that their children will not be better off than they are."

So where are the bold new solutions?

Republicans like to talk about education, skipping over the question of how better schools could help struggling workers in their 40s and 50s. Democrats have become fond of trade barriers, which don't exactly have a good record of lifting a country's living standards.

I'm not suggesting the answers are easy. But if we can agree that globalization and technological innovation have made the country richer -- and they have, enormously -- then we should be able to talk about how the winners can do a better job of compensating the losers.

An immigration policy that lets in fewer low-wage workers, but more doctors and scientists, might be a start, notes Benjamin M. Friedman, the author of "The Moral Consequences of Economic Growth." So might tax cuts for the middle class -- paid for by tax increases on the well-off, who have done very nicely of late.

There will, inevitably, be huge fights over the solution to any one of these issues. At times, the fights will get nasty, and people will come forward to decry the lack of civility in American politics. So be it. Economies, like democracies, can thrive without civility. They don't thrive if they try to ignore their biggest problems forever.

Source: David Leonhardt, "Election's Over. Now to Tackle the Realities," *ECONOMIX*, Business/Financial Desk, Sec. C, Col. 1. Copyright © 2006 The New York Times Company.

Part Five

International Economics and Finance

With each passing decade, the nations of the world grow increasingly interdependent. When weighing various macroeconomic policy options, U.S. decision makers must consider international economic conditions. In the past, economists were primarily concerned with domestic monetary and fiscal policy and any perceived impact international activities might have on these policies. As far as international issues were concerned, decision makers examined the value of a nation's currency, or its exchange rate; the balance of payments; and perhaps protectionist tendencies that might exist in the world economy. Today, however, more complex questions arise involving volatile exchange rates; the economic power of an increasingly unified Europe; the integration of Eastern Europe and the former Soviet Union into the Western market system; China and India's rapid economic growth; the changes in various international institutions such as the International Monetary Fund, the World Bank, and the World Trade Organization; the outcome of the UN's Millennium Development Goals focused on reducing global poverty and arresting the global HIV/AIDS pandemic; the world's challenge to reduce its dependence on nonrenewable energy, especially petroleum, and to develop renewable and sustainable energy resources; and the world's need to address the pressing environmental challenges from global warming and climate change to issues dealing with fishing, grazing, soil, water, food, air pollution, and biodiversity. All of this is in the context of global instability and uncertainty related to the U.S. war in Iraq and terrorism. These trends and questions challenge the dynamics of twenty-first-century globalization.

In Chapter 2 we saw how global economic activity has become more integrated by technological change transforming production, finance, trade, information systems, and communications throughout the world. These changes have caused economic and financial markets to become more integrated, and this increased interdependence has affected national political decisions, social and environmental policy, and culture.

In Part 5 we will explore all of these issues and questions. Chapter 20, "International Trade and Interdependence," examines; the recent history of world trade, the role of trade in the U.S. economy, the theory of free trade, the case for protectionism, and the recent experience with trade integration and liberalization. Chapter 21, "International Finance," explores the concepts of the international balance of payments and exchange rates including the recent history of the U.S. dollar. Chapter 22, "Economic Problems of Developing Nations," focuses on the reality of global poverty, the basic economic problems of developing nations, and competing schools of thought on development and underdevelopment. Finally, Chapter 23, "Economies in Transition," will revisit the concepts of capitalism and socialism, explore the transition of the former Soviet Union, Eastern Europe, Japan, the People's Republic of China, and India. The concept of sustainability will be examined in the context of the world's environmental and energy challenges. The final "Thinking Critically" section focuses on the issues related to the future of globalization.

CHAPTER TWENTY

International Trade and Interdependence

◼ Introduction

As we have noted previously, interdependence among nations is a major feature of the modern world economy, and this will be a salient theme throughout the remainder of this book. To understand this concept properly and apply it to the problems we will be examining, we must be more specific. By the term economic interdependence, we mean that all countries are affected by the events of an economic nature that occur in many other countries. For example, many industrialized nations rely on developing nations for raw materials and other resources. In turn, many developing nations import manufactured finished goods from industrialized nations. The degree of interdependence is, of course, different for every nation. For example, the Japanese economy is seriously affected by increased oil prices yet relatively unaffected by Costa Rica's decision to increase banana prices. On the other hand, the Costa Rican economy, also strongly affected by an oil price increase, has the flexibility to shift its imports of steel from the United States to Japan.

Economic interdependence describes the effect of the complex international flow of goods, services, and capital among nations. It helps us understand how individuals, businesses, and nations must first exchange their currencies before exchanging goods and services. To acquire Japanese Toyotas, a U.S. auto importer must first exchange dollars for yen in a currency market. Then, the automobile transaction can be completed.

Financial markets are interdependent as well. For example, if real interest rates fall in Germany and at the same time rise in the United States, investors are likely to sell their German bonds and invest the proceeds in U.S. bonds generating a better return. If Mexico experiences political instability or increasing inflation, domestic and foreign investors will likely transfer funds from Mexico to the United States or Europe. Information and communications technology has increased both the magnitude and speed of these transfers and facilitated international interdependence.

The nature of this contemporary interdependence involves not only the exchange of goods and services but technology transfers, financial capital movements, and factors affecting the *international division of labor. For the past four centuries, raw materials and resources as well as technology provided the impetus for trade. Indeed, much of the motivation for the geographical explorations of the fifteenth century was the search for trade routes and later for colonies from which raw materials could be exported cheaply. Later, with the Industrial Revolution, the ability to manufacture and export products cheaply became a motivation for trade. While capital has always been highly mobile, seeking the highest profits worldwide, today the transfer of technology has made it very easy to set up operations in places where wages and other production costs are low. Increasingly, industrialized nations are losing jobs and exports to developing countries, which offer an abundance of low-wage labor.*

 1. What other examples of economic interdependence are there?

In this chapter, we shall begin to explore various aspects of this interdependence and its implications: the extent of world trade and international trade theory and policy.

World Trade

The rapid process of globalization and trade liberalization that we examined in Chapter 2 has resulted in a sustained increase in the growth of both world real GDP (Figure 20.1) and the volume of World Trade (Figure 20.2) since 2001. World real GDP growth has been at about an annual average of 4.5 percent and is projected to be so through 2010; and the volume of World Trade has been increasing at an annual average of 7 percent, and this is expected to continue through 2010 as well.

As can be seen in Table 20.1, world exports were more than $11 trillion dollars (with about 80 percent being goods and the other 20 percent services).

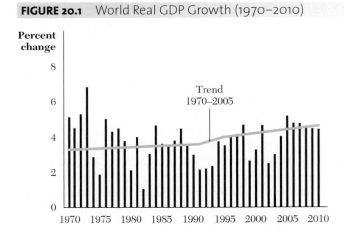

FIGURE 20.1   World Real GDP Growth (1970–2010)

Source: Data from The World Trade Organization, 2006

FIGURE 20.2 World Trade Volume (Goods and Services)

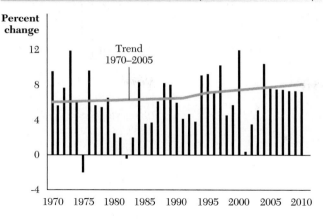

Source: Data from The World Trade Organization, 2006

TABLE 20.1 Share of Goods and Commercials Services in the Total Trade of Selected Regions and Economies, 2004 (Billion dollars and percentage based on balance of payments data).

	Exports			Imports		
	Value	**Share**		**Value**	**Share**	
	Total	**Goods**	**Commercial Services**	**Total**	**Goods**	**Commercial Services**
World	11140	80.9	19.1	11060	81.1	18.9
North America	1709	77.8	22.2	2284	85.3	14.7
Canada	378	87.6	12.4	335	83.3	16.7
Mexico	202	93.1	6.9	216	91.1	8.9
United States	1129	71.8	28.2	1733	85.0	15.0
South and Central America	347	83.9	16.1	293	80.3	19.7
Europe	5032	77.6	22.4	4864	78.9	21.1
Commonwealth of Independent States (CIS)	301	88.9	11.1	222	77.6	22.4
Africa	275	82.7	10.3	258	78.9	21.1
Asia	3060	85.3	14.7	2852	82.1	17.9
China	655	90.5	9.5	606	88.2	11.8
Hong Kong, China*	314	82.9	17.1	299	90.0	10.0
India	117	66.3	33.7	138	70.3	29.7
Japan	634	85.0	15.0	541	75.2	24.8
Korea, Republic of	298	86.6	13.4	269	81.6	18.4

Source: Data from *World Economic Outlook*, 2006, p.25
*Trade in goods includes significant re-exports or imports for e-exports.

TABLE 20.2 Leading exporters and importers in world merchandise trade, 2004 (Billion dollars and percentage)

Rank	Exporters	Value	Share	Annual Percentage Change	Rank	Importers	Value	Share	Annual Percentage Change
1	Germany	912.3	10.0	21	1	United States	1525.5	16.1	17
2	United States	818.8	8.9	13	2	Germany	716.9	7.6	19
3	China	593.3	6.5	35	3	China	561.2	5.9	36
4	Japan	565.8	6.2	20	4	France	465.5	4.9	17
5	France	448.7	4.9	14	5	United Kingdom	463.5	4.9	18
6	Netherlands	358.2	3.9	21	6	Japan	454.5	4.8	19
7	Italy	349.2	3.8	17	7	Italy	351.0	3.7	18
8	United Kingdom	346.9	3.8	13	8	Netherlands	319.3	3.4	21
9	Canada	316.5	3.5	16	9	Belgium	285.5	3.0	22
10	Belgium	306.5	3.3	20	10	Canada	279.8	2.9	14
11	Hong Kong, China	265.5	2.9	16	11	Hong Kong, China	272.9	2.9	17
	domestic exports	20.0	0.2	2		retained imports	27.3	0.3	13
	re-exports	245.6	2.7	17					
12	Korea, Republic of	253.8	2.8	31	12	Spain	249.3	2.6	20
13	Mexico	189.1	2.1	14	13	Korea, Republic of	224.5	2.4	26
14	Russian Federation	183.5	2.0	35	14	Mexico	206.4	2.2	16
15	Taipei, Chinese	182.4	2.0	21	15	Taipei, Chinese	168.4	1.8	32
16	Singapore	179.6	2.0	25	16	Singapore	163.9	1.7	28
	domestic exports	98.6	1.1	24		retained imports	82.8	0.9	30
	re-exports	81.0	0.9	26					
17	Spain	178.6	2.0	14	17	Austria	117.8	1.2	18
18	Malaysia	126.5	1.4	21	18	Switzerland	111.6	1.2	16
19	Saudi Arabia	126.2	1.4	35	19	Australia	109.4	1.2	23
20	Sweden	122.5	1.3	20	20	Malaysia	105.3	1.1	26

Source: International Monetary Fund, *World Economic Outlook*, 2006, p. 21.

North America was responsible for $1.7 trillion (Canada for $378 billion, the United States for $1.1 trillion, and Mexico for $202 billion), South and Central America for $347 billion, Europe for $5 trillion, the Commonwealth of Independent States for $301 billion, Africa for $275 billion, and Asia for $3 trillion (China for $655 billion, Japan for $634 billion, and South Korea for $298 billion).

In 2004 the leading exporters and importers in world merchandise trade (Table 20.2) were Germany and the United States. Germany exported $912 billion of goods (about 10 percent of the world total) while the United States imported $1.5 trillion (or about 16 percent of the total world goods imports). China was ranked third in each category.

The Impact of International Trade on the United States

Since the early 1980s, international trade has continued to become a larger and larger share of the U.S. economy. By 2000, imports of goods represented 13 percent of the GDP and exports of goods represented 8 percent of the GDP, together representing more than 20 percent of the GDP. Since the early 1980s, the United States has experienced a trade deficit. By 1987, the trade deficit had

FIGURE 20.3 U.S.–International Trade (1989–2006)

Source: The Federal Reserve Bank of St. Louis, 2006.

increased to $40 billion. With a change in policies and a determined deprecia-
tion of the U.S. dollar (to make exports more competitive and imports more
expensive), the U.S. trade deficit narrowed in 1991 to less than $10 billion. Yet,
in the 1990s, globalization and the global movement toward the liberalization of
trade and markets along with a returning strong U.S. dollar produced a trend
toward larger trade deficits. This process accelerated from the period 1997 to
the present.

Figure 20.3 shows the share of exports and share of imports as a percentage
of the U.S. GDP. Together, exports and imports were 27 percent by 2006 (16
percent for exports and 11 percent for imports). Yet, while exports as a percentage of GDP peaked in 1997 (11 percent), declined to 9 percent in 2001, and
gradually recovered to 11 percent in 2006, an acceleration in the U.S. appetite
for imports continues. As a consequence, the U.S. trade deficit reached record
levels. By 2006, the U.S. trade deficit was more than $600 billion and was at a
level that represented more than 6 percent of the GDP. (As we will see in
Chapter 21, many experts are concerned that in the long run the United States
cannot finance or sustain this level of trade deficit.) More than two-thirds ($400
billion) of this trade deficit is with China and Japan.

The United States trades with many countries, and Figure 20.4, shows that
Canada is the major trading partner with the United States. In 2005 the United
States exported almost 24 percent of its goods to Canada and imported more
than 17 percent of its goods from Canada.

FIGURE 20.4 U.S. Goods Export and Import Shares, 2005

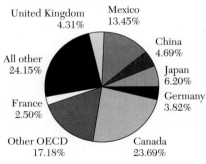

Goods Export Shares, 2005

United Kingdom 4.31%
Mexico 13.45%
China 4.69%
Japan 6.20%
Germany 3.82%
Canada 23.69%
Other OECD 17.18%
France 2.50%
All other 24.15%

(a) Share from United States, 2005

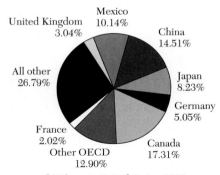

Goods Import Shares, 2005

Mexico 10.14%
United Kingdom 3.04%
China 14.51%
Japan 8.23%
Germany 5.05%
Canada 17.31%
Other OECD 12.90%
France 2.02%
All other 26.79%

(b) Share to United States, 2005

Source: Federal Reserve Bank of St. Louis, 2006.

2. Using the data in Table 20.2, calculate U.S. trade balances with China, Japan, Mexico, Germany, and the United Kingdom.

The Modern Theory of International Trade

Modern economic interdependence and the influence of multinational corporations led to more complex national trade questions in the 1990s. Before examining those questions, however, we need to understand why trade takes place. The simple answer to this question relies on the theory of comparative advantage, which suggests that free trade is most beneficial to world economies. We shall examine the theory behind international trade, a few of the more convincing arguments for protection, and current trends toward free trade as well as the critics of such attempts.

THE BIG PICTURE

Comparative Advantage

The theory of comparative advantage explains why nations gain from specialization in production and trade. Two countries will benefit if they both specialize in producing goods in which they have a relative advantage and trade those goods freely. One way to think about this is by comparing the resources or inputs it takes to produce two goods, textiles and computers, in two countries, the U.S. and Mexico, and examine how each might benefit from specialization and trade.

Suppose that the U.S. is more efficient in producing both textiles and computers than Mexico. (Using the same amount of inputs, the U.S. can produce more computers and textiles). Suppose furthermore that the U.S. is twice as productive in textile production and four times as productive in computer production. We can say that the U.S. has an *absolute* advantage in both goods, that is, it can produce both textiles and computers more efficiently). However, if we look at the relative advantage of each nation, we find that the U.S. has a relative (and absolute advantage) in producing computers, while Mexico has a relative (but not an absolute) advantage in producing textiles.

Production with same resource inputs:

US	Mexico
200 Textiles	100 textiles
400 Computers	100 computers

The U.S. can produce computers relatively more efficiently than it can produce textiles and Mexico can produce textiles relatively more efficiently than it can produce computers – given the same input or resource requirements. Thus, the U.S. has a *comparative* advantage in computers and Mexico has a *comparative* advantage in textiles. Given that the US has limited resources, the U.S. will benefit from specializing in computer production, and importing textiles from Mexico, which should specialize in textile production, and Mexico will benefit from trading textiles for computers. When each country specializes in the good that it is relatively best at producing and trades that good freely, total production or output of both goods increases. After trade occurs, the standard of living in both countries increases.

This is illustrated in Figure 20.BP.1 below. Before trade occurs, both countries produce both goods. Given that the US can produce either 200 Textiles or 400 Computers with its resources, suppose it decides to devote $\frac{1}{4}$ of its resources to producing 50 Textiles and $\frac{3}{4}$ of its resources to producing 300 Computers. Similarly, Mexico can produce either 100 Textiles or 100 Computers, and chooses to produce 25 Textiles and 75 Computers. Total output of both countries is then 75 Textiles and 375 Computers before trade. After trade, the US specializes entirely in computer production, producing 400 Computers, and Mexico specializes entirely in textile production, producing 100 Textiles. Production of both goods has increased, and both countries can now consume more of both goods due to specialization and trade based on comparative advantage.

If this process is extended to more countries, then specialization and trade based on the theory of comparative advantage should increase global efficiency and enhance the standard of living of all trading countries. The section below outlines the theory of comparative advantage in more detail, and then lays out some of the problems with this theory when applied to the modern global economy.

FIGURE 20.BP.1

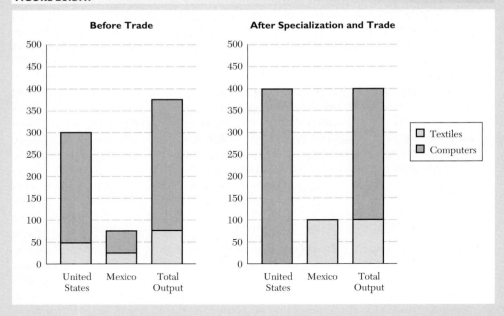

Who Trades What, and Why?

How does an individual nation assume its place in the world economy? Why does one nation specialize in production of groundnuts; a second, textiles; a third, aircraft; and a fourth, financial services? One of the first economists to deal with this question was Adam Smith, and in 1817 David Ricardo refined Smith's ideas to develop the general approach that we still use today. This approach to understanding trade is based on two basic concepts, absolute and comparative advantage.

Some assumptions will greatly facilitate matters by allowing us to deal with the essentials. In our hypothetical world, we have two nations, producing two goods. Perfect competition exists everywhere, there are no transportation costs, and labor and capital cannot move between the two nations. The costs of production in terms of labor hours are assumed to be as follows:

	Cost to Produce 1 Unit (Hours of Labor)	
	Wheat	**Cloth**
United Kingdom	10	20
France	15	45

Under these assumptions, the United Kingdom can produce both goods with less labor cost than can France. The United Kingdom, therefore, has an absolute advantage in producing both wheat and cloth, and France has an absolute disadvantage in each. Having an **absolute advantage** simply means that a nation can produce goods (in this case, both wheat and cloth) more efficiently than another.

This does not mean, however, that the United Kingdom produces and exports both goods and that France produces neither of them. To find out what production and exchange will take place, we must examine the production trade-off ratios between products within each nation; that is, we must see how much cloth must be given up to produce more wheat. In our example, one unit of wheat is produced in the United Kingdom with half the amount of labor time that it takes to produce a unit of cloth; with other factors constant, one unit of cloth will exchange for two units of wheat. In France—again, because of the relative costs of production—one unit of cloth can be exchanged for three units of wheat. This gives us the following internal rates of exchange of cloth for wheat:

$$\text{United Kingdom } 1 \text{ cloth} = 2 \text{ wheat}$$
$$\text{France } 1 \text{ cloth} = 3 \text{ wheat}$$

or

$$\text{United Kingdom } \tfrac{1}{2} \text{ cloth} = 1 \text{ wheat}$$
$$\text{France } \tfrac{1}{3} \text{ cloth} = 1 \text{ wheat}$$

By comparing the internal rates of exchange in each of the two countries, a trader might reason, "If I could buy one unit of wheat in Paris, ship it to London, and exchange it there for cloth, I could get one-half of a unit of cloth; if I exchanged it in France, I would get only one-third of a unit of cloth. My gain from this trade is one-sixth of a unit of cloth. On the other hand, taking one unit of cloth from Paris to London and exchanging it for wheat would bring me only two units of wheat, whereas I could have gotten three units of wheat at home in France. I lose one unit of wheat in the process." Note that taking one unit of cloth from London to Paris results in a gain of one unit of wheat (two units of wheat in the United Kingdom but three units in France).

Our trader would quickly conclude that France has a comparative advantage in the production and export of wheat, even though France has an absolute disadvantage in both goods. By similar reasoning, we conclude that the United Kingdom has a comparative advantage in the production of cloth. A **comparative advantage** means that one nation can produce a product relatively, not absolutely, more efficiently than another nation. (A nation with an absolute advantage can produce a variety of products more efficiently than another.) Trade is expanded when nations produce products where they possess a comparative advantage.

Although the assumptions underlying this theory are "unreal" in today's world, economists since David Ricardo's time have shown that his comparative advantage model is valid for a world of many nations producing many different goods. Other economists have demonstrated that dropping the assumptions of

TABLE 20.3   Total Country Production

	Units per Year		
	Wheat		**Cloth**
Brazil	700	or	700
France	2,400	or	800

perfect competition and zero transportation costs reduces the gain from special-ization and trade but does not invalidate the theory. The only assumption crucial to these results is labor immobility. If workers migrated freely from country to country, we could have exchanges of labor rather than exchanges of products.

Comparative Advantage and Output

In the following example, we can see what happens to total output of two goods (here, units of wheat and cloth) when trade occurs. We can also use a production possibilities curve to help us understand the effect of trade on total output. Unlike our previous example, we don't know the amount of labor involved in the production of each of these outputs, nor do we know the size of the labor forces. While we cannot calculate total output precisely, the production levels shown in Table 20.3 are consistent with our hypothetical costs and rates of exchange.

For the production levels given, France has the absolute advantage in the production of both products. If neither country is involved in international trade, each must use part of its resources to produce some of each product to meet domestic demand. If France uses half of its resources to produce wheat and half to produce cloth, cloth production will be 400 units and wheat production 1,200 units. If Brazil divides its labor resources so that six-sevenths produce wheat and one-seventh produces cloth, 600 units of wheat and 100 units of cloth will be produced. Total world output will be that shown in Table 20.4. Figure 20.5 shows the production possibilities curves for this example.

3. In what product does Brazil have the comparative advantage? Why would France want to trade with Brazil at all?

TABLE 20.4   Total World Output without Trade

	Units per Year	
	Wheat	**Cloth**
Brazil	600	100
France	1,200	400
Total	1,800	500

FIGURE 20.5   Production Possibilities without Trade

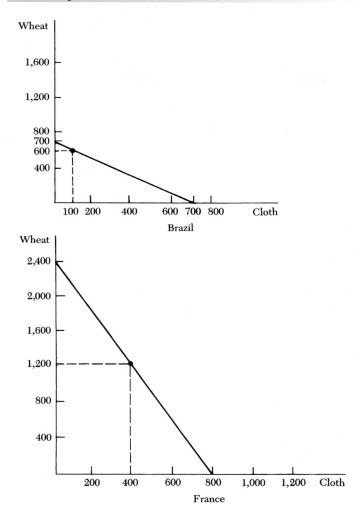

The two countries can expand total output by specializing. France has a comparative advantage in wheat production, and Brazil has a comparative advantage in cloth. If each country produces only its specialty, world output expands as shown in Table 20.5.

With trade, the countries can exchange some of their expanded output so that both countries have both products. Of the wheat France produces, it uses some for domestic consumption and exports the rest. Of the cloth Brazil produces, it

TABLE 20.5 Total World Output with Specialization

	Units per Year	
	Wheat	**Cloth**
Brazil	0	700
France	2,400	0
Total	2,400	700

uses some for domestic consumption and exports the rest. After trading, many results are possible, but we might get a result similar to that shown in Table 20.6. In this case, the countries exchange 1,000 units of wheat from France for 500 units of cloth from Brazil. Figure 20.6 shows the production possibilities curves of Brazil and France with trade.

4. Who has gained what through specialization and trade?
5. In the example just given, what are some other possible combinations of exchange?

Thus, if each nation specializes in the product in which it has a comparative advantage, world output of both commodities is increased—in this case by 600 units of wheat and 200 units of cloth. If specialization and trade result in some reasonable distribution of this gain, both countries are better off than they would be in the absence of trade. This is the essence, then, of the argument for free trade.

Terms of Trade

In the example from the previous section, not only can we determine whether Brazil and France can benefit from specialization and trade, we can also examine exchange ratios or a **terms of trade** in which both will gain. By looking at the

TABLE 20.6 Total World Output with Specialization and Trade

	Units per Year	
	Wheat	**Cloth**
Brazil	1,000	200
France	1,400	500
Total	2,400	700

FIGURE 20.6 Production Possibilities with Trade

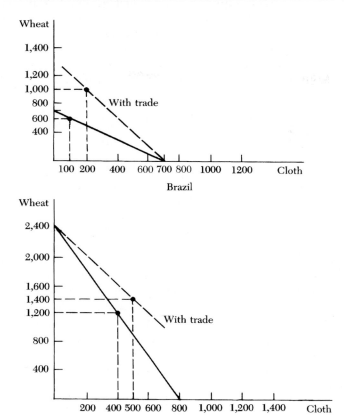

Brazil

France

internal or domestic production ratios within each nation—the production possibilities in Table 20.3—we can determine how much wheat must be given up in order to produce an additional unit of cloth. Brazil can produce 700 units of wheat or 700 units of cloth during a year, so producing an additional unit of wheat necessarily means reducing cloth production by 1 unit. France can produce 2,400 units of wheat or 800 units of cloth, so the internal production trade-off is 3 units of wheat for each additional unit of cloth produced. To produce an additional unit of cloth, French wheat production must be reduced by 3 units.

With the internal production trade-off at 1 unit of wheat for 1 unit of cloth in Brazil (1W:1C) and 3 units of wheat for 1 unit of cloth in France (3W:1C), we can look for a terms of trade somewhere between those two ratios and show that each nation will gain from trade. The simplest trading ratio within that range is

2W:1C. Both nations gain with a 2:1 terms of trade. Brazil is able to exchange 1 unit of cloth for 2 units of wheat (twice as much as domestic production would allow), and France is able to exchange 2 units of its wheat for 1 unit of cloth, rather than sacrificing a full 3 units for an additional unit.

Several other trading ratios are possible in this example. In practice, the final terms of trade will depend on the bargaining strength of each nation as well as other economic and political factors. Each nation will want to negotiate the best possible terms of trade for itself.

To measure the terms of trade, we compare import and export price ratios—that is, we measure the price a country pays for imports and the price it receives for exports. We can express this as an index number:

$$\text{terms of trade} = \frac{\text{index of export prices}}{\text{index of import prices}} \times 100$$

For example, suppose the U.S. export price index was 113 in 1997 and the import price index was 95, both beginning from a base year of 1992 (at 100). In this case, the terms of trade would be $113/95 \times 100 = 119$. The terms of trade over the 1992–1997 period increased from 100 to 119, a 19 percent improvement. This improvement in terms of trade allowed the United States to give up 19 percent less in exports to obtain the same amount of imports.

For developing countries, the terms of trade is a very important influence on their capability to carry out their development plans and strategies. If their terms of trade decline, they have to pay relatively more for imports than they receive for their exports (that is, they must pay greater amounts of exports in return for imports).

Problems with the Theoretical Assumptions of Free Trade

This theoretical model of comparative advantage clearly shows that international trade benefits the trading nations. Since the 1800s, this theory has become the rationale for most economists' belief that free trade is good and anything that interferes with it—such as tariffs, quotas, and other protectionist measures—is, by definition, bad. But the theory itself has serious problems. As is often the case in economic analysis, these problems involve the assumptions of the model.

When Ricardo first developed the theory of comparative advantage, he assumed that costs remain constant no matter what the level of production. Therefore, a nation could increase its production to satisfy the needs of other nations without increasing its own costs. But modern economics has documented, to the satisfaction of most, that since production is subject to diminishing returns, it is also subject to increasing costs—sooner or later, depending on what is being produced. In such a case, the increased costs may cancel out much, if not all, of the benefits of comparative advantage.

Ricardo also did not consider the large transportation costs that may be involved in international trade. These often raise the costs of imported goods considerably over those produced domestically and cancel out some of the benefits of international trade.

Finally, Ricardo assumed that the factors of production that are mobile within a country may be immobile internationally. These days labor still is fairly immobile, but capital funds move freely internationally. It is not so easy, as the modern era has shown, for a country to abandon production of one product and move resources into the production of another without serious reallocation problems. Further, moving resources from one industry to another can cause serious political difficulties beyond the practical economic realities.

Despite these limitations, the theory of comparative advantage does provide a useful perspective for viewing the trading process. However, it cannot alone explain the much more complicated process of the internationalization of world production.

Restrictions to Free Trade: Protectionism

Free trade exists if there are no barriers to the export and import of goods and services. But, historically, when unemployment, job loss, reduced profits, and recession threaten a nation, domestic industry, or region, the predictable response is a call for increased protection of domestic goods and thus domestic jobs.

Nations use several types of trade restrictions, but the most common have been tariffs and quotas. **Tariffs** are simply taxes on goods imported or exported, while **quotas** are limits on the quantities of goods imported or exported. More recently, orderly marketing agreements (OMAs) have been popular. OMAs are nonmonetary barriers that absolutely or quantitatively limit imports and thus limit the choice between imported and domestic goods. Importers reap the profits from the higher prices commanded by the limited supply (assuming that there is a relatively inelastic demand for the product).

In general, tariffs and quotas succeed in their objective—they protect a special interest at the expense of the whole population. In other words, a few people are helped a lot, while all citizens are hurt a little because they pay higher prices for the goods and services on which tariff duties are imposed.

Arguments for Protectionism.
Nations establish trade barriers for many reasons. Most often protectionist measures are designed to protect some interest in the home country. Special interest groups in the United States often appeal to Congress for protection. Industries also seek protection from "unfair trade practices." For example, some governments subsidize particular industries, giving those products a price advantage over other viable producers. Representatives of new industries also use the "infant industries" argument that they need help to gain a foothold in world markets already flush with producers that might "overpower" the infant industry in a

competitive marketplace. This argument is common in developing nations hoping to diversify their primarily agricultural base with a new industry. With time, however, particularly in the industrialized countries, the infant industry might grow to be a major competitor in the market, offering a better product at a better price.

Included in the protectionists' argument is another reason for tariff levies—retaliation. Governments have often increased tariffs in response to increases by trading partners. The 1930 Smoot-Hawley tariff, for example, set off a world-wide round of tariff increases. This "do unto others as they have done unto you" philosophy has also been used simply for the sake of self-esteem. As a result, consumers in both nations pay the higher price. At worst, such retaliation can compound recession into worldwide depression. During the 1930s, international trade almost disappeared—one important factor in the length and depth of the Great Depression. More recently, in the 1990s, the United States threatened retaliatory action against French wine.

At times Congress has considered proposals that it levy tariffs for the purpose of raising revenue, since the proceeds from the tax are collected by the government. This is well and good, but there are many more effective ways of raising revenue. Besides, if the tariff prices the imported good above that of the domestic product, the government will not collect any revenue, since the consumer will be priced out of the import market and will purchase only the domestic product.

Another protectionist argument centers on the need to reduce the competition of cheap foreign labor to protect domestic labor and domestic wage rates.

Protection is also very sensitive to political cycles. For example, during presidential elections, some candidates propose protectionism to win political support from some areas of the United States hurt by exports.

Other arguments on trade policy have run from the rather dry and abstract to the invective. The "national defense" argument falls into both categories. The merchant marine and the oil industry have argued for protection, since they are essential in times of national emergency.

6. Congress adopted import quotas to protect the oil industry for "defense" reasons from 1954 to 1973. How did these protective quotas, designed to encourage U.S. oil production, work during the OPEC oil embargo of 1973? As a consequence, what happened to domestic reserves of oil?

Costs of Protectionism.   Despite the many arguments in support of protectionist policies, an analysis of the consequences for consumers in each nation and the overall international trading system shows that one group may gain while another loses, and the entire trading system often suffers. The practice of protectionism results in all consumers paying higher prices for goods and services. The higher cost of imported goods may contribute to inflationary pressures. Protected jobs and firms may be sheltered from the competitive dynamics of the market, which would normally force them to allocate their scarce resources more efficiently and more productively.

The costs of protectionism can be high. Australia's Center for International Economics in 1990 concluded that if all regions in the global trading system reduced their tariff and nontariff barriers by 50 percent, the total gains from freer trade, measured in terms of increases in worldwide output, would be around $740 billion (more than $130 per person). A 1988 report issued by the Organization for Economic Cooperation and Development (the OECD, which includes the twenty-two advanced Western countries) concluded that agricultural protectionism cost the OECD countries about $72 billion a year. With free trade in agriculture, the study argues, personal incomes would increase by 1 percent, and less than 1 percent of the workforce would be displaced. The cost per farm job saved was estimated at $20,000 per year. In addition, free trade in agriculture would potentially increase Third World nations' agricultural exports by $30 billion a year.

In the 1997 *Economic Report of the President*, the Clinton administration noted the costs and benefits of free trade:

> Defenders of free trade can do it a disservice by promoting it as a way to create more jobs or to reduce bilateral trade deficits. Jobs, the unemployment rate, and the overall balance of payments [see Chapter 21] are ultimately a consequence of macroeconomic policies, not trade barriers. The real objective of free trade is to raise living standards by ensuring that more Americans are working in areas where the United States is comparatively more productive than its trading partners. In a full-employment economy, trade has more impact on the distribution of jobs than on the quantity of jobs.
>
> —*Economic Report of the President*, 1997, p. 21.

International Trade Issues

As the volume of world trade has grown, nations have joined together in agreements to reduce trade barriers between them and to move toward freer trade. These agreements have included establishing trading blocs among a group of specific countries to reduce barriers among themselves (increasing both trade and the size of the market), as well as multinational agreements to reduce barriers throughout the world. Among the trade agreements important to the United States (as well as to the other countries involved) are the North American Free Trade Agreement (NAFTA) signed in 1992, and the Asia-Pacific Economic Cooperation (APEC) agreements joining twelve Asia-Pacific countries. Meanwhile, the integration of Europe continued with the Maastricht Treaty officially establishing the European Union in 1993. The decade of the 1990s brought much progress on the trade front. The WTO advanced the liberalization and globalization dynamics and established an economic and political framework for advancing free markets and along with them the goal of free trade. By the beginning of the twenty-first century, the

.com bubble had burst and the results of the 1990s experience with globalization, trade, and financial liberalization policies documented the winners and losers, with results unevenly distributed. A strong antiglobalization movement emerged at the WTO meetings in Seattle in 1999 with protesters in the streets. Following the terror attacks on September 11, 2001, and subsequent wars in Afghanistan and Iraq (2003), the WTO-led push for enhanced trade liberalization began to crumble. Following the Seattle experience, the Doha Round in 2001 again focused on the importance of linking trade liberalization with the development goals and objectives of developing nations, who argued that trade liberalization was not contributing to their development agenda. The Doha Round encountered nothing but difficulty. The followup meetings in Cancun, Mexico, in 2003 collapsed after the fourth day, with the majority of members from the developing countries walking away in anger. The more recent meetings in Hong Kong in 2005 were no more successful. In 2006 there was a faint-hearted effort to breathe life back into the Doha agenda at the meeting of the World Economic Forum in Davos, Switzerland, but there were no expectations that anything would come of it. In the opinion of many experts, by 2006 it appeared that the era of multilateral trade liberalization was over. However, many critics and experts, like George Stiglitz (author of *Making Globalization Work*, 2006), argue that there is a comprehensive set of proposals for reform that would make it possible for trade liberalization to work. This would effectively mean creating a fair trade environment in which all subsidies and trade restraints are eliminated. His point is that this is not the case today, especially for the advanced countries, even though they claimed to advocate free trade.

Next, we will briefly examine the following topics to explore more fully some aspects of the controversy concerning trade liberalization. First, we will consider the experience of the North American Free Trade Agreement between the United States, Canada, and Mexico. Then we will focus on the issue of U.S. trade with Asia and China.

North American Free Trade Agreement (NAFTA)

In 1992, the North American Free Trade Agreement joined Canada, the United States, and Mexico into a multilateral trading bloc. NAFTA provides guiding principles for the reduction of tariffs on goods traded between these countries over fifteen years, until trade barriers no longer exist among the three. The NAFTA agreement was signed by President Bush in 1992 and ratified by Congress in late 1993, despite considerable debate in the 1992 presidential campaign (with Ross Perot opposing NAFTA and Bill Clinton supporting a modified NAFTA agreement). Some changes were negotiated in the areas of the environment and job loss.

NAFTA was hotly debated. Opponents argued that job losses would offset increased profits to manufacturers and lower consumer prices. Supporters argued that more jobs and increased wealth would result for all three nations. Since implementation in 1994, critics point to data validating their predictions.

In the first two years of the agreement, Mexico imported fewer U.S. goods than in previous years; at the same time the level of Mexican exports to the United States rose dramatically. Even supporters of the agreement have adjusted their earlier prediction of U.S. job growth. A currency crisis in the Mexican peso complicated interpretation of early results of the treaty. While some argue that the jury is still out on NAFTA, others—politicians and economists alike—look ahead to more free trade agreements in South America and the establishment of a Free Trade Area of the Americas (FTAA).

Since NAFTA began, proponents and critics have been studying the experience in order to be able to argue that it has indeed been successful or that it has been a disappointment or, even, a failure. By 2007, there had been several major and highly reputable studies on the performance of NAFTA (the World Bank, Institute for International Economics, AFL-CIO, etc.). Obviously, everyone can make a case for his or her position. Nevertheless, this is a very controversial and important debate as it sheds light not just on the experience of NAFTA but the recent passage of the Central American Free Trade Agreement (CAFTA).

The following article by James Parks, "NAFTA, CAFTA Not Working" (AFL-CIO, September 12, 2006), is an example of the case that critics make of NAFTA and CAFTA.

Free Trade Area of the Americas (FTAA)

In addition to NAFTA and CAFTA, a proposal to expand free trade throughout the Americas is in the works, with discussions to form the Free Trade Area of the Americas (FTAA). This proposed free trade area would encompass some thirty-four countries that currently produce about $11 trillion in GDP and have a total population of 800 million. If these talks succeed, import tariffs among these countries would fall to zero over the next decade or so, and quotas would be reduced over the same period. In early 2001, the Bush administration promoted the enhanced free trade programs and policies at the Third Summit of the Americas in Quebec City. President Bush and his trade representative, Robert B. Zoellick, worked hard to promote the idea of a Free Trade Area of the Americas.

Asia-Pacific Economic Cooperation (APEC) Agreements

As Pacific Rim countries have continued to grow in importance to the world economy, they have established trade agreements among themselves and with some of their traditional trading partners. In 1989, representatives from twelve Asia-Pacific countries—Australia, Canada, Japan, the Republic of Korea, New Zealand, the United States, Brunei, Indonesia, Malaysia, the Republic of the Philippines, Singapore, and Thailand—met to discuss global and regional economic development, global trade liberalization, regional cooperation, and future economic cooperation in the Asia-Pacific region. These formal discussions continue and are called Asia-Pacific Economic Cooperation (APEC). As U.S.

NAFTA, CAFTA Not Working

James Parks

They are the twin pillars of recent U.S. trade policy—NAFTA and DR-CAFTA. And neither of them is working.

After 12 years, NAFTA (North American Free Trade Agreement) has not brought prosperity to working people in Mexico, Canada and United States, as promised.

And like NAFTA and other bad U.S. trade agreements, DR-CAFTA (Dominican Republic—Central American Free Trade Agreement) does not contain enforceable workers' rights or environmental protections. The agreement, which went into effect in January, is already failing after just eight months, according to a report released Tuesday.

In testimony submitted Sept. 11 to the Senate Finance Subcommittee on International Trade for NAFTA hearings, AFL-CIO Policy Director Thea Lee noted that "rather than encouraging sustainable and equitable growth, NAFTA has contributed to the loss of jobs and incomes of workers, while enriching the very few."

> NAFTA's main outcome has been to strengthen the clout and bargaining power of multinational corporations, to limit the scope of governments to regulate in the public interest and to force workers into more direct competition with each other, while assuring them fewer rights and protections. The increased capital mobility afforded by NAFTA has hurt workers, the environment and communities in all three NAFTA countries.

Since 1994, the U.S. combined trade deficit with Mexico and Canada has ballooned from $9 billion to $127 billion, Lee says. The Department of Labor has certified that well over half a million U.S. workers lost their jobs due to NAFTA, and the nonprofit Economic Policy Institute (EPI) estimates the skyrocketing NAFTA trade deficit contributed to the loss of more than 1 million jobs and job opportunities.

Mexican workers haven't fared any better. Real wages in Mexico are actually lower today than before NAFTA went into effect in 1994, and the number of people in poverty grew from 62 million to 69 million through 2003, Lee says.

The NAFTA model was the starting point for CAFTA. In *Monitoring Report: DR-CAFTA in Year One*, prepared by the Stop CAFTA Coalition, Katherine Hoyt of the Nicaragua Network, one of the members of the coalition, says CAFTA has fueled the deterioration of workers' rights. For example, according to the report:

- Few collective bargaining agreements exist with noncompany unions in the free-trade zones of Central America, and corporations continue to fire union leadership in order to quash organizing efforts.

- Despite promises from the El Salvadoran government and the Bush administration, the cost of living is increasing, including the price of food. The White House had assured Salvadoran farmers that increased food exports from the United States would lead to lower food prices.

- In Nicaragua, funds from a program to support farmers are going to rich, powerful large producers, not to small farmers who desperately need them.

- Using a section of CAFTA, El Salvador's government is preparing a new law to privatize the nation's water system, an action that traditionally leads to huge cost increases and the loss of water by poor farmers and workers.

With Congress poised to consider new NAFTA-type trade agreements with Peru and Colombia, lawmakers need to take a look at what has happened in Central America and Mexico, Lee says:

Trade agreements must include enforceable protections for workers' core rights and must preserve our ability to use our domestic trade laws effectively. They must protect our government's ability to regulate in the public interest, to use procurement dollars to promote economic development and other legitimate social goals, and to provide high-quality public services. Finally, it is essential that workers, their unions and other civil society organizations be able to participate meaningfully in our government's trade policy process, on an equal footing with corporate interests.

The success or failure of any future trade and investment agreements will hinge on government's willingness and ability to negotiate agreements that appropriately address all of the social, economic and political dimensions of trade and investment, not just those of concern to corporations. Unfortunately, NAFTA is precisely the wrong starting point.

trade with this region increases, we can expect that these negotiations will grow in importance and expand to include other rapidly growing Pacific Rim economics.

7. What is the case against NAFTA?
8. Can you find information (data) that would support or contradict this argument? What is it?
9. What are the lessons of NAFTA for CAFTA?
10. What would make for a more "fair" agreement?

The WTO and GATT

Despite debates over protectionism, much of the post–World War II period has seen an overall reduction in the excessive protection of the Great Depression years. Nations have, of course, disagreed as to which goods should be exempt from tariff reductions and where tariff levels should be set. Protectionist tendencies are particularly prevalent during periods of severe recession as countries compete for shrinking markets. Still, primarily through international negotiations in organizations such as the **General Agreement on Tariffs and Trade (GATT)**, treaties increase trade through agreed-on reductions in tariffs.

Ninety-nine nations participated in the General Agreement on Tariffs and Trade, Multilateral Trade Negotiations, or the Tokyo Rounds, which concluded in 1979 after five years of negotiation over tariff reductions and the elimination of nontariff impediments and distortions to trade. In 1986, GATT attempted to reduce barriers in Punta del Este, Uruguay, and continued through 1993. Delegates negotiated reductions in both tariff and nontariff barriers, on everything from intellectual property, including patents and copyrights, to services such as telecommunications.

The most controversial part of the Uruguay Round was the agreement to establish the World Trade Organization (WTO) as the institution responsible for governing international trade. The WTO represents more than 120 countries. The WTO has the duty of implementing the agreements in the Uruguay Round by administering the agreements and providing a forum for settling disputes. The WTO replaced GATT as the central institution working to eliminate trade barriers. In its early years of existence, the WTO has had its share of critics and supporters. Critics argue that the WTO oversteps its bounds in issues of national sovereignty. As the WTO makes more decisions, the organization has come under increased scrutiny from its supporters, who want increased powers and enforcement of those powers, and critics, who want to reduce WTO's importance.

European Integration

Twelve European nations with a total population of 320 million and a GDP rivaling that of the United States formally merged into the European Union in 1993. (In 1995 three more countries joined the EU, and in 2004 ten more joined.) The latest in a series of European organizational efforts beginning in 1952 with the European Coal and Steel Community, the EU trading bloc was designed to liberalize trade between member nations, encourage cooperation in intergovernmental and security affairs, and facilitate the movement toward a single currency. The economic goal of the EU is to synchronize economic policies promoting European economic growth and stabilization. Gains from integration are predicted at around 6.2 percent of combined GDP, or $230 billion.

Continued integration efforts are not easy. Strikes by French farmers and German miners emphasize the discord within member nations, as the EU places regional economic decisions above national ones. The EU is opening its doors to trade with the rest of the world, and thus opening a growing European market to U.S. products, even though trade among member nations receives greater emphasis. For U.S. trade, the future direction of EU economic policy is an important one. The majority of EU members moved to a common currency (the euro) in January 2000.

11. If a nation encourages free trade, what happens to the laborer whose job is threatened by increased domestic demand for imported substitutes?

Japan as a Neomercantilist Trading Partner

While NAFTA, APEC, FTAA, the WTO, and the European Union aim at reducing the potential for trade wars, fears of such disputes have not vanished.

In particular, some concern persists regarding Japan's remaining neomercantilist trade policies. Some policy makers working on Japan trade issues have concluded that prior to the mid-1990s, Japan's trade policies were mercantilist in nature and that free trade interrupted their organized markets.

Japanese exports to U.S. markets account for more than half of Japan's total trade surplus. Needless to say, there is concern over Japanese trade policies, which are generally exclusionary and sometimes violate international trade law. The strategies with which the Japanese encourage strategic industries often puts U.S. domestic competitors at a disadvantage.

U.S. government and trade officials and businesspeople have long been frustrated with the Japanese. Intensive rounds of bilateral trade negotiations have increased the frustration on both sides. Tariff barriers *have* fallen over the past few years, but other restrictive practices have made entry into some Japanese markets difficult.

Some Japanese exporters have created special problems. In the late 1980s, some high-technology industries began feeling a competitive pinch, and Japanese firms were found guilty of dumping semiconductors, computer chips, and telephones on the U.S. market. **Dumping** occurs when an exporting nation sells its product at a lower price in an importing country than it does in its own country. In one case, AT&T, the nation's largest manufacturer of telephone equipment, filed an official complaint that accused "Japan, Taiwan, and South Korea of dumping, or selling goods below the cost of production to build market share—a violation of international trade law." In 1987, the United States instituted a protective tariff on $3 billion of Japanese imports to retaliate for semiconductor dumping. Permanent tariff duties were also imposed on the manufacturers of telecommunications equipment after the AT&T decision.

U.S.–Asia Trade Relationship

The robust postwar economic performance of many Asian countries has driven the strong U.S.-Asia trade and economic relationship. In recent years Asian economies have experienced some of the world's highest growth rates and will continue to be key export markets for U.S. firms. Outside of South Asia, trade with the Pacific Rim region represents about 30 percent of U.S. trade with the world. The United States imports different items from the Asian region than it exports. The top imports from the Pacific Rim include electrical machinery, automobiles, toys, furniture, clothing, and footwear. The top U.S. exports to that region include aircraft, chemicals, plastics, agricultural products, automobiles, and pharmaceutical products.

U.S.–China Trade

Since 1995, U.S. trade with China has represented an increasing share of U.S. total trade, reflecting some substitution away from other Pacific Rim trading partners toward China. The United States imports different items from China than it exports to China. In 2004, top import items from China included a wide range of consumer goods, such as toys, sporting goods, apparel, and footwear. Top U.S. export items to China included a number of intermediate components and machinery, aircraft, soybeans, and cotton. Many imports from China now take the place of goods previously imported from other countries. China increasingly is a large and growing market for U.S. goods and services. Since China's accession to the WTO, U.S. exports to China have risen faster than exports to the rest of the world.

Engaging China

The U.S.-Asia trade and economic relationship offers vast opportunities for citizens in all of these countries to prosper, however, China's integration into the global economy will not come without challenges. For instance, WTO membership has offered China new benefits, such as Permanent Normal Trade Relations with the United States and access to the WTO's rules-based dispute-settlement mechanism. China's WTO membership also brings new responsibilities, such as improving the protection of intellectual property, full compliance with trade agreements, and continued progress toward a flexible, market-based exchange-rate regime. China has made strides toward economic reform at all levels of government, but there are areas that require further progress. The United States will continue to work with China to assist its integration as a responsible stakeholder in the international economy and to ensure that bilateral economic relations are mutually beneficial.

FIGURE 20.7   U.S. Exports to China and the World

U.S. exports to China have been growing faster than to the rest of the world. 1990 = 100

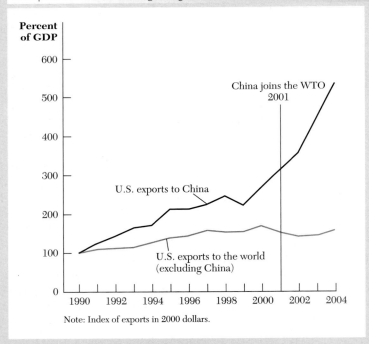

Note: Index of exports in 2000 U.S. dollars.

Source: *The Economic Report of the President*, 2006, pg. 166–167.

12. China's integration into the global economy will not come without challenges. Explain.
13. What are the primary issues for the United States with respect its trading relationship with China?
14. What would you argue to be a sound U.S. trade relationship and policy with China?

Conclusion

With protectionist measures, there is always an undercurrent of possible retaliation and trade wars similar to those of the 1930s, during which time international trade almost disappeared. In the past decade, however, the fear of retaliation seems not to have been an issue. Increasingly more economists are calling for the introduction of trade strategies as an improvement on free trade.

Developing countries are especially concerned about protectionist tendencies. They need to increase their exports in order to earn much-needed dollars and foreign currencies with which to repay the enormous debt that they have accrued in the past. A quota on imported steel would greatly affect a nation such as Brazil, which relies heavily on steel exports to earn foreign exchange. These nations have learned to play the game of protection as well. Several of the developing countries are using import controls as well as export subsidies to improve their trade positions. This trend has been caused by a minimal weakening of inflationary activity and the persistence of high unemployment levels.

Protection or free trade? Retaliation? Negotiated trade agreements? More than forty years ago, in his 1977 presidential address to the twelfth biannual convention of the AFL-CIO, George Meany declared, "Free trade is a joke and a myth, and a government policy dedicated to 'free trade' is more than a joke—it is a prescription for disaster. The answer is fair trade—do unto others as they do unto you—barrier for barrier, closed door for closed door."

The 2001 U.S. economic recession that followed the collapse of the technology bubble and boom of the late 1990s resulted in a worldwide economic slowdown. The critics of globalization, free trade, and economic liberalization gathered more and more influence. This put enormous pressure on the World Trade Organization and other regional economic integration initiatives. By 2003 and into the early months of 2004, WTO trade discussions broke down in Cancun, Mexico, and Miami, Florida. Rising protectionist sentiment was visible throughout the global economy.

There can be no doubt that arguments over free trade will continue in the future, and the effects will be felt on currencies and domestic policies. In the next chapter, we measure international trade and survey the historical development of the institutions that permitted international exchange to develop and flourish in an increasingly interdependent world. We will also see how these institutions sometimes failed to develop appropriate policies for the ever-changing and complex world economy.

Review Questions

1. What linkages among nations have been most important in increasing interdependence in the world economy today?

2. When we say that the world economy is characterized by interdependence, does this mean that all nations are equally dependent on other nations, or are some nations more dominant and others more dependent? Why is that so?

3. What is the logic behind the theory of comparative advantage?

4. What is important about the terms of trade for a country?

5. What is the case for and against free trade?

6. The global economy is becoming more and more integrated. There are several trade blocs and efforts toward economic integration. Explain.

CHAPTER TWENTY-ONE

International Finance

◼ Introduction

Having considered the theory and the recent history of international trade, we shall now turn our attention to issues of international finance and to accounting for the international exchange of goods, services, investment, and other capital flows. Monies flow from one nation to another when citizens or institutions of a given nation decide to lend to or borrow from foreigners and to import or export goods and services.

We begin our examination with a discussion of the **balance of payments,** *which is the accounting scheme that governments and international organizations use for measuring trade and capital flows between nations. We shall then move to a discussion of exchange rates and review how they respond to trade and financial transactions. Our discussion of exchange rates includes how international trade flows alter these rates, and how systems of exchange have changed throughout the century.*

The Balance of Payments

All nations must eventually adjust their national economic policies to meet the demands of the international trading and financial system. Nations commonly keep track of these demands with a mechanism called the balance-of-payments accounting system. A balance-of-payments account is a statement of a nation's aggregate international financial transactions over a period of time, usually one year. The balance of payments is a statement that shows the exchange of a country's currency for foreign currencies for all of the international transactions of a country's citizens, businesses, and government during a year. It helps nations keep track of the flow of goods and services into and out of the country. In this accounting statement, all international economic and financial transactions must have either a positive or a negative effect on a nation's balance-of-payments accounts. Table 21.1 shows the effects of possible transactions.

TABLE 21.1 Credits and Debits in a Nation's Balance of Payments

Credits (+)	Debits (−)
1. Any *receipt* of foreign money	1. Any *payment* to a foreign country
2. Any *earnings* of an investment in a foreign country	2. Any *earnings* on domestic investments by a foreign country
3. Any sale of goods or services abroad (*export*).	3. Any purchase of goods and services from abroad (*import*)
4. Any gift or aid *from* a foreign country	4. Any gift or aid *given* abroad
5. Any *sale* of stocks or bonds abroad	5. Any *purchase* of foreign stocks or bonds
6. Any foreign investment in this country	6. Any investment in a foreign country

The balance-of-payments accounting statement is divided into three major classifications: the current account, the capital account, and the financial account. (In June 1999, the Bureau of Economic Analysis changed the way that it accounts for financial transactions in its international account. The BEA had previously used only a current account and capital account; by adding the financial account, the BEA conforms more closely to the international guidelines of the International Monetary Fund.) For each of these accounts, subtracting payments from receipts results in an account balance.

The Current Account

The **current account** includes the import and export of all goods and services, investment income, and most unilateral transfers during a year. Exports of goods and services create a receipt of income, while imports of goods command payments abroad, resulting in an outflow of income. Table 21.2 shows the magnitude of these components of the current account for 2005.

By far the largest category under the current account is the export and import of merchandise—cars, steel, raw materials, machines, and so forth. In 2005 U.S. merchandise exports totaled $895 billion, and merchandise imports totaled an outflow $1.2 trillion. The balance referred to as the **balance of trade** represents the value of exports of goods and services minus the value of imports. For 2005, the balance of trade was –$717 billion. The balance is negative because payments were larger than receipts in 2005.

Besides merchandise trade, the current account records investment income and services of various types. When we total all of the transactions in the current account, we get the current account balance. For 2005, this balance was –$791–791.5 billion.

Just as we examined the budget deficit within the framework of our leakages and injections model of National Income Accounting, we can look at trade deficits within the same context. In equilibrium, leakages equal injections:

$$\text{leakages} = \text{injections}$$
$$S + Tx + M = I + G + X$$

TABLE 21.2   U.S. International Transactions, 2005

Transaction	Amount (in millions)
Current Account	
(1) Exports of goods and services and income receipts	$1,749,892
(2) Goods, balance-of-payment basis	894,631
(3) Services	380,614
(4) Income Receipts	474,647
(5) Imports of goods and services and income payments	−2,455,328
(6) Goods, balance-of-payment basis	−1,677,371
(7) Services	−314,604
(8) Income Payments	−463,353
(9) Unilateral current transfers, net	−86,072
(10) Balance on current account = (1) + (5) + (9)	−791,508
Capital Account	
(11) Capital Account transactions, net	−4,351
Financial Account	
(12) U.S.-owned assets abroad, net (increase/financial outflow (−))	−426,801
(13) U.S. official reserve assets, net	14,096
(14) U.S. government assets, other than official reserves assets, net	5,538
(15) U.S. private assets, net	−446,436
(16) Foreign-owned assets in the United States, net (increase/financial inflow (+))	1,212,250
(17) Foreign official assets in the United States, net	199,495
(18) Other foreign assets in the United States, net	1,012,755
(19) Balance of capital financial flows = (16) − (12)	785,449
(20) Statistical discrepancy (sum of above items with sign reversed)	10,410
Balance of payments = (1) +(5) + (9) + (11) + (12) + (16) + (20)	0
Balance of trade = (2) + (3) + (6) + (7)	−716,730

Source: Bureau of Economic Analysis, *Survey of Current Business*, June 2006.

Next, we can rewrite the equation in terms of the current account balance, which is in deficit in this case:

$$X - M = S - I - G + Tx,$$

where I is domestic investment, G is government expenditures, $X - M$ is net exports (and here serves as a measure of the current account deficit or surplus), S is private domestic saving, and Tx is domestic tax receipts.

$$(X - M) = S - I - (G - Tx),$$

where $X - M$ is the current account balance and $G - Tx$ is the government deficit. This balance is linked to fiscal and/or saving imbalances.

The Capital Account

The amount in the nation's **capital account** is small. The only transactions included are a few unilateral transfers that had been included in the current account until the Bureau of Economic Analysis changed its accounting for financial transactions in 1999. The BEA provides the following definition:

> The newly defined capital account consists of capital transfers and the acquisition or disposal of nonproduced nonfinancial assets. They are major types of capital transfers and are debt forgiveness and migrant's transfers (goods and financial assets accompanying migrants as they leave or enter the country). "Other" capital transfers include the transfer of title to fixed assets and the transfer of funds linked to the sale or acquisition of fixed assets, gift and inheritance taxes, death duties, uninsured damage to fixed assets, and legacies. The acquisition and disposal of nonproduced nonfinancial assets includes the sales and purchases of nonproduced

U.S. Capital Flow Sustainability

In principle, the United States can continue to receive net capital inflows (and run current account deficits) indefinitely provided it uses these inflows in ways that promote its future growth and help the United States to remain an attractive destination for foreign investment. The key issue concerning U.S. foreign capital inflows is not their absolute level but the efficiency with which they are used. Provided capital inflows promote strong U.S. investment, productivity, and growth, they provide important benefits to the United States as well as to countries that are investing in the United States.

To evaluate the *sustainability* of these inflows, economists often evaluate a country's *external debt burden*. This debt burden can be seen in terms of a *stock* and a *flow* burden. One stock measure that is sometimes examined is a country's *net foreign asset position*. Net foreign assets measure the value of a country's foreign assets relative to the liabilities it owes to foreigners. When foreign assets exceed liabilities, a country is a *net foreign creditor*. When foreign liabilities exceed foreign assets, it is a *net foreign debtor*. Net capital inflows contribute to net foreign debt because some share of these inflows reflect foreign purchases of debt in-

struments. A rising level of net foreign debt may be a warning sign that debt could become unsustainable in the future.

U.S. current account deficits in recent years have caused its level of net foreign debt to rise from negative 4 percent of GDP in 1995 to negative 22 percent in 2004. Other countries vary in their net foreign asset or debt positions. For example, Japan is a net foreign creditor (foreign assets exceeding foreign liabilities) with net foreign assets equivalent to 38 percent of its GDP. In contrast, Australia is a net debtor with net foreign debt equivalent to 64 percent of its GDP. Great Britain's net foreign debt is equivalent to 13 percent of its GDP. While net foreign debt or asset positions can be a useful indicator, however, these figures must be interpreted cautiously since what constitutes an "excessive" amount of net foreign debt is far from clear.

One *flow measure* of the external debt burden is a country's *net foreign income*. Countries either receive or pay foreign income depending on their foreign asset and liability levels as well as the rate of return they earn and pay on these assets and liabilities. When a country receives more in interest, dividends, profit remittances, and

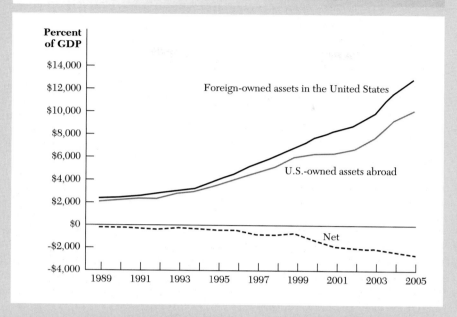

FIGURE 21.1 U.S. Net International Investment Position at Year End
With Direct Investment Positions Valued at Current Cost

The U.S. net international investment position at year end 2005 was –$2,693.8 billion (preliminary) with direct investment valued at current cost, as the value of foreign investments in the United States exceeded the value of U.S. investments abroad. At year end 2004, the U.S. net international investment position was –$2,360.8 billion (revised).

royalties on its foreign assets than it pays on its foreign liabilities, it is a *net foreign income recipient*. When payments exceed receipts, a country makes *net foreign income payments*.

One striking feature of the U.S. balance of payments accounts is that the United States has continued to earn net foreign income despite its rising level of net foreign debt. For example, the United States earned $30 billion in net foreign income in 2004 despite a stock of net foreign debt equivalent to $2.5 trillion. By comparison, Japan received $86 billion in net foreign income payments in 2004 despite the fact that it held $1.8 trillion in net foreign assets. Between 1995 and 2004, the United States earned over $200 billion in net foreign income despite current account deficits that totaled

more than $3 trillion during this period. Therefore, U.S. external debt has not appeared burdensome by this measure because its net foreign income flows have remained positive.

While U.S. capital inflows can continue indefinitely, recent levels of net inflows received are likely to moderate in the future. At more than 6 percent of GDP, U.S. net capital inflows are unusually high by historical standards. While no specific "critical value" exists beyond which a country can no longer necessarily receive net foreign capital inflows, recent growth in U.S. net inflows has attracted substantial attention. The key questions concern the rate and magnitude by which U.S. net inflows moderate in the future....

Source: *Economic Report of the President*, 2006, pp. 144–145.

assets, such as the rights to natural resources, and the sales and purchases of intangible assets, such as patents, copyrights, trademarks, franchises, and leases.

Although these capital account transactions are relatively small in the U.S. accounts, they are more important to other countries and may become more important to U.S. accounts. In 2005, these transactions amounted to –$4.4 billion.

The Financial Account

The financial account includes all financial flows in and out of the United States. U.S. financial outflow represents the purchase of capital assets outside of the United States by the government, citizens, or corporations. The dollars used to purchase these assets flow out of the country. In return, the government, citizen, or business now owns an asset abroad. U.S. citizens or businesses might make bank deposits in other countries, purchase foreign stocks and bonds, or even buy foreign productive facilities (a plant, office, McDonald's franchise, etc.). All of these activities produce an increase in U.S. assets abroad, or an outflow of dollars—a payment in the balance of payments. On the other hand, if U.S. residents were to sell their foreign assets and bring the proceeds back home, this would be recorded as a receipt. In 2005, the net outflow of U.S. private assets amounted to –$446 which represented payments in the financial account. Financial inflow into the United States, which occurs when foreign governments, institutions, corporations, or individuals increase their assets in the United States, amounted to $1.2 trillion in 2005.

1. What do we lose by foreign direct investment in the United States? What do we gain when it occurs?

Balancing the Accounts

The balance of payments always "balances." Whatever surplus (net inflow) or deficit (net outflow) these transactions generate is offset by the use of official reserve assets of the U.S. government and the statistical discrepancy.

The *statistical discrepancy* category is in one sense an accounting mechanism for balancing the accounts. It is simply the total of the items in the current, capital, and financial account measurements with the sign reversed. One reason this account is necessary is that the measurement of all international transactions is extremely complex. The government cannot accurately measure all of these transactions, particularly illegal ones; some transactions, both legal and illegal, will escape measurement. For 2005, the deficit in the U.S. current, capital, and financial account items indicates an outflow of dollars. This number could represent any one or a combination of possible activities. The deficit would put downward pressure on the dollar, reducing its value and "balancing" the deficit. Alternatively, other nations could hold on to the dollars that they had received because of U.S. imports from their countries or U.S. capital flows to their countries. They might want to hold these dollars for future use. Whatever the specifics, to compensate for the imprecision involved in attempting to measure all international economic activities, the statistical discrepancy category mechanically balances the international accounts.

2. If investment by Canada in the United States results in a "receipt" or positive effect on the U.S. balance of payments in the financial account, is this investment necessarily good for the United States? Why or why not?
3. What would be an example of a merchandise export? A government transfer payment? If you took $1,000 out of your bank account in the United States and put it in a bank in London, what effect would it have in the balance of payments accounts?

The U.S. Capital Account Surplus

. . . In 2004 . . . the United States ran a *current account deficit* of $668 billion. This deficit meant the United States imported more goods and services than it exported. The counterpart to the U.S. current account deficit was a U.S. *capital account surplus*. [Here "capital account" includes both the capital and financial accounts in Table 21.1.] This surplus meant that foreign investors purchased more U.S. assets than U.S. investors purchased in foreign assets, investing more in the United States than the United States invested abroad. By economic definition, a country's current and capital account balances must offset one another. Therefore, the U.S. current account deficit was matched by a capital account surplus of $668 billion (including $85 billion in net statistical discrepancies within the capital account, which are included in part to ensure the accounts sum to zero).

Because foreigners invested more in the United States than the United States invested abroad, the United States received *net foreign capital and financial inflows* (hereafter called net capital inflows). Countries like the United States that run capital account surpluses and current account deficits receive net foreign capital inflows. In contrast, countries that run capital account deficits and current account surpluses experience net foreign capital outflows.

Between 1980 and 2004, the United States ran a capital account surplus and a current account deficit in all but three years. More recently, net capital inflows to the United States have risen sharply. The $668 billion in net inflows received in 2004 was nearly $300 billion greater than the level of net inflows received only three years earlier. As a percent of U.S. Gross Domestic Product (GDP), net capital inflows rose from 1.5 percent in 1995 to 4.2 percent in 2000 to 5.7 percent in 2004. In 2005, U.S. net capital inflows are likely to have exceeded 6 percent of GDP and ranged from $700 to $800 billion in dollar terms.

◆ The recent rise in U.S. net capital inflows between 2002 and 2004 in part reflects global economic conditions (such as a large increase in crude oil prices) as well as policies (such as China's exchange rate policy) and weak growth in several other large economies (such as Germany) that led to greater net capital outflows from these countries.

◆ The United States is likely to remain a net foreign capital recipient for a long time.

Trade Deficits

When reporters, economists, and politicians speak of balance-of-payments deficits (outflows of dollars) and surpluses (inflows of dollars), they may be referring only to the transactions in the current account or the current and financial accounts—and not in the balancing cash, gold, or bond transactions. The *basic balance* includes the balance on the current account added to the long-term capital movements. This basic balance normally shows a payments deficit (payments > receipts) or surplus (receipts > payments).

If we look only at the merchandise balance in the current account (the balance of trade), we find that the U.S. "balance" has historically been a surplus. In every year from 1893 until 1971, merchandise exports exceeded merchandise imports. Beginning in the 1970s, however, the balance of trade has shown deficits—large ones in the late 1970s and even larger in the 1980s and late 1990s, after simply large deficits in the early 1990s. The trade deficits of the early to mid-1970s resulted primarily from the large increase in the price of imported oil. During the first half of the 1980s, the trade deficits were caused by a very strong dollar, which made U.S. goods much more expensive than imported goods. This price shift decreased U.S. exports and increased foreign imports. In the latter half of the decade, the value of the dollar fell, and the trade deficit began to decrease in 1988, having reached a record $152.9 billion in 1987. Deficits in the trade balance continued to narrow until 1992. Since 1992 trade deficits climbed to record levels. Figure 21.2 shows the pattern for international transactions balances between 1981 and 2006.

Trade deficits in the current account have been offset by larger financial inflows into the United States, which have reduced the deficit in the basic balance. Until recently the financial account has historically run deficits, since it records U.S. corporate investment in foreign nations.

During the period when imports by Americans do exceed our exports to the rest of the world, foreigners must accept additional dollar securities in exchange for our excess imports. In different words, we finance the excess imports by borrowing from the rest of the world or by selling U.S. assets to foreigners. This accommodating flow of credit or capital to the United States is an inevitable corollary of the trade deficit.

—Martin Feldstein, "Why the Dollar Is Strong," *Challenge,* January/February 1984

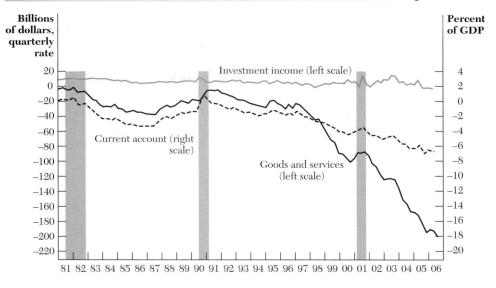

FIGURE 21.2 Current Account, Trade, and Investment Income Balances, 1981–2006

Source: Federal Reserve Bank of St. Louis, 2006.

One of the problems a nation encounters in trade, just as in life, is that it must pay for the goods and services received. An individual can use either cash or an IOU to offset a debt. In the international sphere, several alternatives are available. Payments are accepted in cash (dollars), gold, or special drawing rights (a bookkeeping form of international money).

If a nation's exports exceed its imports, it will have attained a balance-of-trade surplus. The reward for this is increased employment and income at home. The penalty is higher prices. Why? As exports of goods and services rise, income (Y) and hence GDP increase. As income increases, consumption increases. As consumption increases, more dollars are competing for fewer domestic goods, and prices will tend to rise.

A trade deficit (imports greater than exports) earns a nation's economic and political leaders criticism and economic disadvantages. Strains are placed on the value of a nation's currency with respect to other currencies. If these strains become too severe, the country's currency will **depreciate** (be worth less) with respect to other, stronger currencies, so imported goods will cost more. On the other hand, exports should become cheaper and thus more attractive to foreign nations. In following sections of this chapter, we will see how this happens.

A country cannot do away with a trade deficit simply by removing or reducing a "big" item on the balance-of-payments statement. For example, it is not true that, as opponents of foreign aid have argued, this expenditure caused deficits in the basic trade balance for many years. Much foreign aid is "tied"; that is, it must be spent on goods produced in the United States. So if the

United States cut foreign aid by $1 billion, U.S. exports might be reduced by as much as $800 million. The gain would be very small indeed. Many of the items in the balance of payments are related to other items in this way.

It is, however, legitimate to note that when a particular item is in surplus, the country has the freedom to run up a deficit in some other item without creating pressure against its currency. This sort of situation can be created in either of two ways: There may be items that in the working out of "basic economic forces" generate a surplus, or other countries in the world economy may "allow" deficits to exist without exerting pressure for policy measures that would reduce them. An example of the former is the flow of investment income into the United States. In the past, the net income on U.S. investments abroad allowed the United States to, among other things, increase its ownership of factories and mines in other countries and finance military expenditures abroad. An example of the second situation would be the willingness of countries to hold onto dollars accumulated from U.S. deficits because dollars are valuable to them.

Exchange Rates and the Balance of Payments

As we mentioned earlier, trade imbalances can create pressures on a nation's currency. Let's examine how the value (exchange rate) of the dollar is determined and how it influences the balance of payments.

THE BIG PICTURE

Exchange Rates

The supply and demand model (developed in Chapter 8) is used to determine exchange rates. There are a number of determinants that affect exchange rates, and this can make fluctuations in exchange rates difficult to understand. But the logic behind the supply and demand model for exchange rates, and thus behind fluctuations in exchange rates, is straightforward. When international actors (including consumers, investors, businesses, speculators, and governments) want more of a particular country's goods, services, or assets, they will demand more of that country's currency to pay for those goods, services, or assets. As shown in Figure 21.BP.1, any increase in the demand for a nation's currency will cause that currency to increase (or appreciate) in value relative to the currency of its trading partner (whose currency will in turn decrease, or depreciate, in value). When international actors want less of a particular nation's goods, services, or assets, they will demand less of that nation's currency. Any decrease in the demand for a nation's currency will cause that currency to decrease (or depreciate) in value relative to the currency of its trading partner(s). There are, of

FIGURE 21.BP.1 The Market for Dollars Responds to an Increase in Demand

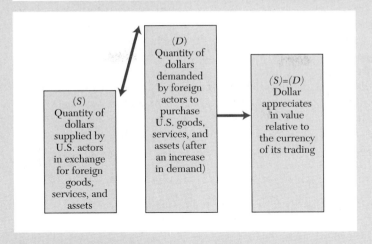

course, a number of variations to this story, and we explore the nuances of changes in exchange rates in the rest of the chapter.

Recall that, as we saw in Chapter 8, the value of a nation's currency, the exchange rate, is determined by the supply of and demand for that currency. The supply of a nation's currency comes from the country's central bank as well as its citizens who desire to purchase foreign goods, services, securities, and other assets. For example, the supply of U.S. dollars would increase if the Fed supplied more dollars in order to purchase foreign currencies, if U.S. citizens wanted to purchase more imported goods, or if U.S. investors wanted to invest in foreign asset markets. Figure 21.3 shows that an increase in the supply of dollars in exchange for euros causes the value of the dollar in terms of foreign currency to depreciate (decrease in price relative to the euro). A depreciation of the dollar means that each U.S. dollar buys less foreign currency than it used to, making foreign goods more expensive to purchase.

The demand for a nation's currency comes from foreign citizens who want to purchase the home country's goods and assets. For example, the demand for dollars would increase if the prices of U.S. goods fell relative to foreign goods (causing foreign citizens to desire more U.S. goods), if foreign citizens wanted to invest more in U.S. bonds, or if foreign citizens wanted to hold more dollars as assets. As Figure 21.4 shows, an increase in the demand for dollars by European citizens would shift the demand curve for the dollar to the right, causing the dollar to appreciate (increase in price relative to the euro). An appreciation of the dollar means that each dollar can purchase more foreign currency than it used to, making foreign goods cheaper to U.S. citizens.

FIGURE 21.3   An Increase in the Supply of Dollars

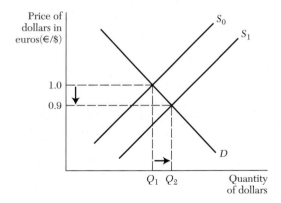

The Dollar and the Euro

In fact, the dollar was strong relative to the euro from 1999 to 2001 and weak from 2001 to 2007. As the U.S. economy slowed in 2001, the stock market plummeted, and the Fed slashed interest rates to try to stave off a recession. Normally, economists would expect declining stock prices and low interest rates on bonds to scare off foreign investors, causing a decrease in the demand for dollars and a depreciation of the dollar.

While the dollar fell with respect to the euro and other European currencies, including the pound and Kroner, Asian currencies held up the sagging dollar—at least for a while. During much of the period from 2003–2007 the United States was very dependent on Asian central banks to finance the current account deficit.

Determinants of Exchange Rates

To understand shifts in the supply and demand curves for a currency, we must understand the determinants of exchange rates. Table 21.3 lists some of the factors that cause shifts in the supply of and demand for a currency. The supply of a

FIGURE 21.4   An Increase in the Demand for Dollars

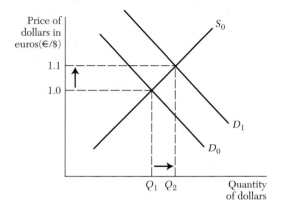

TABLE 21.3 Shifts in the Supply and Demand for a Currency (Dollars)

Determinant Change	Supply of Dollars	Demand for Dollars	Value of the Dollar
U.S. prices increase.	U.S. citizens want cheaper foreign goods; supply of dollars increases.	Foreign citizens want fewer U.S. goods; demand for dollars decreases.	Depreciates
U.S. demand for foreign goods, services, and assets increases.	U.S. citizens want more foreign items; supply of dollars increases.	Foreign citizens do not change the amount of U.S. goods they purchase; demand for dollars does not shift.	Depreciates
Foreign demand for U.S. goods, services, and assets increases.	U.S. citizens do not change the amount of foreign goods they purchase; supply of dollars does not change.	Foreign citizens want more U.S. items; demand for dollars increases.	Appreciates
U.S. productivity increases, lowering the prices of U.S. goods.	U.S. citizens prefer cheaper U.S. goods to many foreign goods; supply of dollars decreases.	Foreign citizens want more U.S. goods now that the price has fallen; demand for dollars increases.	Appreciates
U.S. interest rates increase.	U.S. investors move their money from foreign banks back to U.S. banks to get a higher return; supply of dollars decreases.	Foreign investors put more money in U.S. banks to get a higher return; demand for dollars increases.	Appreciates

currency is affected by the central bank's decisions to supply more or less of the currency, as well as domestic consumer and producer decisions regarding foreign goods, services, and assets. The demand for a nation's currency is affected by the demand for a nation's products and the prices of those products. The lower the price of the products, the greater the demand, and thus the greater the demand for the nation's currency, since currency is needed to purchase the products. Other factors that often influence exchange rates include tastes and preferences for the country's products, productivity increases, the inflation rate, and the domestic interest rate relative to other countries' rates. In Figure 21.5, an increased demand in the United States for Japanese-produced Toyotas increases the demand for yen and thus increases the exchange rate of the yen in terms of dollars. Each dollar will purchase fewer yen as the price of yen in dollars rises. From the opposite perspective, the price of dollars in terms of yen has decreased.

Given the current U.S. trade deficits, we might expect the value of the dollar to be falling with respect to many other currencies, since the demand for U.S. exports is low (contributing to a low demand for dollars) and the demand for imported goods is high (contributing to a large supply of dollars). But other fac-

FIGURE 21.5 Supply and Demand for Toyotas and Yen

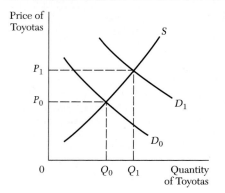

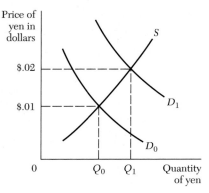

tors affect the demand for a nation's currency. Nontrade pressures, which are not influenced by the demand for a nation's products, might dramatically influence the value, or the exchange rate, of the dollar. Currencies are used not only to purchase goods and services, but also to make money—that is, to earn a rate of return, or interest. The Fed's tightening of monetary policy in the fall of 1979, in late 1989, and from 1997 to 2000 did curb the growth rate of the money supply, but the resulting higher interest rate and a growing confidence that the United States was a "safe haven" for assets created a demand for dollars among foreign corporations and investors.

To illustrate this, we will assume that before the Fed initiative, $1 would purchase 100 yen. In Figure 21.6, a Fed reduction in the growth rate of the

FIGURE 21.6 Supply and Demand for Dollars When U.S. Interest Rates Increase

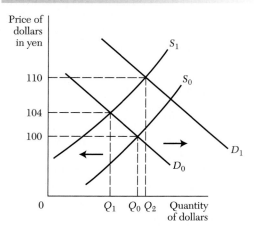

Discount store, Tokyo, Japan.
(Eddie Stanger/SuperStock, Inc.)

money supply is shown by the shift in the supply curve of dollars from S_0 to S_1. A higher interest rate created by the reduced money supply will attract foreign investment and thus increase the demand for dollars. This is shown by a shift in the demand curve from D_0 to D_1.

In this example, the dollar has become very strong. Therefore, it commands or purchases a larger quantity of other foreign currencies and thus more foreign goods and services. Before the Fed's contractionary monetary policy, $1 would purchase 100 yen, but with less supply and greater demand, $1 purchases 110 yen. Japanese products have become relatively cheaper for U.S. consumers. That will tend to increase Japanese (foreign) imports, which increases the tendency for the U.S. balance of trade to run a deficit. At the same time, 1 yen commands fewer dollars, its buying power having fallen from $.010 worth of U.S. products to only $.009 worth. Therefore, each U.S. product costs Japanese consumers more. Even though the prices of U.S. products have not changed in absolute terms, for a Japanese consumer they are relatively higher, since the yen's dollar-purchasing power has declined. As a result, fewer U.S. goods are exported to Japan, leading to further deterioration in the balance of trade. In this example, the dollar has appreciated, or gained in value with respect to the yen, while the yen has depreciated, or lost value with respect to the dollar.

The Value of the Dollar since the 1970s

During the 1970s, the U.S. dollar experienced a spectacular decline in value relative to other major trading currencies. Beginning in the fall of 1979, the dollar began an upward roll, eventually reaching new highs against most European currencies each day in early 1985 (see Figure 21.7). The decline in the 1970s reflected major weaknesses in the U.S. economy: slow growth, an impressive economic challenge by Germany and Japan, and relatively high and continuing inflation in the United States. Factors responsible for sustaining the high dollar value in the 1980s included the high U.S. budget deficits, high real interest rates, and low levels of inflation with respect to those in other industrial nations. The dollar peaked against the yen in 1985 at $1 = 260 yen.

Between 1985 and 1993, the dollar began to drop, particularly in relation to the German mark and the Japanese yen. In September of 1985, the Group of Five (the United States, United Kingdom, France, West Germany, and Japan—also known as G-5), agreed in the Plaza Accord* to intervene in foreign exchange markets to lower the value of the soaring dollar in order to promote more even-handed economic growth.† After 1993, the dollar had fallen to its post–World War II low against the yen at $1 = 100.9 yen. The dollar had depreciated more than 50 percent from its peak in 1985, as interest rates in the United States and oil prices continued to fall. Since 1993, the dollar strengthened against the yen and many other major currencies and by early 1997 had moved to 125 yen per dollar.

The period between 1971 and 1997 shows a complete cycle of exchange rate movements that respond to domestic inflation, interest rates, and intervention in currency markets. Some economists argue that the U.S. merchandise trade balance was not reduced by a greater magnitude during the period of dollar decline because many foreign producers cut their profit margins in order to keep export prices low and thus maintain their share of the market. These economists also point out that the dollar depreciation was much greater with respect to the yen and German mark than to other currencies. Thus, prices of goods imported from those areas remained attractive to U.S. consumers.

4. What kind of sale on U.S.-produced goods were Japanese consumers and businesses treated to with the fall in the value of the dollar between 1985 and 1993? How would U.S. retailers advertise such a deal?

In 1997 the value of the dollar was again turning upward. The threat of increased inflation caused the Fed to institute a somewhat more restrictive mone-

---

*The Plaza Accord was so named after the location of the September 1985 meeting at New York City's Plaza Hotel.

†Currency intervention occurs when a nation (or nations) purchase (or sell) the currency of a particular nation to establish a higher (or lower) rate of exchange. In this case, the G-5 nations agreed to sell dollars so as to lower the dollar's value with respect to other trading currencies. This is truly a managed float!

FIGURE 21.7   Exchange Rates

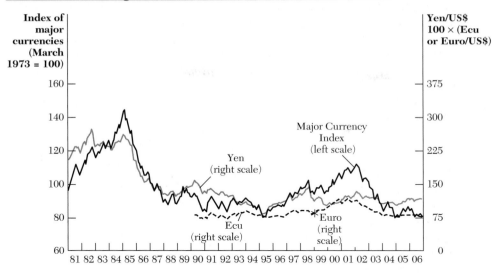

Source: Federal Reserve Bank of St. Louis, 2006.

tary policy and thus an increase in interest rates in the United States. Japanese investors, still concerned with domestic banking and stock market crises, moved some of their funds to the United States and Europe to seek higher yields and perhaps greater stability. As the movement continued, the U.S. trade balance felt increased pressure as imports became more attractive to U.S. consumers and exports lost their exchange advantage in international markets.

The U.S. dollar continued to grow stronger from 1997 to the early months of 2001. As Figure 21.7 illustrates, the weak dollar of the late 1970s gave way to the strong dollar of the early 1980s, only to weaken from 1985 to 1990. From 1990 to 1995, the dollar maintained its general strength but was weaker to the yen and stronger to the euro. From 1995, the dollar began its rise for the remainder of the decade, growing stronger against the yen and the euro. Much of the strength of the dollar was related to the increased demand for dollars generated by the strong foreign demand for U.S. financial instruments and for direct investment in the United States. In addition, the demand for U.S. exports began to increase in the late 1990s.

The U.S. dollar, as measured by the major currency index in Figure 21.6, strengthened from 1999 to the beginning of 2002. After 2002, the dollar declined through 2006 well into 2007. The U.S. economic downturn, along with continued concerns about the U.S. economic recovery, contributed to the dollar's fall. The growing U.S. trade and current account deficit and the domestic budget deficit were also major factors.

Volatile Dollar May Not Be Scary to Washington
Steven R. Weisman

As the dollar tumbled against the euro this week, reflecting fresh concern about a possible weakening of the American economy, Treasury Secretary Henry M. Paulson Jr. issued the usual phrase from the catechism: "A strong dollar is clearly in our nation's best interest."

Treasury secretaries since Robert E. Rubin in the 1990s have, with rare exceptions, offered precisely, that formula whenever the subject comes up.

But many economists say that Mr. Paulson's statement does not reflect what the United States actually seeks right now. For one thing, the Bush administration is in active pursuit of a weaker dollar against China's currency which would probably encourage similar changes with other Asian competitors. The goal would be making American exports there less expensive, and imports more expensive, helping to spur an industrial revival at home.

And though there are high risks if the dollar were to continue to fall rapidly against the euro and the British pound, the United States is generally seen as hoping for the economic gains delivered by a lower dollar as American exports become more competitive against planes, machinery and other goods produced in Europe.

"Paulson has got to like a euro that's appreciating in value," said C. Fred Bergsten, director of the Peterson Institute of International Economics and a longtime advocate of a weak dollar. "He came into office facing an overall American trade deficit that is close to $1 trillion a year. He's got to welcome something that shows the trade deficit likely to go down."

Still, the fluctuations of the dollar have unsettled many in the world of finance this last week, when it sagged about 2 percent against the euro, bringing its decline this year to more than 12 percent. . . .

In Europe, the French finance minister, Thierry Breton, has expressed concern about a weakening dollar, noting that exports have helped Europe's recent economic recovery. But other European finance ministers said this week that at least for now, gains in the euro do not appear to threaten prospects for growth in Europe.

The gyrations of the dollar highlight the sensitivity of Mr. Paulson's role at this particular moment, as he prepares for his biggest overseas trip so far as Treasury chief: a veritable expedition to China, accompanied by five cabinet members and by Ben S. Bernanke, the Federal Reserve chairman.

The goal of the trip, which starts Dec. 14, is to engage China on a range of economic issues but most particularly to press Beijing to let its currency, the yuan, rise in value against the dollar. That would help, American officials hope, to narrow a Chinese trade surplus with the United States that soared past $200 billion last year.

As a former investment banker who lived and breathed the logic of international markets for decades at Goldman Sachs, Mr. Paulson is trying to engineer a kind of correction in which China would cease what American officials say have been currency manipulations aimed at pumping out exports.

Against the background of the rise of the euro, the China trip illustrates the three-cornered complexities of the world economy and of Mr. Paulson's dollar diplomacy.

Suddenly with a declining dollar, Europeans are stepping up their purchases of American goods, and it has become more expensive for Americans to visit Europe as tourists or business officials. American investors overseas, meanwhile, are enjoying the

FIGURE 21.8

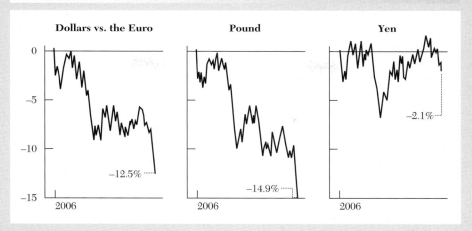

Source: Bloomberg Financial Markets, *The New York Times*

extra kick that a falling dollar delivers on their foreign profits.

The decline of the dollar against the euro, while the dollar-to-yuan ration remains stable, also has the effect of increasing tensions between Europe and China. European businesses, like their American counterparts, are already upset about cheap Chinese exports to Europe. Now these goods are even cheaper because the yuan is declining against the euro, pulled down by the dollar.

The Chinese, meanwhile, are likely to get more nervous than ever that a decline in the dollar against the yuan will damp their exports and reduce the value of their dollar-denominated assets, putting pressure on Chinese banks that are holding those assets.

China has resisted American appeals to let the yuan rise in value, arguing that China is already undertaking painful economic reforms—writing off bad loans and closing money-losing state enterprises—and cannot afford further social disturbance brought on by new difficulties in exports.

"We are committed to a market-based exchange-rate mechanism," said a senior Chinese official, speaking anonymously under Chinese ground rules. "But we will do it in a responsible way—responsible to the health of our country, the United States, Asia and beyond."

Part of the reason for the dollar sell-off, many analysts say has been a recent sense of disappointment about the American economy even as Europe has picked up some momentum, prompting traders to look for more promising investments in markets overseas. The prospect of higher interest rates in Europe while rates remain stuck or drift lower in the United States has also drawn funds out of the dollar.

Some analysts also say that the dollar decline has been partly seasonal—that there is always a decline in investment in dollar-denominated investments at the end of the year, despite the huge need by the United States to finance its current-account and budget deficits. . . .

"It's like musical chairs," [Robert Sinche, head of global currency research and strategy at Bank of America] added. "When the music stops, those who have deficits are going to suffer."

If American policy makers are pleased about the prospect of the dollar's providing a kick for exports, they fear a dollar falling so far and fast that it fuels inflation in the United States. Higher inflation might force the Federal Reserve, which is still concerned that price increases are outside its comfort zone, to raise interest rates, slowing the American economy further.

"The fall of the dollar has both benefits and risks," said Nouriel Roubini, chairman of Roubini Global Economics. "The danger is that the willingness of foreign investors to buy dollars is shrinking. If the fall of the dollar accelerates, investors could start dumping U.S. assets, and you'll get a hardlanding for the economy."

The fear of a loss in the value of its assets is a factor in China's rebuffing American imprecations to let its currency float more flexibly against the dollar, many analysts say. China has amassed $1 trillion in foreign exchange reserves after years of trade surpluses with Europe and the United States.

About $700 billion of those reserves are said by many economists to be in dollars. One reason China does not want a cheaper dollar against the yuan, these economists say, is

that the value of its holdings would decrease, limiting the lending ability of its banks.

Nevertheless, Mr. Paulson's trip is organized around the principle that China needs a bit of a weaker dollar now because its current path of binging on exports will overheat the Chinese economy—it is growing at 10 percent a year—and cause a collapse sooner or later if it is not cooled off slowly.

The dollar has declined about 5 percent against the yuan in the last year and a half, but American policy makers say that the yuan is still artificially low. . . .

Not all economists agree that an upward revaluation of the yuan will benefit the American economy. They note that cheap exports from China are desired by American consumers, and that Chinese imports have not led to rising unemployment, as critics charge.

"Let's say China revalues by 10 percent overnight," Mr. Sinche said. "Then prices at Wal-Mart go up by 10 percent. So we then see worse inflation numbers, the Fed tightens monetary policies, and we end up with higher inflation, higher prices and higher interest rates. Remind me again why that's what we want."

Source: "Volatile Dollar May not Be Seary to Washington," Steven R. Weisman, *The New York Times*, December 2, 2006, section C, p. 1.

The Future of the International Financial System

As the twenty-first century began, global capital markets became more integrated. Economic policy makers and central bankers from all countries realized that their ability to control their respective domestic economies, in the context of rapid global change, was increasingly more difficult and less effective. Capital was highly mobile. It could move quickly. Currency values were increasingly volatile.

The countries with the eight largest industrial economies (the United States, Canada, United Kingdom, France, Germany, Italy, Russia and Japan), together known as the G-8 countries, responded by voluntarily coordinating some of their economic policies. Their ongoing effort to cooperate has been mildly successful. Still, without the discipline of an enforcement mechanism, countries tend to do only what is self-serving and politically expedient. Annual economic summits have served largely to bring together the members of the G-8 for public relations, ritual identification of the problems they face collectively, and only moderate cooperation.

By 2006, the global economy was marked by rapid and dramatic forces of change. Developing countries in Asia, Latin America, and Africa were moving toward market economies and democratic governments. Other nations in transition in Eastern Europe, Central Europe, and the Commonwealth of Independent States were also following the path toward establishing market economies, drawing enormous attention to the potential opportunities afforded by these emerging market economies. In these countries there is a new interest in stock and bond markets. There have been investment scandals, such as the one in Albania in 1997, which produced riots and a governmental crisis. Increased capital flows in the form of direct private foreign investment in these countries have led many international commercial banks and investment banks to aggressively establish themselves there.

From the 1990s to the early years of the twenty-first century, China and India emerged as powerful new players in the global economy. Western Europe has continued to adapt to the changes and challenges of European economic integration and monetary union for most of the EU members. West Germany's integration with East Germany slowed the locomotive for European economic growth a bit. And while all this has been taking place, the competitive pressures of the marketplace are pushing even more rapid change.

The mid-1990s found Japan coming out of three years of recession, only to have its economy collapse again in 1998 as fears of a currency crisis gripped Asia and spread to Latin America. In 2001, Japan continued to try to solve many internal financial and political problems as well as confront new competitive pressures in its own backyard. By the early months of 2004, the United States and the global economy were entering a period of synchronized growth and economic recovery. But the U.S. occupation of Iraq, the terrorist train bombing in Madrid, and the continued instability in the Middle East provided a context for an underlying concern about the prospects for continued growth and stability. Oil prices increased to more than $75 per barrel, causing continued concern. There were expectations that the dollar would continue to decline and result in a much needed soft-landing for the dollar. Europe and Japan were concerned that their export-driven recoveries would be constrained by the cheaper U.S. dollar.

Exchange Rate Systems: An Historical Perspective

Some type of international financial system is required to deal with the "imbalances" in the balance-of-payments positions among nations. If the United States, for example, has an overall balance-of-trade deficit with the rest of the world, some mechanism must exist for "balancing" that deficit. Throughout the history of modern world capitalism, several different systems have existed for accomplishing this task, including fixed and fluctuating exchange standards.

The Gold Standard

Gold served as the external form of payment in the international system from the Middle Ages until the twentieth century. Under a gold standard, a country's currency is convertible into gold at a fixed price. The price of the currency expressed in terms of gold is known as its parity value. The United States and the United Kingdom once defined their currencies in terms of gold. As a result, surpluses and deficits in the balance of payments were equivalent to a certain amount of gold.

This mechanism was relatively simple and had some attractive results. The flow of gold from the United Kingdom would reduce the money supply in the United Kingdom and increase it in the United States. As an automatic reaction, prices would fall in the United Kingdom and rise in the United States, since less (more) money would tend to force prices downward (upward) and since gold was a part of the money supply. Consumers in each country would then respond to the price changes. Exports of U.S. goods would tend to fall, and those of the United Kingdom would tend to increase. Consequently, the balance-of-payments surplus of the United States would tend to decline, all without any government intervention.

The concept of liquidity is vital to trade in that transactions require some standard of "moneyness" that is universally accepted, and the trading parties must have this liquidity. Under the gold standard, if countries do not have enough gold reserves (or gold mines) to facilitate trade or if output of goods and services outstrips the output of gold, a liquidity crisis results. The health of domestic economies is therefore at the mercy of the world's ability to produce gold. In practice, the gold standard limited the amount of international trade that could be financed and tended to restrict some domestic economies. As nations and trade grew, the limited gold resources could not satisfy the needs of world trade.

The International Monetary Fund and the Bretton Woods System

Two world wars separated by the Great Depression dealt fatal blows to the gold standard. The framework for the system that forms the official organizational structure of today's international financial negotiations was formulated in 1944 at a conference in Bretton Woods, New Hampshire, and became known as the **Bretton Woods system**. The institutional arrangements settled on were to be overseen by a new organization, the **International Monetary Fund (IMF).** The IMF was established to provide an institutional framework for monetary cooperation and consultation when problems arose. It was charged with facilitating expansion and balanced growth of trade with high levels of domestic income and employment.

To accomplish this goal, the participants established a system of fixed exchange rates. Under the fixed exchange system, currencies were defined in terms of one another. The IMF was to provide for stable exchange rates between currencies. Consistency was assured, with each nation defining its currency in terms of both gold and the U.S. dollar. The U.S. dollar maintained a passive role in the Bretton Woods system because it was chosen to serve as the key or reserve currency, making it as acceptable as gold in international transactions. The Bretton Woods system functioned with this fixed exchange system until 1973.

International Monetary Crisis

The IMF was created and designed to guarantee the working of the Bretton Woods system, but problems sent the fixed exchange system into periods of confusion and disarray, never quite fulfilling the dreams of its creators. According to the design of the Bretton Woods system, exchange rate adjustments should occur in cases of persistent balance-of-payments difficulties. However, because the dollar was the reserve currency and essential for international liquidity, necessary dollar adjustments were avoided. In addition, more serious trouble lay deeper than this. Currency realignments were rare under the Bretton Woods system. Many believed depreciation was a sign of national weakness, while appreciation was viewed not as a sign of strength but as a compromise to a weaker economic position. Many nations' exchange rates were out of kilter, since they remained at essentially the same parity rates that existed at the end of World War II.

With ever-increasing deficits in the balance of payments, U.S. policy remained much the same during the 1960s. During this period, the IMF virtually conceded its operations to the Group of Ten, consisting of the ten most economically powerful countries in the world. At their meetings they discussed and acted at any indication of weakness in currency operations—but prompt realignment of parity rates did not occur. A system of emergency capital flows developed, with funds being shuttled from one weak currency to the next. This led only to greater instability within the Bretton Woods system.

In August 1971, President Nixon introduced the New Economic Policy (NEP), which, along with domestic wage and price controls, called for a temporary 10 percent surcharge on all imports as well as a "temporary" halt in the convertibility of dollars into gold. (This temporary condition still exists, and it is now understood that August 15, 1971, marked the complete end of the gold exchange standard. Although U.S. citizens have not been able to exchange their dollar holdings for gold from the U.S. Treasury since 1934, foreign dollar holders continued to exchange dollars for gold until this suspension.) Under the burden of inflation and the high costs of the war in Vietnam, the U.S. balance-of-payments deficit was larger and more pressing than it had been at any time in the nation's history.

Floating Exchange Rates

On December 18, 1971, President Nixon committed what a few years earlier would have been political suicide and devalued the dollar. The "historic" Smithsonian agreement called for an 8 percent devaluation of the dollar and a realignment of other currencies to reflect the lower value of the dollar. As pressures continued, nations began to let their currencies float (adjust to daily changes in the supply of and demand for each currency).

Since 1973, *de facto* currency depreciations or appreciations occur without official IMF sanction. The overvalued dollar was allowed to seek its own worth in the somewhat free international currency markets. The IMF was given the power to "oversee the exchange rate regime, adopt principles to guide national policies, and encourage international cooperation."

In the years since the introduction of floating exchange rates, the international monetary system has adjusted surprisingly well, even though the central banks of most major industrial countries have intervened at one time or another to "manage" or intervene in their exchange rates. Floating exchange rates have presented special problems for developing economies, however. Because few of these nations had well-developed currency markets, they tied or pegged their currency to that of their major industrial trading partner. A developing nation whose currency was pegged to the British pound found that its currency, like the pound, depreciated by almost 25 percent between mid-1975 and the end of 1976. These kinds of exchange rate movements can cause severe inflationary pressures in developing countries where inflation is often a persistent problem.

Conclusion

With all of these changes taking place, what will become of the international financial system? A number of factors currently drive this system with interactive effects. The context of these changes is a competitive system characterized by deregulation, free markets, and innovation. Deregulation and innovation have generated exchange rate volatility as financial entities have applied new computer and information system technologies to their operations and the development of new products and services.

Clearly, these issues confound simple Keynesian solutions to macroeconomic problems. As we move further into this millennium, global policy makers will continue to be challenged to find workable solutions that promote worldwide economic stability.

Review Questions

1. What is the international balance of payments? What does it mean to have a balance-of-payments surplus or deficit?

2. What kinds of activities contribute positive credits (+) to a nation's balance of payments?

3. How can you use the National Income Accounting framework to illustrate a trade deficit?

4. What has been the experience of the United States with trade deficits and current account deficits since 1990?

5. What has been the experience of the U.S. dollar since 1975? What is the situation for the U.S. dollar today?

6. What are the primary determinants of the value of a nation's currency (exchange rate)?

7. What can explain the appreciation of the dollar? The depreciation of the dollar?

8. What have been the yen/dollar and euro/dollar relationship since 1999? What is your analysis of these relationships?

CHAPTER TWENTY-TWO

The Economics of Developing Nations

◾ Introduction

A *ccording to the United Nations, by the year 2020 approximately 80 percent of the world's population (an estimated 8 billion) will be living in developing countries. What will this mean in terms of global poverty? The competition for global resources? The economic growth and development needs of these countries? Relations between the more-developed and less-developed countries?*

By the early 1960s, it had become common practice to refer to nations as being part of either the First, Second, or Third World. Those in the First World were the Western industrialized market economies, while those in the Second World were members of the socialist planned economies. The remaining nations fell into the category of the Third World. The member nations of the Third World were the developing nations of Asia, Africa, the Middle East, and Latin America. Most of these nations had achieved political independence by the early 1960s and found themselves caught between the First and Second Worlds in terms of both the Cold War and their own quest for economic development.

By 1960 the economic gap between the developed and developing world had widened to such an extent that the United Nations declared the 1960s to be the "Development Decade." Since then, the global community and many international institutions such as the World Bank and the International Monetary Fund have devoted considerable resources to an attempt to bring about economic development in the Third World over the last forty-five years. These efforts, as we shall see, have produced mixed results, great controversy, and an emerging consensus on the future direction of development.

Common Characteristics of Developing Nations

Despite great diversity among developing nations, they share a set of common characteristics. A developing nation typically has the following attributes:

- ◆ Low standard of living
- ◆ Low level of labor productivity

◆ High rate of population growth
◆ High and rising level of unemployment and underemployment
◆ Dependency on agricultural production and primary product exports
◆ Vulnerability in international political, economic, and financial relations

Global Poverty

At the end of the twentieth century, about 1.2 billion people lived in abject poverty (surviving on $1 a day or less). As shown in Table 22.1, the number of people living on less than $2 a day increased from 2,654 million in 1990 to 2,739 million in 1999. In 2002, 50 percent of the world's population lived in poverty, with 77.8 percent of the population of South Asia classified as living in poverty and 74.9 percent of sub-Saharan Africa classified as poor. By comparison, Latin America and the Caribbean had a poverty rate of 24.0 percent and Europe and Central Asia only 16.1 percent. Although poverty rates have improved significantly East Asia, sub-Saharan Africa and South Asia continue to see increases in the number of people in poverty, and Eastern Europe has seen a tripling of the poverty rate during its difficult transition period.

Global poverty on such a scale is even more dramatic when looked at in terms of the *distribution* of global income. A 2005 IMF study revealed that 77 percent of the world's people earn 15 percent of its income.

Underdevelopment: The Reality and Significance

It is difficult—if not impossible—for those of us living in a modern advanced nation such as the United States to understand what it would be like to live in poverty in a developing nation. Denis Goulet, a professor at the University of Notre Dame, has put it eloquently:

> Underdevelopment is shocking: the squalor, disease, unnecessary deaths, and hopelessness of it all! No man understands if underdevelopment remains for him a mere

TABLE 22.1   Number of Extremely Poor People in the World

Region	Number of People Living on Less than $2 per day (millions)		
	1990	1999	2002
East Asia and Pacific	1,116	900	748
China (new field)	825	627	533
Europe and Central Asia	23	113	76
Latin America and the Caribbean	125	127	123
Middle East and North Africa	51	70	61
South Asia	958	1,039	1,091
Sub-Saharan Africa	382	489	516
Total	2,654	2,739	2,614

Source: Data from *World Bank, World Development Indicators,* 2006.

statistic reflecting low income, poor housing, premature mortality, or underemployment. The most empathetic observer can speak objectively about underdevelopment only after undergoing, personally or vicariously, the "shock of underdevelopment." This unique cultural shock comes to one as he is initiated to the emotions which prevail in the "culture of poverty." The reverse shock is felt by those living in destitution when a new self-understanding reveals to them that their life is neither human nor inevitable. The prevalent emotion of underdevelopment is a sense of personal and societal impotence in the face of disease and death, of confusion and ignorance as one gropes to understand change, of servility toward men whose decisions govern the course of events, of hopelessness before hunger and natural catastrophe. Chronic poverty is a cruel kind of hell, and one cannot understand how cruel that hell is merely by gazing upon poverty as an object.

—Denis Goulet, *The Cruel Choice*, Atheneum, 1975

1. Have you ever been to a developing country? Did you see the kind of underdevelopment described in the quotation? If not, can you imagine this kind of reality?

Underdevelopment is an economic as well as human condition. In economic terms, we tend to think of an underdeveloped country as having a low per capita income and a low per capita gross domestic product. A developing country usually has a large percentage of its labor force in agriculture. It typically has a shortage of domestic savings, so it must rely on external capital and technology to stimulate investment and economic growth. Such a country usually depends on a small number of primary exports (raw materials and food crops) and some manufactured goods. It typically has balance-of-payments problems that stem from current account deficits (deficits in trade and investment income). In addition to the climate disaster, poverty and AIDS and other diseases developing countries also suffer from large external debts, which require sizable debt servicing (interest and principal payments). Payment of the debt involves outflows of interest and principal to foreign creditors.

While many economists tend to discuss underdevelopment in economic terms, others have expanded the economic aspect to include categories such as productivity, equity, sustainability, and empowerment. The box on page 530 emphasizes each of these categories as a part of a more fully developed definition of what constitutes not just economic development but human development. (This paradigm has been developed by the United Nations.)

Basic Economic Problems of Developing Nations

To complete our basic profile of a developing country, we turn to a more detailed discussion of the basic economic problems of developing nations. These problems include economic growth, population, macroeconomic instability, international trade and finance, and environmental problems.

Economic Growth

The primary consideration for developing countries is increasing the rate of economic growth. The essence of seeking higher levels of economic growth is to produce more goods and services to improve the population's material standard of living. Economic development, in its most basic sense, is the process of improving standards of living and well-being by raising per capita income.

As we have seen, economic growth depends on a number of factors. In a macroeconomic context, it involves increasing consumption, investment, government spending, and trade. In a microeconomic context, it involves physical resources, labor resources, and technology as applied to production. Microeconomic concerns oblige us to think in terms of efficiency and productivity. Macroeconomic issues require us to think in terms of savings flowing to investments in productive activities. Taken separately or together, these two perspectives on economic growth frame a context for understanding the challenges of economic development.

As Table 22.2 shows, the economic growth experience of developing nations has been encouraging in some areas, especially Asia, while discouraging in others, especially Latin America, sub-Saharan Africa, and the Arab states. This, as we shall see, has serious implications for the goal of reducing poverty in the face of enormous environmental and population growth pressures.

Population: Undermining Economic Growth

In 2000, the world's population had reached the 6.0 billion mark. The United Nations and the World Bank projected that global population would reach 8.8 billion by the year 2030. Of these, 7.4 billion (or 84 percent) of humanity will be living in the low- and middle-income countries.

Table 22.3 illustrates the growth of world population from 1975 to 2001, with projections for the year 2015. The low- and middle-income countries have

TABLE 22.2   Growth of per capita GDP in Low- and Middle-income Countries (by Region)

	1985–1989	1990–1994	1995–9	2000–2004	2005*	2006*
High Income	3.0	1.5	2.2	1.6	1.9	2.0
Low-income Countries	2.4	1.4	3.3	3.2	5.3	4.7
East Asia and Pacific	0.9	4.6	5.0	5.0	6.1	5.2
Europe and Central Asia	1.4	−14.4	−0.7	4.9	3.2	4.5
Latin America and the Caribbean	−4.0	−4.0	1.7	0.0	1.5	0.6
Middle East and North Africa	8.1	−1.6	3.3	0.6	0.4	0.3
South Asia	3.6	2.7	4.0	3.7	5.4	4.8
Excluding India	2.2	2.1	1.7	2.5	4.8	3.8
India	4.0	2.8	4.6	4.1	5.5	5.1
Sub-Saharan Africa	0.2	−1.8	1.1	1.4	3.0	3.8
Middle-income Countries	1.5	1.2	2.7	4.0	4.9	4.6
East Asia and Pacific	6.4	8.1	5.9	7.1	7.4	7.1
Excluding China	3.8	5.5	1.0	3.4	3.0	3.7
China	8.2	9.6	8.1	8.4	8.6	8.0
Europe and Central Asia	1.3	−5.8	1.8	5.4	5.2	5.0
Latin America and the Caribbean	0.2	1.7	0.9	0.8	3.1	2.5
Middle East and North Africa	−1.0	1.8	2.0	2.9	3.1	3.7
South Asia	1.5	4.3	3.9	3.0	3.5	4.8
Sub-Saharan Africa	−0.4	−2.4	1.1	2.3	3.6	3.3
Developing Countries	1.4	0.9	2.5	3.6	4.7	4.5

Source: Data from World Bank staff estimates
*f = forecast

made some progress in reducing the average annual population growth rate from 2.5 percent between 1965 and 1975 to 2.1 percent for low-income countries and 1.4 percent for middle-income countries between 1975 and 2003. Yet this reduction has not been enough to halt the rapid increase in population growth from 2.4 billion in 1965 to 4.1 billion in 1990 to 6.3 billion in 2003. The age structure (number of persons in specific age groups) in the least developed countries is such that 35 to 50 percent of the population is under age 15, and the women in this category are in or entering their peak fertility years. So, even if the average annual population growth rate is declining, say from 2.5 percent to 1.7 percent as is projected, the absolute size of the population is still increasing dramatically.

Even more striking is the situation in much of Africa. In sub-Saharan Africa, the average annual population growth rate has been about 3 percent for more than 25 years. This is more than a full percentage point above the world average and more than three times the average for high-income countries, where the population growth rate is less than 1.0 percent.

2. What do these data mean in the context of economic development and the economic growth data examined earlier?

TABLE 22.3 Population

	Total Population* (millions)			Annual Population Growth Rate (%)	
	1975	2003	2015	1975–2003	2003–2015
Developing Countries	2,967.1	5,022.4	5,885.6	1.9	1.3
Least Developed countries	355.2	723.2	950.1	2.5	2.3
Arab States	144.6	303.9	386.0	2.7	2.0
East Asia and the Pacific	1,310.4	1,928.1	2,108.9	1.4	0.7
Latin America and the Caribbean	318.4	540.7	628.3	1.9	1.3
South Asia	838.7	1,503.4	1,801.4	2.1	1.5
Sub-Saharan Africa	313.1	674.2	877.4	2.7	2.2
Central and Eastern Europe and the CIS	366.6	406.3	396.8	0.4	−0.2
High Income	781.8	948.3	1,005.6	0.7	0.5
Middle Income	1,849.6	2,748.6	3,028.6	1.4	0.8
Low Income	1,440.9	2,614.5	3,182.5	2.1	1.6
World	4,073.7*	6,313.8*	7,219.4*	1.6	1.1

Source: United Nations, *Human Development Report*, 2005, http://hdr.undp.org/statistics/data/pdf/hdr05_table_5.pdf.

The population growth and pressure in the poorest nations will continue in the context of a projected slowdown in the growth of the global economic system. With more mouths to feed as the number of the world's poor increases, the ability of nations to realistically increase their standard of living by increasing the real per capita GDP will be all the more difficult, if not impossible. Any improvement requires major changes on many different fronts, not the least of which is population control.

The basic issue is that for economic progress to take place, the rate of economic growth has to exceed the rate of population growth. This has not been happening in the Third World.

Macroeconomic Instability

Developing nations share with everyone the same basic overall goal of sustained economic growth with price stability. Yet, unlike the more advanced industrialized countries, their ability to practice traditional Keynesian stabilization policies has proven to be more limited. Many analysts have pointed out that the basic Keynesian theoretical and policy framework evolved out of unique circumstances—the crisis of a well-developed capitalist market economy in the 1930s—and it has been refined in that context ever since. In many developing nations, however, the state of development of free markets and other economic institutions presents unique complexities when it comes to developing policy prescriptions for inflation and unemployment. In other words, traditional

Keynesian stimulus policies (increased government spending, lower taxes, lower interest rates, etc.) may not be sufficient to trigger higher growth.

Moreover, in developing nations, inflation rates may be as high as 25 percent to more than 1,000 percent. High rates of inflation have the same negative consequences on the economy as in advanced market economies, but to a greater degree. From a policy perspective, developing countries typically resort to conventional Keynesian stabilization policies: reducing government spending, increasing taxes, and reducing government deficits. These usually result in slower growth and higher unemployment, neither of which poor developing countries can tolerate. Contractionary fiscal policy is usually matched with a tight monetary policy, but reducing the growth rate of the money supply and increasing interest rates only worsens the contraction of the economy.

Unemployment in developing countries is also a critical problem, and official government unemployment statistics tend to understate its severity. This is a result of political considerations, as well as different methods of determining unemployment than in more advanced market economies. When a country announces that its unemployment rate is only 6 percent, the actual rate may be closer to 30 percent or even more in rural areas. The difficulty in measurement comes from the fact that large numbers of people work outside of formal labor markets. In the informal labor market, there is no official record of work, wages, or taxes. People working in the informal labor market may exchange labor for goods and/or services, or they may work occasionally for cash for which there is no official record.

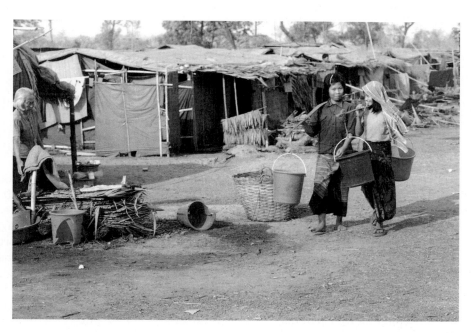

Poverty in South Asia: Thai sisters in their primitive village.
(Mark Richards/PhotoEdit)

Furthermore, while formal unemployment is a problem, *underemployment* is a much greater problem. Many people working in the formal labor market are working only a few days or hours a week while seeking full-time employment. In many developing countries, underemployment rates are estimated to be in the range of 40 to 50 percent.

Government policies to address unemployment and underemployment are usually the standard Keynesian expansionary prescription: increase government spending, lower taxes, increase the money supply, and lower interest rates. But these policies are difficult to implement because inflation is severe and governments confront large internal deficits and demanding external debts. For this reason, many leaders champion the growth of the informal sector.

International Trade

In the international sector, developing nations have been trying to reduce their historic current account and balance-of-payments deficits. In addition, virtually all developing countries are trying to diversify their export sectors by moving away from traditional dependence on one or several primary commodity exports (such as oil, coffee, and cotton).

The nations that have been implementing export diversification strategies with some success are called **newly industrializing countries (NICs).** This group includes Hong Kong, Taiwan, Singapore, Malaysia, the Philippines, South Korea, Brazil, Mexico, and Argentina. These countries have allowed foreign firms to set up operations that have generated a sizable export capability in manufactured goods and hence contributed to increased employment and income.

Policies to promote export growth and reduce imports are designed to improve the overall trade balance. But many developing countries have argued that the terms of trade—the price of *developed* countries' exports relative to the price of *developing* countries' exports—has turned against them. The deteriorating terms of trade, they contend, contributes to their current account deficit and the balance-of-payments deficit.

Table 22.4 shows the percentage change in the total dollar value in goods for developing countries for the Period 2000–2005, along with projected percentage changes for 2006 and 2007 and ten-year averages from 1988–1997 and 1998–2007. For trade in fuel, the annual average is projected to grow to 14.1 percent for exports and 10.7 percent for imports between 1998 and 2007. Trade in nonfuel merchandise is projected to grow an average of 12.4 percent per year for exports and 11.4 percent per year for imports. Trade in primary products are expected to average a growth of 7.4 percent per year for exports and 5.9 percent per year for imports. For the period of 1998–2007, the terms of trade are expected to be 7.4 for fuel, –0.3 percent for nonfuel, and 1.8 percent for primary products.

Table 22.5 reflects the payments balances on the current accounts of developing nations from 2000–2005 with estimations for the years 2006 and 2007. The current account had been in deficit until 2000 when it reached $91.1 billion. The primary source of this surplus was $70.0 billion from the Middle

TABLE 22.4 Other Emerging Market and Developing Countries—By Source of Export Earnings: Total Trade in Goods (*Annual percent change*)

	Ten-year Averages		2000	2001	2002	2003	2004	2005	2006	2007
	1988–1997	1988–2007								
Fuel										
Value in U.S. dollars										
Exports	5.5	14.1	48.3	−8.9	4.6	24.6	32.1	38.2	17.6	6.4
Imports	3.8	10.7	10.5	13.1	10.4	17.7	23.6	24.5	17.6	11.4
Volume										
Exports	4.4	5.0	8.4	1.7	3.1	9.1	9.9	6.0	6.6	5.3
Imports	1.3	9.0	13.5	15.3	8.9	6.4	14.4	19.4	16.2	10.3
Unit value in U.S. dollars										
Exports	1.6	9.0	36.4	−10.5	2.3	13.9	20.5	30.8	10.5	1.0
Imports	3.1	1.5	−2.5	−2.0	1.6	10.9	8.3	4.5	1.2	0.7
Terms of trade	−1.5	7.4	39.8	−8.7	0.6	2.7	11.3	25.2	9.2	0.3
Nonfuel										
Value in U.S. dollars										
Exports	10.6	12.4	18.3	0.7	10.2	21.8	27.8	19.9	14.3	11.7
Imports	11.5	11.4	19.1	−0.8	7.0	22.5	29.5	18.3	15.3	12.6
Volume										
Exports	8.9	10.2	16.0	3.1	8.9	12.1	16.0	12.5	11.6	12.0
Imports	9.5	8.9	15.2	1.4	6.1	12.6	17.1	10.7	12.3	12.8
Unit value in U.S. dollars										
Exports	2.3	2.2	2.1	−2.4	1.2	8.9	10.5	6.8	2.6	−0.1
Imports	2.7	2.5	3.5	−2.0	0.8	9.0	10.7	6.8	2.8	0.1
Terms of trade	−0.4	−0.3	−1.4	−0.3	0.5	−0.1	−0.2	−0.1	−0.2	−0.2
Primary Products										
Value in U.S. dollars										
Exports	5.3	7.4	4.6	−5.0	2.6	18.4	37.3	16.5	14.9	0.1
Imports	5.8	5.9	5.1	−0.8	2.1	14.2	26.1	20.5	10.6	5.9
Volume										
Exports	6.0	4.4	2.2	3.8	0.8	4.3	14.2	1.8	2.4	7.3
Imports	4.8	5.1	3.4	4.2	3.4	6.1	12.6	12.5	9.7	6.2
Unit value in U.S. dollars										
Exports	0.9	3.0	2.3	−8.3	1.9	13.5	19.7	14.8	12.1	−6.4
Imports	1.5	1.2	2.3	−4.7	−1.3	9.6	12.2	7.4	1.0	−0.2
Terms of trade	−0.6	1.8	—	−3.8	3.3	3.5	6.6	6.8	11.0	−6.2

Source: Data from *World Economic Outlook*, April 2006, Statistical Appendix,
http://www.imf.org/external/pubs/ft/weo/2006/01/pdf/statappx.pdf.

East, Malta, and Turkey. This amount came essentially from the large Middle East oil revenue derived from the years of oil prices in the range of $28 to $35 per barrel. The current account balances of India and China are interesting as each in the early years of the twenty-first century have become stronger players in the international economy and the global trading system. The plight of the net debtor countries is also quite important as this category of countries continues to struggle particularly with the slowdown in the global economy that took place from 2000 to 2003 and the rise in global petroleum prices.

TABLE 22.5 Other Emerging Market and Developing Countries: Payments Balances on Current Account

	2000	2001	2002	2003	2004	2005	2006	2007
				Billions of U.S. dollars				
Other emerging market and developing countries	91.1	44.2	84.5	148.5	219.8	423.3	486.7	473.2
Regional groups								
Africa	7.2	0.5	−7.5	−2.5	0.9	15.2	23.5	25.9
Sub–Sahara	−0.7	−7.4	−12.6	−12.2	−10.8	−6.6	2.2	5.9
Excluding Nigeria and South Africa	−5.8	−9.7	−7.9	−8.4	−6.7	−9.0	−4.4	−4.0
Central and eastern Europe	−32.4	−16.2	−24.0	−37.1	−59.2	−63.1	−72.2	−77.0
Commonwealth of Independent States	48.3	33.1	30.2	35.8	62.4	90.3	112.4	109.4
Russia	46.8	33.9	29.1	35.4	58.6	86.6	106.0	99.0
Excluding Russia	1.4	−0.8	1.1	0.4	3.8	3.7	6.4	10.4
Developing Asia	46.1	40.6	72.2	86.3	94.7	155.4	159.5	171.9
China	20.5	17.4	35.4	45.9	68.7	158.6	173.3	189.6
India	−4.6	1.4	7.1	8.8	1.4	−19.0	−26.1	−28.7
Excluding China and India	30.2	21.8	29.7	31.6	24.6	15.8	12.3	11.0
Middle East	70.0	39.8	29.5	59.0	103.4	196.0	240.9	235.6
Western Hemisphere	−48.1	−53.6	−16.0	7.1	17.7	29.6	22.7	7.5
Brazil	−24.2	−23.2	−7.6	4.2	11.7	14.2	10.5	2.6
Mexico	−18.6	−17.6	−13.5	−8.6	−7.2	−5.7	−5.5	−6.8

Source: Data from *World Economic Outlook*, April 2006, Statistical Appendix, http://www.imf.org/external/pubs/ft/weo/2006/01/pdf/statappx.pdf.

These factors are evident in the continuous growth in the level of total external debt of developing countries since 2000. As can be seen in Table 22.6, the total external debt of all developing countries grew from 2.5 trillion in 2000 to more than 3.2 trillion in 2005. As of 2005, the Western Hemisphere alone is responsible for $808.4 billion; developing Asia for $828.0 billion; and Central and Eastern Europe for $604.6 billion. The total external debt of developing countries was more than $3.2 trillion in 2005.

International Finance and Development

As we saw in the previous chapter, when a currency is depreciated, exports are cheaper and thus more competitive and imports are more expensive. The theoretical result is an increase in exports, a decrease in imports, and an improvement in the trade balance, the current account, and the overall balance of payments.

Many developing countries have been and continue to be confronted by a huge external debt. The total external debt of developing countries was more than $3.2 trillion in 2005. The debt service on these loans is an enormous burden. Their external debt has put additional pressure on developing countries to increase their export earnings in order to earn the foreign exchange needed to service the external debt. Critics argue that this outflow of scarce foreign exchange hampers governments from spending and investing domestically to produce economic growth.

TABLE 22.6 Summary of External Debt and Debt Service

	1998	1999	2000	2001	2002	2003	2004	2005	2006	2007
External Debt						*Billions of U.S. dollar*				
Other emerging market and										
developing countries	2,550.5	2,597.0	2,523.6	2,519.5	2,612.6	2,852.5	3,083.9	3,224.3	3,410.1	3,575.2
Regional groups										
Africa	282.7	281.3	269.9	258.5	271.1	294.6	305.8	282.1	265.4	265.3
Central and eastern Europe	269.8	286.7	309.9	316.0	368.2	460.5	553.8	604.6	656.5	706.2
Commonwealth of Independent States	222.8	219.0	199.2	194.4	199.8	239.9	281.0	331.4	374.7	419.4
Developing Asia	695.0	693.1	656.5	661.2	665.2	697.7	751.0	828.0	909.6	967.5
Middle East	290.9	302.5	304.6	306.4	313.1	324.9	347.4	370.0	381.7	386.6
Western Hemisphere	789.4	814.5	783.4	782.9	795.3	834.7	844.7	808.4	822.3	830.4
External Debt						*Percent of exports of goods and service*				
Other emerging market and										
developing countries	174.2	167.7	132.8	134.5	128.6	115.8	97.3	82.1	75.4	71.6
Regional groups										
Africa	236.3	219.7	171.4	172.5	175.6	151.7	123.5	91.2	74.2	68.1
Central and eastern Europe	118.6	134.1	127.7	121.6	127.6	125.2	116.7	109.3	108.4	106.2
Commonwealth of Independent States	175.2	177.2	120.9	117.2	111.9	107.1	93.0	86.1	84.3	89.1
Developing Asia	129.1	119.7	94.2	95.8	84.6	73.2	60.6	54.2	50.5	46.3
Middle East	183.3	149.8	108.4	116.8	112.4	95.1	79.8	63.4	56.3	53.7
Western Hemisphere	269.4	269.0	218.8	226.5	229.9	218.4	179.9	142.3	129.6	125.2
Analytical groups										
By external financing source										
Net debtor countries	220.1	219.9	185.3	185.1	183.4	169.5	143.6	121.1	111.0	105.4
of which, official financing	305.4	312.4	265.6	274.0	277.3	268.5	228.3	191.5	176.1	169.6
Net debtor countries by										
debt-servicing experience										
Countries with arrears and/or rescheduling during 1999–2003	360.7	349.8	274.8	284.8	281.4	256.8	212.6	166.3	143.6	132.4

Source: Data from *World Economic Outlook*, April 2006

TABLE 22.6 Summary of External Debt and Debt Service *(continued)*

	1998	1999	2000	2001	2002	2003	2004	2005	2006	2007
				Percent of exports of goods and service						
Debt-service Payments										
Other emerging market and										
developing countries	25.8	26.4	24.3	23.6	21.0	19.8	15.4	14.8	11.9	11.3
Regional groups										
Africa	21.3	19.8	16.7	17.5	13.8	13.2	11.5	11.2	7.0	6.7
Central and eastern Europe	24.2	27.1	26.5	28.5	26.8	26.2	22.0	22.2	22.9	21.9
Commonwealth of Independent States	23.3	21.9	36.8	23.4	26.2	28.2	23.9	18.9	13.7	14.4
Developing Asia	18.5	16.2	14.0	15.3	14.6	11.9	7.9	7.0	6.6	6.1
Middle East	15.0	11.9	8.6	10.2	6.6	7.6	6.6	7.0	6.5	6.4
Western Hemisphere	49.2	59.5	52.9	49.8	42.9	42.8	33.3	35.6	24.1	22.8

Source: International Monetary Fund, *World Economic Outlook*, April 2006, Statistical Appendix, Table 37.

Since the mid-1980s, private commercial banks in the advanced countries significantly reduced the level of loans to developing nations. This created a net resource transfer (the difference between new loans and debt service) on the order of approximately $30 billion a year flowing out of developing nations to the creditors in the advanced countries. In response, creditors and creditor governments developed initiatives in the early 1990s to reduce the level of debt and debt service without making large new loans. Creditors renegotiated loans at reduced interest rates or reduced the amount of the original loan. They also devised some creative financial schemes like debt-for-equity swaps, which essentially allow creditor banks to sell a portion of a country's debt to a buyer who purchases the debt on the secondary market at a discount and then uses it as investment capital in the country.

In spite of several well-intended responses on the part of commercial banks, the International Monetary Fund, and the World Bank, the external debt of developing countries still exists at a level that exacts an enormous opportunity cost in terms of the debt service burden. The external debt grew from $1.9 trillion in 1995 to $3.2 trillion in 2005. The debt service payments (interest and amortization) skyrocketed from $175 billion in 1995 to a high of $581.1 billion in 2005 and are predicted to remain approximately $550.0 billion both in 2006 and 2007. The irony for developing countries is that between 2000 and 2005 they paid $2.9 trillion in debt service on an external debt of approximately $3 trillion, yet they still owe approximately $3 trillion. If they had not had this debt, it is reasonable to assume that these countries would have had an additional $3 trillion to spend on pressing social and economic priorities such as health, education, infrastructure, technology, and the environment. In recent years, debt service as a percentage of exports of goods and services has ranged from a high of 24.3 percent in 2000 to a low of 14.8 percent in 2005.

Indeed, since the 1980s many groups have supported debt relief and debt forgiveness as a way for the advanced nations and their commercial banking institutions to relieve the burden of the developing countries' external debt. The pressure to service this external debt becomes even more pronounced in periods of slowing global economic growth, or in periods of financial crisis. Since the 1990s, several countries, including Mexico, Russia, Turkey, Argentina, Brazil, Indonesia, and the Philippines, experienced economic and financial crises that threatened their ability to service their external debts.

Environmental Problems

Population growth provides several strains on the environment. It increases the demand for goods and services. More people mean more wastes. To feed more people, more land must be put into cultivation, and land currently under cultivation must be farmed more efficiently and productively. This requires more water and often more resource inputs, with consequences for human health and the long-term viability of the land itself.

The existence of large numbers of poor people exacerbates environmental problems. In many countries, the pressure to increase nontraditional exports to improve the trade balance and service external debt has resulted in policies that encourage deforestation to permit creation of large cotton and cattle farms. The result is tremendous environmental degradation: not only deforestation, but species extinction, soil depletion and erosion, water contamination, and air pollution.

This issue was one of several addressed at the Earth Summit held in Rio de Janeiro, Brazil, in June 1992. This conference, sponsored by the United Nations, established the link among population growth, poverty, and the environment. It concluded that preservation of the environment and establishment of a framework for sustainable development depend on significantly reducing poverty and population growth in the developing countries. Sustainable development—a goal that had nearly unanimous support at the Earth Summit—is a model of economic growth that respects the integrity of Earth's physical life support system. It means developing a production system that does not degrade or undermine the ability of Earth's life support system to regenerate and cleanse itself. People must use resources in a way that permits renewable resources to renew themselves.

Explanations and Solutions for Underdevelopment

As we saw at the beginning of this text, the basic economic problem is essentially one of producing an economic surplus beyond immediate consumption needs. The more efficient and productive a society, the greater the level of economic surplus or savings for investment. And investment promotes growth in the output of goods and services.

Underdevelopment complicates this problem by creating a cycle of poverty that is hard to break. The existence of high levels of poverty builds a base of people with low incomes, most often subsistence incomes that allow for little if any savings. Yet low-income families tend to have more children. The higher birthrates drive population growth, which slows the rate of economic growth. Higher population growth rates also contribute to higher unemployment and underemployment, especially in a slow-growing economy. Productivity is hampered by other consequences of poverty: poor health and nutrition among the population, a low level of savings (which contributes to the low investment level), and a low level of education. The resulting low level of productivity contributes to the low level of income, and the cycle repeats itself.

3. How can the cycle of poverty be broken?

While there is widespread agreement among economists about what constitutes development and underdevelopment, there is no consensus with regard to what caused this condition to emerge, what perpetuates it, and what should be done to overcome it. Most economists believe solving underdevelopment requires that the low level of savings be offset by savings injections from external sources. These resources must come from the government in the form of direct income transfers or investment in enterprises and **infrastructure** (roads, bridges, airports, seaports, potable water, electricity, education, etc.). The funds for such investments must come from private foreign investment or from borrowing. This capital and the technology that it would bring can act as the primary stimulus for breaking the cycle of poverty and underdevelopment. With regard to more specific solutions, there are three distinct competing perspectives (schools of thought or paradigms): the neoliberal, structuralist, and dependency models.

The Neoliberal Model

According to the **neoliberal model,** developing nations must adopt modern capital and technology to have strong economic growth. Underdevelopment is assumed to be a natural condition characterized by backward and archaic institutions and values. This condition of underdevelopment must give way to progress and modernization characterized by industrialization, the mechanization of agriculture, urbanization, secular values, and political stability.

This model explains underdevelopment as a consequence of geography, culture, lack of capital and technology, and the vicious cycles of unproductive labor and poverty. In this overall context, the model asserts, a developing nation must create dynamic markets in land, labor, and capital. The emergence of dynamic and smoothly functioning markets along with the expansion of free trade are thus the road to progress. Together, the inflow of foreign capital and the transfer of modern technology are the catalyst necessary to provide the stimulus for sustained growth.

The neoliberal view is that only a free and open private market economy can overcome the vicious cycle of underdevelopment. Because foreign (external) capital, emerging financial markets, and technological change are the stimulants for sustained economic growth in this view, it emphasizes the positive role that multinational firms (corporations) and international financial institutions can and need to play in this process. From the perspective of economic policy, the neoliberal model offers the following prescription:

◆ A conservative fiscal policy that shrinks domestic deficits by reducing state spending and increasing taxes

◆ A conservative monetary policy of higher interest rates to reduce inflation

◆ The promotion of free trade and open-market economic policies that invite the free flow of goods, services, and capital. This will often require an adjustment in the currency's exchange rate through an official devaluation or a commitment to free flexible floating exchange rates.

The Structuralist Model

In the late 1960s and early 1970s, many economists advanced a perspective on underdevelopment that modified the traditional view. This group, led by Raul Prebish, a Brazilian economist then with the United Nations Economic Commission on Latin America, argued that the basic economic problem of underdevelopment exists for all countries but must be understood in the proper historical context. For Latin American, Asian, and African countries, their respective states of underdevelopment had to be understood in the context of their historic relationship to the European countries, which conquered them and transformed them into colonies. These countries' economies were therefore shaped by the economic needs of the colonial powers. Only this historical view explains the inequality in the distribution of income and wealth, the concentration in land ownership, the historic dependence on primary export products, the linking of foreign capital with the industrial and finance capital of domestic elites, and the frequent inappropriateness of Keynesian theories and policies to the circumstances of developing nations.

This **structuralist model** did not deny the basic economic analysis of the traditional view but saw domestic political and economic factors as obstacles to development. The structuralists also viewed the international economic and financial system of the 1960s and 1970s as serving the economic interests of the developed nations while reinforcing the dynamics of underdevelopment for the developing nations.

The contemporary proponents of the structuralist view emphasize the importance of a free and open market economy. They support constructive and responsible foreign investment and the transfer of technology from developed countries. Yet they also emphasize the importance of the following measures:

◆ A more genuine and equitable distribution of productive land
◆ A more diversified economy less reliant on primary commodity exports
◆ Government policies that realistically address the problem of poverty and income distribution
◆ An active role for government in the economy
◆ Strong environmental policies
◆ Relief from the burden of external debt
◆ Changes in the international trading and financial system designed to bring about a more equitable integration of developing countries into the global economy

The essence of the structuralist view is that breaking the cycle of underdevelopment requires much more than free and open markets supported by foreign capital and technology.

The Dependency Model

In the 1960s, the **dependency model** challenged the traditional and structural theories by using Marxian analysis to look at the problem of underdevelopment. The dependency model assumed that we must view underdevelopment as a consequence of the historical evolution of capitalism and the integration of developing countries into the expanding sphere of capitalist production globally. This model is based upon a generalized application of a Marxist methodology drawn from philosophy, history, sociology, political science, and economics. The character and structure of a developing country's economic and political system, as well as its class and social stratification system, are explained by its historical experience with colonialism and the subsequent expansion of capitalism.

Such a historical analysis locates the primary dynamic for change in the economic sphere as it represents at any time a historically specific mode of production. This mode of production characterizes the way in which land, labor, and capital are brought together on a domestic as well as global level.

Dependency analysis argues that development can best be understood as a natural product of the process of capitalist development and expansion worldwide. The theory asserts that as capitalism spread from the European countries in the fifteenth century, it exploited the countries in Latin America, Asia, and Africa. The exploitation of labor and natural resources allowed for a transfer of wealth from the now-developing countries to the then-industrializing European countries. The process of capital accumulation systematically required the exploitation and subjugation of the Third World nations. Colonialism was the political and military dimension that enforced this process. Therefore, dependency analysis argues, this process transformed these countries' economies into vehicles that served the primary needs of the advanced countries. The character of this interdependence produced a dependence, in which the economies of less-developed countries were conditioned by the development and expansion of the advanced country's economy.

Proponents of the dependency view focus their analysis on the way a developing country's economy is integrated with the global economy. Dependency theorists examine everything from the banking system to the communications system to the educational system, focusing on the role and behavior of the direct foreign investment of multinational firms and the role and behavior of multilateral institutions such as the International Monetary Fund (IMF) and the World Bank. They argue that these institutions are the instruments and vehicles for the exploitation, domination, and perpetuation of underdevelopment in these countries. They do not deny that some degree of progress, modernization, and economic development result from the spread of capitalism, but they insist that the development is uneven and distorted.

For many years (the 1960s to the 1980s), dependency theorists believed that only a more democratic and socialistically organized society could bring genuine development to these countries by breaking the forms of dependency. The dominating capitalist institutions would need to be replaced. Socialism was seen as one alternative development path. In theory, this was attractive to some, but in practice it proved to be difficult, if not impossible. By the late 1990s, whatever the analytical merit of the dependency view, historic events had spelled, for the time being, the end of socialism in practice in Eastern Europe and the Soviet Union. Coming off the dismal economic decade of the 1980s, the majority of developing nations entered the 1990s and the early twenty-first century in pursuit of market capitalist development strategies.

Recent Economic Trends

Developing countries, confronted with the problems of debt, population, poverty, and the environment, are rapidly adopting variants of the neoliberal model—free and open-market economic strategies for development. Nowhere is this more evident than in Latin America. Among many countries, Mexico is one of the most dramatic examples of the cyclical character of the experience with the neoliberal strategy. The new Mexican development strategy, which began in 1982 and has been in practice since, involves the following actions:

◆ Privatizing state-owned enterprises
◆ Opening the economy to foreign investment
◆ Opening the economy by eliminating tariff and nontariff trade barriers
◆ Stabilizing the economy by reducing inflation and domestic deficits
◆ Reducing the level and debt service demands of external debt
◆ Entering into free trade agreements with other nations
◆ Diversifying exports

The success or failure of this strategy will depend on many internal and external factors. It remains to be seen whether enough capital will ultimately flow to these countries to generate rapid development, if the new market-driven economies are efficient and productive enough to compete on a global scale, and if the new democratic governments can manage to maintain political stability and order as their people wait patiently for the results to spill over to them.

Much of the implementation of the neoliberal model involves the relationship between the IMF, international commercial banks, and host government. The IMF and commercial banks expect, if not require, governments to implement conservative monetary and fiscal policies in order to provide economic stability (reduce inflation and eliminate budget deficits) and sound economic fundamentals so that capital will flow into the country (and domestic capital will not leave) in order to promote economic growth. In official circles, this kind of economic policy is called "structural adjustment." Many critics of this policy orientation and the IMF's role argue that these policies do not promote growth but induce economic stagnation and reduce the population's standard of living, while serving the vested interests of the domestic financial class and multinational institutions. In some countries, structural adjustment policies have had a major impact on employment and pay, especially for women.

The impact of the free trade policies demanded by the International Monetary Fund and governments such as Mexico that adhere to the neoliberal (structural adjustment) program can be seen in the following article that details the negative consequences of the North American Free Trade Agreement for Mexico.

Why Mexico's Small Corn Farmers Go Hungry
Tina Rosenberg

Mexico City—Macario Hernández's grandfather grew corn in the hills of Puebla, Mexico. His father does the same. Mr. Hernández grows corn, too, but not for much longer. Around his village of Guadalupe Victoria, people farm the way they have for centuries, on tiny plots of land watered only by rain, their plows pulled by burros. Mr. Hernández, a thoughtful man of 30, is battling to bring his family and neighbors out of the Middle Ages. But these days modernity is less his goal than his enemy.

This is because he, like other small farmers in Mexico, competes with American products raised on megafarms that use satellite imagery to mete out fertilizer. These products are so heavily subsidized by the government that many are exported for less than it costs to grow them. According to the Institute for Agriculture and Trade Policy in Minneapolis, American corn sells in Mexico for 25 percent less than its cost. The prices Mr. Hernández and others receive are so low that they lose money with each acre they plant.

In January, campesinos from all over the country marched into Mexico City's central plaza to protest. Thousands of men in jeans and straw hats jammed the Zócalo, alongside horses and tractors. Farmers have staged smaller protests around Mexico for months. The protests have won campesino organizations a series of talks with the government. But they are unlikely to get what they want: a renegotiation of the North American Free Trade Agreement, or NAFTA, protective temporary tariffs and a new policy that seeks to help small farmers instead of trying to force them off the land.

The problems of rural Mexicans are echoed around the world as countries lower their import barriers, required by free trade treaties and the rules of the World Trade Organization. When markets are open, agricultural products flood in from wealthy nations, which subsidize agriculture and allow agribusiness to export crops cheaply. European farmers get 35 percent of their income in government subsidies, American farmers 20 percent. American subsidies are at record levels, and last year, Washington passed a farm bill that included a $40 billion increase in subsidies to large grain and cotton farmers.

It seems paradoxical to argue that cheap food hurts poor people. But three-quarters of the world's poor are rural. When subsidized imports undercut their products, they starve. Agricultural subsidies, which rob developing countries of the ability to export crops, have become the most important dispute at the W.T.O. Wealthy countries do far more harm to poor nations with these subsidies than they do good with foreign aid.

While such subsidies have been deadly for the 18 million Mexicans who live on small farms—nearly a fifth of the country—Mexico's near-complete neglect of the countryside is at fault, too. Mexican officials say openly that they long ago concluded that small agriculture was inefficient, and that the solution for farmers was to find other work. "The government's solution for the problems of the countryside is to get campesinos to stop being campesinos," says Victor Suárez, a leader of a coalition of small farmers.

But the government's determination not to invest in losers is a self-fulfilling prophecy. The small farmers I met in their fields in Puebla want to stop growing corn and move into fruit or organic vegetables. Two years ago Mr. Hernández, who works with a farming cooperative, brought in thousands of peach plants. But only a few farmers could buy them. Farm credit essentially does not exist in Mexico, as the government closed the rural bank, and other bankers do not want to lend to small farmers. "We are trying to get people to rethink and understand that the traditional doesn't work," says Mr. Hernández. "But the lack of capital is deadly."

The government does subsidize producers, at absurdly small levels compared with subsidies in the United States. Corn growers get about $30 an acre. Small programs exist to provide technical help and fertilizer to small producers, but most farmers I met hadn't even heard of them.

Mexico should be helping its corn farmers increase their productivity or move into new crops—especially since few new jobs have been created that could absorb these farmers. Mexicans fleeing the countryside are flocking to Houston and swelling Mexico's cities, already congested with the poor and unemployed. If Washington wants to reduce Mexico's immigration to the United States, ending subsidies for agribusiness would be far more effective than beefing up the border patrol.

Source: "Why Mexico's Small Corn Farmers Go Hungry," Tina Rosenberg, *New York Times,* 3/3/03. Copyright © 2003 New York Times Co. Used with permission.

4. Given this problem, what do you think the appropriate response should be from the U.S. and Mexican governments? Why?

Conclusion

The early years of the twenty-first century have served to reinforce the seriousness of global poverty and underdevelopment. As we have seen, these problems are growing larger and more complicated. The demographic dynamics and trends provide an enormous challenge. The global public health crisis, led by the HIV/AIDS pandemic that generates on average 3 million more people per year with the virus and about 3 million deaths from the virus, could be helped with a modest financial commitment to support the necessary programs as presented by the United Nations. But with the global war on terrorism and global spending on defense at a level of $900 billion a year, there is a fierce competition for competing resources.

As we will see in the last chapter, the economies of China and India are integrating into the global system at a swift pace. As their economies grow, their demand for fossil fuel energy (petroleum) also is growing and pushing up the demand for and consequently the price of oil. Worldwide, we are seeing intensified pressure not only for fossil fuels but water, food, minerals, timber, and other resources. Indeed, the goal of sustainable development is the new global agenda.

This set of problems and pressures present an incredible challenge for the global community and for global capitalism.

Review Questions

1. What are several of the most common characteristics of a developing country?

2. What is the World Bank's classification scheme for the world's nations? Do you think that this is a useful way to group the world's nations?

3. What is the character and magnitude of global poverty? In what ways is poverty more than an economic problem?

4. What are the five basic categories of economic problems of developing nations? How would you rank them in order of importance?

5. What is the relationship between the problems of economic growth and population? Between population and the environment?

6. What is the basic economic explanation for poverty and underdevelopment in the developing world?

7. Of the three competing views of underdevelopment, which do you find to be the most convincing? Why?

8. By the early 1990s, the governments of developing nations apparently were adopting development strategies with a discernible trend. What was this trend? What do you think are the strengths of this strategy? What do you think are or could be some problems with the strategy?

9. At the Earth Summit in 1992, a consensus emerged on the need for all nations to pursue strategies of sustainable development. What does this mean for developing nations? Advanced nations?

CHAPTER TWENTY-THREE

Economies
in Transition

■ Introduction

A   *s the twentieth century drew to a close, the centrally planned socialist economies of Eastern Europe and the former Soviet Union had collapsed and started a transition to reliance on free markets. In other parts of the world from Latin America to Asia, countries were swiftly moving toward free and open-market economies and away from economies with strong government roles. In the early years of this century, these trends continue. Why is this happening? What does this mean? Do these changes represent the end of socialism and the triumph of capitalism?*

In this chapter, we will review the global historical experience with socialism and capitalism. In particular, we will examine the experience of the former Soviet Union, Eastern Europe, the People's Republic of China, Japan, and the United States. Contemporary globalization dynamics and trends have dramatically changed the landscape of the global economy and the reality for these major economies. At the same time, the global community is becoming increasingly aware of the consequences of the dependency of the world's dominant economies on fossil fuels, especially petroleum. The increased demand pressures on nonrenewable resources and the fragility of renewable resources have raised critical questions about the sustainability of the current character of global economic growth. Demographic trends and growing pressures on food production, water use, deforestation, overfishing, and overgrazing appear to be laying the foundation for future resource scarcity and resource conflicts. This complex set of problems presents to the international community the challenge of creating a global political and economic system that is able to resolve these problems in the context of sustainable long-term growth.

Looking Backward

At the end of World War II, the Bretton Woods system provided the structure and rules for a new international economic and financial system. The International Monetary Fund oversaw this international monetary system, which positioned the U.S. dollar as the key reserve currency. The system was designed to promote trade and facilitate capital flow among

550

nations, thereby promoting growth. As we saw in the last chapter, the system survived until the early 1970s. Since its creation in 1944, the Bretton Woods system had been challenged to adjust to changes in the global system and its components. The process of constant adjustment during and since has been difficult, yet remarkably successful in many ways.

The most dynamic agents of transformation have been the phenomenal changes in technology—in production of goods and services, communications, transportation, and information—which have dramatically altered the character of the global economic and financial system. These changes have placed enormous pressure on institutions—governments, businesses, financial institutions, and many others—to adapt.

The rapid growth of multinational (transnational) firms in the 1960s was and continues to be fueled by technological change and the pursuit of profit. It is now possible to transfer technology to any part of the globe, utilizing local labor and other resources to produce all or any part of a product. The character of modern production systems in a computer age, combined with the mobility of capital and the interchangeability of human labor, has profoundly changed the character of national economies and the international economic system itself. The globalization of production and the internationalization of capital have pushed the global economic system to a level of development unimaginable fifty years ago.

Financial institutions and financial markets have expanded and changed their roles to deal with this globalization. U.S. banks have branches throughout the world, and foreign banks have offices in the United States. Communication and information technology have allowed these financial markets and institutions to expand their operations. The Group of Eight nations (the United States, Canada, United Kingdom, France, Germany Italy, Russia and Japan) have—with varying degrees of success—embarked upon a path of voluntary policy coordination. And the group has called upon central banks in these countries to monitor their macroeconomic stabilization policies so as to pursue coordinated stability in the international economic and financial system.

With the conclusion of the General Agreement of Tariffs and Trade negotiations and the establishment of the World Trade Organization, nations have endorsed the goal of freer trade rhetorically but cling to protectionist policies in practice. The past several decades have seen the emergence of Japan and the successful newly industrializing countries (NICs) as economic powers. Yet, just as the WTO pushs for a global free trade system, the world is splitting into trade blocs: Europe, the Pacific Basin, and North America. The movement toward political democratization and economic liberalization (market economies) in Eastern Europe and the former Soviet Union has created enormous challenges for the global economy. And, finally, the formal economic integration of Western Europe, which began in 1992 with the Treaty of Maastricht, has set into motion forces that will challenge the structure and operation of the European Monetary Union (EMU) and a common European currency.

Along with these trade efforts have come significant changes in other dimensions of the economy. The Cold War economic and military tension between the United States and the former Soviet Union has come to an end. Poverty levels in the developing world have continued to expand. And nations have recognized the environmental challenges associated with the need for sustainable development. Together, these changes have brought the international system to a historic turning point. Clearly, the end of the twentieth century marked the end of one era and the beginning of another.

1. Do you agree that the global community is indeed at the beginning of a new era? Explain.

Economic Systems Revisited: Capitalism and Socialism

Capitalism and socialism were the two predominant models of economic systems in the twentieth century. But now most nations are attempting to find the right combination of free markets and government policies to achieve stable economic development. Throughout the world, this may produce very different kinds of mixed economies and market-government institutions.

Most would argue that socialism has met with economic and political failure. The desire for individual freedom and political democracy, along with the inability of authoritarian and bureaucratic socialist economies to provide for an increased standard of living, resulted in widespread revolutionary changes in Eastern Europe and the former Soviet Union in the 1990s. At the beginning of this century, China, Vietnam, North Korea, and Cuba remain the predominant countries committed to making a variant of market socialism work.

Capitalism, as we have seen, is characterized by the private ownership of the factors of production. This system relies primarily on markets to allocate scarce resources. The free-market system allows prices to be determined by the interaction of supply and demand. Socialism, on the other hand, is characterized by the public (social) ownership of capital and natural resources. The following lists contrast the major characteristics of these two systems.

Socialism relies upon social ownership and the process of planning to make decisions about resource allocation. Some socialist countries have utilized both planning and the market system to allocate scarce resources. Such market socialism is intended to utilize the best from each basic system. In practice, this usually produced a mixed economy that included both private and public ownership of the means of production and a private market economy supported by government planning. These ideal—theoretical—types of economic systems do not exist anywhere in the world today. Yet every nation today has an economy that combines some elements of these systems.

The primary distinction between national economies generally comes down to the character of property relations, that is, between private or public ownership of the factors of production and the role of free markets. In capitalism, private ownership prevails, with corporations and other businesses making decisions about production based on profit expectations. In socialism, the goal of production of enterprises is influenced by state (social) objectives.

Capitalism and Socialism

Capitalism

- Private ownership of the means of production
- A market in labor
  a. Workers are divorced from ownership.
  b. Workers are without control over the process of production or choice of product produced.
  c. The price of labor (wage) is determined by the supply and demand for labor.
- A market for land and natural resources
- Income distribution based on market-determined returns to owned factors of production (land, labor, and capital)
- Markets in essential commodities (basic needs)
- Control of the means of production (capital) and the production process by owners of capital or their managerial representatives, with profit as the main objective

Socialism

- Public (social) ownership of the means of production
- Labor markets determined by planning decisions
  a. Workers participate in self-management and/or shared decision making.
  b. The price of labor is determined by planners in accordance with a market wage (supply and demand) in combination with a social wage that incorporates the free provision of many basic needs (health, education, transportation, housing, etc.).
- Government allocation of land and natural resources
- Income distribution based on a market-determined wage, guided by government planning, in accordance with a social wage and government goals of reducing inequalities in the distribution of income (rather than income related to the ownership of capital or the exploitation of labor)
- Provision of basic needs at no charge or at government-subsidized prices (social wage), with the goal of maximizing public welfare
- Full employment of human resources, utilizing moral and material incentives for increasing output and efficiency, guided by planning

The End of the Cold War and the Movement Toward Economic Liberalization and Global Capitalism

The 1980s was an economic disaster for developing nations. The long U.S. recession of the early 1980s spilled over into the entire global economic system. The economic slowdown exacerbated the external debt problems of developing nations. The United States and the Soviet Union intensified their Cold War conflict with accelerated arms spending and talk of a potential limited nuclear war.

By the late 1980s, political movements in Eastern Europe, especially in Poland, began to push for a larger role in the economy for workers and a more democratic political system. The leadership in the Soviet Union by the late 1980s was also pushing for an opening up (liberalization) of the economy and a more democratic political system.

The story of the end of the Cold War is long and rich. Suffice it to say that by 1991, the Soviet Union had collapsed and given way to the emergence of the

Commonwealth of Independent States (made up of the former states of the Soviet Union, with Russia being the largest and most powerful). This, along with the transition toward economic liberalization in the former Soviet-dominated Easter Bloc countries, paved the way for the 1990s, a decade of globalization and economic liberalization. The widespread assumption was that capitalism was beginning a new era of growth and expansion.

The 1990s ushered in a decade of dramatic and fast-paced change all over the globe. Europe continued its efforts toward economic and monetary integration and unification. Eastern Europe accelerated its transition toward economic liberalization and integration with Western Europe. The countries of the Commonwealth of Independent States began to move toward variants of market capitalism and various experiments with political democracy. The Pacific Basin region of Asia and South Asia began to grow rapidly and develop, even as Japan's economy entered a period of stagnation that would last almost fifteen years. In this context, China would emerge as the fastest-growing country in the world. Latin America began a decade-long experiment with economic liberalization pushed by the International Monetary Fund and supported by the United States. In this context of globalization, growth, and optimism, Africa remained the one part of the global system seemingly ignored as it confronted a multitude of economic, political, and social challenges, not the least of which were poverty and a public health crisis shaped by the HIV/AIDS pandemic.

While the 1990s proved to be very positive for the U.S. economy, other parts of the world signaled some of the costs and consequences of unrestrained global capitalism. The Mexican economy suffered the Peso Crisis in 1994. Several Asian Economics temporarily collapsed during the Asian Financial Crisis of 1997. The globalization dynamic of the 1990s was called into question by a growing antiglobalization movement toward the end of the 1990s, with the now famous conference in Seattle in 1999.

With so much going on all over the world during this time period, there is probably no story more important to examine than the rapid growth and emergence of the People's Republic of China. That story to which we now turn.

By 2007, the global economic system was confronting the current and future realities of both China and India. Then the article on, "A New World Economy: The Balance of Power Will Shift to the East as China and India Evolve," Pete Engardio makes the argument that these two countries are now and will continue to fundamentally transform the global economic system for the remainder of this century. Let us examine his assessment.

A New World Economy
Pete Engardio

It may not top the must-see list of many tourists. But to appreciate Shanghai's ambitious view of its future, there is no better place than the Urban Planning Exhibition Hall, a glass-and-metal structure across from People's Square. The highlight is a scale model bigger than a basketball court of the entire metropolis—every skyscraper, house, lane, factory, dock, and patch of green space—in the year 2020.

There are white plastic showpiece towers designed by architects such as I.M. Pei and Sir Norman Foster. There are immense new industrial parks for autos and petrochemicals, along with new subway lines, airport runways, ribbons of expressway, and an elaborate riverfront development, site of the 2010 World Expo. Nine futuristic planned communities for 800,000 residents each, with generous parks, retail districts, man-made lakes, and nearby college campuses, rise in the suburbs. The message is clear. Shanghai already is looking well past its industrial age to its expected emergence as a global mecca of knowledge workers. "In an information economy, it is very important to have urban space with a better natural and social environment," explains Architectural Society of Shanghai President Zheng Shiling, a key city adviser.

It is easy to dismiss such dreams as bubble-economy hubris—until you take into account the audacious goals Shanghai already has achieved. Since 1990, when the city still seemed caught in a socialist time warp, Shanghai has erected enough high-rises to fill Manhattan. The once-rundown Pudong district boasts a space-age skyline, some of the world's biggest industrial zones, dozens of research centers, and a bullet train. This is the story of China, where an extraordinary ability to mobilize workers and capital has tripled per capita income in a generation, and has eased 300 million out of poverty. Leaders now are frenetically laying the groundwork for decades of new growth.

Invaluable Role

Now hop a plane to India. It is hard to tell this is the world's other emerging superpower. Jolting sights of extreme poverty abound even in the business capitals. A lack of subways and a dearth of expressways result in nightmarish traffic.

But visit the office towers and research and development centers sprouting everywhere, and you see the miracle. Here, Indians are playing invaluable roles in the global innovation chain. Motorola, Hewlett-Packard, Cisco Systems, and other tech giants now rely on their Indian teams to devise software platforms and dazzling multimedia features for next-generation devices. Google principal scientist Krishna Bharat is setting up a Bangalore lab complete with colorful furniture, exercise balls, and a Yamaha organ—like Google's Mountain View (Calif.) headquarters—to work on core search-engine technology. Indian engineering houses use 3-D computer simulations to tweak designs of everything from car engines and forklifts to aircraft wings for such clients as General Motors Corp. and Boeing Co. Financial and market-research experts at outfits like B2K, Office-Tiger, and Iris crunch the latest disclosures of blue-chip companies for Wall Street. By 2010 such outsourcing work is expected to quadruple, to $56 billion a year.

Even more exhilarating is the pace of innovation, as tech hubs like Bangalore spawn companies producing their own chip designs, software, and pharmaceuticals. "I find Bangalore to be one of the most exciting places in the world," says Dan Scheinman, Cisco Systems Inc.'s senior vice-president for corporate development. "It is Silicon Valley in 1999." Beyond Bangalore, Indian companies are showing a flair for producing high-quality goods and services at ridiculously low prices, from $50 air flights and crystal-clear 2¢-a-minute cell-phone service to $2,200 cars and cardiac operations by top surgeons at a fraction of U.S. costs. Some analysts see the beginnings of hypercompetitive multinationals. "Once they learn to sell at Indian prices with world quality, they can compete anywhere," predicts University of Michigan management guru C.K. Prahalad. Adds. A. T.

FIGURE 23.1   The Strengths and Weaknesses

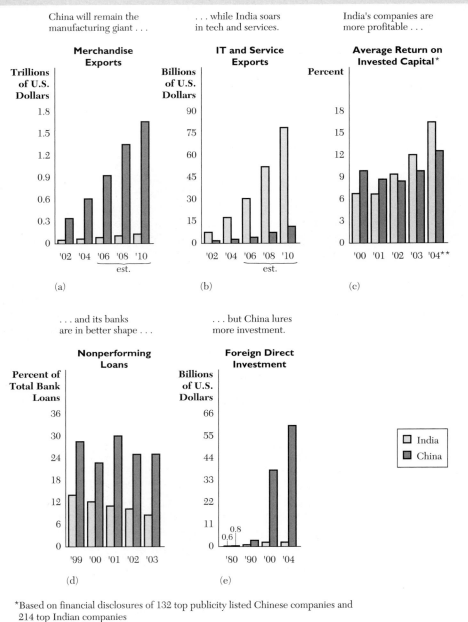

China will remain the
manufacturing giant . . .

. . . while India soars
in tech and services.

India's companies are
more profitable . . .

**Merchandise
Exports**

**IT and Service
Exports**

**Average Return on
Invested Capital***

(a)   (b)   (c)

. . . and its banks
are in better shape . . .

. . . but China lures
more investment.

**Nonperforming
Loans**

**Foreign Direct
Investment**

☐ India
■ China

(d)   (e)

*Based on financial disclosures of 132 top publicity listed Chinese companies and
 214 top Indian companies
**Data for 2004 Fiscal year incomplete

Source: Data from *Business Week*, August 22/29, 2005

FIGURE 23.2 Handicapping the race

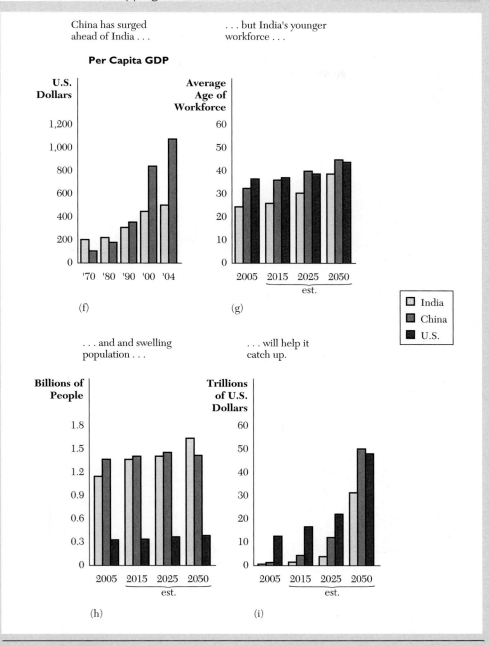

China has surged
ahead of India . . .

. . . but India's younger
workforce . . .

Per Capita GDP

(f)

(g)

India
China
U.S.

. . . and and swelling
population . . .

. . . will help it
catch up.

(h)

(i)

Source: Data from *Business Week*

Kearney high-tech consultant John Ciacchella: "I don't think U.S. companies realize India is building next-generation service companies."

Simultaneous Takeoffs

China and India. Rarely has the economic ascent of two still relatively poor nations been watched with such a mixture of awe, opportunism, and trepidation. The postwar era witnessed economic miracles in Japan and South Korea. But neither was populous enough to power worldwide growth or change the game in a complete spectrum of industries. China and India, by contrast, possess the weight and dynamism to transform the 21st-century global economy. The closest parallel to their emergence is the saga of 19th-century America, a huge continental economy with a young, driven workforce that grabbed the lead in agriculture, apparel, and the high technologies of the era, such as steam engines, the telegraph, and electric lights.

But in a way, even America's rise falls short in comparison to what's happening now. Never has the world seen the simultaneous, sustained takeoffs of two nations that together account for one-third of the planet's population. For the past two decades, China has been growing at an astounding 9.5% a year, and India by 6%. Given their young populations, high savings, and the sheer amount of catching up they still have to do, most economists figure China and India possess the fundamentals to keep growing in the 7%-to-8% range for decades.

Barring cataclysm, within three decades India should have vaulted over Germany as the world's third-biggest economy. By mid-century, China should have overtaken the U.S. as No.1. By then, China and India could account for half of global output Indeed, the troika of China, India, and the U.S.—the only

industrialized nation with significant population growth—by most projections will dwarf every other economy.

What makes the two giants especially powerful is that they complement each other's strengths. An accelerating trend is that technical and managerial skills in both China and India are becoming more important than cheap assembly labor. China will stay dominant in mass manufacturing, and is one of the few nations building multibillion-dollar electronics and heavy industrial plants. India is a rising power in software, design, services, and precision industry. This raises a provocative question: What if the two nations merge into one giant "Chindia?" Rival political and economic ambitions make that unlikely. But if their industries truly collaborate, "they would take over the world tech industry," predicts Forrester Research Inc. analyst Navi Radjou.

In a practical sense, the yin and yang of these immense workforces already are converging. True, annual trade between the two economies is just $14 billion. But thanks to the Internet and plunging telecom costs, multinationals are having their goods built in China with software and circuitry designed in India. As interactive design technology makes it easier to perfect virtual 3-D prototypes of everything from telecom routers to turbine generators on PCs, the distance between India's low-cost laboratories and China's low-cost factories shrinks by the month. Managers in the vanguard of globalization's new wave say the impact will be nothing less than explosive. "In a few years you'll see most companies unleshing this massive productivity surge," predicts Infosys Technologies CEO Nandan M. Nilekani.

To globalization's skeptics, however, what's good for Corporate America translates into layoffs and lower pay for workers. Little wonder the West is suffering from future shock. Each new Chinese corporate takeover bid or revelation of a major Indian outsourcing deal elicits howls of protest by U.S. politicians. Washington think tanks are publishing thick white papers charting China's rapid progress in microelectronics, nanotech, and aerospace—and painting dark scenarios about what it means for America's global leadership.

Such alarmism is understandable. But the U.S. and other established powers will have to learn to make room for China and India. For in almost every dimension—as consumer markets, investors, producers, and users of energy and commodities—they will be 21st-century heavyweights. The growing economic might will carry into geopolitics as well. China and India are more assertively pressing their interests in the Middle East and Africa, and China's military will likely challenge U.S. dominance in the Pacific.

One implication is that the balance of power in many technologies will likely move from West to East. An obvious reason is that China and India graduate a combined half a million engineers and scientists a year, vs. 60,000 in the U.S. In life sciences, projects the McKinsey Global Institute, the total number of young researchers in both nations will rise by 35%, to 1.6 million by 2008. The U.S. supply will drop by 11%, to 760,000. As most Western scientists will tell you, China and India already are making important contributions in medicine and materials that will help everyone. Because these nations can throw more brains at technical problems at a fraction of the cost, their contributions to innovation will grow.

Consumers Rising
American business isn't just shifting research work because Indian and Chinese brains are young, cheap, and plentiful. In many cases, these engineers combine skills—mastery of

FIGURE 23.3   China's Hunger for Raw Materials

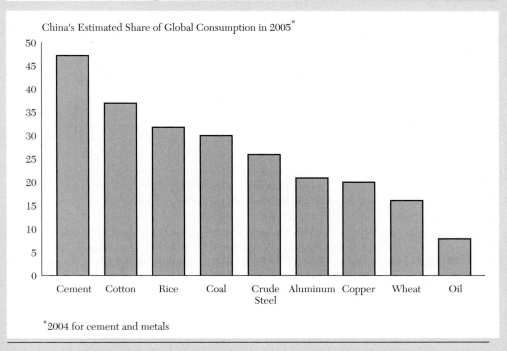

China's Estimated Share of Global Consumption in 2005°

°2004 for cement and metals

Source: Data from *Business Week,* August 22/29, 2005

the latest software tools, a knack for complex mathematical algorithms, and fluency in new multimedia technologies—that often surpass those of their American counterparts. As Cisco's Scheinman puts it: "We came to India for the costs, we stayed for the quality, and we're now investing for the innovation."

A rising consumer class also will drive innovation. This year, China's passenger car market is expected to reach 3 million, No. 3 in the world. China already has the world's biggest base of cell-phone subscribers—350 million—and that is expected to near 600 million by 2009. In two years, China should overtake the U.S. in homes connected to broadband. Less noticed is that India's consumer market is on the same explosive trajectory as China five years ago. Since 2000, the number of cellular subscribers has rocketed from 5.6 million to 55 million.

What's more, Chinese and Indian consumers and companies now demand the latest technologies and features. Studies show the attitudes and aspirations of today's young Chinese and Indians resemble those of Americans a few decades ago. Surveys of thousands of young adults in both nations by marketing firm Grey Global Group found they are overwhelmingly optimistic about the future, believe success is in their hands, and view products as status symbols. In China, it's fashionable for the upwardly mobile to switch high-end cell phones every three months, says Josh Li, managing director of Grey's Beijing office, because an old model suggests "you are not getting ahead and updated." That means these nations will be huge proving grounds for next-generation multimedia gizmos, networking equipment, and wireless Web services, and will play a greater role in setting global standards. In consumer electronics, "we will see China in a few years going from being a follower to a leader in defining consumer-electronics trends," predicts Philips Semiconductors Executive Vice-President Leon Husson.

For all the huge advantages they now enjoy, India and China cannot assume their role as new superpowers is assured. Today, China and India account for a mere 6% of global gross domestic product—half that of Japan. They must keep growing rapidly just to provide jobs for tens of millions entering the workforce annually, and to keep many millions more from crashing back into poverty. Both nations must confront ecological degradation that's as obvious as the smog shrouding Shanghai and Bombay, and face real risks of social strife, war, and financial crisis. Increasingly, such problems will be the world's problems. Also, with wages rising fast, especially in many skilled areas, the cheap labor edge won't last forever. Both nations will go through many boom and harrowing bust cycles. And neither country is yet producing companies like Samsung, Nokia, or Toyota that put it all together, developing, making, and marketing world-beating products.

Both countries, however, have survived earlier crises and possess immense untapped potential. In China, serious development only now is reaching the 800 million people in rural areas, where per capita annual income is just $354. In areas outside major cities, wages are as little as 45¢ an hour. "This is why China can have another 20 years of high-speed growth," contends Beijing University economist Hai Wen.

Very impressive. But India's long-term potential may be even higher. Due to its one-child policy, China's working-age population will peak at 1 billion in 2015 and then shrink steadily. China then will have to provide for a graying population that has limited retirement benefits. India has nearly 500 million people under age 19 and higher fertility rates. By mid-century, India is expected to have 1.6 billion people—and 220 million more workers than China. That could be a source for instability, but a great advantage for growth if the government can provide education and opportunity for India's masses. New Delhi just now is pushing to open its power, tele-com, commercial real estate and retail sectors to foreigners. These industries could lure big capital inflows. "The pace of institutional changes and industries being liberalized is phenomenal," says Chief Economist William T. Wilson of consultancy Keystone Business Intelligence India. "I believe India has a better model than China, and over time will surpass it in growth."

For its part, China has yet to prove it can go beyond forced-march industrialization. China directs massive investment into public works and factories, a wildly successful for-mula for rapid growth and job creation. But considering its massive manufacturing out-put, China is surprisingly weak in innovation. A full 57% of exports are from foreign-invested factories, and China underachives in software, even with 35 software colleges and plans to graduate 200,000 software engineers a year. It's not for lack of genius. Microsoft Corp.'s 180-engineer R&D lab in Beijing, for example, is one of the world's most productive sources of innovation in computer graphics and lan-guage simulation.

While China's big state-run R&D institutes are close to the cutting edge at the theoreti-cal level, they have yet to yield many com-mercial breakthroughs. "China has a lot of capability," says Microsoft Chief Technology Officer Craig Mundie. "But when you look un-der the covers, there is not a lot of collabora-tion with industry." The lack of intellectual property protection, and Beijing's heavy role in building up its own tech companies, make many other multinationals leery of doing se-rious R&D in China.

China also is hugely wasteful. Its 9.5% growth rate in 2004 is less impressive when you consider that $850 billion—half of GDP—was plowed into already-glutted sec-tors like crude steel, vehicles, and office buildings. Its factories burn fuel five times less efficiently than in the West, and more than 20% of bank loans are bad. Two-thirds of China's 13,000 listed companies don't earn back their true cost of capital, esti-mates Beijing National Accounting Institute President Chen Xiaoyue. "We build the roads and industrial parks, but we sacrifice a lot," Chen says.

FIGURE 23.4 Reshaping the Global Economy

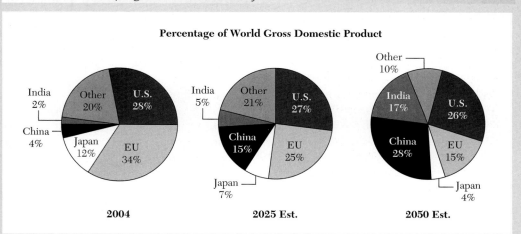

Percentage of World Gross Domestic Product

2004

India 2%
China 4%
Other 20%
U.S. 28%
Japan 12%
EU 34%

2025 Est.

India 5%
Other 21%
U.S. 27%
China 15%
EU 25%
Japan 7%

2050 Est.

Other 10%
India 17%
U.S. 26%
China 28%
EU 15%
Japan 4%

Source: Data from Keystone India

India, by contrast, has had to develop with scarcity. It gets scant foreign investment, and has no room to waste fuel and materials like China. India also has Western legal institutions, a modern stock market, and private banks and corporations. As a result, it is far more capital-efficient. A *BusinessWeek* analysis of Standard & Poor's Compustat data on 346 top listed companies in both nations shows Indian corporations have achieved higher returns on equity and invested capital in the past five years in industries from autos to food products. The average Indian company posted a 16.7% return on capital in 2004, vs. 12.8% in China.

Small-batch Expertise

The burning question is whether India can replicate China's mass manufacturing achievement. India's info-tech services industry, successful as it is, employs fewer than 1 million people. But 200 million Indians subsist on $1 a day or less. Export manufacturing is one of India's best hopes of generating millions of new jobs.

India has sophisticated manufacturing knowhow. Tata Steel is among the world's most-efficient producers. The country boasts several top precision auto parts companies, such as Bharat Forge Ltd. The world's biggest supplier of chassis parts to major auto makers, it employs 1,200 engineers at its heavily automated Pune plant. India's forte is small-batch production of high-value goods requiring lots of engineering, such as power generators for Cummins Inc. and core components for General Electric Co. CAT scanners.

What holds India back are bureaucratic red tape, rigid labor laws, and its inability to build infrastructure fast enough. There are hopeful signs. Nokia Corp. is building a major campus to make cell phones in Madras, and South Korea's Pohang Iron & Steel Co. plans a $12 billion complex by 2016 in Orissa state. But it will take India many years to build the highways, power plants, and airports needed to rival China in mass manufacturing. With Beijing now pushing software and pledging intellectual property rights protection, some Indians fret design work will shift to China to be closer to factories. "The question is whether China can move from manufacturing to services faster than we can solve our infrastructure bottlenecks," says President Aravind Melligeri of Bangalore-based QuEST, whose 700 engineers design gas turbines, aircraft engines, and medical gear for GE and other clients.

However the race plays out, Corporate America has little choice but to be engaged—heavily. Motorola illustrates the value of leveraging both nations to lower costs and speed up development. Most of its hardware is assembled and partly designed in China. Its R&D center in Bangalore devises about 40% of the software in its new phones. The Bangalore team developed the multimedia software and user interfaces in the hot Razr cell phone. Now, they are working on phones that display and send live video, stream movies from the Web, or route incoming calls to voicemail when you are shifting gears in a car. "This is a very, very critical, state-of-the-art resource for Motorola," says Motorola South Asia President Amit Sharma.

Companies like Motorola realize they must succeed in China and India at many levels simultaneously to stay competitive. That requires strategies for winning consumers, recruiting and managing R&D and professional talent, and skillfully sourcing from factories. "Over the next few years, you will see a dramatic gap opening between companies," predicts Jim Hemerling, who runs Boston Consulting Group's Shanghai practice. "It will be between those who get it and are fully mobilized in China and India, and those that are still pondering."

In the coming decades, China and India will disrupt workforces, industries, companies, and markets in ways that we can barely begin to imagine. The upheaval will test America's commitment to the global trade system, and shake its confidence. In the 19th century, Europe went through a similar trauma when it realized a new giant—the U.S.—had arrived. "It is up to America to manage its own expectation of China and India as either a threat or opportunity," says corporate strategist Kenichi Ohmae. "America should be as open-minded as Europe was 100 years ago." How these Asian giants integrate with the rest of the world will largely shape the 21st-century global economy.

2. What does the future of Shanghai look like?
3. Engardio argues that China and India have different economic models, but given their relative advantages and flaws, both are expected to deliver very high growth for decades. What are the strengths and weaknesses of each country?
4. China presents some interesting challenges to the United States in the coming years. What are the geopolitical challenges?
5. What energy and ecological challenges do China and India present?
6. Engardio concludes that "How these Asian giants integrate with the rest of the world will largely shape the 21st-century global economy." Do you agree? Why or why not?

The People's Republic of China

We should not interpret the collapse of socialism in Eastern Europe and the former Soviet Union as the downfall of socialism or communism everywhere. In China, one-fifth of humanity is still living in an economically functioning socialist country—evidence that a variant of socialism is still with us. Economic and foreign policy analysts must consider China's political and economic role in the present and emerging global system.

China has one of the longest cultural, political, and economic histories of any country in the world. It was a relatively developed and sophisticated society centuries before Columbus discovered the New World. Yet, as Europe emerged from the Middle Ages and grew into a modern economy, China stood still. By the time the communist revolutionary Mao Tse-tung came to power in 1949 after a peasant-led revolution, China was still basically a feudalistic agricultural society.

The primary thrust of the Chinese Revolution was to reform the agricultural system. This meant taking land from rich landowners and redistributing it to peasants, who would work the land collectively and share in the fruits of their labor. With economic aid and technology from the Soviet Union in the 1950s, China began to transform both the agricultural and industrial sectors of its economy. These efforts met with mixed results between the late 1950s and the mid-1960s. The debates over economic strategy and policy centered around work incentives. Proponents of moral incentives argued that the workers' revolutionary consciousness ought to be enough to motivate them to produce for the general welfare. Proponents of material incentives argued that workers' revolutionary consciousness alone would not increase economic output for the general social welfare. Higher wages, salaries, bonuses, and promotions would need to be a part of the approach to economic production. Those who argued for material incentives also supported the liberalization of the economy and the introduction of free-market practices. These reforms would have introduced market prices and decentralized the planning process.

Mao regenerated support for the ideals of the socialist revolution and the primacy of moral incentives. From 1965 to the mid-1970s, under Mao's leadership, China entered a period known as the Great Proletarian Cultural Revolution. Those who favored material incentives were denounced. Professionals were sent from urban areas to work in the countryside. Universities were closed down, and students spread out all over the country, carrying the word of Mao. People who resisted the government or were considered enemies of the state were arrested, often tortured, and in some cases murdered. This period of revolutionary upheaval caused the economy to stagnate. The per capita income and production gains made in the 1950s and early 1960s were lost. Only after Mao's death in 1976 did the Cultural Revolution end and the country begin to revive economically.

In 1978, the Chinese Central Committee under the leadership of Deng Xiaoping brought forward dramatic reforms. These reforms took place in agriculture, industry, and the character of property rights. In 1979, Deng ended the agricultural commune system. Workers who did own land individually and worked for the collective welfare were now able to actually own their own parcel of land. They could sell any agricultural surplus they produced and keep the income for themselves. Peasant farm families could work for wages (wage labor) outside the family plot. The use of material incentives generated greater production and began to reduce the role of the state. Finally, Deng's reforms allowed for the emergence of small private enterprises. These new private enterprises were allowed to compete with state enterprises, especially in the retail sector. This change unleashed an entrepreneurial spirit throughout China.

By the late 1970s, the Chinese economy was opened up to Western influences for the first time since 1948. Tourists and those interested in trade and investment opportunities were permitted to travel in China and deal with government officials. Chinese students were permitted to study abroad. A new era had begun.

The Chinese economy continued to grow and expand in the 1980s under Deng's leadership and the leadership of Zhao Ziyang, the prime minister. Their strategy was to rely on centralized economic planning to direct economic activity in the major sectors of the economy, such as heavy industry, but at the same time to introduce elements of a market economy into the economy. The introduction of private ownership in agriculture and in small enterprises set into motion a silent economic revolution that grew rapidly and carried with it the additional demand of political democracy.

Deng's political power base was in the urban centers, where most of the large-scale, heavy industrial state enterprises are located. With his reforms, the state began to change the character and composition of its role, and the state's fiscal role changed radically. In 1978, state government expenditures were almost 35 percent of GNP, and tax revenues were about the same. By 1989 government expenditures had dropped to 23 percent of GNP, and tax revenues to 21 percent of GNP.

In May 1989, thousands of university students and workers gathered in Tiananmen Square in Beijing to challenge the authority of the government. This political unrest was related to the desire for more political freedom and democracy. The protest continued until June 3, when the government sent tanks and troops into the square to clear the demonstrators. Many people were killed, others arrested and tortured, and some executed. World opinion turned against the repressive Chinese government, and the democracy movement was driven underground.

The years after Tiananmen Square have seen political stability and economic growth return to China. In 1991, the real GDP grew at a rate of 10 percent. Yet there is a strong sense among many analysts that China's economic liberalization trend, along with a repressed desire for political democracy, will eventually bring about tremendous changes.

In 1991, state enterprises produced only 50 percent of the nation's industrial output, compared to 80 percent in 1979. The state sector is shrinking, less efficient, and costly to support. The Chinese workforce seems to be infected with new and growing ambitions and expectations with respect to the private economy, especially in rural areas.

The state has less and less revenue with which to maintain the costly state enterprises and their workforce. State workers receive generous benefits for education, housing, and medical care. More than one-third of the government's budget supports subsidies, and almost 50 percent of these subsidies are absorbed by the state-owned enterprises.

The economic tension between the rural agricultural sector and the declining urban industrial sector appears to be on a collision course. The inherent political conflict and consequences seem also to be predictable. In the meantime, China continues to grow and appears stable. Yet this apparent calm cannot erase the fact that, although China's saving rate is 40 percent of its GDP, the country has no financial system capable of utilizing these savings in a productive manner. The nation's infrastructure is in terrible condition and in need of expansion. Energy and raw materials are in short supply all over the country. Other challenges are a growing appetite for consumption goods and an emerging environmental crisis (especially air pollution) in cities.

Will China maintain this unique variant of socialism or in time yield to the economic and political pressures calling for a market economy and political democracy? The rest of the world will be watching with great interest. Will China continue to develop rapidly, or will growth slow as China faces shortages on skilled labor, infrastructure and resources? Will production shift from China to other countries as its costs rise?

The Coming Energy Revolution and the Challenge of Global Warming and Climate Change

As the global community confronts the early years of the twenty-first century, there is probably no greater challenge than finding a way to reduce our use and dependence upon nonrenewable fossil fuels. Ending global poverty and bringing about global peace are high on the list but the immediate and long-term consequences of energy use are at the core of the question of the long-term environmental sustainability of the planet and its people.

Since the beginning of the U.S. war in Iraq, world petroleum prices have increased from $20 per barrel in 2003 to a high of $78 per barrel in 2006. It was not a surprise to anyone that Exxon earned record profits of $39.5 billion in 2006 on revenues of $377 billion (following its record profits of $36 billion in 2005). As can be seen in Figures 23.5 and 23.6 and Table 23.1, world oil consumption has been steadily increasing from just over 40 million barrels per day in 1970 to just over 60 million barrels per day in 1980, to more than 80 million barrels per day in 2006. At current rates of use and expectations for increased demand, the world will be using more than 120 million barrels per day by 2020. Where is this oil going to come from? Who will control it? What will it cost? How will the global economic and financial system absorb this reality? These are vital questions to consider.

In early 2007, world petroleum consumption was more than 80 million barrels per day. The United States was using 20 million barrels per day and importing 12 million barrels per day, or about 60 percent of its petroleum consumption. At $60 per barrel, the United States was spending $1.2 billion a day for its total petroleum consumption, or $438 billion a year, with $262 billion spent on imported petroleum. In using more than 80 million barrels per day, the world was spending $4.9 billion a day or $1.8 trillion a year. Petroleum is a non-

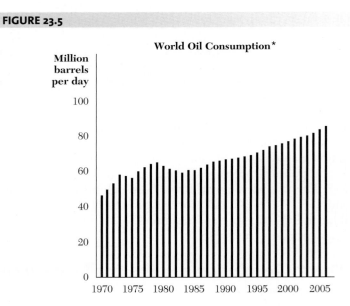

FIGURE 23.5

World Oil Consumption*

Sources: Energy Information Administration; Rocky Mountain Institute.

*Prices are for Saudi Arabian light crude, which typically sells at a discount to West Texas Intermediate, adjusted for inflation.

FIGURE 23.6

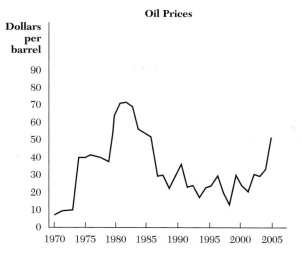

Oil Prices

Sources: Energy Information Administration; Rocky Mountain Institute.

renewable fossil fuel that will run out toward the end of this century. More importantly, the supply and demand dynamics will tighten over the next critical decades. There is enormous pressure on the global community to begin a transition toward the serious conservation (reduce use and enhanced efficiency) of nonrenewable energy and the rapid development of renewable energy technologies and sources. Continuing to depend on and use fossil fuels, especially petroleum and coal, will only further accelerate the already serious problem of global warming and global climate change. This problem is not only a resource

TABLE 23.1 Global Oil Demand by Region
(Millions of barrels a day)

	Demand	
	2004	**2005**
North America	25.34	25.43
Europe	16.33	16.30
OECD Pacific	8.53	8.63
China	6.43	6.59
Other Asia	8.56	8.72
Former Soviet Union	3.76	3.80
Middle East	5.62	5.91
Africa	2.81	2.90
Latin America	4.86	4.99
World	82.23	83.25

Source: International Energy Agency, *Oil Market Report*, March 2006.

FIGURE 23.7 U.S. Energy Overview   Fossil Fuels

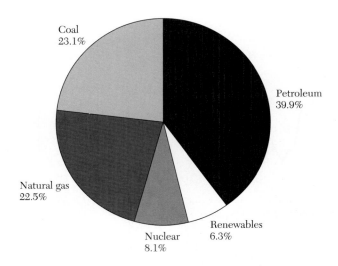

Share of U.S. energy consumption, 2006

Coal
23.1%

Petroleum
39.9%

Natural gas
22.5%

Nuclear
8.1%

Renewables
6.3%

Total consumption: 101.27 quadrillion BTUs

Source: Energy Information Administration.

FIGURE 23.8 U.S. Demand for Oil Imports

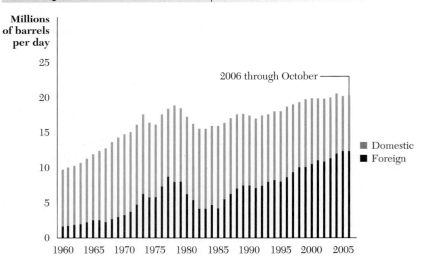

Millions
of barrels
per day

2006 through October

■ Domestic
■ Foreign

Source: Energy Information Administration.

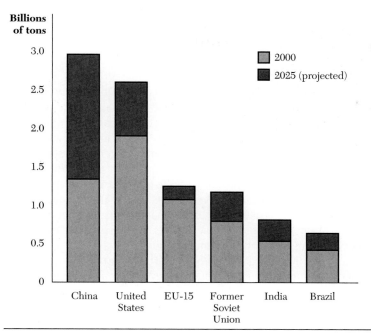

Source: From Gryenier, *Global Energy Revolutions: A Blueprint for Solving Global Warming,* © copyright 2007 Greenpeace (http://www.greenpeace.org/usa)

and environmental problem but a reality that has incredible consequences for the global economic and financial system.

As Figure 23.9 makes clear, the World Resources Institute projected 2025 level of contributions to greenhouse-gas emissions (billion of tons of carbon equivalent) will double from the 2000 levels for China. The top six contributors will be China, followed by the United States, the EU-15, the former Soviet Union, India, and Brazil.

In February 2007, Intergovernmental Panel on Climate Change announced its latest report on the status of Global Warming and Climate Change. The panel predicted temperature rises of 1.1 to 6.4°C (2 to 11.5°F) by 2100. On sea levels, the report predicted rises of 7 to 23 inches by the end of the century. The report said that man-made emissions of greenhouse gases can be blamed for these problems. The study group indicated that it was 90 percent confident in its assessment. This report put to rest the years of scientific debate about whether the problem was real or not and in particular was it caused by human use of fossil fuels.

In the following excerpt from Greenpeace's 2006 publication, *Global Energy Revolution: A Blueprint for Solving Global Warming*, we can consider their case for the coming energy revolution and, more importantly, what they recommend can be done to accomplish this transition to sustainability.

The Energy [R]evolution

The climate change imperative demands nothing short of an Energy Revolution. At the core of this revolution will be a change in the way that energy is produced, distributed, and consumed. The good news is that America is blessed with some of the best renewable energy resources in the world and after initial success with energy efficiency following the oil crisis in the 70s, there is still enormous potential for improvement in the United States.

This report shows that we have a choice: we can cut carbon dioxide (CO_2) emissions in the United States nearly 75% by 2050 without relying on dangerous nuclear power or expensive new coal technologies. With rapid deployment of energy efficiency and renewable energy we can stop global warming.

Spurred by oil-price volatility and the war in Iraq, the issue of energy security is now at the top of the energy policy agenda. One reason for price increases is that supplies of all fossil fuels—oil, gas, and coal—are becoming scarcer and more expensive to produce. The days of cheap oil and gas are coming to an end. At the same time green energy is booming business in America, and this growth has to continue if we are going to stop global warming. Renewable energy technologies can deliver the energy we need, as this report shows, but only with consistent support based on an understanding that solving global warming is our top energy priority.

The solution to our future energy needs lies in greater use of renewable energy sources for both heat and power. Nuclear power is not the solution. There are multiple threats to people and the environment from its operations.

These include the risks and environmental damage from uranium mining, processing, and transport the risk of nuclear weapons proliferation; the unsolved problem of nuclear waste; and the potential hazard of a serious accident. In addition, uranium, the fuel for nuclear power, is a finite resource. By contrast, the reserves of renewable energy that are technically accessible globally are large enough to provide many times more power than the world currently consumes—forever.

Renewable energy technologies vary widely in their technical and economic maturity, but there is a range of technologies that offer increasingly attractive options. These include wind, biomass, solar, geothermal, ocean, and hydroelectric power. Their common feature is that they produce little or no greenhouse gases, and rely on virtually inexhaustible natural sources for their "fuel." Some of these technologies are already competitive, and their economics will continue to improve as they develop technically. The price of fossil fuels, on the other hand, continues to rise.

At the same time there is enormous potential for reducing our energy consumption, while providing the same level of energy services. This study details a series of energy efficiency measures that together can substantially reduce demand in industry, homes, business, and transportation.

The challenges posed by global warming are great and they require new ways of thinking about energy. At the core of the Energy Revolution will be a change in the way that energy is produced, distributed, and con-

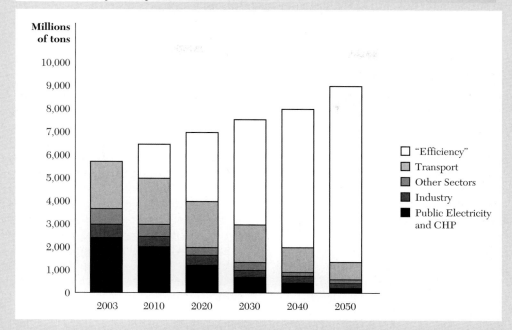

sumed. The five key principles behind this shift are:

1. respecting the natural limits of the environment,

2. implementing renewable solutions, especially through decentralized energy systems,

3. phasing out dirty, unsustainable energy sources,

4. decoupling economic growth from the consumption of fossil fuels, and

5. creating greater equity in the use of resources.

Two contrasting scenarios are outlined in this report, the Reference Scenario and the Energy [R]evolution Scenario. The Reference Scenario is based on the reference scenario published by the International Energy Agency (IEA) in World Energy Outlook 2004, and extrapolated forward from 2030. In its report the IEA suggests that global CO_2 emissions will almost double as energy demand grows and most of that demand is met with coal, gas, and oil.

The first goal of the Energy [R]evolution Scenario is to cut global carbon dioxide emissions in half by mid-century. The second objective is to achieve these reductions while phasing out nuclear energy. This report shows how the United States can achieve these goals. It outlines how the U.S. can more fully exploit the large potential for reducing energy demand through energy efficiency, to ensure we are using our energy resources wisely. At the same time, cost-effective renewable energy sources are accessed for heat, electricity generation, and the production of biofuels.

The Energy [R]evolution Scenario describes a development pathway to transform the present situation into a safe, sustainable energy supply. The key findings of the scenario are as follows:

◆ The electricity sector can pioneer renewable energy development. By 2050, nearly 80% of electricity can be produced from renewable energy sources. In the Energy [R]evolution Scenario 34% is generated by wind, 18% by solar, 14% by hydro, and 9% biomass. There is a smaller amount of ocean energy and geothermal power, as well as nearly 20% fossil generation, 85% of which is natural gas.

◆ Under our Energy [R]evolution Scenario total carbon dioxide emissions are reduced 72% without resorting to an increase in dangerous nuclear power or new coal technologies.

◆ In the heat supply sector, the contribution of renewables will grow to more than 60% by 2050. Fossil fuels will be increasingly replaced by more efficient modern technologies, in particular biomass, solar, and geothermal technologies.

◆ America's oil use can be cut over 50% by 2050 with much more efficient cars and trucks potentially including new plug-in hybrids, use of biofuels, and greater reliance on electricity for public transportation.

We have a long way to go. Today in America less than 10% of electricity is generated renewably, while the contribution of renewables to heat supply is only 8%. More than 95% of America's primary energy supply still comes from fossil fuels and CO_2 emissions are projected to increase by more than 50% under the Reference Scenario.

The United States faces a significant increase in expenditure on electricity supply under the Reference Scenario. The undiminished growth in demand for electricity, increase in fossil fuel prices, and cost of CO_2 emissions will all result in North America's electricity supply costs rising from $290 billion per year to $750 billion per year in 2050. The Energy [R]evolution Scenario, on the other hand, not only meets global CO_2 reduction targets but also helps to stabilize energy costs and thus relieves the economic pressure on society. Increasing energy efficiency and shifting energy supply to renewable energy resources reduces the net long-term costs for electricity supply by 40% compared to the Reference Scenario. In other words, following stringent environmental targets in the energy sector makes not only good environmental sense, but good economic sense, as well.

To make the energy revolution real and to avoid dangerous climate change, Greenpeace recommends that the United States:

◆ phase out of all subsidies for fossil fuels and nuclear energy,

◆ set legally binding targets for renewable energy,

◆ provide defined and stable returns for renewable energy investors,

◆ guarantee priority access to the grid, and

◆ institute strong efficiency standards for all appliances, buildings, and vehicles.

Source: From Grynier, *Global Energy Revolution: A Blueprint for Solving Global Warming*, 2007 Greenpeace (http://www.greenpeace.org/usa.

Sustainable Development and the Environmental Crisis

As you have seen throughout this book, an unregulated market economy produces market failure, or negative externalities, when it comes to the physical environment. Even a regulated market system only succeeds at setting a particular level of pollution that is determined to be acceptable (based on an assessment of cost and risk). The pollution and degradation of the environment continue nevertheless. Many critics have argued that preventing current and future environmental degradation requires a new world view that focuses on developing environmentally sustainable ways to produce, consume, distribute, and dispose of goods and services. This argument recognizes the need for global economic growth, but in a way that does not violate or degrade our Earth capital—the physical life-support systems of the planet.

Many experts argue that we have already pushed beyond critical thresholds in our use and degradation of renewable and nonrenewable resources. As the growth of the global population (particularly in developing countries) continues, we can witness many symptoms of damage: early stages of global climate change, or global warming (the greenhouse effect); atmospheric change and ozone depletion; water scarcity; declining water quality; declining per capita grain production; soil erosion; overfishing; overgrazing; air and water pollution; and the loss of species and biodiversity.

While particular environmental problems are unique, they typically stem from economic growth fueled by resources that are nonrenewable, notably petroleum, natural gas, coal, and uranium. Environmental experts believe that the global community is nearing (if it has not already surpassed) many of Earth's physical limits. Their concern is that this kind of industrial economic growth is unsustainable.

This overall perspective is easiest to understand in the context of the following two figures reproduced from a best-selling environmental science textbook, *Living in the Environment*, by G. Tyler Miller. In Figure 23.11, Earth capital, in the center of the diagram is the foundation upon which Earth's life support system is based. Degrading or destroying this foundation undermines the ability to sustain life and the quality of that life. Economic growth that destroys Earth capital is unsustainable. Figure 23.12 identifies the social, political, economic, and environmental problems that derive in part from Earth's environmental and resource problems. Miller takes the position that human beings must adopt a new worldview of sustainability and create the kinds of practices and institutions necessary to preserve Earth's biological and physical integrity.

Global Restructuring and the Future of Capitalism

In the face of the economic, political, and environmental challenges confronting the global community in a time of rapid change and transformation, it is predictable that there are many competing perspectives on the character of this change and where it will lead in the twenty-first century. Let's examine three distinct perspectives.

FIGURE 23.11   Solar and Earth Capital

Solar and Earth capital consists of the life-support systems provided by the sun and the planet for use by humans and other species. These two forms of capital support and sustain all life and all economies on the Earth.

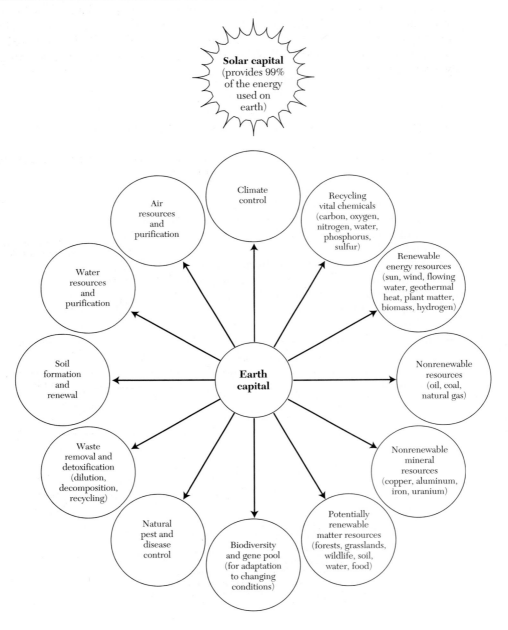

Source: From Miller,G. Tyler. *Living in the Environment*. © 2001. Reprinted with permission of Brooks/Cole, a division of Thomson Learning: www.thomsonrights.com

Many proponents of the free-market system view this transition, even with its problems, as a necessary adjustment period. The spread of the market system across the world and the global economic and financial integration taking place will lay the foundation for a long period of economic growth for all nations. Their view is that this strong growth will provide the necessary resources to solve many social, economic, health, and environmental problems. This optimistic future anticipates the rapid development of new technologies and the ongoing emergence of political democracy across the globe. This mainstream conservative view sees market capitalism as an economic system that is strong, dynamic, and adaptable.

FIGURE 23.12 Factors Causing Environmental and Social Problems

Environmental, resource, and social problems are caused by a complex, poorly understood mix of interacting factors, as illustrated by this simplified model.

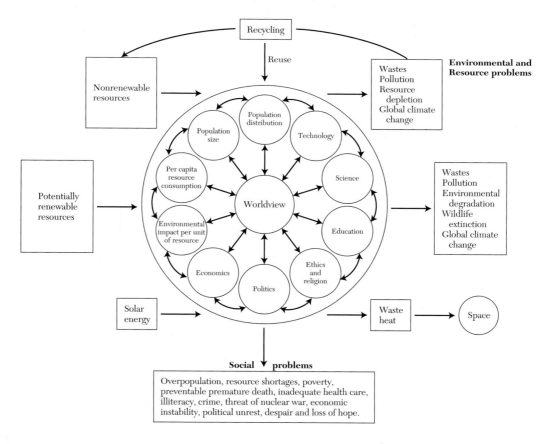

Source: Reprinted with permission of Brooks/Cole, a division of Thomson Learning: www.thomsonrights.com

Pedestrians in the shopping district of Macao, China
(Paul Conklin/PhotoEdit)

A more liberal view accepts many of the global changes taking place as necessary and welcome but recognizes that an unrestrained market system will continue to produce undesirable social, political, economic, and environmental outcomes unless the government (or state) plays a more active role in the domestic economy. This view recognizes the need to yield some economic sovereignty at the international level in order to be able to solve many of the economic, financial, and environmental problems that nation-states confront. This view accepts the basic principles of a capitalist market economy but envisions a very different role for the state to play in the future—a role that would involve greater planning, public investment, and a stronger involvement with the private sector.

A more radical view criticizes market capitalist institutions and blames most of the planet's problems on the unrestrained growth and expansion of industrial and finance capital across the global community. This view holds that global capitalism not only exploits labor but destroys the earth as well, producing poverty and inequality, economic insecurity, and uneven growth and development. Proponents of this perspective advocate a more responsive model of socialism than that which was and currently is practiced throughout the world. This view acknowledges the failures and excesses of a bureaucratic and authoritarian (nondemocratic) socialism but envisions a new kind of democratic and market socialism that would bring forward a sustainable model of economic growth. The radical view sees the current dynamics of economic and financial integration as part of a strategic global restructuring of capitalism. This restructuring is a necessary response on the part of capitalists to adapt and maintain their structures of capital accumulation so that the inherent dynamic of capitalism—capital accumulation—can continue unabated while avoiding the system's tendency to move toward economic crisis.

Conclusion

Early in the twenty-first century, we have the opportunity to reflect upon our study of introductory economics. What have we learned that helps us to understand our past, our present, and our future? Will the basic economic questions of today always be the basic economic questions? Will the microeconomic tool kit continue to help us make the kinds of decisions we need to make as educated consumers? Will firms be able to make critical decisions using competitive market microeconomic tools and concepts? Will governments be able to adapt traditional macroeconomic policy to the changing microeconomic, macroeconomic, and international realities of a global system challenged by rapid and unprecedented technological change? Can the economic systems of all nations responsibly manage the environmental, energy, and natural resource challenges of this new century? Can human society conduct its economic affairs peacefully?

Review Questions

1. What are the fundamental differences between capitalism and socialism as economic systems?

2. How would you characterize China's experience with socialism and its current economic transition? What kinds of economic problems does China face today?

3. Describe the major changes occurring in India and China. To what extent do these changes provide difficulties or opportunities for U.S. businesses?

4. What can developing countries learn from the successes of China and India?

5. Why does Greenpeace think we need a "Global Energy Revolution"? How might Conservatives, Liberals and Radicals react to their proposals?

6. What is Earth capital? There are two distinct worldviews in terms of the global environment. What are they? What do you understand sustainable economic growth to be?

7. Global capitalism is in transition. What are three distinct views of this transition? Which do you feel is the most accurate? Why?

THINKING CRITICALLY

Globalization in the Twenty-first Century

As you have seen in Chapters 20 through 23, the international economic and financial system has undergone a profound transformation since the post–World War II days of the late 1940s and the Bretton Woods system. Global trade has exploded, and the world of international finance has made it difficult for many nations to manage their own economies. Much of this change has been made possible by rapid technological change. The dominant industrial advanced countries have struggled to adapt to these changes and have in many cases moved in the direction of economic and financial integration. By the late 1980s, the socialist experience of the former Soviet Union and the Eastern European countries collapsed, and the movement toward market economies began. The developing countries of Asia, Latin America, and Africa found themselves drawn more tightly into this new global system with unique challenges having to do with population pressures, external debt, and balance of payments deficits, to name a few. And surrounding this entire process of change is what many experts argue to be an unprecedented environmental crisis that calls for a new direction toward sustainable development.

Case: The Future of Outsourcing?

In a January 2006 issue of *Business Week* magazine, Pete Engardio wrote a special report on "The Future of Outsourcing: How It's Transforming Whole Industries and Changing the Way We Work." This is an excellent article to use as a final integrative exercise in Thinking Critically. The focus on work in a global context allows us to revisit the early reading we did on economic history and economic philosophers (Smith, Marx, Schumpeter, and Keynes), the role of the firm, the role of the government (state), the international system, and the energy and environmental challenges pertaining to sustainability.

The Future of Outsourcing:
Pete Engardio
How It's Transforming Whole Industries and Changing the Way We Work
– –

Globalization has been brutal to midwestern manufacturers like the Paper Converting Machine Co. For decades, PCMC's Green Bay (Wis.) factory, its oiled wooden factory floors worn smooth by work boots, thrived by making ever-more-complex equipment to weave, fold, and print packaging for everything from potato chips to baby wipes.

But PCMC has fallen on hard times. First came the 2001 recession. Then, two years ago, one of the company's biggest customers told it to slash its machinery prices by 40% and urged it to move production to China. Last year, a St. Louis holding company, Barry-Wehmiller Cos., acquired the manufacturer and promptly cut workers and nonunion pay. In five years sales have plunged by 40%, to $170 million, and the workforce has shrunk from 2,000 to 1,100. Employees have been traumatized, says operations manager Craig Compton, a muscular former hockey player. "All you hear about is China and all these companies closing or taking their operations overseas."

But now, Compton says, he is "probably the most optimistic I've been in five years." Hope is coming from an unusual source. As part of its turnaround strategy, Barry-Wehmiller plans to shift some design work to its 160-engineer center in Chennai, India. By having U.S. and Indian designers collaborate 24/7, explains Vasant Bennett, president of Barry-Wehmiller's engineering services unit, PCMC hopes to slash development costs and time, win orders it often missed due to engineering constraints—and keep production in Green Bay. Barry-Wehmiller says the strategy already has boosted profits at some of the 32 other midsize U.S. machinery makers it has bought. "We can compete and create great American jobs," vows CEO Robert Chapman. "But not without offshoring."

Come again? Ever since the offshore shift of skilled work sparked widespread debate and a political firestorm three years ago, it has been portrayed as the killer of good-paying American jobs. "Benedict Arnold CEOs" hire software engineers, computer help staff, and credit-card bill collectors to exploit the low wages of poor nations. U.S. workers suddenly face a grave new threat, with even highly educated tech and service professionals having to compete against legions of hungry college grads in India, China, and the Philippines willing to work twice as hard for one-fifth the pay.

Workers' fears have some grounding in fact. The prime motive of most corporate bean counters jumping on the offshoring bandwagon has been to take advantage of such "labor arbitrage"—the huge wage gap between industrialized and developing nations. And without doubt, big layoffs often accompany big outsourcing deals.

The changes can be harsh and deep. But a more enlightened, strategic view of global sourcing is starting to emerge as managers get a better fix on its potential. The new buzzword is "transformational outsourcing." Many executives are discovering offshoring is really about corporate growth, making better use of skilled U.S. staff, and even job creation in the U.S., not just cheap wages abroad. True, the labor savings from global sourcing can still be substantial. But it's peanuts compared to the enormous gains in efficiency, productivity, quality, and revenues that can be achieved by fully leveraging offshore talent.

Thus entrepreneurs such as Chapman see a chance to turn around dying businesses, speed up their pace of innovation, or fund development projects that otherwise would have been unaffordable. More aggressive outsourcers are aiming to create radical business models that can give them an edge and change the game in their industries. Old-line multinationals see offshoring as a catalyst for a broader plan to overhaul outdated office operations and prepare for new competitive battles. And while some want to downsize, others are keen to liberate expensive analysts, engineers, and salesmen from routine tasks so they can spend more time innovating and dealing with customers. "This isn't about labor cost," says Daniel Marovitz, technology managing director for Deutsche Bank's global businesses. "The issue is that if you don't do it, you won't survive."

The new attitude is emerging in corporations across the U.S. and Europe in virtually every industry. Ask executives at Penske Truck Leasing why the company outsources dozens of business processes to Mexico and India, and they cite greater efficiency and customer service. Ask managers at U.S.-Dutch professional publishing giant Wolters Kluwer why they're racing to shift software development and editorial work to India and the Philippines, and they will say it's about being able to pump out a greater variety of books, journals, and Web-based content more rapidly. Ask Wachovia Corp., the Charlotte (N.C.)-based bank, why it just inked a $1.1 billion deal with India's Genpact to outsource finance and accounting jobs and why it handed over administration of its human-resources programs to Lincolnshire (Ill.)-based Hewitt Associates. It's "what we need to do to become a great customer-relationship company," says Director of Corporate Development Peter J. Sidebottom. Wachovia aims to reinvest up to 40% of the $600 million to $1 billion it hopes to take out in costs over three years into branches, ATMs, and personnel to boost its core business.

Here's what such transformations typically entail: Genpact, Accenture, IBM Services, or another big outsourcing specialist dispatches teams to meticulously dissect the workflow of an entire human resources, finance, or info tech department. The team then helps build a new IT platform, redesigns all processes, and administers programs, acting as a virtual subsidiary. The contractor then disperses work among global networks of staff ranging from the U.S. to Asia to Eastern Europe.

In recent years, Procter & Gamble, DuPont, Cisco Systems, ABN Amro, Unilever, Rockwell Collins, and Marriott were among those that signed such megadeals, worth billions. In 2004, for example, drugmaker Wyeth Pharmaceuticals transferred its entire clinical-testing operation to Accenture Ltd. "Boards of directors of virtually every big company now are insisting on very articulated outsourcing strategies," says Peter Allen, global services managing director of TPI, a consulting firm that advised on 15 major outsourcing contracts last year worth $14 billion. "Many CEOs are saying, `Don't tell me how much I can save. Show me how we can grow by 40% without increasing our capacity in the U.S.,'" says Atul Vashistha, CEO of outsourcing consultant neoIT and co-author of the book *The Offshore Nation*.

Some observers even believe Big Business is on the cusp of a new burst of productivity growth, ignited in part by offshore outsourcing as a catalyst. "Once this transformation is done," predicts Arthur H. Harper, former CEO of General Electric Co.'s equipment management businesses, "I think we will end up with companies that deliver products faster at lower costs, and are better able to compete against anyone in the world." As executives shed more operations, they also are spurring new debate about how the future corporation will look. Some management pundits theorize about the "totally disaggregated corporation," wherein every function not regarded as crucial is stripped away.

Processes, Now on Sale

In theory, it is becoming possible to buy, off the shelf, practically any function you need to run a company. Want to start a budget airline but don't want to invest in a huge back office? Accenture's Navitaire unit can manage reservations, plan routes, assign crew, and calculate optimal prices for each seat.

Have a cool new telecom or medical device but lack market researchers? For about $5,000, analytics outfits such as New Delhi-based Evalueserve Inc. will, within a day, assemble a team of Indian patent attorneys, engineers, and business analysts, start mining global databases, and call dozens of U.S. experts and wholesalers to provide an independent appraisal.

Want to market quickly a new mutual fund or insurance policy? IT services providers such as India's Tata Consultancy Services Ltd. are building software platforms that furnish every business process needed and secure all regulatory approvals. A sister company, Tata Technologies, boasts 2,000 Indian engineers and recently bought 700-employee Novi (Mich.) auto- and aerospace-engineering firm Incat International PLC. Tata Technologies can now handle everything from turning a conceptual design into detailed specs for interiors, chassis, and electrical systems to designing the tooling and factory-floor layout. "If you map out the entire vehicle-development process, we have the capability to supply every piece of it," says Chief Operating Officer Jeffrey D. Sage, an IBM and General Motors Corp. veteran. Tata is designing all doors for a future truck, for example, and the power train for a U.S. sedan. The company is hiring 100 experienced U.S. engineers at salaries of $100,000 and up.

Few big companies have tried all these options yet. But some, like Procter & Gamble, are showing that the ideas are not farfetched. Over the past three years the $57 billion consumer-products company has outsourced everything from IT infrastructure and human resources to management of its offices from Cincinnati to Moscow. CEO Alan G. Lafley also has announced he wants half of all new P&G products to come from outside by 2010, vs. 20% now. In the near future, some analysts predict, Detroit and European carmakers will go the way of the PC industry, relying on outsiders to develop new models bearing their brand names. BMW has done just that with a sport-utility vehicle. And Big Pharma will bring blockbuster drugs to market at a fraction of the current $1 billion average cost by allying with partners in India, China, and Russia in molecular research and clinical testing.

Of course, corporations have been outsourcing management of IT systems to the likes of Electronic Data Systems, IBM, and Accenture for more than a decade, while Detroit has long given engineering jobs to outside design firms. Futurists have envisioned "hollow" and "virtual" corporations since the 1980s.

It hasn't happened yet. Reengineering a company may make sense on paper, but it's extremely expensive and entails big risks if executed poorly. Corporations can't simply be snapped apart and reconfigured like LEGO sets, after all. They are complex, living organisms that can be thrown into convulsions if a transplant operation is botched. Valued employees send out their résumés, customers are outraged at deteriorating service, a brand name can be damaged. In consultant surveys, what's more, many U.S. managers complain about the quality of offshored work and unexpected costs.

But as companies work out such kinks, the rise of the offshore option is dramatically changing the economics of reengineering. With millions of low-cost engineers, financial analysts, consumer marketers, and architects now readily available via the Web, CEOs can see a quicker payoff. "It used to be that companies struggled for a few years to show a 5% or 10% increase in productivity from outsourcing," says Pramod Bhasin, CEO of Genpact, the 19,000-employee back-office-processing unit spun off by GE last year. "But by offshoring work, they can see savings of 30% to 40% in the first year" in labor costs. Then the efficiency gains kick in. A $10 billion company might initially only shave a few million dollars in wages after transferring back-office procurement or bill collection overseas. But better management of these processes could free up hundreds of millions in cash flow annually.

Those savings, in turn, help underwrite far broader corporate restructuring that can be truly transformational. DuPont has long wanted to fix its unwieldy system for administering records, payroll, and benefits for its 60,000 employees in 70 nations, with data scattered among different software platforms and global business units. By awarding a long-term contract to Cincinnati-based Convergys Corp., the world's biggest call-center operator, to redesign and administer its human resources programs, it expects to cut costs 20% in the first year and 30% a year afterward. To get corporate backing for the move, "it certainly helps a lot to have savings from the outset," says DuPont Senior Human Resources Vice-President James C. Borel.

Creative new companies can exploit the possibilities of offshoring even faster than established players. Crimson Consulting Group is a good example. The Los Altos (Calif.) firm, which performs global market research on everything from routers to software for clients including Cisco, HP, and Microsoft, has only 14 full-time employees. But it farms out research to India's Evalueserve and some 5,000 other independent experts from Silicon Valley to China, the Czech Republic, and South Africa. "This allows a small firm like us to compete with McKinsey and Bain on a very global basis with very low costs," says CEO Glenn Gow. Former GE exec Harper is on the same wavelength. Like Barry-Wehmiller, his new five-partner private-equity firm plans to buy struggling midsize manufacturers and use offshore outsourcing to help revitalize them. Harper's NexGen Capital Partners also plans to farm out most of its own office work. "The people who understand this will start from Day One and never build a back room," Harper says. "They will outsource everything they can."

Some aggressive outsourcers are using their low-cost, superefficient business models to challenge incumbents. Pasadena, (Calif.)-based IndyMac Bancorp Inc., founded in 1985, illustrates the new breed of financial services company. In three years, IndyMac has risen from 22nd-largest U.S. mortgage issuer to No. 9, while its 18% return on equity in 2004 outpaced most rivals. The thrift's initial edge was its technology to process, price, and approve loan applications in less than a minute.

But IndyMac also credits its aggressive offshore outsourcing strategy, which Consumer Banking CEO Ashwin Adarkar says has helped make it "more productive, cost-efficient, and flexible than our competitors, with better customer service." IndyMac is using 250 mostly Indian staff from New York-based Cognizant Technology Solutions Corp. to help build a next-generation software platform and applications that, it expects, will boost efficiency at least 20% by 2008. IndyMac has also begun shifting tasks, ranging from bill collection to "welcome calls" that help U.S. borrowers make their first mortgage payments on time, to India's Exlservice Holdings Inc. and its 5,000-strong staff. In all, Exlservice and other Indian providers handle 33 back-office processes offshore. Yet rather than losing any American jobs, IndyMac has doubled its U.S. workforce to nearly 6,000 in four years—and is still hiring.

Superior Service

Smart use of offshoring can juice the performance of established players, too. Five years ago, Penske Truck Leasing, a joint venture between GE and Penske Corp., paid $768 million for trucker Rollins Truck Leasing Corp.—just in time for the recession. Customer service, spread among four U.S. call centers, was inconsistent. "I realized our business needed a transformation," says GFO Frank Cocuzza. He began by shifting a few dozen data-processing jobs to GE's huge Mexican and Indian call centers, now called Genpact. He then hired Genpact to help restructure most of his back-office. That relationship now spans 30 processes involved in leasing 216,000 trucks and providing logistical services for customers.

Now, if a Penske truck is held up at a weigh station because it lacks a certain permit, for example, the driver calls an 800 number. Genpact staff in India obtains the document over the Web. The weigh station is notified electronically, and the truck is

TABLE V.1 Hot Players in the Offshore Outsourcing World

Consultant Gartner Inc.'s clients ask most about these companies' offshore offerings. For estimates of outsourcing revenues, areas of specialty, and location of operations, go to www. businessweek. com/ go/ outsourcing.

Business Services	Software Development	Call Centers
1 Hewitt Associates U.S.	1 Tata Consultancy Services INDIA	1 Convergys U.S.
2 ACS U.S.	2 Infosys Technologies INDIA	2 Wipro INDIA
3 Accenture U.S.	3 Wipro INDIA	3 CIC OneSource INDIA
4 IBM U.S.	4 Accenture U.S.	4 ClientLogic U.S.
5 EDS U.S.	5 IBM U.S.	5 24/7 Customer INDIA
6 Hewlett-Packard U.S.	6 Cognizant Technology Solutions U.S.	6 SR. Teleperformance FRANCE
7 Wipro INDIA	7 Satyam INDIA	7 eTelecare International U.S.
8 HCL Technologies INDIA	8 Patni Computer Systems INDIA	8 SITEL U.S.
9 Tata Consultancy Services INDIA	9 EDS U.S.	9 Teletech U.S.
10 WNS Global Services INDIA	10 CSC U.S.	10 Customer Corp. U.S.

Data: Gartner Inc. Ranking based on frequency of queries from Gartner's 10,000 global clients.

back on the road within 30 minutes. Before, Penske thought it did well if it accomplished that in two hours. And when a driver finishes his job, his entire log, including records of mileage, tolls, and fuel purchases, is shipped to Mexico, punched into computers, and processed in Hyderabad. In all, 60% of the 1,000 workers handling Penske back-office process are in India or Mexico, and Penske is still ramping up. Under a new program, when a manufacturer asks Penske to arrange for a delivery to a buyer, Indian staff helps with the scheduling, billing, and invoices. The $15 million in direct labor-cost savings are small compared with the gains in efficiency and customer service, Cocuzza says.

Big Pharma is pursuing huge boosts in efficiency as well. Eli Lilly & Co.'s labs are more productive than most, having released eight major drugs in the past five years. But for each new drug, Lilly estimates it invests a hefty $1.1 billion. That could reach $1.5 billion in four years. "Those kinds of costs are fundamentally unsustainable," says Steven M. Paul, Lilly's science and tech executive vice-president. Outsourcing figures heavily in Lilly's strategy to lower that cost to $800 million. The drugmaker now does 20% of its chemistry work in China for one-quarter the U.S. cost and helped fund a startup lab, Shanghai's Chem-Explorer Co., with 230 chemists. Lilly now is trying to slash the costs of clinical trials on human patients, which range from $50 million to $300 million per drug, and is expanding such efforts in Brazil, Russia, China, and India.

Other manufacturers and tech companies are learning to capitalize on global talent pools to rush products to market sooner at lower costs. OnStor Inc., a Los Gatos (Calif.) developer of storage systems, says its tie-up with Bangalore engineering-services outfit HCL Technologies Ltd. enables it to get customized products to clients twice as fast as its major rivals. "If we want to recruit a great engineer in Silicon Valley, our lead time is three months," says CEO Bob Miller. "With HCL, we can pick up the phone and get somebody in two or three days."

Such strategies offer a glimpse into the productive uses of global outsourcing. But most experts remain cautious. The McKinsey Global Institute estimates $18.4 billion in global IT work and $11.4 billion in business-process services have been shifted abroad so far—just one-tenth of the potential offshore market. One reason is that executives still have a lot to learn about using offshore talent to boost productivity. Professor Mohanbir Sawhney of Northwestern University's Kellogg School of Management, a self-proclaimed "big believer in total disaggregation," says: "One of our tasks in business schools is to train people to manage the virtual, globally distributed corporation. How do you manage employees you can't even see?"

The management challenges will grow more urgent as rising global salaries dissipate the easy cost gains from offshore outsourcing. The winning companies of the future will be those most adept at leveraging global talent to transform themselves and their industries, creating better jobs for everyone.—With Michael Arndt in Green Bay, Wis., and Dean Foust in Charlotte, N.C.

Source: "The Future of Outsourcing: How It's Transforming Whole Industries and Changing the Way We Work," Pete Engardio, *Business Week*, January 30, 2006.

Exercises

1. What would be Adam Smith's reaction to this article? Marx's? Schumpeter's? Keynes's?

2. What was your initial reaction after reading this article?

3. What is meant by the term *labor arbitrage*?

4. What does the author mean by the term *transformational outsourcing*?

5. What would be a totally disaggregated corporation?

6. How does the offshore option change the economics of re-engineering?

7. Who are the hot players in the offshore–outsourcing world?

8. What are some of the new challenges for management education?

9. What is a plausible case against offshoring?

10. How might offshoring fundamentally change the nature of global capital-ism for workers, firms, and governments?

GLOSSARY

Absolute advantage In international trade, a condition in which one nation can produce more of a particular commodity with the same amount of resources as another nation uses for producing that commodity.

Aggregate demand The total quantity of goods and services demanded by households, businesses, government, and the international sector at various prices.

Aggregate supply The total quantity of goods and services producers are willing to supply at varying price levels.

Alienation The condition resulting from the separation of the worker from the means of production. Alienation from the worker's point of view results from no control over the product, no control of the means of producing it, and an antagonistic relationship of workers and owners.

Antitrust policy Laws that attempt to limit the degree of monopoly in the economy and to promote competition. In the United States, the passage, interpretation, and enforcement of antitrust laws have involved varying degrees of emphasis on market performance, market conduct, and market structure. See *Sherman Antitrust Act*.

Appreciation of currency The relative strengthening of a currency in a flexible exchange rate system. The appreciated currency rises in cost and value relative to the depreciated currency.

Assumption A proposition that is accepted as true. Economists use simplifying assumptions in building economic models.

Average cost Total cost divided by the number of production units.

Average fixed cost Total fixed cost divided by total units of output.

Average propensity to consume (APC) Total consumption divided by total disposable income. This is the average consumption income ratio.

Average propensity to save (APS) Total saving divided by total disposable income.

Average revenue Total revenue divided by total output.

Average variable cost (AVC) Total variable cost divided by total output.

Balance of payments A summary record of a country's transactions that typically involves payments and receipt of foreign exchange. Credit items and debit items must balance, since each good that a country buys or sells must be paid for in one way or another.

Balance of trade The difference between the value of exports and the value of imports of visible items (goods and services).

Barriers to entry Obstacles to a firm's entry into new industries or markets. These obstacles may be political (such as tariffs or trade restrictions), economic (economies of scale or limited resources, especially in oligopolies), or legal (patents, copyrights, or monopoly).

Board of Governors A seven-member group members are appointed by the U.S. president and approved by the Congress to head the Federal Reserve. The board coordinates and regulates the nation's money supply. See *Federal Reserve System*.

Breakeven point (1) In national income accounting, the amount of income corresponding to consumption of the entire income. There is no saving or dissaving. (2) For an individual business, the amount of revenue corresponding to a production level at which revenues exactly equal costs. There are no profits or losses.

Bretton Woods Agreement (1944) The international agreement that formed the basis for today's international financial organizations. After World War II, the Allied nations agreed that international financial affairs would be overseen by the International Monetary Fund. GATT and the World Bank were also outcomes of Bretton Woods.

Budget deficit   The amount by which government expenditures exceed government revenues during the accounting period.

Built-in stabilizers   Automatic, nondiscretionary forms of fiscal policy that compensate for particular trends of aggregate changes in national income.

Business cycle   Recurrent ups and downs of business activity, shown in a host of business indicators. Expansion and contraction phases are both thought to have certain cumulative features. They may also contain the seeds of the turning points at the cycle's peak and trough.

Capital   A factor of production, along with labor and land; the stock of a society's produced means of production, including factories, buildings, machines, tools, and inventories of goods in stock.

Capital account   Unilateral and capital transfers in balance-of-payment accounting, capital transfers of nonproduced, nonfinancial assets.

Capitalism   An economic system in which the basic resources and capital goods of the society are privately owned. Decisions are usually made by individual units, which may be relatively small (pure competition) or quite large (monopoly/oligopoly). Decisions tend to be based on profitability in the case of businesses, or, in the case of individuals, on economic self-interest.

Cartel   An organization of producers designed to limit or eliminate competition among its members, usually by agreeing to restrict output in an effort to achieve noncompetitive prices. An example is OPEC.

Central bank   A Federal Reserve Board operation that serves the nation's banks. Besides its major responsibility—control of the money supply—it conducts some restriction, regulation, and investigation of the banking industry.

Ceteris paribus   Literally, "other things being equal"; a term used in economics to indicate that all variables except the ones specified are assumed not to change.

Change in demand   A shift in the demand curve due to a change in one of the determinants of demand.

Change in supply   A shift in the supply curve due to a change in one of the determinants of supply.

Class   In an economic sense, a group of people defined in terms of their relationship to production. For example, under capitalism, one class of people (proletariat) works the means of production, and another class (capitalists, bourgeoisie) owns the means of production. This concept was used largely by Karl Marx.

Classical economics   A school of economics that usually refers to the doctrines of the British Classical School of the late eighteenth and early nineteenth centuries, especially those of Adam Smith and followers. They emphasized competition, free trade, and minimal state intervention in the economy.

Classical liberalism   A doctrine stressing the importance of rationality, property rights, individual freedom, and laissez-faire.

Collusion   Agreements to avoid competition or to set prices.

Commodity   Marketable item produced to satisfy wants. Commodities may be either tangible goods or intangible services. Marx considered labor under the wage contract a commodity because it orders wage contracts and responds to supply-and-demand conditions.

Communism   An economic system characterized by socialization of labor, centralization of the ownership of the means of production, centralized coordination of production, centralization of credit policy through a central bank, and reduction of alienation and exploitation of the worker.

Comparative advantage   In international trade, a country's productive advantage with respect to a particular commodity, based on its ability to give up fewer other commodities to produce a unit of the commodity than another country would have to give up. This relative cost of production is most significant in determining mutually beneficial patterns of trade among nations.

Competition Theoretically, competition exists in a perfect and an imperfect form; the former is known as perfect competition, the latter as monopoly oligopoly, and monopolistic competition.

Concentration ratio The percentage of total sales in an industry that is accounted for by a specific number of firms.

Conglomerate merger Companies in unrelated industries merge.

Conservative economist An economist who advocates classical theory, classical liberalism, and classical economics (i.e., that government should intervene only when necessary, and then only minimally).

Consumer Price Index (CPI) A government statistic that measures inflation in terms of the weighted average composite of goods and services commonly consumed by average families.

Consumer sovereignty The doctrine that the market follows the dictates of consumers, and is driven solely by consumer tastes and preferences. Producers respond to consumer demand.

Consumption Expenditures by households and individuals on consumer goods.

Corporation A form of business organization with a legal existence separate from that of the owners, in which ownership and financial responsibility are divided, limited, and shared among any number of individual and institutional shareholders.

Cost-push inflation A general increase in prices associated with increases in the cost of production. Categorized as supply inflation.

Creative destruction The process of the transformation of industries due to extraordinary innovations in which the most innovative actors tend to succeed while non-innovating establishments are destroyed.

Crowding out Loss of funding as a result of the competition between economic units for the use of limited funds. The term usually refers to the federal budget deficit and the continued borrowing of the U.S. Treasury. Funds used to finance government spending deprive businesses of necessary capital, thus crowding out investment.

Currency Any recognized material accepted as national money; almost always paper or coin.

Current accounts In balance-of-payments accounting, the accounts that summarize the flow of goods and services between one nation and the rest of the world.

Cyclical (budget) deficit The part of the federal deficit that fluctuates with the state of the economy. It increases when there is a downturn of the business cycle.

Cyclical unemployment Measure of unemployment due to decreased demand during the troughs of business cycles, when output is curtailed. Workers who are cyclically unemployed are expected to be reinstated as the cycle moves upward.

Deficit spending Government spending when net government revenues are less than net government expenditures.

Demand (1) Quantity demanded. (2) The whole relationship of the quantity demanded to variables that determine it, such as tastes, income, population, and price. (3) The demand curve.

Demand curve A hypothetical construction depicting how many units of a particular commodity consumers would be willing to buy over a period of time at all possible prices, assuming that the prices of other commodities, money incomes of consumers, and other factors are unchanged.

Demand deposits Checking accounts in commercial banks. These deposits can be turned into currency "on demand," i.e., by writing a check. Demand deposits are a main form of money in the United States.

Demand, law of A principle concerning the relationship between price and quantity demanded: All other things constant, the lower the price, the higher the quantity demanded. In other words, price and quantity demanded are inversely related.

Demand-pull inflation A general increase in prices arising from increasing excess demand for a given level of output.

Dependency model A model that assumes that underdevelopment is a consequence of the historical evolution of capitalism and the integration of developing countries into the expanding sphere of capitalist production globally.

Depreciation (1) Loss of value in capital equipment due to use or obsolescence. (2) The loss of value in any valuable good or commodity due to use or market forces (such as currency exchange rates).

Depression A prolonged downswing of economic activity exemplified by mass unemployment, a level of national income well below the potential level, and great excess capacity. A depression is more severe and longer lasting than a recession. The economic breakdown of the industrialized world in the 1930s was called the Great Depression. See *Recession*.

Derived demand Demand of a good for use in the production of goods and services.

Devaluation A downward revision in the value at which a country's currency is pegged in terms of a foreign currency.

Dialectics The study of the contradictions within the essence of things; an exchange of a thesis and antithesis that results in a synthesis; the struggle of opposing forces in the economy that, according to Karl Marx, drives economic change.

Discount rate Interest rate charged on loans from the Federal Reserve Bank to its member banks. The rate is pegged to the fed funds rate.

Discretionary fiscal policy A fiscal policy designed to respond to a particular situation in the macroeconomy. These policies are implemented to achieve specific goals, usually high output, high employment, and stable prices.

Diseconomies of scale The phenomenon of disproportional increasing costs as a firm's long-run productive capacity grows. Simply put, the growth of production costs in an expanding firm outstrips the growth in production.

Disintermediation Resource allocation, particularly investment, by a firm that excludes intermediary institutions such as savings and loan institutions, banks, or brokerage firms.

Disposable personal income Amount of personal income remaining after payment of various federal, state, and local taxes and other nontax payments.

Dissaving Deficit or negative spending; that is, borrowing or drawing down other financial assets in order to consume.

Distribution (of income) The division of the total product of a society among its members. The distribution is sometimes described by a classification according to income size or by a classification including factor payments.

Division of labor Subdivision of a productive process into its component parts, which are then handled by specially skilled or trained laborers. Adam Smith believed it was a major source of increased productivity over time.

Dumping Sale by an exporting nation of its product at a lower price in an importing country than in its own country. Dumping tends to ruin the importer's domestic industry while strengthening the exporter's market share.

Economic dependence The relationship of unequal interdependence, endured by the less advanced countries with the developed countries. Theoretically, a country is in a state of economic dependence if the expansion of its economy depends on that of another country. See *Imperialism*.

Economic development Progressive changes in a society's ability to meet its economic tasks of production and distribution. Development is characterized by increasing output and the growth of economic institutions, relationships, and methods that facilitate society's ability to generate economic growth.

Economic growth Increase in productive capabilities beyond the necessary elements of survival. Expansion creates more jobs, goods, and income.

Economic planning The planning of investment, consumption, and similar decisions by one or another bodies. Several variants (among which are corporate planning, command planning, and indicative planning) demonstrate variety in what is to be planned and who does the planning.

Economic profits A return to capital above "normal profit"; profit remaining after opportunity costs have been taken into account.

Economic system The "mode of life" of a society; the manner in which people organize themselves for production and distribution.

Economic theory A theory of economics or resource allocation. Examples are Marxist, classical, and Keynesian theory. See *Theory*.

Economics The study of the allocation of resources, the production of goods and services, and their distribution in societies.

Economies of scale The phenomenon of decreasing average costs in large-scale production (usually oligopolistic production). The growth of production in an expanding firm outstrips the growth in costs.

Efficiency In economics, allocation of scarce resources to best meet the needs and wants of society.

Elasticity A function that describes the sensitivity of demand or supply of a product to changes in its price. Elasticity equals the percentage change in quantity demanded (supplied) divided by the percentage change in price.

Employment Act of 1946 U.S. federal law that created a Council of Economic Advisers to advise the president on the state of the economy and on how best to achieve the goal of full employment.

Enclosure movement In England during the Middle Ages, a series of parliamentary acts by which the feudal nobility fenced off or enclosed lands formerly used for communal grazing, destroying feudal ties and creating a large, new "landless" labor force.

Entrepreneur In the classical liberal sense, an innovator and owner of the means of production. In the modern corporate world, a businessperson is often considered an entrepreneur.

Equation of exchange The quantity theory of money, expressed as $MV = PQ$, where M is the money stock, V is velocity of money, P is price level, and Q is real national income. It is a tautology, because V is defined as PQ/M.

Equilibrium A state of balance in which there are no endogenous pressures for change. A market equilibrium is said to exist at the price where the quantity demanded equals the quantity supplied.

Exchange rate The price of a nation's currency in terms of another nation's currency.

Exhaustive spending Governmental purchases of goods and services.

Exports Any unit of production that leaves the country where it was produced for sale in another country.

Externalities Costs of productive activity that the firm is not obliged to bear. The costs are borne by the public as social costs of production. Also known as third-party effect. Externalities may be detrimental (external costs) or beneficial (external benefits).

Factor of production Any implement or agent whose services are used in the production of economic goods and services. Three basic factors are land, labor, and capital.

Federal Reserve System (Fed) An independent agency of the federal government and instrumental in determining monetary policy. Its main tools are altering reserve requirements, and conducting open-market purchases and sales of governmental securities. See *Discount rate; Monetary policy; Reserve requirements; Open Market Operations*.

Fed funds rate The interest rate that banks charge when they lend reserves to other banks for short periods of time; the Federal Reserve currently targets the fed funds rate and uses policy tools to achieve the stated target.

Feudalism The economic system that preceded capitalism. Relations of class were between lord and serf. Feudalism existed in a society in which tradition and ceremony played the major roles.

Financial account In Balance of Payments Accounting, all financial flows in and out of a country.

Financial intermediaries Institutions such as banks, savings and loans, insurance companies, mutual funds, pension funds, and finance companies that borrow funds from people with savings and then make loans to others (borrowers).

Financial intermediation Use of financial institutions to deposit or acquire funds from the public. Such institutions pool numerous funds and then provide them to businesses, governments, or individuals.

Firm Unit that makes decisions regarding the employment of factors of production and production of goods and services.

Fiscal policy Governmental policy concerned with the tax and expenditure activities of the federal government, including the size of public spending and the balancing or unbalancing of the federal budget. This policy is designed to promote certain macroeconomic objectives—usually full employment, stable prices, economic growth, and balance-of-payments equilibrium.

Fixed exchange rate A rate at which a currency is fixed (set) to establish its price relative either to a universal exchange (gold) or to another currency.

Floating exchange rate A currency exchange rate that rises or falls in response to the forces of international supply and demand. See *Exchange rate.*

Forces of production All of the necessary elements—tools, machines, factories, means of transportation, labor, science, technology, skills, knowledge, etc.—required to produce goods and services.

Fractional reserve system A banking system under which commercial banks are required to maintain reserves equal to a prescribed percentage of their demand or other deposits. See *Reserve requirement.*

Free trade A situation in which all commodities can be freely imported and exported without special taxes or restrictions being levied because of their status as imports or exports.

Frictional unemployment Loss of jobs caused by temporary mismatching of laborers with jobs due to differences between the needs of business and skills of labor.

Full employment A condition under which those who wish to work at the prevailing wage are able to find work. In the United States, full employment is defined as 4 percent unemployment.

General Agreement on Tariffs and Trade (GATT) An association of countries that "sets and regulates the code of international trade conduct and promotes free trade."

Gini coefficient A measure of inequality in income distribution derived from the Lorenz curve. To calculate it for a population, find the difference in area between a 45° line and the population's Lorenz curve, and divide the difference by the entire area below the 45° line.

Glut An excess of production over the amount purchased. This usually leads to a decline in production and possibly a recession.

Gross domestic product (GDP) The market value of all final goods and services produced in an accounting period by factors of production located within a country.

Gross national product (GNP) The market value of all final goods and services produced in an accounting period by factors of production owned by citizens of that country.

Hidden unemployment Workers who are unemployed or underemployed but are not counted in official unemployment statistics. Includes discouraged workers who are unemployed but have given up looking for a job, and workers who are working part-time but would like more hours of work.

Historical materialism Developed by Karl Marx, an in-depth historical study of material relations of people. The basis of social and economic change resides in class relations of people. The base of a society is its mode of production, and all class struggle emanates out of the relations of people to the mode of production. The superstructure, which is determined by the base, includes the philosophy, religion, ideology, etc. of the specific epoch.

Horizontal merger Companies in the same industry merge.

Imperialism One country's economic, social, political, and cultural dominance over another country. Imperialism, as developed by Lenin, Sweezy, Baran, Magdoff, and many others, is a historical problem and directly related to the growth and development of capitalism.

Imports Goods brought into a country for sale, having been produced elsewhere.

Income elasticity of demand The percentage change in quantity demanded divided by the percentage change in income. It measures how much the demand for a product changes when income changes.

Income flow The path that income follows in the economy. Businesses pay rents, wages, interest, and profits to households, which in turn spend their incomes to continue the flow.

Incomes policy A governmental policy designed to limit inflation by instituting direct and indirect controls over prices, wages, profits, and other types of income.

Income velocity of money The rate of turnover of money in the economy. From the equation of exchange, velocity is GDP divided by the money supply. See *Equation of exchange.*

Index number A weighted average of a given variable with a specified base number, usually 100.

Indirect business taxes Taxes imposed on the production and sale of goods. Examples include sales tax, excise tax, custom duties, and property taxes.

Industry The collective group of producers of a single good or service or closely related goods or services.

Inefficiency in production A condition in a noncompetitive market in which output is not at minimum average cost.

Inefficiency in resource allocation A condition in a noncompetitive market in which the good's price does not equal marginal cost.

Infant industry An industry that has recently been established in a country and has not yet had time to exploit possible economies of scale and other efficiencies. Such industries provide one of the traditional arguments for tariff protection.

Inflation A general rise in the average level of all prices in an economy as defined by some index (Consumer Price Index, wholesale price index, or GDP price deflator).

Infrastructure Necessary supports for development, such as transportation routes and social services.

Innovation A change for the better in technology or production. A change is considered "better" if it involves higher efficiency and/or lower production costs.

Institutional economics An approach to studying the economy that focuses on understanding the role and evolution of human-made institutions in shaping the economy and economic behavior.

Institutionalist Economists practicing institutional economics.

Interest (1) The price of borrowing money. (2) The rate of return to owners of financial capital.

Interest rate The amount of interest expressed as a percentage of the initial sum.

International Monetary Fund (IMF) International organization founded with the goal of encouraging trade by establishing an orderly procedure for stabilizing foreign exchange rates and for altering those rates in the case of fundamental balance-of-payments disequilibrium.

International trade   Buying and selling of goods and services across national borders. The country that sells is the exporter, and the country that buys is the importer.

Inventories   Stocks of goods kept on hand to meet orders from other producers and customers.

Investment   An addition to a firm's or society's stock of capital (machines, buildings, inventories, etc.) in a certain period of time.

"Invisible hand"   Term coined by Adam Smith to suggest that individuals who are motivated only by private (not social) interest will nevertheless be guided invisibly by the market to actions and decisions beneficial to the welfare of society.

Kanban   The "just-in-time" system in which services and supplies are produced and delivered only when needed.

Keiretsu   A production relation between a large core firm and its subsidiaries that allows for a stable, mutually beneficial long-term relationship.

Keynesian economics   Theory characterized by its emphasis on macroeconomic problems, the special role of aggregate expenditure in determining national income, and the possibility of unemployment equilibrium; its attempt to synthesize real and monetary analysis; and its argument for a greater government involvement in the economy.

Keynesian multiplier (k)   The number of dollars by which a $1 increase in spending ($C, I, G$) will raise the equilibrium level of national income. Represented as k, it can be expressed mathematically in relation to the marginal propensity to consume (MPC) or the marginal propensity to save (MPS):

$$k = \frac{1}{1 - \text{MPC}} \quad k = \frac{1}{\text{MPS}}$$

Labor   The physical and mental contributions of humans to the production process. Collectively, labor refers to all workers.

Labor force participation rate   Percentage of actual civilians participating in the labor force compared with the total number of civilians of working age.

Labor theory of value   Theory held by Marx (and Smith in differing form) that the value of a commodity is proportional to the labor embodied in its production.

Laissez-faire   A doctrine that the state should largely leave the economy to its own devices. Associated with Adam Smith.

Land   A means of production that includes raw materials and the land upon which productive activity takes place (i.e., factory, farm).

Law of diminishing returns   Principle that in the production of any commodity, as more units of a variable factor of production are added to a fixed quantity of other factors of production, the amount that each additional unit of the variable factor adds to the total product will eventually begin to diminish.

Law of specialization   The tendency for productivity to increase when laborers specialize in one particular task.

Liberal economist   An economist who accepts capitalism and advocates government intervention when market failures occur.

Liquidity   The ease with which an asset can be converted into cash. Considerations in measuring liquidity include the time necessary to acquire cash, the cost of conversion, and the predictability of the asset's value.

Liquidity preference   Demand for money as a function of the interest rate; the willingness to hold money on hand.

Liquidity trap   In Keynesian theory, the point in the economy when all economic agents desire to keep each additional dollar on hand. To them, the existing interest rate does not warrant the acquisition of bonds. The demand for money is thus perfectly elastic or horizontal, and monetary policy is completely ineffective in stimulating aggregate expenditures.

Long run Any extended period, usually longer than three to five years. For a firm, the time necessary to effect changes in "fixed" resources. Economists view the long run as the period in which equilibrium is reached.

Lorenz curve Graphs the extent of income inequality by charting the cumulative percentage of income against the cumulative percentage of families.

Macroeconomics The branch of economics concerned with large economic aggregates such as GDP, total employment, overall price level, and how these aggregates are determined.

Malthus, Thomas Economist who developed a theory that population tends to grow at a geometric rate while food supplies can, at best, grow at an arithmetic rate. Thus, in Malthus's eyes, extreme poverty, famine, plague, and war would continually beset humanity.

Marginal cost (MC) The change in total cost resulting from raising the rate of production by one unit.

Marginal factor cost The cost of an additional resource or factor of production (which in competition equals the price of the resource).

Marginal physical product (of labor) The additional output realized when one more unit of a variable input is used, assuming all other input levels are held constant.

Marginal propensity to consume (MPC) The change in consumption divided by the change in income (MPC $= \Delta C/\Delta Y$).

Marginal propensity to save (MPS) The change in saving divided by the change in income that brought it about (MPS $= \Delta S/\Delta Y$).

Marginal revenue (MR) The change in a firm's total revenue arising from the sale of one additional unit.

Marginal revenue = marginal cost In microeconomics, the point at which profits are maximized for a firm.

Marginal revenue product The additional revenue realized when one more unit of a variable input is used, assuming all other input levels are held constant.

Market (1) An area over which buyers and sellers negotiate the exchange of a well-defined commodity. (2) From the point of view of a household, the firms from which it can buy a well-defined product. (3) From the point of view of the firm, the buyers to whom it can sell a well-defined product.

Market economy An economy functioning largely through market forces (supply, demand, etc.).

Market failure The inability of the market to produce an efficient (or acceptable) result.

Market power A condition in which the firm can exercise control over the price of a good or service because the firm supplies the total quantity.

Marxian economics School of economics aimed at understanding the class system (or private property system), the methods of production and commodity exchange under capitalism.

Materialism In Marxian economics, the notion that production of goods and services for survival is the essential human activity in all societies. This activity colors and structures all other aspects of life.

Medium of exchange The function of money as intermediary. Since money is accepted in payment for goods and services and is valued for the goods and services it buys, money is a medium of exchange.

Mercantilism A characteristic European economic doctrine in the sixteenth to seventeenth centuries, emphasizing the role of money and trade in economic life and the desirability of active state intervention in the economy.

Microeconomics Branch of economics that deals with the interrelationships of individual businesses, firms, industries, consumers, laborers, and other factors of production that make up the economy. Focuses on markets.

Mixed economy An economy in which there are substantial public and private sectors, in which private enterprise and the market are significant determining factors, but in which the state also takes on certain basic economic responsibilities (e.g., full employment and business regulation). See *Capitalism*.

Mode of production In Marxian economics, the major economic structure, or base, of society, composed of the forces of production and the relations of production.

Monetary aggregates Various measures of the money supply used by the Federal Reserve System and include M_1 and M_2.

Monetary policy Governmental policy concerned with the supply of money and credit in the economy and the rate of interest. This policy is designed to promote certain macroeconomic objectives, usually full employment, stable prices, economic growth, stable exchange rates, or balance-of-payments equilibrium.

Money Anything that is generally accepted in payment for goods and services and in the repayment of debts.

Monopolistic competition A market structure in which each firm is relatively small, but each has a monopoly on its particular version of the product in question. Competition in such a framework includes advertising, easy entry product differentiation, limited price control and other forms of non-price competition.

Monopoly A market structure in which there is a single seller of a commodity or service that has no close substitutes.

Monopoly capitalism An economy that marks the dominance of imperfect competition; productive forces or factors are extremely concentrated, and markets are imperfect. See *Capitalism*.

Multinational corporation A corporation that operates within more than one country.

Multiplier See *Keynesian multiplier; Transfer multiplier*.

National debt The net accumulation of federal budget deficits; the total indebtedness of the federal government.

National income The total income of factors of production in the current productive period.

Neoliberal model A model that assumes that developing nations must adopt modern capital and technology to have strong economic growth.

Net national product (NNP) Total output of final goods and services produced in an economy in a given period of time, including net rather than gross investment. NNP = GDP – depreciation or capital consumption allowances.

Newly Industrializing Countries (NIC) A group of countries (Hong Kong, Taiwan, Singapore, Malaysia, the Philippines, South Korea, Brazil, Mexico, and Argentina) that have allowed foreign firms to set up operations favorably and have generated sizable export capabilities.

Oligopoly A market structure in which a few large firms dominate the industry. Some of these industries produce an undifferentiated product, others a differentiated product. In either case, a special feature of oligopoly is that the firms recognize their interdependence.

Open-market operations Federal Reserve purchases and sales of government securities on the open market. These activities are an important instrument of monetary policy because sales of government securities reduce the money supply, while purchases increase it. See *Federal Reserve System*.

Opportunity cost The cost of an economic good as measured in terms of the alternative goods one must forgo to secure it.

Organization of Petroleum Exporting Countries (OPEC) Organization of oil-producing nations, largely in the Middle East, that have joined together for the purpose of controlling the production, export, and price of petroleum.

Orthodox economics The mainstream approach to economic theory, which emphasizes the rational, calculating nature of human behavior and seeks to model that behavior quantitatively and scientifically.

Paradigms A set of assumptions, concepts, values, practices, and so forth that inform a specific discipline (e.g. orthodox economics, Marxian economics, or institutional economics) during a particular period of time.

Paradox of thrift Economic principle, identified by Keynes, that an increase in the desire to save decreases output, even though investment may also increase.

Peak (of business cycle) The height of the business cycle; characterized by greatest economic activity and followed by contracting economic activity.

Per capita income Total national income divided by total population.

Perfect competition The market structure characterized by large numbers of small firms producing and selling a homogeneous product in a competitive market with easy entry and exit.

Petrodollars Dollars and currency in the form of monetary reserves controlled by the oil-exporting (largely OPEC) nations, accumulated by selling petroleum.

Phillips curve Graph showing the relationship between inflation and unemployment.

Political business cycle Distortion of the basic business cycle caused by the actions and policies of politicians bidding for reelection. Usually a four-year cycle in sequence with presidential elections.

Political economy Social science dealing with political policies and economic processes, their interrelationships, and their mutual influence on social institutions.

Possessions Personal items people own and use, including home, farm, or tools. Private property, in contrast, reflects ownership of impersonal property used by the owner only to collect rent on land, interest, and profits on capital; it is used (worked) by others.

Postindustrial society A society that has encountered the processes of industrialization and has gone beyond industrialization in terms of benefits accruing to the people. Some people consider the United States a postindustrial society.

Praxis Practical activity with an added twist, i.e., the dialectical interrelation of thought and practice. The term was used by the young Hegelians and especially Marx.

Precautionary demand for money Holding money in order to cover unexpected or temporary expenses or losses of income.

Present value The value today of a sum to be received or paid in the future, adjusted by a prevailing or assumed interest rate.

Price An amount of money that guides resource allocation and reflects the value of a good or service. Prices are transmitted by markets through which producers make decisions about what factors of production to use, and consumers decide what to consume.

Price ceiling A legally set, maximum price (price control), designed to keep prices in a particular market below the equilibrium price.

Price elasticity of demand The sensitivity of demand for a product to changes in its price.

Price elasticity of supply The sensitivity of supply of a product to changes in its price.

Price index See *Consumer Price Index; Index number.*

Price leadership The practice of a single firm in an industry announcing a price change and other firms following suit.

Price stability Price policy that aims to counter wide fluctuations in aggregate price levels. During a period of high inflation, for example, governments seeking price stability adopt anti-inflationary measures such as credit withdrawal, higher interest rates, and decreased government spending (or increased taxes).

Price wars Progressive price cutting to increase sales.

Primitive accumulation A way of accumulating wealth that fuels class conflict. In particular, the early formation of capital that accompanied the development of capitalism, often characterized by piracy and plunder.

Product differentiation Business strategy in which substitute products retain some distinctive difference. Means of differentiating products include brand names, coloring, packaging, or advertising.

Production possibilities curve Graph that illustrates scarcity and opportunity cost by showing that whenever society chooses to have more of one type of good, it must sacrifice some of another type of good.

Productivity (of labor) The output produced per unit of input (output per hour of work).

Profits Excess of revenues over costs. Normal profits are equal to the opportunity costs of management. Economic profits are the profits above the normal profit. Theoretically, in pure competition, economic profits equal zero in the long run. However, in imperfect market structures, they do not.

Progressive income tax Tax that claims an ever-increasing percentage of income as the income level rises.

Property Tangible or intangible possession that may be used to produce some product or aid in the selling of the product. Certain legal rights are attached to this "private property."

Property rights In capitalism, where productive property is privately owned, owners' rights to control the use of these productive resources. See *Possessions*.

Protectionism Policy that institutes high tariffs on incoming goods, so as to preserve domestic industry. Protectionism was prevalent during mercantilism. See *Infant industry; Tariff*.

Public debt The amount of outstanding federal debt held by individuals, corporations, and nonfederal government agencies.

Public goods Goods or resources that benefit the general public and are not necessarily directly paid for by all those who use them. Examples are street signs and public schools.

Public sector Local, state, and federal governmental offices, organizations, and institutions.

Putting-out system Labor system in which an owner would give workers the necessary materials and pay the worker to make a finished product. Replaced the handicraft type of industry and marked the emergence of private capital.

Quantity demanded The specific number of units of a product in the economy that is desired by economic agents at a given price level.

Quantity supplied The specific number of units of a product in the economy that is provided by producers at a given price level.

Quantity theory of money Theory that the quantity of money in the economy largely determines the level of prices. Stated as $MV = PQ$, where M is the quantity of money, V is the income velocity of money, P is the price level, and Q is real national income. The theory postulates that V is largely determined by institutional factors and Q is determined by factor supplies and technology; hence changes in M will be reflected in proportionate changes in P.

Quotas Limits on the quantities of goods imported or exported.

Radical economists Economists who are critical of classical and neoclassical theory and view economic problems as resulting directly from the capitalist system itself. Thus, the only serious relief to these problems is a change of economic system.

Rational expectations An economics-based theory about the nature of economic agents, stating that all agents are rational, logical, and aware of what is best for them and what the consequences of decisions and developments in the economy will mean for their well-being. Agents will act logically to take advantage of changes in the economy and enhance their position.

Real wages   Wages measured from a specific point; wages that reflect the rate of inflation. If a worker's wage level increases 10 percent and inflation increases 10 percent in the same period of time, then we say that the real wage remains the same. Usually contrasted with money wages, which in the example would reflect only the 10 percent increase in the worker's wage.

Recession   A slowing down of economic activity, resulting in an increase in unemployment and in excess industrial capacity. Less severe than a depression. Sometimes defined in the United States in terms of a decline in GDP for two or more successive quarters of a year.

Regulation Q   Federal regulation placing a ceiling on interest rates payable by banks on deposits. This regulation has been phased out.

Relations of production   The relationships among people in the production process, especially the class structure (i.e., slave/slaveowner, serf/lord, laborer/capitalist).

Rent   (1) Payment for the services of a factor of production. (2) Payment for the use of land.

Reserve army (industrial)   A term developed by Marx to describe the functioning of capitalism in which worker strength was greatly decreased, in proportion to the amount of unemployment.

Reserve currency   A currency that is accepted in settlement of international exchanges.

Reserve requirement   In banking, the fraction of public deposits that a bank holds in reserves.

Ricardo, David   One of the reformers of classical liberalism, developed by Adam Smith. Ricardo's analysis was based on an economy composed of many small enterprises.

Savings   All income received by households and not spent on the consumption of goods and services.

Say's law   The doctrine (named after J. B. Say) that "supply creates its own demand."

The production of one good adds to both aggregate supply and aggregate demand. In this nonmonetary world, depression and mass unemployment are not possible.

Scarcity   Inability of a society to produce or secure enough goods to satisfy all the wants, needs, and desires people have for these goods.

Seasonal unemployment   Joblessness created by changing seasonal conditions or demand.

Services   Duties (or work) for others that do not necessarily render a good but are nevertheless worth payment.

Sherman Antitrust Act   A major U.S. antitrust law passed in 1890 prohibiting "every contract, combination in the form of trust or otherwise or conspiracy, in restraint of trade or commerce," and prescribing penalties for monopoly.

Shortage   Disequilibrium situation wherein quantity demanded exceeds quantity supplied. In such a situation, price will tend to rise until it reaches an equilibrium level (where quantity supplied equals quantity demanded).

Shortrun   For a firm, the period in which some inputs are fixed.

Smith, Adam   Economist who in 1776 published *The Wealth of Nations*, noting the foundation of a new individualist philosophy, classical liberalism.

Socialism   An economic system in which property and the distribution of wealth are subject to control by the community.

Special Drawing Rights (SDRs)   A bookkeeping device created by the International Monetary Fund to increase international liquidity. SDRs may be drawn by each country in proportion to its original fund contribution.

Specialization (of labor)   Methods of production in which individual workers specialize in particular tasks rather than making everything for themselves.

Speculative demand for money   Function that describes the amount of assets held by households and firms in the form of money, relative to the interest rate.

Stagflation Term coined in the 1970s to describe the coexistence of unemployment (stagnation) and inflation afflicting the United States and other countries.

Standard of deferred payment Acceptability as future payment; a characteristic of money.

Stock Shares of ownership in a corporation. May be common stock and/or preferred stock.

Store of value An asset that holds value into the future. Money has this characteristic.

Structural (budget) deficit The federal budget deficit which remains if the economy is at full employment.

Structural unemployment Type of permanent unemployment that stems from shifting demand and/or technological changes requiring new skills for workers. Disparities in geographic locations of workers and jobs also contribute to this phenomenon.

Structuralist model A model that assumes that domestic political and economic factors affect development.

Superstructure Society's ideals, institutions, and ideologies, including laws, politics, culture, ethics, religions, morals, and philosophy, that, according to Marx, support the economic base of society and the existing mode of production.

Supply The amount of goods or services produced and available for purchase.

Supply curve The set of all points representing the amount of goods or services that will be offered at different price levels.

Supply shock Events that are unexpected and that limit the aggregate supply of goods and services.

Supply, law of Economic principle that says the lower the price, the lower the quantity supplied, all other things being constant. Price and quantity supplied are positively related.

Surplus A state of disequilibrium wherein quantity supplied exceeds quantity demanded. Price will tend to fall until it reaches an equilibrium (where quantity supplied equals quantity demanded).

Surplus value In Marxian terms, the amount by which the value of a worker's output exceeds his or her wage. Hence, a source of profit for the capitalist.

Tariff A tax applied to imports.

Terms of trade The prices of a country's exports in relation to its imports. Any improvement in a country's terms of trade means a relative increase in its export prices, while a deterioration in its terms of trade indicates a relative increase in its import prices.

Theory A cogently expressed group of related propositions declared as principles for explanation of a set of phenomena.

Total cost The cost of all factors of production involved in producing one good.

Total fixed costs The sum of all costs that do not change with varying output (in the short run). A firm incurs these costs regardless of production levels.

Total revenue The amount of funds credited to the firm for sales of its output; price multiplied by units sold.

Total variable costs The sum of all costs that fluctuate in relation to the activity of the firm and the productive process. The two major variable costs are labor and resources.

Transactions demand for money Function that indicates the amount of money balances that individuals desire for purchasing purposes. Considered relatively constant, given a level of income and consumption pattern.

Transfer multiplier The ratio that relates the change in the equilibrium level of income to a change in government transfer payments.

Transfer payments Government payments to individuals that are not compensation for currently productive activity.

Trough (of business cycle) The low point of the business cycle, representing the slowest level of business activity. Following this low point, the cycle begins an upward swing.

Unemployed   A person sixteen years of age or older who is not working and is available for work and has made an effort to find work during the previous four weeks.

Unemployment   A condition wherein workers who are ordinarily part of the labor force are unable to find work at prevailing wages. May take any of five specific forms: (1) Frictional unemployment arises from workers changing jobs, etc.; all labor markets have this kind. (2) Seasonal unemployment results from changing seasonal demand and supply for labor. (3) Structural unemployment results from changing or shifting product demand; i.e., it is a function of geographic and job skill mobility. (4) Cyclical unemployment arises from changes in demand of labor during the business cycle. (5) Hidden unemployment consists of frustrated potential workers who have given up looking for a job.

Unemployment rate   The number of people unemployed expressed as a percentage of the total number of people in the labor force.

Unit of account   A measure of value or the standard way of quoting prices and keeping accounts in an economy.

Value added   Strictly, the value of a final product less the cost of production.

Variable costs   Costs that fluctuate due to the activity of the firm and the productive process. The two major variable costs are labor and resources.

Vertical merger   Companies in different stages of an industry merge.

Wage and price controls   Mandatory regulation of wages and prices by the government in order to contain inflation. The U.S. government applied such controls to certain segments of the economy with varying force from 1971 to 1974.

Wages   The price paid for units of labor or service supplied in the market per unit of time.

World Bank   A bank that assists poor countries by lending or by insuring private loans to finance development projects. Officially the International Bank for Reconstruction and Development (IBRD) established after World War II to promote postwar reconstruction and development of underdeveloped countries.

NAME INDEX

Jordan, Michael, 265

Keen, Maurice, 51
    The Outlaws of Medieval Legend, 51
Kennedy, John F., 295
Kerry, John, 13
Keynes, John Maynard, 10, 11, 87, 93–95, 97, 103,
    339, 346–372, 392, 446
    The End of Laissez–Faire, 94
    *The General Theory of Employment, Interest, and
        Money*, 339, 348, 368, 399–400, 418
Khrushchev, Nikita, 474
King Harold, 50
King John, 50–51
Kollar-Kotelly, Colleen, 292
Kroc, Ray, 205
Krugman, Paul, 13
    *The Great Unraveling: Losing Our Way in the
        New Century*, 13
Kuhn, Thomas, 9
    The Structure of Scientific Revolutions, 9

Lafley, Alan G., 581
Lee, Thea, 496, 499
Leonhardt, David, 471

Malthus, Thomas, 67–68
    Principles of Political Economy, 67
Mao Tse-tung, 563
Marovitz, Daniel, 580
Marshall, Alfred, 7
    Principles of Economics, 7
Marx, Karl, 11, 40, 41, 71–85, 103, 104, 105, 348
    Capital, 72, 74, 81
    The Communist Manifesto, 71, 72, 73, 77, 79, 80,
        81, 84
    Critique of Political Economy, 76
    dialectics, 73–74
    The Economic and Philosophic Manuscripts of 1844,
        78
    The German Ideology, 40, 72
    The Grundrisse, 78
    Theories of Surplus Value, 78
    Wage Labor and Capital, 78
McCain, John, 12
McCloskey, Deidre, 347
McNally, David,
    Political Economy and the Rise of Capitalism,
        49
Meany, George, 503
Melligeri, Aravind, 562
Mellon, Andrew, 346, 347
Mill, John Stuart, 71, 338
    Principles of Political Economy, 71
Miller, Bob, 584
Miller, G. Tyler, 573

Morgan, J.P., 91
Mundie, Craig, 561

Nader, Ralph, 14
Newton, Isaac, 105
Nilekani, Nandan M., 558
Nixon, Richard M., 526
Nordhaus, William, 461

O'Connor, Sandra Day, 293
Ohmae, Kenichi, 563
O'Neill, June, 301

Parks, James, 495–497
Paul, Steven M., 584
Paulson, Henry M., 522
Pei, I.M., 555
Perot, Ross, 495
Phelps, Edmund, 457
Phillips, A.W., 456
Pitt, Brad, 238
Polanyi, Karl, 54, 59
    The Great Transformation, 54, 59
Pollin, Robert, 14
Powell Jr., Lewis F., 305
Prahalad, C.K., 555
Prebish, Raul, 541
Proudhon, Pierre Joseph, 53–54
    What is Property, 53

Queen Victoria, 87

Radjou, Navi, 556
Reagan, Ronald, 12, 98–99, 119, 227, 242, 260,
    272, 277, 292, 387, 427, 465, 473
Reynolds, R.J., 452
Ricardo, David, 26, 338, 486, 487, 492–493
Roberts, Julia, 360
Robinson, Joan, 8, 200
    Freedom and Necessity, 8
Rockefeller, John D., 87, 91
Roosevelt, Franklin D., 94
Rose, Stephen J., 242
Rosenberg, Tina, 546
Roubini, Nouriel, 524
Rowe, Jonathan, 333
Rubin, Robert E., 522
Ruskin, John, 87–88
    "Traffic," 88
Russell, Bertrand, 347

Sage, Jeffrey D., 581
Samuelson, Paul, 456
Sawhney, Mohanbir, 584
Say, Jean Baptiste, 10, 57, 66–68
    A Treatise on Political Economy, 87–88

SUBJECT INDEX

Knights of Labor, 257–258

Labor, 42, See also Workers
    early development of labor force, 55
    influence of labor incomes, 235–238
    in Quantity Theory of Money, 340–341
    in radical analysis of capitalism, 13
Laborers, 63
Labor market, 219, 260–261
Labor theory of value, 78
    Marx's use of, 78
Labor unions, 256
    and corporations in the 21st century, 267–269
    economic effects of, 260–265
    growth of, 264
    history of, 257–260
    problems with, 257
    future of, 265
Lags,
    action lag, 422
    implementation, 381
    inside lag, 422
    in fiscal policy, 381
    legislative, 381
    in monetary policy, 422
    outside lag, 422
    reaction lag, 382
    recognition lag, 381, 422
Laissez–faire, 57, 68–69, 348
    definition of, 57
    flowering of, 87
    and free trade, 68
    Keynesian critique of, 93–95
    socialist critique of, 53, 71–85
    in the United States, 91–93
    in the Victorian Age, 87–88
Land, 42
Landowners (landlords), 63
Law of diminishing returns, 160
Law of specialization, 160
Leakages, 353–354
    in the money creation process, 412–413
Less developed countries (LDCs), 529–542
    economic condition, 529–542
    and protectionism, 27
Liberal economics, 12
    and changes in the global community,
        576
    elements of, 12–13
    and government regulation, 273
Limited liability, 249
Liquidity, 400
Liquidity preference, 400
Liquidity trap, 400–401, 417–418
Long run, 159

Lorenz curve, 231–235

Macroeconomic goals, 313–321
Macroeconomic policy, 322
Macroeconomics, 311
    defined, 311, 313
    goals of, 313–321
    tools of, 322
Magna Carta, 50
Managed float, 524
Manor, 44–45
    decline of, 48–49
Margin requirement, 419
Marginal cost, 161, See Cost
    pricing, 290
Marginal external benefit, 282
Marginal factor cost, 222, See Cost
Marginal physical product, 222
Marginal product of labor, 161
Marginal propensity,
    to consume (MPC), 358–360
    to save (MPS), 360–361
Marginal revenue, 165, See Profit maximization
Marginal revenue product, 222
Marginal social benefit, 283
Marginal social cost, 284–285
Market failure, 281
Market power, 192
Market rate of interest, See Interest rates
Markets, 57, 61, 124, 179–180
    capitalism, 124
    emergence of, 57–59
    in equilibrium, 137–139
    and exchange and division of labor, 61
    noncompetitive, 189–218
    price determination, 124, 126
    regulation of, 404–407
    and resource allocation, 111–120
    theory of, 124
Marxian analysis of capitalism, 77–81
Marxian critique,
    of capitalism, 77–81
    of laissez–faire, 71–72
Marxian economics, 10
    assessment of, 83–85
Marxian theory of instability, 79
Marxism, 100, 71–85
Materialism, 74–75
Material concept of history, See Historical
    materialism
Medieval merchants, 46–47
Medium of exchange,
    money as, 398
Mercantilism, 55
Mergers, 256

New Economic Policy (NEP),
  of Nixon administration, 527
New Deal, 97, 276
New Keynesians, 463
Newly industrialized countries (NICs), 24, 255,
  536, 551
Noncompetitive markets, See Markets
North American Free Trade Agreement (NAFTA),
  33, 495–499
NOW accounts, 408

Occupational segregation, 239–243
Office of Management and Budget, 375
Oil industry, 5, See OPEC
Oligopoly, 190–191, 206, 211–212, 280
  characteristics of, 206
Open Market Committee of the Federal Reserve
  System, 402
Open market operations, 418, 420
Operation Desert Storm, 30
Opportunity cost, 26, 113, 158
  of college, 121
  guns vs butter, 114
  of Harrison Ford, 26
  of unemployment, 319
Orderly Market Agreement (OMAs), 491
Organic composition of capital, See Capital
Organization of Petroleum Exporting Countries
  (OPEC), 30, 144, 208, 209, 211, 321, 443,
  457
Orthodox economics, 10
Outlaws, 51
Output,
  and the quantity theory of money, 340
Outsource, 252, 578–584
Ownership, See Private property

Paradigm, 9
  Copernican and Ptolemaic, 9
  of human development, 530
Pax Americana, 322–324
Peasants, 44–45, 52
Partnership, 248
Peace dividend, 118
People's Republic of China, 554–565
  Chinese revolution, 563
  Cultural Revolution, 302, 564
  modernization program, 563–564
  political realities, 564–565
Perfect competition, 157, 190–191
Personal consumption of GDP, 330
Personal dividend income, 331
Personal income, 235, 331
Personal interest income, 331
Personal possessions vs private property, 54
Personal savings, 331, See Saving

Personal taxes, 331, See Tax(es) and taxation
Personal wealth,
  distribution of, 234–235
Phillips curve, 456
Pin factory, 59–60
Plaza Accord, 516
Policy,
  advisory groups and, See Fiscal policy,
    Monetary policy
Political economy, 8
Positive economics, 6
Possessions, 54
Poverty, 294
  anti–poverty programs, 238–239
  children and, 244–245
  and government intervention, 238–239
  global, 530–531
  and income redistribution, 294–296
  level of, 530–531
Poverty line, 294
Poverty rate, 294
Precautionary demand for money, 399
Prices, 124
  determination of, 126–147
  elasticity, 148
  equilibrium, 137
  monetary policy and, 423–424
  price leadership, 211
  price stability, 211
  and the quantity theory of money, 340
  regulation of (price controls and price ceiling),
    144–145
  of related goods, 130
Price leadership, 211, See Prices
Price stability, 211
Price wars, 206, 207
Private property, 52–54, 234
  personal possessions, 54
  and the poor, 234–235
Private property rights, 50, 51, 53, 54
Procyclical policy, 375, 382
Producer sovereignty, 189
Product Accounting, 326–336
Production, 42
  factors of, 42
  inefficiency in, 196
  internationalization of, 19–24
  mode of, 75
  and prices, 124
  process as a source of surplus value, 78
Production possibilities curve, 114
Productivity, 90, 446–449
  decline in, 447
  and GDP, 446
  and labor, 446–447
  measurement, 446–447

cyclical, 316
defined, 316
frictional, 316
hidden, 316
and inflation trade–off, 455–459
involuntary part–time, 318
opportunity cost of, 319
seasonal, 316
structural, 316
Unit of account,
money as, 399
United Nations Children's Fund (UNICEF), 244
United States economic history,
after WWII, 24, 96–101, 116, 118–119, 251,
272–273, 322–326, 405, 425–429,
456–459, 520–521
1970s energy crisis, 111
overview of the 1980s, 98–100, 323–325,
406–407
overview of the 1990s, 100–101, 325–326,
406–407
Urban economics, 7
Urbanization and feudalism, 46
Uruguay Round, 500
Uses of money, See Money

Value,
added counting, 332
labor theory of, 78
Velocity of money, 340
Vertical merger, 291

Vietnam War,
failure in, 97
fiscal and monetary policies, 321
Victorian Age, 87–89

Wage–price spiral,
and inflation, 428–429
Wages, 64
Wagner Act, 259
Wants, 112–113
Women,
discrimination and, 242–243
income inequality and, 1, 242–243
and the labor force, 242–243
and work, 237, 242–243
Workers,
in classical economics, 59–63
involuntary part time, 318
World Com, 101, 254
World trade, 19, 25–29, 480–504
World Trade Organization (WTO), 34, 495–496,
500, 551
World War II, 116, 275, 314, 315, 316
demise of gold standard and, 526–527
parity exchange rates after, 527
U.S. economy after, 96–98, 116, 118–119,
525–526
world economy after, 526–527, 550–552

Yen, 146
exchange rate of, 28, 145–146, 519–521